Blue Book of Airguns™

Seventh Edition

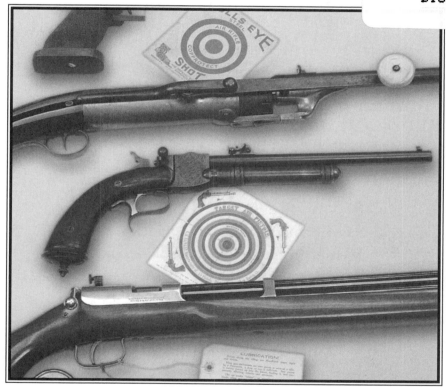

by Dr. Robert D. Beeman & John B. Allen
Edited by S.P. Fjestad

$29.95
Publisher's Softcover
Suggested List Price

$44.95
Publisher's Hardcover
Suggested List Price

Blue Book of Airguns™
Seventh Edition

This book is the result of continual airgun research performed by attending shows and communicating with airgun dealers, collectors, company historians, contributing editors, and other knowledgeable industry professionals worldwide each year. This book represents an analysis of prices for which airguns have actually been selling during that period at an average retail level. Although every reasonable effort has been made to compile an accurate and reliable guide, airgun prices may vary significantly, depending on such factors as the locality of the sale, the number of sales we were able to consider, and economic conditions. Accordingly, no representation can be made that the airguns listed may be bought or sold at prices indicated, nor shall the author or publisher be responsible for any error made in compiling and recording such prices and related information.

All Rights Reserved
Copyright 2008
Blue Book Publications, Inc.
8009 34th Avenue South, Suite 175
Minneapolis, MN 55425 U.S.A.
Orders Only: 800-877-4867
Phone: 952-854-5229
Fax: 952-853-1486
Email: bluebook@bluebookinc.com
Website: http://www.bluebookinc.com

Published and printed in the United States of America
ISBN: 1-886768-77-3
ISBN 13: 978-1-886768-77-2

TABLE OF CONTENTS

ACKNOWLEDGEMENTS

Barry Abel
José Roberto Romerio Abrahão
Marv Adams
Sue Adams
Trevor Adams
Ingvar Alm
Jörg Altenburger
Reiner Altenburger
Dieter Anschütz
Dennis Baker
Geoffrey Baker
Gary Barnes
Toshiko Beeman
Larry Behling
Sharon Bell
Justin "JB" Biddle
Randall Bimrose
Adam Blalock
Monika Bräutigam
George Brenzovich
Gurney Brown
Kathy Brown
Gordon Bruce
Dr. Bruno Brukner
Robert Buchanan
Phil Bulmer
Mandy Cardoniga
Steve Cary
Michale Chao
Jim & Ann Coplen
Colin Currie
Amanda Davis
Peter DeRose

Mike Driskill
Fred Ehrlich
Ulrich Eichstädt
S.P. Fjestad
Ralph Heize Flamand
Dean Fletcher
John Ford
Kenth Friberg
Bo Fred
Gregory Fuller
Susan Gardner
Tom & Edith Gaylord
Carolyn Gilman
John Griffiths
John Groenewold
Yvette Hicks
Tony Hall
Matts Hammer
Larry Hannusch
Will Hartlep
Don Howard
Tom Gaylord
Greg Glover
Jon Jenkins
Susan Johnston
Paul Kanieski
John Knibbs
David Kosowski
Fred Liady
Steve Loke
Rick MacHale
Juan Manual
Tim McMurry

Dani Navickas
Dave Nemanic
Ed Niccum
Jon Oakleaf
Ted Osborn
Eyck Pflaumer
Wulf-Heinz Pflaumer
Sue Piedmont
Scott Pilkington
Eduardo Poloni
Kurt Pottiez
Wes Powers
Neal Punchard
Don Raitzer
Lewis Reinhold
Ron Sauls
Otwin Sayle
Tim Saunders
Phillip Schreier
Davis Schwesinger
Tom Slocum
Robert Spielvogel
Bruce Stauff
Bruce Stauff Jr.
David Swan
Guillermo Sylianteng Jr.
Frank Turner
Steve Upham
Tod Utter
John Walter
Hans-Hermann Weihrauch
Hans Weller
André Wirth

ABOUT THE COVER & CREDITS

Daystate LTD, Competa Model .22 caliber PCP pistol, manufactured in Stone, Staffordshire, England from 1980 to 1995. This fine example is the rather unique Midas Brass Model, with its name coming from the polished brass air reservoir. Stamped with serial number CP18 indicates this air pistol is very early production. In like new condition, this pistol in the hands of a competent sharpshooter would shoot the center out of the Bulls Eye target below it.

Charles Bunge located in Geneva, NY was the maker of this .28 caliber Upstate New York type spring air Gallery rifle. While popular during the 1870s as repeating Gallery airguns few of them wherever manufactured and even fewer still survived the decades since their use. These spring air rifles where cocked by pulling up and back on the round ivory handle to compress the spring and then manually revolving the cylinder to a loaded chamber.

Giffard Gas Pistol manufactured by Francaise d' Armes et Cycles located in St. Étienne, France circa 1880s. This 6mm caliber single shot tap loading CO_2 pistol is a great example of the airgun maker's art during the 1880s. From the high-grade finely checkered walnut grip with fancy grip cap and trigger guard, to the adjustable rear sight, to the removable gas cylinder, to the hammer, to the power adjuster, to the tap loader all affixed to the fancy engraver frame.

If you recognized this target and turned to this page to confirm your suspicions, congratulations, it is a reduced copy of the long lost Hawley Kalamazoo target. Read that $1,500-$2,000 for a mint original.

Sheridan Products Inc. Model A .22 caliber PCP rifle? Then you look closer and realize the stock forearm split is missing and think (Could this be the one that got away?), then you read this and the light comes on, Sheridan did not make this. You guessed it; it's a Tim Jones Sheridan Model A .22 caliber PCP special complete with precision Lothar Walther barrel and stock carved from original Sheridan blank.

Back Cover: Excellent Phantom Model (4.4mm lead ball caliber only) Pistol manufactured in Stockholm, Sweden circa 1953-1959. Total production of this spring piston pistol was approximately 4,572 and because of a design flaw in the muzzle, area the survival number is very low. To find one complete with box and ammo in this condition is unheard of and the asking price of $1,250 is sure to bring even the healthiest of collectors to their knees.

Cover airguns courtesy of Ingvar Alm
Cover design and layout - Clint H. Schmidt & John Allen
7th Edition credits:
Art Dept. - Clint H. Schmidt
Research & Contribution Coordinators - Dr. Robert Beeman & John Allen
Proofing/Copyediting - Kelsey Fjestad & Sara Lange
Cover & Text Printing - Bang Printing, located in Brainerd, MN

While many of you have probably dealt with Blue Book Publications, Inc. for years, it may be helpful for you to know a little bit more about our company, including information on how to contact us regarding our various titles, software programs, and other informational services.

Blue Book Publications, Inc.
8009 34th Avenue South, Suite 175
Minneapolis, MN 55425 USA
Phone No.: 952-854-5229 • Orders Only (domestic and Canada): 800-877-4867, ext. 3
Fax No.: 952-853-1486 (available 24 hours a day)
Web site: www.bluebookinc.com
General Email: bluebook@bluebookinc.com - we check our email at 9am, 12pm, and 4pm M - F.
Office hours are: 8:30am - 5:00pm CST, Monday - Friday (except major U.S. holidays)

Voice mail extensions and email addresses on all employees are provided below:

Extension 10 - Beth Schreiber	beths@bluebookinc.com	Extension 17 - Zachary R. Fjestad	zachf@bluebookinc.com
Extension 11 - Katie Sandin	katies@bluebookinc.com	Extension 18 - Tom Stock	toms@bluebookinc.com
Extension 12 - John Andraschko	johnand@bluebookinc.com	Extension 19 - Cassandra Faulkner	cassandraf@bluebookinc.com
Extension 13 - S.P. Fjestad	stevef@bluebookinc.com	Extension 22 - Kelsey Fjestad	kelseyf@bluebookinc.com
Extension 15 - Clint H. Schmidt	clints@bluebookinc.com	Extension 27 - Shipping	
Extension 16 - John Allen	johna@bluebookinc.com		

Additionally, an after-hours message service is available for ordering - please use ext. 3. All orders are processed within 24 hours of receiving them, assuming payment and order information is correct. Depending on the product, we typically ship Media Mail, Priority Mail, DHL or UPS. Expedited shipping services are also available domestically for an additional charge. Please contact us directly or check our website for an expedited shipping method that suits you best.

Online subscriptions and individual download services for the *Blue Book of Gun Values*, *Blue Book of Airguns*, *Blue Book of Modern Black Powder Arms*, *Blue Book of Pool Cues*, *Blue Book of Electric Guitars*, *Blue Book of Acoustic Guitars*, and the *Blue Book of Guitar Amplifiers* are available.

As this edition goes to press, the following titles/products are currently available. Many of these softcover editions are also available in hardcover deluxe editions. Please check our website for more information, including the most current availability, pricing, and S/H charges on all titles.

Blue Book of Gun Values, 29th Edition by S.P. Fjestad
Blue Book of Gun Values, 29th Edition CD-ROM
Blue Book of Guns Inventory Software Program CD-ROM (ISP) (includes the databases from 29th Edition *Blue Book of Gun Values*, 5th Edition *Blue Book of Modern Black Powder Arms* and 7th Edition *Blue Book of Airguns*, plus inventory software program)
Gianfranco Pedersoli - Master Engraver by Dag Sundseth, edited by S.P. Fjestad & Elena Micheli-Lamboy
5th Edition *Blue Book of Modern Black Powder Arms* by John Allen
7th Edition *Blue Book of Airguns* by Dr. Robert Beeman & John Allen
Parker Gun Identification & Serialization, compiled by Charlie Price and edited by S.P. Fjestad
American Gunsmiths by Frank Sellers (Late 04/08 release date)
The Ammo Encyclopedia by Michael Bussard (04/08 release date)
Blue Book of Pool Cues, 3rd Edition, by Brad Simpson
Blue Book of Electric Guitars, 11th Edition, by Zachary R. Fjestad, edited by S.P. Fjestad
Blue Book of Acoustic Guitars, 11th Edition, by Zachary R. Fjestad, edited by S.P. Fjestad
Blue Book of Guitar Amplifiers, 3rd Edition, by Zachary R. Fjestad, edited by S.P. Fjestad
2nd Revised Edition *Gibson Flying V* by Zachary R. Fjestad & Larry Meiners
Blue Book of Guitars CD-ROM , 11th Edition
Blue Book of Guitar Amplifiers CD-ROM, 3rd Edition
The Nethercutt Collection - the Cars of San Sylmar by Dennis Adler

If you would like to get more information about any of the above publications/products, simply check our web site: www.bluebookinc.com. We would like to thank all of you for your business in the past - you are the reason we are successful. Our goal remains the same - to give you the best products, the most accurate and up-to-date information for the money, and the highest level of customer service available in today's marketplace. If something's right, tell the world over time. If something's wrong, please tell us immediately - we'll make it right.

MEET THE STAFF

Editor & Publisher S.P. Fjestad

Many of you may want to know what the person on the other end of the telephone/fax/email looks like, so here are the faces that go with the voices.

John B. Allen – Author & Associate Editor Arms Division

Cassandra Faulkner – Executive Assistant Editor

Tom Stock – CFO

Clint H. Schmidt – Art Director

Beth Schreiber Operations Manager

Katie Sandin Operations

Kelsey Fjestad Operations/Proofing

Sara Lange Operations/Proofing

Ricky McNamara Operations/Shipping

Zachary R. Fjestad – Author/Editor Guitar & Amp Division

John Andraschko - Technology Director

HOW TO USE THIS BOOK

The prices listed in this edition of the *Blue Book of Airguns* are based on the national average retail prices a consumer can expect to pay. This is not an airguns wholesale pricing guide (there is no such thing). More importantly, do not expect to walk into a gun/pawn shop or airgun/gun show and think that the proprietor/dealer should pay you the retail price listed within this text for your gun. Resale offers on most models could be anywhere from near retail to 50% less than the values listed. These prices paid will be depending upon locality, desirability, dealer inventory, and potential profitability. In other words, if you want to receive 100% of the price (retail value), then you have to do 100% of the work (become the retailer, which also includes assuming 100% of the risk).

Percentages of original finish, (condition factors with corresponding prices/values, if applicable) are listed between 20% and 100%.

Please refer to "Anatomy of an Airgun" to learn more about the various airgun parts and terminology. Also, you may want to check the Glossary and the Abbreviations for more detailed information about both nomenclature and airgun terminology.

A Trademark Index listing the current airgun manufacturers, importers, and distributors is provided. This includes the most recent emails, websites, and other pertinent contact information for these individuals and organizations. The Index is a handy way to find the make/model you're looking for in a hurry. To find an airgun in this text, first look under the name of the manufacturer, trademark, brand name, and in some cases, the importer (please consult the Index if necessary). Next, find the correct category name(s), typically Pistols, Rifles, and Shotguns.

Once you find the correct model or sub-model under its respective subheading, determine the specimen's percentage of original condition, and find the corresponding percentage column showing the price of a currently manufactured model or the value on a discontinued model.

Since this publication consists of 504 pages, you may want to take advantage of our index as a speedy alternative to going through the pages, and our comprehensive Trademark Index for a complete listing of airgun manufacturers, importers, and distributors. Don't forget to read the editorial, including articles by Tom Gaylord and Jim Carmichel, long time shooting editor for *Outdoor Life*.

For the sake of simplicity, the following organizational framework has been adopted throughout this publication.

1. **Manufacturer Name or Trademark** - brand name, importer, or organization is listed alphabetically in uppercase bold face type.

2. **Manufacturer Status** - This information is listed directly beneath the trademark heading, providing current status and location along with importer information for foreign trademarks.

3. **Manufacturer Description** - These notes may appear next under individual heading descriptions and can be differentiated by the typeface. This will be specific information relating to the trademark or models.

4. **Category Name** - (normally, in alphabetical sequence) in upper case (inside a screened gray box), referring mostly to an airguns configuration.

5. **Category Note** - May following a category name to help explain the category, and/or provide limited information on models and values.

6. **Category Price/Value Adjustment** - The last potential piece of information that may appear below a category name (above a model name) is a category price/value adjustment. These may be included here only if the adjustment applies to all models in the category.

7. **Model Name and Description** - appear flush left, are bold faced, and all upper-case letters, either in chronological order (normally) or alphabetical order (sometimes, the previous model name and/or close sub variation will appear at the end in parentheses) and are listed under the individual category names. These are followed by the model descriptions and usually include descriptive information about the model.

10 —
GRADING	100%	95%	90%	80%	60%	40%	20%

C 142 *COLT'S MANUFACTURING COMPANY, INC.*

1 — # COLT'S MANUFACTURING COMPANY, INC.

2 — Current manufacturer located in Hartford, CT. Colt airguns are currently imported and serviced exclusively by Umarex USA located in Fort Smith, AR beginning 2007. Previously imported and serviced exclusively by Crosman Corp. located in East Bloomfield, NY 2003-2006 andby Daisy Manufacturing Company located in Rogers, AR.

3 — Colt airguns are manufactured by Umarex, the current owner of Walther. Colt airguns are faithful copies of the famous Model 1911 A1. With the size and weight of a real Colt, five versions are available, including a special 160th Anniversary model. Many of the same precision options offered for the cartridge pistols have been available for the airguns, including a barrel compensator, competition (tuning set with speed hammer, rapid release double thumb safety, beavertail grip safety, grip with thumb guard, backstrap, sights) features, and Colt Top Point (Red Dot) heads-up sighting scope. All models are pre-drilled for the Serendipity SL optical sight.

For more information and current pricing on both new and used Colt firearms, please refer to the *Blue Book of Gun Values* by S.P. Fjestad (also available online).

4 — ## PISTOLS

7 — **GOVERNMENT MODEL 1911 A1** - .177 cal., CO_2, semi-auto, SA and DA, eight-shot rotary magazine, 5 in. rifled steel BBL, 425 FPS, blade front/adj. rear sight, trigger safety, grip safety, blue or nickel finish, checkered black plastic or smooth wood grips, 8.6 in. OAL, 2.38 lbs.

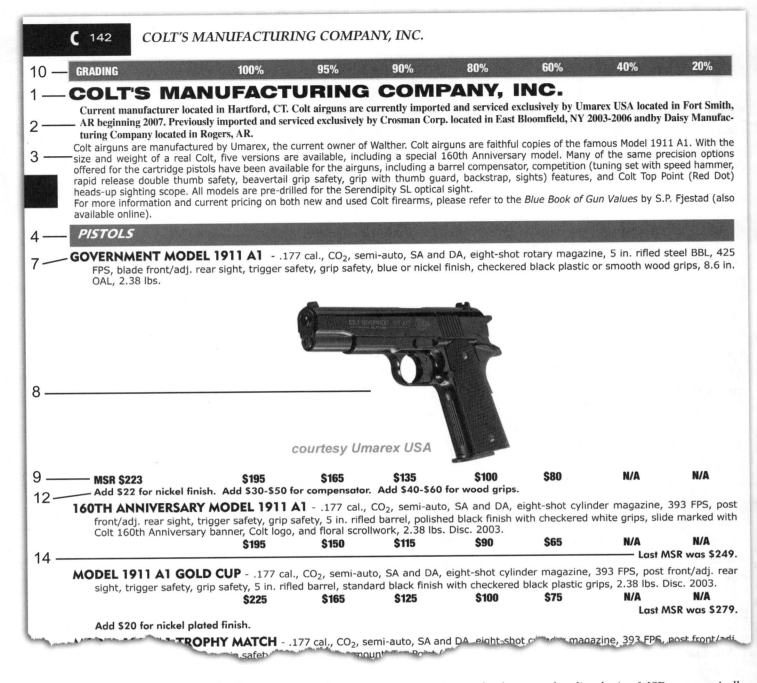

courtesy Umarex USA

9 —
MSR $223	$195	$165	$135	$100	$80	N/A	N/A

12 — Add $22 for nickel finish. Add $30-$50 for compensator. Add $40-$60 for wood grips.

160TH ANNIVERSARY MODEL 1911 A1 - .177 cal., CO_2, semi-auto, SA and DA, eight-shot cylinder magazine, 393 FPS, post front/adj. rear sight, trigger safety, grip safety, 5 in. rifled barrel, polished black finish with checkered white grips, slide marked with Colt 160th Anniversary banner, Colt logo, and floral scrollwork, 2.38 lbs. Disc. 2003.

	$195	$150	$115	$90	$65	N/A	N/A

14 — Last MSR was $249.

MODEL 1911 A1 GOLD CUP - .177 cal., CO_2, semi-auto, SA and DA, eight-shot cylinder magazine, 393 FPS, post front/adj. rear sight, trigger safety, grip safety, 5 in. rifled barrel, standard black finish with checkered black plastic grips, 2.38 lbs. Disc. 2003.

	$225	$165	$125	$100	$75	N/A	N/A

Last MSR was $279.

Add $20 for nickel plated finish.

TROPHY MATCH - .177 cal., CO_2, semi-auto, SA and DA, eight-shot cylinder magazine, 393 FPS, post front/adj.

---

8. **Image** - Next in this long line of information may (but not always) follow an image with credit of the model. A picture truly can say a thousand words.

9. **Price/Value line** - This information will either follow directly below the model name and description or, if there is an image, below the image. The information appears in descending order from left to right with the values corresponding to a condition factor shown in the Grading Line near the top of the page. 100% price on a currently manufactured airgun also assumes not previously sold at retail. In a many cases, N/As (Not Applicable) are listed and indicate that the condition is not frequently encountered so the value is not predictable. On a currently manufactured airgun, the lower condition specimens will bottom out at a value, and a lesser condition airgun value will approximate the lowest value listed. An MSR automatically indicates the airgun is currently manufactured, and the MSR (Manufacturer's Suggested Retail) is shown left of the 100% column. Recently manufactured 100% specimens without boxes, warranties, etc., that are currently manufactured must be discounted slightly (5%-20%, depending on the desirability of make and model). On vintage airguns, you may see N/As in the 100%-90% condition categories, as these original older guns are rarely encounter in 90%+ condition, and cannot be accurately priced. Higher condition factors may still exist, but if the only known sales have been of examples in 90% condition, a very desirable/collectible airgun may double or triple in value in the next higher condition range, so the value is not predictable. A currently manufactured airgun without a retail price published by the manufacturer/importer will appear as MSR N/A.

10 —

GRADING	100%	95%	90%	80%	60%	40%	20%

4 — **RIFLES: MODIFIED REAR/UNDER LEVER COCKING**

5 — See also Lincoln in the "L" section of this book for the Lincoln underlever rifles from which BSA underlever air rifles were developed.

6 — Subtract 20% for specimens equipped with gas-spring unit (sometimes inappropriately called "gas ram" or "gas strut"). Such modification makes the gun non-original, voids the manufacturer's warranty and may cause cumulative injury to gun. Length measurements may vary by about 0.25 in. or so within models.

7 — **AIRSPORTER** - .177, .22, or .25 cal., UL, SP, SS, 1020/800/550 FPS, tap loader, tapered breech plug, blued finish, 8 lbs.

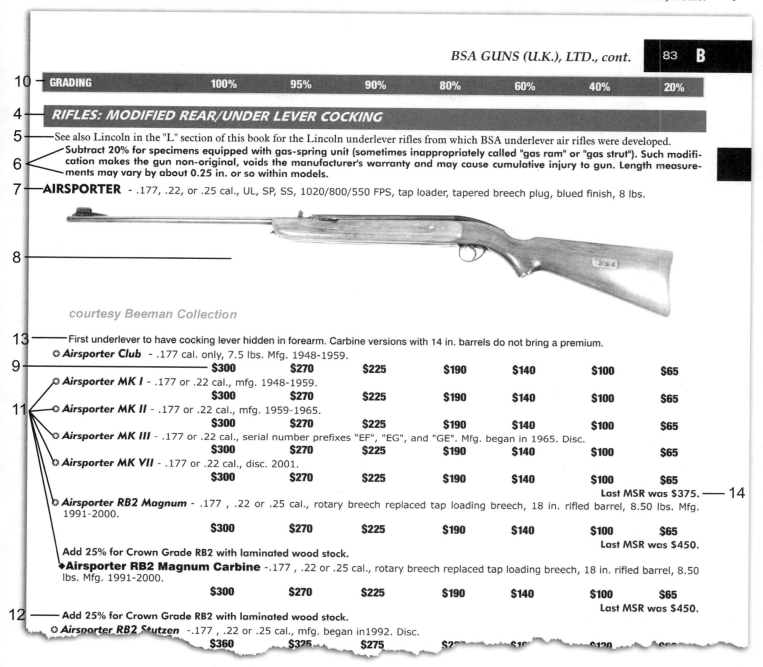

8 —

courtesy Beeman Collection

13 — First underlever to have cocking lever hidden in forearm. Carbine versions with 14 in. barrels do not bring a premium.

⊙ *Airsporter Club* - .177 cal. only, 7.5 lbs. Mfg. 1948-1959.

9 —

	$300	$270	$225	$190	$140	$100	$65

⊙ *Airsporter MK I* - .177 or .22 cal., mfg. 1948-1959.

	$300	$270	$225	$190	$140	$100	$65

11 — ⊙ *Airsporter MK II* - .177 or .22 cal., mfg. 1959-1965.

	$300	$270	$225	$190	$140	$100	$65

⊙ *Airsporter MK III* - .177 or .22 cal., serial number prefixes "EF", "EG", and "GE". Mfg. began in 1965. Disc.

	$300	$270	$225	$190	$140	$100	$65

⊙ *Airsporter MK VII* - .177 or .22 cal., disc. 2001.

	$300	$270	$225	$190	$140	$100	$65

Last MSR was $375. — 14

⊙ *Airsporter RB2 Magnum* - .177 , .22 or .25 cal., rotary breech replaced tap loading breech, 18 in. rifled barrel, 8.50 lbs. Mfg. 1991-2000.

	$300	$270	$225	$190	$140	$100	$65

Last MSR was $450.

Add 25% for Crown Grade RB2 with laminated wood stock.

♦**Airsporter RB2 Magnum Carbine** -.177 , .22 or .25 cal., rotary breech replaced tap loading breech, 18 in. rifled barrel, 8.50 lbs. Mfg. 1991-2000.

	$300	$270	$225	$190	$140	$100	$65

Last MSR was $450.

12 — **Add 25% for Crown Grade RB2 with laminated wood stock.**

⊙ *Airsporter RB2 Stutzen* -.177 , .22 or .25 cal., mfg. began in1992. Disc.

	$360	$325	$275	$2~~	$1~~	$120	$6~~

10. Grading Line - Grading lines will normally appear at or near the top of each page.

11. Sub-model and Sub-Sub-mode Name - Variations within a model appear as sub-models, or sub-sub-models, they are differentiated from model names because they are preceded by a bullet, indented, and are in upper and lower case type, and are usually followed by a short description of that sub-model. These sub-model descriptions have the same typeface as the model descriptions.

12. Model Price/Value Adjustments - Extra cost features/special value orders and other value added/subtracted features are placed directly under individual price lines or in some cases, category names. These individual lines appear bolder than other descriptive typeface. On many guns less than 15 years old, these add/subtract items will be the last factory MSRs (manufacturer's suggested retail price) for that option.

13. Model Note - Manufacturer and other notes/information appear in smaller type, and should be read since they contain both important and other critical, up-to-date information.

14. On many discontinued models/variations, a line may appear under the price line, indicating the last manufacturer's suggested retail price (MSR) or vintage era retail price (RP) flush right on the page.

FOREWORD - THE HISTORY

Wulf Pflaumer (l), President & CEO of Umarex, Monika Bräutigam, Assistant to the President, and S.P. Fjestad at the recent SHOT Show in Las Vegas.

A PREMATURE INFANT IS BORN

One of the best parts of my job is watching a project like this as it slowly grows up from infancy, and feeling proud once it crawls, then talks, and finally moves freely empowered by the strength of its own legs. The tiny infant in this case was a 5-page airgun section which had little announcement or fanfare when it was unceremoniously dumped into the back of the 4th Edition *Blue Book of Gun Values* in 1983. Why include such a small, seemingly unimportant section?

Looking back, it was like a premature baby fighting to stay alive. It received no accolades or special nourishment, and I'm sure most readers never even noticed it hiding in the back of a firearms book. Realizing the opportunity I had with the gun book, which was sparked by my early interest in BB guns while growing up on a small Midwestern dairy farm, airguns helped develop my shooting skills more than anything else. Airguns simply deserved a section in the book - they meant too much to me to be left out.

NURTURING THE BABY

Slowly but surely the section grew up within the protective custody of the *Blue Book of Gun Values*. Patrick Lucking took over the section in 1990, and during his watch, it put on some much needed weight and reached a whopping 33 pages before Dennis Adler took over as airgun editor in 1998. This growing section remained in relative obscurity, so we decided it had enough critical mass to break out of the gun book and become a separate title with some additional help.

THE CHILD LEAVES THE CRIB

The 1st Edition of the *Blue Book of Airguns* was published during 2001, with Dennis Adler as the author, and Dr. Robert Beeman and myself as co-editors. The retail price on this 160 page 6x9 in. book was $9.95, and nobody told us it was overpriced. The cover featured a Beretta 92 FS air pistol, Jeanne Adler's Daisy "A Christmas Story" Red Ryder BB gun, and my Feinwerkbau Model 300 Running Boar that I paid almost $900 for in the late 1980s. More importantly, Dr. Robert Beeman, the undisputed godfather of the airgun industry, had agreed to become the co-editor. Beeman had (and still has) the largest airgun collection in the world, and what better way to get source information? A dream team of sorts had been put together, and maybe the best part of the

1st Edition was the editorial, which consisted of important articles by Tom Gaylord, Dennis Adler, and Dr. Beeman.

THE 'TWEEN MAKES 2ND GRADE

The 2nd Edition was written by John Allen & Dr. Beeman, and edited by myself, as Dennis Adler was too busy attending to his automotive titles. The 3rd Edition, featuring a new 8 ½ x 11 format and published in 2003, remains my favorite cover, and the two hardcover deluxe editions may never be equaled for coolness. Another major breakthrough was that it included hundreds of images from the fabled Beeman collection. This publication had now come of age and simply could not be ignored any longer by airgun enthusiasts. We were rapidly filling the void of information that was sorely needed. There simply wasn't another single airgun title as informative on currently manufactured and vintage airguns.

The 4th Edition, published in 2004, expanded the successful formula used in the 3rd Edition, with many more sections and images being added. Expanded to 384 pages, Dr. Beeman and John Allen continued to work as a team with Allen now specializing on currently/recently manufactured airguns, while Dr. Beeman focused on vintage airguns and company histories. Fortunately, Beeman is also a great photographer, and we have been lucky enough to use many images of the airguns in his extensive collection. Tom Gaylord, one of the airgun industry's most gifted writers, continued his "Airgun Powerplants" series and provided another "Gaylord Reports" summarizing all the most recent products, innovations, and trends available to airgunners.

A HEALTHY ADOLESCENT EMERGES

The 5th Edition, published in 2005, grew faster than a major league baseball player on steroids, reaching 440 pages. The biggest indicator of any book, regardless of how good you think it is, is determined by how well it sells. And the 472 page 6th Edition published last year was originally scheduled to last for 2 years. Instead, it sold out in half the time, which explains why you have this new 7th Edition in your hands now instead of next year. Our refined and improved formula has remained the same, but this edition broke the 500 page landmark, and remains the best single publication available on airguns.

In closing, I would like to thank everyone for supporting this project, even when it was a 5- page section. Make sure you don't miss the latest article by Tom Gaylord on "Benjamin's Discovery" and my old friend Jim Carmichel's serious account of pigeon shooting in Tennessee. Once again, we look forward to providing you with the best airgun information you can get in years ahead.

Sincerely,

S.P. Fjestad
Editor & Publisher
Blue Book Publications, Inc.

PS - Older editions are now collectible for their information and articles, which aren't available anywhere else. Please visit www.bluebook-inc.com for more information, availability and pricing, including an online subscription or downloads to the entire airgun database, including color images. *And get a third edition hardcover if you can find one!*

Co-author John Allen, researching another "you got a what?" question. Big questions deserve a big library, and thankfully, the Blue Book Publications, Inc. reference library is one of the largest in the world for guns, airguns, and guitars.

First, a big THANK YOU to all you readers that purchased a Sixth Edition at a pace that made a two-year print run sell out in one year making this new edition necessary. Looking back to mid-December, the thought of a completely new Seventh Edition *Blue Book of Airguns* seemed almost impossible. Now here we are in early March (after ten days in mid-January spent on the road to Las Vegas, NV for the Thirtieth SHOT Show) finalizing the last few pages for the printer. 2008 is presenting more new airguns designs and new airgun products than ever before, and it is no wonder this has become one of the fastest growing industries in the great outdoors and indoor arenas.

How can all this information be assembled into one book is a common question by readers, and the answer is on page 4 with a list of our great contributing editors. In fact, for this edition we have more contributing editors than ever before. These people deserve the most thanks because without them this book would still be in its infant stages. Most contributing editors work in this industry in one form or another, and everyone fills an important part of this book with information. Contributing editors come from many different backgrounds including Product, Sales, and Marketing managers for the major airgun manufacturers as well as dealers and collectors of many different airguns.

Probably the biggest news this year came out of Crosman/Benjamin with the introduction of their new Dual Fuel (CO₂ or Compressed Air) Air Rifle called the Discovery. Do not miss Tom Gaylord's editorial on this. Other news includes that Webley & Scott, LTD. is back and being imported and distributed exclusively by Legacy Sports International. They have six new models of air rifles and one new air pistol. Airguns of Arizona/Precision Airgun Distribution has hit the street running, importing and distributing BSA, Daystate, FX Airguns, Rohm Twinmaster, and Parker Hale. Gamo has been very busy also introducing six new models including their new Whisper VH that looks like more fun than any grown man

should ever have. Unless of course, you are thinking about the new Baikal MP-661K Drozd Blackbird, a CO₂ and battery powered rifle with electronic trigger and select fire. Anschütz introduced their new S2 version PCP target rifles. The S2 has improved airflow characteristics and needs about 50% less impact energy to open the valve when firing the shot. Thus, the air rifle barreled action is subjected to almost no vibrations. This only scratches the surface of the great many new airguns that will hit the market in 2008.

Other new features of the Seventh Edition include that over two hundred new detailed images have been added. A completely revised Photo Grading System has also been added with descriptions that should help the reader understand condition rather than simply showing examples that they look like. The percentage of original finish on an airgun (its condition) can be measured, but once the science of how to look at airgun condition is understood, the actual measuring part will become easier. "How to Use This Book" is in a new format that should also be easier for the user/reader to digest and understand how the *Blue Book of Airguns* works. Both the Glossary and Abbreviations sections are expanded to include more information that is also needed to properly use this book. Last, but by far not the least, is the part of the book that everybody pays the money for and works the pages to a frazzle looking through. The A-Z sections of the Seventh Edition have grown by another thirty-four pages over the Sixth Edition.

When finally finishing a project like this, it is not hard to be proud of all the hard work performed by everyone involved. This includes people working at the front lines in the office, on the phones, proofing, and at the shows: Beth, Cassandra, Katie, Kelsey, and Sara. John is our programmer who created and maintains our data input tool and with a few key strokes he can output the data in a number of different formats (book, CD-ROM, online subscriptions, etc.). Clint, is our production manager/art director that takes the data and makes it look like anything we want it to be. S.P., the Editor and Publisher, who pioneered an airgun database with prices in 1983, is the whip when needed, pushes us content providers when we need pushing, pulls up the loose ends when they need pulling, and makes everything happen on time (if we're on time) so we can move on to the next project. There are also a couple people behind the scenes (Tom and Zach) that provide support to this machine (this team) in so many ways that can not be counted. A really large thank you goes out to all.

As always, this project is a Work-in-Progress and as such will never be a perfect manuscript. We want to hear from you with any corrections or additions needed to make this a better title. After all with out you this project would not be as successful as it is. Thank you!

John B. Allen
Co-author – *Blue Book of Airguns*

WELCOME TO THE SEVENTH EDITION!

Dr. Robert D. Beeman, Co-author, *Blue Book of Airguns*

It was a delightful surprise when S.P. Fjestad, the head honcho and publisher at Blue Book Publications, notified me that the Sixth Edition *Blue Book of Airguns*, despite a larger printing run, had sold out a year ahead of its expected life, meaning a new edition would be needed only a year after its publication, rather than the expected span of two years! This apparently is due, not only to ever more universal use of the *Blue Book of Airguns* in the USA, but to a rapidly increasing dependence on this reference all over the world. The world's airgun collectors, dealers, and airgunners plus gun writers and editors from the big prestigious gun journals such as *VISIER* and *DWJ* in Germany, *Airgun World* and *Airgunner* in the UK, and *American Rifleman* in the USA, to smaller gun publications from the Americas to India to Australia and back to Scandinavia have begun to notice that despite much increased coverage of USA airguns, this book had grown in scope to the point where it now covers even more foreign models than domestic.

Unlike a blue book of used cars which covers every model of the last few years (which is as interesting as last year's phone book when a new edition comes out), the *Blue Book of Airguns* is noted for its historical articles, depth of model identifications, illustrations, specifications, as well as maker history. It is directed to those who want information as well as those who simply need lists of values! And while it covers models back a century or more and, unlike a Blue Book of used cars, it adds more old models with every edition. It is gratifying to learn that many airgun fans and collectors strive to obtain complete series of the *Blue Book of Airguns*. Airgun literature specialists, such as Doug Law, find more persons willing to pay well over the original cover price for older editions – up to $100 dollars or more!

This is a critical period in the roughly six centuries of airgun development. Not only are there more exciting technical developments than ever, but public awareness of airguns, both pro and con, is increasing at an amazing rate. Airgunners need to be more aware of what is happening, not just technical developments, but perhaps even more critical are political developments. The United Kingdom, long a leader in the area of adult airguns, has governmental forces that increasingly seek to unreasonably regulate, even eliminate, many or all airguns. The UK's Justice Secretary Kenny MacAskill, has called "to clamp down on the sale of weapons such as airguns." He lists gun control campaigners first among those to be involved – there is a virtually complete lack of input invited from airgunners! He stresses that "firearm casualties rose 25% last year" and that "cases of attempted murder involving firearms are almost three times that of a decade ago." Note the lack of distinction between firearms and airguns! Airgunners have an obligation to educate their legislators.

American and other airgunners should take serious note of the above! Some such legislative attention is caused by the airgunners themselves by referring to airguns via the jargon of firearms. British airgunners often harmfully refer to airguns as "weapons." American airgunners also cast a negative light on their guns by such terminology, and even more with the use of silencers, which are of very doubtful legal status and almost universally seen as sinister by the general public and legislators. Careless and inconsiderate use of airguns hurts airgunners the world around!

We have submitted literally hundreds of updates, corrections, and additions to this Seventh Edition, but this represents only a fraction of the international airgun research carried on by Mrs. Beeman and myself. Much of that work is reported on our website: www.beemans.net. This includes information on airgun collecting and selection, care and feeding, legal problems, hunting, ballistics, inside stories, and what is perhaps the biggest airgun news EVER – the probable identification of the .46 caliber repeating "assault" air rifle carried on the Lewis and Clark Expedition of 1803-06! In addition to being so interesting on its own, this matter gives the airgun field a huge credibility boost.

Finally, if you find an error in these Blue Books, or have additional information, it is UP TO YOU to let us know for the good of all future readers! There are only two of us, we can't read every detail of every gun publication and it would be incredibly inefficient to extract bits of solid information from forums, etc. Please send your positive inputs on current models to John Allen at guns@bluebookinc.com at the Blue Book Publication offices in Minnesota. Inputs on older models should be sent directly to me in California at BlueBookEdit@Beemans.net.

Robert D. Beeman
Co-author – *Blue Book of Airguns*

Benjamin's Discovery

This innovative new rifle from an old American airgun maker will have the airgunning world standing at attention!

by Tom Gaylord

What you are about to discover isn't just a new airgun from Benjamin. There are plenty of those. This report is about an entirely new type of airgun that could only have been developed in the United States. In fact, I believe it could only have been developed by the Crosman Corporation, owners of Benjamin Sheridan, because they had the ideal starting point, the will to succeed, and a management team dedicated to developing new products.

In October 2006, I attended a writer's conference hosted by Crosman for the American airgun press. They brought us to the factory in East Bloomfield and shared their vision of the products they would roll out in the coming year. What surprised me was the corporate willingness and desire to innovate. They were actually talking airguns there in northern New York. What a sharp contrast to other manufacturers who have little or no idea of how to use their products or, indeed, of who their customers actually are. If you ask them, they'll say Wal-Mart and Dick's Sporting Goods. Those companies are not customers of anything. They are in the supply chain, but modern business has taken the view that if Wal-Mart says they want something a certain way, why they must have it! Just ask Remington, who had to buy back a huge unsold inventory, how sound that idea is.

CROSMAN IS DIFFERENT

Crosman is aware of the real customers-the actual shooters who will buy their guns. Sure, they sell to the big box stores, too, but they haven't lost sight of the real reason they're in business, which is not to pump pallets of SKUs out the back door regardless of what they are. Those products have to come to rest in owners' hands or the whole thing falls apart.

I saw this attitude at the writer's conference, which lead me to propose an entirely new precharged pneumatic (PCP) of novel design. To my delight, they were already discussing PCPs for their future and were eager to listen.

A DIFFERENT DRUMMER

The normal entry into PCPs is to get an outside manufacturer to produce something the company can put their name on. It's quick off the line, but it leaves the company lacking technical expertise. What I proposed was an in-house development.

Fundamental to my proposal were these key points about the rifle:

- Developed on an existing CO_2 platform.
- Operate on 1,800 psi of air instead of 3,000 psi.
- Get at least 25 good shots per fill.
- Achieve at least 710-730 f.p.s. in .22 caliber.

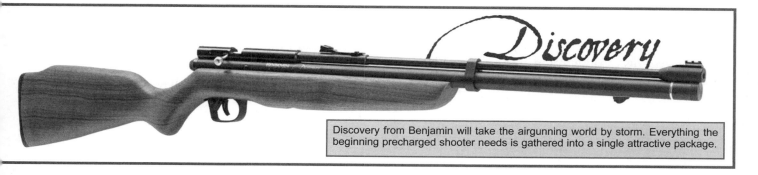

Discovery

Discovery from Benjamin will take the airgunning world by storm. Everything the beginning precharged shooter needs is gathered into a single attractive package.

- Sold in a package with a hand pump and pellets. There should be nothing more to buy.
- Have a steel receiver with a long 11mm scope rail.
- Price for the entire package (gun, pump and pellets) would be affordably low.

Crosman invited me to present my proposal. They took time to consider what I had said, and to my delight, several weeks later they agreed to proceed.

I went to East Bloomfield in February 2007 for what I thought was a round of discussions. I took a proof of concept mockup of the new rifle, based on the Benjamin AS392T CO_2 rifle. It was a simplistic model that used an external scuba tank to power the rifle for demonstrations. I estimated velocity with the .22-caliber Crosman Premier pellet at 710-730 f.p.s. with the rifle's standard valve running on 1,200 psi air. This wasn't the new rifle-it was just a means to demonstrate my ideas for lower air pressure and the use of an existing gun.

I was all set to walk Crosman engineers through the operation of that rifle, when their lead engineer, Ed Schultz, trumped me with two 2260 rifles he had already converted to air! When he brought those rifles into conference room, my first look told me Crosman had gotten it right.

Schultz had upped the proposed air pressure from 1,800 psi to 2,000 psi and modified a valve to handle it. He admitted surprise when his testing revealed the prototypes had shot more pellets than expected before needing to be refilled. The velocity of the .177 model was bumping the magic velocity of 1,000 f.p.s., making this the fastest gas gun Crosman and Benjamin had ever made.

With the .22-caliber rifle he was getting velocities of almost 800 f.p.s. Clearly, he had surpassed my proposal and had entered the realm of world-class PCPs. But that wasn't the last or even the biggest of his surprises.

DUAL FUEL

Schultz had also tried both rifles with bulk CO_2 gas and discovered that they worked perfectly! He coined the term "dual fuel" for this capability, and I knew instinctively that Crosman had just created the Rosetta Stone of airguns—a universal gateway rifle to bring the masses to airgunning!

Thousands of shooters use CO_2 in their airguns but refuse to try high-pressure air for many reasons. They don't want

With open sights or a scope, the Discovery has everything you need in an affordable PCP.

the expense of a scuba tank. They say that a hand pump is too difficult to use. Many are afraid of things they've heard or think they've heard about the danger of air at high pressure. They saw the movie "Jaws" and they remember the shark blowing up with the scuba tank in its mouth.

But, the Benjamin Discovery is also a CO_2 rifle! Not only that, it's the most powerful CO_2 rifle in the Crosman and Benjamin Sheridan lineup. CO_2 followers can buy the rifle and fill it from standard paintball bulk tanks by means of an inexpensive, optional adapter. Then, someday, when they're either bored or feeling especially brave, they can drain the CO_2 and fill the rifle with air, using the hand pump that comes with it. They'll be delighted to learn that high-pressure air offers even greater velocity than CO_2 and still gets a fair number of shots per fill. Not the 100 plus of CO_2, but about 35 good shots, which equates to more than one shot per pump stroke!

Eventually, they'll realize that 2,000 psi is not so different than the 900 psi of CO_2, plus the thinner air flows through the valve much faster than CO_2. That's where the extra power comes from. Crosman simply keeps the valve open longer, so the relatively lower-pressure air can act on the pellet for a longer time.

HAND PUMP

The hand pump was essential to my concept because it eliminated the complaints of needing a scuba tank and a dive shop. Because the new rifle needs only 2,000 psi of air instead of 3,000, pumping is now possible for people who formerly could not handle it. A modern high-pressure hand pump is fairly easy to operate until the pressure passes 1,500 psi. At that point, the effort required for each pump stroke starts increasing. Up to 2,000 psi the additional effort is still light

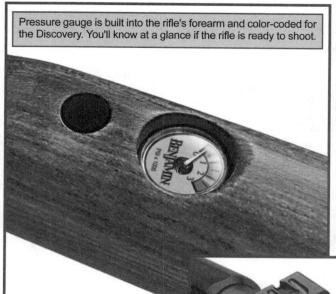

Pressure gauge is built into the rifle's forearm and color-coded for the Discovery. You'll know at a glance if the rifle is ready to shoot.

Front sight is a raised ramp with a fiber optic bead.

The pump that comes with the rifle is a full-fledged PCP pump. Pump gauge is color-coded for the pressures of the Discovery.

Williams supplied both front and rear fiber optic sights. Rifle also has a 9-inch, 11mm scope rail.

enough that a healthy teen boy or girl can operate it. Above 2,000 psi, the effort required increases rapidly, until you reach 2,500 psi, when it becomes noticeably difficult. There's another step-up in effort around 2,700 psi that holds all the way to 3,000. The Discovery does away with all of that, giving the world the first sporting PCP that's easy to pump.

Crosman will also offer their own version of a high-pressure air tank for shooters who don't want to fuss with the pump at all. Those who already use scuba tanks for other PCPs will discover that they get far more fills at 2,000 psi than they do at 3,000.

ADDITIONAL FEATURES

That initial gun was already incredible, but Crosman wasn't finished with it. They added an onboard manometer (air pressure gauge) forward of the triggerguard, so the shooter would know the status of pressure in the reservoir. With CO_2, the pressure doesn't matter (CO_2 pressure changes with the temperature); with air, it's vital to know the amount of pressure remaining. There are PCPs costing twice what the Discovery costs that do not have manometers, so this is a big deal.

To keep dirt out of the reservoir, they installed a fine particle filter behind the inlet nipple. Dirt is the enemy of seals in pneumatic and gas guns, yet only about half the upscale makers install filters to keep it out.

I wanted open sights on the gun because I wanted it to be

shootable right out of the box, but Crosman went beyond that. They installed Williams fiber optic sights front and rear.

The dual fuel capability meant the rifle had to be emptied of one type of gas before the other was introduced. Also, I was concerned that new users might overfill their guns in hopes of getting more power, when it would actually lock up the valve. There had to be a way to get the air or CO_2 out, so Crosman engineers designed a unique tool that enters the breech and depresses the valve stem, dumping the contents of the reservoir. This is the first time I've seen such a tool, though all PCPs need it sooner or later.

Finally, Crosman went the extra ten yards and stocked the Discovery with real walnut! That's right—a PCP that already costs less than any PCP ever sold and comes with its own hand pump, is stocked in walnut and has more features than most $700 European wunderboomers.

BUT HOW DOES IT SHOOT?

That was the question on everyone's mind. We expected the accuracy to be similar to that of a 2260-the rifle that had served as the prototype and starting point. But, the 2260 has never been used at long range because it's powered by CO_2.

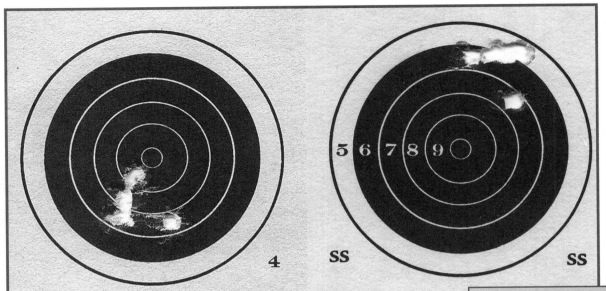

Target on the left took five .22-caliber JSB Exacts at 50 yards-0.374 inches. On the right, five .177 Crosman Premiers went into this 0.458-inch group.

Out to 35 yards, it's a fine rifle, but what would it do at 50? No one knew until I took it to the range and found out.

The first outing was in my backyard at just 21 yards, to get sighted in and to know what to expect. I expected small groups at such short range, but I wasn't prepared for what I got. The Discovery wasn't just accurate, it was a tack-driver! If only that would hold out to at least 35 yards, we'd have a great little starter PCP.

The next test was at a rifle range. First, I checked zero on the 25-yard range. The groups were just as small as at 21 yards, with several coming in smaller! The best group from the .177 rifle was five JSB Exacts that measured just 0.234 inches.

I was switching the one Leapers 8-32x56mm scope between the two rifles at the range, but sight-in was never a problem. The Discovery has no bad habits as far as scope-mounting goes.

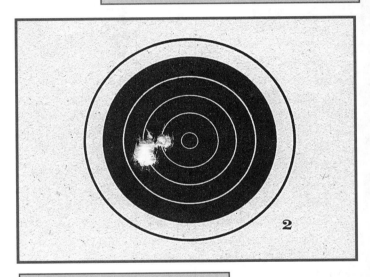

Five .177 JSB Exacts passed through this hole measuring 0.234 inches at 25 yards.

THE ACID TEST-50 YARDS

This is where a rifle will fall apart if it's going to. Was there any reason to believe that an American-made PCP selling for so very little could hope to pull it off? Well, frankly, no. However, someone forgot to tell both rifles. They shot numerous groups, the largest coming in at around one inch, but several were a half-inch or smaller. And, the .22 shot the best group of the session, a blistering 0.384-inch five-shot group of JSBs. The .177 was close behind with 0.486 inches for five Crosman Premier heavies.

WORLD-CLASS

The Benjamin Discovery is a world-class PCP. It may not have all the refinements of an $800 European rifle, but it will shoot just as well and you can buy it with a hand pump for less than half that price. I predict this rifle will open the gate for firearms shooters to take up airgunning.

Great Jonesboro Pigeon Shoot

by Jim Carmichel
Shooting Editor for *Outdoor Life*.
Reprinted from *The Compleat Just Jim*,
by Jim Carmichel

The whole thing got started when Bob Jenkin's second oldest daughter was accused of shoplifting a brassiere at Maude and Mabel's Discount Variety Store. Bob (whose full name is Robert E. Lee Jenkins), like most folks who live on the lower end of the county, took his daughter's troubles to Fry (for Friedman L.) Bacon, a lawyer of some local repute. Fry Bacon is one of the last of that dwindling species of attorneys once admitted to the Bar after a period of having "read law," but with no other formal training. This shortcoming has been of no noticeable difficulty to Fry Bacon who describes himself as a "champion of poor people's causes" and, in return for legal services, has been known to take in chickens, coon hounds and enough odd parcels of land to make him the county's biggest property owner.

Not one to let textbook law interfere with a good courtroom battle, Fry Bacon's favorite tactic is to open his Bible to some random page, wave it in the faces of judge and jury, shout that there is no higher law than the law of God, then have the jury get down on its collective knees while he leads a prayer for his dear misguided client who, he claims, has just recently been washed in the blood of the lamb and aims to spend the rest of his life doing kind deeds and "helping out wider wimmin."

Fry Bacon was just the man to represent Robert E. Lee Jenkin's daughter.

In Fry Bacon's opinion, the theft of a brassiere was truly a delicate subject and hardly one to be discussed before a mixed courtroom audience. The word brassiere was abhorrent to him under such circumstances, and so was the diminutive form "bra." Thus he substituted the phrase "set of briars," thumping his clinched fists to his chest, whenever necessary, to indicate their approximate purpose and his own apparent meaning.

The case did not go well for Fry Bacon. His assertion that the poor girl was feeble minded did not produce the desired effect, nor did his pleas that the lass was "with child" by a stranger last seen two years before. Seeing no hope in this line of defense, he turned to attacking the two eyewitnesses as "godless sinners," and

"short-skirted harlots" and was just warming to this line of reasoning when it happened.

Six tons of pigeon manure came cascading through the courtroom ceiling. It covered the jury, it covered the godless harlots, it covered His Honor the judge and it covered Fry Bacon. It covered them with six tons of dry, dusty, choking pigeon droppings that had been accumulating in the courthouse attic for decades, straining the ceiling rafters and needing only the shock wave of Fry Bacon's rhetoric to set it free.

"Ladies and gentlemen of the jury," Fry Bacon is reputed to have said when the dust cleared somewhat, "Behold the wrath of The Lord …"

The case was dismissed and the courthouse closed for six weeks because, as one Jonesboro wag put it, "The wheels of justice can't turn in that stuff."

The episode was not without some warning. About fifteen years earlier Bill Bowman, a leading Jonesboro humanitarian, had noted that the pigeons had so gummed up the courthouse clockworks that each hour was lasting about eighty minutes. The matter had been brought up at the City Council meeting where Virgil Meeks noted that the additional time was probably a good thing and the clock should not be tampered with. The Council agreed with his logic and voted eleven to one to leave the clock alone. The one dissenting vote came from Pearlie Goode, the church organist, who complained that the clock's once silvery chimes were sounding more like a pig sloshing through a mud hole.

But now with the collapse of the courtroom ceiling, something clearly had to be done. The first order of business was how to clear out the existing mess and that in itself brought about a political scandal which almost brought down the county government. The lowest bid to haul away the pigeon manure ran into some thousands of dollars, enough to cause a county-wide financial crisis. At the last minute Mort Screeb, who owns a tomato farm down by the Chucky River, stepped in and said that the stuff was great tomato fertilizer and that he would haul it off for nothing. His one condition, however, was that he be allowed to take it as he needed it, which, further questioning disclosed, might cover a period of three or four years.

In the end a clean-up crew was hired to carry it off but the ensuing political fight, with Screeb screaming kickback, produced a shakeup in Washington County politics which continues even to this day. Area newspapers called it the Pigeon Krap Kickback Kaper with the courthouse insiders becoming known as the Kounty Krap Klan. The local chapter of the KKK objected to this and threatened to burn a cross on a reporter's lawn until they discovered he lived in an apartment owned by the regional Grand Wizard.

Despite all the uproar, a few cool heads noted that nothing was being done about the pigeons. They were as happy as ever, perching on the belfry railing, roosting in the clockworks, building more nests, hatching babies and contributing hourly to another avalanche.

The first step in correcting the pigeon problem was to hire professional exterminators. They rigged a cannon-like affair which made a burping noise - guaranteed to frighten pigeons and starlings and other such winged creatures. The Jonesboro pigeons loved it. It would burp and they would coo and in winter they warmed their feet on its outstretched muzzle. Obviously, stronger measures were called for. That's when I arrived on the scene.

Living in Jonesboro is not quite like living anywhere else on earth. It's a beautiful little town nestled in the wooded valleys of East Tennessee. It was home to a scrappy young lawyer by the name of Andy Jackson and now, after two hundred years of existence, is one of the best preserved towns of its kind to be found anywhere. No power or telephone lines ensnare its streets, no parking meters clutter its curbs, and old-fashioned street lamps cast a warm glow on brick-paved sidewalks.

In the town square is the county courthouse where swell Jonesboro's pigeons. Even though it was completed in 1912 it is still called the "new" courthouse by most of Jonesboro's citizens who will remember the "old" courthouse, and probably even the one before that. Two Jonesboro dowagers have not spoken for thirty years because each believes she is the original Scarlett O'Hara and the other an imposter. Another is convinced she is Alice in Wonderland and at any given time can produce at least twenty corroborating witnesses to that effect.

Stray dogs, camels and pack mules eventually find their way home, and it is no different with wandering Jonesboroites. After several years of living in the far west and exploring lands far beyond, I returned to Jonesboro to spend my declining years near the poor dirt farm where I grew up.

Citizens of Jonesboro seldom leave town except in a state of acute disgrace, so it was naturally assumed when I left town years before that there must have been a substantial stigma attached to my departure. Of course I was eyed with some suspicion when I reappeared on the village green. But I opened up a downtown office just as bold and brass, looked up old girlfriends, and settled back in place as easily as a pup taking a nap. Whatever crimes or indiscretions that vivid imaginations may have reckoned for my departure were apparently forgotten. Even old Aunt Bessie, who used to slip up behind me and hit me with her cane, now smiled sweetly and said if I would bring her a pumpkin she'd make me a pie. (Not for a million bucks would I eat one of that mean old woman's pies.)

It was a comfortable reunion but, alas, too good to last. When I moved into my second story office directly across from the courthouse and laid eyes on all those grinning pigeons lined up on the balcony, I knew fate had caught up with me.

No one could argue that the courthouse needed to be rid of the pigeons and it was equally clear that the only way to solve the problem was to shoot them. Their clock tower fortress was apparently impregnable to all other forms of attack. But until my arrival no one had possessed both the will and the means of dealing with them, and my second story office window provided the perfect sniper's roost. Destiny surely planned the whole thing.

As discretely as enthusiasm permitted, I passed the word that I wouldn't mind taking a few pot shots at the pests "just to keep my eye in practice." And just as discretely the word came back that it was my "bound civic duty to rid the town of the damnable beasts." Even the sheriff, H.H. Hackmore, who is in charge of courthouse maintenance, stopped by to bestow his blessing on the project.

Second only to the speed of light is the blazing speed of Jonesboro gossip. In no time at all everyone knew that a big game hunter had come to do in the courthouse pigeons. Billy Graham couldn't have caused a bigger stir.

The distance, as measured to the peak of the clock tower, was forty-one yards and the choice of weapons was my old pump-up pellet rifle. I figured this was the only safe equipment for the job even though it might handicap me a bit. I didn't know just how much of a handicap this was to be until I tried adjusting the aperture sight for a forty-one yard dead-on point of impact. The pellets hit everywhere except dead on, with the group sizes ranging upward of ten to twelve inches.

I'd made the mistake of announcing that I would begin knocking off the pigeons on the following Monday morning. I say mistake because when I arrived at work, pellet rifle in hand, a crowd of onlookers had already gathered in the street. It was going to be a memorable day in Jonesboro history, and they wanted to see it happen. There was a smattering of applause as I entered the ancient building and I think I heard Harry Weems, who runs Harry's Men's Shop downstairs, offering to cover all bets.

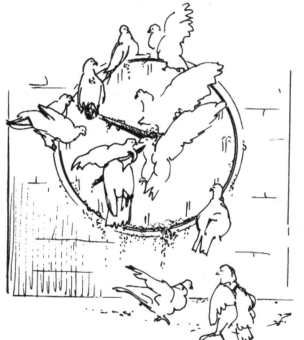

Filling the rifle's air reservoir with ten full strokes of the pump handle, I fed a pellet into the chamber and, taking a rest on the window sill, leveled the sights on a particularly plump pigeon. The crowd below held its breath. PLUFFT went the air rifle. SPLAT went the wayward pellet on an ornate piece of concrete scroll work. COO went the pigeon. I'd missed clean. A chuckle rippled through the throng.

Feverishly I pumped the rifle and fed in another pellet. PLUFFT, SPLAT, COO. The chuckle became a collective guffaw. PLUFFT, SPLAT, COO, again and again I tried. No results. Someone shouted from below, "If them was lions they'd be pickin' their teeth about now." PLUFFT, SPLAT, COO. Even the pigeons joined in the fun, waddling over to the roof's edge for a better view of the sorry spectacle.

By then my audience was drifting off by twos and threes, telling each other it was the biggest disappointment since Jack Hicks' hanging was called off in the Spring of 1904. Harry Weems paid off his losses and my disgrace was complete.

That day I called Dr. Robert Beeman, the country's leading dealer and importer of quality air rifles and accessories, and ordered a German-made Feinwerkbau Model 124 rifle and a supply of special pointed-pellets. The FWB-124 was the hottest thing going on in hunting-type air rifles. It gives a muzzle velocity of better than 800 feet per second - close to a .22 Rimfire Short - and is accurate enough to hit a dime - or a pigeon's head - at 41 yards. "Send it airmail," I told Bob, "I've got to salvage my reputation." Revenge would be mine, I told everyone, describing the fancy new air rifle I'd ordered. But sometimes the airmails fly slowly and it was weeks before the FWB-124 arrived. By then the whole town was laughing about the "wonderful pigeon gun" that existed only in my imagination.

But it did arrive and my first few test shots showed it to be more accurate than I dared hope. Topped off with a ten-power scope and zeroed dead-on at 41 yards, I cut a neat little group about the size of a shirt button.

The next morning a small crowd of onlookers gathered to watch the next chapter in Carmichel's disgrace. Even the pigeons seemed interested and about twenty lined up on the balcony railing to see what was happening. I started on the right end of the row and worked my way to the left.

The first bird toppled off with scarcely a flutter. His neighbor noted his demise with idle curiosity, but no particular concern. When the next two or three went over the edge the others began to get somewhat more curious and COOed at the stricken forms with some amazement. In fact, as more pigeons fell the remainder reacted with increasing perplexity, those on the far left end having to lean far out from their perch, wings aflutter, in order to watch the peculiar behaviors of their brethren.

The first run was fourteen straight kills with Harry collecting bets like mad. The pigeons still hadn't figured out what was going on but apparently they thought it best temporarily to go somewhere else and give it some thought. That day's tally was twenty-seven pigeons and a few stray starlings. Next day would be even better.

But next day disaster arrived in a totally unexpected form. I was brewing a pot of tea and had just killed the first pigeon of the day when "Shorty" Howze, Jonesboro's seven-foot policeman, charged into my office and presented me with a complaint lodged by one of the townspeople. According to the unnamed plaintiff I was "molesting Jonesboro's beloved pigeons."

"Com'on Shorty," I protested, "you've got to be kidding. Everybody wants rid of those pigeons, you told me so yourself. And besides, I have the sheriff's O.K."

"I know," Shorty replied, "The courthouse is county property and you can shoot over there all you want to. But the chief says when you shoot across the street you're violating Jonesboro air space. So the complaint stands."

"Who complained?" I asked.

"I'm not allowed to say."

"I know, but tell me anyway."

"That crazy acting woman that just moved into the old Crookshank's place."

"The one that has all those cats and makes her husband walk the dog at two in the morning?"

"That's the one."

"Thanks for telling me."

"By the way" he said, stopping at the other door and glancing at the air rifle standing by the window, "That's one hell of a pigeon gun."

Except for an occasional guarded shot the rifle stood unused. The pigeons flourished and grew fatter and life in Jonesboro trudged through an uneventful winter. By spring I'd all but forgotten the ill-fated affair. Then a really splashing event occurred that brought the pigeon problem back into brilliant focus. The leading character was not me this time but none other than one Judge Hiram Walpole Justice. It seems that Judge Justice, all decked out in his new tailor-made blue suit, had just handed down an important decision and was on the courthouse lawn discussing it with some reporters when a pigeon swooped down and scored a bullseye on the Judge Justice's jacket. It was seen on live TV by thousands.

The Judge turned on his heel and stalked back into the courthouse muttering something about the futility of "holding court in a damned chickenhouse." That afternoon Judge Justice was in my office learning the finer points of shooting courthouse pigeons with a FWB-124.

Every morning thereafter the Judge would declare a recess at about ten o'clock and rush over to my office to blast a few pigeons, giggling fiendishly every time one plopped on the pavement. His Honor became a very fine marksman.

This had been going on for about two weeks when one morning Shorty, backed up by the mayor and two constables, crashed into my office and waved a warrant at the backside of the judge. "Ah ha," yelled the mayor, "we know what you've been up to, Carmichel. This time we've got you dead to rights."

With his judicially robed backside to the door, the judge was kneeling on the floor, taking a careful aim with the rifle rested on the window sill. So intent was he to his purpose that he didn't even look up, but continued aiming.

"That ain't me," I said, stepping out of the washroom. "That's Judge Justice. And if I was you I wouldn't bother him right now."

All worthy projects must end and by late summer the judge had pretty well wiped out the pigeon population, firing something near fifteen hundred pellets in the process. In all probability the whole thing would have reached a happy conclusion had it not been for one of those freak, clod-dissolving August cloudbursts. The creek overflowed its banks, poured into the streets of Jonesboro and, for the first time in history, flooded the courthouse basement where two-hundred years of moldy Jonesboro records are kept. The devastation to the voting records, in particular, was total. Wiped out.

An official inquiry was launched in order to discover the causes of the unprecedented flooding and the final ruling was that:

"One Jim Carmichel, a citizen of Jonesboro, is known to have shot pigeons on the courthouse roof and thereby stopped up the underground drainpipes and thus contributed to the flooding."

There's a new crop of pigeons living in the clock tower now. I can see them grinning this way…

CORRESPONDENCE/ APPRAISALS/INFORMATION

AIRGUN QUESTIONS/APPRAISALS POLICY

Whether we wanted it or not, Blue Book Publications, Inc. has ended up in the driver's seat as the clearinghouse for information. To ensure that the research department can answer every question with an equal degree of thoroughness, a library, hundreds of both new and old factory brochures, price sheets, and dealer inventory listings are maintained and constantly updated. It's a huge job, and we answer every question like we could go to court on it. We have extended all of the following services to our website at www.bluebookinc.com.

POLICY FOR INQUIRES

For information on your airguns, the charge is $10 per question, payable by a major credit card. Value information will be given within a range only, since in many cases, a condition factor can only be accurately assessed in person. We must have a complete description including manufacturers name, model, serial number, gauge/caliber, and barrel length. All Inquiries will be put in a FIFO system (first in, first out). Make sure you include the proper return email address, return mailing address and phone/fax number.

APPRAISAL INFORMATION

If you wish to have a airgun(s) appraised accurately based on the correct condition factor(s), we must have good quality photos (digital color images are preferred) with a complete description including manufacturers name, model, serial number, gauge/caliber, barrel length (a complete Airguns Appraisal Form must be filled out for each airgun). On some airguns (depending on the trademark and model), a factory letter may be necessary. The accuracy of the appraisal is directly dependent on the quality of your images and the information you provide. Our charge for a written appraisal is $20 per gun up to $1,000 of retail value. Once the appraised retail value for a single airgun reaches $1,000 or more, the charge will be 2% of the appraised value. Please allow 2-3 weeks response time per appraisal request.
The accuracy of the appraisal is directly dependent on the quality of your images and the information you provide.

Digital Photo Specifications:
72 pixel/inch or better
JPEG
Quality: 5-Medium, Baseline Optimized.
RGB
Photos should include an overall shot of each side, special engraving options, proof marks, grips/stock/forearm, etc. Photos may be emailed as attached files to Guns@BlueBookInc.com or mailed to the address at the top of this page.

We hope that you can appreciate this policy regarding airgun questions and/or appraisals. Just as millions of computer users are now paying for reliable and speedy hardware/software support, it is time to take a similar service approach ensuring that the most accurate and up-to-date airgun information is provided to you on a professional and reliable basis.

ADDITIONAL SERVICES

Individuals requesting a photocopy of a particular page or section from any edition of the *Blue Book of Airguns* for insurance or reference purposes will be billed at $5 per page, up to 5 pages, and $3.50 per page thereafter.

ANATOMY OF AN AIRGUN

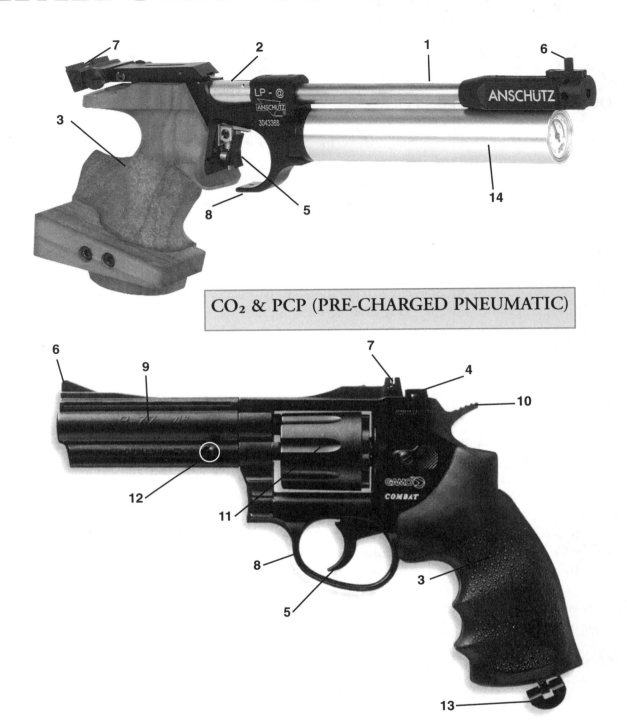

CO₂ & PCP (PRE-CHARGED PNEUMATIC)

1. Barrel	6. Front Sight	11. Cylinder
2. Breech Area	7. Adjustable Rear Sight	12. Cylinder Catch
3. Grip	8. Trigger Guard	13. CO₂ Cylinder Retaining Screw
4. Safety	9. Barrel Housing	14. Compressed Air Cylinder
5. Trigger	10. Hammer	

ANATOMY OF AN AIRGUN

CO_2

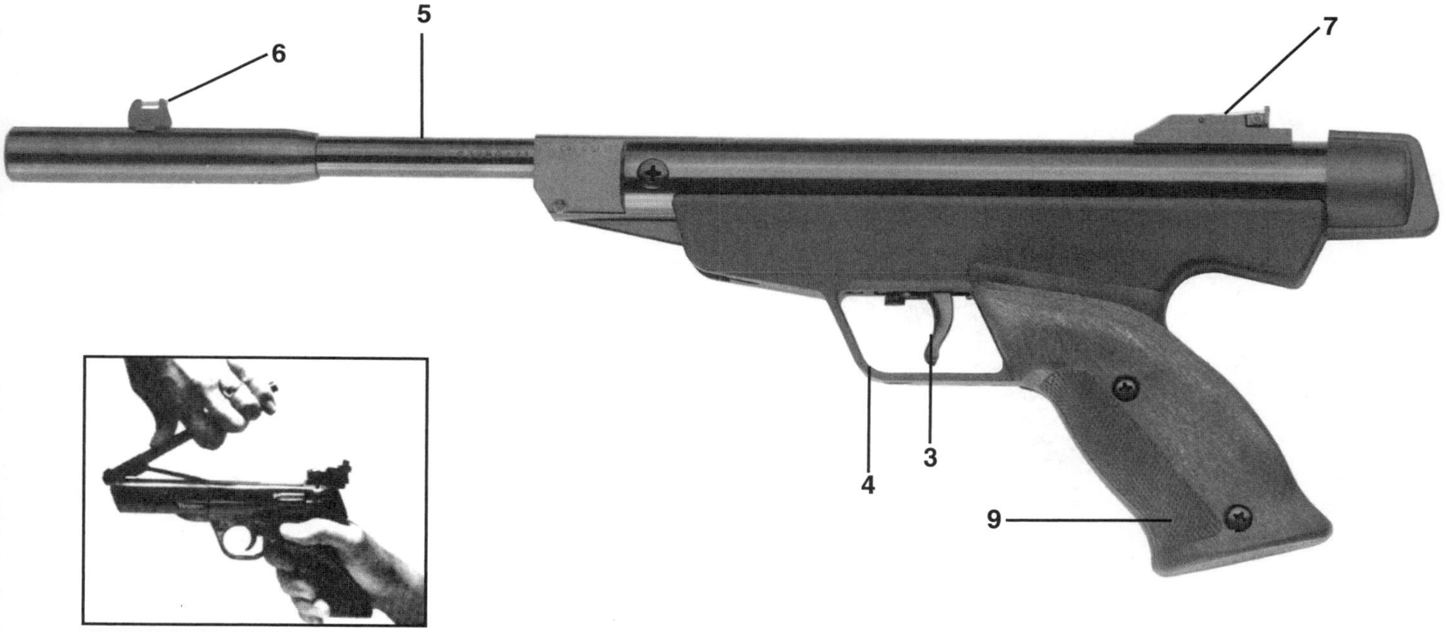

Barrel Cocking

1. Safety
2. CO_2 Cylinder Retaining Screw
3. Trigger
4. Trigger Guard
5. Barrel
6. Front Sight
7. Adjustable Rear Sight
8. Rear Sight
9. Grip
10. Picatinny Rail (for accessories mounting)

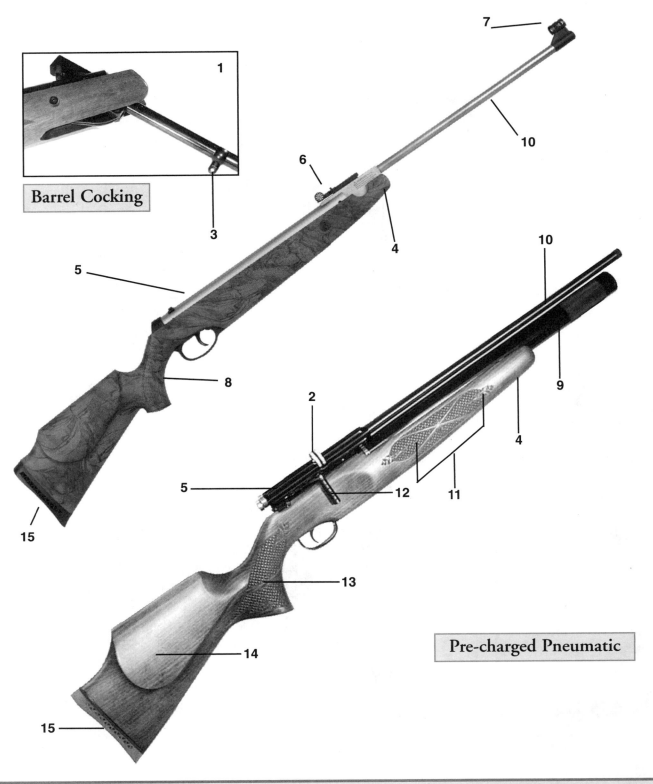

Barrel Cocking

Pre-charged Pneumatic

1. Barrel Cocking (barrel is pulled downward)
2. Rotary Mag
3. Sling Swivel Studs
4. Forend
5. Grooved Receiver
6. Adjustable Rear Sight
7. Globe Front Sight
8. Semi-Pistol Grip
9. Tube Air Reservoirs
10. Barrel
11. Checkered Forearm
12. Bolt Handle
13. Full Pistol Grip
14. Monti Carlo Check Piece
15. Ventilated Recoil Pad

ANATOMY OF AN AIRGUN

Side-Lever Cocking

Under-Lever Cocking

1. Adjustable Buttplate
2. Adjustable Cheekpiece
3. Vertical/Horizontal Scope Adjustments
4. Scope
5. Side-Lever For Cocking (lever is pulled out to the side)
6. Muzzle Weight
7. Stippling
8. Trigger
9. Thumbhole Stock Design
10. Knob for Adjusting Cheekpiece
11. Monte Carlo Cheekpiece
12. Stock Checkering
13. Trigger Guard
14. Safety
15. Grooved Receiver
16. Adj. Rear Sight
17. Front Sight
18. Under-Lever (for cocking)
19. Vent. Recoil Pad.
20. Under-Lever Cocking (under-lever pivots downward)

GLOSSARY

ACTION
The working heart of an airgun; generally all of the working parts other than the stock, barrel, and sights (may or may not include the air compression or gas/air storage system).

AIRGUN
A gun that utilizes compressed air or other gas to launch the projectile.

AIRSOFT
Also called Soft Air, is a different configuration than an airgun in that airsoft shoots round plastic balls of 6mm and 8mm diameter. These balls are called BBs, and are powered by spring-piston, by electrically-driven spring piston (automatic electric gun), by low-pressure gasses like green gas and by CO_2. Many airsoft pistols and rifles are replicas of famous firearm makes and models. Used by competition shooters, including both target shooting and simulated war games, and by collectors.

APERTURE SIGHT
Typically, a front or rear sight assembly consisting of a hole (aperture) located in an adjustable base through which the sights and target are aligned.

BB
"Air Rifle Shot" balls of lead or steel, which are used as projectiles in airguns. Restricted to 0.173 in. to 0.180 in. diameter.

BACK STRAP
The part of the revolver or pistol frame which is exposed at the rear of the grip.

BARREL
The steel tube which a projectile travels through.

BARREL BAND
A metal band, either fixed or adjustable, around the forend of a gun that holds the barrel to the stock.

BARREL COCKING
Also known as "break barrel." The action of pivoting the barrel downward or upward compresses the mainspring of a spring-piston action into firing position.

BARREL SHROUD
An outer metal tube that encloses the true barrel within it. Often used to conceal and protect the tiny tube that is the real barrel in BB guns-the real barrel in such guns may be more correctly known as the "shot tube." The barrel shroud is sometimes incorrectly referred to as the barrel.

BEAVERTAIL FOREND
A wider than average forend.

BLUING
The chemical process of artificial oxidation (rusting) applied to gun parts so that the metal attains a dark blue or nearly black appearance.

BOLT ACTION
The breech closure is: in line with the bore at all times; manually reciprocated to load, unload and cock; and is locked in place by breech bolt lugs engaging abutments usually in the receiver. There are two principle types of bolt actions, i.e., the turn bolt and the straight pull type.

BORE
Internal dimensions of a barrel (smooth or rifled) which can be measured using the metric system (ie. millimeters), English system (i.e. inches), or by the gauge system (see gauge). On a rifled barrel, the bore is measured across the lands. Also, the traditional English term is used when referring to the diameter of a shotgun muzzle ("gauge" in U.S. measure).

BOTTLE-FED
A pre-charged pneumatic airgun with a removable gas/air tank.

BREAK-OPEN
A type of gun action which is cocked by "breaking open" the gun in the mid-line, generally just about over the trigger. In break-open BB guns, this causes internal rods to be pulled back and cock the piston.

BREECH
The opening to the rear chamber portion of the barrel.

BREECH SEAL
A seal which is designed to prevent propulsive gases from leaking out from behind the projectile. Usually an o-ring, circle of leather, or synthetic material. (Called a "barrel washer" in England.)

BULK FILL
CO_2 guns filled from large tanks.

BULL BARREL
A heavier than normal barrel with little or no taper.

BUTT
(Pistols) Bottom part of the grip. (Rifles) Rear of shoulder end of stock, which rests against shooter's shoulder.

BUTTPLATE
A protective plate attached to the butt of the buttstock. May be metal, plastic, or rubber. Sometimes airgun makers use a rubber recoil pad although the recoil dampening effect may not be needed.

BUTTSTOCK
Usually refers to the portion of a long gun that comes in contact with the shooter's shoulder.

CALIBER
The diameter of the bore (measured from land to land). It does not designate bullet diameter.

CHAMBER
The cavity at the breech end of the barrel bore that has been formed to accept and support a specific pellet.

CHECKERING

A functional decoration consisting of pointed pyramids cut into the wood. Generally applied to the pistol grip and forend/forearm areas affording better handling and control.

CHEEKPIECE

A raised part of the side of the stock of a shoulder-arm against which the shooter rests his face. Usually associated with a Monte Carlo-type stock. Its purpose is to raise the shooter's eye to the height necessary to maintain the triangle of force.

COCKING INDICATOR

Any device which the act of cocking moves into a position where it may be seen or felt in order to notify the shooter that the gun is cocked.

COLOR CASE HARDENING

A method of hardening steel and iron while imparting colorful swirls as well as surface figure. Normally, the desired metal parts are put in a crucible packed with a mixture of charcoal and finely ground animal bone to temperatures in the 800° C to 900° C range, after which they are slowly cooled, and then submerged into cold water.

COMB

The portion of the stock on which the shooter's cheek rests.

COMPENSATOR

A recoil-reducing device that mounts on the muzzle of a gun to deflect part of the propelling gases up and rearward. Also called a "muzzle brake."

COMPRESSED AIR

Air at greater than atmospheric pressure. Guns which use compressed air include hose-fed airguns, spring-piston airguns, pump pneumatics, and pre-charged pneumatics.

CONCENTRIC PISTON

An arrangement in spring piston airguns where the barrel serves as a piston guide for a compression piston which encircles and rides on the barrel.

CROWNING

The rounding or chambering normally done to a barrel muzzle to ensure that the mouth of the bore is square with the bore axis and that the edge is countersunk below the surface to protect it from impact damage. Traditionally, crowning was accomplished by spinning an abrasive-coated brass ball against the muzzle while moving it in a figure-eight pattern, until the abrasive had cut away any irregularities and produced a uniform and square mouth.

CYLINDER

In airguns, especially spring piston airguns, it is the cylinder-shaped main body or reciever. In such guns it is also known as the body tube or receiver.

DETENT

A spring-loaded cam which aids in holding an airgun mechanism, especially the barrel, in the closed position.

DIABOLO

A term used when referring to the style of pellets with a constricted waist.

DIOPTER

European term for aperture or peep sight. Usually refers to a target grade sight.

DOUBLE ACTION

The principle in a revolver or auto-loading pistol wherein the hammer can be cocked and dropped by a single pull of the trigger. Most of these actions also provide capability for single-action fire.

DOUBLE ACTION ONLY

Hammer no longer cocks in single action stage.

DOUBLE-BARRELED

A gun consisting of two barrels joined either side by side or one over the other.

DOUBLE-SET TRIGGER

A device that consists of two triggers, one to cock the mechanism that spring-assists the other trigger, substantially lightening trigger pull.

DOVETAIL

A flaring machined or hand-cut slot that is also slightly tapered toward one end. Cut into the upper surface of barrels and sometimes actions, the dovetail accepts a corresponding part on which a sight is mounted. Dovetail slot blanks are used to cover the dovetail when the original sight has been removed or lost; this gives the barrel a more pleasing appearance and configuration.

DRY FIRING

Aiming and firing the rifle without a pellet in it. This is an excellent technique to improve marksmanship skills. Some rifles recommend not dry firing, so check with your rifles instructions before trying it.

ENGLISH STOCK

A straight, slender-gripped stock.

ENGRAVING

The art of carving metal in decorative patterns. Scroll engraving is the most common type of hand engraving encountered. Much of today's factory engraving is rolled on, which is done mechanically. Hand engraving requires artistry and knowledge of metals and related materials.

ETCHING

A method of decorating metal gun parts, usually done by laser etching acid or photo engraving.

EYE RELIEF

The distance that the eye is positioned behind the ocular lens of the telescopic sight. A two-to three-inch distance is average. The shooter adjusts the eye relief to ensure a full field of view. This distance is also necessary to prevent the telescope from striking the shooter face during recoil in some rifles.

FIXED SIGHTS

Non-adjustable sights.

FOREARM (FOREND)

Usually a separate piece of wood in front of the receiver and under the barrel used for hand placement when shooting.

FOREND (FOREARM)

Usually the forward portion of a one-piece rifle or shotgun stock, but can also refer to a separate piece of wood.

FRONT STRAP

That part of the pistol grip frame that faces forward and often joins with the trigger guard.

GAS-SPRING SYSTEM

The type of operating system in which the main spring is replaced by (and uses) a gas-filled cylinder with a piston to generate the energy to move a projectile through the barrel (inappropriately sometimes called "gasram" or "gas strut").

GRAVITY FEED MECHANISM

A magazine which feeds projectiles, generally round balls or BBs, to the projectile feeding area by the simple, dependable action of gravity.

GRIP

The handle used to hold a handgun, or the area of a stock directly behind and attached to the frame/receiver of a long gun.

GRIPS

Can be part of the frame or components attached to the frame used to assist in accuracy, handling, control, and safety of a handgun. Some currently manufactured handguns have grips that are molded with checkering as part of the synthetic frame.

GROOVE

The spiral cuts in the bore of a rifle or handgun barrel that give the bullet its spin or rotation as it moves down the barrel.

GROOVED RECEIVER

The straight cuts in the upper portion of the receiver used when attaching a scope.

HEEL

Back end of the upper edge of the buttstock at the upper edge of the buttplate or recoil pad.

HOODED SIGHT

A front sight that is equipped with a metal canopy. Designed to eliminate light reflections, as well as to protect the sight pillar.

LAMINATED STOCK

A gunstock made of many layers of wood glued together under pressure. Together, the laminations become very strong, preventing damage from moisture, heat, and warping.

LANDS

Portions of the bore left between the grooves of the rifling in the bore of a firearm. In rifling, the grooves are usually twice the width of the land. Land diameter is measured across the bore, from land to land.

LENGTH OF PULL

The distance from the forward center of the trigger curve to the rear surface of the buttplate. A pull of about 13.5 inches is a typical adult size on rifles.

LOADING GATE

The area on an airgun which, when opened, allows for the insertion of the projectile.

LOADING TAP

An airgun mechanism into which single projectiles may be loaded and then moved into firing position. Varieties include: pop-up, turning (faucet), and swinging.

MAGAZINE (mag.)

The container within or attached to an airgun which holds projectiles to be fed into the gun's chamber.

MAINSPRING

The spring which, when compressed and then released, generates the energy to move a projectile through the barrel.

MANNLICHER STOCK

A full-length slender stock with slender forend extending to the muzzle (full stock) affording better barrel protection.

MICROMETER SIGHT

A finely adjustable sight.

MODERATOR

A device designed to reduce muzzle report on an airgun by moderating the air released when firing. See Silencer.

MONTE CARLO STOCK

A stock with an elevated comb, used primarily for scoped rifles.

MUZZLE

The forward end of the barrel where the projectile exits.

MUZZLE BRAKE

A recoil-reducing device attached to the muzzle. Some "muzzle brakes" do not actually reduce recoil, but rather mainly are used as cocking aids.

MUZZLE ENERGY

The energy of a projectile as it departs from the muzzle of a gun. Derived from the formula: 0.5 x mass x velocity squared.

MUZZLE WEIGHT

A weight (usually adjustable) equalizing device attached at muzzle end of the barrel used to balance and stabilize the barrel.

OPEN SIGHTS

Rear sight of traditional "leaf" type with open-topped V-notch or U-notch, as distinct from a scope or aperture (peep) sight.

PARALLAX

Occurs in telescopic sights when the primary image of the objective lens does not coincide with the reticle. In practice, parallax is detected in the scope when, as the viewing eye is moved laterally, the image and the reticle appear to move in relation to each other.

PARKERIZING

Matted rust-resistant oxide finish, usually matte or dull gray, or black in color, usually found on military guns.

PEEP SIGHT

Rear sight consisting of a hole or aperture through which the front sight and target are aligned.

PELLET

An airgun projectile that is not a ball. Available in many styles, including wadcutter (target and high impact), pointed (high penetration), round nose (general use), and hollow point (expands on impact).

PICATINNY RAIL

A serrated flat rail attached to a forward portion of pistols and rifles used to clamp (Weaver Style Mount) accessories on.

PNEUMATIC

A term referring to the use of air/gas pressure as an energy source. In airguns it propels the BB or pellet out of the barrel.

PRE-CHARGED PNEUMATIC SYSTEM

The type of operating system that uses an externally charged chamber (either integral or removable) of compressed air or gas to generate the energy to move a projectile through the barrel.

PUMP UP AIRGUN

Airgun powered by air compressed by a pump integral to the gun. Usually all of the compressed air is discharged when the gun is fired for a single shot per air charge.

RECEIVER

The central area of an airgun's mechanism which serves to house or connect some or all of these parts: trigger mechanism, power mechanism, barrel, stock. A round airgun receiver generally is referred to as the body tube, cylinder, compression tube, or receiver. In air pistols, it generally is referred to as the frame.

RECOILLESS

A mechanical design that allows an airgun to be shot with little or no felt recoil.

REGULATOR

Device that steps the pressure in the air cylinder down to a lower level to maintain consistent pressure for the airgun to fire from. Often found on match grade rifles to ensure absolute consistency.

REPEATER/REPEATING

A term used when referring to an airgun being capable of firing more than one shot without having to manually reload.

RESERVOIR

Storage area for airgun projectiles. Generally not connected to the projectile feeding area or magazine.

RIB

A raised sighting plane affixed to the top of a barrel.

RIFLING

The spirally cut grooves in the bore of a rifle or handgun. The rifling stabilizes the bullet in flight. Rifling may rotate to the left or the right, the higher parts of the bore being called lands, the cuts or lower parts being called the grooves. Most U.S.-made barrels have a right-hand twist, while British gun makers prefer a left-hand twist. In practice, there seems to be little difference in accuracy or barrel longevity.

SCHNABEL FOREND

The curved/carved flared end of the forend that resembles the beak of a bird (Schnabel in German). This type of forend is common on Austrian and German guns, and was popular in the U.S., but the popularity of the Schnabel forend/forearm comes and goes with the seasons.

SIDE LEVER

The lever located on the side of an airgun used for cocking the mainspring into firing position.

SIDE-LEVER COCKING

The action of pivoting the side lever compresses the mainspring of a spring-piston action into firing position.

SILENCER

A device designed to slow and dissipate the sudden expansion of the gas that propels a projectile up the bore of a gun. Buyers of airguns equipped with a silencer (or any built-in or added device, which reduces discharge sound) are advised to obtain a federal permit for the silencer part ($200) and check their state and local laws very carefully. See warning at www.beemans.net.

SINGLE ACTION

A design which requires the hammer to be manually cocked for each shot.

SINGLE STAGE TRIGGER

Typical American hunting trigger that breaks upon application of pressure.

SKIRT

The flaring, thin area of diabolo-style pellets that engages the rifling in a barrel and acts as an air seal.

SLING SWIVELS

Metal loops affixed to the gun on which a carrying strap is attached.

SOUND MODERATOR ("Silencer")

Device which reduces the discharge sound by one decibel or more. All versions, including built-in models, probably are illegal in the United States, unless accompanied by a $200 federal permit and, if required, a state permit. (See www.beemans.net.)

SPRING-FED MAGAZINE

A projectile storage area which is designed to feed the projectiles to the firing or loading area by means of a spring-loaded projectile follower.

SPRING-PISTON SYSTEM

Airgun operating system that uses a metal or gas mainspring to push a piston, which in turn uses a cushion of air to push the projectile through the barrel.

STIPPLING

The roughening of a surface (with the use of a special punch or tool) to provide the shooter with a better grip.

STOCKS

See grip.

TAKEDOWN

A gun which can be easily taken apart in two sections for carrying or shipping.

TANG(S)

The extension straps of the receiver to which the stock is attached.

TARGET TURRETS

Raised adjuster knobs on a scope that can easily be turned by hand without use of tools.

TIROLERSCHAFT

Tyrolean style stock.

TOP LEVER

The lever located on the top of an airgun used for cocking the mainspring into firing position.

TOP-LEVER COCKING

The action of pivoting the top lever (generally found on air pistols) upward compresses the mainspring of a spring-piston action into firing position.

TWO STAGE TRIGGER

Small amount of take up is the first stage, coming to a complete stop. Second stage breaks and releases trigger with any further pressure.

UNDER LEVER

The lever located under an airgun used for cocking the mainspring into firing position.

UNDER-LEVER COCKING

The action of pivoting the under lever downward compresses the mainspring of a spring-piston action into firing position.

VELOCITY

The speed at which the ammunition is being propelled. Normally calculated as Feet-Per-Second (fps).

YOUTH DIMENSIONS

Usually refers to shorter stock dimensions and/or lighter weight enabling youth/women to shoot and carry a lighter, shorter airgun.

WUNDHAMMER SWELL

A swelling of the pistol grip area of a rifle stock, intended to give support to the palm of the firing hand.

English/American Translations of Airgun Terms

English	American
Horizontal Sight Adjustment	Windage
Vertical Sight Adjustment	Elevation
Joint Washer, Barrel Washer	Breech Seal
Loading Lever	Cocking Arm
Fixing Screw	Lock Screw
Kit	Equipment
Barrel Fixing Plunger, Barrel Latch	Detent
Cranked Spring	Spring w/Straight Leg(s)
Back Block	Receiver End Cap
Bead	Front Sight
Receiver Sight	Peep Sight
Mains Line Tension	House Current
Fore-end	Forearm
Cylinder, Body	Receiver, Body Tube
Grub Screw	Headless Screw
Calibre	Caliber
Arrestor Projections	Scope Stop
Anti-Clockwise	Counter Clockwise
Nought	Zero (the number)
Strip	Disassemble
Fix (a design)	Finalize a Design
Sort Out	Fix, figure out, Organize
Knackered	Needs Repair
One Off (on orders)	One On (on orders)
Brilliant	Excellent
Spot On	Absolutely Appropriate
One Off	Unique

ABBREVIATIONS

AA	Addictive Airgunning
AAG	American Air Gunner
adj.	Adjustable
AG	Airgunnner
AGNR	*Air Gun News & Report* Magazine
AH	Airgun Hobby
AL	*Airgun Letter*
AR	*Airgun Revue* Magazine
AW	*Airgun World* Magazine
B	Blue
BA	Bolt Action
BACS	Brocock Air Cartridge System
BB	Air Rifle Shot
BBC	Break Barrel Cocking
BBL	Barrel
BC	Barrel Cocking
BF	Bulk Fill or Bottle Fed
BO	Break Open
BP	Buttplate
BT	Beavertail
ca.	Circa
cal.	Caliber
CC	Case Colors
CDT	Capacitve Discharge Technology, Harper patent
CH	Cross Hair
CO_2	Carbon Dioxide
COMP	Compensated/Competition
CP	Concentric Piston
CYL	Cylinder
DA	Double Action
DB	Double Barrel
DISC	Discontinued
DST	Double Set Triggers
DT	Double Triggers
DWJ	*Deutsches Waffen Journal*
EXC	Excellent
FA	Forearm
FPS	Feet per Second
Ft/lbs	Foot pounds
g./ gm.	Gram
ga.	Gauge
GC	Grip Cocking
GD	Gun Digest
GOVT	Government
gr.	Grain
GR	Guns Review
GS	Gas Spring
HB	Heavy Barrel
HC	Hard Case
intro.	Introduced
LA	Lever Action
LH, LHS	Left Hand
LOP	Length of Pull
LT	Light
Mag.	Extra Powerful; Magnum
mag.	Magazine or Clip

MC	Monte Carlo
ME	Muzzle Energy
MFC	Muzzle Flip Compensator
MFG/ mfg.	Manufactured/Manufacture
MK	Mark
MMC	Micro-Movement Cocking System
MSR	Manufacturer's Suggested Retail
MV	Muzzle Velocity
N	Nickel
N/A	Not Applicable or Not Available
NIB	New in Box
No.	Number
OA	Overall
OAL	Overall Length
OB	Octagon Barrel
OCT	Octagon
OD	Outside Diameter
OIR	Optic-illuminated Reticle
PCP	Pre-Charged Pneumatic
PG	Pistol Grip
POR/ P.O.R.	Price on Request
PSI	Pounds per Square Inch
PIPS	Power Intesification Piston System
PP	Pump Pneumatic
QD	Quick Detachable
RB	Round Barrel
RH, RHS	Right Hand
REC	Receiver
RPM	Rounds Per Minute
S/N, SN	Serial Number
SA	Single Action
SG	Straight Grip
SL	Side Lever
SP	Spring Piston
SPEC	Special
SPG	Semi-Pistol Grip
Spl.	Special
SR	Semi-recoilles
SS	Single Shot or Stainless Steel
SSP	Single Stroke Pneumatic
ST	Single Trigger
TBD	To Be Determined
TD	Takedown
TGT	Target
TL	Top Lever
TT	Target Trigger
UIT	Union Internationale de Tir
UL	Under Lever
USA	United States of America or U.S. Airguns
VG	Very Good
V/Visier	*VISIER* magazine
w/	With
w/o	Without
WD	Wood
WFF	Watch for Fakes
WO	White Outline
WW	World War

AIRGUN GRADING CRITERIA

The following descriptions are provided to help evaluate condition factors for both vintage and currently/recently manufactured airguns. **Please refer to the following eight-page color Photo Grading System (PGS) to determine the correct grade for your airgun(s).** Once the percentage of original condition has been determined, getting the correct value is as simple as finding the listing and selecting the correct condition factor. Also included are both the NRA Modern and Antique Condition Standards for firearms as a comparison, including a conversion chart for converting percentages to NRA Modern Standards. "N/As" throughout this book are used to indicate that values can't be accurately established because of rarity, lack of recorded sales, or other factors that may preclude realistic pricing within a condition factor. **All digital photos in the following Photo Grading System are courtesy of Dr. Robert D. Beeman.**

100% - all original parts, 100% original finish, perfect condition in every respect, inside and out. On currently manufactured airguns, the 100% value assumes not previously sold at retail.

95% - all original parts, near new condition, very little use; minor scratches or handling dings on wood, metal bluing near perfect, except at muzzle or sharp edges.

90% - all original parts, perfect working condition, some minor wear on working surfaces, no corrosion or pitting, minor surface dents or scratches, sharp lettering, numerals and design on metal and wood; unmarred wood, fine bore.

80% - good working condition, minor wear on working surfaces, no broken or replacement parts, sharp lettering, numerals and design on metal and wood, some surface freckling/light rust (especially on vintage airguns).

60% - safe working condition, sharp lettering, numerals and design on metal and wood, some scratches, dings, and chips in wood, good bore, may have some corrosion and pitting.

40% - well-worn, perhaps requiring replacement of minor parts or adjustments, sharp lettering; numerals and design on metal and wood, on older airguns, major surface rust and pitting may be present, but do not render the airgun unsafe or inoperable.

20% - most of original finish is gone, metal may be seriously rusted or pitted, cleaned or reblued, principal lettering, numerals and design on metal still legible, wood may have serious scratches, dings, and may be refinished and/or cracked, both minor and major repairs may be present.

NRA MODERN CONDITION DESCRIPTIONS

New - not previously sold at retail, in same condition as current factory production.

Perfect - in new condition in every respect.

Excellent - new condition, used but little, no noticeable marring of wood or metal, bluing near perfect (except at muzzle or sharp edges).

Very Good - in perfect working condition, no appreciable wear on working surfaces, no corrosion or pitting, only minor surface dents or scratches.

Good - in safe working condition, minor wear on working surfaces, no broken parts, no corrosion or pitting that will interfere with proper functioning.

Fair - in safe working condition, but well-worn, perhaps requiring replacement of minor parts or adjustments which should be indicated in advertisement, no rust, but may have corrosion pits which do not render article unsafe or inoperable.

CONVERTING TO NRA MODERN STANDARDS

When converting from NRA Modern Standards, the following rules generally apply:

New/Perfect - 100% with or without box. Not mint - new (i.e., no excuses). 100% on currently manufactured firearms assumes NIB condition and not sold previously at retail.

Excellent - 95%+ - 99% (typically).

Very Good - 80% - 95% (should be all original).

Good - 60% - 80% (should be all original).

Fair - 20% - 60% (may or may not be original, but must function properly and shoot).

Poor - under 20% (shooting not a factor).

NRA ANTIQUE CONDITION DESCRIPTIONS

Factory New - all original parts; 100% original finish; in perfect condition in every respect, inside and out.

Excellent - all original parts; over 80% original finish; sharp lettering, numerals and design on metal and wood; unmarred wood; fine bore.

Fine - all original parts; over 30% original finish; sharp lettering, numerals and design on metal and wood; minor marks in wood; good bore.

Very Good - all original parts; none to 30% original finish; original metal surfaces smooth with all edges sharp; clear lettering, numerals and design on metal; wood slightly scratched or bruised; bore disregarded for collectors firearms.

Good - some minor replacement parts; metal smoothly rusted or lightly pitted in places, cleaned or reblued; principal lettering, numerals and design on metal legible; wood refinished, scratched, bruised or minor cracks repaired; in good working order.

Fair - some major parts replaced; minor replacement parts may be required; metal rusted, may be lightly pitted all over, vigorously cleaned or reblued; rounded edges of metal and wood; principal lettering, numerals and design on metal partly obliterated; wood scratched, bruised, cracked or repaired where broken; in fair working order or can be easily repaired and placed in working order.

Poor - major and minor parts replaced; major replacement parts required and extensive restoration needed; metal deeply pitted; principal lettering, numerals and design obliterated, wood badly scratched, bruised, cracked, or broken; mechanically inoperative, generally undesirable as a collector's firearm.

AIR PISTOLS

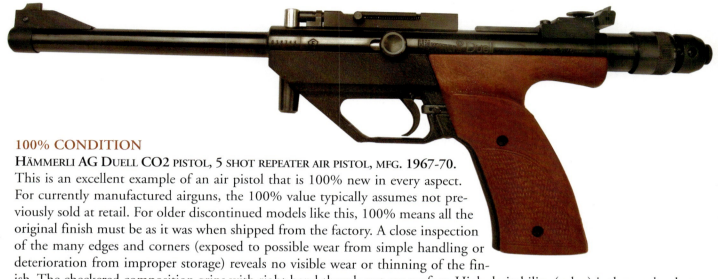

100% CONDITION

HÄMMERLI AG DUELL CO2 PISTOL, 5 SHOT REPEATER AIR PISTOL, MFG. 1967-70.
This is an excellent example of an air pistol that is 100% new in every aspect.
For currently manufactured airguns, the 100% value typically assumes not previously sold at retail. For older discontinued models like this, 100% means all the
original finish must be as it was when shipped from the factory. A close inspection
of the many edges and corners (exposed to possible wear from simple handling or
deterioration from improper storage) reveals no visible wear or thinning of the fin-
ish. The checkered composition grips with right hand thumb rest are perfect. High desirability (value) is the result when
the right combination of many factors (trademark, condition, configuration, year of manufacture, total number produced, number of variations, etc.) comes together. This pistol would be a prize in any collection.

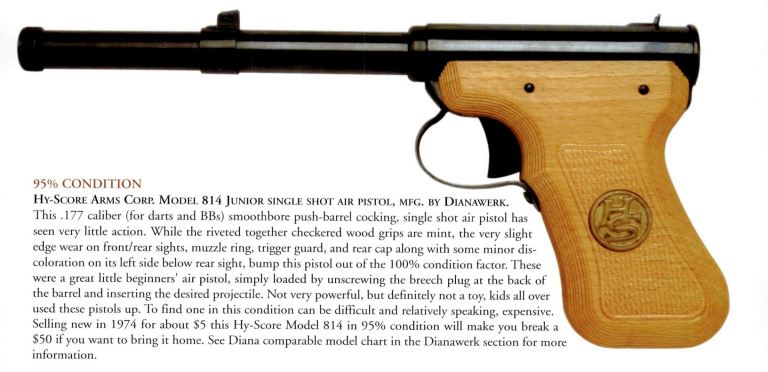

95% CONDITION

HY-SCORE ARMS CORP. MODEL 814 JUNIOR SINGLE SHOT AIR PISTOL, MFG. BY DIANAWERK.
This .177 caliber (for darts and BBs) smoothbore push-barrel cocking, single shot air pistol has
seen very little action. While the riveted together checkered wood grips are mint, the very slight
edge wear on front/rear sights, muzzle ring, trigger guard, and rear cap along with some minor discoloration on its left side below rear sight, bump this pistol out of the 100% condition factor. These
were a great little beginners' air pistol, simply loaded by unscrewing the breech plug at the back of
the barrel and inserting the desired projectile. Not very powerful, but definitely not a toy, kids all over
used these pistols up. To find one in this condition can be difficult and relatively speaking, expensive.
Selling new in 1974 for about $5 this Hy-Score Model 814 in 95% condition will make you break a
$50 if you want to bring it home. See Diana comparable model chart in the Dianawerk section for more
information.

AIR PISTOLS

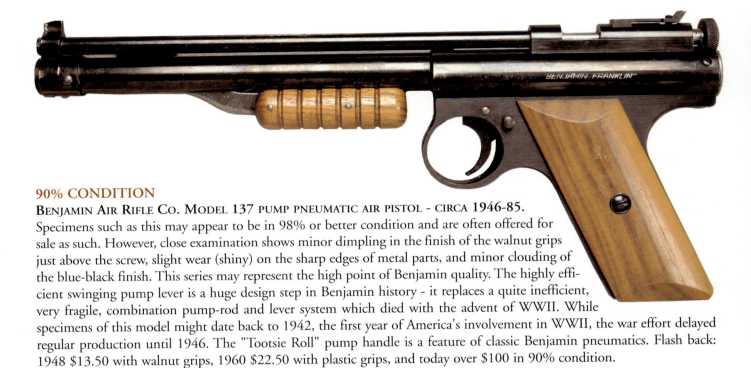

90% CONDITION

BENJAMIN AIR RIFLE CO. MODEL 137 PUMP PNEUMATIC AIR PISTOL - CIRCA 1946-85.
Specimens such as this may appear to be in 98% or better condition and are often offered for sale as such. However, close examination shows minor dimpling in the finish of the walnut grips just above the screw, slight wear (shiny) on the sharp edges of metal parts, and minor clouding of the blue-black finish. This series may represent the high point of Benjamin quality. The highly efficient swinging pump lever is a huge design step in Benjamin history - it replaces a quite inefficient, very fragile, combination pump-rod and lever system which died with the advent of WWII. While specimens of this model might date back to 1942, the first year of America's involvement in WWII, the war effort delayed regular production until 1946. The "Tootsie Roll" pump handle is a feature of classic Benjamin pneumatics. Flash back: 1948 $13.50 with walnut grips, 1960 $22.50 with plastic grips, and today over $100 in 90% condition.

80% CONDITION

BENJAMIN AIR RIFLE CO. MODEL 112 LEVER-ACTIVATED PUMP ROD PNEUMATIC PISTOL FROM CIRCA 1938-1941.
The original black nickel finish shows considerable wear from finger contact above the grips and on the body tube, where the pumping hand rubs the gun. Also note the few small surface blemishes, but lack of surface freckling or light pitting. The pump linkage design on this model used an inefficient "grasshopper" system, drawing out the pump rod and putting great strain on the pump/rod linkage. This model is frequently found with that linkage broken, but this specimen's linkage is in fine condition. The forward body band screws show minor dings, probably from adjustments being performed with the wrong size screwdriver. The wooden grips are very good with only minor nicks.

AIR PISTOLS

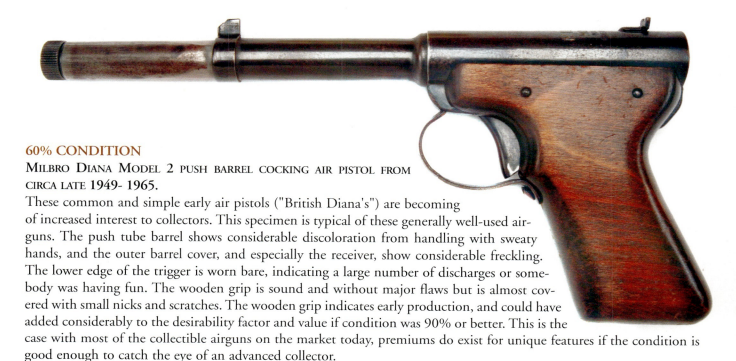

60% CONDITION

MILBRO DIANA MODEL 2 PUSH BARREL COCKING AIR PISTOL FROM CIRCA LATE 1949- 1965.

These common and simple early air pistols ("British Diana's") are becoming of increased interest to collectors. This specimen is typical of these generally well-used airguns. The push tube barrel shows considerable discoloration from handling with sweaty hands, and the outer barrel cover, and especially the receiver, show considerable freckling. The lower edge of the trigger is worn bare, indicating a large number of discharges or somebody was having fun. The wooden grip is sound and without major flaws but is almost covered with small nicks and scratches. The wooden grip indicates early production, and could have added considerably to the desirability factor and value if condition was 90% or better. This is the case with most of the collectible airguns on the market today, premiums do exist for unique features if the condition is good enough to catch the eye of an advanced collector.

40% CONDITION

TITAN MARK 5 PUSHROD-COCKING, SPRING PISTON PISTOL, MFG. CIRCA 1920.

At first glance, this specimen's condition may appear better than it really is. The visible wear and missing finish on barrel and air chamber are the result of an amateur using steel wool. This was performed in an attempt to remove some pitting and as usual, resulted in bright shinny metal instead of the normal thinning blue or brown patina. Fortunately the amateur was not too aggressive, only hitting the high sides of the air chamber front half saved better than half the original blue. Unfortunately, the pitting that remains along with additional dings and dents in the front grip frame along with what appears to be some work performed between the air chamber and breech block move the condition down to the 40% or possibly even less range. Vintage airguns in this condition should be functional, if it doesn't shoot it should get priced accordingly. Non-functional airguns can result in a 20%-80% reduction in value, depending on its overall desirability factor.

AIR PISTOLS

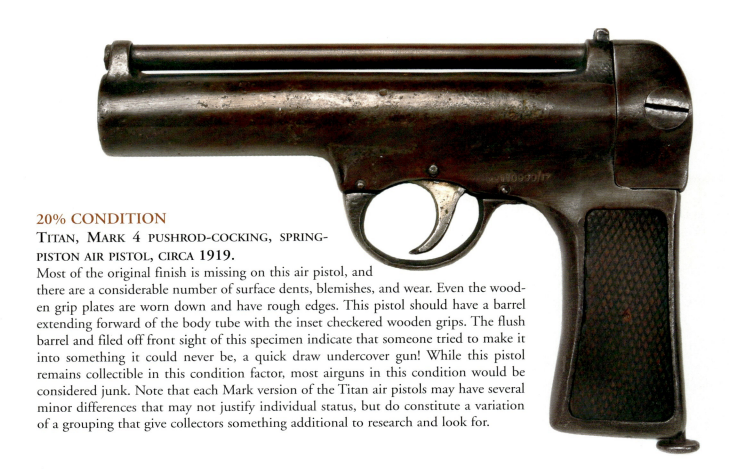

20% CONDITION

TITAN, MARK 4 PUSHROD-COCKING, SPRING-
PISTON AIR PISTOL, CIRCA 1919.
Most of the original finish is missing on this air pistol, and
there are a considerable number of surface dents, blemishes, and wear. Even the wood-
en grip plates are worn down and have rough edges. This pistol should have a barrel
extending forward of the body tube with the inset checkered wooden grips. The flush
barrel and filed off front sight of this specimen indicate that someone tried to make it
into something it could never be, a quick draw undercover gun! While this pistol
remains collectible in this condition factor, most airguns in this condition would be
considered junk. Note that each Mark version of the Titan air pistols may have several
minor differences that may not justify individual status, but do constitute a variation
of a grouping that give collectors something additional to research and look for.

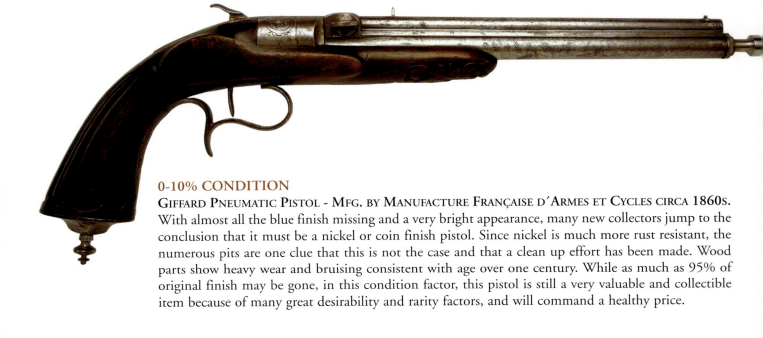

0-10% CONDITION

GIFFARD PNEUMATIC PISTOL - MFG. BY MANUFACTURE FRANÇAISE D´ARMES ET CYCLES CIRCA 1860S.
With almost all the blue finish missing and a very bright appearance, many new collectors jump to the
conclusion that it must be a nickel or coin finish pistol. Since nickel is much more rust resistant, the
numerous pits are one clue that this is not the case and that a clean up effort has been made. Wood
parts show heavy wear and bruising consistent with age over one century. While as much as 95% of
original finish may be gone, in this condition factor, this pistol is still a very valuable and collectible
item because of many great desirability and rarity factors, and will command a healthy price.

AIR RIFLES

100% CONDITION

WEIHRAUCH MODEL HW 55T BREAK BARREL COCKING (BBC) SPRING PISTON (SP) RIFLE, MFG. CIRCA 1978.

This relatively recently manufactured air rifle is perfect in every aspect, with no wear on either the metal surfaces or Tyrolean wood stock. When determining upper condition factors on airguns, always inspect the area(s) where wear will accumulate first when using - in this case, where the barrel pivots when cocking and the muzzle and wrist area of the stock where a shooter will hold the rifle during cocking. Also, check any edges or high spots that could be subject to wear from handling or storage.

95% CONDITION

TYROL MODEL CM1, CO2 POWERED, MILITARY TRAINER, MFG. BY TIROLER SPORTWAFFENFABRIK UND APPARATEBAU GMBH IN KUFSTEIN, AUSTRIA IN 1959.

Because of the history behind this semi-auto rifle (developed to be a military trainer), an experienced collector at a glance can determine it is unused. The stock does show some almost unnoticeable minor handling marks and the metalwork has some microscopic freckling and discoloration. The presence of these condition factors on a very common airgun like a 1980s-1990s Daisy, Crosman, Marksman, Gamo, etc. can almost make them un-sellable (reduce their value by 30%-50%), while on a collectable airgun the value only changes by 5%-10%.

AIR RIFLES

90% CONDITION

CHALLENGER ARMS CORP. PLAINSMAN GAS RIFLE MODEL CO2 POWERED RIFLE, MFG. 1953-1958.

This gun's condition factor is 90% plus, mostly due to the knurled knob, trigger and guard, muzzle, and light discoloration of metal bluing on the barrel and air chamber. Wear (nicks, dings, and even light scratches) on the stock does not affect overall condition nearly as much as metal wear. This airgun shows normal wear and tear for its vintage, and still operates perfectly, which is another key when trying to determine overall condition and value. If it doesn't shoot, how much will a buyer have to spend to make it shoot?

80% CONDITION

H. QUACKENBUSH MODEL 5, VARIETY 3, COMBINATION GUN, MFG. 1884-1913.

The blued metal edges of this specimen are beginning to show some brightness combined with the plum patina on the barrel and a scratch on the receiver put overall, about 20% to 25% of the metal finish worn or thinning. The stock is in somewhat better condition than the metal and when one part of the gun is better than another, it is necessary to consider whether any refinishing has taken place. Even excellent refinishing will reduce the value. Careful examination of the edges of the stock varnish give every indication that this finish is absolutely original. Thus, opposite to the usual situation, this stock actually upgrades the overall condition a bit. Special features also count: if the "patchbox" is missing the removable firing pin, a value reduction must be made.

AIR RIFLES

60% CONDITION

KESSLER MODEL PNEUMATIC PUMP RIFLE, MFG. 1948-1950.

The receiver finish edge deterioration (nicks) on this air rifle is classic and a good example to show the new person on the block what we mean by edge wear. Freckling on barrel, bolt handle, and knurled knob along with darkening of the stock, and cracked forearm all add up to an overall condition of 60%. This gun was not only used quite a bit, but also abused occasionally, in addition to not being properly maintained. In most cases, a middle of the road (40%, 60%, and 80%) condition factor is far simpler to determine than high-end condition (95% or better). The middle of the road is also where the item's eye appeal can also affect the retail value as much as actual condition.

40% CONDITION

BENJAMIN MODEL 352 CO2 RIFLE, MFG. MID-1950S.

This little rifle is one we all can relate to for one reason or another. The configuration of the barrel over air chamber set into a plain stock appears across many trademarks and finish wear patterns are predictable. Note how the barrel and air chamber finish have turned a brownish patina because of wear and original bluing oxidation. The plain stock also has the normal handling marks with some dark spots that may clean off if attempted by a professional. These types of finish problems can drastically affect overall eye appeal and make a $50-$60 air rifle a tough sale at $40. Considering this gun is almost a half century old should not let the buyer be talked into spending more than what is fair.

AIR RIFLES

20% CONDITION

DAISY MODEL 25 VARIANT 4, LONG-LEVER ELBOW-SLIDE COCKING BB RIFLE CIRCA 1920S-30S.
The wear on the stock and metal of this gun is very consistent. There are considerable areas displaying original blue, but almost all are marked with small patches and freckling of rust. The stock finish obviously is original, but marked with some major blemishes, scratches, and even a small burn mark. It is interesting that the bluing does not seem to show much wear; its degradation seems to have been almost entirely due to poor storage conditions over the several decades of this gun's life. The total drop in condition from new is about 80%. Still a nice specimen in one of the most popular series Daisy ever produced. Over twenty million of the hard-hitting Model 25 airguns went through about 58 variants over 65 years - Daisy's longest lived model.

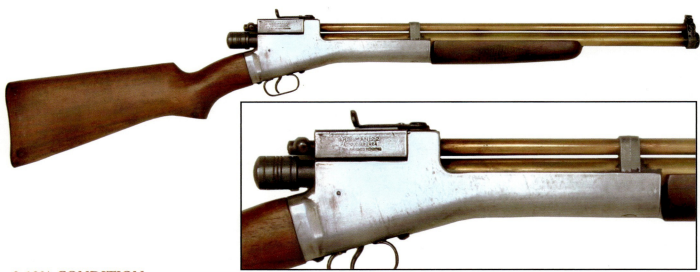

0-10% CONDITION

CROSMAN MODEL 102 PUMP PNEUMATIC REPEATER, MFG. 1929-50.
This is a special, all-too-common condition. To the novice this gun may be beautiful. Its black lacquer finish has completely been removed, probably by steel wool, and the underlying aluminum and brass have been polished. The stock may have been cleaned and refinished. The removal of all metal finish has earned this gun a condition rating reduction of 90+%. Restoration generally is to be reserved for extreme cases, such as this, but must be done very carefully and can only lift a gun to a middle condition value that generally does not cover the expense of restoration.

A SECTION

ABT

Previous manufacturer located at 715-727 North Kedzie St., Chicago, Illinois circa 1925-1958. The company name is an acronym of the founders' names: Gus Adler, Jack Bechtol, and Walter Tratsch. Producers of carnival and shooting gallery BB pistols, BB rifles, and supplies. Developed Air-O-Matic airgun design, patented April 19, 1932, pat. no. 1854605 and Oct. 6, 1942, pat. no. 2297947. Other patents to 1949.

Most of the known ABT guns are pistols which were captive mounted in highly decorated wooden boxes serving as miniature, coin-operated firing ranges. These were used for entertainment and as covert/rigged games of chance. These game guns were manufactured from 1925 to about 1958. There are no production records from about 1941 to 1946 due to WWII. The shooting box part of the company's history is detailed at www.crowriver.com/abt.htm.

It is not clear when hose-fed compressed air ABT airguns were made, but the patents run from 1932 through 1949. ABT apparently applied for Arrow-Matic as a trademark, and so marked at least some guns, but were granted the Air-O-Matic trademark for semi-automatic airguns that are fed from a patented, pre-loaded fiber tube of BBs that was inserted into a unique rear- or top-feeding loading chute when the gun was opened by pulling back the top of the receiver or a side bolt. At least three versions of shoulder-fired, hose pneumatic rifles and one similar pistol are known. Also known is a sliding pump action rifle, unmarked, but with exactly the same unusual, complex, loading chute.

Virtually all ABT specimens are well worn from hard shooting gallery use, but are very durable due to rugged, excellent construction. Carnival airguns are now becoming more popular with airgun collectors, and values can be expected to rise accordingly.

GRADING	100%	95%	90%	80%	60%	40%	20%

PISTOLS

CAPTIVE SHOOTING BOX PISTOL - .40 cal., spring action, tube-fed repeater, 2.6 in. smoothbore blue barrel, 8.7 in. OAL, 2.9 lbs., no safety. Mfg. 1925-1958.

courtesy Beeman Collection

	N/A	N/A	$180	$150	$100	$75	$50

AIR-O-MATIC GALLERY PISTOL - .173 cal., hose pneumatic, semi-automatic repeater, patented pop-up loading chute loaded by insertion of patented, fiber, pre-loaded tube of BBs, 7.1 in. smoothbore barrel, 12.7 in. OAL, 2.6 lbs., no safety. Probably mfg. 1930s to 1940s.

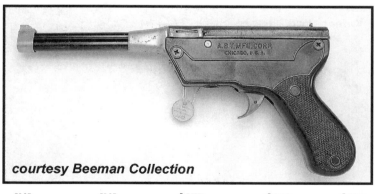

courtesy Beeman Collection

	N/A	N/A	$275	$210	$195	$175	$150

RIFLES

AIR-O-MATIC REAR LOADER - .173 cal., hose pneumatic, semi-auto repeater, loading chute pops out of rear of receiver for insertion of patented, fiber, pre-loaded tube of BBs, approx. 16 in. smoothbore barrel within longer barrel shroud, stamped with 1932 patent date, model name cast in plastic buttplate. No safety, approx. 42 in. OAL, approx. 5 lbs.

GRADING	100%	95%	90%	80%	60%	40%	20%

✿ *Air-O-Matic Rear Loader Variant I* - large sheet metal receiver extends almost to bottom edge of the middle of the stock.

courtesy Beeman Collection

	N/A	N/A	N/A	$300	$225	$150	$100

✿ *Air-O-Matic Rear Loader Variant II* - small receiver in line with barrel above one piece stock.

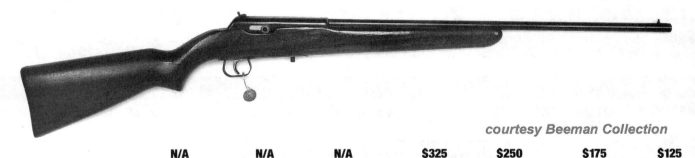

courtesy Beeman Collection

	N/A	N/A	N/A	$325	$250	$175	$125

AIR-O-MATIC TOP LOADER - .173 cal. semi-auto repeater, hose pneumatic, loading chute pops out of top of receiver for insertion of patented, fiber, pre-loaded tube of BBs, approx. 23 in. smoothbore barrel within larger barrel shroud which is topped by a small full-length tube, Metal box-like receiver divides stock into two pieces, stamped with 1942 and 1949 patent dates, model name cast in plastic buttplate, no safety, approx. 42 in. overall, approx. 5.6 lbs.

✿ *Air-O-Matic Top Loader Knob Variant* - short, straight-pull knob. Early.

	N/A	N/A	N/A	$300	$225	$150	$100

✿ *Air-O-Matic Top Loader Bolt Variant* - long, lifting bolt. Later.

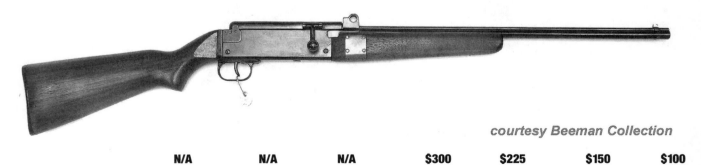

courtesy Beeman Collection

	N/A	N/A	N/A	$300	$225	$150	$100

GRADING	100%	95%	90%	80%	60%	40%	20%

AIR-O-MATIC SLIDE ACTION - .173 cal., hose pneumatic, repeater, pop up loading chute loaded by insertion of patented, fiber, pre-loaded tube of BBs, 23 in. smoothbore barrel, unusual two diameter sliding forearm, no safety, no markings, 42.5 in. OAL, 7.1 lbs. Probable mfg. 1940s.

courtesy Beeman Collection

	100%	95%	90%	80%	60%	40%	20%
	N/A	N/A	N/A	$275	$200	$125	$75

ARS (AIR RIFLE SPECIALISTS)

Current importer located in Pine City, NY. Dealer or consumer direct sales.

ARS previously imported airguns from Shin Sung, located in Korea, and Farco airguns from the Philippines. For information on Farco airguns, see the "F" section.

PISTOL

HUNTING MASTER AR-6 - .22(.177 or .20 special order) cal., PCP, SS, 12 in. rifled steel barrel, six-shot rotary mag., approx.twenty shots at 20 ft./lb. ME on one charge. 18.3 in. OAL, 3 lbs. Mfg. Duk Il in Seoul, Korea. Disc.

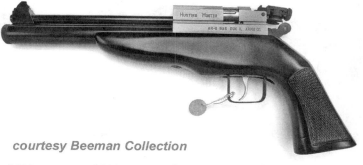

courtesy Beeman Collection

	100%	95%	90%	80%	60%	40%	20%
	$650	$600	$550	$500	$450	N/A	N/A

RIFLES

ADVENTURE DB - .22 cal., PCP, removable mag., pistol gip stock, 41.3 in. QAL, 8.2 lbs. Mfg. 1990s.

courtesy Beeman Collection

	100%	95%	90%	80%	60%	40%	20%
	$550	$475	$395	$325	$250	N/A	N/A

CAREER II (CAREER 707) - .22 cal., PCP, six-shot (or side-loading SS) lever action, 22.75 in. blue barrel, 1000 FPS, adj. diopter rear sight, hooded front sight, checkered walnut stock and forearm, 7.75 lbs. Mfg. in Korea; new 1995.

	100%	95%	90%	80%	60%	40%	20%
	$450	$365	$285	$235	$175	N/A	N/A

Last MSR was $580.

FIRE 201 - 9mm cal., PCP, SL, smooth bore or rifled barrel, 900 FPS, beech stock. Mfg. in Korea, 2000.

	100%	95%	90%	80%	60%	40%	20%
	$450	$365	$285	$235	$175	N/A	N/A

Last MSR was $595.

HUNTING MASTER AR6 - .177, .20, .22, or .25 (disc.) cal., PCP, exposed cocking hammer, six-shot rotary mag., 25.5 in. blue finish barrel, 1000+- FPS (.22), adj. rear peep sight, grooved receiver, checkered Monte Carlo walnut stock, rubber butt pad, 6.75 lbs., 41.25 OAL. Mfg. in Korea.

	100%	95%	90%	80%	60%	40%	20%
	$450	$365	$285	$235	$175	N/A	N/A

Last MSR was $580.

Add $20 for extra six-shot cylinder. Add $50 for charging unit. Add 10% for .20 cal.

GRADING	100%	95%	90%	80%	60%	40%	20%

HUNTING MASTER AR6 MAGNUM - .22 cal., PCP, six-shot rotary mag., 22.75 in. blue finish barrel, alloy receiver with gold burnish finish, 1000 FPS, adj. rear sight, checkered walnut stock and forearm, 6.75 lbs. Mfg. in Korea, disc.

	100%	95%	90%	80%	60%	40%	20%
	$425	$350	$275	$195	$150	N/A	N/A

Last MSR was $580.

Add $20 for extra six-shot cylinder.   Add $50 for charging unit.

HUNTING MASTER 900 - 9mm cal., PCP, 26.8 in. BBL, 900 FPS, wood stock. Mfg. by Duk Il, disc. 1999.

courtesy Beeman Collection

	100%	95%	90%	80%	60%	40%	20%
	$1,000	$800	$650	$500	$400	N/A	N/A

Last MSR was $1,000.

KING HUNTING MASTER - .22 cal., PCP, five-shot rotary mag. Mfg. in Korea, disc.

	100%	95%	90%	80%	60%	40%	20%
	$425	$350	$275	$195	$150	N/A	N/A

Last MSR was $580.

MAGNUM 6 - .22 cal., CO_2 or PCP, six-shot, similar to the King Hunting Master. Mfg. in Korea, disc.

courtesy Howard Collection

	100%	95%	90%	80%	60%	40%	20%
	$425	$350	$275	$195	$150	N/A	N/A

Last MSR was $500.

QB 77 - .177 or .22 cal., CO_2, SS, 21.5 in. barrel, hardwood stock, 5.5 lbs. Mfg. in China, disc. 2001.

	100%	95%	90%	80%	60%	40%	20%
	$150	$115	$80	$65	$50	N/A	N/A

Last MSR was $149.

ABAS MAJOR

Previously manufactured by A.A. Brown & Sons located at 1 Snake Lane, Alvechurch Birmingham, England, circa 1945-1946.
Albert Arthur Brown and his sons, Albert Henry Brown and Sydney Charles Brown were co-patentees and partners in developing and producing the Abas Major air pistol. (ABAS = initials of A. Brown and Sons.)

PISTOLS

ABAS MAJOR - .177 cal., concentric piston SP action, tap loading, trigger guard and forward edge of grip frame swings forward under the 7.6 in. barrel to cock the mainspring, counterclockwise rifling, blue, black crinkled paint, or aluminum finish, no safety. Walnut Grip Variant: smooth walnut grips, blued, some with black crackle paint, earliest production with lever release button on bottom of grip. Smooth Plastic Grip Variant: smooth brown composition grips, blued, most common variant. Checkered Plastic Grip Variant: checkered brown plastic grips, 8.1 in. OAL, 2.7 lbs. Less than 1870 known of all variants, mfg. 1946-49. Ref: AW: 1978, Apr. 1982.

courtesy Beeman Collection

	100%	95%	90%	80%	60%	40%	20%
	$800	$725	$650	$575	$500	$450	$400

Add 10% for release button on bottom of grip.   Add 10% for black enamel.   Add 15% for Walnut Grip Variant.   Add 20% for original factory box with Abas Major pellets.

GRADING	100%	95%	90%	80%	60%	40%	20%

ABBEY ALERT

For information on Abbey Alert airguns, see Produsit in the "P" section.

ACCLES & SHELVOKE LTD.

Previous manufacturer located at Talford Street Engineering Works, Birmingham, Warwickshire, England. Founded by James Accles and George Shelvoke in 1913.

Accles & Shelvoke originally produced humane cattle killers patented by James Accles and Charles Cash. Before WWII, the firm manufactured the Warrior, an air pistol developed and patented by association of Frank Clarke and Edwin Anson. They may have also produced the prototypes of the Titan air pistols for Frank Clarke. After WWII, the company produced the Acvoke air pistol, designed by John Arrowsmith. They were still recorded as making humane cattle killers in 2005. Air pistols were produced from 1931 to 1956. The authors and publisher wish to thank John Atkins for his valuable assistance with the following information in this edition of the *Blue Book of Airguns*.

PISTOLS

ACVOKE - .177 cal., SP, SS, concentric piston, cocked by pivoting grip forward with the aid of a lever which folds down from grip backstrap, 8 in. rifled BBL, blue finish, vertically ribbed plastic grips marked "ACVOKE" in an oval logo, 8.6 in. OAL, 2.0 lbs. Mfg. c. 1946-1956. Ref: GR Oct. '80.

courtesy Beeman Collection

$550	$500	$450	$350	$300	$250	$175

Add 20% for original factory box. Add 10% for cork adapter.

WARRIOR - .177 or .22 cal. SL, SP, SS, 8 in. rifled barrel, blue or nickel finish. Concentric bbl. and piston. Chamfered Lever Variant: Outer front corner of cocking lever chamfered (mfg. 1930-33). Square Cocking Lever Variant: curvedouter front corner of cocking lever is squarish, recurved trigger guard, serial numbered and marked "Accles & Shelvoke LTD", 8.6 in. OAL, 2.2 lbs. Mfg. 1933-39. Ref. GR Apr. 80 and AW Sept 81.

courtesy Beeman Collection

$900	$850	$800	$750	$700	$550	$450

Add 25% for Chamfered Lever Variant. Add 40% for nickel finish.   Add 30% for .22 cal. Add 25% for Abercrombie and Fitch markings (MONOGRAM label stamped on LHS). Add 20% for factory box.

ACRO

For information on ACRO airguns, see Ampell in the "A" section.

ACVOKE

For information on Acvoke, see Accles & Shelvoke Ltd. above.

AERON CZ s.r.o.

Current manufacturer located in Brno, Czech Republic. Currently imported and/or distributed by Top Gun Air Guns Inc., located in Scottsdale, AZ. Previously imported by Airguns of Arizona located in Gilbert, AZ, Pilkington Competition Equipment LLC located in Monteagle, TN, Pyramyd Air, Inc. located in Bedford Heights, OH, by Euro-Imports, located in Pahrump, NV, Century International Arms, Inc., located in St. Albans, VT, and Bohemia Arms, located in Fountain Valley, CA.

For information on Tau model pistols and rifles previously manufactured by Aeron, see Tau BRNO in the "T" section.

GRADING	100%	95%	90%	80%	60%	40%	20%

PISTOLS

MODEL B95 - .177 cal., CO_2 refillable from tank or 12-gram capsule, SS, 8.3 in. Lothar Walther barrel, 425 FPS, adj. rear sight, adj. trigger, adj. barrel weight, adj. pistol grip, 2.4 lbs. Disc. 2004.

	100%	95%	90%	80%	60%	40%	20%
	$350	$250	$200	$145	$100	N/A	N/A

Add 5% for left-hand grip.

MODEL B96 - .177 cal., CO_2 bulk fill or 12-gram cylinder, five shot, 8.3-10 in. Lothar Walther barrel, 443 FPS, adj. rear sight, adj. trigger, adj. barrel weight, adj. pistol grip, 2.4 lbs. Disc. 2006.

courtesy Aeron CZ

	100%	95%	90%	80%	60%	40%	20%
	$575	$450	$350	$250	$150	N/A	N/A

Add 10% for left-hand model.

B97 CHAMELEON - .177 cal., CO_2, similar to Model B96 except SS.

courtesy Aeron CZ

	100%	95%	90%	80%	60%	40%	20%
	$375	$295	$235	$195	$150	N/A	N/A

MODEL B98 - .177 cal., PCP, five shot, 8.3 in. Lothar Walther barrel, 443 FPS, adj. sights, adj. trigger, adj. barrel weight, adj. pistol grip, 2.4 lbs. Disc. 2007.

courtesy Aeron

	100%	95%	90%	80%	60%	40%	20%
	$849	$750	$650	N/A	N/A	N/A	N/A

Add 5% for left-hand grip.

MODEL B99 - .177 cal., PCP, SS, 8.3 in. Lothar Walther barrel, 425 FPS, adj. rear sight, adj. trigger, adj. barrel weight, adj. pistol grip, 2.4 lbs. Disc. 2006.

	100%	95%	90%	80%	60%	40%	20%
	$695	$550	$450	$300	$245	N/A	N/A

Add 5% for left-hand grip.

GRADING	100%	95%	90%	80%	60%	40%	20%

MODEL B100 - .177 cal., PCP, SS, competition target pistol.

	$735	$600	$495	$400	$325	N/A	N/A

Add 5% for left-hand grip.

MODEL ACZ101 JUNIOR - .177 cal., PCP, SS, 8 in. Lothar Walther barrel, 443 FPS, adj. sights, adj. trigger, adj. barrel weight, adj. pistol grip, 2.4 lbs.

MSR N/A	$850	$735	$600	N/A	N/A	N/A	N/A

Add 5% for left-hand grip.

MODEL ACZ101 SPIDER - .177 cal., PCP, SS, 10 in. Lothar Walther barrel, 443 FPS, adj. sights, adj. trigger, adj. barrel weight, adj. pistol grip, 2.4 lbs.

courtesy Aeron

MSR N/A	$850	$735	$600	N/A	N/A	N/A	N/A

Add 5% for left-hand grip.

RIFLES

MODEL B40/B41/B41-5 - .177 (Model B40 and B41) or .22 (Model B41-5) cal., CO_2, SS (Model B41 and B41-5) or five shot (Model B40), 15.75 in. barrel, 476-410 FPS, UIT target model, adj. sight, adj. trigger, adj. cheek piece, adj. buttplate, wood stock, 9.5 lbs. Disc. 2005.

	$210	$185	$150	$115	$85	N/A	N/A

MODEL B40J/B41J/B41J-5 - .177 (Model B40J and B41J) or .22 (Model B41J-5) cal., CO_2, SS (Model B41J and B41J-5) or five shot (Model B40J), 15.75 in. barrel, 476-410 FPS, UIT target model, adj. sight, adj. trigger, adj. cheek piece, adj. buttplate, wood stock, 9.5 lbs. Disc. 2005.

	$210	$185	$150	$115	$85	N/A	N/A

AIR ARMS

Current manufacturer located in East Sussex, England. Currently imported by Pomona Air Guns located in Victorville, CA, Pyramyd Air, Inc. located in Bedford Heights, OH, Straight Shooters Precision Airguns in St Cloud, MN, and Top Gun Air Guns, Inc., located in Scottsdale, AZ. Previously imported by Dynamit Nobel-RWS, Inc. Dealer or consumer direct sales.

Air Arms is a division of its parent company NSP Engineering Ltd. and has been manufacturing airguns since the mid-1980s. The latest Air Arms models, S300, S310, S400, S410, and the Pro-Target (designed by three-time world champion Nick Jenkinson and gunsmith Ken Turner), are pre-charged pneumatics that can be filled from a SCUBA tank, allowing many shots to be fired from one charge. The remaining models, Pro-Sport, TX200 Mk III, TX200 HX, and Pro-Elite are spring piston rifles. All Air Arms models feature Walther barrels.

RIFLES

BORA/BORA AL - .177 or .22 (Bora AL) cal., SL, SP, SS, with (Bora AL) or w/o 35 shot mag. over barrel, 11 in. rifled steel barrel, blue finish, 625 FPS, two-stage adj. trigger, sling swivels, beech Monte Carlo stock with checkered PG and vent. recoil pad, 35.5 in. OAL, 7.7 lbs.

	$275	$225	$175	$125	$75	N/A	N/A

Add 20-40% for Bora AL.

CAMARGUE/CAMARGUE AL - .177 or .22 (Camargue AL) cal., SL, SP, SS, with (Camargue AL) or w/o 35 shot mag. over barrel, tap-loading, 15 in. rifled steel barrel, blue finish, 625 FPS, two-stage adj. trigger, sling swivels, walnut Tyrolean-style stock with checkered PG and vent. recoil pad, 39.8 in. OAL, 7.94 lbs.

	$450	$375	$325	$275	$225	N/A	N/A

Add 20-40% for Camargue AL.

GRADING	100%	95%	90%	80%	60%	40%	20%

EV2 - .177, PCP, SS, side lever loading, 16.15 in. rotary swaged barrel, black finish, quick release charging connector, adj. trigger, silver color multi-adj. cheekpiece, forearm, and butt plate, competition stock, spirit level, wind indicator, approx. 40.5 in OAL, 9.12 lbs. New 2004.

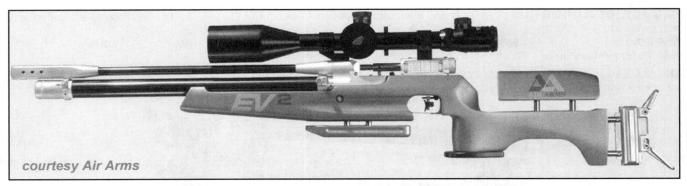

courtesy Air Arms

	100%	95%	90%	80%	60%	40%	20%
MSR N/A	$1,950	$1,750	$1,550	$1,250	N/A	N/A	N/A

Add $60 for blue/silver or red/silver laminated stock.

KHAMSIN/KHAMSIN AL - .177 or .22 (Khansin AL) cal., SL, SP, SS, with (Khansin AL) or w/o 35 shot mag. over barrel, tap-loading, 15 in. rifled steel barrel, specially polished blue finish, 625 FPS, two-stage adj. trigger, sling swivels, walnut thumbhole stock with checkered PG and vent. recoil pad, 39.8 in. OAL, 7.94 lbs.

			100%	95%	90%	80%	60%		
			$400	$325	$275	$225	$175	N/A	N/A

Add 20-40% for Khamsin AL.

MISTRAL/MISTRAL AL - .177 or .22 (Mistral AL) cal., SL, SP, SS, with (Mistral AL) or w/o 35 shot mag. over barrel, 15 in. rifled steel barrel, blue finish, 625 FPS, two-stage adj. trigger, sling swivels, beech Monte Carlo stock with checkered PG and vent. recoil pad, 39.8 in. OAL, 7.94 lbs.

courtesy Beeman Collection

	100%	95%	90%	80%	60%	40%	20%
	$350	$275	$225	$175	$125	N/A	N/A

Add 20-40% for Mistral AL.

NJR100 - similar to the TM200, except has hand-picked barrel for accuracy, adj. cheekpiece, forearm, and shoulder pad, 10.75 lbs.

	100%	95%	90%	80%	60%	40%	20%
	$1,525	$1,300	$1,100	$795	$550	N/A	N/A

Last MSR was $2600.

Add 5% for left-hand.

PRO-ELITE - .177 or .22 cal., BBC, SP, 18 ft/lbs. (.177), 22 ft/lbs. (.22), 14 in. Walther barrel, beech Monte Carlo stock with cheekpiece, 9.3 lbs.

	100%	95%	90%	80%	60%	40%	20%
	$469	$350	$280	$225	$180	N/A	N/A

PRO-SPORT - .177 or .22 cal., SP, 9.7 in., 12-groove Walther barrel, multi-adj. two-stage trigger, sound moderator, ergonomically designed high comb beech or walnut sporter stock, 9 lbs.

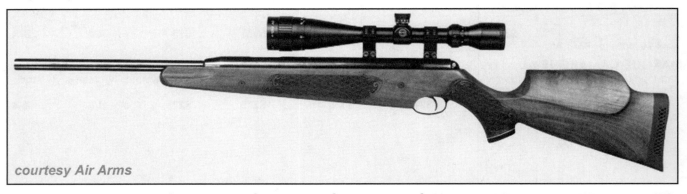

courtesy Air Arms

	100%	95%	90%	80%	60%	40%	20%
MSR N/A	$690	$550	$450	$350	N/A	N/A	N/A

Add 20% for walnut stock.

GRADING	100%	95%	90%	80%	60%	40%	20%

PRO-TARGET/PT MK III/ HUNTER - .177 or .22 cal. (Hunter), PCP, sliding bolt action, 12-groove 16 in. Walther barrel, multi-adj. trigger system, quick release charging connector, free-floating barrel (MK III), competition adj. cheekpiece, wood grain laminate, or optional red or blue laminate stock with multi-adj. butt pad, 6.6 lbs. Disc. 2001.

	100%	95%	90%	80%	60%	40%	20%
	$850	$675	$550	$450	$350	N/A	N/A

Last MSR was $1,150.

Add 15% for MK III Model or for optional laminate stock.

SM100 - .177 or .22 cal., PCP, 22 in. barrel, adj. two-stage trigger, beech stock, 8.5 lbs. Disc. 1994.

	100%	95%	90%	80%	60%	40%	20%
	$700	$600	$480	$365	$275	N/A	N/A

Last MSR was $975.

Add 10% for left-hand variation.

S200 - .177 or .22 cal., PCP, BA, SS, built-in pressure gauge, 18.9 in. rotary swaged barrel, black finish, two-stage adj. trigger, beech stock and forearm, vent. recoil pad, 35.7 in. OAL, 6.17 lbs. New 2004.

	100%	95%	90%	80%	60%	40%	20%
MSR N/A	$565	$475	$375	$275	$225	N/A	N/A

S200T - .177 cal., PCP, BA, SS, built-in pressure gauge, 18.9 in. rotary swaged barrel, black finish, two-stage adj. trigger, beech stock with adj. cheekpiece and butt pad, beech forearm,34.3-36.5 in. OAL, 6.61 lbs. New 2004.

	100%	95%	90%	80%	60%	40%	20%
MSR N/A	$625	$550	$450	$350	$275	N/A	N/A

S300 - .177 cal. or .22 cal., PCP, bolt action, 12-groove 19.7 in. Walther barrel, multi-adj. two-stage trigger, quick release charging connector, beech or walnut stock with Monte Carlo-style cheekpiece, 6.6 lbs. Disc. 2001.

	100%	95%	90%	80%	60%	40%	20%
	$350	$275	$225	$175	$125	N/A	N/A

Last MSR was $469.

Add 30% for optional deluxe thumbhole version and gold-plated trigger.

S310 - .177 cal. or .22 cal., similar to S300, except has ten-shot magazine. Disc. 2001.

	100%	95%	90%	80%	60%	40%	20%
	$450	$375	$325	$275	$225	N/A	N/A

Last MSR was $569.

Add 30% for optional deluxe thumbhole version and gold-plated trigger.

S400 (CARBINE/CLASSIC/XTRA HI-POWER) - .177 or .22 cal., PCP, side lever action, single shot, built-in pressure gauge, 12-groove 15.4 (Carbine) or 19.7 in. Walther barrel, multi-adj. two-stage trigger, quick-release charging connector, beech or walnut stock with Monte Carlo-style cheekpiece, hand checkered forearm and pistol grip, approx. 6.6 lbs. New 2001.

	100%	95%	90%	80%	60%	40%	20%
MSR N/A	$690	$550	$450	$350	N/A	N/A	N/A

S400 MPR - .177, PCP, BA, SS, built-in pressure gauge, 12-groove 18.63 in. BBL, 540 FPS, diopter sights, black finish, multi-adj. two-stage trigger, quick-release charging connector, ambidextrous beech stock with Monte Carlo-style cheekpiece, approx. 6.9 lbs, 36.4 OAL. New 2007.

courtesy Air Arms

	100%	95%	90%	80%	60%	40%	20%
MSR N/A	$975	$850	$725	$575	N/A	N/A	N/A

☉ S400 MPR-FT - .177, PCP, BA, SS, built-in pressure gauge, 12-groove 18.63 in. BBL, 540 FPS, diopter sights, black finish, multi-adj. two-stage trigger, quick-release charging connector, ambidextrous beech stock with Monte Carlo-style cheekpiece, approx. 6.9 lbs, 36.4 OAL. New 2007.

courtesy Air Arms

	100%	95%	90%	80%	60%	40%	20%
MSR N/A	$1,125	$950	$800	$625	N/A	N/A	N/A

GRADING		100%	95%	90%	80%	60%	40%	20%

S410 (CARBINE/CLASSIC/XTRA HI-POWER) - .177 or .22 cal., PCP, side lever action, ten-shot mag., built-in pressure gauge, 12-groove 15.4 (Carbine) or 19.7 in. Walther barrel, multi-adj. two-stage trigger, quick-release charging connector, beech or walnut stock with Monte Carlo-style cheekpiece, hand checkered forearm and pistol grip, approx. 6.6 lbs. New 2001.

courtesy Air Arms

MSR N/A		$690	$550	$450	$350	N/A	N/A	N/A

Add 10% for Classic or Xtra Hi-Power. Add 25% walnut stock. Add 30% for optional deluxe thumbhole walnut stock.

S410 ERB - .177 or .22 cal., PCP, side lever action, ten-shot mag., similar to S410 except hasadj. power. New 2005.

courtesy Air Arms

MSR N/A		$800	$650	$550	$450	N/A	N/A	N/A

Add10% for walnut stock. Add 20% for optional deluxe thumbhole walnut stock.

S410TDR (TAKE DOWN RIFLE) - .22 cal., PCP, side lever action, ten-shot mag., modular format with 14 in. barrel, takedown buttstock (no tools needed), two-stage adj. trigger, adj. butt pad, pressure gauge, trigger safty, and carrying case, 34.25 OAL, 5.5 lbs. New 2005.

MSR N/A		$950	$825	$700	$550	$350	N/A	N/A

TM100 - similar to XM100, except with adj. cheekpiece and shoulder pad, target-style stock, 8.75 lbs.

		$1,000	$850	$680	$475	$350	N/A	N/A

Last MSR was $1,650.

Add 5% for left-hand model.

TX200/TX200SR - .177 or .22 cal., UL, SP, 15.75 in. barrel, 913/800 FPS, 9.2 lbs.

		$460	$400	$310	$250	$175	N/A	N/A

Last MSR was $560.

Add15% for walnut stock. Add 10% for left-hand variation. Add 20% for recoilless S.R. model.

✿ **TX200 MK III** - .177 or .22 cal., UL, SP, 14.1 in. Walther barrel, sound moderator, beech or walnut stock with Monte Carlo-style cheek piece, latest version of the TX200 Series, 9.25 lbs.

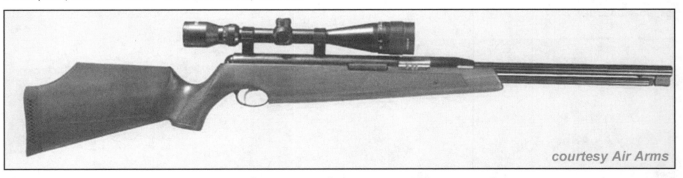

courtesy Air Arms

MSR N/A		$565	$475	$375	$275	$225	N/A	N/A

GRADING	100%	95%	90%	80%	60%	40%	20%

✿ ***TX200 HC*** - .177 or .22 cal., UL, SP, 7 in. Walther barrel, beech or walnut stock with Monte Carlo-style cheekpiece, carbine version of TX200 MK III. 8.5 lbs.

	100%	95%	90%	80%	60%	40%	20%
MSR N/A	$565	$475	$375	$275	$225	N/A	N/A

XM100 - similar to the SM100, except has quick-release tank connector and walnut stock, 8 lbs. Disc. 1994.

	100%	95%	90%	80%	60%	40%	20%
	$800	$680	$540	$400	$300	N/A	N/A

Last MSR was $1,260.

Add 10% for left-hand variation.

AIRBOW

Previous trademark used by Robin Parks for a pneumatic rifle which fires special hollow arrows.
Research is ongoing with this trademark, and more information may be included both in future editions and online.

RIFLES

AIRBOW - .38 cal. arrows inserted into barrel shroud over the barrel, PCP, SS, black composition body, detachable buddy bottle, red plastic safety, Daisy spot sight, extendable stock of M16 carbine style, 35 in. OAL with stock extended, 5.0 lbs.

courtesy Beeman Collection

	100%	95%	90%	80%	60%	40%	20%
	$425	$375	$300	$235	$150	N/A	N/A

AIR CANES

As the name suggests, these are canes containing an airgun mechanism.

AIR CANE BACKGROUND

Air canes are a whole collecting field in themselves, but they form a delightful and key part of most quality airgun collections. Wolff´s book (1958) has one of the few fairly good discussions regarding these intriguing guns. He points out that while cane firearms were novelty weapons of no great practical value, air canes were one of the pinnacles of airgun effectiveness and utility- and certainly stand as some of the finest examples of wonderfully intricate and beautifully made airgun mechanisms. In most specimens, the gun function was concealed, but some bear trigger guards, shoulder stocks, or other obvious evidence as to their nature. Most apparently were designed for self-defense or as a method of carrying a hunting arm while out walking- in those days, the transition between town and country could come rather quickly.
The Golden Age of air canes came in the 1800s when English air canes dominated the field. Key makers of London and Birmingham included John Blanch, Edward Reilly, and James Townsend. An airgun was part of the attire of many a well-dressed English gentleman of the late 1800s. Most specimens were sold in wonderfully fitted cases with their pump and accessories. These accessories often included a rifle-style, buttstock-shaped air reservoir or skeleton wooden buttstock which could be carried in the huge pockets of a gentleman's "great coat" until extra air volume and/or steadiness of fire were needed from the air cane.

AIR CANE CONFIGURATIONS

The mechanism almost always was pneumatic, usually being charged by numerous strokes from a separate pump. A few have a self-contained pump and a few use pre-charged air cartridges, and extremely rare variantsfeatured a spring-piston mechanism. The typical pattern was two parts: the rear half of the gun was the tubular air reservoir and valve mechanism; the forward half contained the barrel and lock mechanism. These lock mechanisms were often jewel-like in their detail and operation.
Rather commonly, there were two barrels, a smooth bore in which a rifled barrel was nestled, or vice versa. The rifled barrels usually were brass, bearing an elegantly scalloped rifling of twenty-two or more shallow, low-friction grooves. A ramrod was housed within the nest of barrels, with its handle forming the screw-off base tip of the cane. The trigger, typically, issimply a button which protrudes only when the gun is ready to be put up to your cheek, aimed, and fired. Sights and even a trigger guard
may be present externally. Weight varied from 1.5 to over 8 pounds; calibers generally were in the .30 to .36 area, but ranged from .177 to .75! The projectiles of air canes generally were lead balls, cast from the molds included in cased outfits. However, imagination seemed to be the only limit as to what could be fired from these amazing guns. Shot, darts, arrows, bullets,and even harpoons and multipronged fish and frog spears have been utilized!

AIR CANES RECENTLY MANUFACTURED

There recently has been a small renaissance in air canes. In the 1980s, Harper produced some wonderful modern air canes in England. As these utilized the Brocock air cartridges instead of a built-in air reservoir, they could be made very slim and truly elegant. The handles sometimes were wonderfully carved dogs' heads or other figures. Fold-out triggers were virtually undetectable in the fine engraving. In the United States, also in the 1980s, the famed airgun maker Gary Barnes produced an amazingly intricate and functionally astonishing full automatic air cane!

AIR CANES CUE BALL TYPE

Cue Ball CO_2 Air Canes are configuration of air canes made to resemble a black metal cane with a billiard ball for its knob. These air canes fire a CO_2 cylinder as the projectile, with astonishing force and range. Firing causes the seal on the CO_2 cylinder to be pierced. Pressure builds until the cylinder itself is propelled from the muzzle. The cylinder, as a projectile, gathers additional velocity from jetting action. The inventor apparently wishes to remain anonymous because of the mistaken idea that these air canes would be considered as "destructive devices" by the BATF because they are over .50 caliber. Actually, BATF has no jurisdiction over these air canes because they are not firearms! John Caruth obtained six of these air canes and had twenty-five of them reproduced by Tom Allison in the 1990s. The original maker also made a few specimens which retain the CO_2 cylinder but fire a conventional .45 caliber lead ball. The original price for these Cue Ball CO_2 Air Canes was $350. Values now run from about $150 to $450 for the cylinder-shooting Cue Ball CO_2 air canes and about $200 to $500 for the ball-firing Cue Ball CO_2 air canes. The authors and publisher wish to thank Mr. John Caruth for assistance on Cue Ball Air Cane information in this edition of the Blue Book of Airguns.

AIR CANE VALUES

Values of air canes vary greatly, but a typical British air cane in good condition generally will sell for $600 to $1,200. A cased Air Cane w/ accessories (original pump, bullet mold, cocking key, and disassembly tool) and in fine condition will sell in the $3,000 plus range.

A variety of air canes (top to bottom):
American aircane with built in pump, dogs head handle made of horn.
Giant British aircane with trigger guard.
British aircane with knobby branch surface - concealing nature of gun.
British aircane - slim, muzzle-loading version.
British breech loading aircane.
British muzzle-loading aircane - the most common aircane type.
Courtesy of Beeman Collection

AIRFORCE AIRGUNS

Current manufacturer and distributor located in Fort Worth, TX. Dealer and consumer direct sales.
The project to design and produce the AirForce Talon began in 1994. Shipping began in the U.S. during 1999. The Talon Series has pre-charged single shots with variable power. They were first marketed in England under the name Gun Power Stealth, and they are manufactured in Fort Worth, TX, by designer John McCaslin.

GRADING	100%	95%	90%	80%	60%	40%	20%

RIFLES

CONDOR - .177, 20 (new 2007), or .22 cal., single shot, PCP (490cc compressed air bottle doubles as shoulder stock), external thumb-pressure-operated adj. power system allows 600-1,300 FPS (depending on cal. and pellet weight), 24 in. Lothar Walther barrel (interchangeable for cal.), aircraft-grade aluminum alloy and polymer construction with three integrated dovetail rails for accessories, two-stage adj. trigger, black anodized finish, 6.5 lbs. (gun and bottle), 38.75 in., OAL. New 2004.

courtesy Airforce Airguns

MSR $608	$575	$495	$395	$300	N/A	N/A	N/A

Add $65 for fiberoptic open sights or refill clamp. Add $134 for 4-16x50mm scope and one inch high rings. Add $185 for refill clamp, 4-16x50mm scope, and one inch high rings.
AirForce Airguns offers accessories for all models (too many to list). Contact AirForce Airguns (see Trademark Index) for price and availability.

TALON - .177 or .22 cal., single shot, PCP (compressed air bottle doubles as shoulder stock), external thumb-pressure-operated adj. power system allows 400-1000 FPS (depending on cal. and pellet weight), 18 in. Lothar Walther barrel (interchangeable for cal.), aircraft-grade aluminum alloy and polymer construction with three integrated dovetail rails for accessories, two-stage adj. trigger, black anodized finish, 5.5 lbs. (gun and bottle), 32.6 in., OAL. New 1998.

MSR $495	$465	$375	$275	$225	N/A	N/A	N/A

Add $65 for fiberoptic open sights or refill clamp. Add $113 for 3-9x40mm scope and one inch high rings. Add $165 for refill clamp, 3-9x40mm scope, and one inch high rings.
AirForce Airguns offers accessories for all models (too many to list). Contact AirForce Airguns (see Trademark Index) for price and availability.

TALON SS - .177 or .22 cal., similar to Talon, except has 12 in. Lothar Walther barrel in an extended shroud with muzzle cap sound moderator system, 5.25 lbs. (gun and bottle), 32.75 in., OAL. New 2000.

MSR $515	$485	$395	$300	$250	N/A	N/A	N/A

Add $65 for fiberoptic open sights or refill clamp. Add $145 for 4-16x50mm scope and one inch high rings. Add $195 for refill clamp, 4-16x50mm scope, and one inch high rings. Add $937 for Ultimate Condor Combo.
AirForce Airguns offers accessories for all models (too many to list). Contact AirForce Airguns (see Trademark Index) for price and availability.

GRADING	100%	95%	90%	80%	60%	40%	20%

AIRGUNAID

Previous manufacturer located in Chelmsford, Essex, Great Britain circa 1980-82.

Research is ongoing with this trademark, and more information will be included both in future editions and online. Basically these are Scottish Diana rifles fitted with a .20 cal. barrel. It took the Brits a while to pick up on this caliber, which was introduced to precision spring piston airguns by the Beeman company in the 1970s. Average original condition specimens are typically priced in the $100 to $200 range.

AIRGUN EXPRESS, INC.

Previous importer with retail catalog sales located in Bedford Heights, Ohio, previously located in Montezuma, IA. In July, 2006 Airgun Express was sold to and has been integrated with Pyramyd Air in Bedford Heights, Ohio.

Mail order and catalog sales of many major brand airguns including Beeman, Crosman, Daisy, Gamo, Mendoza (importer), RWS, and others. Please contact the company directly for more information and prices of their products (see Trademark Index listing).

AIR GUN INC.

Previous importer and distributor located in Houston, TX.

Air Gun Inc. previously imported Industry Brand airguns (disc. 2006). Please refer to the "I" section of this book for information on these airguns.

AIR LOGIC

Previous manufacturer and distributor located in Forest Row, Sussex, England. Air Logic had limited importation into the U.S.

RIFLES

GENESIS - .22 cal., SL, single-stroke pneumatic, 630 FPS, bolt-action sliding barrel by Lothar Walther, recoilless, adj. trigger, 9.50 lbs. Mfg. began in 1988. Disc.

	100%	95%	90%	80%	60%	40%	20%
	$575	$450	$360	$295	$225	N/A	N/A

Last MSR was $750.

AIR MATCH

Previous trademark manufactured in Italy circa 1980s. Previously imported by Kendall International located in Paris, KY.

PISTOLS

MODEL 400 - .177 cal., SL, single-stroke pneumatic, adj. trigger, UIT target model, 2 lbs.

	100%	95%	90%	80%	60%	40%	20%
	$320	$260	$180	$105	$60	N/A	N/A

MODEL 600 - .177 cal., SL, single-stroke pneumatic, adj. sights, adj. trigger, UIT target model, 2 lbs.

	100%	95%	90%	80%	60%	40%	20%
	$350	$280	$200	$125	$80	N/A	N/A

AIRROW

Current registered trademark of Swivel Machine Works, Inc., currently located in located in Newtown, CT, previously located in Milford, CT.

Swivel Machine Works, Inc., started manufacturing arrow-firing rifles and pistols in 1990, and has recently started manufacturing pellet-firing air rifles. Contact the manufacturer directly for information and prices on their arrow-firing models.

PISTOLS

AIRROW PISTOL ABS 013 - arrow firing, PCP, SS, takes down to watertight case (provided), 24.8 in. OAL, 5 lbs. Mfg. 1990-2005.

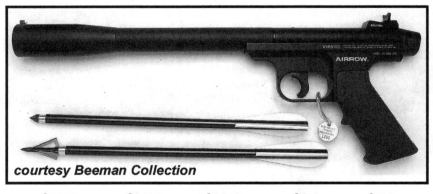

courtesy Beeman Collection

	100%	95%	90%	80%	60%	40%	20%
	$1,500	$1,250	$1,000	$750	$500	N/A	N/A

GRADING	100%	95%	90%	80%	60%	40%	20%

RIFLES

AIRROW MODEL A-8SRB STEALTH - 177, .22, or .38 cal., CO_2 or PCP, SS or nine-shot mag., 20 in. rifled BBL, 1100 FPS, scope rings included, 35 in. OAL, 7.5 lbs.

courtesy Airrow

MSR $2,299	$2,299	$1,995	$1,650	$1,250	$995	N/A	N/A

Many options available.

AIRROW ARCHERY MODEL A-8S1P STELTH - arrow firing, PCP, 7 oz. cylinder w/ valve, SS, air trigger, 16 in. BBL., Car stock,scope rings, takes down to watertight case (provided). Mfg.1990-date.

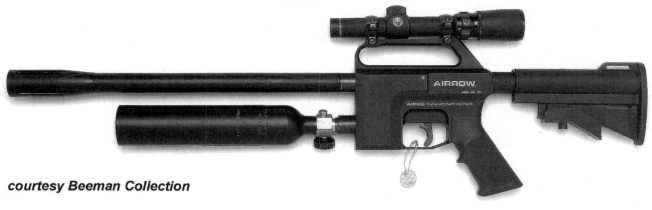

courtesy Beeman Collection

MSR $1,699	$1,500	$1,250	$1,000	$750	$500

Performs to 2,000 PSIG above or below water level.

AIR SOFT

Term currently used to identify a configuration of gun copies primarily manufactured in the Orient.

In the last two decades a new type of gun has appeared. The so-called Air Soft guns originally were designed to be a type of non-gun for customers whose local laws highly restricted or forbade the ownership of actual firearms. Generally, they are made in the styling (sometimes very exact styling)of well-known firearms. Models ranged from copies of famous handguns to heavy machine guns. They soon became popular with customers who wanted to collect, and even have the sensation of firing, guns which were too expensive, too highly regulated, or too dangerous for general ownership. Most fire relatively harmless 6 mm diameter light plastic balls at muzzle velocities below 300 FPS. Even those which fire at somewhat higher power generally are not capable of inflicting serious injury to humans or property. Balls filled with paint or made of aluminum sometimes are available but have not been very popular and may be difficult to buy locally. Many of the Air Softguns are not designed to fire paintballs or metal balls and may be damaged or ruined by their use.

The classification of Air Softguns has led to some interesting legal questions. Without a doubt, they are not firearms and are not dangerous or lethal weapons. In fact, they are not weapons in any sense unless one might use them as a club. They may use carbon dioxide, compressed air, or mechanical means, including electrical micro-motors to propel their projectiles – so some are not even truly airguns. Federal law requires the versions firing plastic balls to have at least their muzzle areas conspicuously marked with blaze orange color, but illegal unmarked imports often appear.

From a safety standpoint, by far the largest caution is to not brandish them where they might be mistaken for dangerous weapons. There have been cases were individuals used such guns in holdups or pointed them at police officers in dark alleys or where several teenagers wearing ski masks appeared with exact lookalikes of AK 47s, Thompson sub-machine guns, M16 rifles, etc. at their schools – distinctly unwise moves. But certainly over 99.9% are used and enjoyed harmlessly – often as enjoyable substitutes for potentially harmful real guns. Production of Air Soft guns, mainly in the Orient, has become a huge market. They range from toy-like, almost insulting imitations to very sophisticated, expensive copies of heavy machine guns which may use well-made metal or even original parts from deactivated real automatic weapons. This is now a collecting field in itself and not be covered in this guide unless a specimen has special historical significance. Values run from a couple of

GRADING	100%	95%	90%	80%	60%	40%	20%

dollars for plastic specimens which only suggest their design origin to hundreds of dollars for those sophisticated specimens with well-made, or even original, metal parts. There is a great deal of information on Air Soft guns available on the Web. Two examples are illustrated: Left (very realistic example): A Daisy copy of an Uzi sub-machine gun, with replica cartridges and magazine (produced before the requirement for blaze orange markings). Right (caricature, toy-like example): representation of AK-47 rifle. Note that the package of the projectiles is labeled: BB BULLET – but the contents are neither BBs nor bullets! Ref. *Blue Book of Airguns*, edition 4.

courtesy Beeman Collection

ALFA - PROJ spol. sr.o.

Current manufacturer located in Brno, Czech Republic. Currently imported and/or distributed by Top Gun Air Guns Inc., located in Scottsdale, AZ. Previously imported (until 2007) by Pyramyd Air, Inc. located in Bedford Heights, OH.

PISTOLS

ALFA CO$_2$ SPORT - .177 cal., CO$_2$, SS, adj. sights, adj. trigger, 450 FPS. New 2006.

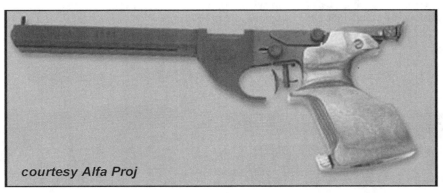

courtesy Alfa Proj

	100%	95%	90%	80%	60%	40%	20%
No MSR.	$465	$395	$350	N/A	N/A	N/A	N/A

RIFLES

ALFA CO$_2$ TARGET - .177 cal., CO$_2$, SS, adj. sights, adj. cheeckpiece, adj. butt plate. New 2006.

	100%	95%	90%	80%	60%	40%	20%
No MSR.	$495	$450	$395	N/A	N/A	N/A	N/A

ALROS

Current manufacturer of CO$_2$ and PCP rifles located in Staffs, United Kingdom. 1993 - present. No current U.S. importation.

The authors and publisher wish to thank Mr. Tim Saunders for assistance with this information.

RIFLES

SHADOW - .177, .20, or .22 cal., PCP, SS or eight-shot mag., BA (RH or LH), blue finish, beech or walnut stock, with or without thumbhole. Sporting rifles infour variants(three with built-in air reservoir): M60 Hunter, M100 Carbine, M140 Standard, and the Shadow 400 variant with removable 400 cc buddy bottle, 39/40 in. OAL, 7-7.5 lbs. Mfg. beginning in 1997.

	$650	$575	$500	$400	$300	$250	$200

Add 10% for Shadow 400. Add 20% for eight-shot magazine. Add 10% for walnut stock. Add 25% for thumbhole walnut stock.

STARFIRE - similar to Shadow, except has two 12 gm. CO$_2$ cylinders, power level set at UK 12 ft. lb. limit, approx forty shots per charge.

Current values not yet determined.

TRAILSMAN - .177, .20, or .22 cal., PCP, SS, BA (RH or LH), 16mm Lothar Walther barrel, blue finish, adj. tubular stock, composition grips, takedown construction. Two variants: Trailsman Standard with built-in reservoir under barrel, 5 lbs. Trailsman 400 with removable 400 cc buddy bottle reservoir, 6 lbs. New late 1990s.

	$530	$450	$375	$300	$225	$175	$125

Add 10% for Trailsman 400.

GRADING	100%	95%	90%	80%	60%	40%	20%

AMERICAN ARMS, INC.

Previous manufacturer and importer located in North Kansas City, MO until 2000.

Even though American Arms, Inc. imported Norica airguns, they are listed in this section because of their private label status. Importation began in late 1988 and was discontinued in 1989. For more information and current pricing on imported American Arms, Inc. firearms, please refer to the *Blue Book of Gun Values* by S.P. Fjestad (also available online).

PISTOLS

IDEAL - .177 cal., BBC, SP, 400 FPS, adj. sights, 3 lbs.

	100%	95%	90%	80%	60%	40%	20%
	$75	$60	$45	$30	$20	N/A	N/A

Last MSR was $105.

RIFLES

JET RIFLE - .177 cal., BBC, SP, 855 FPS, adj. double-set triggers, hardwood stock, 7 lbs.

	100%	95%	90%	80%	60%	40%	20%
	$100	$85	$70	$55	$40	N/A	N/A

Last MSR was $160.

Subtract $35 for Junior Model.

COMMANDO - .177 cal., BBC, SP, 540 FPS, adj. sights, 5 lbs.

	100%	95%	90%	80%	60%	40%	20%
	$80	$65	$50	$40	$25	N/A	N/A

Last MSR was $115.

AMERICAN GALLERY AIRGUNS

This is a group of fairly well-defined airguns which were produced by American gunsmiths just before and after the U.S. Civil War (1861-65).

Travel to the country was difficult for city folks at the time these guns were made. These airguns, typically provided by concessionaires in indoor ranges, provided a means of satisfying the desire to shoot. Again, Wolff (1958) has one of the few good discussions of these interesting airguns which had been unappreciated for a long time. Now they are becoming increasingly hard to acquire as demand and understanding has soared. These airguns are highly stylized from European patterns, such as those made by Josef Rutte of Bohemia around 1830. All have a huge central spring cylinder ahead of the trigger guard, containing a double volute mainspring system. All have leather piston seals and smoothbore barrels. The two main cranking methods are by a crank handle ("Kurblespanner") or by a lever pivoted at the buttplate and typically shaped into the trigger guard in the forward end ("Bügelspanner"). And while virtually all are breech loaders, the particular methods of loading and cocking are classified into several groups.

1. Primary New York: Apparently among the earliest of American gallery airguns, these seem to have developed from European forms which use a detachable crank handle to cock the mainspring. The European forms have a tip-up breech; the American forms developed an unusual breech which opened by twisting the receiver. Famous makers include David and Joseph Lurch, G. Fisher, and August Mock.
2. Secondary New York: A small group featuring the twist-breech loading of the Primary forms, but cocked by a cocking lever formed by a rearward extension of the trigger guard. A gun of this type by John Zuendorff has been credited as being used in the draft riots of the American Civil War.
3. Upstate New York: A small, special group. The main feature is a hand-operated revolving cylinder with the barrel attaching to the receiver with a pin, wedge, and bottom strap in a manner and styling very similar to an open-top Colt revolver. 12- or 13-shot cylinders are known. The only makers listed by Wolff are Charles Bunge and C. Werner.
4. St. Louis: The key characteristic is a long cocking lever of which the forward end is formed by the trigger guard and the remainder concealed in a groove in the under edge of the buttstock. The barrel tips up for breech loading. The stocks have separate buttstock and forearm sections. A large group; famous makers include Bandle, Blickensdoerfer, and Stein.
5. New England: The buttstock and forearm are one piece. A fixed, two-piece cocking lever along the forward side of the receiver swings up and back for cocking. The barrel tips up or twists to a loose open position for loading. Two known makers are Eggers and Tonks.
6. Top Lever Gallery Air Rifle: Cocks by pulling back on heavy lever inserted into comb of rifle. Illustration shows the lever partially up for clarity.
7. Pop Up: Loads via a pop-up breech block in top of receiver.

About 1870 the gallery gun design, so well-developed in America, migrated to Europe and was continued as the European "Bügelspanner" for almost a century by several makers, most notably Oscar Will of Zella-Mehlis, Germany. Will frequently marked his guns as "Original Will" to distinguish them from the many copies -- some of these copies, amusingly, were then marked as "Original". Unmarked copies are rather common.

Values of American Gallery Airguns have escalated from a few hundred dollars only a decade ago, to $1,000 or $2,000 more recently, and especially rare forms, such as Upstate New York models, bear asking prices of up to five thousand dollars. The later European "Bügelspanner" generally sells for $200 to $300, with the "Original Will" marking and better condition adding to the price.

Primary New York

Secondary New York

GRADING	100%	95%	90%	80%	60%	40%	20%

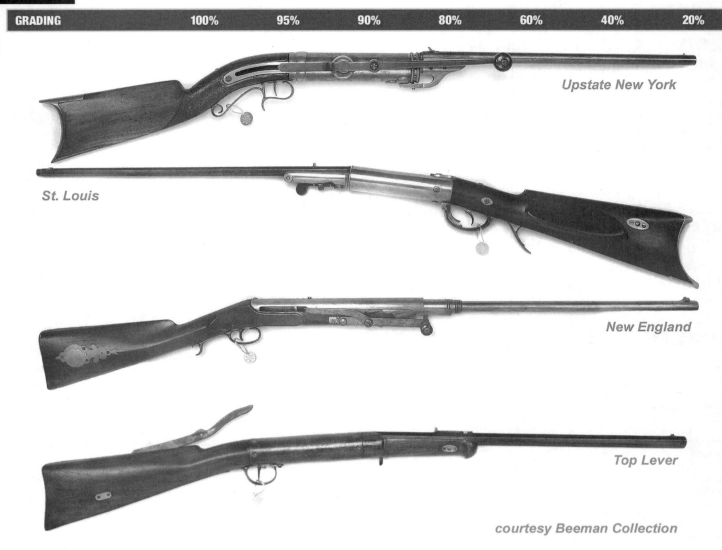

Upstate New York

St. Louis

New England

Top Lever

courtesy Beeman Collection

AMERICAN LUGER

For information on American Luger airguns, see Schimel in the "S" section.

AMERICAN TOOL WORKS

Previous manufacturer of BB guns in Chicago, IL. This company purchased other BB gun makers and produced BB guns under American, Sterling, Upton, and Wyandotte trademarks.

The authors and publisher wish to thank Dennis Baker and John Groenewold for their valuable assistance with the following information in this edition of the *Blue Book of Airguns*. Most guns by American Tool Works were typical SP, LA, BB rifles of rather plain appearance, except for the big 1000-shot repeaters with an octagonal barrel tube, walnut stock, and bright nickel plating. The factory tools went from buyer to buyer and finally ended up with Markham-King in 1929. King dumped the tools in the Detroit River and Daisy finally consumed King and the designs and patents. Guns were made circa 1891-1928 (see Dunathan, 1971). Additional research is underway on this complex group. Information given here must be considered as tentative. Information and illustrations from other collectors is solicited at bluebookedit@Beemans.net.

RIFLES

AMERICAN DART RIFLE - BB/.174 cal., SP, LA, SS, loaded with feathered darts through a cover plate under the barrel, all sheet metal, barrel marked "American Dart Rifle, Upton Machine Company, St. Joseph, Michigan. Ca. 1912-20".

N/A	$800	$650	$500	$350	$225	$150

STERLING SINGLE SHOT There appear to be three variations. This model is under research, and more information will be made available in future editions of this guide.

GRADING	100%	95%	90%	80%	60%	40%	20%

STERLING MODEL D - BB/.174 cal., SP, LA, 1000 shot, octagon barrel tube, nickel or blue finish, 32.2 in. OAL, 2.4 lbs.

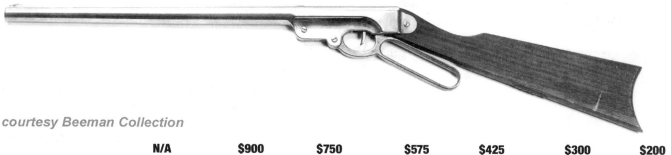

courtesy Beeman Collection

	N/A	$900	$750	$575	$425	$300	$200

Sold by Sears for $1.68 in 1917.

STERLING MODEL G - BB/.174 cal., 1000 shot, SP, LA, octagon barrel tube, nickel or blue finish, barrel marked "American Tool Works". 36 in OAL, 2.4 lbs.

courtesy Beeman Collection

	N/A	$900	$750	$575	$425	$300	$200

UPTON SPECIAL - BB/.174 cal., similar to Sterling Model G, except marked "Upton", 500-shot repeater.

	N/A	$450	$375	$300	$225	$150	$85

Offered by Sears.

UPTON SINGLE SHOT - BB/.174 cal., similar to Sterling Single Shot, except marked "Upton".

	N/A	$250	$200	$150	$100	$75	$50

Offered by Sears in 1922 for $1.15.

UPTON MODEL 10 - BB/.174 cal. . BBC, SS, ring trigger versions of Daisy 20 Variant 3 and Markham number 10 variant 3. 29.5 in. OAL.

	N/A	$900	$750	$575	$425	$300	$200

UPTON MODEL 20 - BB/.174 cal., SP, LA, SS, round barrel cover with distinctive humped ridge under barrel cover ahead of trigger guard, straight grip, slab sided stock, marked as made by Upton Machine Co. in St. Joseph, Michigan, patent dates of 1914 and 1923, 32.3 in., OAL.

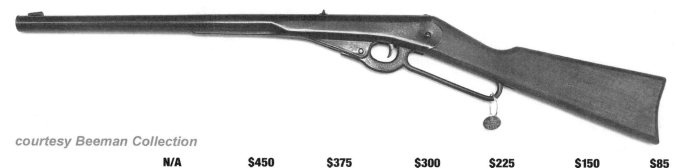

courtesy Beeman Collection

	N/A	$450	$375	$300	$225	$150	$85

UPTON MODEL 30 (350 SHOT) - SP, LA, SS, round barrel cover with humped ridge under barrel cover ahead of trigger guard, straight grip, slab side stock, marked as made by Upton Machine Co. in St. Joseph, Michigan. Patent dates of June 13, 1914 Others Pending. 32.3 in. OAL.
  Current values not yet determined.

UPTON MODEL 40 - BB/.174 cal., similar to Upton Model 20, except 1000 shot.

	N/A	N/A	$500	$375	$250	$175	$100

Sold by Sears in 1922 for $1.48.

UPTON MODEL 50 (500 SHOT) - SP, LA, SS, round barrel cover with humped ridge under barrel cover ahead of trigger guard, straight grip, slab side stock, marked as made by Upton Machine Co.in St. Joesph, Michigan. Patent dates of 1914 and 1923, 32.3 in.OAL.
  Current values not yet determined.

GRADING	100%	95%	90%	80%	60%	40%	20%

UPTON MODEL 1000 - BB/.174 cal. 1000 shot repeater, LA, 35.5 in. OAL. Similar in size, shape, and appearance to Upton Model 40.

	N/A	N/A	$625	$500	$350	$225	$150

UPTON MODEL C - BB/.174 cal., SP, LA, very Daisy-like styling with pistol grip stock.

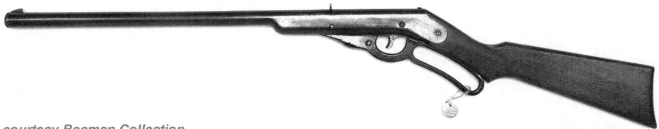

courtesy Beeman Collection

	N/A	$250	$200	$150	$100	$75	$50

UPTON MODEL D - BB/.174 cal. LA, SS, muzzle loader. 32.3 in OAL. Similar in size, shape, and appearance to Upton Model 50.

	N/A	N/A	$575	$450	$350	$250	$150

UPTON MODEL F (500 SHOT) - SP, LA, SS, 32.3in.OAL.
   Current values not yet determined.

WYANDOTTE - BB/.174 cal., similar to Upton Model 40, except marked "All Metal Products, Wyandotte, Michigan".

	N/A	$450	$375	$300	$225	$150	$85

Also made under the Sears name as the Ranger Repeating Air Rifle.

AMPELL

Previous trade name of air and gas guns manufactured by Playtime Products located at 48 E. Main Street, Honeoye, NY, circa 1968-1975. Some production in Canada.

PISTOLS

ACRO 1/S-177/S-220 - .175/BB or .22 cal., CO_2, SS pellet or lead ball (S-177 or S-220) or 80-shot gravity feed mag., cocking gun also loads gun for each shot, all exposed parts cast metal with matte black finish, combination cocking knob/manual safety -- cannot be reset to safe after moving to fire position, 350 FPS, 11.5 in. OAL, 2.6 lbs.

courtesy Beeman Collection

$85	$65	$55	$45	$40	$35	$25

Add 20% for single-shot pellet pistols. Add 20% for original factory kit with Ampell pellets and CO_2 cylinders and papers.

RIFLES

BB MAGNUM M44 - .174/BB cal., SSP, lead or steel BB, 48-shot gravity feed magazine, 350+ FPS, swinging forearm cocks, charges, and loads gun, wood stock, styled like Winchester M-1894 but without cocking lever, combination cocking knob/manual safety -- cannot be reset to safe after moving to fire position, 38 in. OAL, 4.5 lbs.

courtesy Beeman Collection

$175	$150	$125	$100	$75	$50	$40

Add 15% for original factory box and papers.

GRADING	100%	95%	90%	80%	60%	40%	20%

ANICS GROUP

Current manufacturer established in 1990, and located in Moscow, Russia. Currently imported by European American Armory Corp. located in Rockledge, FL. Previously imported by Air Rifle Specialists located in Pine City, NY and Compasseco located in Bardstown, KY. Anics Group was originally an importer of Western-made airguns and firearms. In 1996, they began manufacturing their own line of CO_2 guns, semi-autos, and revolvers.

PISTOLS

MODEL A-101 - BB/.175 cal., CO_2, semi-auto, fifteen-shot mag., 450 FPS, checkered plastic grips, blue or silver finish, wooden checkered grips on silver models, adj. rear sight. Disc. 2006.

	$100	$75	$50	$35	$20	N/A	N/A

MODEL A-101M (MAGNUM) - BB/.175 cal., CO_2, semi-auto, fifteen-shot, 490 FPS, compensator, checkered plastic grips, blue or silver finish, wooden checkered grips on silver models, adj. rear sight. Disc. 2006.

	$100	$75	$50	$35	$20	N/A	N/A

MODEL A-111 - BB/.175 cal., CO_2, semi-auto, fifteen-shot, 450 FPS, contoured plastic grips, blue or silver finish, adj. rear sight. Disc. 2006.

	$100	$75	$50	$35	$20	N/A	N/A

MODEL A-112/A-112L (LASER) - BB/.175 cal., CO_2, semi-auto, fifteen-shot, 490 FPS, adj. rear sight, or with built-in laser housed in barrel lug automatically activated with slight pull of the trigger, contoured plastic grips, blue or silver finish. Disc. 2006.

	$100	$75	$50	$35	$20	N/A	N/A

Add $50 for Model A-112L (Laser).

MODEL A-3000 SKIF - BB/.175 or .177 cal., CO_2, SA or DA, 28-shot rotary mag., 500 FPS, thumb-release safety, grooved trigger guard, ambidextrous mag. release, three-dot adj. target sights, fiberglass-reinforced polyamide frame and grip, matte black or matte black with silver finish slide, hard plastic carrying case, loading tool, and spare rotary magazine, 1 lb. 9 oz. New 2001.

courtesy Howard Collection

MSR $167	$160	$125	$80	$65	$40	N/A	N/A

Add 10% for silver slide (Model A-3000 Silver). Add 20% for long barrel (Model A-3000 LB).

MODEL A9000S BERETTA - BB/.175 or .177 cal., CO_2, SA or DA, 22-shot rotary mag., 470 FPS, thumb-release safety, grooved trigger guard, ambidextrous mag. release, three-dot fixed sights, fiberglass-reinforced polyamide frame and grip, matte black, hard plastic carrying case, loading tool, and spare rotary magazine, 1 lb. 9 oz. New 2007.

courtesy Anics Group

MSR $178	$170	$135	$100	$75	$45	N/A	N/A

REVOLVERS

MODEL A-201 - BB/.175 cal., CO_2, SA or DA, thirty-shot, 410 FPS, loaded through cylinder (five BBs in each chamber), adj. rear sight, contoured plastic grips, CO_2 cartridge loads through base of grip, cylinder rotates when gun is fired, blue or silver finish. Disc.

	$120	$95	$80	$65	$40	N/A	N/A

GRADING	100%	95%	90%	80%	60%	40%	20%

MODEL A-201 MAGNUM - BB/.175 cal., CO_2, SA or DA, thirty-shot, 460 FPS, loaded through cylinder (five BBs in each chamber), adj. rear sight, contoured plastic grips, CO_2 cartridge loads through base of grip, cylinder rotates when gun is fired, blue or silver finish.

	100%	95%	90%	80%	60%	40%	20%
	$125	$105	$80	$65	$40	N/A	N/A

ANSCHÜTZ

Current manufacturer (J. G. ANSCHÜTZ GmbH & Co. KG) established in 1856, and located in Ulm, Germany. Currently imported and/ or distributed by Champion´s Choice, located in LaVergne, TN, Champion´s Shooter´s Supply, located in New Albany, OH, Gunsmithing, Inc., located in Colorado Springs, CO, and International Shooters Service, located in Fort Worth, TX. Previously imported by Pilkington Competion Equipment LLC located in Monteagle, TN.

Models 2001 and 2002 were previously imported by Precision Sales Intl., Inc. Models 333, 335, and 380 were previously imported by Crosman from 1986 to 1988. Model 380 was also previously imported by Marksman. Research is ongoing with this trademark, and more information will be included both online and in future editions. For more information and current pricing on both new and used Anschütz firearms, please refer to the *Blue Book of Gun Values* by S.P. Fjestad (also available online).

PISTOLS

DOLLA MARK II - .177 cal., SP, SS, push-barrel cocking, may be stamped "KEENFIRE" or w/ "JGA" or "Dolla" medalion on wooden grips, no barrel shroud, mainspring visible around barrel when not cocked, nickel-plated finish, load by unscrewing plug at back end of barrel,8.1 in. OAL (uncocked), 0.6 lbs. Mfg. 1929-1939.

courtesy Beeman Collection

	100%	95%	90%	80%	60%	40%	20%
	N/A	N/A	$195	$150	$125	$95	$75

Add 30% for "KEENFIRE" marking (for American market only).
More primitive, but better materials, than JGA - sometimes with Dolla medallions.

JGA (MODEL 100) - .177 cal. darts, pellets, or shot, SP, SS, push-barrel cocking, mainspring covered by barrel shroud, black plastic body with JGA molded into brown plastic checkered grips, nickel plating on barrel shroud, trigger guard, and trigger, load by unscrewing plug at back end of barrel. 8.3 in. OAL uncocked, 0.5 lbs. Mfg. early 1950s to early 1960s.

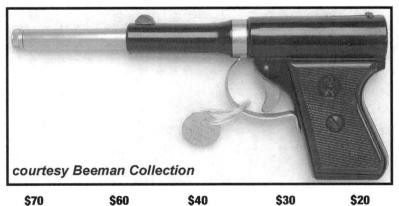

courtesy Beeman Collection

	100%	95%	90%	80%	60%	40%	20%
	$70	$60	$40	$30	$20	N/A	N/A

Also known as IGA.

MODEL M5 JUNIOR - .177 cal., PCP, similar to Model M10, except shorter and lighter.

	100%	95%	90%	80%	60%	40%	20%
	$600	$500	$400	$300	$200	N/A	N/A

GRADING	100%	95%	90%	80%	60%	40%	20%

MODEL LP@ ANSCHÜTZ - .177 cal., PCP, UIT match pistol, 8.93 in. barrel with compensator, internal stabilizer, adj. trigger, adj. sights, adj. Morini grip, 2.47 lbs. 16.54 OAL. New 2001.

courtesy Anschütz

MSR N/A	$1,450	$1,250	$995	$875	$695	N/A	N/A

☸ *Model LP@ ANSCHÜTZ Junior* - .177 cal., PCP, UIT match pistol, 7.5 in. barrel with compensator, internal stabilizer, adj. trigger, adj. sights, adj. Morini grip, 1.92 lbs. 13.98 OAL. New 2004.

MSR N/A	$1,285	$1,150	$995	$875	$695	N/A	N/A

☸ *Model LP@ ANSCHÜTZ Light* - .177 cal., PCP, UIT match pistol, similar to Model LP@ ANSCHÜTZ except has extra small (XS) grip, 2.05 lbs. 16.54 OAL. New 2005.

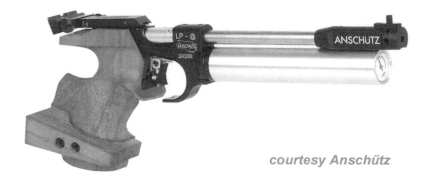

courtesy Anschütz

MSR N/A	$1,285	$1,150	$995	$875	$695	N/A	N/A

MODEL M10 - .177 cal., PCP, 492 FPS, 9.50 in. barrel with compensator, adj. trigger, sights and pistol grip, special dry firing mechanism, walnut grips. Mfg. by SAM in Switzerland 1997-98.

	$700	$550	$475	$400	$300	N/A	N/A

Last MSR was $1,395.

RIFLES

Note: Anschütz has issued a recall of some aluminum air cylinders for target air rifles manufactured prior to December, 2005. This recall only refers to the aluminum air cylinders and not to the complete target air rifle. For more information go to the Anschütz website at http://jga.anschuetz-sport.com.

Durring late 2007 Anschütz introduced S2 version PCP target rifles. The S2 has improved air flow characteristics and needs about 50 % less impact energy to open the valve when firing the shot. Thus the air rifle barreled action is subjected to almost no vibrations. This could be reached by changing the following components:
1. Valve body and valve (the valve body is coated with gold).
2. Action head (visible from the golden coating).
3. Improved cocking piston.
4. New stabilizer which has a higher mass and an extended adjusting range.
5. New spring box.
6. New pressure regulator.

MODEL 35 - .175 cal., BBC, SP, SS, 17.7 in. BBL, blue finish, adj. two-stage trigger, adj. rear and hooded ramp front sights, walnut stained checkered PG stock w/ rubber butt plate, 42.5 in. OAL, 7.4 lbs.
    At the time of publishing MSR and pricing N/A.

MODEL 220 - .177 cal., SL, SP, SS, suppressed recoil system, twin metal piston rings, 18.5 in. barrel, no safety, precision match stock, aperture sight, 44.3 in. OAL, 10.4 lbs. Approx. 11,000 mfg.1959-1967.

	$475	$385	$325	$250	$175	N/A	N/A

MODEL 250 - .177 cal., SL, SP, SS, suppressed recoil system using unique oil pot designed by Hermann Wild, precision match stock, aperture sight. 18.5 in. BBL, 44.7 in. OAL, 10.9 lbs. Mfg. 1968 to the early 1980s.

	$450	$365	$315	$235	$150	N/A	N/A

GRADING	100%	95%	90%	80%	60%	40%	20%

MODEL 275 - .173 (4.4 mm) lead balls cal., Schmeisser system BA, six or twelve round removable box magazine, 17.3 in. barrel, Mauser-style swinging manual safety, 41.7 in. OAL, 5.9 lbs. Intro. mid-1950s.

courtesy Beeman Collection

	100%	95%	90%	80%	60%	40%	20%
	$350	$250	$200	$145	$100	N/A	N/A

MODEL 275 REPEATING AIR RIFLE - .173 (4.4 mm) No. 9 lead balls cal., BA, repeater, six or twelve round removable mag., 17.3 in. BBL, adj. rear and ramp front sights, two-stage trigger, walnut stained Monti Carlo style hardwood stock w/ BP, manual safety, 41.3 in. OAL, 5.7 lbs.

courtesy Anschütz

At the time of publishing MSR and pricing N/A.

MODEL 330 - .177 cal., BBC, SP, SS, Junior version of Model 335 sporter, 16.5 in. BBL, 40.6 in. OAL, 6.3 lbs.

	100%	95%	90%	80%	60%	40%	20%
	$150	$125	$100	$75	$50	N/A	N/A

MODEL 333 - .177 or .22 cal., BBC, SP, 700 FPS, adj. trigger, 18 in. barrel, 6.75 lbs.

	100%	95%	90%	80%	60%	40%	20%
	$180	$125	$90	$75	$60	N/A	N/A

Last MSR was $175.

MODEL 335 - .177 or .22 cal., BBC, SP, 700 FPS, adj. trigger, 18.50 in. barrel, 7.50 lbs. Disc. 2003.

	100%	95%	90%	80%	60%	40%	20%
	$275	$225	$190	$140	$100	N/A	N/A

Last MSR was $200.

Add $10 for Model 335 Mag. .22 cal.

MODEL 380 - .177 cal., UL, SP, 600-640 FPS, match model, removable cheekpiece, adj. trigger, stippled walnut grips. Disc. 1994.

	100%	95%	90%	80%	60%	40%	20%
	$750	$595	$475	$375	$295	N/A	N/A

Last MSR was $1,250.

Subtract 10% for left-hand variation. Add 10% for Moving Target Model.

MODEL 2001 - .177 cal., SL, single stroke pneumatic, 10 lbs. 8 oz.

	100%	95%	90%	80%	60%	40%	20%
	$1,250	$920	$815	$625	$500	N/A	N/A

Last MSR was $1,800.

Subtract 10% for left-hand variation. Add $80 for Running Target Model.

MODEL 2002 - .177 cal., PCP, 26 in. barrel, adj. buttplate and cheekpiece, 10.50 lbs. Mfg. 1997-2006.

courtesy Anschütz

	100%	95%	90%	80%	60%	40%	20%
	$1,150	$995	$850	$700	$550	N/A	N/A

GRADING	100%	95%	90%	80%	60%	40%	20%

✪ **Model 2002 ALU** - .177 cal., PCP, single shot, easy-exchange 350-shot air cylinder with manometer, 25.2 in. barrel, aluminum alloy stock features adj. laminate pistol grip and laminate forearm, adj. alloy cheekpiece, shoulder stock and buttplate attach to alloy frame, 42.5 in. OAL, 10.8 lbs. Mfg. 2000-2006.

| | $1,350 | $1,200 | $1,00 | $825 | $625 | N/A | N/A |

✪ **Model 2002 Club** - .177 cal., PCP, SS, 25.2 in. barrel, Walnut stock with adj. cheekpiece and buttplate, 42.5 in. OAL, 10.8 lbs. Mfg. 2000-05.

| | $915 | $800 | $675 | $550 | $450 | N/A | N/A |

Last MSR was $1,065.

✪ **Model 2002 D-RT** - .177 cal., PCP, SS, Running Target Model, 33.8 in. BBL, 51.5 in. OAL, 9.2 lbs. Disc. 2006.

| | $1,295 | $1,150 | $935 | $775 | $595 | N/A | N/A |

✪ **Model 2002 Junior** - .177 cal., PCP, SS, 20.8 in. barrel, similar to Model 2002, except 35 in. OAL, 7.9 lbs. Disc. 2005.

| | $915 | $800 | $675 | $550 | $450 | N/A | N/A |

Last MSR was $1,065.

MODEL 2002 SUPERAIR
- .177 cal., SL, SSP, SS, 25.2 in. BBL, aluminum alloy or color laminated wood stock with adj. buttplate and cheekpiece, 42.5 in. OAL, 10.50 or 11 (aluminum) lbs. Mfg. 1992-2006.

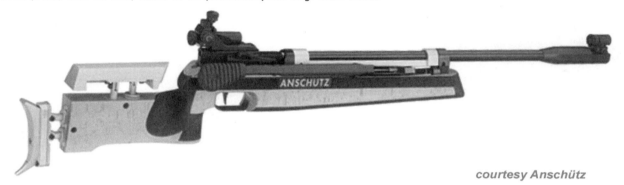

courtesy Anschütz

| | $1,150 | $995 | $850 | $700 | $550 | N/A | N/A |

Add $200 for ALU stock.

MODEL 2020 FIELD
- .177 cal., PCP, SS, similar to Model 2002 CA ALU, 25.2 in. barrel, 690 FPS, 10.36 lbs. Disc. 2006.

courtesy Anschütz

| | $1,350 | $995 | $850 | $700 | $550 | N/A | N/A |

MODEL 2025 FIELD
- .177 cal., PCP, SS, 25.2 in. barrel, similar to Model 2020 Field, 803 FPS. 10.36 lbs. Disc. 2006.

courtesy Anschütz

| | $1,395 | $1,075 | $850 | $700 | $550 | N/A | N/A |

GRADING	100%	95%	90%	80%	60%	40%	20%

MODEL 2027 BIATHLON - .177 cal., PCP, straight pull action, five-shot mag., 24 in. barrel, fully adj. sights, adj. match trigger, walnut stock with adj. cheek/butt plate and four mag. holder, 803 FPS. 9 lbs. Mfg. 2003-2005.

	100%	95%	90%	80%	60%	40%	20%
	$1,295	$1,115	$875	$725	$575	N/A	N/A

Last MSR was $1,400.

MODEL 8001 - .177 cal., PCP, SS, 23 in. barrel, adj. aperture sighs, walnut stock w/ adj. cheekpiece and adj. rubber but plate, 40.16 in. OAL, 8.58 lbs. Mfg. 2008-current.

courtesy Anschütz

At the time of publishing MSR and pricing N/A.

MODEL 8002 - .177 cal., PCP, single shot, easy-exchange 350-shot air cylinder with manometer, 25.2 in. barrel, color laminate wood stock features adj. laminate pistol grip and laminate forearm, adj. alloy cheekpiece, 42.5 in. OAL, 9.2 lbs. Mfg. 2005-07.

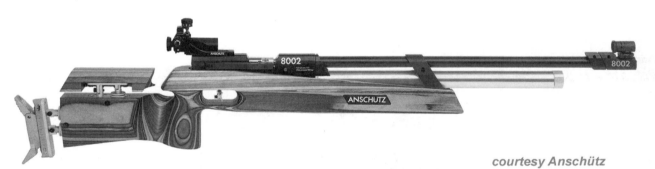

courtesy Anschütz

	100%	95%	90%	80%	60%	40%	20%
	$1,795	$1,645	$1,350	$1,050	$850	N/A	N/A

✪ *Model 8002 Alu* - .177 cal., PCP, single shot, easy-exchange 350-shot air cylinder with manometer, 25.2 in. barrel, aluminum alloy stock features adj. laminate pistol grip and laminate forearm, adj. alloy cheekpiece, shoulder stock and buttplate attach to alloy frame, 42.5 in. OAL, 9.24 lbs. Mfg. 2005-07.

courtesy Anschütz

	100%	95%	90%	80%	60%	40%	20%
	$1,850	$1,740	$1,450	$1,250	$950	N/A	N/A

GRADING	100%	95%	90%	80%	60%	40%	20%

○ *Model 8002 Alu Benchrest* - .177 cal., PCP, single shot, easy-exchange 350-shot air cylinder with manometer, 25.2 in. barrel, aluminum alloy stock features adj. laminate pistol grip and laminate forearm, adj. alloy cheekpiece, shoulder stock and buttplate attach to alloy frame, 42.5 in. OAL, 9.92 lbs. Mfg. 2006-07.

courtesy Anschütz

$1,850	$1,740	$1,450	$1,250	$950	N/A	N/A

○ *Model 8002 Club* - .177 cal., PCP, single shot, similar to Model 8002 except has walnut stock, 42.5 in. OAL, 8.8 lbs. Mfg. 2005-07.

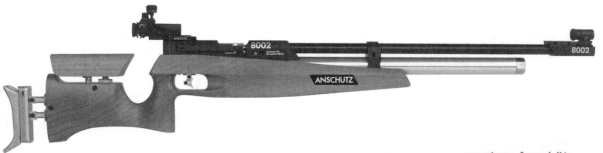

courtesy Anschütz

$1,150	$995	$850	$700	$550	N/A	N/A

○ *Model 8002 Junior* - .177 cal., PCP, single shot, similar to Model 8002 except has laminated stock, 37.4 in. OAL, 7.94 lbs. New 2006.

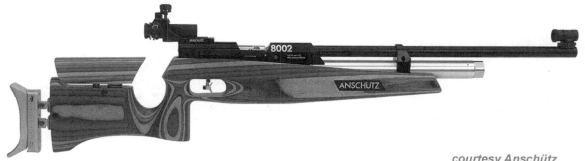

courtesy Anschütz

$1,150	$995	$850	$700	$550	N/A	N/A

MODEL 8002 S2 - .177 cal., PCP, SS, similar to Model 8002 except, S2 up-grade. Mfg. 2008-current.

At the time of publishing MSR and pricing N/A.

○ *Model 8002 S2 Alu* - .177 cal., PCP, SS, similar to Model 8002 ALU except, S2 up-grade. Mfg. 2008-current.

At the time of publishing MSR and pricing N/A.

○ *Model 8002 S2 Club* - .177 cal., PCP, single shot, similar to Model 8002 except has walnut stock, 42.5 in. OAL, 8.8 lbs. Mfg. 2007-current.

At the time of publishing MSR and pricing N/A.

GRADING	100%	95%	90%	80%	60%	40%	20%

○ *Model 8002 S2 Junior* - .177 cal., PCP, SS, similar to Model 8002 Junior except, S2 up-grade. Mfg. 2008-current.

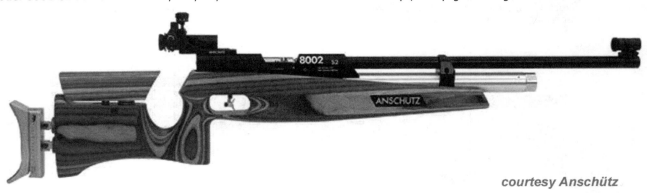

courtesy Anschütz

At the time of publishing MSR and pricing N/A.

○ *Model 8002 S2 Walnut Benchrest* - .177 cal., PCP, cocking lever action, SS, easy-exchange 350-shot air cylinder with manometer, 25.2 in. barrel, adj. aperture rear w/ extention and hooded front sights, walnut stock w/ non-slip PG, extended benchrest cheekpiece, adj. alloy butt plate, S2 up-grade, 41.34 in. OAL, 9.2 lbs. Mfg. 2008-current.

At the time of publishing MSR and pricing N/A.

◆ *Model 8002 S2 Benchrest Start* - .177 cal., PCP, cocking lever action, SS, similar to Model 8002 S2 Walnut Benchrest, except non-slip rubber buttplate adj. for length. Mfg. 2008-current.

At the time of publishing MSR and pricing N/A.

MODEL 9003 PREMIUM - .177 cal., PCP, tension-free connection and vibration dampening of the barreled action in aluminum stock w/ Soft Link® shock absorber pads, adj. buttplate, adj. cheekpiece, adj. forend, 9.9 lbs. Mfg. 2004-07.

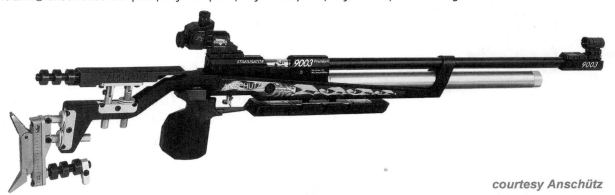

courtesy Anschütz

$2,495	$2,295	$1,895	$1,495	$1,150	N/A	N/A

○ *Model 9003 Premium 150th ANSCHÜTZ Anniversary* - .177 cal., PCP, SS, cocking lever action, similar to Model 9003 Premium, except Compressed air cylinder, PRO-Grip equipment, rear sight knobs and front sight are in Royal ANSCHÜTZ Blue finish, 150 years logos on stock and compressed air cylinder, and selected Limited Edition accessories. Mfg. 2007.

courtesy Anschütz

At the time of publishing MSR and pricing N/A.

Accessories include rear sight 7002, the ahg front sight SWING PLUS, rear sight elevation 6817-U1 and black, heavy steel columns, 3 plastic apertures in blue, 1 safety rod, 2 eye shields, 1 ANSCHÜTZ key pendant, 1 pellet box as well as various 150 years logos, pins and an anniversary certificate.

GRADING	100%	95%	90%	80%	60%	40%	20%

☼ **Model 9003 Premium Benchrest** - .177 cal., PCP, similar to Model 9003 Premium except, adj. benchrest fore-end stock, rubber buttplate, seven stock decoration stickers and box w/ accessories, 9.9 lbs. Mfg. 2005-07.

courtesy Anschütz

	$2,495	$2,295	$1,895	$1,495	$1,150	N/A	N/A

MODEL 9003 S2 PREMIUM - .177 cal., PCP, SS, cocking lever action, similar to Model 9003 Premium, except S2 upgrade, walnut adj. fore-end stock, PG, and cheekpiece. Mfg. 2008.

courtesy Anschütz

At the time of publishing MSR and pricing N/A.

☼ **Model 9003 S2 Premium 150th ANSCHÜTZ Anniversary** - .177 cal., PCP, SS, cocking lever action, similar to Model 9003 S2 Premium, except Compressed air cylinder, PRO-Grip equipment, rear sight knobs and front sight are in Royal ANSCHÜTZ Blue finish, 150 years logos on stock and compressed air cylinder, and selected Limited Edition accessories. Mfg. 2008.

courtesy Anschütz

At the time of publishing MSR and pricing N/A.

Accessories include rear sight 7002, the ahg front sight SWING PLUS, rear sight elevation 6817-U1 and black, heavy steel columns, 3 plastic apertures in blue, 1 safety rod, 2 eye shields, 1 ANSCHÜTZ key pendant, 1 pellet box as well as various 150 years logos, pins and an anniversary certificate.

☼ **Model 9003 S2 Premium Benchrest** - .177 cal., PCP, SS, cocking lever action, similar to Model 9003 Premium Benchrest, except S2 upgrade. Mfg. 2008.

At the time of publishing MSR and pricing N/A.

GRADING	100%	95%	90%	80%	60%	40%	20%

HAKIM MILITARY TRAINING RIFLE - .22 cal., UL, SP, SS, rifled, tap-loading, full military style stock and sights, receiver ring marked with skull and Arabic markings for National Union Youth Movement, other Arabic markings for: "Training Airgun, Anschütz, Germany 1955", Caliber 5.5mm, 10.5 lbs. Approx. 2800 mfg. 1954. Ref: AR2 :27-29.

courtesy Beeman Collection

		N/A	N/A	$400	$300	$200	$150	$75

Built 1955 for Egyptian Government; based on Anschütz Model 1954 air rifle.

ANSON, E. & CO.

Previous manufacturer located in Birmingham, England circa 1890-1945.

Edwin Anson and Company was a gunsmithing business, previously active from about 1890 to 1945. Models produced were the Ansonia air rifle (apparently a copy of the MGR rifle of Mayer & Grammelspacher), Star air pistols, and small numbers of the Firefly air pistol. They designed, with Frank Clarke, but did not produce, the Westley Richards Highest Possible air pistols and the Accles & Shelvoke Warrior air pistol. Ref: AW-May 1984.

PISTOLS

STAR - .177 cal., underlever, SS, SP, smoothbore, Vulcanite grips w/ "FC" monogram, First variant: marked "The Star", Second Variant: unmarked or w/ "Anson Star", approx. 100 mfg. 1926- mid 1930s. Ref. AGW March, 2003.

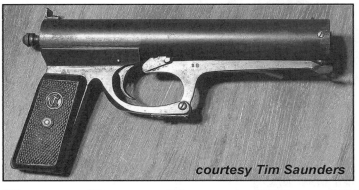

courtesy Tim Saunders

	N/A	N/A	N/A	$2,100	$1,500	$1,000	$750

Add 20% for original box.

FIREFLY - .177 cal., push-barrel cocking, SP, smoothbore, concentric mainsprings, wooden barrel cover, frame and grip are heavy cast iron, marked "O.K." on left side of trigger, "ANSON" on the right side, and "FIREFLY" on frame above trigger. Mfg. 1925-1933.

courtesy Beeman Collection

$375	$325	$275	$225	$175	$150	$125

Add 40% for factory box.

Distributed by the Midland Gun Company (later absorbed by Parker and Hale), Birmingham, England.

GRADING	100%	95%	90%	80%	60%	40%	20%

RIFLES

ANSONIA - .177 cal., BBC, SP, 17 in. octagonal barrel with nine-groove RH rifling, adj. sights, barrel screwed into barrel block, lever detent like MGR but two-piece barrel marked "The Ansonia", 41.5 in. OAL, 7.5 lbs. Mfg.1905-10.

courtesy Beeman Collection

	$900	$825	$750	$675	$600	$500	$400

ANSONIA Mk.2 - similar to Ansonia, except simpler, fixed sight, and the barrel and barrel block are one piece.
Values TBD

APACHE (aka FIRE-BALL)

Previous trademark manufactured by Burhans and Associates of CA, or one of their subsidiaries, in 1948-1949.

APACHE BACKGROUND

The authors and publisher wish to thank Jon Jenkins and John Groenewold for their valuable assistance with the following information in this edition of the Blue Book of Airguns.

The Apache rifle evidently is California's first publicly marketed airgun and is one of the shortest lived of all American airgun designs, apparently having been produced only in 1948 and 1949.

In 1949, the Apache tooling was acquired by Standard Interstate Machine Company (SIMCO) in Glendale, CA. By June of 1949, SIMCO had begun manufacturing an Apache-type model air rifle marked on the buttplate as the Texan. Apparently, the Apache tooling and parts were also used to produce the SIMCO rifles. These generally were marked "SIMCO" in an oval on the front left side of the receiver. Guns are known with both the SIMCO marking on the receiver and an Apache marking on the pump tube plug. Some SIMCO guns are not marked at all. Apparently, Apache parts were simply utilized until exhausted, but SIMCO guns generally are identifiable by their careful finishing. The final preparation of the metalwork is better and the finishing itself is of a greater consistency than the former Apache production. The stock lacquer is darker and more opaque than on Apache rifles and is more carefully applied. SIMCO rifles have a walnut stock with the word "Texan" on the buttplate. This buttplate marking appears to be the exception. Manufacturing of the Apache/Simco line seems to have ceased in 1949.

There are no known examples of SIMCO pistols. The last address for SIMCO was on Hollywood Way in Burbank, CA. Ref: AGNR - Apr. 1986.

APACHE CONFIGURATION

Apache airguns were available in various design configurations, but there is some interesting confusion about which variations were actually produced. What was advertised does not always match what is actually seen in known specimens. The original rifle was advertised as always having a .175 caliber insert barrel, but there are a number of specimens which do not have any threads at the muzzle. Such a lack makes it impossible to fix a sub-caliber barrel. They were also advertised as having a hollow space in the buttstock for a tube of ammunition, but apparently none were made with this feature. Eight-shot .175 caliber Fireball rifles were advertised in 1948, but none have been reported. A version called the SIMCO Texan was specified in 1949 dealer literature as taking regular .22 caliber pellets, but only .24 (No. 4 Buckshot) specimens are known. And the pistols were promoted as coming in real wooden boxes, but rather fragile cardboard factory cartons seem to have been the reality. If you have clear evidence of the existence of presently unknown features or models, please contact Blue Book Publications or email: bluebookedit@Beemans.net.

Early production Apache rifles used a plastic stock and forearm. Plastic technology was only beginning at the time, and these plastic stocks were prone to frequent breakage. Production was switched to Walnut stocks as early as March 1948. Since both were available at the same time, it is possible to find mismatched guns. Two buttstock attachment techniques were used with no clear definition between production runs. Attaching the buttstock with a bolt through the pistol grip is the least common variation. The standard, most common arrangement is a long bolt, hidden by the buttplate, running through the length of the buttstock. The steel barrel and brass pump tube were chemically treated/ blued. On both the rifles and pistols only the .24 (No. 4 Buckshot) caliber barrel was rifled. Apache rifles are known with all possible combinations and variations of parts. Apparently, any parts handy at assembly time were used. Guns with various screws in the receiver, a plastic buttstock and a wooden forearm, completely unmarked, and/or with poor finishing of the metalwork were produced and should not be considered prototype efforts or mistakes.

It is clear that the first versions of the rifle were single shot. The second form of the rifle had a ten-shot magazine assembly. These rifles omit the .24 (No. 4 Buckshot) loading port on the top of the frame and can only be fired with .24 (No. 4 Buckshot) balls using the magazine. Some rifles were sold as .24 (No. 4 Buckshot) repeaters only and some included the .175 barrel. These seem to require muzzle loading in the early versions, but later versions could be loaded through a small hole in the top of the receiver. All non-repeater guns equipped with the .175 barrel liner had to be muzzle-loaded when the liner was being used. Bolt handles on the non-repeater guns were fragile and specimens often have this item broken or missing. In the spring of 1948, a pistol was added to the Apache line. Available first as a single shot in , the .24 (No. 4 Buckshot) pistol was soon offered as a six-shot repeater with the same interchangeable caliber feature and spring-fed magazine as the rifles. The first production models of the pistols had heavy die-cast frames, similar to the rifles; later production featured an aluminum frame. These frames generally were polished to give the appearance of chrome plating, but some were painted black. Grips on the pistols were either wood (common), black, or ivory plastic (scarce). The .175 insert for the pistol attached using the same type of threaded muzzle arrangement as the

GRADING	100%	95%	90%	80%	60%	40%	20%

rifle. There are rare examples of the pistols with a friction fit, rather than a threaded arrangement, for the insert. The pump tube is thin-wall brass tubing prone to failure at the pivot points. The performance of the pistols was rather moderate in both calibers.

APACHE MARKINGS

Apache guns are marked on the forward pump tube plug (if at all) with "Burhans and Associates" or "National Cart Corporation", or just the word "Fire-ball", or "Apache". Some markings included an address with the word "Fire-ball" or "Apache" but not the company name. Charles Burhans operated the National Cart Corporation, so these various markings imply the same origin. Although not precision airguns, the genius of the Apache rifle lay in using the larger .25 caliber barrel and the ability to quickly change calibers.

PISTOLS

APACHE - FIRE-BALL PISTOL - BB/.175 and .24 (No. 4 Buckshot) cal. dual cal., or .24 (No. 4 Buckshot) cal. only, UL multi-pump pneumatic, smooth or rifled (.24 (No. 4 Buckshot)), walnut or plastic grips, die-cast zinc or aluminum frame, polished or all blue paint finish. Mfg. 1948-1949.

courtesy Beeman Collection

⚬ *Apache - Fire-Ball Pistol First Variation* - heavy cast zinc receiver (similar to rifle), usually .24 (No. 4 Buckshot) cal. SS only, 8.25 in. rifled barrel, 225 FPS.1.9 lbs, 11.9 in. OAL.

	100%	95%	90%	80%	60%	40%	20%
	$350	$295	$250	$195	$150	$95	$65

Add 25% for factory box and literature. Add 10% for painted receiver. Add 10% for ivory-colored grips. Add 50% for press-fit inner barrel. Subtract 10% for missing name. Subtract 15% for missing .175 barrel insert on guns with threaded muzzle rings.

⚬ *Apache - Fire-Ball Pistol Second Variation* - .24 (No. 4 Buckshot) cal., SS or repeater with six-round spring fed mag., aluminum receiver, polished or painted blue, 8.25 in. rifled barrel with removable smoothbore .175 cal. liner (may attach via screw threads in end of barrel or press-fit), wooden or plastic (ivory or black) grips. 1.3 lbs without barrel liner.

	100%	95%	90%	80%	60%	40%	20%
	$350	$295	$250	$195	$150	$95	$65

Add 25% for factory box and literature. Add 10% for painted receiver. Add 10% for ivory-colored grips. Add 50% for press-fit inner barrel. Subtract 10% for missing name. Subtract 15% for missing .175 barrel insert on guns with threaded muzzle rings.

RIFLES

APACHE - FIRE-BALL - TEXAN - BB/.175 and .24 (No. 4 Buckshot) cal. dual cal., or .24 (No. 4 Buckshot) cal. only, SS, UL multi-pump pneumatic, smooth or rifled (.24 (No. 4 Buckshot)), 540 FPS, plastic and/or walnut stock and forearm, black finish,die-cast zinc or aluminum frame,36.3 in. OAL, 5.5-6.5 lbs. Mfg. 1948-1949.

courtesy Beeman Collection

⚬ *Apache - Fire-Ball - Texan First Variation* - .24 (No. 4 Buckshot) cal., withround loading port in top of receiver, may include .175 threaded barrel insert, SS, plastic or walnut buttstock and forearm.

	100%	95%	90%	80%	60%	40%	20%
	$275	$225	$175	$140	$100	$80	$60

Add 25% for factory box and literature. Add 20% for "Texan" w/ walnut stock and forearm, MSR was $14.95. Add 10% for .24 (No. 4 Buckshot) cal. only. Add 100% for chrome plating on all metalwork. Subtract 25% for missing .175 barrel insert on guns with threaded muzzle rings. Add 30% for "SIMCO" marked guns.

GRADING	100%	95%	90%	80%	60%	40%	20%

✿ **Apache - Fire-Ball - Texan Second Variation** - .175 or .24 (No. 4 Buckshot) cal., SS with .175 cal. threaded barrel insert loaded from the muzzle, later versions have a small round loading port in the top, or side of receiver or six-shot repeater, walnut buttstock attached via a bolt through bottom of pistol grip.

courtesy Beeman Collection

	$275	$225	$175	$140	$100	$80	$60

Add 25% for factory box and literature. Add 20% for "Texan" w/ walnut stock and forearm, MSR was $14.95. Add 10% for .24 (No. 4 Buckshot) cal. only. Add 100% for chrome plating on all metalwork. Subtract 25% for missing .175 barrel insert on guns with threaded muzzle rings. Add 30% for "SIMCO" marked guns.

Transitional guns -- either buttstock or forearm of contrasting material (hardwood or plastic) priced as Variation Two or Three depending on method of buttstock attachment.

✿ **Apache - Fire-Ball - Texan Third Variation** -similar to Second variation, except has walnut buttstock attached by long bolt running from under buttplate.

	$260	$200	$150	$120	$80	$65	$45

Add 25% for factory box and literature. Add 20% for "Texan" w/ walnut but stock and forearm, MSR was $14.95. Add 10% for .25 cal. only. Add 100% for chrome plating on all metalwork. Subtract 25% for missing .175 barrel insert on guns with threaded muzzle rings. Add 30% for "SIMCO" marked guns.

ARMIGAS (ARMIGAS-COMEGA)

Previous manufacturer located at Via Valle Inzino, Brescia, Italy.
Associated with Atillio Zanoletti. Maker of gas-powered rifles, circa 1961 to early 1980s.

PISTOLS

OLIMPIC - SS or repeater variations known, additional details and values TBD.

RIFLES

ARTEMIA - 8 mm cal., CO_2, BA, additional details and values TBD.

OLIMPIC - .177 cal., CO_2, repeater, 80-shot spring-fed magazine removes for loading, tends to jam during operation, bulk feed CO_2 valve at muzzle end, 22 in. barrel, no safety, marked with Armigas brand, Olimpic name, and "BREV. INTERN" ("International Patent"), 4.5 mm, 38 in. OAL, 5.5 lbs.

courtesy Beeman Collection

	N/A	$750	$600	$500	$400	$300	N/A

Some how related to TyRol COmatic rifle in Austria (see "T" section), COmatic Rifle of Ventyrini of Argentina (see "V" section) and Fionda rifle of Brazil (see "F" section).

SHOTGUNS

HUNTER MOD. S66 8mm shot capsule (no. 11/12 birdshot) or 8 mm lead ball, SS, two CO_2 tanklets provide about 20 shots, exterior hammer, 39 in. OAL, 6.4 lbs. Additional details and values TBD.

GRADING	100%	95%	90%	80%	60%	40%	20%

ARMSCOR

Current trademark manufactured by Arms Corporation of the Philippines, located in Manila, Philippines. No current importation, previously imported by Armscor Precision International, located in Las Vegas, NV. For more information and current pricing on both new and used Arms Corporation of the Philippines firearms, please refer to the *Blue Book of Gun Values* by S.P. Fjestad (also available online).

PISTOLS

ARMSCOR PISTOL - .22 cal., CO_2, SL, 7.50 in. barrel, 500 FPS, fixed sights, 2.2 lbs. Disc. 2002.

	100%	95%	90%	80%	60%	40%	20%
	$165	$125	$85	$60	$45	N/A	N/A

Last MSR was $112.

RIFLES

ARMSCOR EXECUTIVE - .22 cal., CO_2, bolt action, 22 in. barrel, 700 FPS, leaf-type rear sight, hooded front sight, beech stock with checkered grip and forearm, manual safety, 5.75 lbs. Disc. 2002.

courtesy Howard Collection

	100%	95%	90%	80%	60%	40%	20%
	$145	$115	$90	$70	$50	N/A	N/A

Last MSR was $120.

ARMSCOR STANDARD - .22 cal., CO_2, bolt action, 22 in. barrel, 700 FPS, leaf-type rear sight, hooded front sight, beech stock, manual safety, 5.75 lbs. Disc. 2002.

	100%	95%	90%	80%	60%	40%	20%
	$135	$95	$80	$65	$50	N/A	N/A

Last MSR was $112.

ARMSCOR RETRACTABLE - .22 cal., CO_2, bolt action, 22 in. barrel, 700 FPS, leaf-type rear sight, hooded front sight, retractable composite shoulder stock with pistol grip, 6 lbs. Disc. 2002.

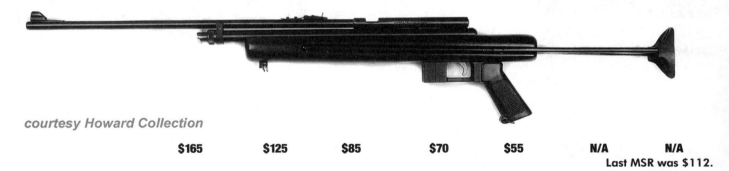

courtesy Howard Collection

	100%	95%	90%	80%	60%	40%	20%
	$165	$125	$85	$70	$55	N/A	N/A

Last MSR was $112.

ARROW

Previous trademark used by a few different manufacturers including Friedrich Langenham located in Zella - St. Blasii, Thüringen, Germany, the State Industry Factory located in Shanghai, China, and William Heilprin located in Philadelphia, PA.

These are completely unrelated makers. Please see the individual makers' names in this guide.

ARTES de ARCOS

Previous manufacturer located in Madrid and Barcelona, Spain.

GRADING	100%	95%	90%	80%	60%	40%	20%

ASAHI

Previous trademark manufactured by Kawaguchiya located in Japan circa 1948-1955.

Research is ongoing with this trademark, and more information will be included both online and in future editions. Copy of pre-WWII German "Millicia Style" rifles e.g. Diana Model 27. Average original condition specimens are typically priced in the $100 range. The most recent specimens with a modern-looking half stock are rare and typically command an extra $50.

courtesy Beeman Collection

ATLAS AIR GUN MANUFACTURING CO.

Previous manufacturer located in Ilion, NY circa 1889.

See Atlas Gun Co.

ATLAS AIR RIFLE MANUFACTURING CO.

Previous manufacturer located in Ilion, NY circa 1953-56.

Manufacturer of a pump-up pneumatic rifle. Research is ongoing with this trademark, and more information will be included both online and in future editions.

ATLAS GUN CO.

Previous manufacturer located in Ilion, NY circa 1886-1906.

The Atlas Gun Company of Ilion, New York is another of the links between key parts of the world airgun developmental picture. It was founded around 1886 by George P. Gunn of the Haviland & Gunn Company whose designs were the foundation of most modern production airguns. The Atlas company was then consumed by Daisy in 1906 as part of their aggressive program to eliminate competition.

The first Atlas gun was the 1886 model, a break-open BB gun using an unusual gravity repeater mechanism incorporating three iron rods as a BB raceway. Gunn was granted a patent for the design in 1895. The last of the Atlas BB guns have peculiar ring lever cocking arms which extend forward instead of back from the trigger and have a finger ring instead of the traditional loop. These guns typically have the name "ATLAS" cast into the frame, which also has a special shape. The combinations of these features are so distinctive that these models may be identified from quite far away. The Dandy BB gun that appeared in the 1897 Sears mail order catalog had these beacon features, but is without the Atlas marking. It almost surely was produced by Atlas.

RIFLES

1886 ATLAS BREAK-OPEN REPEATER - .180 cal., BB, BC, SP, brass smoothbore barrel, break-open action, gravity-fed magazine, sheet metal frame and grip frame, wire trigger guard, nickel finish. Walnut stock with deep crescent butt, stamped in a circle: "Atlas Gun Company, Pat. Mar. 9, 1886. USE B.B. SHOT. Ilion, New York, Patent applied for". No safety. Circa 1886-1890.

	N/A	N/A	$1,500	$1,200	$900	$600	$450

1899 VICTOR BREAK-OPEN REPEATER - .180 cal., BB, BC, SP, brass smoothbore barrel, break-open action, gravity-fed magazine, sheet metal frame and grip frame, wire trigger guard, nickel finish. Walnut stock with deep crescent butt, stamped "VICTOR". No safety. Circa 1899-1906.

	N/A	N/A	$1,200	$900	$600	$400	$300

1900 ATLAS LEVER ACTION REPEATER - .180 cal., BB, BC, SP, brass smoothbore barrel, distinctive lever action with ring lever ahead of trigger, gravity-fed magazine, sheet metal barrel sheath, cast iron cocking lever, receiver frame and grip frame. Walnut stock with crescent butt. Lettering cast into grip frame: "ATLAS". No safety. First version circa 1900-03.

courtesy Beeman Collection

	N/A	N/A	$1,150	$850	$550	$350	$250

Add 20% for brass frame. Subtract 20% for last version -- simpler frame with Atlas name in script. Circa 1903-06.

GRADING	100%	95%	90%	80%	60%	40%	20%

DANDY LEVER ACTION REPEATER - .180 cal. BB, BC, SP, brass smoothbore barrel, distinctive lever action with ring lever ahead of trigger, gravity-fed magazine, sheet metal barrel sheath, cast iron cocking lever, receiver frame and grip frame. Walnut stock with crescent butt. No lettering on frame. No safety. Sears mail order version (Dandy evidently was a trade name for Sears and other sellers). Circa 1892.

		N/A	N/A	$1,050	$750	$450	$250	$150

NEW DANDY - gravity-fed repeater similar to Dandy, same cast iron parts, cocking lever, and action, nickel finish. The only marking is on the RHS of slab sided stock: "NEW DANDY MODEL 94". 32.2 in. OAL, 2.5 lbs. Mfg. circa 1894.

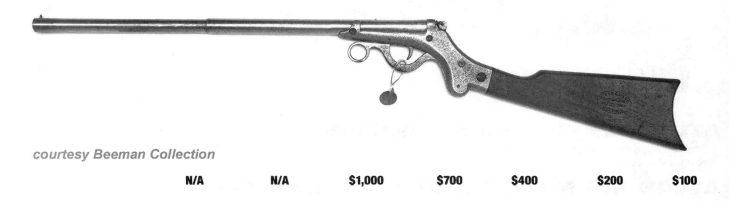

courtesy Beeman Collection

		N/A	N/A	$1,000	$700	$400	$200	$100

B SECTION

BAM (BEST AIRGUN MANUFACTURER IN CHINA)

Current trademark manufactured by Jiang Su Xin Su Machinery Manufacturing Co. Ltd. located in WuXi, JiangSu Province, China. Currently imported and distributed by Xisico USA, Inc. located in Houston, TX.

GRADING	100%	95%	90%	80%	60%	40%	20%

RIFLES

MODEL KL-3B - .177 or .22 cal., SL, SP, 15.5 in. barrel, 850/650 FPS, black parkerized finish, semi-pistol grip Monte Carlo wood stock with buttplate, hooded front and adj. rear sights, trigger safety, 6.8 lbs. Disc. 2007.

	100%	95%	90%	80%	60%	40%	20%
MSR $65	$60	$50	$40	N/A	N/A	N/A	

MODEL XS-B3-1 - .177 or .22 cal., SL, SP, 15 in. barrel, 540/410 FPS, black finish, metal collapsible buttstock, grooved pistol grip and forearm, hooded front and adj. rear sights, trigger safety, 7.15 lbs.

	100%	95%	90%	80%	60%	40%	20%
MSR $95	$80	$70	$60	$50	N/A	N/A	N/A

MODEL XS-B4-2 - .177 or .22 cal., UL, SP, 17.5 in. barrel, 630/480 FPS, black finish, semi-pistol grip wood stock with buttplate, hooded front and adj. rear sights, sling swivels, trigger safety, 7 lbs.

	100%	95%	90%	80%	60%	40%	20%
MSR $50	$35	$30	$25	$20	N/A	N/A	N/A

MODEL XS-B7 - .177 or .22 cal., SL, SP, 15 in. barrel, 540/410 FPS, black finish, semi-pistol grip wood stock with buttplate, hooded front and adj. rear sights, scope rail, trigger safety, 7 lbs. Disc. 2006.

	100%	95%	90%	80%	60%	40%	20%
	$60	$50	$40	$30	N/A	N/A	N/A

MODEL XS-B9-1 - .177 cal., SL, SP, 10 shot mag., 16.5 in. barrel, black polymer forend and pistol grip butt stock, take down design, black finish bbl., 4x32 scope, trigger safety, 32 in. OAL, 6.2 lbs. New 2007.

	100%	95%	90%	80%	60%	40%	20%
MSR $110	$95	$80	$70	$60	N/A	N/A	N/A

MODEL XS-B5-10 - .177 cal., multi-pump pneumatic, 15.3 in. barrel, 10 shot, 500 FPS, black finish, metal collapsible buttstock, pistol grip, hooded front and adj. rear sights, trigger safety, 20-30 in. OAL, 4.4 lbs. New 2007.

	100%	95%	90%	80%	60%	40%	20%
MSR $120	$110	$95	$80	$70	N/A	N/A	N/A

MODEL XS-B11 - .177 cal., BBC, SP, 16.38 in. barrel, 590 FPS, black finish, semi-pistol grip Monte-Carlo wood stock, hooded front and adj. rear sights, trigger safety, 6 lbs. New 2006.

	100%	95%	90%	80%	60%	40%	20%
MSR $120	$99	$80	$70	$60	$50	N/A	N/A

MODEL XS-B12 - .177 cal., BBC, SP, 16.38 in. barrel, 590 FPS, black finish, semi-pistol grip Monte-Carlo wood stock, hooded front and adj. rear sights, trigger safety, 6 lbs.

	100%	95%	90%	80%	60%	40%	20%
MSR $120	$99	$80	$70	$60	$50	N/A	N/A

MODEL XS-B15 - .177 cal., BBC, SP, 14.4 in. barrel, 480 FPS, black finish, semi-pistol grip wood stock with buttplate, hooded front and adj. rear sights, trigger safety, 5.5 lbs.

	100%	95%	90%	80%	60%	40%	20%
MSR $95	$80	$70	$60	$50	N/A	N/A	N/A

MODEL XS-B18 - .177 or .22 cal., BBC, SP, 16.38 in. barrel, 850/650 FPS, black parkerized finish, semi-pistol grip Monte Carlo wood stock with buttplate, hooded front and adj. rear sights, trigger safety, 6.9 lbs. Disc. 2006.

	100%	95%	90%	80%	60%	40%	20%
	$90	$75	$50	$40	N/A	N/A	N/A

MODEL XS-B20 - .177 cal., BBC, SP, 16 in. barrel, 930 FPS, blue finish, semi-pistol grip Monte Carlo wood stock with recoil pad, hooded front and adj. rear sights, Rekord trigger and auto-safety, 7.26 lbs. Disc. 2006.

	100%	95%	90%	80%	60%	40%	20%
	$135	$105	$90	$75	N/A	N/A	N/A

MODEL XS-B21 - .177 or .22 cal., SL, SP, 19.5 in. barrel, 950/715 FPS, blue finish, semi-pistol grip Monte Carlo wood stock with recoil pad, adj. hooded front and adj. rear sights, double automatic trigger safety, 9.68 lbs.

	100%	95%	90%	80%	60%	40%	20%
MSR $180	$150	$115	$95	$85	N/A	N/A	N/A

MODEL XS-B26 - .177 cal., BBC, SP, 16 in. barrel, 880-1000 FPS, blue finish, semi-pistol grip Monte Carlo wood stock with recoil pad, hooded front and adj. rear sights, adj. trigger and auto-safety, 43 in. OAL, 7.3 lbs. New 2006.

	100%	95%	90%	80%	60%	40%	20%
MSR $195	$175	$140	$110	$95	N/A	N/A	N/A

Add 10% for Thumbhole stock (Model XS-B26-2). Add 20% for 4x32 AO Scope (Model XB-26-2C).

MODEL XS-B28 - .177 cal., BBC, SP, 19.5 in. barrel, 1000-1250 FPS, blue finish, semi-pistol grip Monte Carlo wood stock with recoil pad, hooded front and adj. rear sights, adj. trigger and auto-safety, 48 in. OAL, 8 lbs. New 2007.

	100%	95%	90%	80%	60%	40%	20%
MSR $275	$250	$210	$175	$150	N/A	N/A	N/A

Add 10% for Thumbhole stock (Model XS-B26-2). Add 20% for 4x32 AO Scope (Model XB-26-2C).

MODEL XS-B30 - .177 or .22 cal., SL, SP, 17.3 in. barrel, 1100/900 FPS, blue finish, semi-pistol grip Monte Carlo wood stock with recoil pad, adj. trigger, adj. hooded front and adj. rear sights, double automatic trigger safety, 44.5m OAL, 9.4 lbs. New 2005.

	100%	95%	90%	80%	60%	40%	20%
MSR $195	$175	$140	$110	$95	N/A	N/A	N/A

MODEL XS-B40 - .177 or .22 cal., UL, SP, 14.1 in. barrel, 1050/850 FPS, black finish, adj. trigger, Monte Carlo semi-pistol grip wood stock with recoil pad, hooded front and adj. rear sights, sling swivels, trigger safety, 41.3 OAL, 9.3 lbs. New 2005.

	100%	95%	90%	80%	60%	40%	20%
MSR $375	$295	$250	$195	$150	N/A	N/A	N/A

GRADING	100%	95%	90%	80%	60%	40%	20%

MODEL XS-B50/MODEL XS-B51 - .177 or .22 cal., PCP, 18.5 in. barrel, 1000 FPS, blue finish, semi-pistol grip or thumbhole (Model XS-B51, new 2005) Monte Carlo wood stock with recoil pad, manual safety. New 2003.

MSR $425	$395	$345	$255	$200	N/A	N/A	N/A

Add 15% for Model XS-B51 (thumbhole stock). Add 5% for .22 cal.

BBM

For information on BBM air pistols, see Steiner in the "S" section.

BRNO

See Aeron CZ s.r.o. listing in the "A" section.

BSA GUNS (U.K.), LTD.

Current manufacturer, BSA Guns (UK), Ltd., previously known as "The Birmingham Small Arms Co. Ltd." and "BSA GUNS Ltd.," founded in 1861 in Birmingham, England. The original factory was destroyed by bombing during the period of August to November 1940. As a result they moved the operations to Marshall Lake Road, Shirley, Warwickshire from 1942 to 1964. From 1964 to 1967 it was located at Redditch, Warcestershire. In 1967 the factory was moved to it's present address Armory Road, Small Heath, Birmingham. Presently owned by Gamo of Spain. Currently exclusively imported/distibuted by Precision Airgun Distribution/Airguns of Arizona located in Gilbert, AZ. Previously imported by Compasseco, Inc. located in Bardstown, KY, Precision Sales, Westfield, MA (1995-2002), Dynamit-Nobel/RWS, Ithaca Gun Co. (1975-1979), Marksman, Savage Arms, and others.

For information and current pricing on both new and used BSA firearms, please refer to the *Blue Book of Gun Values* by S.P. Fjestad (also available online).

For additional information on the origin of Lincoln Jeffries and BSA underlever air rifles, see "Lincoln" in the "L" section of this text.

BSA also manufactured firearms: military, sporting, and target rifles and shotguns. These are discussed in *The Golden Century* by John Knibbs.

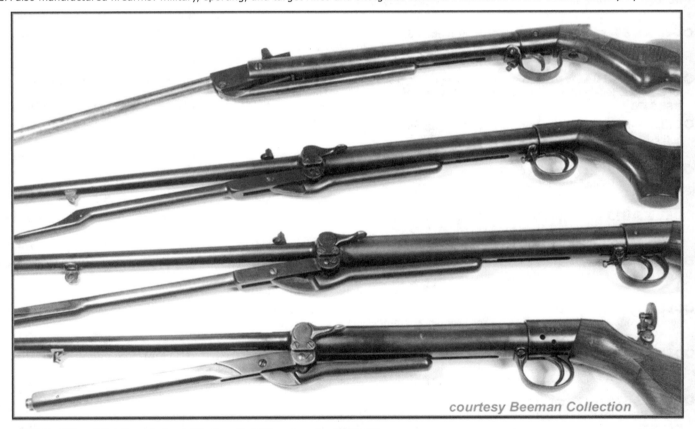

courtesy Beeman Collection

TOP: "The BSA Breakdown Pattern" .177 cal., mfg. 1933-39.
SECOND: "The BSA Air Rifle Improved Model D", 2nd pattern showing cocking lever with side fences mfg. 1908-1921.
THIRD: "The BSA Air Rifle Standard Pattern" showing side button catch mfg. 1912-1914.
BOTTOM: "The BSA Standard Air Rifle" mfg. 1919-1939.

BSA BACKGROUND

The history of BSA air rifles is based on the patents of, and the early marketing of, airguns by Lincoln Jeffries. Therefore, the introduction to the Lincoln section of this book is prerequisite to this section. The serious study of BSA airguns absolutely requires reference to the BSA books by John Knibbs. The authors and publisher wish to thank John Groenewold and John Knibbs for their assistance with the following

GRADING	100%	95%	90%	80%	60%	40%	20%

information in this edition of the *Blue Book of Airguns*.

The Lincoln Jeffries underlever air rifle made by BSA proved so successful that by 1906 BSA had begun marketing them under their own name and in several different models. The air rifles commonly referred to as "Lincoln Jeffries," "Lincoln patent," "Lincoln," "H," and "Light" models are actually stamped "H The Lincoln Air Rifle" or "L The Lincoln Air Rifle" and should be easy to identify. See Lincoln in the "L" section of this guide.

The bayonet type underlever cocking handle was the original Lincoln Jeffries design. The front end of this lever bears a small handle, or "bayonet" dropping down from, but parallel to, the barrel. Original bayonet underlevers just had a bend where they engaged the latch mechanism. Later ones were strengthened by additional metal bracing ("fillets or fences") on the sides of the bend area. The bayonet underlever was replaced by the much more reliable and less obtrusive side button underlever in 1911. Beginning in 1919, BSA started to replace side button underlevers with front button underlevers. Old-style underlevers were sometimes replaced with newer versions during repairs and modifications, and this may confuse present identification.

BSA MODEL IDENTIFICATION

Although well-designed and well-built, the early BSA air guns can be difficult to identify. Early practice at the factory was to use up existing old parts wherever possible on new models. Hence numerous variations exist. Several duplicate names for different models of different sizes and configurations also exist.

The designations of Improved Model B and Improved Model D bring up the question: "Where are the Models A through D?" A great deal of study seems to rather conclusively show that there never were any such models, except perhaps as developmental steps in the minds and long-lost notes of BSA airgun designers. The existing models certainly represent improvements over developmental steps that never came into production. Furthermore, the BSA designers made additional improvements in their "Improved Models" B and D, without changing the public designations. They probably did this with the idea that they were avoiding confusion, but the result was that vendors, customers, and repair shops could not be sure of what parts they were ordering or what would be shipped to them. This type of confusion was not well controlled until new models were produced after WWII.

Serial numbers and their prefixes are very important as they designate the model variation of the gun, date of manufacture, sear mechanism, and/or the caliber. In mid-1914 BSA started to mark new air cylinders by photo etching. However, some air rifles were assembled from parts with stamped lettering long after that date. The photoetching process was not perfected then. Many guns which originally had photoetched markings now appear unmarked because the etching has been worn off or buffed off during refinishing. Additionally, many different models were assembled using old parts from stock; thus there are considerable variations, even within a single model. The serial number and its prefix generally will allow cross-referencing to factory records and published lists, but often caliber and physical measurements must also considered. Specimens may be up to almost 100 years old; many have been repaired or modified with parts that may not even resemble the original parts. Using the information given here and some ingenuity, it should be possible to fairly well identify most BSA airguns. For serial number lists, production information, and a great deal of additional detail, one must consult the BSA references by John Knibbs. (His book sales partner in the USA is JG Airguns LLC.)

BSA MARKINGS

BSA airguns made prior to 1939 were marked with a single-digit "bore" size. These are not to be confused with model numbers. The bore size usually is marked on top of the gun near the piled arms symbol and loading port. Number 1 bore is .177 in. (4.5 mm). Number 2 is referred to as .22 in. (5.5 mm) but is actually 5.6 mm. Conventional 5.5 mm German and American .22 inch caliber pellets generally would not give optimal performance in Number 2 bore airguns. In the 1980s, Beeman Precision Airguns, then Webley's exclusive agent in the large USA market, insisted that Webley standardize their ".22 or No. 2 bores" to fit the German .22 in./5.5 mm precision pellets. Webley complied and BSA quietly followed suit soon after. Number 3 bore is .25 in. cal. (6.35 mm).

PISTOLS

240 MAGNUM - .177 or .22 cal., TL, SP, SS, 510/420 FPS, 6 in. barrel, two-stage adj. trigger, adj. rear sight, sights separate from barrel on up-swinging top receiver unit, integral scope rail, one-piece walnut grip, automatic safety, 9 in. OAL, 2 lbs. Mfg. 1994-2000.

courtesy Tim Saunders

$260	$220	$190	$150	$115	$75	N/A

Last MSR was $259.

GRADING	100%	95%	90%	80%	60%	40%	20%

SCORPION - 177 or .22 cal., BBC, SP, SS, 7.9 in barrel, 510/380 FPS, automatic safety, 3.4 lbs., 15.3 in. OAL. Mfg. 1973-1993.

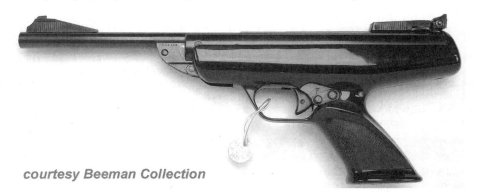

courtesy Beeman Collection

○ **Scorpion MK I** - KEMATEL sights. Mfg. 1973-1985.

	$225	$200	$175	$150	$125	$100	$75

Add 25% for boxed with all accessories. Subtract 10% for missing cocking aid.

○ **Scorpion MK II** - integral scope groove, steel and plastic sights. Mfg. 1985-1993.

	$250	$225	$200	$175	$150	$125	$100

Last MSR was $190.

Add 25% for boxed with all accessories. Subtract 10% for missing cocking aid.

RIFLES: BARREL COCKING

Subtract 20% for specimens equipped with gas-spring unit (sometimes inappropriately called "gas ram" or "gas strut"). Such modification makes the gun non-original, voids the manufacturer's warranty, and may cause cumulative injury to gun. Length measurements may vary by about 0.25 in. or so within models.

BREAKDOWN PATTERN - .177 cal., BBC, SP, SS, 18.5 in. barrel, marked "Breakdown Pattern", no serial number prefix from 1933 to 1936, "B" prefix after 1936, 41.5 in. OAL. Mfg. 1933-1939.

	N/A	$350	$300	$200	$150	$100	N/A

BSA´s first barrel cocking air rifle.

BUCCANEER - .177 or .22 cal., BBC, SP, SS, similar to Scorpion MK II pistol, except black, brown, or camouflage composite thumbhole stock, 18.5 in. rifled barrel, marked "BUCCANEER" on top of compression tube, 35.5 in. OAL. Mfg. 1977-1983.

courtesy Howard Collection

	$400	$350	$295	$250	$195	N/A	N/A

Add 25% for boxed with all accessories.

CADET - .177 cal., BBC, SP, SS, rifled or smooth bore (mfg. for various export markets w/ "S.B." serial number suffix) barrel, blue finish, 37.5 in. OAL, 4.75 lbs. Mfg. 1946-1959.

	$200	$180	$160	$140	$120	$100	$60

○ **Cadet Major** - .177 cal., BBC, SP, SS, rifled or smooth bore (mfg. for various export markets w/ "S.B." serial number suffix) barrel, blue finish, 42 in. OAL, 5.5 lbs. Mfg. 1947-1959.

	$200	$180	$160	$140	$120	$100	$60

COMET - .177 or .22 cal., BBC, SP, SS, 17.5 in. rifled barrel, blue finish, 825-570 FPS, adj. bridge style rear and fixed front sights, scope grooves,anti-beartrap, manual safety, black synthetic stock w/buttpad, 42.5 in. OAL, 5.9 lbs. Mfg. 2007.

	$310	$275	$225	$175	N/A	N/A	N/A

Last MSR was $324.

GRADING	100%	95%	90%	80%	60%	40%	20%

LIGHTNING - .177 or .22 cal., BBC, SP, SS, 10 (British version) or 15 in. rifled barrel, blue finish, variation of the Supersport, 39.5 in. with Volumetric sound moderator or 33 in. w/o Volumetric sound moderator OAL, 6.1 lbs. Mfg. 1997-2007.

courtesy Precision Airgun Distribution

	$515	$425	$359	$300	N/A	N/A	N/A

Last MSR was $540.

British version with 10 in. barrel and BSA Volumetric sound moderator (requires $200 federal transfer tax in USA).

☉ **Lightning XL** - .177 or .22 cal., BBC, SP, SS, 10 (British version) or 15 in. rifled barrel, blue finish, similar to Lightning except, redesigned stock and adj. two-stage trigger. Mfg. 2005-current.

MSR N/A	$505	$480	$400	$335	$275	N/A	N/A

MERCURY - .177 or .22 cal., BBC, SP, SS, 18.5 in. rifled barrel, blue finish, 700/550 FPS, serial number prefixes "W" and "Z," adj. rear and globe front sights, 43.5 in. OAL, 7.25 lbs. Mfg. 1972-1980.

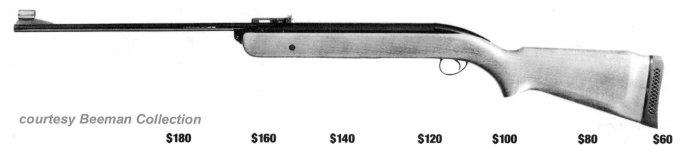

courtesy Beeman Collection

	$180	$160	$140	$120	$100	$80	$60

☉ **Mercury S** - .177 or .22 cal., BBC, SP, SS, 18.5 in. rifled barrel, blue finish, 825-600 FPS, adj. rear and globe front sights, oil finished and checkered walnut stock, thicker barrel, 44.5 in. OAL. 7.25 lbs. New 1980-disc.

	$230	$200	$170	$150	$125	N/A	N/A

MERCURY CHALLENGER - .177 or .22 cal., BBC, SP, SS, 18.5 in. rifled barrel, blue finish, 850-625 FPS, adj. rear and globe front sights, Maxi-Grip scope rail, redesigned stock, 43.5 in. OAL, 7.25 lbs. Mfg. 1983-1997.

	$250	$225	$200	$185	$160	N/A	N/A

Last MSR was $205.

MERCURY TARGET - .177 cal., BBC, SP, SS, 18.5 in. rifled barrel, blue finish, simalar to Mercury except, ramp on trigger block for Anschutz aperture target rear sight, tunnel front sight, approx. 2,000 mfg. 1975.

	$375	$350	$295	$245	$195	N/A	N/A

MERLIN MK I - .177 or .22 cal., BBC, SP, SS, 14.25 in. rifled barrel, blue finish, plastic pellet loading block, 36 in. OAL, 3.5 lbs. Mfg. 1962-64.

	$250	$225	$200	$185	$160	N/A	N/A

☉ **Merlin MK II** - .177 or .22 cal., BBC, SP, SS, 14.25 in. rifled barrel, blue finish, metal pellet loading block, anti-bear-trap device, 36 in. OAL, 3.5 lbs. Mfg. 1964-1968.

	$250	$225	$200	$185	$160	N/A	N/A

METEOR - .177 or .22 cal., BBC, SP, SS, 18.5 in. rifled or smoothbore barrel, blue finish, 650-500 FPS, adj. rear and fixed front sights, 6 lbs. New 1959.

☉ **Meteor MK I** - .177 or .22 cal., BBC, SP, SS, 18 in. rifled or smoothbore barrel, blue finish, 650-500 FPS, adj. rear and fixed front sights, 41 in. OAL, 5.25 lbs. Mfg. 1959-1962.

	$180	$160	$140	$120	$100	$80	$60

☉ **Meteor MK II** - .177 or .22 cal., BBC, SP, SS, 18 in. rifled or smoothbore barrel, blue finish, 650-500 FPS, more streamlined appearance, improved adj. rear and fixed front sights, first use of plastic rear body tube cap, 41 in. OAL, 5.25 lbs. Mfg. 1962-68.

	$180	$160	$140	$120	$100	$80	$60

☉ **Meteor MK III** - .177 or .22 cal., BBC, SP, SS, 18 in. rifled or smoothbore barrel, blue finish, 650-500 FPS, more robust stock with squared-off forearm, adj. rear and fixed front sights, 41 in. OAL, 6 lbs. Mfg. 1969-1973.

	$180	$160	$140	$120	$100	$80	$60

☉ **Meteor MK IV** - .177 or .22 cal., BBC, SP, SS, 18.5 in. rifled barrel, blue finish, 650-500 FPS, adj. bridge style and fixed front sights, 41 in. OAL, 6 lbs. Mfg. 1973-77.

	$180	$160	$140	$120	$100	$80	$60

GRADING	100%	95%	90%	80%	60%	40%	20%

⊙ *Meteor MK V* - .177 or .22 cal., BBC, SP, SS, 18.5 in. rifled barrel, blue finish, 650-500 FPS, adj. bridge style and fixed front sights, 41 in. OAL, 6 lbs. Mfg. 1977-1994..

	$180	$160	$140	$120	$100	$80	$60

⊙ *Meteor MK 6* - .177 or .22 cal., BBC, SP, SS, 17.5 in. rifled barrel, blue finish, 760-580 FPS, adj. trigger, adj. bridge style and fixed front sights, scope grooves, anti-beartrap, manual safety, rubberbuttpad, 42 in. OAL, 7.5 lbs. Mfg. 1993-2007.

	$320	$270	$195	$150	N/A	N/A	N/A

Last MSR was $350.

◆**Meteor MK 6 Carbine** - .177 or .22 cal., BBC, SP, SS, 15 in. rifled barrel, blue finish, 760-580 FPS, adj. trigger, adj. bridge style and fixed front sights, scope grooves, anti-beartrap, manual safety, rubber buttpad, 39 in. OAL, 5.7 lbs. Mfg. 1993-2007.

	$350	$295	$245	$195	N/A	N/A	N/A

Last MSR was $375.

⊙ *Meteor Super* - .177 or .22 cal., BBC, SP, SS, 19 in. rifled or smoothbore barrel, blue finish, 650-500 FPS, Monte Carlo stock, adj. rear and fixed front sights, vent. recoil buttpad, 41 in. OAL, 6 lbs. Mfg. 1967-1973.

	$210	$185	$160	$140	$115	$90	$70

SHADOW - .177 or .22 cal., BBC, SP, SS, rifled barrel, blue finish, same action as Scorpion MK II pistol with black, brown, or camouflage (Trooper) thumbhole composite stock, marked "SHADOW" on compression tube, cocking aid, 27 in. OAL. Mfg. 1985-86.

	$450	$425	$400	$375	$350	$325	$300

Add 25% for boxed with all accessories. Add 25% for Trooper model.

SUPERSPORT - .177, .22, or .25 cal., BBC, SP, SS, 850/625/530 FPS, 18 in. rifled barrel, blue finish, Monte Carlo stock with vent. recoil pad, anti-beartrap, manual safety, 41 in. OAL, 6.6 lbs. New 1986.

⊙ *Supersport America* - .177, .22, or .25 cal., BBC, SP, black finish, 850/625/530 FPS, black Monte Carlo composite stock with vent. recoil pad.

	$250	$225	$200	$185	$160	N/A	N/A

⊙ *Supersport Custom* - .177 or .22, cal., BBC, SP, SS, 990/665 FPS, 18.5 in. rifled barrel, blue finish, rotating breech for loading pellets, large diameter air cylinder, nylon parachute piston seal, checkered walnut stock w/ cheekpiece and vent. recoil pad, Maxigrip sight rail, heavy barrel, adj. metal two stage trigger, manual safety on RHS, 43.8 in. OAL, 7.8 lbs. Mfg. 1987-1992.

	$500	$425	$375	$300	$250	N/A	N/A

⊙ *Supersport MK I* - .177, .22, or .25 cal., BBC, SP, rifled barrel, blue finish, 850/625/530 FPS. Mfg. 1986-87.

	$230	$200	$170	$150	$125	N/A	N/A

Last MSR was $279.

⊙ *Supersport MK I Carbine* - .177, .22, or .25 cal., BBC, SP, rifled barrel, blue finish, 850/625/530 FPS, 14 in. barrel. Mfg. 1986-87.

	$255	$225	$185	$160	$145	N/A	N/A

Last MSR was $279.

⊙ *Supersport MK2 E/E (Magnum)* - .177, .22, or .25 (disc.) cal., BBC, SP, 18.50 in. rifled barrel, blue finish, 950/750/600 FPS, 42 in. OAL, approx. 6.6 lbs. Mfg. 1987-2007.

	$405	$335	$285	$235	N/A	N/A	N/A

Last MSR was $428.

⊙ *Supersport MK2 SS Carbine E/E* - .177, .22 or .25 cal., BBC, SP, SS, 950/750/650 FPS, 15.5 in. barrel, 39 in. OAL, 6.2 lbs. Mfg. 1987-2007.

	$405	$335	$285	$235	N/A	N/A	N/A

Last MSR was $428.

⊙ *Supersport XL* - .177, .22, or .25 cal., BBC, SP, 18.50 in. rifled BBL, 900/650/600 FPS, adj. rear and ramp front sights, groved for scope mounting, blue finish, adj. two-stagew trigger, checkered Monte Carlo style stock w/ rubber recoil pad, hardwood 42 in. OAL, approx. 6.8 lbs. Mfg. 2007-current.

MSR N/A	$439	$405	$335	$285	$235	N/A	N/A

MODEL 635 MAGNUM - .25 cal., BBC, SP, SS, rifled barrel, blue finish, 850-625 FPS, 7.25 lbs.

	$300	$260	$230	$200	$175	$135	$95

XL TACTICAL - .177, .22, OR .25 cal., BBC, SP, SS, 14.5 in. rifled barrel, blue finish, similar to Lightning except, synthetic stock and adj. two-stage trigger. OAL 37.5, 6.6 lbs. New 2007.

courtesy Precision Airgun Distribution

MSR N/A	$505	$480	$400	$335	$275	N/A	N/A

GRADING	100%	95%	90%	80%	60%	40%	20%

RIFLES: MODIFIED REAR/UNDER LEVER COCKING

See also Lincoln in the "L" section of this book for the Lincoln underlever rifles from which BSA underlever air rifles were developed.

Subtract 20% for specimens equipped with gas-spring unit (sometimes inappropriately called "gas ram" or "gas strut"). Such modification makes the gun non-original, voids the manufacturer's warranty and may cause cumulative injury to gun. Length measurements may vary by about 0.25 in. or so within models.

AIRSPORTER - .177, .22, or .25 cal., UL, SP, SS, 1020/800/550 FPS, tap loader, tapered breech plug, blued finish, 8 lbs.

courtesy Beeman Collection

First underlever to have cocking lever hidden in forearm. Carbine versions with 14 in. barrels do not bring a premium.

✪ **Airsporter Club** - .177 cal. only, 7.5 lbs. Mfg. 1948-1959.

	$300	$270	$225	$190	$140	$100	$65

✪ **Airsporter MK I** - .177 or .22 cal., mfg. 1948-1959.

	$300	$270	$225	$190	$140	$100	$65

✪ **Airsporter MK II** - .177 or .22 cal., mfg. 1959-1965.

	$300	$270	$225	$190	$140	$100	$65

✪ **Airsporter MK III** - .177 or .22 cal., serial number prefixes "EF", "EG", and "GE". Mfg. began in 1965. Disc.

	$300	$270	$225	$190	$140	$100	$65

✪ **Airsporter MK VII** - .177 or .22 cal., disc. 2001.

	$300	$270	$225	$190	$140	$100	$65

Last MSR was $375.

✪ **Airsporter RB2 Magnum** - .177 , .22 or .25 cal., rotary breech replaced tap loading breech, 18 in. rifled barrel, 8.50 lbs. Mfg. 1991-2000.

	$300	$270	$225	$190	$140	$100	$65

Last MSR was $450.

Add 25% for Crown Grade RB2 with laminated wood stock.

♦**Airsporter RB2 Magnum Carbine** -.177 , .22 or .25 cal., rotary breech replaced tap loading breech, 18 in. rifled barrel, 8.50 lbs. Mfg. 1991-2000.

	$300	$270	$225	$190	$140	$100	$65

Last MSR was $450.

Add 25% for Crown Grade RB2 with laminated wood stock.

✪ **Airsporter RB2 Stutzen** -.177 , .22 or .25 cal., mfg. began in1992. Disc.

	$360	$325	$275	$225	$165	$120	$80

✪ **Airsporter S** - .177 or .22 cal., oil finish, checkered walnut stock; heavier barrel, 0.5 inch longer.Mfg. began in1979. Disc.

	$345	$310	$260	$215	$160	$115	$75

✪ **Airsporter Stutzen** - .177 or .22 cal., full length stock. Mfg. 1985-1992.

	$360	$325	$275	$225	$165	$120	$80

Last MSR was $540.

AIRSPORTER S CENTENARY (COMMEMORATIVE) - .177 or .22 cal., SP, UL, SS, tap marked "BSA Piled Arms Centenary 1982 - One of One Thousand" on top of air chamber, blue finish, three-quarter length Stutzen-style checkered walnut stock with Schnabel forend (cocking lever contained in forend) and PG cap with trademark, Mk. X 4x40mm scope, QD sling swivels and leather sling, shooting kit, BSA patch, BSA gun case, and certificate numbered to rifle. Mfg. 1982 only.

	$1,000	$950	$800	N/A	N/A	N/A	N/A

Last MSR was $650.

Add 10% for gun case, accessories and all literature.

Mfg. in 1982 to commemorate 100 years of BSA "Piled Arms" symbol, three Martini Henry .577 SS rifles piled in military fashion.

BSA AIR RIFLE - .177 cal., UL (bayonet style), SP, SS, faucet tap loading, Marked: "THE BSA AIR RIFLE" (1905) or "THE BSA AIR RIFLE (Lincoln Jeffries Patent)" (1906-1907), 43.5 in. OAL. Mfg. 1905-07.

	$500	$450	$400	$325	$275	$200	$100

BSA IMPROVED PATTERN - .177 cal., UL (bayonet style), SP, SS, tap loading, new patented breech plug retaining plate and larger chamber in the breech plug, breech plates marked "P. Par.," 43.5 in. OAL. Mfg. 1906-1907.

	$500	$450	$400	$325	$275	$200	$100

This model may have been what would have been called the Model C or D.

GRADING	100%	95%	90%	80%	60%	40%	20%

GOLDSTAR - .177 or .22 cal., UL, SP, 18.50 in. barrel, two-stage adj. trigger, hardwood stock, ten-shot rotary magazine, 950/750 FPS, 8.50 lbs. Mfg. 1991-2001.

	$500	$450	$400	$300	$200	N/A	N/A

Last MSR was $847.

Magazine was developed from VS2000.

⊙ *Goldstar E/E (Magnum)* - .177 or .22 cal., UL, SP, 1020/625 FPS, 17.50 in. barrel, two-stage adj. trigger, hardwood stock, ten-shot rotary magazine, 8.50 lbs. Disc. 2001.

	$450	$400	$350	$300	$200	N/A	N/A

Last MSR was $700.

E/E = "Export Extra"- power above 12 ft. lb., the British legal limit.

GUN LAYING TEACHER - .177 cal., UL (modified to rear), SP, SS, very special variation of Improved Model D underlever air rifle. Cocked by lever behind breech. Instead of a stock it had a system of heavy rails to allow function as a miniature artillery piece for teaching military artillery crews. Known as the Admiralty Pattern guns. Most were fired by pulling a lanyard attached to the firing mechanism, the later production models, had a solenoid-operated trigger mechanism. Second unmarked ("Improved Model" or "Inside Barrel Model") variation made in the early 1940s;were the ones with the Solenoid operated trigger. There were made for use in the Valentine Model tank used in New Zealand; used into the 1950s. It fits inside a tank's cannon barrel for training tank gunners. Mfg. 1911 - circa 1943. Ref. USA (Feb. 1995).

courtesy Beeman Collection

	N/A	N/A	$3,750	$3,000	$2,000	$1,500	$1,200

This gun was designed in 1911, was first delivered in June of 1915, and the last of the only 212 produced was delivered in January of 1916. The entire period of production wasseven months.

IMPROVED MODEL B - .177 cal., UL (bayonet style), SP, SS, tap loading, marked with "Improved Model B", Standard version: 43.3 in. OAL, Light version: 39 in. OAL. Mfg. 1907-1908.

	$800	$700	$600	$400	$300	$200	$150

IMPROVED MODEL D - .177, .22, or .25 (1908-1918 only) cal., SP, SS, UL (bayonet, side button, end button styles), 1.125 (Juvenile) or 1.25 in. dia air cylinder.

Approximately 600 total 25 cal. mfg. in Ordinary and Light versions. Most .25 cal. were sent to India where they saw rough use; very few exist today. There are five size variations (not marked as such) plus the Military models. Size may vary by about 0.25 in.

⊙ *Improved Model D (Junior)* - .177 cal.,1.25 in. OD, 34.25 in. OAL. Approx. 1097 mfg. 1912-14.

	$800	$700	$600	$500	$400	$300	$200

⊙ *Improved Model D (Juvenile)* - .177 cal., air cylinder 1.125 in. OD, folding leaf rear sight, 34.25 in. OAL. Approx. 600 mfg. 1913-14.

	$1,000	$900	$800	$700	$600	$400	$300

⊙ *Improved Model D (Light)* - .177, or .25 cal., 39 in. OAL, mfg. 1908-1918.

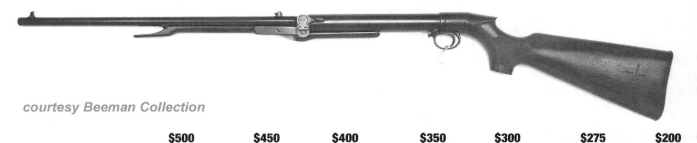

courtesy Beeman Collection

	$500	$450	$400	$350	$300	$275	$200

Add 500% for original .25 cal. barrels.
Less then 20 mfg. in .25 cal.

GRADING	100%	95%	90%	80%	60%	40%	20%

✪ *Improved Model D (Military Model)* - .177 or .22 cal., UL, SP, SS, very special variation of Improved Model D for military training; duplicated size, balance, and sights of the Long Lee-Enfield Territorial Model 303 military rifles. Variation one: .177 cal., simple bayonet cocking lever. Variation two: .177 or .22 cal., bayonet underlever cocking lever with side reinforcements ("fillets or fences") at bend point. Variation three: .22 (No. 2 bore) cal., side button cocking lever. Approx. 430 total of all variations mfg. 1907-1914.

courtesy Beeman Collection

	N/A	N/A	$3,500	$2,500	$1,500	$850	N/A

✪ *Improved Model D (Ordinary)* - .177, .22, or .25 (1908-1918) cal., 43.5 in. OAL.

	$500	$450	$400	$350	$300	$275	$200

Add 500% for original .25 cal. barrels.

✪ *Improved Model D (Sporting)* - .22 (No. 2 bore) cal., 45.5 in. OAL. Mfg. 1909-1917.

	$500	$450	$400	$350	$300	$275	$200

STANDARD - .177 or .22 (No. 2) cal., UL, SP, SS, marked "STANDARD". Mfg. 1919-39.

All air rifles made between WWI and WWII were marked "STANDARD".

✪ *Standard Variant 1* - Giant or "Long Tom" (common nicknames, not marked as such), S or T serial number prefixes, 45.5 in. OAL.

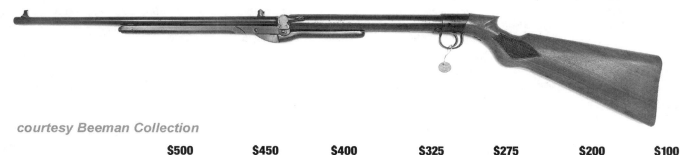

courtesy Beeman Collection

	$500	$450	$400	$325	$275	$200	$100

Add 25% for T serial number prefix.

✪ *Standard Variant 2* - Light (not marked as such) - L or A serial number prefixes.

courtesy Beeman Collection

	$500	$450	$400	$325	$275	$200	$100

Add 25% for A serial number prefix.

✪ *Standard Variant 3* - .177cal. only, comes in two verisons.Club No. 1 version: "CLUB" markings. 45.5 in. OAL. Mfg. 1922-30. Club No. 4 version: "CLUB NO. 4" markings, C or CS serial number prefixes, 45.25 in .OAL. Mfg. 1930-39.

courtesy Beeman Collection

	$500	$450	$400	$325	$275	$200	$100

Add 25% for C serial number prefix.

CLUB model designations and world wide patent details photoetched on top of the compression tube.

GRADING	100%	95%	90%	80%	60%	40%	20%

STUTZEN MK 2 - .177, .22 cal., or .25 cal., concealed UL, SP, rifled barrel, blue finish, 1020/800/675 FPS, 14 in. barrel, rotating breech, Monte Carlo stock with cheek piece and rosewood Schnabel fore cap, Maxi Grip scope rail, 6.25 lbs. Mfg. 1997-2000.

	$560	$485	$380	$335	$285	N/A	N/A

Last MSR was $700.

SUPERSTAR - .177, .22, or .25 cal., UL, SP,SS, 1020/800/675 FPS, 18.5 in. rifledbarrel, blue finish, rotating breech for loading pellets, checkered beech stock, Maxi Grip scope rail, two-stage trigger, 43 OAL, 7.75 LBS. Mfg. 1992-94.

	$420	$375	$315	$260	$185	$125	N/A

Last MSR was $470.

☉ *Superstar Carbine* - .177, .22, or .25 cal., UL, SP, SS, 850/625/530 FPS, 14 in. rifled barrel, blue finish, rotating breech for loading pellets, checkered beech stock, Maxi Grip scope rail, two-stage trigger, 39.5 OAL. Mfg. 1992-94.

	$420	$375	$315	$260	$185	$125	N/A

Last MSR was $470.

SUPERSTAR MK2 E/E - .177, .22, or .25 cal., UL, SP, 18.5 in. rifled barrel, blue finish, 950/750/600 FPS, rotating breech for loading pellets, Monte Carlo stock, Maxi Grip scope rail, adj. two-stage trigger, 43 in. OAL, 8.50 lbs. Mfg. 1994-2001.

	$480	$450	$350	$275	$215	N/A	N/A

Last MSR was $350.

E/E = "Export Extra"- power above 12 ft. lb., the British legal limit.

☉ *Superstar MK2 Carbine E/E* - .177, .22, or .25 cal., UL, SP, SS, 950/750/600 FPS, 14 in. rifled barrel, blue finish, rotating breech for loading pellets, Monte Carlo stock, Maxi Grip scope rail, adj. two-stage trigger, approx. 8. lbs. Mfg. 1994-2001.

	$480	$410	$350	$275	$215	N/A	N/A

Last MSR was $350.

E/E = "Export Extra"- power above 12 ft. lb., the British legal limit.

☉ *Superstar MK2 Magnum* - .177, .22, or .25 cal., UL, SP, 18.5 in. rifled barrel, blue finish, 1020/800/675 FPS, rotating breech for loading pellets, Monte Carlo stock, Maxi Grip scope rail, adj. two-stage trigger, 43 in. OAL, 8.50 lbs. Mfg. 2001-2003.

	$480	$450	$350	$275	$215	N/A	N/A

Last MSR was $540.

RIFLES: PRECHARGED PNEUMATICS

FIREBIRD - .177 or .22 cal., PCP, UL rotating breech action, SS, 1100/800 FPS, 17.5 in. barrel, adj. trigger and power level, beech Monte Carlo stock with vent. recoil pad, 42 in. OAL, 7.25 lbs. Mfg. 2001-03.

	$300	$250	$200	$150	$100	N/A	N/A

$350.

☉ *Firebird Carbine* - .177 or .22 cal., PCP, UL rotating breech action, SS, 1100/800 FPS, 13 in. barrel, adj. trigger and power level, beech Monte Carlo stock with vent. recoil pad, 39 in. OAL, 7.5 lbs. Mfg. 2001-03.

	$350	$300	$225	$175	$125	N/A	N/A

Last MSR was $395.

HORNET - .22 cal., PCP,SS, micro-movement cocking mechanism, SLC pressure regulator, 18.5 in. match grade free-floating barrel, 850 FPS,blue finish, adj. two-stage trigger, checkered beech Monte Carlo stock with vent. recoil pad, 37.5 in. OAL, 7.9 lbs. Mfg. 2003-07.

	$875	$750	$650	$550	$450	N/A	N/A

Last MSR was $923.

HORNET CARBINE - .22 cal., PCP,SS or ten-shot mag. (new 2004), micro-movement cocking mechanism, pressure regulator, 15.75 in. match grade free-floating barrel,850 FPS,blue finish, adj. two-stage trigger, checkered beech Monte Carlo stock with vent. recoil pad,34 in. OAL, 7.5 lbs. Mfg. 2003-07.

courtesy Precision Airgun Distribution

	$875	$750	$650	$550	$450	N/A	N/A

Last MSR was $923.

GRADING	100%	95%	90%	80%	60%	40%	20%

HORNET CARBINE MULTISHOT - .22 cal., PCP, ten-shot mag., micro-movement cocking mechanism, pressure regulator, 15.75 in. match grade free-floating barrel, 850 FPS, blue finish, adj. two-stage trigger, checkered beech Monte Carlo stock with vent. recoil pad, 34 in. OAL, 7.5 lbs. Mfg. 2004-07.

	$960	$875	$750	$650	N/A	N/A	N/A

Last MSR was $1,035.

HORNET MULTI SHOT - .22 cal., PCP, ten-shot mag., micro-movement cocking mechanism, SLC pressure regulator, 18.5 in. match grade free-floating barrel, 850 FPS, blue finish, adj. two-stage trigger, checkered beech Monte Carlo stock with vent. recoil pad, 37.5 in. OAL, 7.9 lbs. Mfg. 2004-07.

	$960	$875	$750	$650	N/A	N/A	N/A

Last MSR was $1,035.

LONE STAR - .22 or .25 cal., PCP, SS, MMC, 750 fps. (.25 cal.), 18.5 (.22 cal.) or 23 in. BBL, beech Monte Carlo stock with vent. recoil pad, manual safty, 37-41.5 in. OAL, 7.6-7.8 lbs. Mfg. 2008-current.

courtesy Precision Airgun Distribution

MSR N/A	$687	$575	$450	$385	N/A	N/A	N/A

SCORPION - .177 or .22 cal., PCP, SS, BA, 988-815 fps., 18.5 in. barrel, beech Monte Carlo stock with vent. recoil pad, 37 in. OAL, 7.8 lbs. New 2007.

MSR N/A	$875	$825	$755	$650	$550	N/A	N/A

SCORPION CARBINE - .177 or .22 cal., PCP, SS, BA, 988-815 fps., 15 in. barrel, beech Monte Carlo stock with vent. recoil pad, 33.5 in. OAL, 6.8 lbs. New 2007.

MSR N/A	$875	$825	$755	$650	$550	N/A	N/A

SCORPION T-10 BULL BARREL - .177 or .22 cal., PCP, BA, ten-shot metal mag., 988-815 fps., 18.5 in. barrel, adj. two-stage trigger, beech Monte Carlo stock with vent. recoil pad, 44.5 in. OAL, 8 lbs. Mfg. 2008-current.

MSR N/A	$1,154	$875	$825	$755	$650	N/A	N/A

SPITFIRE - .177 or .22 cal., PCP, SS, 1100/800 FPS, 17.5 in. barrel, beech Monte Carlo stock with vent. recoil pad, 40.5 in. OAL, 7.2 lbs. Mfg. 1999-2006.

	$450	$350	$285	$225	$185	N/A	N/A

Last MSR was $465.

○ *Spitfire Carbine* - .177 or .22 cal., PCP, SS, 1100/800 FPS, 14.5 in. barrel, beech Monte Carlo stock with vent. recoil pad, 39 in. OAL, 7.25 lbs. Mfg. 1999-2006.

	$495	$395	$325	$265	$215	N/A	N/A

Last MSR was $526.

○ *Bisley Spitfire* - .177 or .22 cal., PCP, SS, similar to Spitfire except lower power designed for 10-Meter Match use with rear match aperature sight with an interchangeable front sight. Mfg. 2005-2006.

	$625	$550	$450	$350	$250	N/A	N/A

Last MSR was $641.

SPORTSMAN HV - .177 or .22 cal., PCP, SS, BA, 18.5 in. barrel, beech Monte Carlo stock with vent. recoil pad, 37 in. OAL, 7.8 lbs. New 2007.

courtesy Precision Airgun Distribution

MSR N/A	$875	$825	$755	$650	N/A	N/A	N/A

GRADING	100%	95%	90%	80%	60%	40%	20%

SUPERTEN - .177 or .22 cal., PCP, BA, 200cc bottle, ten-shot rotary mag., 1000/800 FPS, 17.25 in. rifled barrel, match grade trigger, beech or walnut Monte Carlo stock with adj. pad, 37.5 in. OAL, approx. 7.75 lbs. New 1996.

  ○ *SuperTEN MK1* - .177 or .22 cal., PCP, BA, ten-shot rotary mag., 1000/800 FPS, 17.25 in. rifled barrel, match grade trigger, beech or walnut Monte Carlo stock with adj. pad, 37.5 in. OAL, approx. 7.75 lbs. Mfg. 1996-2001.

	100%	95%	90%	80%	60%	40%	20%
	$750	$600	$525	$475	$425	N/A	N/A

Last MSR was $880.

  ○ *SuperTEN MK2* - .177 or .22 cal., PCP, BA, ten-shot rotary mag., 1250/1050 FPS, 17.25 in. rifled free-floating matchgrade barrel, adj. match grade trigger, checkered beech or walnut Monte Carlo stock with adj. pad, 37.5 in. OAL, Approx. 7.9 lbs. Mfg. 1999-2001.

courtesy Precision Airgun Distribution

	100%	95%	90%	80%	60%	40%	20%
	$950	$850	$700	$625	N/A	N/A	N/A

Last MSR was $880.

Add 30% for walnut stock.

  ○ *SuperTEN MK2 Carbine* - .177 or .22 cal., PCP, BA, ten-shot rotary mag., 1050/850 FPS, 13.25 in. rifled free-floating matchgrade barrel, adj. match grade trigger, checkered beech or walnut Monte Carlo stock with adj. pad, 33.5 in. OAL, Approx.6.6 lbs. Mfg. 1999-2001.

	100%	95%	90%	80%	60%	40%	20%
	$950	$900	$750	$625	N/A	N/A	N/A

Last MSR was $880.

Add 30% for walnut stock.

  ○ *SuperTEN MK3* - .177 or .22 cal., PCP, BA, ten-shot rotary mag., 1250/1050 FPS, 17.25 in. rifled standard or Bull(new 2004)free-floating matchgrade barrel, adj. match grade trigger, checkered beech or walnut Monte Carlo stock with adj. pad, 37.5 in. OAL, Approx. 7.9 lbs. New 2001.

	100%	95%	90%	80%	60%	40%	20%
MSR N/A	$1,154	$1,095	$995	$850	$700	$625	N/A

Add 30% for walnut stock. Add 20% for Bull barrel.

  ○ *SuperTEN MK3 Carbine* - .177 or .22 cal., PCP, BA, ten-shot rotary mag., 1050/850 FPS, 13.25 in. standard or Bull(new 2004)rifled free-floating matchgrade barrel, adj. match grade trigger, checkered beech or walnut Monte Carlo stock with adj. pad, 33.5 in. OAL, Approx.6.6 lbs. Mfg. 2001-07.

	100%	95%	90%	80%	60%	40%	20%
	$1,225	$1,050	$900	$750	$625	N/A	N/A

Last MSR was $1,277.

Add 30% for walnut stock. Add 20% for Bull barrel.

TECH STAR - .22 cal., PCP,SS, 100cc reservoir, micro-movement cocking mechanism, pressure regulator, 18.5 in. barrel,1000 FPS,blue finish,adj.rear fixed front sights, adj. two-stage trigger, checkered beech Monte Carlo stock with vent. recoil pad,37 in. OAL,6.6 lbs. Mfg. 2004-07.

	100%	95%	90%	80%	60%	40%	20%
	$650	$535	$450	$375	$325	N/A	N/A

Last MSR was $687.

ULTRA - .177 or .22 cal., PCP, SS, MMC, 706 fps. (.22 cal.), 14 in. barrel, beech Monte Carlo stock with vent. recoil pad, 32 in. OAL, 5.7 lbs. New 2007.

	100%	95%	90%	80%	60%	40%	20%
MSR N/A	$739	$655	$550	$450	$385	N/A	N/A

ULTRA MULTISHOT - .177 or .22 cal., PCP, 10 shot mag., MMC, 706 fps. (.22 cal.), 14 in. barrel, beech Monte Carlo stock with vent. recoil pad, 32 in. OAL, 5.7 lbs. New 2007.

courtesy Precision Airgun Distribution

	100%	95%	90%	80%	60%	40%	20%
MSR N/A	$839	$765	$655	$550	$450	N/A	N/A

GRADING	100%	95%	90%	80%	60%	40%	20%

RIFLES: SIDE LEVER COCKING

VS 2000 - .177 or .22 cal., SL, SP, nine-shot repeater, rifled barrel, blue finish, 850-625 FPS, 9 lbs. Approx. ten were mfg. Disc. 1986.

N/A	N/A	$3,000	$2,800	N/A	N/A	N/A

Last MSR was $330.

B.S.F. "BAYERISCHE SPORTWAFFENFABRIK"

Previous manufacturer located in Erlangen, Germany. Previously imported by Kendell International located in Paris, KY, and by Beeman Precision Arms under the Wischo label.

B.S.F. (Bayerische Sportwaffenfabrik) is the base brand for airguns marked B.S.F., Bavaria, and Wischo. B.S.F. was founded in 1935 and produced a few airguns before the pressures of WWII took over. Production began again in 1948 and put an emphasis on solid, simple construction. The Model S54 remains asa classic of solid, elegant construction for a sporter air rifle. B.S.F.´s own production was generally sold under the Bavaria label. The Wischo Company of Erlangen, one of Europe´s leading gun distributors, distributed large numbers, especially to Beeman Precision Airguns in the USA, under the Wischo label. The collapse of their British agent, Norman May & Co, in 1980 resulted in the dismissal of most of the 130 workers. The Schütt family sold the business to Herbert Gayer, who refined the production considerably. However, this was not enough to prevent further decline of the company. It was then purchased by the Hermann Weihrauch Company in nearby Mellrichstadt in the late 1980s. By incorporating some HW design and cosmetic features and parts, a surprisingly good line of upper economy level airguns was developed to supplement the top-of-the-line, regular HW models. Weihrauch manufactures versions of B.S.F. models for Marksman (Marksman Models 28, 40, 55, 56, 58, 59, 70, 71, 72, and 75).

PISTOLS

B.S.F. (WISCHO) MODEL S-20 - .177 cal., BBC, 450 FPS, 2.5 lbs. Mfg. 1950-1985.

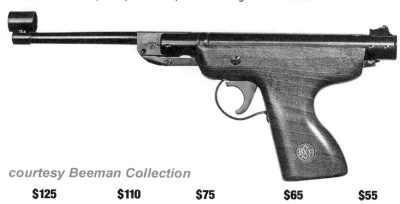

courtesy Beeman Collection

$125	$110	$75	$65	$55	N/A	N/A

Last MSR was $130.

Some Model S-20 pistols were assembled from components and sold by Weihrauch through 1988.

B.S.F. (WISCHO) MODEL CM - similar to Model S-20 except is target style. Disc. in 1988.

courtesy Beeman Collection

$150	$125	$90	$75	$65	N/A	N/A.

RIFLES

BAVARIA MODEL 35 - .177 cal., BBC, SP, 500 FPS, 4.50 lbs.

$150	$120	$100	$75	$50	N/A	N/A

Last MSR was $125.

BAVARIA MODEL 45 - .177 cal., BBC, SP, 700 FPS, 6 lbs.

$165	$125	$105	$85	$60	N/A	N/A

Last MSR was $125.

GRADING	100%	95%	90%	80%	60%	40%	20%

BAVARIA MODEL 50 - .177 cal., BBC, SP, 700 FPS, 6 lbs.

	100%	95%	90%	80%	60%	40%	20%
	$175	$130	$110	$85	$60	N/A	N/A

BAVARIA MODEL S 54 - .177 or .22 cal., UL, SP, 685/500 FPS, 8 lbs.

courtesy Beeman Collection

	100%	95%	90%	80%	60%	40%	20%
	$235	$175	$135	$95	$75	N/A	N/A

Subtract 10% for Sport Model w/ plain stock (discontinued 1986). Add 10% for M Model. Ref: ARG: 37-44.

☼ ***Model S 54 Deluxe*** - .177 or .22 cal., UL, SP, 19.1 in. rifled barrel (12 grooves RH), tap-loader, hand checkered walnut stock, cast aluminum buttplate, 46.8 in. OAL, 8.6 lbs., no safety.

courtesy Beeman Collection

	100%	95%	90%	80%	60%	40%	20%
	$495	$425	$375	$250	$150	N/A	N/A

Add 20% for pre-1980 stock, forearm round in cross section, hand checkering.

BAVARIA MODEL S 55/55 N - .177 or .22 cal., BBC, SP, 16.1 in. rifled barrel (12 grooves, RH), 870/635 FPS, no safety, 40.6 in. OAL, 6.4 lbs. Disc. 1986.

courtesy Beeman Collection

	100%	95%	90%	80%	60%	40%	20%
	$180	$140	$105	$80	$60	N/A	N/A

Add $15 for Deluxe Model. Add $30 for Special Model 55 N (N = "Nussbaum," German for walnut).

BAVARIA MODEL S 60 - .177 or .22 cal., BBC, SP, 800/570 FPS, 6.50 lbs.

courtesy Beeman Collection

	100%	95%	90%	80%	60%	40%	20%
	$180	$140	$105	$80	$60	N/A	N/A

BAVARIA MODEL S 70 - .177 or .22 cal., BBC, SP, 19.1 in. barrel, 855/610 FPS, checkered Monte Carlo stock, ventilated rubber buttplate, 7 lbs.

	100%	95%	90%	80%	60%	40%	20%
	$265	$225	$185	$145	$105	N/A	N/A

GRADING	100%	95%	90%	80%	60%	40%	20%

BAVARIA MODEL S 80 - .177 or .22 cal., BBC, SP, 800/570 FPS, 8.25 lbs.

	100%	95%	90%	80%	60%	40%	20%
	$210	$180	$140	$105	$80	N/A	N/A

Last MSR was $185.

BAHCO

Previous manufacturer, Aktiebolaget Bahco (AB Bahco), has roots dating back to 1862 as a metal working business in Stockholm and Enköping, Sweden. No longer produces airguns.

BAHCO, which, due to a strange font used in the stamping of the name, appears to read as "BAMCO" and is so listed in many places, is a brand name of Aktiebolaget Bahco (AB Bahco).

This Swedish firm has roots dating back to the founding of a steel works in 1862 by Göran Fredrik Göransson, which developed exceptional quality saws under the same Fish & Hook brand that their tools bear today. Their most famous products, based on 118 patents granted to Johan Johansson from 1888 to 1943, are the adjustable spanner wrench (Crescent wrench) and adjustable pipe wrench (monkey wrench). They have produced over 100 million examples of those world famous tools. According to Walter (2001) they also formerly specialized in bayonets and military equipment and produced gas-powered rifles under the Excellent brand from 1906 to 1915 with the patents of Ewerlöf and Blómen. Today the Bahco name can be found on garden and other tools in almost any large hardware or warehouse store, but no longer on airguns.

The Bahco Model S1 air rifle is very similar to the Excellent C2 air rifle and is sometimes listed with it. The Bahco Model 1S clearly is the older design. The full relationship of the Bahco and Excellent brand airguns has yet to be determined. (See Excellent in the "E" section of this guide.)

RIFLES

MODEL S1 - 4.5 mm cal., SS, trombone-style slide action pump pneumatic, smoothbore octagonal BBL, breech block swings to side to load, no safety. Mfg. circa 1900.

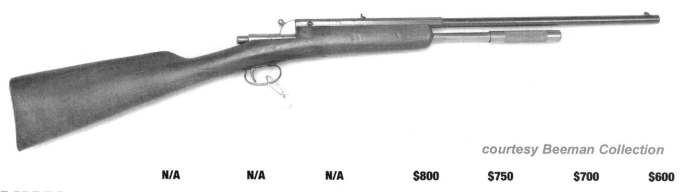

courtesy Beeman Collection

	100%	95%	90%	80%	60%	40%	20%
	N/A	N/A	N/A	$800	$750	$700	$600

BAIKAL

Current trademark of products manufactured by the Russian State Unitary Plant "Izhevsky Mechanichesky Zavod" (SUP IMZ), located in Russia. Currently imported by European American Armory, located in Sharpes, FL; Compasseco, located in Bardstown, KY; and Pyramyd Air, Inc., located in Pepper Pike, OH. Dealer sales. For more information and current pricing on both new and used Baikal firearms, please refer to the *Blue Book of Gun Values* by S.P. Fjestad (also available online).

First known to American airgunners after WWII by the Baikal IZh 22, a typical Russian simple, but fairly sturdy, break barrel .22 cal. air rifle. Baikal also manufactures many models that are not currently available in the American marketplace.

PISTOLS

IZH 46/46M - .177 cal., UL, SSP, SS, 410 FPS (IZh 46 disc.) or 460 FPS (IZh 46M w/ larger compressor), micrometer fully adj. rear target sight, adj. international target grip, five-way adj. trigger, 10 in. hammer-forged rifled barrel, 2.4 lbs.

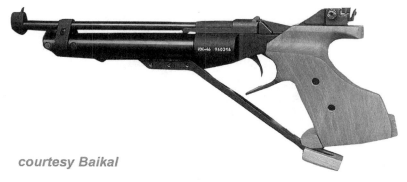

courtesy Baikal

	100%	95%	90%	80%	60%	40%	20%
MSR $430	$375	$325	$275	$200	$150	N/A	N/A

Subtract 25% for IZh 46.

GRADING	100%	95%	90%	80%	60%	40%	20%

IZH 53 - .177 cal., BBC, SP, SS pistol, black plastic stock with thumb rest and finger grooves.

courtesy Beeman Collection

	$75	$65	$55	$50	$40	$30	$20

IZH 53M - .177 cal., BBC, SP, SS, 360 FPS, adj. rear sight, adj. trigger, rifled 8.8 in. barrel, black plastic target grip, 16.3 in OAL, 2.4 lbs.

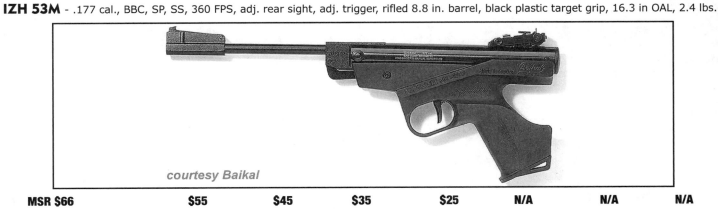

courtesy Baikal

MSR $66	$55	$45	$35	$25	N/A	N/A	N/A

MP-651K - .177 cal, CO_2 semi-auto repeater, 8 or 12 g. cylinders, DA, 8-round mag., 5.9-in. BBL, 340 FPS, adj rear blade front sights, black finish, cast aluminium and synthetic, 1.54 lbs. 9.45 OAL. Mfg. 2007 - current.

courtesy Baikal

MSR N/A	$85	$70	$55	$40	N/A	N/A	N/A

MP-654K (MAKAROV SEMI-AUTO) - .177 cal, CO_2 (capsule loads in magazine), single or double action, thirteen-shot, 3.8 in. barrel, 380 FPS, 1.6 lbs. Importation disc. 2003.

courtesy Baikal

	$100	$85	$70	$55	$40	N/A	N/A

Last MSR was $120.

GRADING	100%	95%	90%	80%	60%	40%	20%

MP-661K DROZD - .177 BB cal., battery and 8 or 12 g. cylinder CO_2, electronic trigger rapid-fire (one, three, and six round rapid-fire busts), 30 round mag., 10 in. BBL, 330 FPS, black high-strength plastic construction. Mfg. 2006 - current.

courtesy Baikal

MSR $264	$235	$180	$140	$90	N/A	N/A	N/A

Add $55 for extra 30 round mag.

MP-672 - .177 cal., PCP, SS, micrometer fully adj. rear target sight, adj. target grip, adj. trigger, 10 in. hammer-forged rifled barrel, 2.6 lbs. Mfg. 2008-current.

courtesy Baikal

At the time of publishing MSR and pricing N/A.

RIFLES

IJ 22 - .177 cal., BBC, SP, SS, 17.90 in. rifled barrel, 410-498 FPS, vertical lever breech-lock on LHS of barrel, brass lined, rifled barrel, blued finish, trigger guard, grip cap and buttplate of dark red plastic hardwood stock with unique shoulder up behind end cap, plastic inset marked "IJ 22", typically sold new with extra mainspring and seals, 40.8 OAL, 5.2 lbs. Mfg. in USSR circa 1970s.

courtesy Beeman Collection

	$75	$65	$55	$50	N/A	N/A	N/A

Also sold internationally as Vostok, in Britain as Milbro G530, and in USA as HyScore 870 Mark 3.

IZH 60 - .177 cal., SL, SP, 460 FPS, 16.50 in. barrel, telescoping stock, 5 lbs. 6 oz. Disc.

courtesy Baikal

	$90	$80	$65	$50	$40	N/A	N/A

Last MSR was $140.

GRADING	100%	95%	90%	80%	60%	40%	20%

IZH 61 - .177 cal., SL, SP, five-shot mag., 490 FPS, 17.80 in. barrel, polymer telescoping stock, 6.4 lbs.

courtesy Baikal

MSR $121	$110	$80	$65	$50	N/A	N/A	N/A

IZH 32BK - .177 cal., SL, SP, 541 FPS, integral rail for scope mount, adj. buttplate, adj. cheek piece, adj. trigger, walnut stock, 11.68 in. barrel, 12.13 lbs. Mfg. 1999-2002.

	$750	$650	$525	$425	$275	N/A	N/A

Last MSR was $1,100.

This model is designed for ten-meter running target competition.

IZH 38 - .177 cal., BBC, SP, SS, 410-498FPS MV, very short pull, 40.8 in OAL, 5.2 lbs.
Current values not yet determined.

IZH DROZD - .177 BB cal., battery and CO_2, rapid-fire (one, three, and six round rapid-fire busts), 30 round mag., 10 in. BBL, 330 FPS, adj rear sight, black and yellow color high-strength plastic construction, detachable stock. Mfg. 2003-06.

	$220	$180	$140	N/A	N/A	N/A	N/A

Last MSR was $239.

This model became the MP-661K Drozd Blackbird circa 2007.

MP-661K DROZD BLACKBIRD - .177 BB cal., battery and 12 g and larger CO_2, or air cylinder, electronic trigger with switch allows SS or automatic-fire (300, 450, or 600 rpm), 400 round mag., 10 in. BBL, 330 FPS, adj rear sight, black color high-strength plastic construction. Mfg. 2007 - current.

courtesy Baikal

MSR $285	$265	$220	$180	$140	N/A	N/A	N/A

Add $10.50 for speed loader.

MP-512 - .177 cal., BBC, SP, SS, 490 FPS, integral rail for scope mount, adj. sights, polymer stock redesigned w/ grip enhancing inserts (New 2008), 17.70 in. barrel, 6.20 lbs. Mfg. 1999-current.

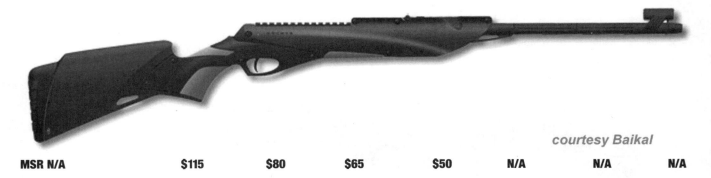

courtesy Baikal

MSR N/A	$115	$80	$65	$50	N/A	N/A	N/A

GRADING	100%	95%	90%	80%	60%	40%	20%

MP-512M - .177 or .22 cal., BBC, SP, SS, 970-820 FPS, integral rail for scope mount, adj. sights, birch or polymer stock, 17.70 in. barrel, 6.20 lbs. Mfg. 2006-current.

courtesy Baikal

MSR N/A	$100	$75	$60	$45	N/A	N/A	N/A

MP-513/MP-513M - .177 or .22 (New 2006) cal., BBC, SP, SS, 1000 FPS, integral rail for scope mount, adj. sights, European wood stock, 17.70 in. barrel, 6.20 lbs. New 2003.

courtesy Baikal

MSR $198	$175	$140	$100	$75	N/A	N/A	N/A

Add 5% for .22 cal. MP-513M new 2006.

MP-514k - .177 cal., BC, SP, eight-shot mag., 558FPS, 16.54 in. rifled BBL, adj. rear post front sights, polymer stock, auto-safety, 6.2 lbs., 25.6 in. OAL. Mfg. 2007-current.

MSR N/A	$150	$125	$95	$75	N/A	N/A	N/A

MP-532 - .177 cal., SL, SP, 15.75 in. rifled streel BBL, 427 FPS, adj. rear and hooded front sight, adj. butt pad, adj. trigger, 9.26 lbs. Imported 1999-2007.

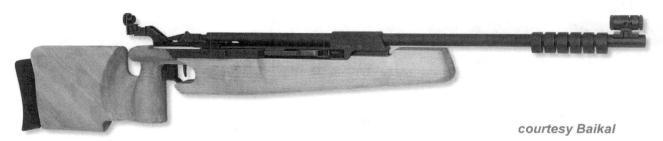

courtesy Baikal

	$495	$400	$325	$265	$165	N/A	N/A

Last MSR was $599.

MP-532T RUNNING BOAR - .177 cal., SL, SP, 15.75 in. rifled steel BBL, 427 FPS, scope rail, adj. butt pad, adj. trigger, 47.24 in. OAL, 11 lbs. No current importation. Mfg. 2007-current.

courtesy Baikal

At the time of publishing MSR and pricing N/A.

GRADING	100%	95%	90%	80%	60%	40%	20%

MP-571 BIATHLON - .177 cal., PCP, lever cocking repeater, includes four five-shot mags., 15.75 in. rifled steel BBL, adj. rear and hooded front sights, adj. buttplate and cheek rest, adj. trigger, 41.7 in. OAL, 9.26 lbs. No current importation. Mfg. 2008-current.

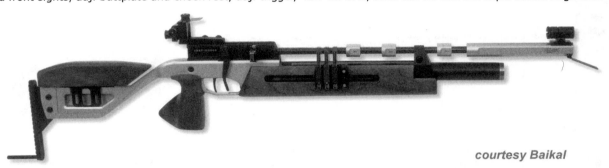

courtesy Baikal

At the time of publishing MSR and pricing N/A.

MP-572 SPORTING - .177 cal., PCP, lever cocking SS, 17.75 in. rifled steel BBL, adj. rear and hooded front sights, adj. buttplate and cheek piece, adj. trigger, 46 in. OAL, 10.34 lbs. No current importation. Mfg. 2008-current.

courtesy Baikal

At the time of publishing MSR and pricing N/A.

BAILEY

For information on Bailey airguns, see Columbian in the "C" section.

BALCO-SUB

Manufacturer of CO_2 spear pistols at 6 Menexelon Street, Kato Kifisia, Greece.

PISTOL

BALCO PRO - CO_2, SS, heavy plastic, aluminum, and stainless steel. 22.9 in. OAL, 2.3 lbs.

courtesy Beeman Collection

	$250	$225	$200	$150	$100	N/A	N/A

Add 10% for factory plastic sheath.

BARNES PNEUMATIC

Current custom manufacturer located in New Windsor, MD.

Circa 2007 Gary Barnes is drawing on 30 years of experience, 22 as a master Bladesmith. Barnes applies unique artistic skill and design as well as mechanical creativity to his airguns. Specializing in large bore, high accuracy airguns, often with exotic styling and decoration of which all parts, including barrels are designed and manufactured in his shop. Various base models are listed on his website, but all are produced per-individual request. The following are examples of his craftsmanship. Contact Mr. Barnes directly (see Trademark Index) for price and availability. Please Note: On December 22, 2007 Gary Barnes ceased accepting new airgun orders. All airgun orders placed before December 22, 2007 will be filled as ordered.

AIRCANES

Contact Mr. Barnes directly (see Trademark Index) for price and availability.

AUTOCANE - .27 in. cal., 800 psi traditional PCP, full-automatic 500 rpm, 12 shot magazine, rosewood handle w/ gold lip pearl, sterling silver cap, acid etched body, deeply engraved top. 39.8 OAL, 4.7 lbs. Ref. USA (Nov-Dec 1997). Manf. 1997.

courtesy Fred Liady

PISTOLS

Contact Mr. Barnes directly (see Trademark Index) for price and availability.

HERITAGE CLASS 32 .32 in. cal. (0 buckshot ball), SS, PCP, frictionless hammer, 2 stage match trigger, 11 mm scope dovetail, high pressure breech, dueling style stock.

courtesy Gary Barnes

RIFLES

Contact Mr. Barnes directly (see Trademark Index) for price and availability.

APPALOOSA - .32 in. cal. PCP w/ quick fill reservoir, SS, solid brass barrel shroud. Mfg. 2005.

courtesy Gary Barnes

FIRST MODEL - .45 cal., traditional 500 psi PCP, magazine fed cross block repeater, adj. power, set trigger, deluxe walnut stock, acid-etched decoration, sterling silver shields, jeweled detail, 48 IN. OAL, 10 lbs Ref. USA (Jan. 1997). Mfg. 1996.

courtesy Fred Liady

GRADING	100%	95%	90%	80%	60%	40%	20%

HIGH PLAINS CARBINE - .375 in. cal., PCP, SS, LA, "Shear Ring" breech size each round during loading. Claro walnut stock, brass rear sight, 850 fps, 36 in. OAL, 6.2 lbs. Mfg. 1997. Ref. AR 3: p.35.

courtesy Fred Liady

BARNETT INTERNATIONAL

Research is ongoing with this trademark, and more information will be included both online and in future editions. Average original condition specimens on most common Barnett models are typically priced in the $150-200 range.

BARON MANUFACTURING COMPANY

Previous manufacturer located in Burbank, CA, ca. 1945-1949. Purchased by Healthways Corporation, Los Angeles, CA, in 1947 (Distributed by Healthways as Sportsman. Jr. after 1947. Also private labeled as Wright Target Shot Jr. air pistol 1947-49).

PISTOL

SPORTSMAN JR - .177 cal., SS, SP, 2.5 in smoothbore bbl. unscrews for rear loading of BBs, darts, pellets; removes for shooting corks, 8.1 in OAL, 1.0 lb. Cocks by pulling knob at rear of compression tube. Checkered grip panels.

courtesy Beeman Collection

$150	$125	$100	$80	$60	$40	$20

Last MSR was $3.49.

Add 20% for box and literature.

BARTHELMS, FRITZ (FB RECORD)

For information on Fritz Barthelms, please refer to FB Record in the "F" section.

BASCARAN, C. y T. SRC

Previous manufacturer located in Eibar, Guipuzcoa, Spain.

Bascaran, C. y T. SRC manufactured airguns under the Cometa tradename. Research is ongoing with this trademark, and more information will be included both in future editions and online. Average original condition specimens on most common Bascaran, C. y T. SRC models are typically priced in the $75-$125 range.

BAVARIA

For information on Bavaria airguns, see B.S.F. "Bayerische Sportwaffenfabrik" in this "B" section.

GRADING	100%	95%	90%	80%	60%	40%	20%

BAYARD

Previously manufactured by Anciens Éstablissements Pieper in Herstal Liége, Belgium.

This company is best known for their semi-auto pistol manufacture. They produced a .177 cal., SP, BBC, SS air rifle for HyScore of New York, post-WWII. A mounted knight logo and "Bayard" may be stamped on the side of thebody tube. Has a buttplate with cast letters "BELGIUM" in a vertical row. There are two known versions. One has a spring-loaded J-shaped pellet seating device on top of the breech. Very well made with hand checkered hardwood stock. Very good condition specimens sell in the $100-$200 range. Add $50 for pellet seating model.

courtesy Beeman Collection

BEC EUROLUX AIRGUNS

Previous trademark distributed by BEC Inc., located in Alhambra, CA.

RIFLES

MODEL BEC 15AG - .177 cal., BBC, SP, SS, 14.5 in. barrel, 500 FPS, black finish, walnut-tone hardwood stock, 5.5 lbs. Disc. 2006.

100%	95%	90%	80%	60%	40%	20%
$60	$50	$40	$30	$20	N/A	N/A

Last MSR was $69.

MODEL BEC 18AG - .177 or .22 cal., BBC, SP, SS, 16.5 in. barrel, 850/700 FPS, black finish, walnut-tone hardwood stock, 6.9 lbs. Disc. 2006.

100%	95%	90%	80%	60%	40%	20%
$85	$60	$50	$40	$30	N/A	N/A

Last MSR was $99.

MODEL BEC 21AG - .177 or .22 cal., BBC, SP, SS, 20 in. barrel, 1000/800 FPS, black finish, walnut-tone hardwood stock, 9.9 lbs. Disc. 2006.

100%	95%	90%	80%	60%	40%	20%
$160	$115	$85	$60	$50	N/A	N/A

Last MSR was $189.

BEDFORD

Previous maker and distributor of air pistols. 45 High Street, Boston, Mass. Founded by American engineer, Augustus Bedford, about 1875.

Evidently operated without a partner at first, manufacturing or, at least, selling the Henry Quackenbush designed "Rifle Air Pistol". Bedford later developed airgun patent 172,376, issued January 18, 1876, covering moving the barrel more forward and loading an airgun with a cam sealing bolt action. He joined with George W. Walker who had patent 179,984, issued July 18, 1876, which further improved the bolt action, to form Bedford and Walker, to produce a new design airgun, known as the Bedford & Walker Eureka. Ref. Groenewold (2000).

PISTOL

BEDFORD RIFLE AIR PISTOL - .21 cal. smoothbore, SS, SP., cast iron frame nickel-plated or Japan black, 12.75 in. OAL, 1.5 pounds. Barrel above compression tube. Cocked by pulling barrel forward. Loaded w/ dart when barrel is moved forward for cocking. Saw handle grip w/ embossed checkering. Rear edge of grip casting has a 5/16 in. hole for insertion of a wire shoulder stock. Marked: MANF'D BY A. BEDFORD. 45 HIGH ST. BOSTON. PATD. JUNE 6. DEC. 26, 1871. on LHS upper panel of frame. Stamped w/ SN on upper LHS of frame; production apparently low - this specimen is SN 11. Apparently identical to Quackenbush Rifle Air Pistol which bears these same patent dates. Mfg. 1878-1880.

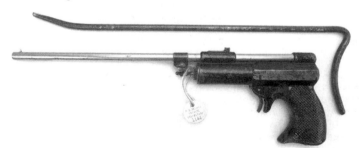

courtesy Beeman Collection

100%	95%	90%	80%	60%	40%	20%
N/A	N/A	$2,150	$1,500	$1,050	$750	$450

Add 10% for wire shoulder stock. Add 20% for nickel finish. Add 25% for original factory box and instructions.

GRADING	100%	95%	90%	80%	60%	40%	20%

BEDFORD & WALKER

Previous manufacturer located in Boston, MA circa 1880s.

Former gunmaking partnership of Augustus Bedford and George A. Walker in Boston, MA, USA. Manufactured the Eureka air pistol based on the Quackenbush push-barrel design with a loading bolt patented by Walker in 1876. Production started in Bedford's Eureka Manufacturing Co. circa 1876, then went to the Pope Brothers & Company plant, and finally transferred to the H.M. Quackenbush plant from the 1880s until 1893. Quackenbush featured the pistol in his catalogs and listed a sale of seventy-four Eureka air pistols in 1886. (Bedford worked in the Quackenbush factory for several years and he, Pope, Walker, and Quackenbush were close associates -- so there is a good deal of overlap and confusion about the origin, production, and sales of their designs). Last sales occurred circa 1893.

PISTOLS

EUREKA STANDARD - .21 cal., SP, SS push-plunger, Japan black or nickel finish.

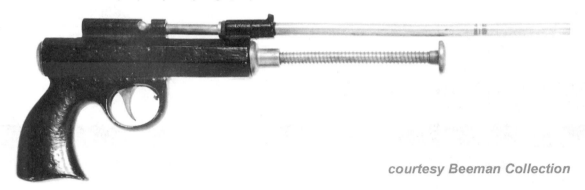

courtesy Beeman Collection

$795	$745	$700	$625	$550	$475	N/A

Add 10% for nickel finish. Add 20% for wire shoulder stock.

EUREKA DELUXE - .21 cal, SP, SS push-plunger, nickel finish, rosewood inserts on flared grip, hardwood case with locking lid, wire shoulder stock, wrench, and box of slugs or darts.

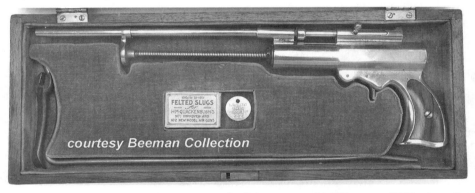

courtesy Beeman Collection

N/A	N/A	$1,750	$1,250	$750	$500	$350

BEEMAN PRECISION AIRGUNS

Current manufacturer and importer located in Huntington Beach, CA. Dealer and consumer direct sales.

The Beeman company was founded by Robert and Toshiko Beeman in 1972 in San Anselmo, CA. Originally named Beeman´s Precision Airguns, the company began by importing airgun models and pellets from Weihrauch, Feinwerkbau, Webley, Dianawerk, Handler and Natermann, Hasuike, and other overseas companies. After moving to San Rafael, CA, circa 1975 the name of the company was changed to Beeman Precision Airguns, Inc. They began to design their own models of airguns and airgun pellets to be produced by Weihrauch, Webley, Norica, Handler and Natermann, and Hasuike. Among the many airgun items introduced by the Beemans were the first telescopic sights built especially for high power sporting air rifles and the first hollow point airgun pellets. By the late 1970s, the Beeman company was importing over 90% of the adult airguns brought into the USA.

Although several other companies, notably Winchester and Hy-Score, had previously attempted to introduce adult airguns to the American shooting market, Beeman is credited with the first successful, commercial development of the adult airgun market in the United States. Tom Gaylord, founder and former editor of *Airgun Letter*, *Airgun Revue*, and *Airgun Illustrated Magazine*, recorded in his book *The Beeman R1* that "the Beeman R1 is the rifle that brought America fully into the world of adult airguns." (Versions of the Beeman R1, generally lower in power or less deluxe, are marketed in other parts of the world as the Weihrauch HW 80.) Other models were produced for Beeman by Norica, Erma, FAS, Record, Sharp, Air Arms, Titan, Gamekeeper, and others. Circa 1983 Beeman moved to Santa Rosa and added certain precision firearms to its line and changed its name to Beeman Precision Arms, Inc. On April 3, 1993, Robert and Toshiko sold most of the assets of their company to S/R Industries of Maryland. S/R moved the company to Huntington Beach, CA to be near one of its other holdings, Marksman Industries, and restored the name of Beeman Precision Airguns. The company has continued to feature the very high quality airguns which had become synonymous with the Beeman name and added an economy line for mass marketers.

Beeman has exclusive rights to any airguns officially marketed in the U.S. under the names Beeman, Feinwerkbau, and Beeman designed models manufactured by Weihrauch and others. Some models, marketed by Beeman in the late 1970s and early 1980s, were manufactured in

GRADING	100%	95%	90%	80%	60%	40%	20%

Germany by Mayer & Grammelspacher (Dianawerk). Early production of those airguns used Diana model numbers under the Beeman's Original brand, but later shipments were marked with the Beeman name and model numbers. Very small stampings on the Dianawerk receivers indicate the month and year of manufacture.

Beeman imported Feinwerkbau and Weihrauch Airguns, whichappear under their respective headings in this section. Beeman/Webley airguns are incorporated into this section, as are economy airguns that are only promoted through chain stores under the Beeman name.

Additional material on the history of the Beeman company, the Beemans, the history of airguns, the development of the airgun market in the USA, and a wide range of other airgun information is available at www.Beemans.net.

For more information and current values on used Beeman firearms, please refer to the *Blue Book of Gun Values* by S.P. Fjestad (also available online).

PISTOLS

ADDER - .177, .20, .22 or .25 cal., 940/850/775/630 FPS, 14 to 20 ft. lbs. ME, PCP, SS, bolt action, grip, trigger guard, and forearm from one piece of select hardwood, smooth grips, scope grooves, blue receiver end cap, 10.5 in. barrel, 16.5 in. OAL, manual safety, 2.75 lbs. Ten mfg. in England by Titian 1992.

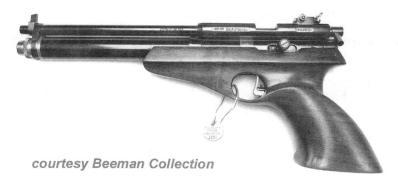

courtesy Beeman Collection

	N/A	$800	$700	$550	$350	N/A	N/A

Last MSR was $530.

Add 10% for .20 cal.

FAS 604 - .177 cal., TL, SP, SS, 380 FPS, 2.2 lbs. Mfg. in Italy. Disc. 1988.

	$295	$250	$195	$150	$100	N/A	N/A

Last MSR was $495.

Add 10% for left-hand variation.

HW 70/HW70A/HW70S - .177 cal., BBC, SP, 440 FPS, two-stage adj. trigger, 6 in. rifled steel barrel, blue/black epoxy or silver (HW 70S, mfg. 1992 only) finish, hooded front and adj. rear (scope grooves added to rear sight base HW 70A 1992) sights, one-piece composition grip and forearm. 2.4 lbs. Mfg. in Germany with importation beginning in 1972.

MSR N/A	$175	$135	$105	$90	$75	N/A	N/A

Add 20% for HW70S with silver finish. Subtract 20% for safety. Add 10% for Santa Rosa address.

Early versions did not have a retainer screw in the side of the rear body plug. The plug may come loose and fly out (recalled).

HURRICANE - .177 or .22 (disc.) cal., TL, SP, SS, 500 FPS, plastic grips with RH thumbrest, adj. rear sight supplied with adapter which replaced rear sight with scope mounting dovetail, hooded front sight, aluminum grip frame cast around steel body tube, RH manual safety, black epoxy finish, 8 in. button rifled barrel, 11.2 in. OAL, 2.4 lbs. Mfg. in England with importation beginning in 1990.

	$235	$195	$150	$115	$95	N/A	N/A

Last MSR was $275.

Add 10% for wood grips. Add 15% for finger groove Beeman "combat" wood grips. Add 20% for Beeman factory markings with San Rafael address. Add 10% for Beeman factory markings with Santa Rosa address. Add 20% for large deluxe factory box with form-fitting depressions, including depression for mounted scope, in hard plastic shell with red flocked surface. Add 10% for factory box with molded white foam support block. Add 20% for Model 20 scope combo.

MODEL 700 - .177 cal., BBC, SP, 460 FPS, 7 in. barrel, 3.1 lbs. Disc. 1981.

	$125	$100	$75	$50	$40	N/A	N/A

Last MSR was $122.

Add 20% for left-hand grip. Add 20% for Beeman walnut stock. Add 50% for Beeman folding metal shoulder stock.

Mfg. for Beeman in Germany by Mayer & Grammelspacher. First imports marked "Beeman's Original Model 5".

GRADING	100%	95%	90%	80%	60%	40%	20%

MODEL 800 - .177 cal., BBC, SP, SS, 460 FPS, 7 in. barrel, Giss patent double opposing piston recoilless mechanism, 3.2 lbs. Disc. 1982.

courtesy BeemanCollection

	100%	95%	90%	80%	60%	40%	20%
	$225	$175	$150	$125	$100	N/A	N/A

Last MSR was $191.

Add 10% if stamped "Beeman's Original". Add 20% for left-hand grip. Add 20% for Beeman walnut stock. Add 50% for Beeman folding metal shoulder stock.

Mfg. for Beeman in Germany by Mayer & Grammelspacher. First imports marked "Beeman's Original Model 6".

MODEL 850 - similar to Model 800 with same rotating barrel shroud as the Model 900. Disc. 1982.

courtesy Beeman Collection

	100%	95%	90%	80%	60%	40%	20%
	$295	$250	$200	$150	$125	N/A	N/A

Last MSR was $225.

Add 20% for left-hand grip or scope mount (shown in picture). Add 20% for Beeman walnut grip (shown in picture). Add 50% for Beeman metal wire shoulder stock (fitting shown in picture).

Mfg. in Germany for Beeman by Mayer & Grammelspacher.

MODEL 900 - .177 cal., BBC, SP, 490 FPS, 7.1 in. barrel, double opposing piston recoilless mechanism, rotating barrel shroud, target model with adj. walnut match grips, match micrometer sights, 3.3 lbs. Disc. 1981.

	100%	95%	90%	80%	60%	40%	20%
	$375	$295	$250	$195	$145	N/A	N/A

Last MSR was $445.

Add 10% if stamped "Beeman's Original". Add 10% for left-hand grip. Add 20% for fitted factory case.

Mfg. in Germany for Beeman by Mayer & Grammelspacher. First imports marked "Beeman's Original Model 10".

NEMESIS - .177 or .22 cal., TL, SS, single-stroke pneumatic, 385/300 FPS, two-stage adj. trigger, black or brushed chrome finish, manual safety, adj. open sights, integral scope rail, 2.2 lbs. Mfg. in England. 1995-disc.

	100%	95%	90%	80%	60%	40%	20%
	$150	$125	$110	$90	$75	N/A	N/A

Last MSR was $200.

Add 10% for brushed chrome finish.

P1 MAGNUM - .177, .20, .22 (disc.1995) cal., TL, SP, SS, single (.22) or dual power action, 600/480 FPS in .177, 500/420 FPS in .20, two-stage trigger, scope groove, barrel and sights in same unit, walnut grips, Colt 1911A1 styling, accepts any custom grips designed for the 1911A1. Mfg. in Germany with importation beginning in 1985.

courtesy Beeman Collection

MSR N/A	100%	95%	90%	80%	60%	40%	20%
	$375	$325	$265	$225	$175	N/A	N/A

Add 10% for .22 cal. Add 10% for Santa Rosa address. Add 15% for grooved Combat grips (shown in picture). Add 30% for Beeman shoulder stock (walnut) - designed by R. Beeman. Add 100% for gold plating. Add 30% for stainless steel style or blue/stainless dual finish. Add 100% for Commemorative Model, enameled 20th year logo inletted into deluxe rosewood grip (25 mfg. 1992 only).

Designed by Robert Beeman; engineered by H.W. Weihrauch Company. The P1 was the predecessor of the Weihrauch HW 45.

GRADING	100%	95%	90%	80%	60%	40%	20%

P2 - .177 or .20 (mfg. 1990-93) cal., TL, SSP, SS, similar to Beeman P1 except single-stroke pneumatic, not dual power, 435/365 FPS, two-stage adj. trigger, walnut grips. Mfg. in Germany with importation 1990-2001.

courtesy Beeman Collection

	$275	$235	$190	$165	$125	N/A	N/A

Last MSR was $385.

Add 20% for match grips. Add 30% for .20 cal. Add 10% for Santa Rosa address.

P3 - .177 cal., TL, SSP, 410 FPS, cocking the hammer allows the top frame to swing up as a charging lever, automatic safety and beartrap prevention, adj. rear sight, rifled steel barrel, built-in muzzle brake, two-stage trigger, anatomical polymer composite grip, 1.7 lbs. Mfg. in Germany with importation beginning in 1999.

courtesy S.P. Fjestad

MSR N/A	$175	$145	$115	$90	$75	N/A	N/A

Add 20% for Millennium Model with gold trigger, hammer, and safety. Add 50% for P3 Combo with 5021 scope and accessories.

TEMPEST - .177 or .22 (disc.) cal., TL, SP, SS, 500/400 FPS, plastic grips with RH thumb rest, adj. rear sight, aluminum grip frame cast around steel body tube, compact version of Hurricane (Tempest bodies produced by grinding off rear section of Hurricane castings), RH manual safety, 6.87 in. button rifled barrel, black epoxy finish, 9.2 in. OAL, 2.0 lbs. Mfg. in England 1981 to date.

	$195	$155	$125	$95	$80	N/A	N/A

Last MSR was $235.

Add 10% for Beeman wood grips. Add 15% for finger groove Beeman "combat" wood grips. Add 20% for Beeman factory markings with San Rafael address. Add 10% for Beeman factory markings with Santa Rosa address. Add 20% for large factory box 11.6 x 8.6 inches, black with logo. Add 10% for medium factory box 10.2 x 6.6 inches, black with logo.

WOLVERINE - .177 or .25 cal., PCP, SS, BA, 10.5 in. barrel, 940/630 FPS (14 to 20 ft. lbs. ME), similar to Adder except has stippled grip select walnut, solid brass rear receiver cap, match trigger, scope grooves, 16.5 in. OAL, manual safety, 3.0 lbs. Ten mfg. in England by Titian 1992.

courtesy Beeman Collection

	N/A	$800	$700	$550	$350	N/A	N/A

Last MSR was $700.

GRADING	100%	95%	90%	80%	60%	40%	20%

RIFLES

MODEL 100 - .177 cal., BBC, SP, 660 FPS, 18.7 in. barrel, 6.0 lbs. Disc. 1980.

	100%	95%	90%	80%	60%	40%	20%
	$125	$95	$80	$65	$55	N/A	N/A

Last MSR was $155.

Add 10% if stamped "Beeman's Original".
Mfg. in Germany by Mayer & Grammelspacher. First imports marked "Beeman's Original Model 27".

MODEL 200 - .177 cal., BBC, SP, 700 FPS, 19 in. barrel, 7.1 lbs. Disc. 1979.

	100%	95%	90%	80%	60%	40%	20%
	$125	$95	$80	$65	$55	N/A	N/A

Last MSR was $197.

Add 10% if stamped "Beeman's Original".
Less than 100 mfg. in Germany by Mayer & Grammelspacher. First imports marked "Beeman's Original Model 35".

MODEL 250 - .177, .20, or .22 cal., BBC, SP, 830/750/650 FPS, 20.5 in. barrel, 7.8 lbs. Disc. 1981.

courtesy Beeman Collection

	100%	95%	90%	80%	60%	40%	20%
	$275	$225	$175	$145	$100	N/A	N/A

Last MSR was $217.

Add 50% for Commemorative model (shown), Diana emblem in stock (approx. 20 Beeman 250s were so marked). Add 30% for Long Safety version - safety bolt projects 1.225 in. (29 mm) from rear end of receiver and is not stamped "N". Such guns were recalled as a hazard and a shorter safety, stamped "N", installed. Add 60% for .20 cal. version (approx. 40 were produced).
Manufactured in Germany by Mayer & Grammelspacher.

MODEL 400 - .177 cal., SL, SP, 650 FPS, 19 in. barrel, target model with match micrometer aperture sight, 10.9 lbs. Disc. 1981.

	100%	95%	90%	80%	60%	40%	20%
	$800	$700	$600	$450	$300	N/A	N/A

Last MSR was $615.

Add 10% if stamped "Beeman's Original". Add 15% for left-hand stock and lever. Add 15% for Universal model (adj. cheekpiece).
Mfg. in Germany by Mayer & Grammelspacher. First imports marked "Beeman's Original Model 75".

MODEL GH500 COMBO - .177 cal., BBC, SP, SS, Belgium Matte finish, ported muzzle brake, 525 FPS, Monte Carlo sporter style composite stock, automatic safety, adj. 3-7x20 Beeman scope, 38.5 in. OAL, 5 lbs. Mfg. in USA. Mfg. 2004-06.

	100%	95%	90%	80%	60%	40%	20%
	$75	$60	$50	$40	N/A	N/A	N/A

Last MSR was $90.

MODEL GH650 - .177 cal., BBC, SP, 650 FPS, sporter trigger, automatic safety, walnut stained beech Monte Carlo stock with recoil pad, ported muzzle brake, 4x32mm Beeman scope, 41.5in. OAL, 5.9 lbs. Mfg. 2003-06.

	100%	95%	90%	80%	60%	40%	20%
	$165	$135	$105	$80	$50	N/A	N/A

Last MSR was $190.

MODEL GH1050/GH1050 COMBO - .177 or .22 cal., BBC, SP, 812/1000 FPS, rifled steel barrel, fiberoptic sights with fully adj. rear, or 3-9x32 scope with muzzle brake (GH1050 Combo), two-stage adj. trigger, ambidextrous black synthetic stock with recoil pad, automatic safety, 45.67 in. OAL, 6.4 lbs. New 2005.

	100%	95%	90%	80%	60%	40%	20%
MSR N/A	$195	$170	$125	$95	$65	N/A	N/A

Add 25% for GH1050 Combo Model.

MODEL GS700 - .177 cal., BBC, SP, 700 FPS, two-stage trigger, automatic safety, walnut stained beech stock, 6.9 lbs. Mfg. in Spain, disc. 2001.

	100%	95%	90%	80%	60%	40%	20%
	$100	$90	$80	$70	$55	N/A	N/A

Last MSR was $149.

MODEL GS950 - .177 or .22 cal., BBC, SP, 950/750 FPS, blue finish, adj. rear and fixed front fiberoptic sights, two-stage trigger, automatic safety, walnut stained Monte Carlo stock, 46.25 in. OAL, 7.25 lbs. Mfg. in Spain, 2001-06.

	100%	95%	90%	80%	60%	40%	20%
	$210	$175	$145	$110	$90	N/A	N/A

Last MSR was $250.

☼ **Model GH950 Combo** - .177 or .22 cal., BBC, SP, 950/750 FPS, includes Model GS950 with ported muzzle brake, either 4x32mm or 3-9x32mm Beeman scope with adj. objective and target turrets with caps, and 250-count tin of hollow point pellets. Mfg. 2003-06.

	100%	95%	90%	80%	60%	40%	20%
	$265	$215	$175	$125	$95	N/A	N/A

Last MSR was $320.

Add 10% for GH950 Combo with 3-9x32mm Beeman scope.

GRADING	100%	95%	90%	80%	60%	40%	20%

MODEL GS1000 - .177 or .22 cal., BBC, SP, 1000/765 FPS, micrometer adj. rear and blade front sights, two-stage adj. trigger, automatic safety, checkered European sporter style walnut stained stock with PG and recoil pad, 46.75 OAL, 7.5 lbs. Mfg. in Spain, mfg. 2001-06.

courtesy Beeman Collection

	$235	$190	$135	$105	$85	N/A	N/A

Last MSR was $280.

○ *Model GH1000 Combo* - .177 or .22 cal., BBC, SP, 1000/765 FPS, includes Model GS1000 with ported muzzle brake, either 3-9x32mm or 3-12x40mm Beeman scope with adj. objective and target turrets with caps, and 250-count tin of hollow point pellets. Mfg. 2003-06.

	$335	$275	$215	$175	$145	N/A	N/A

Last MSR was $420.

Add 5% for 3-12x40mm Beeman scope.

MODEL GT600 - .177 cal., BBC, SP, 600 FPS, sporter trigger, automatic safety, walnut stained beech stock, 5.9 lbs. Mfg. in Spain, disc. 2001.

	$80	$70	$60	$50	$40	N/A	N/A

Last MSR was $119.

MODEL GT650 - .177 cal., similar to Model GT600. Mfg. in Spain 2001-2002.

	$90	$85	$80	$70	$50	N/A	N/A

Last MSR was $135.

MODEL HW30 - .177 or .20 (disc.) cal., BBC, SP, SS, 675/600 FPS, two-stage non-adj. trigger, plain beech stock with or w/o buttplate, automatic safety, 40.0 in. OAL, adj. rear sight (early versions all metal), 5.5 lbs. 40.0 in. OAL. Mfg. in Germany new 1972.

MSR N/A		$245	$195	$155	$115	$80	N/A	N/A

Add 10% for no safety. Add 20% for .20 caliber. Add 10% for San Rafael or Santa Rosa address. Add 20% for early M versions - stock with cheekpiece, deep forearm, and rubber buttplate.

MODEL HW50 - .177 cal., BBC, SP, SS, 700 FPS, non-adj. trigger, plain beech stock w/o cheekpiece or buttplate, automatic safety, heavy machined receiver cap, front sight with interchangeable posts, 43.1 in. OAL, 6.9 lbs. Mfg. in Germany 1972-95.

courtesy Beeman Collection

	$250	$200	$190	$165	$140	N/A	N/A

Subtract 25% for sheet metal receiver cap (post 1994 mfg.). Add 10% for no safety. Add 20% for early M versions - stock w/cheekpiece, deep forearm, and rubber buttplate.

HW55SM/HW55MM/HW55T - .177 cal., BBC, SP, 660-700 FPS, match aperture sight, with beech stock checkered pistol grip (HW55SM), walnut stock with checkered grip, forearm and cheekpiece (HW55MM), or deluxe Tyrolean walnut stock with deep dish cheekpiece (HW55T), 43.7 in OAL, 7.8 lbs.

	$495	$425	$325	$250	N/A	N/A	N/A

Add 20% for HW55MM. Add 50% for HW55T, 25 Beeman specimens made and imported.

MODEL HW 77 - .177, .20, or .22 cal., UL, SP, SS, 830/770 FPS, blue finish, automatic safety, two-stage adj. trigger, beech high comb Monte Carlo hand cut checkered PG sporter stock, white-lined grip cap and rubber recoil pad, factory stamped with Santa Rosa address, automatic safety, 43.7 in OAL (carbine version 39.7 in. OAL), 8.7 lbs. Mfg. in Germany 1983-1998.

	$395	$375	$350	$295	$225	$150	$125

Last MSR was $600.

Add 10% for left-hand variation. Add 15% for .20 cal. Add 50% for Tyrolean stock (deep cup cheekpiece, RH only).
Beginning in 1995, the Model HW 77 can be upgraded to the power of the Model HW 77 Mk II.

○ *Model HW 77 MKII Carbine* - .177 cal., SP, UL, SS, 930 FPS, similar to Model HW 77, except 11.5 in. barrel, Huntington Beach address, 39.7 in. OAL, 8.7 lbs. Mfg. in Germany new 1999.

MSR N/A		$575	$450	$350	$295	$245	$180	$115

GRADING	100%	95%	90%	80%	60%	40%	20%

MODEL HW97 - .177 or .20 cal., UL, SP, 800/750 FPS, automatic safety, two-stage adj. trigger, beech stained Monte Carlo stock with high cheekpiece, 44.1 in. OAL, 9.2 lbs. Mfg. in Germany new 1995.

⊙ *Model HW97 MKI* - .177 or .20 cal., UL, SP. Mfg. 1995-1998.

	100%	95%	90%	80%	60%	40%	20%
	$475	$395	$325	$250	$175	N/A	N/A

Add 5% for .20 cal. Add 15% for .177 cal. Centennial Model with blue/gray laminate stock.

⊙ *Model HW97 MKII* - .177 or .20 cal., UL, SP, similar to Model HW97 MKI except velocity increased to 930 FPS for .177 and 820 FPS for .20 cal. Mfg. 1999-2001.

	100%	95%	90%	80%	60%	40%	20%
	$475	$395	$325	$250	$175	N/A	N/A

Add 20% for .20 cal. Millennium Model with blue/gray laminate stock.

⊙ *Model HW97 MKIII* - .177 or .20 cal., UL, SP, similar to Model HW97 MKII, except shortened barrel to improve appearance, balance, and lock time, 40.25 in. OAL, 9.2 lbs. Mfg. in Germany new 2002.

	100%	95%	90%	80%	60%	40%	20%
MSR N/A	$575	$475	$395	$305	$225	N/A	N/A

MODEL R1/R1-AW/R1 CARBINE - .177, .20, .22, or .25 (disc.) cal., BBC, SP, SS, 19.3 in. barrel, blue or nickel plated (R1-AW) finish, 1000/610 FPS, new design using some Weihrauch Model HW 35 parts with designed changes to greatly increase power, speed, cocking ease and efficiency, beech Monte Carlo stock, hand cut checkered pistol grip with palm swell and white lined grip cap, forearm extends to front end of barrel block, white lined rubber buttplate with molded BEEMAN lettering, solid steel receiver cap, 14.3 in. LOP, 45.2 in. OAL, 8.5 lbs. Mfg. in Germany 1981 to date.

courtesy Beeman Collection

	100%	95%	90%	80%	60%	40%	20%
MSR N/A	$565	$485	$415	$325	$245	N/A	N/A

Add 20% for Santa Rosa address. Add 90% for custom grade. Add 25% for Field Target Model. Add 400% for Goudy/Beeman custom stock. Add 105% for X fancy stock. Add 10% for left-hand variation. Add 25% for blue/silver finish. Add 50% for Tyrolean stock (less than 25 mfg.). Add 60% for commemorative model (50 mfg. 1992 only - 20th year commemorative medallion inlaid into stock, silver/blue metal finish, deluxe). Add 20% for AW Model with electroless nickel finish and black Kevlar/graphite/fiberglass stock, available in .20 cal. carbine only, 9.7 lbs. Deduct 20% for gas spring retrofit (inappropriately called gas ram or strut).

  Chrome and gold-plated variations of the R1 with RDB prefix serialization may exceed retail values by 150%-300%. This is the first spring piston airgun to reach 1000 FPS MV. Designed by Robert Beeman, stock design by Robert Beeman and Gary Goudy; engineered by H.W. Weihrauch. Predecessor of Weihrauch HW 80 and considered as first successful start of adult airgun market in USA. Ref: Gaylord, 1995, *The Beeman R1*.

MODEL R1 LASER® - .177, 20, .22, or 25 cal., similar to Model R1, except Laser® spring piston unit for up to an additional 200 FPS, laminated sporter stock inlaid with baked enamel Beeman Laser® logo. Mfg. 1988-2001.

⊙ *Model R1 Laser® MK I* - metal pistol grip gap replaced by rosewood in 1994. Mfg. 1988-1995.

	100%	95%	90%	80%	60%	40%	20%
	$1,200	$1,000	$900	N/A	N/A	N/A	N/A

Add 25% for Mark 1 with Santa Rosa address. Add 10% for metal grip cap.

⊙ *Model R1 Laser® MK II* - similar to Model R1 Laser® MK I, except no pistol grip cap. .25 cal. disc. Mfg. 1995-99.

	100%	95%	90%	80%	60%	40%	20%
	$1,000	$950	$850	N/A	N/A	N/A	N/A

⊙ *Model R1 Laser® MK III* - similar to Model R1 Laser® MK II, except gas spring version. Mfg. 1999-2001.

	100%	95%	90%	80%	60%	40%	20%
	$900	$850	$800	N/A	N/A	N/A	N/A

MODEL R5 - .20 cal., BBC, SP, SS, similar to Feinwerkbau Model 124, except upgraded deluxe stock, receiver incorrectly factory stamped "Model 125, 5.mm/.22 cal." Four mfg. in Germany 1981.

courtesy Beeman Collection

Rarity precludes accurate pricing.
  Ref: Beeman (1998) AR3:61-62.

GRADING	100%	95%	90%	80%	60%	40%	20%

MODEL R6 - .177 cal., BBC, SP, SS, 815 FPS, two stage trigger, automatic safety, plain beech stock, rubber buttplate, automatic safety, 41.8 in OAL, 7.1 lbs. Mfg. in Germany. 1995-2001.

	$225	$195	$150	$125	$95	N/A	N/A

Last MSR was $285.

Add 150% for custom grade.

MODEL R7 - .177 or .20 cal., BBC, SP, SS, 700/620 FPS, two-stage adj. trigger, beech stock with Monte Carlo comb, forearm extending to front end of barrel block, 14.3 in. LOP, scope grooves, hand checkered pistol grip, rubber buttplate with molded "BEEMAN", all metal sights, automatic safety, 40.2 in. OAL, 6.1 lbs. Mfg. in Germany 1983 to date. Ref: AA, (March 2003).

MSR N/A		$325	$265	$210	$165	$110	N/A	N/A

Add 15% for .20 cal. Add 20% for San Rafael or Santa Rosa address. Add 10% for no safety (new 1986). Add 20% for RDB versions, early production, soft rubber buttplate with Beeman name, cheekpieces with sharp edges and sweeping outline, greater detailing.

MODEL R8 - .177 cal., BBC, SP, SS, 720 FPS, two-stage adj. trigger, beech stock similar to Model R7, except sharply defined cheekpiece, 14.3 in. LOP, solid steel receiver cap, metal sights, scope grooves, automatic safety, 43.0 in. OAL, 7.1 lbs. Mfg. in Germany 1983-1997.

courtesy Beeman Collection

	$320	$250	$225	$195	$135	N/A	N/A

Last MSR was $380.

Add 20% for Santa Rosa address. Add 20% for RDB versions, early production, soft rubber buttplate with Beeman name, cheekpieces with sharp edges and sweeping outline, greater detailing.

MODEL R9/R9 COMBO - .177 or .20 cal., BBC, SP, SS, 1000/800 FPS, adj. trigger, automatic safety, beech stock, with or without (Model R9 Goldfinger) adj. rear and globe front sights, receiver cut for scope mounts, 4x32mm or 3-9x32mm (Model R9 Combo new 2003) Beeman scope, muzzle brake (Model R9 Goldfinger Combo new 2003), 43.0 in. OAL, 7.3 lbs. Mfg. in Germany new 1995.

courtesy Beeman Collection

MSR N/A		$365	$295	$235	$185	$135	$95	N/A

Add $80 for Model R9-Deluxe with hand checkered grip, white lined grip cap and buttplate. Add 25% for laminate stock. Add 5% for "Goldfinger" version with gold-plated trigger. Add $70 for Model R9 Combo with 4x32mm Beeman adj. objective scope with target turrets with caps and tin of pellets. Add $100 for Model R9 Combo with 3-9x32mm Beeman adj. objective scope with target turrets with caps and tin of pellets. Add $100 for Model R9 Goldfinger Combo with 4-12x40mm Beeman adj. objective scope with target turrets and caps.

MODEL R10 - .177, .20, or .22 cal., BBC, SP, SS, 1000/750 FPS, smooth walnut finished beech stock, forearm ends at barrel pivot, solid steel machined receiver cap, automatic safety, 45.8 in. OAL, 7.5 lbs. Mfg. in Germany 1986-1995.

	$395	$350	$300	$195	$150	N/A	N/A

Last MSR was $400.

Add 25% for Model R10 Deluxe, hand checkered grip, white lined grip cap and buttplate, forearm extends to forward end of barrel block. Add 15% for .20 cal. Add 100% for Laser Model (laminated stock). Add 95% for custom grade walnut stock. Add 100% for custom fancy walnut stock. Add 110% for extra fancy walnut stock. Subtract 5% for left-hand variation. Add 20% for RDB versions, early production, soft rubber buttplate with Beeman name, cheekpieces with sharp edges and sweeping outline, greater detailing.

MODEL R11 - .177 cal., BBC, SP, SS, 925 FPS, 19.6 in. barrel with sleeve, adj. cheekpiece and buttplate, adj. trigger, scope ramp on receiver, no sights, 43.5 in. OAL, 8.75 lbs. Mfg. in Germany 1994-95.

	$425	$400	$350	$300	$250	N/A	N/A

GRADING	100%	95%	90%	80%	60%	40%	20%

○ *Model R11 MK II* - .177 cal., BBC, SP, SS, 925 FPS, similar to Model R11, except has dovetailed receiver for scope mounting, improved trigger and end cap. Mfg. in Germany with importation beginning in 1995.

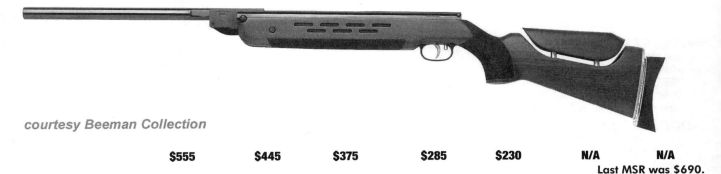

courtesy Beeman Collection

	$555	$445	$375	$285	$230	N/A	N/A

Last MSR was $690.

MODEL RX - .177, .20, .22, or .25 cal., BBC, Theoben GS, SS, 1125/960/810/650 FPS, adj. velocity, deluxe Monte Carlo beech stock with cheekpiece, forearm extends to forward end of barrel block, hand checkering and white-lined PG cap, white-lined rubber buttplate with molded BEEMAN letters, all metal sights, scope grooves, automatic safety, 45.7 in. OAL, 8.7 lbs. Mfg. in Germany 1990-1992.

	$350	$300	$250	$200	$150	N/A	N/A

Last MSR was $470.

Add 15% for .20 and .25 cal. Add 50% for Field Target version with adj. cheekpiece. Add 10% for left-hand variation. Add 25% for Power Adjustment Pump.
This model's GAS-SPRING piston system sometimes is inappropriately referred to as a "gas-ram" or "gas strut" system.

MODEL RX-1 - similar to Model RX, except adj. two-stage trigger and stamped with small "1" on rear of receiver. Mfg. in Germany 1992-2001.

courtesy Beeman Collection

	$475	$420	$380	$325	$225	N/A	N/A

Last MSR was $590.

Add 10% for left-hand variation. Add 15% for Santa Rosa address. Add 30% for hand checkered walnut "Luxury" stock. Add 50% for Commemorative model with 20th Anniversary disc inlaid into stock. Add 25% for Power Adjustment Pump.

MODEL RX-2 - .177, .20, or .22, cal., similar to Model RX-1, except laminated stock and improved non-adj. trigger,. 9.8 lbs., Mfg. in Germany new 2001.

courtesy Beeman Collection

MSR N/A	$665	$575	$450	$365	$275	N/A	N/A

MODEL S-1 - .177 cal., BBC, SP, SS, 900 FPS, two-stage adj. trigger, automatic safety, beech stock, 45.5 in OAL, 7.1 lbs. Mfg. in Spain 1995-1999.

	$150	$100	$75	$60	$40	N/A	N/A

Last MSR was $210.

GRADING	100%	95%	90%	80%	60%	40%	20%

MODEL SLR-98 - .22 cal., GS, UL, similar to Model UL-7, blue finish, 780 FPS, seven-shot removable mag., automatic safety, 39 in. OAL, 7.9 lbs. Mfg. in Germany 2001-04.

courtesy Beeman Collection

	100%	95%	90%	80%	60%	40%	20%
	$1,195	$950	$750	$600	$485	N/A	N/A

Last MSR was $1,385.

MODEL SS550 TARGET/SS550 HUNTER COMBO - .177 cal., BBC, SP, SS, Belgium Matte finish,550 FPS, ambidextrous Monte Carlo sporter style composite stock with pad, sporter grade trigger, automatic safety, diopter rear and hooded front sights or 4x20 scope with ported muzzle brake (SS550 Hunter Combo), 36.5-38.5 in. OAL, 5 lbs. New 2005.

	MSR N/A	$55	$40	$30	$20	N/A	N/A	N/A

Add 30% for SS550 Hunter Combo.

MODEL SS650/SH650 HUNTER COMBO - .177 cal., BBC, SP,700 FPS, sporter trigger, automatic safety, walnut stained beech stock with recoil pad, fiberoptic sights or ported muzzle brake and 4x32mm Beeman scope (SH650 Hunter Combo), 39.5-41in.OAL, 5.9-8.7 lbs. Mfg. 2005-06.

	$85	$65	$55	$45	$35	N/A	N/A

Last MSR was $100.

Add 20% for SH650 Hunter Combo.

MODEL SS1000/SH1000 HUNTER COMBO - .177 or .22 cal., BBC, SP, 1000/800FPS, adj. fiberoptic sights or 3-9x32 AO/TT scope (SH1000 Combo), two-stage adj. trigger, automatic safety, sporter style walnut stained stock with PG and recoil pad, 44.5 OAL,9-10 lbs. Mfg. 2005-06.

	$145	$115	$85	$65	$45	N/A	N/A

Last MSR was $170.

Add 20% for SH1000 Combo Model.

MODEL SS1000T - .177 cal., BBC, SP, 1000 FPS, ported muzzle brake, 3-9x32mm AO Beeman scope with adj. objective and target turrets with caps, hardwood Monti-Carlo stock, adj. two-stage trigger, auto-safety, 47.25 in. OAL, 10.5 lbs. New 2007.

	MSR N/A	$175	$145	$125	$95	N/A	N/A	N/A

AIR WOLF - .20, .22, or .25 cal., 940/822/660 FPS, PCP, SS, BA, light high comb walnut stock, hand checkered PG, white-lined rubber recoil pad, 20.8 in. barrel, blue finish, no sights, scope grooves, manual safety, 37 in. OAL, 5.6 lbs. Mfg. in England 1992 only.

	$950	$850	$750	$650	$550	N/A	N/A

Last MSR was $680.

Add 5% for .20 cal. Add 10% for charging adapter with gauge.
Approx. 10-20 mfg.

BEARCUB - for information on this model, see Webley & Scott, LTD. in the "W" section.

CARBINE C1 - field carbine with shotgun butt and straight grip.

courtesy Beeman Collection

For information on this model, see Webley & Scott, LTD. in the "W" section.

CLASSIC MAGNUM - .20 or .25 cal., 910/680 FPS, BBC, GS, SS, 15 in. barrel, automatic lever safety, checkered walnut stock with angular forearm extending just forward of barrel base block, 44.5 in. OAL, 8.3 lbs. Mfg. in England 1992 only.

	$890	$750	$590	$475	$350	N/A	N/A

Last MSR was $895.

Add 5% for .20 cal. Add 15% for power adjustment pump.

GRADING	100%	95%	90%	80%	60%	40%	20%

CROW MAGNUM I - .20 or .25 cal., 1060/815 FPS, BBC, GS, SS, 16 in. barrel, automatic safety (thin metal piece), smoothly curved trigger, built-in scope base, no sights, polished steel muzzle weight, 46 in. OAL, 8.6 lbs. Mfg. in England 1992-1993.

	100%	95%	90%	80%	60%	40%	20%
	$850	$750	$625	$500	$350	N/A	N/A

Add 5% for .20 cal. Add 15% for power adjustment pump.

CROW MAGNUM II - .20 or .25 cal., 1060/815 FPS, BBC, GS, SS, 16 in. barrel, automatic safety (rugged metal strip), "beak shaped" trigger centered in guard, Dampa Mount scope rings provided for built-in scope rail, no sights, polished steel muzzle weight, 46.0 in. OAL, 8.6 lbs. Mfg. in England 1993-1995.

	100%	95%	90%	80%	60%	40%	20%
	$950	$750	$600	$450	$300	N/A	N/A

Last MSR was $1,220.

Add 15% for power adjustment pump.

CROW MAGNUM III - .20, .22, or .25 cal., BBC, GS, 1060/1035/815 FPS, 16 in. barrel, similar to Crow Magnum II, except two stage adj. trigger, redesigned piston with steel face and O-rings, extended compression cylinder, deluxe hand checkered Hyedua ambidextrous stock, 46.0 in. OAL, 8.6 lbs. Mfg. in England. 1995-2001.

	100%	95%	90%	80%	60%	40%	20%
	$1,000	$800	$650	$500	$350	N/A	N/A

Last MSR was $1,220.

Add 15% for power adjustment pump.

CROW MAGNUM IV - .20, .22, or .25 cal., BBC, GS, 1060/1035/815 FPS, 16 in. barrel, similar to Crow Magnum III, except automatic safety with protective "bump" inside forward curve of trigger guard, trigger has straighter profile and is moved back in guard, 46.0 in. OAL, 8.6 lbs. Mfg. in England, 2001-04.

courtesy Beeman Collection

	100%	95%	90%	80%	60%	40%	20%
	$1,150	$950	$750	$550	$400	N/A	N/A

Last MSR was $1,355.

ECLIPSE - for information on this model, see Webley & Scott, LTD. in the "W" section.

FALCON 1 - .177 cal., BBC, SP, SS, 640 FPS, 43 in. OAL, 6.7 lbs. Mfg. in Spain 1981-1984.

courtesy Beeman Collection

	100%	95%	90%	80%	60%	40%	20%
	$150	$125	$115	$95	$75	N/A	N/A

FALCON 2 - .177 cal., BBC, SP, SS, 580 FPS, 41 in. OAL, 5.9 lbs. Mfg. in Spain 1981-1984.

courtesy Beeman Collection

	100%	95%	90%	80%	60%	40%	20%
	$120	$85	$65	$55	$45	N/A	N/A

Last MSR was $110.

GRADING	100%	95%	90%	80%	60%	40%	20%

FWB 124 - see the Feinwerkbau entry in the "F" section of this guide for FWB Model 124 designed for the USA market, plus special Beeman versions such as Custom, and Custom Deluxe.

Lewis & Clark Commemorative courtesy Beeman Collection

FX 1 - similar to Falcon 1. Mfg. in Spain 1985-1992.

	$155	$125	$105	$75	$45	N/A	N/A

Last MSR was $140.

FX 2 - similar to Falcon 2. Mfg. in Spain 1985-1992.

	$125	$100	$85	$65	$45	N/A	N/A

GAMEKEEPER - .25 cal., PCP, SS, quick-change air cylinder, 15 in. barrel, 680 FPS, steel receiver, composition detachable buttstock, stock, barrel, and air cylinder remove to pack gun into briefcase, steel barrel weight, no sights, scope grooves, manual lever safety, 36.3 in. OAL, 8.2 lbs. Mfg. in England by Coltester 1992-93.

courtesy Beeman Collection

Last MSR was $990.

Total of five imported, value is in the $1,250-$1,500 range.

KODIAK - .22 or .25 cal., BBC, SP, 17.50 in. barrel, 865/775 FPS, deluxe Monte Carlo stock with cheekpiece, grip cap and rubber buttplates with white line spacers, PTFE, muzzle threaded for Beeman Air Tamer or Webley Silencer, automatic safety, 45.6 in. OAL, 8.9 lbs. Mfg. in England, new 1993.

courtesy Beeman Collection

MSR N/A	$600	$525	$415	$315	$220	N/A	N/A

Add 10% for Air Tamer (muzzle unit without baffles). Add 10% for Webley Silencer.
Muzzle threaded for silencer on this model (if silencer is present). Transfer to qualified buyer requires $200 federal tax in USA.

MAKO - .177 cal., PCP, SS, BA, 930 FPS, hand cut checkered beech stock, adj. trigger, manual safety, 38.5 in. OAL, 7.3 lbs. Mfg. in England 1995-2002.

	$750	$650	$795	$400	$295	N/A	N/A

Last MSR was $1,000.

Add 50% for FT Model with checkered thumbhole stock.

MAKO MKII - .177 or .22 cal., PCP, SS, BA, 1000/860 FPS, checkered walnut stock, two stage adj. trigger, scope grooves, no sights, manual safety, 37 in. OAL, 5.5 lbs. Mfg. in England, 2003-06.

	$825	$700	$550	$450	$325	N/A	N/A

Last MSR was $999.

GRADING	100%	95%	90%	80%	60%	40%	20%

MANITOU FT - .177 cal. PCP, SS, 21 in. barrel, angular stock with adj. cheekpiece, 36.3 in. OAL, 8.75 lbs. Mfg. in England 1992 only.

courtesy Don R.

	100%	95%	90%	80%	60%	40%	20%
	$895	$750	$565	$495	$350	N/A	N/A

Last MSR was $995.

Add 20% for left-hand variation. Add 10% for charge adapter with gauge.
Total of ten guns were imported into the U.S.

OMEGA - for information on this model, see Webley & Scott, LTD. in the "W" section.

SILVER BEAR COMBO (SB500) - .177 cal., BBC, SP, SS, Belgium Matte finish, ported muzzle brake, 500 FPS, Monte Carlo sporter style composite stock, vented recoil pad, automatic safety, adj. 4x20 Beeman scope, 37 in. OAL, 5 lbs. Mfg. in USA, mfg. 2002-06.

	100%	95%	90%	80%	60%	40%	20%
	$65	$55	$45	$35	N/A	N/A	N/A

Last MSR was $72.

SUPER 7 - .22 or .25 (1994 only) cal., PCP, seven-shot mag., quick-change 280 cc air cylinder (bottle), 19 in. barrel, 990 FPS (.22 cal.), checkered walnut stock, manual safety, 41 in. OAL, 7.25 lbs. Mfg. in England 1992-94.

	100%	95%	90%	80%	60%	40%	20%
	$1,100	$950	$800	$650	$500	N/A	N/A

Last MSR was $1,575.

Add 5% for .25 cal.

SUPER 12 - .20, .22 or .25 cal., PCP, twelve-shot mag., 850 FPS (.25 cal.), quick-change air cylinder (bottle), checkered walnut stock, manual safety, 41.7 in. OAL, 7.8 lbs. Mfg. in England 1994-2001.

courtesy Beeman Collection

	100%	95%	90%	80%	60%	40%	20%
	$1,400	$1,195	$975	$795	$595	N/A	N/A

Last MSR was $1,675.

Add 5% for .20 cal. or .25 cal.

SUPER 12 MKII - .20, .22 or .25 cal., similar to Super 12, except match trigger assembly and new style stock. Mfg. 2001-04.

	100%	95%	90%	80%	60%	40%	20%
	$995	$900	$750	$600	$450	N/A	N/A

Last MSR was $2,015.

SUPER 17/17FT - .177 cal., PCP, seventeen-shot rotary mag., 1090 FPS, quick-change air cylinder (bottle), laminated target stock, adj. match trigger, adj. buttplate, optional adj. cheekpiece. Mfg. in England 1998-2002.

	100%	95%	90%	80%	60%	40%	20%
	$1,400	$1,225	$995	$875	$595	N/A	N/A

Last MSR was $1,675.

Add 40% for Field Target model.

UL-7 - .22 cal., UL, GS, 12 in. barrel, 780 FPS, manual safety, seven-shot rotary mag., checkered walnut stock, 39 in. OAL, 8.1 lbs. Mfg. in England 1992-93.

	100%	95%	90%	80%	60%	40%	20%
	$1,195	$995	$775	$650	$495	N/A	N/A

Last MSR was $1,560.

Add 10% for power adjustment pump.
Approx. eight were imported to the U.S. 1992-93.

VULCAN I - for information on this model, see Webley & Scott, LTD. in the "W" section.

GRADING	100%	95%	90%	80%	60%	40%	20%

VULCAN II - for information on this model, see Webley & Scott, LTD. in the "W" section.

VULCAN III - for information on this model, see Webley & Scott, LTD. in the "W" section.

WOLF PUP - .20, .22, or .25 cal.,PCP, SS, BA, 13.5 in. barrel, 910/800/645 FPS, light high comb walnut stock, hand checkered grip, white-lined rubber recoil pad, no sights, scope grooves, manual safety, 31.5 in. OAL, 5.0 lbs. Approx. 10-20 mfg. in England by Titian 1992 only.

courtesy Beeman Collection

	N/A	$675	$595	$545	$450	N/A	N/A

Last MSR was $680.

Add 5% for .20 cal. Add 10% for charging adapter with gauge. Add 25% for Deluxe Model with thumbhole stock and match trigger.

MODEL SS1000H - .177 or .22 cal., BBC, SP, 1000/800FPS, 3-9x32 scope, two-stage adj. trigger, automatic safety, sporter style walnut stained stock with PG and recoil pad, 46.5 OAL, 10 lbs. New 2007.

MSR N/A	$145	$115	$85	$65	$45	N/A	N/A

BENELLI

Current manufacturer located in Urbino, Italy. Benelli USA, located in Accokeek, MD, was formed during late 1997 and is currently importing all Benelli shotguns. Benelli air pistols are currently imported by Larry's Guns, located in Portland, ME.

For more information and current pricing on both new and used Benelli firearms, please refer to the *Blue Book of Gun Values* by S.P. Fjestad (also available online).

PISTOLS

KITE - .177 cal., PCP, match pistol, 9.45 in. barrel, 475 FPS, adj. trigger, adj. sights, adj. wood grip, 16.89 in. OAL, 2.36 lbs. New 2003.

MSR N/A	$969	$869	$750	$595	$465	N/A	N/A

KITE YOUNG - .177 cal., PCP, match pistol, 7.48 in. barrel, 475 FPS, adj. sights, adj. wood grip 14.82 OAL, 2.13 lbs. New 2003.

MSR N/A	$939	$799	$650	$550	$425	N/A	N/A

BENJAMIN AIR RIFLE COMPANY (BENJAMIN)

Current Benjamin trademark manufactured by Crosman Corp. located in East Bloomfield, NY. Previous manufacturer located in Racine, WI. The Benjamin trademark was purchased in January 1992 by Crosman Air Guns, located in East Bloomfield, NY. Dealer and consumer direct sales.

BENJAMIN AIR RIFLE COMPANY BACKGROUND

The Benjamin Air Rifle Company has its roots in the St. Louis Air Rifle Company, founded by Walter Benjamin in 1899. The St. Louis Air Rifle Company produced several unique, but unreliable, air rifles until 1901. Because of low production, and the propensity of these guns to break and become unrepairable, very few specimens of St. Louis air rifles exist today. Sales of these air rifles are too infrequent to establish price levels. Some replicas were produced in the 1990s.

The Benjamin Air Rifle Company was formed in 1902 when Walter Benjamin purchased the patent rights from the defunct St. Louis Air Rifle Company. Production from 1902 to 1904 and from 1906 to 1986 was in St. Louis, MO (extremely limited production of the Single Valve Model "B" by the W.R. Benjamin Company from 1904 to 1906 was in Granite City, IL). Regular production facilities were not established until 1908 when the Benjamin Air Rifle and Manufacturing Company became a wholly owned subsidiary of the Wissler Instrument Co. In 1977, the Benjamin Air Rifle Company purchased Sheridan Products in Racine, WI, and moved production there from 1986 to 1994. In 1991, they started to merge the Benjamin and Sheridan pistol designs, as the pistol models shifted to a Sheridan-type design and were marketed as Benjamin/Sheridan.

CROSMAN PURCHASES BENJAMIN

Crosman Airguns purchased the combined companies in February 1992, and marketed the Benjamin CO_2 rifles as Benjamin/Sheridan 1993-1998, in addition to the Benjamin pump-up rifles 1994-98. During 1998-2000, the Crosman company began to again catalog and promote the .177 and .22 caliber guns under the Benjamin brand and the .20 caliber guns under the Sheridan name.

The only name to appear on some of the guns made during the interesting decade of the 1990s is in the required warning that cautions users to contact the "Benjamin Sheridan" offices in New York for an owner´s manual. Many gun authorities would not consider such an address in a warning as a brand designation, any more than they would consider these guns to be Crosmans, because the Crosman Company is now using the Crosman name in the contact address.

GRADING	100%	95%	90%	80%	60%	40%	20%

Thus there is a period of about seven years, which to some degree continues to be unclear, where there is some confusion as to the names under which these various airguns were known. It is clear that the shooting public, and most dealers, continued their perception of these guns as Sheridans or Benjamins and never really accepted the Benjamin/Sheridan brand. As noted, Crosman recognized this brand perception and wisely began to again market the guns under the well-known separate Sheridan and Benjamin names. Now this guide is forced to consider all of the current models of these two lines under the poorly accepted name of Benjamin/Sheridan, even including such models as the Sheridan Blue and Silver Streak .20 caliber rifles, or to allow current shooters and dealers to find a particular model and learn its probable value by following each model series under their best known names. Since the concept of the Benjamin/Sheridan designation was a Benjamin idea, most models will be considered in the Benjamin section. Thus, this guide is following the designations used by the manufacturer´s marketing department, the current catalogs, and virtually all shooters and dealers by considering the .177 and .22 caliber guns as Benjamins, and the .20 caliber guns as Sheridans. At this time, this really is only of academic interest because the guns produced since 1991 generally are purchased only as shooters; buyers of current models usually are not concerned with the nuances of name designations.

BENJAMIN AIR RIFLE COMPANY MARKINGS

There surely will come a time in the future, especially for the Sheridan PB and HB20 models, and the HB17 and HB22 pistols made in WI, where the manufacturing address and markings will be of importance in determining values. The marking of "Benjamin Franklin" (which began circa 1936) on some older models evidently has no significance, except as a marketing ploy.

From about 1935 until recently, Benjamin used a model numbering system for both its air rifles and pistols. Model numbers ending in 0 are smooth bore for lead or steel BBs and .177 caliber pellets or darts; model numbers ending in 7 are rifled for .177 caliber pellets or darts; model numbers ending in 2 are rifled for .22 caliber pellets or darts. To keep things interesting, it is apparent that the ever-frugal A.P. Spack and his son, who ran the company during most of its early history, might not have bothered to change stamping dies when they changed model numbers in their advertisements and bulletins. So a gun advertised and sold as a Model 107 might have come out of the factory stamped as Model 177, etc. Such situations evidently were confined to guns which actually were the same, but were under different model numbers, i.e. apparently no guns were stamped with incorrect numbers. Ref: AAG - July 1991.

BENJAMIN AIR RIFLE COMPANY VALUES

Values on Benjamin models are based on guns in good working order with no missing parts. Guns that have had their finish removed and the brass polished have their value reduced to one half or less of the 90% value.

PISTOLS

Although the Benjamin Air Rifle Company is best known for its pneumatic rifles, pneumatic pistols had been added to the line by 1935. There is mention of air pistols on Benjamin letterheads as early as 1908, but actual pistols probably were not introduced until about 1935 when *Popular Science Monthly* illustrated a Series 100 air pistol as a new high-power air "pistol." Evidently, Walter Benjamin did not invent the Benjamin air pistols. He certainly would have patented them, but no patents for the Benjamin air pistols have been uncovered. The air pistols may have come out of the efforts of Milhalyi and Spack to fill time during the Depression.

The Benjamin air pistols began with the simple pump rod-at-the-muzzle design. By 1938, an intriguing but mechanically weak hand lever mechanism had been added to some of the pistol models to operate the muzzle-based pump rod. Both of these rod-at-the-muzzle designs disappeared with the entry of the USA into WWII in 1941. Benjamin pneumatic air pistols reappeared in 1945 with the now familiar swinging arm pump handle mechanism. All single-shot pistols are bolt action and breech-loading.

MODEL 100 SERIES (MODELS 100, 122, AND 177) - BB/.175, .177 or .22 cal., rod-at-the-muzzle pump-up pneumatic, SS, rifled or smoothbore barrel, black nickel finish, wood grips. Mfg. 1935-1941.

courtesy Beeman Collection

	N/A	$125	$105	$90	$55	N/A	N/A

Add 25% for box and instruction sheet.

When the Models 110, 117, and 122 were introduced, the catalog designation of the Model 177 was changed to 107, and the catalog designation of the Model 122 was changed to 102. However, apparently no guns were ever marked as 102 or 107.

GRADING	100%	95%	90%	80%	60%	40%	20%

MODEL 110 SERIES (MODELS 110, 112, AND 117)

- BB/.175, .177 or .22 cal., combination rod-at-the-muzzle/lever hand ("grass-hopper") pump-up pneumatic, SS, rifled or smoothbore barrel, black nickel finish, wood grips. Mfg. 1938-1941.

courtesy Beeman Collection

N/A	$150	$120	$110	$65	N/A	N/A

Subtract 25%-75% for broken or incomplete pump/rod linkages. Add 25% for box and instruction sheet.

MODEL 122 - see Model 100.

MODEL 130 SERIES (MODELS 130, 132, AND 137)

- BB/.175, .177 or .22 cal., pump-up pneumatic, SS, rifled or smoothbore barrel, with swinging lever hand pump, black nickel or matte finish, wood or plastic grips. Mfg. 1946-85.

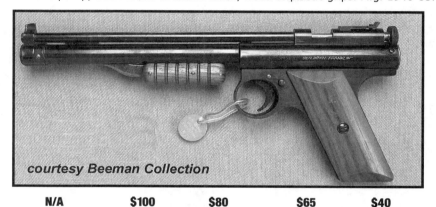

courtesy Beeman Collection

N/A	$100	$80	$65	$40	N/A	N/A

Last MSR was $85.

Add 10% for wood grips. Add 30% for black nickel. Add 15% for box and instruction sheet of plastic grip versions. Add 35% for box and instruction sheet of wood grip versions.

MODEL 150

- BB/.175 cal., pump-up pneumatic, smoothbore, repeating eight-shot, combination rod-at-the-muzzle/lever hand pump, black nickel finish, wood grips. Mfg. 1938-41.

courtesy Beeman Collection

N/A	$225	$200	$160	$125	N/A	N/A

Subtract 25%-75% for broken or incomplete pump/rod linkages. Add 25% for box and instruction sheet.

GRADING	100%	95%	90%	80%	60%	40%	20%

MODEL 160 - BB/.175 cal., pump-up pneumatic, smoothbore, repeating, eight-shot, swinging lever hand pump, black nickel finish, wood grips. Mfg. 1947-60.

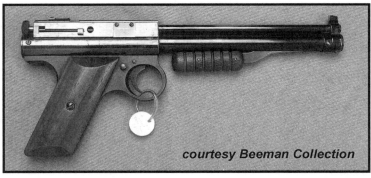

courtesy Beeman Collection

	N/A	$250	$195	$145	$100	N/A	N/A

Add 25% for box and instruction sheet.

MODEL 177 - see Model 100.

MODEL 232 SERIES (MODELS 232 AND 237) - .177 or .22 cal., pump-up pneumatics, SS, BA, swinging lever hand pump, rifled barrel, black matte finish, plastic or wood grips. Mfg. 1985 only.

$115	$105	$85	$75	$45	N/A	N/A

Add 10% for wood grips. Add 15% for box and instruction sheet.

MODEL 242 SERIES (MODELS 242 AND 247) - .177 or .22 cal., pump-up pneumatics, SS, BA, swinging lever hand pump, rifled barrel, black matte finish, wood or plastic grips. Mfg. 1986-92.

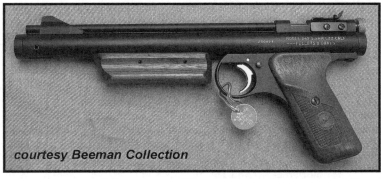

courtesy Beeman Collection

$110	$100	$80	$70	$50	N/A	N/A

Last MSR was $95.

Add 10% for wood grips. Add 5% for box and instruction sheet.

MODEL 250 SERIES (MODEL 250, 252, AND 257) - BB/.175 smoothbore, .177 or .22 cal., 8-gram CO_2 cylinder, single-shot, rifled barrel, compact model, black nickel finish, wood grips. Mfg. 1952-56 (Model 250), and 1953-56 (Models 252 and 257).

courtesy Beeman Collection

N/A	$130	$110	$95	$65	N/A	N/A

Add 10% for no serial number. Add 20% for Models 252 or 257. Add 35% for box and instruction sheet.

MODEL 260 "ROCKET" SERIES (MODELS 260, 262, AND 267) - BB/.175 smoothbore, .177 or .22 cal., 8-gram CO_2 cylinder, single-shot, rifled barrel, blue finish, plastic grips. Mfg. 1957-64 (Model 260), 1956-64 (Model 267), and 1956-73 (Model 262).

$125	$110	$100	$90	$45	N/A	N/A

Add 25% for box and instruction sheet. Add 50% for Benjamin Target Practice Outfit and bell target.

GRADING	100%	95%	90%	80%	60%	40%	20%

MODEL 422 - .22 cal., semi-auto, ten-shot, 8-gram CO_2 cylinder, black finish, plastic grips. Mfg. 1969-73.

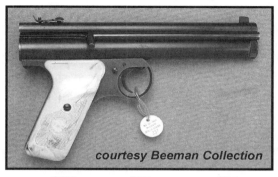

courtesy Beeman Collection

	$115	$100	$95	$80	$55	N/A	N/A

Add 25% for box and instruction sheet.

MODEL 1300 SERIES (MODELS 1300 AND 1320) - BB/.175 smoothbore or 22 cal., rifled barrel, pump-up pneumatic with swinging lever, fifty-shot (Model 1300) BB/.175 smoothbore, or thirty-five-shot (Model 1320, .22 cal.), black finish, plastic grips. Mfg. 1959-64.

	$220	$200	$180	$160	$120	$100	$75

Add 25% for Model 1320. Add 30% for box and instruction sheet.

MODEL 2600 SERIES (MODELS 2600 AND 2620) - BB/.175 smoothbore, .22 cal., 8-gram CO_2 cylinder, thirty-five-shot, blue finish, plastic grips. Mfg. 1959-64.

	$250	$220	$200	$180	$140	$110	$90

Add 25% for Model 2620. Add 25% for box and instruction sheet.

MODEL H17 SERIES (MODELS H17, HB17, HB20, AND HB22) - .177 (Model H17 disc. 1999 and HB17), .20 (Model HB20 disc. 1998), or .22 (Model HB22) cal., single shot pump-up pneumatics, BA, 9.38 in. rifled brass barrel, 525/460 FPS, bright nickel (H17 Model, disc. 1999) or matte black (HB Models), walnut grips, 2.5 lbs. New 1991.

courtesy Benjamin

MSR $211	$185	$145	$85	$65	$40	N/A	N/A

Add 10% for Wisconsin address. Add 15% for bright nickel finish, Model H17. Add 5% for box and instruction literature.

This Series replaced the Benjamin 242 Series, marketed under the Benjamin/Sheridan name from 1991 to 1998. The HB17 and HB22 are currently manufactured and marketed under the Benjamin name by Crosman. The HB20 was manufactured and marketed under the Sheridan name.

MODEL E17 SERIES (MODELS EB17, E17, EB20, E20, EB22, AND E22) - .177, .20, or .22 cal., CO_2, BA, single-shot, 6.38 in. rifled brass barrel, 500/425 FPS, matte black (EB) or bright nickel (E) finish, walnut grips, 1.75 lbs. New 1992.

courtesy Benjamin

MSR $187	$165	$125	$95	$70	$50	N/A	N/A

Add 15% for bright nickel finish. Add 25% for nickel finish and walnut grips. Add 5% for box and instruction literature. Add $20-$30 for factory holster in 95%+ condition.

This Series was marketed under the Benjamin/Sheridan name from 1992 to 1998. The EB17is currently manufactured and marketed under the Benjamin name by Crosman. The EB20 was manufactured and marketed under the Sheridan name by Crosman. (See Introduction to Benjamin section for information on guns produced during the 1990s.) See also: SHERIDAN.

RIFLES

The designation of early Benjamin models is confusing, partly because Walter Benjamin tended to categorize his airguns by patents, rather than external features or appearance. Evidently, no guns are marked as models A, B, C, or D. The first appearance of any Benjamin letter model, in original Benjamin literature, was the model C.

Benjamin Models 300, 310, 312, 317, 360, 367, 700, 710, 720, 3030, 3100, 3120, 3600, and 3620 were recalled by Crosman in 1998.

ST. LOUIS 1899 - one of the predecessors to the Benjamin air rifles, made by the Walter Benjamin's St. Louis Air Rifle Company. Single-shot pneumatic, bicycle-type air pump under the barrel, muzzle loading. Octagonal barrel is blackened wood over a brass tube, smoothbore brass barrel liner. Simple trigger pinches shut a rubber tube serving as air reservoir. 35.8 in. OAL, 1.5 lbs.

    Rarity precludes accurate pricing.

    Russ Snyder, circa 1997 made replicas this model, see Snyder in the "S" section.

ST. LOUIS 1900 - single-shot pneumatic. The big evolutionary step forward in this model is the incorporation of the hand pump into the body tube of the gun. A wooden rod, bearing a washer, has been inserted into the body tube over the barrel. Multiple in and out strokes of this rod charge the gun. This gun uses the same curved barrel found in the 1899 model and the same simple rubber air supply hose pinched shut by the trigger action. This gun is marked on the slab sided buttstock with the logo of the St. Louis Air Rifle Company.

    Rarity precludes accurate pricing.

    Made by Walter Benjamin's St. Louis Air Rifle Company, also known as Improved St. Louis or St. Louis No. 2.

    Russ Snyder, circa 2002 made replicas this model, see Snyder in the "S" section.

MODEL "A" (MODEL 1902) - BB/.175 cal. (smoothbore), barrel under the body tube, wooden pumping rod with operation instructions pasted onto it, receiver with a flat, vertical rear face, trigger guard cast as part of receiver, stock stamped: "Benjamin Air Rifle Company". Extremely rare.

    courtesy Beeman Collection

This is the first Benjamin – referred to as "The Benjamin Air Rifle" by Walter Benjamin.

Evidently, there were at least three other very different appearing, unsuccessful variations of the Model "A" patent in the 1903-06 period. These were designated by Walter Benjamin as the Models 9 and 10, numbers which refer to design levels beginning in the St. Louis Air Rifle Company, and the "Benjamin Repeating Air Rifle." These variations use the same valve arrangement, and also have the barrel underneath the body tube, but have a gently sloping top surface behind the body tube. These variations presently are known only from Walter Benjamin´s scrapbook.

Extreme rarity precludes accurate pricing on this model.

MODEL "B" SINGLE VALVE MODEL - BB/.175 cal. (smoothbore), barrel above body tube, large conspicuous external figure-seven-shaped trigger lever. Extremely rare. Mfg. 1904-08.

    courtesy Beeman Collection

    Rarity precludes accurate pricing.

    Caution: the breech cap may fail explosively if these guns are charged. The 1904-06 variation, identifiable by a solid cast metal breech cap was produced by the W.R. Benjamin Co. The 1908 variation, mfg. by the reorganized Benjamin Air Rifle & Manufacturing Company, has a sheet metal breech cap.

MODEL C (1908) - BB/.175 cal. (smoothbore), same valve arrangement as the Model "B" but with a patented safety trigger to prevent dangerous bursting, gun can fire without the trigger being pulled, smaller trigger lever visible on top, but enclosed by receiver at back, breech cap stamped with "Benjamin Air Rifle & Manufacturing Co.", and 1899 to 1906 patents, not stamped with any model designation, sides of upper rear receiver unit without projections to side, short barrel version stops short of front end of body tube, very rare. Regular barrel version, rare.

    courtesy Beeman Collection

Rarity precludes accurate pricing.

The above early Benjamins are single-shot (except for the unknown Repeater model), rod-at-the-muzzle, smoothbore, muzzle-loading, pump-up pneumatic air rifles with walnut quarter stocks. The reader is referred to *The St. Louis and Benjamin Air Rifle Companies, D.T. Fletcher– Publisher, 1999, ISBN-1-929813-04-X*. There apparently is no "Model D" Benjamin. An unsuccessful attempt to put a conical exhaust valve in a "Model C" may have represented the "Model D."

MODELS E AND F
- BB/.175 cal. (smoothbore), rod-at-the-muzzle, pump-up pneumatics, muzzle-loading, walnut quarter stock, nearly identical to the Model C, but with a flat exhaust valve rather than a ball valve, Model E is the patent pending version, round turret-like unit projects to each side of upper rear receiver unit, rear sight about even with front end of one-piece stock, front sight is a triangular blade soldered to top of barrel, Model F was produced after the patent was issued, round turret-like unit projects to each side of upper receiver unit, rear sight about 1 in. back from front end of stock, front sight is a thin metal blade straddling each side of the barrel, Model E guns are the first Benjamins marked with a model letter; they use the Model C flat breech cap over-stamped around the edge: "MODEL E PAT. PENDING", Model F breech cap is stamped as such and bears 1906-17 patent dates.

courtesy Beeman Collection

	N/A	$195	$165	$135	$110	N/A	N/A

Add 40% for box and instruction sheet. Add 50% for Model E.

The Models E and F are the first really successful and reasonably safe production pneumatic air rifle models (by any manufacturer) and were extremely popular for 25 years, from 1910 to 1935.

MODEL G (MODEL 200)
- similar to Models E and F, BB/.175 cal. smoothbore, muzzle loading, rod-at-the-muzzle, rear sight is a peep sight hole in a metal flange at rear end of receiver, walnut half stock, black nickel finish.

courtesy Howard Collection

	N/A	$190	$160	$125	$100	N/A	N/A

Add 40% for box and instruction sheet.

The single-shot Model 200 and the Benjamin Automatic (Model 600) repeater introduced the very different 1928 Mihalyi in-line valve design which is the basis for all later Benjamin valve systems. This is the first model to correct the accidental discharge problems of the Models C through F.

MODEL AUTOMATIC (MODEL 600)
- BB/.175 cal., semi-auto, twenty-five-shot, magazine-fed smoothbore for lead air rifle shot, rod-at-the-muzzle, similar valves as the single-shot Model 200, walnut half stock with pistol grip, black nickel finish, early versions are marked "Automatic" on the side plate.

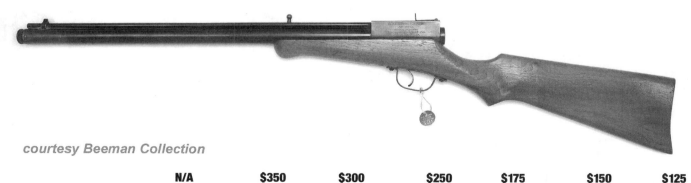

courtesy Beeman Collection

	N/A	$350	$300	$250	$175	$150	$125

Add 15% for "Automatic" marking. Add 35% for box and instruction sheet.

GRADING	100%	95%	90%	80%	60%	40%	20%

MODEL 300 SERIES (MODELS 300, 317/307, AND 322/302) - BB/.175 smoothbore, .177 or .22 cal., single-shot, bolt action, pump-up pneumatics with rod-at-the-muzzle, rifled barrel, black finish, walnut stock. Mfg. 1934-1940.

courtesy Howard Collection

	N/A	$195	$170	$145	$100	N/A	N/A

Add 100% for "one-piece bolt" variation, marked as "Model 300" on the side of the body tube (approx. 12 mfg.). Add 30% for black nickel. Add 25% for box and instruction sheet.

This Series was the first Benjamin to use spring action triggers. The Model 317, with its muzzle pump rod, was later marketed, but not marked, as the Model 307, after a new Model 317, here known as the "317 PH" version, with a swinging pump handle. To be "consistent," the Model 322 was then marketed as the 302. The "Models" 302 and 307 almost surely exist only as catalog and owner's manual designation variations of guns marked as Models 322 and 317. Model 317 shown has later series stock.

MODEL 310 SERIES (MODEL 310, 312 AND 317) - BB/.175 smoothbore, .177 or .22 cal., single-shot, bolt-action, breech-loading, pump-up pneumatic with swinging pump handle, rifled barrel, black nickel finish, walnut stock. Mfg. 1940-1969.

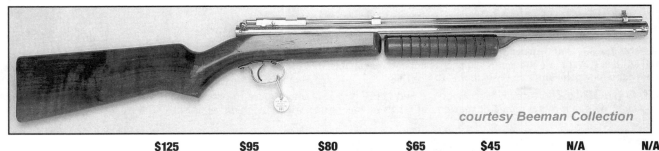

courtesy Beeman Collection

$125	$95	$80	$65	$45	N/A	N/A

Add 20% for CS versions with custom deluxe walnut stock. Add 20% for two-piece cocking bolt. Add 25% for box and instruction sheet.

Note: this version of the Model 317, with its swinging pump handle, is known as the "317PH"; a different Model 317, with a pump rod at the muzzle, was marketed as the "307" but not marked "307", after this new version was introduced. Example shown is polished bright with no original black nickel finish remaining.

MODEL 340 SERIES (MODELS 340, 342, AND 347) - BB/.175 smoothbore, .177 or .22 cal., SS, rifled barrel, similar to Model 310 series but has centrally positioned tang safety, traditional grooved "corn-cob," checkered, or smooth walnut pump handle. Mfg. 1969-86 (Model 340), and Mfg. 1969-92 (Models 342 and 347).

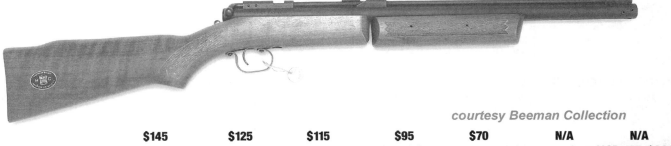

courtesy Beeman Collection

$145	$125	$115	$95	$70	N/A	N/A

Last MSR was $110.

Add 15% for traditional grooved, "corn-cob" pump handle. Add 10% for Williams peep sight. Add 10% for 4x15 scope. Add 10% for box and instruction sheet. Add 20% for two-piece cocking bolt.

MODEL 352 - .22 cal., single shot, 8-gram CO_2 cylinder, bolt-action carbine, rifled barrel, rotating ring safety, black finish, walnut stock.

courtesy Beeman Collection

$195	$175	$155	$120	$85	N/A	N/A

Add 35% for box and instruction sheet.

GRADING	100%	95%	90%	80%	60%	40%	20%

MODEL 360 SERIES (MODELS 360, 362, AND 367)

- BB/.175 smoothbore, .177 or .22 cal., 8-gram CO_2 cylinder, SS, BA, rifled barrel, breech-loading, black finish, 21 in. walnut half stock, manual safety latch. New 1956-57.

courtesy Beeman Collection

	$195	$165	$130	$100	$75	N/A	N/A

Add 20% for CS versions with 24.5 in. deluxe walnut custom stock. Add 20% for rounded outer edge of muzzle, with recessed end of barrel liner (typical form is flat muzzle with slightly protruding brass barrel liner). Add 25% for box and instruction sheet.

MODELS 392 AND S392

- .22 cal., multi-pump pneumatic, bolt-action, single-shot, 19.38 in. rifled brass barrel, 700 FPS, black matte or nickel (Model S397 Disc. 1994) finish, adj. rear sight, American hardwood stock and forearm, 5.5 lbs. New 1992.

courtesy Howard Collection

MSR $250	$215	$175	$125	$90	$65	N/A	N/A

Add 10% for nickel finish. Add 10% for Williams peep sight. Add 15% for 4x15 scope. Add 5% for box and instruction sheet.

The S versions have a silver color finish. Marketed under the Benjamin name 1994-1998. The Model S392 is discontinued the Model 392 is marketed under the Benjamin name. (See Benjamin introduction section.)

MODEL AS392T

- .22 cal., CO_2,88g AirSource cylinder, SS, rifled steel barrel, 610 FPS, black finish, American hardwood stock, ramp front and adj. rear sights,36.5 in. OAL, 5.25 lbs. Mfg. 2004-07.

courtesy Benjamin

	$165	$140	$115	$85	$60	N/A	$40

Last MSR was $180.

MODELS G392 AND GS392

- .22 cal., CO_2, bolt-action, single-shot, 19.38 in. brass rifled barrel, 500 FPS, black (Model G392) or nickel (Model GS392 Disc. 1994) finish, American hardwood stock, adj. rear sight, 5 lbs. Mfg. 1991-98.

	$155	$130	$95	$80	$65	N/A	N/A

Last MSR was $180.

Add 10% for nickel finish (S versions). Add 10% for Williams peep sight. Add 15% for 4x15 scope. Add 5% for box and instruction sheet.

Model G392 was marketed under the Benjamin name 1993-1998. The S prefix indicates silver finish. A .20 cal. version, the Model F9, was marketed under the Sheridan name 1993-1998 (see Benjamin introduction and Sheridan Model F section).

MODELS 397, S397, AND 397C

- .177 cal., multi-pump pneumatic, bolt-action, single-shot, 19.38 in. rifled brass barrel, 750 FPS, black matte or nickel (Model S397 Disc.1994) finish, adj. rear sight, American hardwood stock and forearm, 5.5 lbs. Mfg. 1992-current.

MSR $250	$215	$175	$125	$90	$65	N/A	N/A

Add 10% for nickel finish. Add 20% for Model 397C disc. Add 10% for Williams peep sight. Add 15% for 4x15 scope. Add 5% for box and instruction sheet.

The S versions have a silver color finish. The Model 397C is a carbine version, 3 in. shorter and over a pound lighter. Marketed under the Benjamin name 1994-1998. All models are discontinued except the 397, which is marketed under the Benjamin name. (See Benjamin introduction section.)

GRADING	100%	95%	90%	80%	60%	40%	20%

MODELS G397 AND GS397 - .177 cal., CO_2, bolt-action, single-shot, 19.38 in. brass rifled barrel, 600 FPS, black (Model G397) or nickel (Model GS397 Disc. 1994) finish, American hardwood stock, adj. rear sight, 5 lbs. Mfg. 1991-98.

	$155	$130	$95	$80	$65	N/A	N/A

Last MSR was $180.

Add 10% for nickel finish (S versions). Add 10% for Williams peep sight. Add 15% for 4x15 scope. Add 5% for box and instruction sheet.

Model G397 was marketed under the Benjamin name 1993-1998. The S prefix indicates silver finish. A .20 cal. version, the Model F9, was marketed under the Sheridan name 1993-1998 (see Benjamin introduction and Sheridan Model F section).

MODEL 600 - see Model Automatic.

courtesy Howard Collection

MODEL 700 - BB/.175 cal. smoothbore, pump-up pneumatic with rod-at-the-muzzle pump, twenty-five-shot magazine, black nickel finish, walnut stock. Disc. 1939.

courtesy Howard Collection

	N/A	$200	$180	$170	$150	$125	$100

Add 10% for early versions marked 700 on left side (later versions marked 700 on end cap). Add 35% for box and instruction sheet.

MODELS 710 AND 720 - BB/.175 cal. smoothbore, pump-up pneumatic with swinging pump handle, twenty-five-shot magazine, black nickel finish, walnut stock. Model 710 mfg. 1940-1947, Model 720 mfg. 1947-1962.

courtesy Howard Collection

	N/A	$165	$145	$125	$100	N/A	N/A

Add 30% for Model 710 w/ extended air reservoir mounted under stock. Add 25% for box and instruction sheet.

Image is a Model 720 post-WWII.

MODEL 3030 - BB/.175 cal. smoothbore, 8-gram CO_2 cylinder, breech-loading, bolt action, thirty-shot, black finish, walnut half stock. Mfg. circa 1962-1976.

courtesy Howard Collection

	N/A	$110	$85	$65	$45	N/A	N/A

Add 25% for box and instruction sheet.

GRADING	100%	95%	90%	80%	60%	40%	20%

MODEL 3100 SERIES (MODELS 3100 AND 3120)

- BB smoothbore 100-shot (Model 3100) or .22 cal. lead ball, rifled 85-shot (Model 3120), pneumatic with swinging pump handles. The 3100 was first produced in 1958 followed by the 3120 in 1959. These dates seem to apply to all four of this type: 2600; 2620, 1300; 1320, 3100; 3120, and 3600; 3620. Benjamin offered .22 cal. lead balls, but the BB guns were much more popular, because BBs were more widely available. Mfg. 1959-1985.

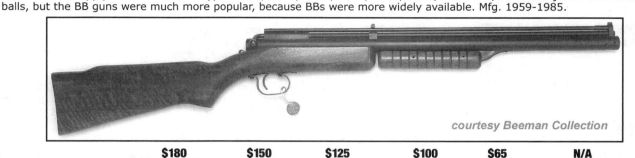

courtesy Beeman Collection

	100%	95%	90%	80%	60%	40%	20%
	$180	$150	$125	$100	$65	N/A	N/A

Add 20% for box and instructions. Add 30% for .22 cal (Model 3120).

MODEL 3600 SERIES (MODELS 3600 AND 3620)

- BB smoothbore 100-shot or .22 cal. lead ball, rifled 85-shot, CO_2, 8-gram cylinders. Mfg. 1959-64.

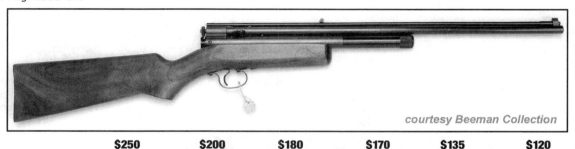

courtesy Beeman Collection

	100%	95%	90%	80%	60%	40%	20%
	$250	$200	$180	$170	$135	$120	$100

Add 25% for box and instructions. Add 50% for .22 cal. (Model 3620). Add 30% for custom grade stock (24.5 in.).

MODEL RM622

- .22 cal., BBC, SP, SS, rifled steel barrel, blue finish, 825 FPS, checkered Monte Carlo hardwood stock, swivel sling mounts, rubber butt pad, hooded front and adj. rear peep sights, 7.5 lbs. Mfg. 2002-04.

	100%	95%	90%	80%	60%	40%	20%
	$200	$185	$165	$145	$120	N/A	N/A

MODEL RM777

- .177 cal., BBC, SP, SS, rifled steel barrel, blue finish, 1100 FPS, checkered Monte Carlo hardwood stock, swivel sling mounts, rubber butt pad, hooded front and adj. rear peep sights, 8.4 lbs. Mfg. 2002-04.

	100%	95%	90%	80%	60%	40%	20%
	$200	$185	$165	$145	$120	N/A	N/A

LEGACY 822 MODEL B8M22

- .22 cal., BBC, SP, SS, rifled steel barrel, blue finish, 800 FPS, checkered Monte Carlo style hardwood stock, vented rubber butt pad, fiberoptic front and adj. rear peep sights, 43 in. OAL, 6.5 lbs. Mfg. 2004-07.

courtesy Benjamin

	100%	95%	90%	80%	60%	40%	20%
	$125	$100	$85	$25	N/A	N/A	N/A

Last MSR was $140.

LEGACY 1000 MODEL B1K77/B1K77X/B1K77XRT

- .177 cal., BBC, SP, SS, rifled steel barrel, blue finish, 1000 FPS, checkered Monte Carlo style hardwood (Legacy Models B1K77 and B1K77X) or Realtree Hardwoods (B1K77XRT New 2005) stock, vented rubber butt pad, fiberoptic front and adj. rear peep sights, 4x32 scope (Legacy Model B1K77X), 43 in. OAL, 6.5 lbs. Mfg. 2004-07.

courtesy Benjamin

	100%	95%	90%	80%	60%	40%	20%
	$235	$205	$175	$145	$120	N/A	N/A

Last MSR was $260.

Add 10% for Legacy Model B1K77X with scope.

GRADING	100%	95%	90%	80%	60%	40%	20%

LEGACY 1000X MODEL B5M77X - .177 cal., BBC, SP, SS, rifled steel barrel, blue finish, 495 FPS, checkered Monte Carlo style hardwood stock, vented rubber butt pad, fiberoptic front and adj. rear peep sights and 4x32 scope, 43 in. OAL, 6.5 lbs. Mfg. 2004-07.

	100%	95%	90%	80%	60%	40%	20%
	$125	$100	$85	$25	N/A	N/A	N/A

Last MSR was $140.

SUPER STREAK MODEL B1122BTM - .22 cal., BBC, SP, SS, blue finished rifled steel barrel w/ fluted muzzle break, upto 1500 FPS w/ lead free pellet, checkered thumbhole hardwood stock, vented rubber butt pad, hooded front and micro adj. rear sight, 4-16x40mm AORG CenterPoint™ scope, manual safty, and 50 lead free pellets. 8.5 lbs., 49.75 in. OAL. Mfg. 2008-current.

MSR $492	$425	$350	$275	$200	N/A	N/A	N/A

SUPER STREAK MODEL B1500BTM - .177 cal., BBC, SP, SS, blue finished rifled steel barrel w/ fluted muzzle break, 1200 FPS w/ 7.9 grain pellet, upto 1500 FPS w/ lead free pellet, checkered thumbhole hardwood stock, vented rubber butt pad, hooded front and micro adj. rear sight, 4-16x40mm AORG CenterPoint™ scope, manual safty, and 50 lead free pellets. 8.5 lbs., 49.75 in. OAL. Mfg. 2008-current.

MSR $492	$425	$350	$275	$200	N/A	N/A	N/A

SUPER STREAK MODEL B1500STM - .177 cal., BBC, SP, SS, silver finished rifled steel barrel w/ fluted muzzle break, 1200 FPS w/ 7.9 grain pellet, upto 1500 FPS w/ lead free pellet, checkered trumbhole hardwood stock, vented rubber butt pad, hooded front and micro adj. rear sight, 4-16x40mm AORG CenterPoint™ scope, manual safty, and 50 lead free pellets. 8.5 lbs., 49.75 in. OAL. Mfg. 2008-current.

MSR $522	$450	$375	$250	$175	N/A	N/A	N/A

DISCOVERY 22 MODEL BP1K22PSL - .22 cal., BA, CO_2 or compressed air Duel Fuel PCP, SS, blue finished rifled steel barrel, up to 900 FPS w/ lead free pellet, walnut PG stock w/ built- in pressure gauge, buttplate, Williams fiber optic adj. sights, cross bolt safety, comes w/ three stage high pressure hand pump and 50 lead free pellets. 5.1 lbs., 39 in. OAL. Mfg. 2008-current.

MSR $399	$385	$300	$225	$150	N/A	N/A	N/A

DISCOVERY 22 MODEL BP1K77PSL - .177 cal., BA, CO_2 or compressed air Duel Fuel PCP, SS, blue finished rifled steel barrel, up to 900 FPS w/ lead free pellet, walnut PG stock w/ built- in pressure gauge, buttplate, Williams fiber optic adj. sights, cross bolt safety, comes w/ three stage high pressure hand pump and 50 lead free pellets. 5.1 lbs., 39 in. OAL. Mfg. 2008-current.

MSR $399	$385	$300	$225	$150	N/A	N/A	N/A

COMMEMORATIVE EDITION RIFLES

MODEL 87 (CENTENNIAL MODEL) - .177 or .22 cal., pump-up pneumatic, single-shot, breech loading, rifled barrel, polished brass finish, full-length walnut stock with inset bronze medallion, approx. 400 mfg. Mfg. 1987 only.

	100%	95%	90%	80%	60%	40%	20%
	$395	$325	$310	$250	$175	$125	$100

Last MSR was $250.

Add 20% for .177 cal. Subtract 25% for missing factory soft side case marked "Benjamin" and manual.

Beware of "seconds" that have standard serial numbers instead of the special 00XXXX sequence. Offered during 1987 as a limited edition "Centennial" issue, the real Centennial for Benjamin was in 2002.

BENJAMIN

Previous marketing name used by the Benjamin Air Rifle Co. and Crosman Corp. from 1991 to about 1998.

See the introduction to the "Benjamin" section.

BENYAMIN

Unknown maker, possibly of the Philippines or the U.S., mid-20th century.

Not a copy of Benjamin features. Multiple stroke pump pneumatic with swing metal pump lever. SS, faucet-style breech. Marked "Benyamin Super" with horse head figures. Full width receiver with slab sides bearing figure of rearing horse. Adult scale buttstock with Monte Carlo comb, cheekpiece, and checkering. Sling swivels on left side of gun. Extreme rarity precludes accurate pricing on this model.

courtesy Beeman Collection

BERETTA, PIETRO

Current manufacturer located in Brescia, Italy. Currently imported and distributed by Umarex USA loccated in Fort Smith, AR beginning March, 2006. Previously imported by Beretta USA Corp., located in Accokeek, MD. Previously distributed by Crosman Corp. located in East Bloomfield, NY 2003-2006. Previously distributed by Beretta USA Corp., located in Accokeek, MD 2000-2003. Dealer sales.

Beretta USA Corp. was formed in 1977, and has been the exclusive importer of Beretta firearms since 1980. Beretta introduced a complete line of air pistols in 2000, which are identical in size, appearance, and model designation to the 9mm Model 92FS. Although the Model 92FS air pistol

GRADING	100%	95%	90%	80%	60%	40%	20%

is identical in appearance to the Beretta 9mm semi-auto, it is not a semi-auto air pistol, but rather utilizes the traditional eight-shot rotary clip loaded at the breech and functions in the same way as a single or double action revolver. The barrel is recessed within a 9mm size muzzle, making this one of the most authentic-looking air pistols (firearm-copy) in production today. The slide is marked "Pietro Beretta Gardone V.T." on the left along with the PB logo, and marked "Carl Walther Alexandria/VA." on the right side. The airguns are manufactured for Beretta by Umarex Sportwaffen GmbH, the present owner of Walther. For more information and current pricing on both new and used Beretta firearms, please refer to the *Blue Book of Gun Values* by S.P. Fjestad (also available online).

PISTOLS

MODEL 92FS - .177 cal., CO_2, SA or DA, eight-shot cylinder mag., 4.5 in. rifled steel barrel, 425 FPS, fixed front, interchangeable rear sight, ambidextrous safety, plastic grips or optional checkered wood grips, available in blue or nickel finish, standard, match, and trophy (disc. 2003) versions, includes carrying case and two rotary mags., 8.3 in. OAL, 2.78 lbs. to 3.0 lbs. New 2000.

courtesy Umarex USA

MSR $217	$180	$150	$100	$75	N/A	N/A	N/A

Add $24 for nickel finish. Add $54 for nickel finish and wood grips. Add $25 for Model 92FS Match with compensator. Add $243 ($265 in nickel) for Model 92FS Trophy with compensator, scope, and mount (disc. 2003).

MODEL 92FS XX-TREME - .177 cal., CO_2, SA/DA, eight-shot rotary mags., 4.5 in. rifled steel barrel, 425 FPS, tactical accessory mount, top point sight, compensator, manual safety, black tactical finish, includes carrying case and two rotary mags. 12.6 in. OAL, 3.6 lbs. New 2008.

courtesy Umarex USA

MSR $288	$280	$245	$200	$150	N/A	N/A	N/A

MODEL ELITE II - .177 BB cal., CO_2, DA, eighteen-shot mag., 4.8 in. rifled steel barrel, 480 FPS, fixed sights, ambidextrous safety, black plastic replica. 1.5 lbs. New 2007.

MSR $50	$45	$35	$25	N/A	N/A	N/A	N/A

MODEL PX4 STORM - .177 cal., CO_2, DA, sixteen-shot mag., 4 in. rifled steel barrel, 380 FPS, fixed sights, ambidextrous safety, black plastic replica. 1.6 lbs. New 2007.

courtesy Umarex USA

MSR $95	$85	$65	$45	$35	N/A	N/A	N/A

GRADING	100%	95%	90%	80%	60%	40%	20%

MODEL PX4 STORM RECON - .177 cal., CO_2, SA/DA, blowback action, sixteen-shot mag., 4.1 in. rifled steel barrel, 380 FPS, Shot Dot™ point sights, ambidextrous safety, brown plastic, compensator, tactical accessory rail mount, Walther tactical flashlight w/ cord switch. 11.64 in. OAL, 2.2 lbs. New 2008.

courtesy Umarex USA

MSR $170	$150	$115	$85	$50	N/A	N/A	N/A

RIFLES

MODEL CX4 STORM - .177 CAL., 88g CO_2, semi-auto blowback action, 30 shot mag., 17.5 in. BBl, 495-600 fps., adj. front and rear sights, top integrated accessory rail, black synthetic stock, manual safety, 30.7 in. OAL, 5.6 lbs. Mfg. 2007-current.

courtesy Umarex USA

MSR $296	$275	$250	$205	$165	N/A	N/A	N/A

MODEL CX4 STORM XT TACTICAL - .177 CAL., 88g CO_2, semi-auto blowback action, 30 shot mag., 17.5 in. BBl, 495-600 fps., adj. front and rear sights, top integrated accessory rail, black synthetic stock, BiPod, 4x32mm tactical scope, compensator, manual safety, 30.7 in. OAL, 5.6 lbs. Mfg. 2008-current.

courtesy Umarex USA

MSR $427	$375	$325	$250	$205	N/A	N/A	N/A

BIG CHIEF
Previous tradename used by unknown British maker for a folded metal BB gun believed to be pre-WWII. For information on Big Chief airguns, see Produsit in the "P" section.

BIJOU
For information on Bijou airguns, see Plymouth Air Rifle Company in the "P" section.

BISLEY

For information on Bisley airguns, see Lincoln Jefferies in the "L" section.

BLACK MAJOR

For information on Black Major airguns, see Milbro in the "M" section.

BOBCAT

For information on Bobcat airguns, see Milbro in the "M" section.

BONEHILL, C.G.

See Britannia listing.

BOONE

Previous trademark manufactured for a few years by Target Products Corp. located in Jackson, MI. beginning 1947.

PISTOLS

BOONE AIR PISTOL - .173 cal., gravity-fed magazine, and a rearward-moving spring piston. Research is ongoing with this trademark, and more information will be included both online and in future editions.

courtesy Beeman Collection

Average original condition specimens on most common Boone models are typically priced in the $45-$95 range. Add 20% for original box.

BOWKETT, JOHN

Current airgunsmith and designer, located in England.

Beginning in the 1970s to date, John Bowkett has been one of Europe's leading airgun designers. He is famous for individual production of advanced design bulk filled CO_2 air pistols and rifles. Bowkett designed airguns for Titan in the 1990s.

RIFLES

BOLT ACTION 25 - .25 cal, 650 FPS, SS, PCP, bolt action, 44 in. OAL, 8 lbs. Mfg. early 1980s.
    Values TBD.

BOLT ACTION 32 - .32 cal., 600 FPS, SS, PCP, bolt action, 42 in. OAL, 8.3 lbs. Mfg. early 1980s.

courtesy Tim Saunders

Values TBD.

BRITANNIA

Previous trademark manufactured by C.G. Bonehill located in Birmingham, England circa 1903-08.

The Britannia name has also been used for a small British push-barrel air pistol of unknown origin, probably made in the 1930s, having a value in the $75 range for gun only or, in the $150 range with original box.

RIFLES

Massive, heavily built airguns which could be considered as the ultimate development of the Gem line of airguns (See the "Gem" entry in the "G" section of this guide). Notable for a huge end plug on bottom end of the buttstock compression chamber.

GRADING	100%	95%	90%	80%	60%	40%	20%

BRITANNIA ANGLO-SURE SHOT MK I - .177, .22, or .25 cal., BBC, SP, SS air rifles with the SP located in the buttstock, 21 in. rifled BBL, dual power by moving the sear stop screw allows different levels of mainspring compression, first small production in Germany with variations in sights, breech latch, and power adjustments but total production probably less than 3500, 35.5 in. OAL, 6.5 lbs. Mfg. circa 1905-1908.

courtesy Beeman Collection

	N/A	$1,100	$800	$600	$450	$350	$250

Add 20% for .22 caliber.

IMPROVED BRITTANIA - .25 cal., BBC, SP, 13 in. barrel, clumsy arrangement of pulling the entire barrel/receiver unit upwards from the frame for cocking, pellet loading via inefficient curved chute with rotating cover, 44.5 in. OAL. Mfg. 1908-09.

courtesy Beeman Collection

	N/A	$1,800	$1,550	$1,200	$850	$650	$450

BRITISH CHIEF

For information on British Chief airguns, see "Big Chief" in this section.

courtesy Beeman Collection

BRITISH CUB

For information on British Cub, see Dolla in the "D" section.

BRITON

Previous trademark ascribed to the T.J. Harrington Company of Walton, Surrey, England, or Edwin Anson or Frank Clark, both of Birmingham, England.

A brand of telescoping barrel, spring-piston air pistol. Research is ongoing with this trademark, and more information will be available both online and in future editions. Average original condition specimens on most common models are typically priced in the $295 range.

GRADING	100%	95%	90%	80%	60%	40%	20%

PISTOLS

BRITON AIR PISTOL -telescoping barrel, spring-piston air pistol. Research is ongoing with this trademark, and more information will be available both online and in future editions.

courtesy Beeman Collection

Average original condition specimens on most common models are typically priced in the $295 range. Add 15% for spring tensioned pellet seater.

BROCOCK

Current manufacturer/importer located in Redditch, Worcestershire, England with an engineering company located in Birmingham, England. Due to the legal issues in the UK with selling Air Cartridge System Rifles and Pistols, Brocock discontinued manufactuer of ACS arms. Previously imported and distributed exclusively by Airguns of Arizona. Brocock was formed in 1989. Some of Brocock´s airguns are manufactured (under contract to specifications) by other manufacturers including Cuno Melcher (ME Sportwaffen), Weihrauch Sport, A. Uberti & C., and Pietta. Dealer and consumer direct sales.

Brocock is currently (2008) working on design and manufacture of a PCP rifle named the Brocock Enigma Model and a BBC rifle named the Brocock Independent Model. All recent production Brocock air pistols and rifles use the dedicated BACS (Brocock Air Cartridge System). This unique system based on the .38 BAC uses a compressed air cartridge which contains a sophisticated valve system which when filled with air and loaded with a pellet, enables these airguns to feel, function, and look like real breech loading firearms.

Brocock was formed by the Silcock brothers (hence the name) to buy the liquidated Saxby and Palmer company in 1989. Brocock manufactured an air cartridge system whose roots go back to a British patent of 1872 used in a Giffard gas gun. The modern form, initially known as a 'TAC' (Tandem Air Cartridge, so called because of the twin sealing arrangement either end of the valve stem) later became 'BACS' (Brocock Air Cartridge System). An air cartridge is a manganese bronze, cartridge-like case that holds air pressure at around 2,700 psi. A spring loaded exhaust valve is opened by the gun's firing pin striking a button located where a primer would be found in a firearm cartridge. The valve opens and the escaping air propels a pellet from a screw-on nosecone.

Air cartridges can be individually charged with a 'Slim Jim' scissor pump. This rather strenuous step, requiring up to six or eight pumps per cartridge, can be avoided by using various devices to charge cartridges quickly and in bulk from SCUBA tanks.

Brocock manufactured the Safari, Predator and Fox rifles in Birmingham but also imported guns especially designed for air cartridges only from Cuno Melcher (ME Sportwaffen), Weihrauch Sport, Aldo Uberti, Pietta and Armi San Marco. The latter three converted some of their replica antique firearm designs into air cartridge airguns.

All air cartridge guns were built so as to make conversion into a firearm very difficult. On early Saxby and Palmer revolvers this included pinning the barrel to prevent its exchange and deleting a portion of the forward end of the cylinder. Pinning the barrels became standard but, during the mid 1990s, the unattractive deletion of the forward end of the cylinders was replaced with machining the spaces between the individual chambers.

Despite the safeguards against conversion, there were a very limited number of cases where criminals using sophisticated machining equipment managed to turn some of these airguns into firearms. Such conversions often were dangerous and these criminals reportedly sometimes lost body parts or their lives when converted guns exploded.

American airgunners take warning!: As of January 2004 the manufacture, importation, sale or transfer of all air cartridge guns was banned by the United Kingdom government. Existing UK owners were given three months in which to apply for a highly restricted Section 1 firearms certificate should they wish continue owning their guns, or to hand them to a police station for destruction without compensation. These guns can't be traded in the UK, or even exported, and thus have no commercial value in the UK.

Brocock is still selling their CO$_2$ and blank firing guns which were unaffected by the 2004 ban. Attempts are being made to have air cartridge guns manufactured outside of the UK and to import them directly into the USA, but development or continued success of such a program seems unlikely.

The authors and publisher wish to thank Mr. Tim Saunders for his assistance with this section of the *Blue Book of Airguns*.

PISTOLS

MODEL PARA PPK 380 - .22 cal., BACS, 3 in. barrel, 300 FPS, seven-shot, blue or nickel finish, black composite or walnut grips, fixed sights, 1.45 lbs., Mfg. by ME Sportwaffen.

$160	$135	$105	$75	$55	N/A	N/A

Last MSR was $175.

Add $30 for nickel finish and walnut grips.

GRADING	100%	95%	90%	80%	60%	40%	20%

REVOLVERS

MODEL 1851 NAVY - .22 cal., BACS, SA, 5 or 7.5 in. barrel, 410 FPS, six-shot, blue with case color frame and brass grip strap frame or nickel finish, walnut grips, fixed sights, 2.4 lbs. Mfg. by Pietta.

courtesy Tim Saunders

100%	95%	90%	80%	60%	40%	20%
$300	$255	$200	$155	$105	N/A	N/A

Last MSR was $343.

Subtract $40 for all-brass frame (Model 1851 Navy Sheriff).

MODEL 1858 REMINGTON ARMY - .22 cal., BACS, SA, 5.5 or 8 in. barrel, 410 FPS, six-shot, blue with brass frame finish, walnut grips, fixed sights, 2.4 lbs. Mfg. by Pietta.

courtesy Tim Saunders

100%	95%	90%	80%	60%	40%	20%
$260	$215	$155	$105	$85	N/A	N/A

Last MSR was $286.

Add $55 for steel frame.

MODEL 1860 NM ARMY - .22 cal., BACS, SA, 6.5 or 8 in. barrel, 410 FPS, six-shot, blue with brass frame finish, walnut grips, fixed sights, 2.75 lbs. Mfg. by Pietta.

100%	95%	90%	80%	60%	40%	20%
$260	$215	$155	$105	$85	N/A	N/A

Last MSR was $286.

Add $55 for steel frame.

MODEL 1862 REB CONFEDERATE - .22 cal., BACS, SA, 5 in. barrel, 410 FPS, six-shot, blue with case color frame finish, brass and walnut grips, fixed sights, 2.4 lbs. Mfg. by Pietta.

100%	95%	90%	80%	60%	40%	20%
$260	$215	$155	$105	$85	N/A	N/A

Last MSR was $286.

MODEL 1873 CATTLEMAN SA - .22 cal., BACS, SA, 4.75, 5.5, or 7.5 in. barrel, 410 FPS, six-shot, blue with color case hardened frame or nickel finish, walnut, polymer pearlite, or polymer ivory grips, brass or steel grip frame, fixed sights, 2.6 lbs. Mfg. by Uberti.

100%	95%	90%	80%	60%	40%	20%
N/A	$550	$495	N/A	N/A	N/A	N/A

Last MSR was $569.

Add $100 for polymer pearlite or ivory grips.
Because of limited availability, call the importer for pricing and availability.

MODEL 1875 REMINGTON SA - .22 cal., BACS, SA, 5.5, or 7.5 in. barrel, 410 FPS, six-shot, blue with color case hardened frame finish, walnut grips, fixed sights, 2.6 lbs. Mfg. by Uberti.
Because of limited availability, call the importer for pricing and availability.

MODEL 1877 THUNDERER SA - .22 cal., BACS, SA, 3, 3.5, 4, or 4.75 in. barrel, 410 FPS, six-shot, blue with color case hardened frame or nickel finish, walnut grips, fixed sights, 2.6 lbs. Mfg. by Uberti.
Because of limited availability, call the importer for pricing and availability.

MODEL BISLEY SA REVOLVER - .22 cal., BACS, SA, 4.75, 5.5, or 7.5 in. barrel, 410 FPS, six-shot, blue with color case hardened frame, walnut grips, fixed sights, 2.6 lbs. Mfg. by Uberti.
Because of limited availability, call the importer for pricing and availability.

GRADING	100%	95%	90%	80%	60%	40%	20%

MODEL BISLEY TARGET FLATTOP - .22 cal., BACS, SA, 4.75, 5.5, or 7.5 in. barrel, 410 FPS, six-shot, blue with color case hardened frame, walnut grips, adj. rear sight, 2.6 lbs. Mfg. by Uberti.

MODEL COMBAT - .22 cal., BACS, SA/DA, 2.5 in. barrel, 380 FPS, six-shot, blue finish, molded grips, fixed sights, 2 lbs. Mfg. by Weihrauch.

	100%	95%	90%	80%	60%	40%	20%
	$290	$245	$195	$145	$95	N/A	N/A

Last MSR was $319.

MODEL COMPACT - .22 cal., BACS, SA/DA, 2.25 in. barrel, 325 FPS, five-shot, blue or nickel finish, molded or walnut grips, fixed sights, 2.24 lbs. Mfg. by ME Sportwaffen.

	$160	$135	$105	$75	$55	N/A	N/A

Last MSR was $175.

   Add $30 for nickel finish and walnut grips.

MODEL MAGNUM - .22 cal., BACS, SA/DA, 3 in. barrel, 350 FPS, five-shot, blue or nickel finish, molded or walnut grips, adj. rear sight, 1.38 lbs. Mfg. by ME Sportwaffen.

	$135	$105	$75	$55	$35	N/A	N/A

Last MSR was $143.

   Add $40 for nickel finish and walnut grips.

MODEL ORION 3 - .22 cal., BACS, SA/DA, 3 in. barrel, 410 FPS, six-shot, blue finish, molded grips, adj. rear sight, 2 lbs. Mfg. by Weihrauch.

	$290	$245	$195	$145	$95	N/A	N/A

Last MSR was $319.

MODEL ORION 6 - .177 or .22 cal., BACS, SA/DA, 6 in. barrel, 550/410 FPS, six-shot, blue finish, molded grips, adj. rear sight, 2.3 lbs. Mfg. by Weihrauch.

	$290	$245	$195	$145	$95	N/A	N/A

Last MSR was $319.

   Add 25% for Model Orion 66, chrome plated.

MODEL POCKET - .177 or .22 cal., BACS, SA/DA, 1.5 in. barrel, 300 FPS, five-shot, blue finish, molded grips, adj. rear sight, 1.2 lbs.

	$135	$105	$75	$55	$35	N/A	N/A

Last MSR was $143.

MODEL SPECIALIST - .22 cal., BACS, SA/DA, 4 in. barrel, 410 FPS, six-shot, blue finish, molded grips, adj. rear sight, 2.24 lbs. Mfg. by Weihrauch.

courtesy Beeman Collection

	$290	$245	$195	$145	$95	N/A	N/A

Last MSR was $319.

MODEL TEXAN - .177 or .22 cal., BACS, SA, 5.5 in. barrel, 550/410 FPS, six-shot, all blue or blue with case color frame and gold-plated trigger guard/grip straps finish, walnut grips, fixed sights, 2.86 lbs. Mfg. by Weihrauch.

	$300	$255	$200	$155	$105	N/A	N/A

Last MSR was $328.

   Add $25 for case color frame and gold plating.
   Because of limited availability, call the importer for pricing and availability.

RIFLES

ENIGMA - .177 or .22cal., PCP, BA, nine-shot rotary magazine indexed and cocked by RHS cocking lever, 16 in. rifled BBL, synthetic stock, two-stage adj. trigger, free floating barrel, 35 in. OAL, 6 lbs. Mfg. 2008.
   Check with manufacturer for current price and availability.

MODEL 1866 YELLOWBOY CARBINE - .22 cal., BACS, six-shot, lever action, 19 in. barrel, 598 FPS, blue finish with brass receiver, walnut stock and forearm, blue forearm barrel band, adj. rear sight, 7.4 lbs. Mfg. by Uberti.
   Because of limited availability, call the importer for pricing and availability.

GRADING	100%	95%	90%	80%	60%	40%	20%

MODEL 1866 SPORTING RIFLE - .22 cal., BACS, twelve-shot, lever action, 24 in. barrel, 598 FPS, blue finish with brass receiver, walnut stock and forearm, brass forearm cap, adj. rear sight, 8.1 lbs. Mfg. by Uberti.

MODEL 1871 ROLLING BLOCK RIFLE - .22 cal., BACS, SS, rolling block action, 17.7 barrel, 598 FPS, blue finish, walnut stock, adj. rear sight, 5.7 lbs. Mfg. by Uberti.

	N/A	$850	$795	N/A	N/A	N/A	N/A

Last MSR was $895.

MODEL 1873 CARBINE - .22 cal., BACS, six-shot, lever action, 19 in. barrel, 598 FPS, blue finish with color case hardened receiver, walnut stock and forearm, blue forearm barrel band adj. rear sight, 7.4 lbs. Mfg. by Uberti.

	N/A	$850	$795	N/A	N/A	N/A	N/A

Last MSR was $895.

Because of limited availability, call the importer for pricing and availability.

MODEL 1873 PISTOL GRIP SPORTING RIFLE - .22 cal., BACS, twelve-shot, lever action, 24 in. barrel, 598 FPS, blue finish with color case hardened or nickel receiver, checkered walnut pistol grip stock and forearm, blue forearm cap, adj. rear sight, 8.1 lbs. Mfg. by Uberti.

MODEL FOX RIFLE - .22 cal., BACS, SS, 14.7 barrel, 598 FPS, blue finish, wire stock, folding trigger, 4X32 scope included, 2.65 lbs. Mfg. by Brocock.

	$275	$225	$185	$145	$95	N/A	N/A

Last MSR was $303.

Because of limited availability, call the importer for pricing and availability.

MODEL REVOLVER CARBINE - .22 cal., BACS, six-shot, SA revolver action, 18 in. barrel, 520 FPS, blue finish, walnut stock, fixed sights, 4.4 lbs. Mfg. by Uberti.

MODEL HERALD RIFLE - .22 cal., BACS, bolt action. Mfg. by Brocock. Disc.

	N/A	$800	$600	$400	$200	N/A	N/A

MODEL PREDATOR RIFLE - .22 cal., BACS, six-shot, bolt action, 17.7 in. barrel, 598 FPS, blue finish, checkered beech stock, two-stage adj. trigger, 5.7 lbs. Mfg. by Brocock.

	$470	$400	$325	$255	$165	N/A	N/A

Last MSR was $515.

MODEL SAFARI RIFLE - .22 cal., BACS, SS, bolt action, 17.7 in. barrel, 598 FPS, blue finish, checkered beech stock, two-stage adj. trigger, 6.5 lbs. Mfg. by Brocock.

	$392	$325	$255	$165	$130	N/A	N/A

Last MSR was $431.

BROLIN ARMS, INC.

Previous importer located in Pomona, CA 1997-99, and previously located in La Verne, CA 1995-97. For more information and current values on used Brolin Arms, Inc. firearms, please refer to the *Blue Book of Gun Values* by S.P. Fjestad (also available online).

RIFLES

SM 1000 - .177 or .22 cal., SL, SP, SS, 1100/900 FPS. adj. front and rear sights, match barrel, automatic safety, Monte Carlo beech stock, 9.125 lbs.

	$155	$130	$115	$85	$55	N/A	N/A

Last MSR was $200.

Add 10% for checkered stock. Add 30% for adj. buttplate.

BROWN, A.A. & SONS

See Abas Major listing in the "A" section.

BROWN

Previously manufactured by O.H. Brown located in Davenport, IA.

GRADING	100%	95%	90%	80%	60%	40%	20%

PISTOLS

STANDARD MODEL BROWN PISTOL - .22 cal., multi-pump pneumatic, 7.5 in. rifled barrel, 17 in. overall, unique pump system behind the barrel compressed air on both push and pull strokes providing very high power, steel parts deep blue finished, select walnut grips, adj. rear sight, exceptionally well made, rare, featured only in 1939 Stoeger catalog, original instructions are an actual engineer's blueprint, 2.4 lb.

courtesy Beeman Collection

N/A	$2,250	$2,000	$1,500	$1,250	$750	N/A

1939 retail price was $12.

Add 25% for original box and blueprint instructions.
Approximate retail for Colt Woodsman Sport Model in 1930 was $32.50.

DELUXE MODEL BROWN PISTOL - .22 cal., similar to Standard Model, except 10 in. barrel and checkered select walnut grips, very rare, 2.5 lb.

courtesy Beeman Collection

N/A	$2,500	$2,250	$2,000	$1,500	$995	N/A

1939 retail price was $20.

Add 25% for original box and blueprint instructions.

BROWNING

Current manufacturer with headquarters located in Morgan, UT.

The Browning Airstar was mfg. by Rutten Airguns SA, located in Herstal-Liege, Belgium. It is the first air rifle with a battery-powered electronic cocking system. Less than 400 examples were available for the U.S. market. For more information and current pricing on both new and used Browning firearms, please refer to the *Blue Book of Gun Values* by S.P. Fjestad (also available online).

RIFLES

BROWNING AIRSTAR - .177 cal., electronic cocking mechanism powered by rechargeable Ni-Cad battery (250 shots per charge), 780 FPS, flip-up loading port, warning light indicates when spring is compressed, electronic safety with warning light, 17.5 in. fixed barrel, hooded front sight with interchangeable sight inserts, adj. rear sight, frame grooved for scope mount, beech wood stock, came in Browning box, 9.3 lbs.

$595	$500	$450	$350	$250	N/A	N/A

Last MSR was $1,000.

Originally marketed in Europe through Browning dealers for $1,000. Was available in the U.S., and marked with both the Browning and Rutten names, and Browning Trademark.

BULL DOG

Previous trademark of unknown British origin, circa Pre-WWII.

The Bull Dog trademark appears on a very small spring piston single shot air pistol with cast metal frame, Birds-head checkered metal grip, and exposed trigger. Pistol is loaded by unscrewing a loading pin on back of frame and cocked by pulling a ring on the forward end of the pistol. Research is ongoing with this trademark, and more information will be included both online and in future editions.

BULLS EYE & SHARPSHOOTER

Previous trademark manufactured by Bull´s Eye Pistol Co. located in Rawlins, WY circa 1928-1960s.

The Bulls Eye catapult air pistol was powered by elastic bands. The Sharpshooter was introduced as a smaller version of the Bulls Eye circa 1938. The production of these models was moved to La Jolla, CA circa 1948, and the company name was changed to Bull´s Eye Mfg. Co. Research is ongoing with this trademark, and more information will be included both online and in future editions. Average original condition specimens of most common Bulls Eye and Sharpshooter Models are typically priced in the $60 range for unboxed models with short body, grip plates, and conventional-looking trigger guard. Early versions with a long body, sheet metal grip, and very thin trigger (which looks like a guard) in original box sell in the $250 range. Ref: AR 1 : 52-54, AR 2 : 54-57, AR4 : 31-39.

courtesy Beeman Collection

BULLS EYE

Previous trademark of Bulls Eye Air Rifle Company, former producer of sheet metal BB guns in Chicago from 1907 to an unknown date.

Produced a lever, gravity feed BB repeater and a single shot break-open BB gun. Both were well built; the lever cocking action used a lever system similar to that of a Colt Model 1860 revolver. The stocks are unusual in being fitted over the grip frames rather than into them. Ref. Dunathan (1957). Research is ongoing with this trademark, and more information will be included both in future editions and online.

BURGO

For information on Burgo, see Weihrauch Sport in the "W" section.

BUSSEY

Previous trademark of airguns previously manufactured by G.G. Bussey and Company located in London, England from 1870 to about 1914.

Based on a 1876 patent awarded to George Gibson Bussey for a simple airgun. The appearance is suggestive of a Quackenbush Model 1 air rifle, but there is almost no similarity in construction. Unusual spring piston action required removal of the barrel for cocking. An accessory plunger was inserted in the open action and used to push the piston backward until engaged by the sear. A pellet or dart was then placed in the breech and the barrel reinserted for firing. Extremely few specimens are known; one measured 29 in. long with a .21 caliber 9.5 in. smoothbore barrel. Research is ongoing with this trademark, and more information may be included both online and in future editions. Rarity precludes accurate pricing at this time.

C SECTION

C Z (CESKA ZBROJOVKA)

Current manufacturer located in Uhersky Brod, Czech Republic, since 1936. No current importation, previously imported by CZ-USA located in Kansas City, KS.

Research is ongoing with this trademark, and more information will be included both online and in future editions. For more information and current pricing on both new and used CZ firearms, please refer to the *Blue Book of Gun Values* by S.P. Fjestad (also available online).

GRADING	100%	95%	90%	80%	60%	40%	20%

PISTOLS

TEX MODEL 3 (CZ-3) - .177 cal., BBC, SP, 400 FPS, 7.50 in. barrel, adj. sights, plastic stock.

	100%	95%	90%	80%	60%	40%	20%
MSR N/A	$80	$70	$60	$50	$40	N/A	N/A

SLAVIA APP661 - 4.5mm round lead ball cal., CO_2, semi-auto repeater, vertical removable mag., Early Version: wood grips, 8 gm CO_2 cylinder, piercing pin in grip cap, Late Version: black plastic grips, 8 or 12 gm CO_2 cylinders, 7.8 in OAL, 1.4 lbs. Mfg. circa 1960-1970.

courtesy Beeman Collection

	100%	95%	90%	80%	60%	40%	20%
	$125	$100	$75	$60	$45	N/A	N/A

Add 50% for early version.

SLAVIA ZVP (Vzduchová Pistole) - .177 in. cal., BBC, SP, SS, very solidly built, blued steel, hand checkered hardwood grips, 13.4 in. OAL, 2.4 lbs. Mfg. 1960-72.

courtesy Beeman Collection

	100%	95%	90%	80%	60%	40%	20%
	$80	$65	$50	$35	$25	N/A	N/A

RIFLES

CZ MODEL Vz-24 - similar to CZ Model Vz-35, except no bayonet lug.

CZ MODEL Vz-35 - 4.40 mm lead ball, SP, rear bolt cocks action, gravity-fed magazine with trap lid, copy of Czech military rifle, with bayonet, 54.1 in. OAL (w/ bayonet), 9.7 lbs (w/ bayonet).

courtesy Beeman Collection

	100%	95%	90%	80%	60%	40%	20%
	N/A	N/A	$450	$350	$250	$150	$65

Add 10% for bayonet.

GRADING	100%	95%	90%	80%	60%	40%	20%

CZ MODEL Vz-36 - 4.40 mm, SP, TL, cocks by swinging lever attached to right side of action up and back, military style stock w/ hand-guards, gravity fed repeater.

  Military trainer, reportedly 4 known. Values TBD.

MILITARY AIRGUN Vz-47 (CZ-BB) - 4.40 mm cal. lead balls, BA, Czech Army training rifle, most w/ military markings and SN but 40 made up late from factory parts do not have typical markings or SNs. 1947-1950.

	100%	95%	90%	80%	60%	40%	20%
	N/A	N/A	$350	$295	$200	$150	$100

CZ 200 - .177 or .22 cal., PCP, BA, SS, 18.92 in. rifled barrel, black finish, beech stock and forearm, adj. trigger, mounting blocks for sight system of choice. New 2001.

courtesy CZ

    While advertised starting in 2001, this model has yet to be manufactured.

CZ 200 S - .177 or .22 cal., similar to CZ 200, except sport stock with recoil pad. New 2001.

courtesy CZ

CZ 200 T - .177 cal., similar to CZ 200, except competition stock with adj. cheek piece and buttplate. New 2001.

courtesy CZ

SLAVIA 236 - .177 in. cal., BBC, SP, SS, hardwood stock with fluted forearm.

courtesy Beeman Collection

	100%	95%	90%	80%	60%	40%	20%
	$80	$65	$50	$35	$25	N/A	N/A

GRADING	100%	95%	90%	80%	60%	40%	20%

SLAVIA 612 - .177 in. cal., BBC, SP, SS, 12 in. rifled steel BBL, all metal except for buttstock, similar to Dianawerk Model 15, 32in. OAL, Mfg.1955-1965.

courtesy Beeman Collection

| | $65 | $40 | $30 | $25 | $20 | N/A | N/A |

SLAVIA 618 - .177 in. cal., BBC, SP, SS, 14.5 in. rifled steel BBL, hardwood PG stock, 35.75 in. OAL, Mfg.1970s.

| | $65 | $40 | $30 | $25 | $20 | N/A | N/A |

SLAVIA 622 - .22 in. cal., BBC, SP, SS, 14.5 in. rifled steel BBL, hardwood PG stock, 35.75 in. OAL, Mfg.1970s.

| | $65 | $40 | $30 | $25 | $20 | N/A | N/A |

SLAVIA 625 - .177 cal., BBC, SP, 450 FPS, 15.75 in. barrel, adj. sights, wood stock, 4 lbs. Disc. 2003.

| | $50 | $40 | $30 | $20 | $10 | N/A | N/A |

Last MSR was $60.

SLAVIA 630 (CZ 77) - .177 cal., BBC, SP, 700 FPS, 21 in. barrel, adj. sights, wood stock, 6.6 lbs.

courtesy C Z

| MSR N/A | $75 | $70 | $60 | $50 | $40 | N/A | N/A |

SLAVIA 631 (CZ 77 LUX) - .177 cal., BBC, SP, 700 FPS, 21 in. barrel, adj. sights, checkered wood or synthetic stock, 6.6 lbs.

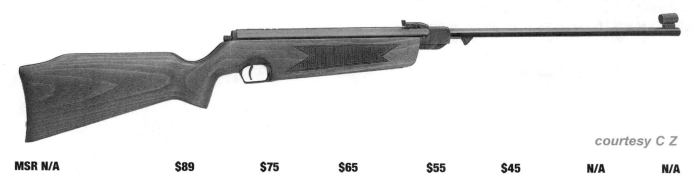

courtesy C Z

| MSR N/A | $89 | $75 | $65 | $55 | $45 | N/A | N/A |

CAP-CHUR EQUIPMENT

For information on CAP-CHUR Equipment tranquilizer guns, see Palmer Chemical & Equipment Co. in the "P" section.

CARBO-JET

For information on Carbo-Jet airguns, see Schimel in the "S" section.

GRADING	100%	95%	90%	80%	60%	40%	20%

CAROLUS

Previous trademark marketed by Hellstedt hardware store, located in Eskilstuna, Sweden.

PISTOL

CAROLUS - 4.5 mm cal. UL, SP, SS, one-piece wood stock, marked LHS with script CAROLUS, blue finish, stamped with a shield design with a contained S. Mfg.1941-1943.

courtesy Beeman Collection

	100%	95%	90%	80%	60%	40%	20%
	$395	$325	$275	$225	$175	N/A	N/A

Add 20% for factory box.

Box is blue with white label and red and black printing, marked Hellsteds Eskilstuna Svensk kvalitéprodukt Refflad pipa, kaliber 4,5 Skottställd på 6 meter Utmärkt övningsvapen LUFTPISTOLEN Carolus ESKILSTUNAFABRIKAT PRIS KR. 19.

CASELMAN

Previous trademark manufactured by Jeff Caselman, located in Cameron, MO circa 1990 to 1994.

Only one or two .308 cal. and one .45 cal. were made. Five or six specimens of the 9mm variety are known. The Caselman airguns are fully automatic and are fed from a 3000PSI bottle which serves as the buttstock. It is perhaps the first successful self-contained, fully automatic airgun. The 9mm guns have a .356in. bore, firing from a twenty-six-round vertical spring-fed magazine. Bullets are 122 grain flat point, soft lead, fired dry at about 750 FPS, MV, about 150 ft./lb. ME. Rate of fire about 600 RPM. The .45 cal. gun firestwenty rounds of 225 grain flat soft lead bullets at a somewhat higher rate of fire. Ad claims: Will saw off a 2x4 at 25 yards! The maker also sold plans and a video for a .30 in. cal. version. Caution: some units may have been built from plans by workers less skilled than this designer/maker. The authors and publisher wish to thank John Caruthfor his valuable assistance with the following information in this edition of the *Blue Book of Airguns*. Ref. Behling (2006).

RIFLES: FULL AUTOMATIC

CASELMAN RIFLE - .308, 9mm, or .45 cal., extremely fine construction, 26 in. bench rest grade barrels and firing from a closed bolt allow great accuracy,48 in. OAL, 16.5 lbs. Values established only for 9mm guns. Mfg. circa 1990-94.

courtesy Beeman Collection

Rarity precludes accurate pricing.

CENTERPOINT

For information on Centerpoint airguns, see Philippines Airguns in the "P" section.

GRADING	100%	95%	90%	80%	60%	40%	20%

CERTUS

Previous trademark manufactured by Cogswell & Harrison (Gunmakers) Ltd., located in London, England. Manufactured in Feltham, Middlesex, England.

Cogswell & Harrison is still one of England´s most prestigious old gunmaking firms. Founded in 1770 by Benjamin Cogswell, the firm was very highly regarded for dueling pistols and military sidearms for officers. Edgar Harrison was granted British patent 330105 for an airgun in June 1930. Pistols relating to this patent were produced only in late 1929 and into 1930.

The Certus is a solid, barrel cocking, spring-piston air pistol with just a superficial resemblance to a Webley air pistol with its barrel running the length of the gun above the compression tube. The Certus has a quite complex mechanism with the barrel pivoting at the rear for cocking, opposite to the Webley front pivot. A 1929 factory catalog indicates both the standard air pistol and the long barrel target version with removable shoulder stock, available in .177 cal. only and rifled. It was all blued finish, except for select walnut grips. Three specimens were reported as known in an August 2002 *Airgun World* article by Tim Saunders, but a very few more do exist. Current retail value in the $2,500-$3,500 range depending on condition and whether original box or case is included. Add 25% for long barrel target version or original shoulder stock.

courtesy Beeman Collection

CHALLENGE

For information on Challenge airguns, see Plymouth Air Rifle Company in the "P" section.

CHALLENGER ARMS CORPORATION

Previous distributor of airguns under the Challenger brand located in Eagle Rock (annexed to City of Los Angeles), CA.

These guns probably were made by Goodenow Manufacturing Company of Eric, PA about 1953-58. They included a pump pneumatic shotgun, a pump pneumatic and CO_2 rifle, a very solidly built pump pneumatic pistol and, finally, an equally well built CO_2 pistol. Construction and design was too good to be competitive at the time. Self-contained valve units, seals, and pump washers were designed for owner replacement. There is considerable confusion about the Plainsman name. It was first applied to the solidly built guns distributed by Challenger Arms Corporation and later used by Healthways for these same guns and then by Healthways for an entirely different, more economical series of CO_2 rifles and pistols. (Healthways probably did not actually manufacture any of the Plainsman airguns listed below, but rather only sold acquired inventory and packaged, perhaps made, shot shells with the Plainsman name combined with the Healthways brand.) Even later, the brand of Plainsmaster was used by Marksman for their Model 1049 CO_2 pistol. Marksman also used the name Plainsman for a slide action BB rifle.

Dunathan´s American BB Gun (1971) first reported two airgun models with the Challenger name. However, the gun he listed as an 1886 Challenger actually represents only a single patent model, perhaps made by the Plymouth Air Rifle Co., and is marked "Challenge". The second gun, listed as an 1887 Challenger, actually was made in small numbers, but its maker is not known (probably not Markham) and there seems to be no justification for referring to it under the Challenger name. The first verified use of the Challenger name for airguns seems to have been by the Challenger Arms Corporation. The Challenger name was again used in 1982-89 by Crosman for their versions of barrel cocking, spring-piston adult air rifles made by Dianawerk and Anschütz and, in 2000, on their own Model 2000 Challenger CO_2 bolt action rifle. Ref: AGNR - Jan. 1986.

For additional information on Plainsman Model airguns, see Healthways, Inc. in the "H" section.

PISTOLS

PLAINSMAN PNEUMATIC PISTOL - .177 or .22 cal., swinging arm pump pneumatic, SS, 300 FPS (.22 cal.) blue finish.

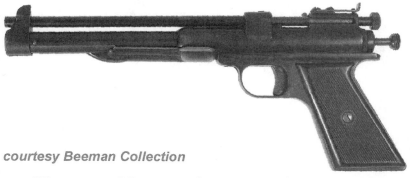

courtesy Beeman Collection

N/A	N/A	$600	$500	$400	$300	$250

Add 20% for .177 cal.

GRADING	100%	95%	90%	80%	60%	40%	20%

PLAINSMAN GAS PISTOL - .177 or .22 caliber, CO_2, SS, 380 FPS (.22 cal.), blue finish.

courtesy Beeman Collection

	N/A	N/A	$300	$225	$150	$100	$50

Add 25% for .177 cal.

RIFLES

PLAINSMAN PNEUMATIC RIFLE - .177 or .22 cal., swinging forearm multiple pump pneumatic, bolt or knurled knob action, SS, hardwood or walnut pump handle/forearm and buttstock.

courtesy Beeman Collection

⊕ *Plainsman Pneumatic Rifle Bolt Handle Variant* - .177 or .22 cal., cocking rod with bolt handle.

	N/A	N/A	$325	$275	$225	$175	$125

Add 50% for .177 cal. Add 15% for walnut.

⊕ *Plainsman Pneumatic Rifle Knurled Knob Variant* - .177 or .22 cal., cocking rod with knurled knob handle.

	N/A	N/A	$325	$275	$225	$175	$125

Add 10% for .177 cal. Add 15% for walnut.

PLAINSMAN GAS RIFLE - .22 cal., CO_2, SS,similar to Plainsman Pneumatic Rifle except, one piece hardwood or walnut stock.

⊕ *Plainsman Gas Rifle Bolt Handle Variant* - .22 cal., CO_2, SS, cocking rod with bolt handle.

courtesy Beeman Collection

	N/A	N/A	$375	$300	$225	$150	$75

Add 20% for bulk fill version. Add 15% for walnut.

GRADING	100%	95%	90%	80%	60%	40%	20%

⊛ *Plainsman Gas Rifle Knurled Knob Variant* - .22 cal., CO_2, SS, cocking rod with knurled knob handle.

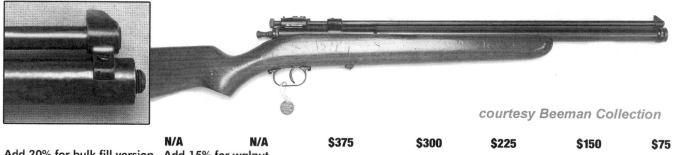

courtesy Beeman Collection

		N/A	N/A	$375	$300	$225	$150	$75

Add 20% for bulk fill version. Add 15% for walnut.

SHOTGUNS

PLAINSMAN AIR SHOTGUN - .28 cal., swinging arm pump pneumatic, similar to Plainsman Pneumatic Rifle, except .28 cal. and marked "S" on RHS, forward side of receiver, uses special pre-packed cardboard shot tubes, hardwood or walnut pump handle/fore-arm and buttstock, five to ten pumps produced enough power to drive a small pattern of shot into a pine board atten meters.

courtesy Beeman Collection

N/A	N/A	$375	$300	$225	$150	$75

CHICAGO COIN MACHINE CO.

Previous manufacturer of coin operated air machine guns for high end shooting galleries. Division of Chicago Dynamic Industries, Inc., 1725 Diversey Blvd., Chicago, Ill. Produced the Commando Air Machine Guns under patent No. 2,837,076 issued June 3, 1958, from about 1958 to the late 1970s. Very well designed, complex, and extremely well built, the 1958 purchase cost of $995, adjusted for inflation to 2007 is about $6900 each! Ref. Behling (2006).

MACHINE GUN

COMMANDO AIR MACHINE GUN - .219 in. steel balls, full-auto in 3 shot bursts, each use adjustable from 130 to 525 shots, 150 rpm. Self contained electric air compressor. 110 volt AC. 8000 round ball hopper. 250 fps. 18 in. smoothbore bbl., 44.3 OAL, 74 lbs. Front post sight, rear circle-on-glass sight. Not marked w/ brand. Fired w/ two hands froma swiveling tripod. 1958 - late 1970s. 12 known specimens.

courtesy Beeman Collection

N/A	N/A	$3,750	$3,000	$2,250	$1,500	N/A

Subtract 15% if without tripod. Add 5 - 10% for wooden case.

CHINESE STATE FACTORIES

In 1987, John Walter wrote in the Fourth Edition of *The Airgun Book*: The Chinese products are usually crudely if reasonably sturdily made, and offer lower power and inferior accuracy than most of their Western European rivals. Some of these products are unauthorized copies of European designs such as the Chinese GLOBE, an imitation Feinwerkbau Model 65 air pistol, illustrated here. The value of this gun would be under $150 in 100% condition, but many of the new specimens are so roughly finished as to appear somewhat worn. While many of the airgun products from the Chinese State Factories have improved since then, the collector and shooter should carefully balance quality, backing, durability, ownership pride, and price.

courtesy Beeman Collection

CLASSIC

For information on Classic airguns, see Gun Toys SRL in the "G" section.

COGSWELL & HARRISON

For information on Cogswell & Harrison airguns, see Certus in this section.
For more information and current pricing on both new and used Cogswell & Harrison firearms, please refer to the *Blue Book of Gun Values* by S.P. Fjestad (also available online).

COLT'S MANUFACTURING COMPANY, INC.

Current manufacturer located in Hartford, CT. Colt airguns are currently imported and serviced exclusively by Umarex USA located in Fort Smith, AR beginning 2007. Previously imported and serviced exclusively by Crosman Corp. located in East Bloomfield, NY 2003-2006 and by Daisy Manufacturing Company located in Rogers, AR.

Colt airguns are manufactured by Umarex, the current owner of Walther. Colt airguns are faithful copies of the famous Model 1911 A1. With the size and weight of a real Colt, five versions are available, including a special 160th Anniversary model. Many of the same precision options offered for the cartridge pistols have been available for the airguns, including a barrel compensator, competition (tuning set with speed hammer, rapid release double thumb safety, beavertail grip safety, grip with thumb guard, backstrap, sights) features, and Colt Top Point (Red Dot) heads-up sighting scope. All models are pre-drilled for the Serendipity SL optical sight.

For more information and current pricing on both new and used Colt firearms, please refer to the *Blue Book of Gun Values* by S.P. Fjestad (also available online).

PISTOLS

GOVERNMENT MODEL 1911 A1 - .177 cal., CO_2, semi-auto, SA and DA, eight-shot rotary magazine, 5 in. rifled steel BBL, 425 FPS, blade front/adj. rear sight, trigger safety, grip safety, blue or nickel finish, checkered black plastic or smooth wood grips, 8.6 in. OAL, 2.38 lbs.

courtesy Umarex USA

MSR $223	$195	$165	$135	$100	$80	N/A	N/A

Add $22 for nickel finish. Add $30-$50 for compensator. Add $40-$60 for wood grips.

GRADING	100%	95%	90%	80%	60%	40%	20%

160TH ANNIVERSARY MODEL 1911 A1 - .177 cal., CO_2, semi-auto, SA and DA, eight-shot cylinder magazine, 393 FPS, post front/adj. rear sight, trigger safety, grip safety, 5 in. rifled barrel, polished black finish with checkered white grips, slide marked with Colt 160th Anniversary banner, Colt logo, and floral scrollwork, 2.38 lbs. Disc. 2003.

	$195	$150	$115	$90	$65	N/A	N/A

Last MSR was $249.

MODEL 1911 A1 GOLD CUP - .177 cal., CO_2, semi-auto, SA and DA, eight-shot cylinder magazine, 393 FPS, post front/adj. rear sight, trigger safety, grip safety, 5 in. rifled barrel, standard black finish with checkered black plastic grips, 2.38 lbs. Disc. 2003.

	$225	$165	$125	$100	$75	N/A	N/A

Last MSR was $279.

Add $20 for nickel plated finish.

MODEL 1911 A1 TROPHY MATCH - .177 cal., CO_2, semi-auto, SA and DA, eight-shot cylinder magazine, 393 FPS, post front/adj. rear sight, trigger safety, grip safety, includes bridge mount, Top Point (red dot) sight, all competition accessories, carrying case and two rotary magazines. Disc. 2003.

	$555	$475	$395	$295	$195	N/A	N/A

Last MSR was $699.

Add $100 for nickel plated finish.

MODEL 1911 A1 TACTICAL - .177 cal., CO_2, semi-auto, SA and DA, eight-shot cylinder magazine, 5 in. BBL, 425 FPS, post front/adj. rear sight, trigger safety, grip safety, includes bridge mount, Top Point (red dot) sight, carrying case and two rotary magazines, 13.75 in. OAL, 2.9 lbs. Mfg. 2007-current.

courtesy Umarex USA

MSR $330	$295	$255	$195	N/A	N/A	N/A	N/A

COLUMBIA

Probably made by the Adams & Westlake Company, Chicago, IL about 1905 to 1915.

One model, a simple push-barrel, single shot, sheet metal BB gun. Marked "COLUMBIA" with Adams & Westlake name and address in a circular logo.

Research is ongoing with this trademark, and more information will be included both online and in future editions.

RIFLES

COLUMBIA - .180 cal. BB, SS, SP. Only one model known, an unusual push-barrel cocking system, sheet metal BB gun. To cock, entire upper body of gun is moved back to cocked position. Unusual tap-loading mechanism looks like an oil lamp part (Adams and Westlake were a large oil lamp manufacturer). Marked "COLUMBIA" in one-inch letters on the side of the buttstock. Stock also with circular logo: "MADE BY ADAMS & WESTLAKE CO. CHICAGO. PAT. APPLD." Nickel-plated metal; slab sided stock. 2.5 lbs., 8.5 in. smoothbore barrel, 33.3 in. OAL.

courtesy Beeman Collection

Good condition examples will retail in the $2,500 range.

Extremely rare, perhaps less than two or three specimens known (much more rare than 1st or 2nd model Daisy!).

GRADING	100%	95%	90%	80%	60%	40%	20%

COLUMBIAN & BAILEY AIRGUNS

This line of airguns began in 1892 with the Bailey BB guns produced by previous manufacturer E.E. Bailey Manufacturing Company in Philadelphia, PA.

The Bailey Company was not successful and only about a dozen Bailey specimens are known today. In 1893 a partnership of Elmer E. Bailey and William G. Smith began to produce airguns under the Columbian trademark. Upon Bailey's death in 1898, the partnership reverted to William Smith. Smith's company was taken over by William Heilprin in 1907 and continued producing airguns until the early 1920s. The airguns of these makers are often referred to as Heilprin airguns, but Heilprin was not involved with most of the Columbian models or most of their production. He produced only the last model of the elite cast iron models and then shifted into sheet medal models- most of those rather quickly expired. The break-open Models L and S, based on Heilprin's patents, were not successful; only a handful of specimens are known today.

Bailey's famous second patent, #507470, issued October 24, 1893, is the key to the Columbian airguns. The patent's key feature, having a reciprocating air chamber enclosed within the gun's frame casting, was central to the Columbian airguns. The 1000 shot design format was a standard of the BB gun industry for over 80 years.

The best known examples of the Columbian line are the heavy, cast metal BB rifles which not only weighed far more than any BB guns of the time but cost much more. When Daisy and other common BB guns were selling for $0.69 to $1.00, the Columbians were the elite airguns, selling for $1.95 to $3.50. Their solid construction, durability, and cost gave a boy who owned one tremendous neighborhood status.

William Johnson's 2002 book "Bailey and Columbian Air Rifles" is the absolute key to this complex line of airguns. We will follow his organization of the early, heavy, cast iron models into 11 types and the final sheet metal models into three lever action and two break open models. Not only must we stop referring to these guns as Heilprins, we must stop referring to some as the Squirrel Model, the Buffalo model, etc. The animal figures can help narrow down the choices, BUT there are three different squirrels in 4 different type groups for a grand total of 9 "squirrel" models. There are two different stag's heads in two different type groups for a total of 4 models and two full buffalos in two different type groups. This section probably can lead to the identification of almost all models, but only Johnson's book and CD can confirm the ID and give you the known variations and the many details.

Most of the models do not trade often enough to clearly establish meaningful values. Johnson's rarity ratings have been translated here into estimated numbers of existing specimens per model. Values can be estimated to a fair degree by comparing rarity factors with the few fairly well established values.

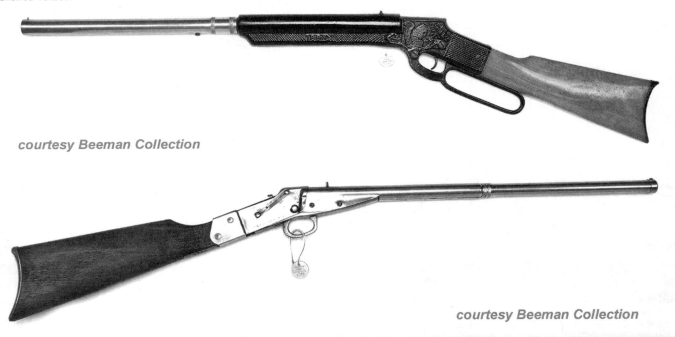

courtesy Beeman Collection

courtesy Beeman Collection

CAST IRON RIFLES

Unless otherwise noted, all were genuine gravity-fed, 1000 shot, repeating BB rifles, large BB/.180 in. cal. w/ smoothbore brass barrels, Winchester-style cocking levers, nickel plated barrel shrouds, and heavy cast iron frames, painted black or nickeled, with ornate raised decorative designs. Johnson has classified the guns into 11 frame types - decorative designs, including the types of bird or mammal shown, within a type are identical except for dates cast in the date panels- unless otherwise noted. (Specifications given are for the Beeman Collection specimens illustrated - specifications of the same model may vary with bbl length, etc.)

TYPE I – BAILEY FIRST MODEL - Frame open at top, no decoration, 1000 shot. Perhaps made 1892-95. No specimens known.

TYPE II – BAILEY SECOND MODEL - similar to First Model, but w/ embossed floral, animal designs, and checkering over entire frame. Large stag's head embossed just ahead of trigger. Barrel w/ shot tube often broken free of frame. Several variations. Usually marked: BAILEY 1000 SHOT AIR RIFLE, PAT'D NOV. 29,'92. Retail: $4.00 black paint, $5.00 nickel frame. Early variation - Rear sight cast into frame, bbl. usually 14", only nickel-plated. Late variation - Rear sight screws into frame, bbl. usually 12.6", nickel or black frames.

N/A	$3,500	$2,750	$2,250	$1,750	$1,250	$750

TYPE III – COLUMBIAN MODEL 1893 - Frame closed along top (as are all future models). Plain frame w/o markings or embossed designs. 13" brass bbl.

GRADING	100%	95%	90%	80%	60%	40%	20%

TYPE IV – COLUMBIAN MODEL 1894 - Sitting squirrel embossed above trigger. Date not cast on gun. First use of sliding loading sleeve cover.

TYPE V – COLUMBIAN MODELS 1895 – 1899 - Sitting squirrel embossed above trigger. Date cast on LHS of iron forearm.

- **Model 1895** - 15-25 specimens known.
- **Model 1896** - 25-50 known.
- **Model 1897** - 8-10 known.
- **Model 1898** - 25-50 known (inc. 500 shot carbine version stamped JUNIOR on stock) (specimen shown: 4.75 lbs., 34.9 in OAL).

courtesy Beeman Collection

- **Model 1899** - 10-15 known (inc. carbine version), rolled steel barrel.

TYPE VI – COLUMBIAN MODEL 1898 (BIG FRAME) Running Buffalo (Bison) embossed above trigger LHS, standing buck on RHS. 1898 cast on forearm panel. Early production with heavy cast lever. About 10-15 black known, but nickel was offered. Retail: $2.00 black, $2.50 nickel frame.

	N/A	$2,750	$2,250	$1,750	$1,250	$750	$400

TYPE VII – COLUMBIAN JUNIOR MODEL - Sitting squirrel embossed above trigger. Short barrel, 500 shot. Marked JUNIOR on LHS metal forearm. Distinctive cocking lever w/ ring loop at back end. About 6 specimens known. 1897-98.

	N/A	$2,750	$2,250	$1,750	$1,250	$750	$400

TYPE VIII – COLUMBIAN CHAMPION MODEL - Decorations are raised embossing but markings "Champion" or "Junior" are incised. Rabbit and bird figures. Regular Version: Marked CHAMPION on LHS of iron forearm. Early versions w/ brass bbl., later w/ steel bbl. 25-50 specimens known. Retail = $1.75 black, $2.25 nickel. Junior Version: Marked JUNIOR on LHS of iron forearm, 1899 on RHS. Full size cocking lever loop. 30.5 in. OAL. Retail $1.50.

TYPE IX – BARTEN COLUMBIAN MODELS - Sitting squirrel embossed above trigger on both sides of receiver. Slim forearm. Unusual cocking lever w/ loop far behind trigger.36 in.OAL. Only type produced by Joseph Barten under royalty from Cora Bailey after Elmer Bailey's death. Retail: $2.25 black, $2.50 nickel. 1899-1902.

- **Columbian Version** - Embossed COLUMBIAN in large letters LHS of iron forearm. Rifle and carbine lengths. About 15-20 specimens known.

	N/A	$2,750	$2,250	$1,750	$1,250	$750	$400

- **Model 99 Version** - Identical to Columbian version except for name.

TYPE X – COLUMBIAN MODELS 1900, 1906, 1908 - Only model with floral, bird, and snake designs embossed above trigger and tiny foxes and squirrel embossed on iron forearm. Only model with dates cast in LHS panel behind trigger. Rifles and carbines.

- **Model 1900** - perhaps over 200 known. (Shown: 4.25 lbs, 34.8 in OAL).

	N/A	$600	$500	$400	$300	$200	$100

- **Model 1906** - COLUMBIAN cast on LHS of iron forearm. 15-25 known. (Specimen shown: 4.0 lbs. 30 in OAL).

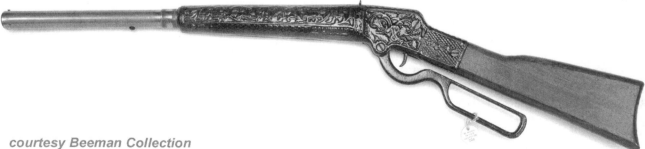

courtesy Beeman Collection

- **Model 1908** - same as 1906 except for cast date. 50-200 known, (early version only w/ OCT. 23, '93 pat. date, later version adds DEC. 8, '08 pat. date).

TYPE XI – COLUMBIAN MODEL 1902 - SS or Repeater, Running Buffalo (Bison) embossed on LHS and Deer on RHS above trigger. No checkering in metal, but the small frame is completely covered with embossed decoration. 27 ½ in OAL. Nickel finish. Mfg. 1901-03.

GRADING	100%	95%	90%	80%	60%	40%	20%

SHEET METAL RIFLES

Sheet metal designs were introduced in 1907 when William Heilprin took over production from William Smith. Several unique features were added, most diagnostic is a thumb operated "safety" which must be held down to fire the gun, a feature of dubious safety value which proved very unpopular in BB guns produced by other makers in the 20th century.

LEVER ACTION RIFLES

All marked HEILPRIN MFG. CO on RHS of receiver w/ 1893, 1908, 1909 patent dates plus the model letter. All Winchester style lever cocking lever, .173 in. BB repeaters, SP, nickel finish.

COLUMBIAN MODEL M - sheet metal cocking lever and trigger resulted in poor survival. About 1909-1911. 10-15 specimens known.

COLUMBIAN MODEL E - Cast iron cocking lever and trigger. Handsome design w/ large nickel plated, shiny areas. 2.9 lbs., 34.6 in. OAL. Mfg. 1912- 1920s, perhaps over 50 specimens known.

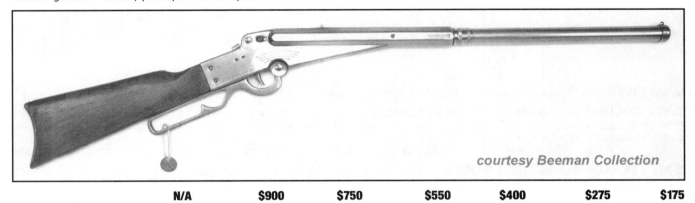

courtesy Beeman Collection

N/A	$900	$750	$550	$400	$275	$175

COLUMBIAN MODEL J - same as Model E but w/ 8 in. bbl and no buttplate. 4-5 known.

BARREL-COCKING RIFLES

Barrel cocking design w/ very touchy Heilprin hold-down safety. Cannot be uncocked. 1913-14.

COLUMBIAN MODEL L - Repeater w/ typical Columbian sliding cover sleeve for loading at rear of barrel. Trigger guard is the trigger. Shaped stock. Same metal buttplate as Model E. Nickel plated. Stamped on top of barrel shroud: COLUMBIAN MODEL L 350 SHOT HEILPRIN MFG. Co. PHILA. PA. U.S.A. PATS. PENDING. One specimen apparently w/o marking. 1.9 lbs., 32 in. OAL. Five known specimens.

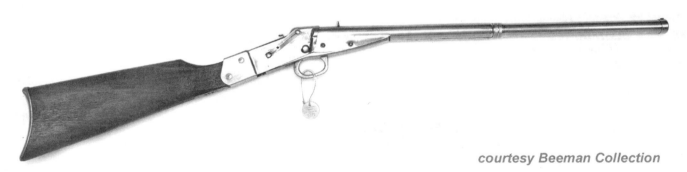

courtesy Beeman Collection

N/A	N/A	$2,150	$1,550	$1,050	$650	$350

Engraved inscription "W.R.A. 3-19-14" indicates specimen is from Winchester Repeating Arms Company airgun collection.

COLUMBIAN MODEL S - similar to Model L except, single shot, no buttplate. Four known.

COMATIC

For information on Comatic airguns, see Venturini in the "V" section.

COMENTO

For information on Comento, see Bascaran in the "B" section.

COMET

For information on Comet airguns, see Milbro in the "M" section.

GRADING	100%	95%	90%	80%	60%	40%	20%

COMPASSECO, INC.

Current importer/distributor located in Bardstown, KY beginning late-1980s. Dealer and consumer direct sales.

Compasseco has been importing/distributing airguns from China since the late-1980s, when most were priced well under $100. During the past several years, the Compasseco airgun line has been considerably improved and expanded. Circa 2008, the Compasseco ecommerce website (see Trademark Index) features airguns from some of the top trademarks world wide with price points for every level of consumer. Also available is virtually every airgun accessory usable.

PISTOLS

TECH FORCE SS2 - .177 cal., SL, SP, 520 FPS, recoilless action, includes carrying case, match adj. trigger, 2.75 lbs. Disc. 2007.

	100%	95%	90%	80%	60%	40%	20%
	$236	$195	$155	$115	$75	N/A	N/A

Last MSR was $295.

TECH FORCE S2-1 - .177 cal., BBC, SP, 2.6 lbs.

	100%	95%	90%	80%	60%	40%	20%
MSR $55	$35	$25	$20	$15	$10	N/A	N/A

TECH FORCE 8 - .177 cal., BBC, SP, 400 FPS, adj. rear sight, ambidextrous polymer grip, 7.25 in. barrel, 2.6 lbs. Disc. 2004.

	100%	95%	90%	80%	60%	40%	20%
	$45	$35	$30	$20	$15	N/A	N/A

Last MSR was $60.

TECH FORCE 35 - .177 cal., UL, SP, 400 FPS., adj. rear sight, 2.8 lbs.

	100%	95%	90%	80%	60%	40%	20%
MSR $40	$30	$25	$20	$15	$10	N/A	N/A

RIFLES

BS-4 OLYMPIC - .177 cal., 640 FPS, SL, SP, recoilless, adj. trigger, micro adj. diopter sight, stippled stock, adj. buttplate, case, 43.3 in. OAL, 10.8 lbs. Disc. 2007.

	100%	95%	90%	80%	60%	40%	20%
	$435	$355	$265	$175	$85	N/A	N/A

Last MSR was $495.

TECH FORCE 6 - .177 cal., SL, SP, 800/750 FPS, all metal, tactical configuration, folding stock, adj. rear sight, 35.5 in. OAL, 6 lbs.

	100%	95%	90%	80%	60%	40%	20%
MSR N/A	$70	$55	$45	$35	$25	N/A	N/A

TECH FORCE 11 - .177 cal., BBC, SP, 600 FPS, trigger safety, Monte Carlo stock, 38.5 in. OAL, 5.5 lbs. Disc. 2007.

	100%	95%	90%	80%	60%	40%	20%
	$30	$20	$15	$10	$5	N/A	N/A

Last MSR was $35.

TECH FORCE 12 - .177 cal., BBC, SP, 750 FPS, trigger safety, Monte Carlo stock, 40 in. OAL, 5.7 lbs. New 2003.

	100%	95%	90%	80%	60%	40%	20%
MSR N/A	$77	$60	$45	$40	$35	N/A	N/A

TECH FORCE 15 - .177 cal., BBC, SP, SS, youth dimensions, 18 in. bbl., 650 FPS, adj. rear and hooded ramp front sights, scope stop, hardwood Monte Carlo style PG stock, 38.4 in. OAL, 5.25 lbs. Mfg. 2008-current.

	100%	95%	90%	80%	60%	40%	20%
MSR N/A	$40	$35	$30	$25	N/A	N/A	N/A

TECH FORCE 20 - .177 or .22 cal., BBC, SP, 1000/750 FPS, dovetail receiver, adj. sights, adj. trigger, trigger safety, Monte Carlo stock, recoil pad, 43 in. OAL, 7.3 lbs. Mfg. 2003-05.

	100%	95%	90%	80%	60%	40%	20%
	$120	$90	$70	$55	$35	N/A	N/A

Last MSR was $150.

TECH FORCE 21 - .177 or .22 cal., SL, SP, 1000/750 FPS, dovetail receiver, adj. sights, adj. trigger, trigger safety, Monte Carlo stock, recoil pad, 46 in. OAL, 9.3 lbs. New 2003.

	100%	95%	90%	80%	60%	40%	20%
MSR N/A	$150	$120	$85	$60	$50	N/A	N/A

TECH FORCE 22 - .177 or .22 cal., BBC, SP, 700/600 FPS, adj. sights, trigger safety, Monte Carlo stock, 43 inb. OAL, 6.4 lbs. Disc. 2007.

	100%	95%	90%	80%	60%	40%	20%
	$30	$25	$20	$15	$10	N/A	N/A

Last MSR was $36.

⊘ *Tech Force 22A* - similar to Tech Force 22, except has ramp front sight. Disc. 2004.

	100%	95%	90%	80%	60%	40%	20%
	$40	$30	$25	$20	$15	N/A	N/A

Last MSR was $46.

TECH FORCE 25 - .177 or .22 cal., BBC, SP, 1000/800 FPS, adj. trigger with safety, Monte Carlo stock, adj. buttplate, 46.2 in. OAL, 7.5 lbs. Disc. 2007.

	100%	95%	90%	80%	60%	40%	20%
	$100	$80	$60	$40	$30	N/A	N/A

Last MSR was $125.

TECH FORCE B26 - .177 or .22 cal., BBC, SP, SS, 16 in. rifled steel BBL, 1000/750 FPS, dovetail receiver, adj. TRUGLO fiber optic sights, adj. trigger, trigger safety, Monte Carlo stock, recoil pad, 43 in. OAL, 7.3 lbs. Mfg. 2008-current.

	100%	95%	90%	80%	60%	40%	20%
MSR N/A	$190	$150	$120	$90	N/A	N/A	N/A

⊘ *Tech Force B26TH* - .177 or .22 cal., BBC, SP, SS, 16 in. rifled steel BBL, 1000/820 FPS, dovetail receiver, adj. TRUGLO fiber optic sights, adj. trigger, trigger safety, thumbhole Monte Carlo style stock, recoil pad, 43 in. OAL, 7.3 lbs. Mfg. 2008-current.

	100%	95%	90%	80%	60%	40%	20%
MSR N/A	$220	$190	$150	$120	N/A	N/A	N/A

GRADING	100%	95%	90%	80%	60%	40%	20%

TECH FORCE 31 - .177 cal., SL, SP, 750/550 FPS, adj. rear sight, folding stock, 36 in. OAL, 7 lbs. Disc. 2007.

	$65	$55	$45	$35	$25	N/A	N/A

Last MSR was $75.

TECH FORCE 3-1 - .177 or .22 cal., SL, SP, SS, 750/550 FPS, adj. rear sight, folding stock, 36 in. OAL, 7 lbs. Mfg. 2008-current.

MSR N/A	$79	$65	$55	$45	N/A	N/A	N/A

TECH FORCE 34 - .177 or .22 cal., UL, SP, 850/650 FPS, trigger safety, Monte Carlo hardwood stock, 41 in. OAL, 7.7 lbs. New 2004.

MSR N/A	$53	$45	$35	$30	$25	N/A	N/A

Add $10 for Tech Force® 34 Scope Combo with a Tech Force® 4x20 scope and rings.

TECH FORCE 36 - .177 cal., UL, SP, 900 FPS, trigger safety, Monte Carlo stock, 7.4 lbs. Disc. 2004.

	$85	$75	$60	$45	$30	N/A	N/A

Last MSR was $95.

TECH FORCE 38 - .177 or .22 cal., UL, SP, 850/650 FPS, trigger safety, hardwood stock, 7 lbs. Disc. 2007.

	$45	$40	$35	$30	$20	N/A	N/A

Last MSR was $53.

✿ *Tech Force 38D* - .177 cal., similar to Tech Force 38, except includes 4x20 scope. Disc. 2004.

	$65	$50	$40	$30	$20	N/A	N/A

Last MSR was $74.

✿ *Tech Force 38GD* - .177 or .22 cal., similar to Tech Force 38, except has Monte Carlo stock and lengthened under-lever. Disc. 2002.

	$45	$35	$30	$20	$15	N/A	N/A

Last MSR was $60.

TECH FORCE B40 - .177 or .22 cal. UL, SP, SS, 17.5 in. rifled steel BBL, 1050/750 FPS, built in sound suppressor, blue finish, Monte Carlo hardwood stock with recoil pad, two-stage adj. trigger with safety, 41.25 in. OAL, 8.5 lbs. New 2005.

MSR N/A	$295	$225	$195	$150	$125	N/A	N/A

✿ *Tech Force 40D* - .177 or .22 cal., BBC, SP, 700/600 FPS, hardwood stock, trigger safety, 43.5 in. OAL, 6.5 lbs. Disc. 2007.

	$32	$25	$20	$15	$10	N/A	N/A

Last MSR was $40.

TECH FORCE 41 - .177 cal., SL, SP, 800 FPS, hardwood Monte Carlo stock, trigger safety, 40.5 in. OAL, 7.2 lbs.

MSR N/A	$53	$40	$35	$30	$20	N/A	N/A

TECH FORCE B50 - .177 or .22 cal., PCP, semi-pistol grip Monte Carlo style wood stock with recoil pad, muzzle brake, manual safety. New 2005.

MSR N/A	$350	$280	$245	$225	$175	N/A	N/A

Add $25 for .22 cal.

TECH FORCE B51 - .177 or .22 cal., PCP, thumbhole Monte Carlo wood stock with recoil pad, muzzle brake, manual safety. New 2005.

MSR N/A	$370	$300	$265	$235	$195	N/A	N/A

Add $25 for .22 cal.

TECH FORCE 51 - .177 cal., BBC, SP, 500 FPS, hardwood/folding stock with pistol grip, automatic safety, adj. sights, 14 in. barrel, 6 lbs. Disc. 2001.

	$60	$50	$40	$30	$20	N/A	N/A

Last MSR was $70.

TECH FORCE 5-10 - .177 cal., UL, multi-stroke pneumatic, 300-750 FPS, ten-shot mag., adj. sights, adj. wire stock, 15 in. BBL, 4.50 lbs.

MSR N/A	$90	$75	$60	$40	$30	N/A	N/A

TECH FORCE 66 - .177 cal., SL, SP, ten-shot mag., 750 FPS, 18 in. barrel, tactical configuration, includes briefcase and 4x32 scope. Disc. 2002, reintroduced 2005.

MRS N/A	$100	$85	$70	$55	$40	N/A	N/A

TECH FORCE 67 - .177 cal., similar to TF 66, except SS, includes briefcase and 4x32 scope. Mfg. 2001-04, reintroduced 2006.

MSR N/A	$120	$90	$70	$50	$30	N/A	N/A

TECH FORCE 78 - .177 or .22 cal., BA, two CO_2 cartridges, 20 in. barrel, adj. rear and ramp front sights, 750/600 FPS, wood stock, adj. trigger, 40 in. OAL, 6.6 lbs.

MSR N/A	$90	$75	$60	$40	$30	N/A	N/A

✿ *Tech Force 78 Gold Series* - .177 or .22 cal., BA, two CO_2 cartridges, 20 in. barrel, adj. rear and ramp front sights, 750/600 FPS, wood stock, adj. trigger, 40 in. OAL, 6.6 lbs.

MSR N/A	$100	$75	$60	$40	$30	N/A	N/A

Add $50 for Tech Force® 78 Gold Series Scope Combo with a Tech Force® 4x32AR Scope and rings.

✿ *Tech Force 78 Gold Series Scope Combo* - .177 or .22 cal., BA, two CO_2 cartridges, 20 in. barrel, adj. rear and ramp front sights, Tech Force® 4x32AR Scope and rings, 750/600 FPS, wood stock, adj. trigger, 40 in. OAL, 6.6 lbs.

MSR N/A	$100	$75	$60	$40	$30	N/A	N/A

GRADING	100%	95%	90%	80%	60%	40%	20%
⚙ *Tech Force 78T* - .177 or .22 cal., CO_2, built in bulk fill adaptor for 88gr cartridge, 20 in. barrel, 700/600 FPS, bolt action, wood stock, adj. trigger, 40 in. OAL, 6.6 lbs. Mfg. 2005-current.							
MSR N/A	$100	$75	$60	$45	$30	N/A	N/A

TECH FORCE 79 - .177 or .22 cal., CO_2, BA, 20.50 in. barrel, 700/520 FPS, grooved receiver, competition style wood stock, adj. trigger, diopter peep sight, 40 in. OAL, 6.6 lbs. New 2001.

	100%	95%	90%	80%	60%	40%	20%
MSR N/A	$180	$145	$125	$85	$65	N/A	N/A

⚙ *Tech Force 79T* - .177 or .22 cal., CO_2, built in bulk fill adaptor, 700/550 FPS, bolt action, 20.50 in. barrel, grooved receiver, competition style wood stock, adj. trigger, diopter peep sight, 40 in. OAL, 7.4 lbs. New 2005.

	100%	95%	90%	80%	60%	40%	20%
MSR N/A	$200	$165	$145	$95	$75	N/A	N/A

⚙ *Tech Force 79 TH* - .177 or .22 cal., CO_2, BA, 20.50 in. barrel, 700/520 FPS, grooved receiver, thumbhole wood stock, adj. trigger, diopter peep sight, 40 in. OAL, 6.6 lbs. New 2006.

	100%	95%	90%	80%	60%	40%	20%
MSR N/A	$180	$145	$125	$85	$65	N/A	N/A

⚙ *Tech Force 79 TACTICAL* - .177 or .22 cal., CO_2, BA, 20.50 in. barrel, 700/520 FPS, grooved receiver, all-weather black tactical thumbhole stock, adj. trigger, diopter peep sight, Tech Force 4X32 AR scope with adjustable objective and target turrets, Tech force Tactical Flash Light and Laser, 40 in. OAL, 6.6 lbs. New 2007.

	100%	95%	90%	80%	60%	40%	20%
MSR N/A	$280	$235	$185	$115	$75	N/A	N/A

TECH FORCE 88 - .177 cal., SL, SP, 850 FPS, 19.50 in. barrel, adj. sights, safety, 7.50 lbs. Disc. 2007.

	100%	95%	90%	80%	60%	40%	20%
	$85	$65	$45	$35	$25	N/A	N/A

Last MSR was $95.

TECH FORCE 89 - .177 cal., SL, SP, bullpup configuration, extending buttplate, 600 FPS, 25 in. overall length. Mfg. 1999-2001.

	100%	95%	90%	80%	60%	40%	20%
	$80	$70	$50	$35	$25	N/A	N/A

Last MSR was $110.

TECH FORCE 97 - .177 or .22 cal., UL, SP, 900/700 FPS, 16 in. barrel, adj. sights, grooved receiver for scope mounting, automatic safety, oil finished Monte Carlo stock with recoil pad, 43 in. OAL, 7.40 lbs. New 1999.

	100%	95%	90%	80%	60%	40%	20%
MSR N/A	$100	$85	$70	$45	$30	N/A	N/A

Add $15 for an installed MacCari spring.

⚙ *Tech Force 97S Scope Combo* - .177 or .22 cal., UL, SP, 900/700 FPS, 16 in. barrel, adj. sights, grooved receiver for scope mounting, TF 4x32AR scope and rings, automatic safety, oil finished Monte Carlo stock with recoil pad, 43 in. OAL, 7.40 lbs. New 1999.

	100%	95%	90%	80%	60%	40%	20%
MSR N/A	$150	$100	$85	$70	$45	N/A	N/A

⚙ *Tech Force 97SC Scope Combo* - .177 or .22 cal., UL, SP, 900/700 FPS, 16 in. barrel, adj. sights, grooved receiver for scope mounting, TF 2-7x32AR scope and rings, automatic safety, oil finished, Monte Carlo stock with recoil pad, 43 in. OAL, 7.40 lbs. New 2007.

	100%	95%	90%	80%	60%	40%	20%
MSR N/A	$160	$115	$95	$75	$50	N/A	N/A

Tech Force® Flat Target Trap, Targets, and 500 rounds of Tech Force Match Pellets, but also a Rifle Case

⚙ *Tech Force 97X Scope Combo* - .177 or .22 cal., UL, SP, 900/700 FPS, 16 in. barrel, adj. sights, grooved receiver for scope mounting, TF 4x32AR scope and rings, automatic safety, oil finished, Monte Carlo stock with recoil pad, Tech Force® Flat Target Trap, Targets, 500 rounds of Tech Force Match Pellets, and rifle case, 43 in. OAL, 7.40 lbs. New 2007.

	100%	95%	90%	80%	60%	40%	20%
MSR N/A	$160	$115	$95	$75	$50	N/A	N/A

TECH FORCE 99 - .177 or .22 cal., UL, SP, 1000/800 FPS, 19.50 in. barrel, MacCari spring, adj. sights, grooved receiver for scope mounting, automatic safety, oil finished Monte Carlo stock with recoil pad, 7.50 lbs. Mfg. 2000-2007.

	100%	95%	90%	80%	60%	40%	20%
	$169	$135	$115	$80	$55	N/A	N/A

⚙ *Tech Force 99 Magnum* - .177 or .22 cal., UL, SP, 1100/900 FPS, 18 in. barrel, adj. sights w/ front sight inserts, grooved receiver for scope mounting, automatic safety, oil finished Monte Carlo stock with recoil pad, anti-beartrap lock and automatic safety, 44.5 in. OAL, 8 lbs. Mfg. 2007-current.

	100%	95%	90%	80%	60%	40%	20%
MSR N/A	$169	$135	$115	$80	$55	N/A	N/A

⚙ *Tech Force 99S Magnum Scope Combo* - .177 or .22 cal., UL, SP, 1100/900 FPS, 18 in. barrel, adj. sights w/ front sight inserts, grooved receiver for scope mounting, 2-7x32AR scope w/ rings, automatic safety, oil finished Monte Carlo stock with recoil pad, anti-beartrap lock and automatic safety, 44.5 in. OAL, 8 lbs. Mfg. 2007-current.

	100%	95%	90%	80%	60%	40%	20%
MSR N/A	$230	$169	$135	$115	$80	N/A	N/A

⚙ *Tech Force 99SC Magnum Scope Combo* - .177 or .22 cal., UL, SP, 1100/900 FPS, 18 in. barrel, adj. sights w/ front sight inserts, grooved receiver for scope mounting, 3-12x44AR scope w/ rings, automatic safety, oil finished Monte Carlo stock with recoil pad, anti-beartrap lock and automatic safety, 44.5 in. OAL, 8 lbs. Mfg. 2007-current.

	100%	95%	90%	80%	60%	40%	20%
MSR N/A	$250	$185	$145	$125	$95	N/A	N/A

⚙ *Tech Force 99SCC Magnum Scope Combo* - .177 or .22 cal., UL, SP, 1100/900 FPS, 18 in. barrel, adj. sights w/ front sight inserts, grooved receiver for scope mounting, 4x32AR scope w/ rings, automatic safety, oil finished Monte Carlo stock with recoil pad, anti-beartrap lock and automatic safety, 44.5 in. OAL, 8 lbs. Mfg. 2007-current.

	100%	95%	90%	80%	60%	40%	20%
MSR N/A	$240	$175	$135	$115	$90	N/A	N/A

⚙ *Tech Force 99 Premier* - .177 or .22 cal., UL, SP, 1100/900 FPS, 18 in. barrel, adj. sights w/ front sight inserts, grooved receiver for scope mounting, built in scope stop, automatic safety, checkered Monte Carlo stock with recoil pad, anti-beartrap lock and automatic safety, 44.5 in. OAL, 8 lbs. Mfg. 2007-current.

	100%	95%	90%	80%	60%	40%	20%
MSR N/A	$190	$155	$135	$85	$60	N/A	N/A

GRADING	100%	95%	90%	80%	60%	40%	20%

⊙ *Tech Force 99PC Premier Scope Combo* - .177 or .22 cal., UL, SP, 1100/900 FPS, 18 in. barrel, adj. sights w/ front sight inserts, grooved receiver for scope mounting, built in scope stop, 4x32AR scope and rins, automatic safety, checkered Monte Carlo stock with recoil pad, anti-beartrap lock and automatic safety, 44.5 in. OAL, 8 lbs. Mfg. 2007-current.

MSR N/A	$240	$190	$155	$135	$85	N/A	N/A

⊙ *Tech Force 99PS Premier Scope Combo* - .177 or .22 cal., UL, SP, 1100/900 FPS, 18 in. barrel, adj. sights w/ front sight inserts, grooved receiver for scope mounting, built in scope stop, 2-7x32AR scope and rins, automatic safety, checkered Monte Carlo stock with recoil pad, anti-beartrap lock and automatic safety, 44.5 in. OAL, 8 lbs. Mfg. 2007-current.

MSR N/A	$250	$200	$165	$145	$95	N/A	N/A

⊙ *Tech Force 99PSC Premier Scope Combo* - .177 or .22 cal., UL, SP, 1100/900 FPS, 18 in. barrel, adj. sights w/ front sight inserts, grooved receiver for scope mounting, built in scope stop, 3-12x44AR scope and rings, automatic safety, checkered Monte Carlo stock with recoil pad, anti-beartrap lock and automatic safety, 44.5 in. OAL, 8 lbs. Mfg. 2007-current.

MSR N/A	$270	$220	$185	$165	$115	N/A	N/A

⊙ *Tech Force 99R5 Scope Combo* - .177 or .22 cal., UL, SP, 1100/900 FPS, 18 in. barrel, adj. sights w/ front sight inserts, grooved receiver for scope mounting, automatic safety, oil finished Monte Carlo stock with recoil pad, anti-beartrap lock and automatic safety, 44.5 in. OAL, 8 lbs. Mfg. 2007-current.

MSR N/A	$169	$135	$115	$80	$55	N/A	N/A

RIFLES: CONTENDER SERIES

MODEL 39 CONTENDER - .177 cal., BBC, SP, SS, youth dimensions, no sights, 4x20 scope and rings, 18 in. bbl., 650 FPS, hardwood Monte Carlo style PG stock, 38.4 in. OAL, 5.25 lbs. Mfg. 2007-current.

MSR N/A	$60	$55	$50	$45	$35	N/A	N/A

Add $3 for TF4x20 scope. Add $10 for TF3-7x20 scope.

MODEL 49 CONTENDER - .177 or .22 cal., BBC, SP, SS, medium dimensions, 18.8 in. bbl., 800/650 FPS, no sights, 4x20 scope and rings, hardwood Monte Carlo style PG stock, 45 in. OAL, 6 lbs. Mfg. 2007-current.

MSR N/A	$80	$75	$70	$55	$45	N/A	N/A

Add $50 for 4x32 scope. Add $60 for 3-9x50 scope.

MODEL 59 CONTENDER - .177 or .22 cal., 17.75 in. bbl., 900/730 FPS, no sights, 4x20 scope and rings, hardwood Monte Carlo style PG stock, 42.3 in. OAL, 7 lbs. Mfg. 2007-current.

MSR N/A	$125	$95	$75	$55	N/A	N/A	N/A

Add $50 for 4x32AR scope. Add $60 for 3-9x50AR scope.

MODEL 89 CONTENDER - .177 or .22 cal., BBC, SP, SS, 17.9 in. bbl., muzzle break, 1000/900 FPS, adj. rear and blade front sights, scope stop, checkered beechwood Monte Carlo style PG stock w/ rubber recoil pad, 46.1 in. OAL, 7.72 lbs. Mfg. 2007-current.

MSR N/A	$190	$150	$115	$85	N/A	N/A	N/A

Add $50 for 4x32AR scope. Add $60 for 2-7x32AR scope. Add $80 for 3-12x44AR scope.

COUGAR

For information on Cougar airguns, see Milbro in the "M" section.

CROSMAN CORP.

Current manufacturer located in East Bloomfield, NY.

CROSMAN BACKGROUND

The Crosman airgun line began with the production of the "First Model" Crosman pneumatic rifle by the Crosman Brothers Co. in June 1923. That rifle was based on a patent by William A. MacLean. In addition to being chauffeur to wealthy heavy construction contractor P.H. Murray, MacLean had developed a tiny business producing "Universal Pellets," .22 caliber diabolo-style pellets. These probably were for American owners of BSA air rifles whose supply of British pellets had been cut off by World War I. MacLean was intrigued by an airgun brought back from Europe by Murray, probably one of those BSA air rifles, and wished to "improve" upon its power source. Apparently he devised the idea of combining a highly accurate rifled barrel firing .22 caliber lead pellets with the then current American airgun pump rod system of the smoothbore Benjamin BB airguns. This pumping system had been well-known in America since the models of Bouron, Hawley (Kalamazoo), and Johnson and Bye in the late 1800s.

The oft-told tale that Murray´s unidentified air rifle, which so impressed MacLean, was a French Giffard pneumatic rifle is controverted by the facts that MacLean was already involved with .22 caliber waisted pellets and that such Giffard guns had not been made for almost a half century. Murray, a pacifist and not at all interested in guns, almost surely would not have purchased a vintage Giffard. It is very probable that he would have brought back a BSA air rifle, then popular all over Europe but not common in America, because he knew that his chauffeur was interested in airguns and had a part-time business making pellets for such guns.

The Crosman Brothers Co., which made those first Crosman air rifles, was an offshoot of the then famous Crosman Brothers Seed Company located in Fairport, NY. Crosman Brothers became the Crosman Rifle Company in August 1923 and then the Crosman Arms Co. in 1925. The Crosman Arms Company later became Crosman Air Guns. The Crosman history has been traced, and its airguns discussed and illustrated, by Dean Fletcher in his excellent books, *The Crosman Rifle*, 1923-1950 (1996), *The Crosman Arms Handbooks* (1996), and *75 Years of Crosman Airguns* (1998).

As with many airguns, originality of parts may be hard to determine. The parts were not serial numbered. Newer parts were often placed, sometimes under company mandate, in older guns during repairs. In older Crosman airguns, the .177 caliber versions generally are much less common, while in the most recent models the .177 caliber is the most common.

Caution: Do not depend on Crosman ads or catalogs to see detailed features. Their ad departments and agencies frequently used illustrations from previous periods.

GRADING	100%	95%	90%	80%	60%	40%	20%

CROSMAN IN THE ADULT AIRGUN MARKET

Crosman expended heroic efforts to develop adult interest in airguns, but ended up a co-leader of the youth market instead. Ironically, it probably was the development of the Crosman pump rifle, and especially the development of mass production, low-cost versions of it, that pre-empted the significant introduction of adult-level spring-piston airguns into the United States. Crosman airguns became a product primarily of interest to, and eventually designed for, youthful shooters. Despite the past efforts of Crosman and others, the development of a significant American adult airgun market was delayed until the 1980s. Crosman´s primary concern over the last few decades has been competition with the other leader of the American youth airgun market, Daisy. Crosman's adult precision airgun line consisted of the Models 6100-6500, from 1982-89. During 2000, the company introduced the Challenger 2000 Series, a single shot, bolt action, CO_2 three position target rifle.

CROSMAN PRIVATE LABEL AND STOREBRAND AIRGUNS

Crosman produced some airguns under the name of their president, P.Y. Hahn, and under several private labels, such as J.C. Higgins and Ted Williams for Sears, Hawthorn for Montgomery Wards, and Revelation for Western Auto. While guns sold to the general public might come back to the factory one by one, private label models had the potential to come back en mass. Thus, the models sold to Sears and Wards usually represented the very best efforts and quality control that Crosman could muster. It is not possible to list all Crosman variations, and surely there are variations, even models, out there that even the factory does not know about. For information on Crosman airguns manufactured for other trademarks, see the Store Brand Cross-Over List at the back of this text.

CROSMAN PRODUCTS NON-FACTORY ALTERED

MODEL SSP-250 (ZZZ TRANQUILIZER DART GUN) - .50 cal., pump pneumatic, single-shot dart gun, modified from Crosman SSP-250 by outside fabricator.

$250	$200	$150	$100	$75	N/A	N/A

JET LINE MODEL 101 (CONDUIT GUN) - CO_2 pistol which fires 12 gram Powerlet carrying wire-pulling fish line through large conduits for electric work (i.e. Powerlet is the projectile!). Produced by Crosman Fabricators with Crosman parts, 10.5 in. OAL (gun only), 1.4 lbs.

courtesy Beeman Collection

$350	$295	$245	$200	$170	$150	$100

Add 20% for factory box. Add 50-100% for original accessories, holster, special spools of line, plastic projectile guides, funnels, box, etc.

⊙ *Jet Line Compact Model 101(Conduit Gun)* - compact version of Model 101 Jet Line pistol. Only marking is a large "C" on each of the orange plastic grip plates. Light gray alloy body. 1.1 lbs. 7.1 in. OAL , gun only.

courtesy Beeman Collection

$175	$125	$100	$60	$45	N/A	N/A

Add 50-100% for original accessories, holster, special spools of line, plastic projectile guides, funnels, box, etc.

GRADING	100%	95%	90%	80%	60%	40%	20%

MODEL 1100 SLUG GUN - .380 bore, CO_2, two Powerlets, SS, non-factory conversion.

Slug-firing conversion
courtesy Beeman Collection

Value will be directly related to the quality of the work performed and condition. Generally not considered collectible.

HANDGUNS

MODEL 36 FRONTIER - BB/.175 cal., CO_2, one Powerlet, SA, chambers hold 6 BBs; spring-fed tubular magazine holds 12 more. Full size, full weight replica of Colt Single Action revolver. Basically a continuation of the Hahn/Crosman Model 45, Series I - Mfg. 1970-1971, Series II - Mfg. 1972-1975.

courtesy Robert Lutter

N/A	$95	$90	$80	$60	N/A	N/A

Add 20% for original factory box. Add 25% for original Western-style holster.

MODEL 38C COMBAT - .177 or .22 cal., CO_2, one Powerlet, SA or DA, six-shot revolving cylinder, 3.5 in. barrel, full size cast alloy metal replica of .38 cal. Smith & Wesson revolver, 350-400 FPS, .177 cal., 2.4 lbs. First Variant: metal rear sight and cylinder, mfg. 1964-1973. Second Variant: plastic rear sight and cylinder, Mfg. 1973-1976. Third Variant: .177 cal., mfg. 1976-1981.

courtesy Robert Lutter

$90	$75	$65	$50	$40	N/A	N/A

Add 20% for original factory box. Add 200%-400% for chrome finish salesman sample.

GRADING	100%	95%	90%	80%	60%	40%	20%

MODEL 38T TARGET - .177 or .22 cal., similar to Model 38C Combat, except 6 in. barrel. First Variant: metal rear sight and cylinder, mfg. 1964-1973. Second Variant: plastic rear sight and cylinder, mfg. 1973-1976. Third Variant: .177 cal., mfg. 1976-1985.

courtesy Beeman Collection

	100%	95%	90%	80%	60%	40%	20%
	$90	$75	$65	$50	$40	N/A	N/A

Add 20% for original factory box. Add 200%-400% for chrome finish salesman sample.

MODEL 44 PEACEMAKER - .177 or .22 cal., CO_2, one Powerlet, single action six-shot revolving pellet, Croswood grips, full size replica of Colt Peacemaker. Series I - mfg. 1970-1971, Series II - mfg. 1972-1975, Series III - mfg. 1976-1981.

courtesy Robert Lutter

	100%	95%	90%	80%	60%	40%	20%
	N/A	$95	$90	$80	$60	N/A	N/A

Add 20% for original factory box. Add 20% for original factory Western low slung holster.

MODEL 45 (HAHN "45") - BB/.175 cal., CO_2, one Powerlet, SA, chambers hold 6 BBs, spring-fed tubular magazine holds 12 more. Full size, full weight replica of Colt Single Action Army revolver. Hahn 45 became Crosman Model 45, but casting dies were not changed, so Crosman Model 45 specimens are marked with the P.Y. Hahn Co. name. Became the Model "Frontier 36" in 1970. Mfg. 1958-1970. Variation: Sears (J.C. Higgins).

courtesy Robert Lutter

	100%	95%	90%	80%	60%	40%	20%
	N/A	$95	$90	$80	$60	N/A	N/A

Add 20% for "Fast Draw" holster. Add 20% for JC Higgins/Sears version. Add 20% for original factory box.

GRADING	100%	95%	90%	80%	60%	40%	20%

MODEL 88 SKANAKER PISTOL - .177 cal., CO_2, 550 FPS, bulk fill tank, SS, target model. Mfg. 1987-1991.

courtesy Beeman Collection

100%	95%	90%	80%	60%	40%	20%
$450	$350	$300	$250	$200	N/A	N/A

Last MSR was $795.

Add $65 for carrying case.

As of Dec. 31, 1991, Crosman liquidated its supply of Skanaker pistols due to expiration of Skanaker name use contract.

MODEL 105 (BULLSEYE) - .177 cal., pneumatic pump, pump lever with one or two open loops, SS, 8.4 in rifled barrel, adj. rear sight, blue finish, checkered tenite grips. 31 oz. Mfg. 1947-1953.

courtesy Robert Lutter

100%	95%	90%	80%	60%	40%	20%
N/A	$90	$80	$75	$70	$50	$30

Add 30% for original factory-marked box.

MODEL 106 (BULLSEYE) - .22 cal., similar to Model 105. Mfg. 1948-1953.

courtesy Robert Lutter

100%	95%	90%	80%	60%	40%	20%
N/A	$90	$80	$75	$70	$50	$30

Add 30% for original factory-marked box.

GRADING	100%	95%	90%	80%	60%	40%	20%

MODEL 111 - .177 cal., CO_2, 10 oz. separate gas cylinder, SS, 8 1/8 in. rifled barrel, adj. rear sight, blue finish, molded tenite grips. 5.50 lbs. Mfg. 1950-1954.

courtesy Robert Lutter

	N/A	$170	$150	$130	$110	$80	$50

Add 30% for original CO_2 tank. (Readers are advised not to charge original Crosman CO_2 tanks used on Models 111, 112,115, and 116). Add 20% for original box. Add 30% for "introduction year" box with gold-colored paper lining and insert cut to hold gun. (Models 111 and 112.) Add 75% for gun with Model A306 dealer display case, tank, bell target, pellets. (Typical premium for such displays in other models.)

These are guns without hose or attached gas tank.

MODEL 112 - .22 cal., similar to Model 111. Mfg. 1950-1954.

courtesy Robert Lutter

	N/A	$170	$150	$130	$110	$80	$50

Add 30% for original CO_2 tank. (Readers are advised not to charge original Crosman CO_2 tanks used on Models 111, 112,115, and 116). Add 20% for original box. Add 30% for "introduction year" box with gold-colored paper lining and insert cut to hold gun. (Models 111 and 112.) Add 75% for gun with Model A306 dealer display case, tank, bell target, pellets. (Typical premium for such displays in other models).

These are guns without hose or attached gas tank.

MODEL 115 - .177 cal., similar to Model 111, except 6 in. barrel. Mfg. 1951-1954.

courtesy Robert Lutter

	N/A	$155	$135	$115	$85	$65	$40

Add 30% for original CO_2 tank. (Readers are advised not to charge original Crosman CO_2 tanks used on Models 111, 112,115, and 116). Add 20% for original box. Add 75% for gun with Model A306 dealer display case, tank, bell target, pellets. (Typical premium for such displays in other models.)

GRADING	100%	95%	90%	80%	60%	40%	20%

MODEL 116 - .22 cal., similar to Model 112, except 6 in. barrel. Mfg. 1951-1954.

courtesy Robert Lutter

	N/A	$155	$135	$115	$85	$65	$40

Add 30% for original CO_2 tank. (Readers are advised not to charge original Crosman CO_2 tanks used on Models 111, 112, 115, and 116). Add 20% for original box. Add 75% for gun with Model A306 dealer display case, tank, bell target, pellets. (Typical premium for such displays in other models.)

MODEL 130 - .22 cal., pneumatic pump, SS. First Variant: with walnut grips and pump handle. Mfg. 1953-1954. Second Variant: with formed metal pump handle. Mfg. 1955-1970.

courtesy Robert Lutter

$85	$65	$55	$45	$35	N/A	N/A

Add 20% for wood cocking handle. Add 40% for original factory-marked box.

MODEL 137 - .177 cal., similar to Model 130. First Variant: with aluminum breech, and fingertip recocking. Mfg. 1954. Second Variant: .177 cal., with formed metal pump handle. Mfg. 1956-1962.

courtesy Robert Lutter

$120	$90	$75	$65	$55	N/A	N/A

Add 20% for wood cocking handle. Add 40% for original factory-marked box.

GRADING	100%	95%	90%	80%	60%	40%	20%

MODEL 150 - .22 cal., 12.5 gm. CO_2 cylinder (Powerlet), SS, Type 1 - with two-piece barrel and breech assembly. First type 1 variation: rotating adj. power cocking knob. Second type 1 variation: non-adjustable power. Mfg. 1954-1956. Type 2 - with one-piece breech/barrel. Mfg. 1956-1967.

courtesy Robert Lutter

	$110	$90	$75	$65	$55	N/A	N/A

Add 20% for Type 1 (except for special versions). Add 150% for Type 1 Sears/J.C. Higgins Model 150 with grey-crinkle finish on frame and loading port. Add 40% for SK (Shooting Kit) version. Add 30% for Sears/Ted Williams version. Add 30% for Wards Model 150. Add 75% for Mexican version. Add 100% for Canadian version. Add 20-40% for standard factory-marked box (five variations).

More than 20 variations are known, plus there are an unknown number of foreign models.

✪ **Model 150C Medalist** - .22 cal., similar to Model 150, except chrome plated and wood presentation box. Mfg. 1957-1961.

	$250	$200	$145	$120	$100	N/A	N/A

✪ **Model 150PK** - .22 cal., similar to Model 150, except has portable metal target backstop. Mfg. 1959-1960.

	$145	$120	$100	$85	$70	N/A	N/A

MODEL 157 - .177 cal., similar to Model 150. Type 1 - with two-piece barrel and breech assembly. First type 1 variation: rotating adj. power cocking knob. Second type 1 variation: non-adjustable power. Mfg. 1954-1956. Type 2 - with one-piece breech/barrel. Mfg. 1956-1967.

courtesy Robert Lutter

	$110	$90	$75	$65	$55	N/A	N/A

Add 75% for Type 1. Add 40% for SK (Shooting Kit) version. Add 30% for Sears/Ted Williams version. Add 75% for Mexican version. Add 100% for Canadian version. Add 20-40% for standard factory marked box (5 variations).

More than 20 variations are known, plus there are an unknown number of foreign models.

MODEL 338 - BB/.175 cal., CO_2, one Powerlet, semi-auto replica of Walther P38 military pistol, twenty-shot magazine, cast metal. Mfg. 1986-1991.

courtesy Robert Lutter

	$45	$40	$35	$30	$20	N/A	N/A

Add 10% for original box.

GRADING	100%	95%	90%	80%	60%	40%	20%

MODEL 357 FOUR - .177 cal. pellets, CO_2, one Powerlet, SA/DA revolver, replica of Colt Python firearm, ten-shot rotary clip, 4 in. rifled barrel, 350 FPS, black finish, adj. rear sight, 27 oz. Mfg. 1983-1997.

courtesy Robert Lutter

	$60	$50	$45	$40	$35	N/A	N/A

Add 10% for factory box. Add 60% for silver finish.

⊛ *Model 357 4GT* - .177 cal., similar to Model 357 Four, except gold color accents and black grips. Mfg. 1997. Disc.

	$60	$50	$45	$40	$35	N/A	N/A

Add 10% for factory box. Add 60% for silver finish.

MODEL 3574W - .177 cal. pellets, CO_2, one Powerlet, SA/DA revolver, ten-shot rotary clip, 4 in. rifled barrel, 435 FPS, black finished, adj. rear sight, 32 oz. Disc. 2004.

	$45	$35	$25	$20	$15	N/A	N/A

Last MSR was $61.

⊛ **MODEL 357GW** - .177 cal. pellets, similar to Model 3574W, except also includes extra 8 in. barrel, three ten-shot rotary clips, five paper targets, red dot sight and mounts, and hard case. Disc. 2004.

	$85	$75	$65	$55	$45	N/A	N/A

Last MSR was $100.

MODEL 357 SIX - .177 cal., similar to Model 357 Four, except has 6 in. barrel. Mfg. 1983-97.

courtesy Robert Lutter

	$60	$50	$45	$40	$35	N/A	N/A

Add 10% for factory box. Add 60% for silver finish.

⊛ *Model 357 6GT* - .177 cal., similar to Model 357 Six, except had gold accents and black grips. Mfg. 1997. Disc.

	$60	$50	$45	$40	$35	N/A	N/A

Add 10% for factory box. Add 60% for silver finish.

MODEL 3576W - .177 cal. pellets, CO_2, one 12g Powerlet, SA/DA revolver, ten-shot rotary clip, 6 in. rifled barrel, 435 FPS, black finished, adj. rear sight, 11.4 in. OAL, 2 lbs.

MSR $91	$80	$60	$45	$35	$25	N/A	N/A

⊛ *Model 357GW* - .177 cal. pellets, CO_2, one Powerlet, SA/DA revolver, ten-shot rotary clip, 6 and 8 in. rifled barrel, 435 FPS, black finished, adj. rear and red dot sights, padded case, 2 lbs. Mfg. 2005-07.

	$85	$75	$65	$50	N/A	N/A	N/A

Last MSR was $100.

GRADING	100%	95%	90%	80%	60%	40%	20%

MODEL 357 EIGHT - .177 cal., similar to Model 357 Four, except 8 in. barrel. Mfg. 1984-96.

courtesy Robert Lutter

	$80	$65	$50	$40	$30	N/A	N/A

Add 10% for factory box. Add 60% for scope or silver finish.

MODEL 380 ROCKET - CO_2, one Powerlet, underwater speargun, one- or two- (early mfg.) piece grips. Mfg. 1959-60.

courtesy Howard Collection

	$500	$475	$450	$400	$300	$225	$150

Add 10% for two-piece grips.

MODEL 451 - CO_2, one Powerlet, semi-auto, six-shot, styled after Colt 45 Automatic. 4.75 in. barrel. Mfg. 1969-70.

courtesy Beeman Collection

	$400	$350	$325	$300	$275	$200	$150

Add 20% for original factory box.

MODEL 454 - BB/.175 cal., CO_2, one Powerlet, semi-auto, styled after Colt Woodsman. sixteen-shot spring-fed magazine, adj. sights, brown Croswood grips. First variant: has coin slot piercing screw. Mfg. 1972-1977. Second variant (BB-Matic): has ring piercing screw lever. Mfg. 1978-1982.

courtesy Robert Lutter

	$50	$45	$40	$35	$25	N/A	N/A

Add 10% for first variant. Add 20% for original factory box.

GRADING	100%	95%	90%	80%	60%	40%	20%

MODEL 455 - .177 cal., CO_2, SS, pellet (Crosman/Blaser 45 conversion unit) converts Colt 45 Automatic firearm (series 70 or earlier) or clones to .177 cal. pellet use, CO_2, single shot. Mfg. in Germany. Mfg.1987-1988.

	100%	95%	90%	80%	60%	40%	20%
	$150	$125	$100	$75	$60	N/A	N/A

Add 10% for original factory box.

MODEL 600 - .22 cal., CO_2, one Powerlet, semi-auto, sophisticated trigger design, ten-round spring-fed magazine, considered by many as the pinnacle of Crosman airgun development, often converted into custom airguns, original specimens are becoming scarce. Variations: three distinct variations based on CO_2 piercing caps. First variant: piercing cap. Second variant: non-piercing cap like Model 160 Standard. Third variant: push button piercing. Sears variant: Sears markings. Mfg. 1960-1970.

courtesy Robert Lutter

	100%	95%	90%	80%	60%	40%	20%
	N/A	$275	$195	$150	$125	$95	$50

Add 75% for Sears variant. Add 20% for original factory-marked box. Add 20% for original holster.

MODEL 677 PLINK-O-MATIC - BB/.175 cal., CO_2, one Powerlet, semi-auto, rare BB version of the Model 600. Mfg. 1961-1964.

	100%	95%	90%	80%	60%	40%	20%
	N/A	$450	$350	$250	$175	$95	N/A

Add 25% for original factory box.

MODEL 971BF (BLACK FANG) - BB/.175, .177 cal., spring piston, seventeen-shot mag. (BB), smooth steel barrel, 250 FPS (BB), black finish, synthetic grip/frame, fixed sights, 10 oz. Mfg. 1996-2002.

	100%	95%	90%	80%	60%	40%	20%
	$15	$10	$5	N/A	N/A	N/A	N/A

MODEL 972BV (BLACK VENOM) - BB/.175 cal., spring piston, .177 cal., seventeen-shot mag. (BB), SS pellet/dart, smooth steel barrel, 270 FPS (BB), 245 FPS (.177 pellet), black finish, synthetic grip/frame, adj. sights, 15 oz. Mfg. 1996-2006.

	100%	95%	90%	80%	60%	40%	20%
	$22	$15	$10	N/A	N/A	N/A	N/A

Last MSR was $25.

MODEL 1008 (REPEATAIR) - .177 cal. pellet, CO_2, one Powerlet, semi-auto, eight-shot mag. SA/DA action, 4.25 in. rifled barrel, 430 FPS, adj. rear sight, replica of Smith & Wesson pistol, 17 oz. Mfg. 1992-1997.

	100%	95%	90%	80%	60%	40%	20%
	$60	$55	$50	$45	$40	N/A	N/A

MODEL 1008B (REPEATAIR) - .177 cal., pellet, CO_2, one Powerlet, eight-shot clip, M-1008B with black frame, 4.25 in. rifled barrel, 430 FPS, adj. rear sight, 17 oz. Mfg. 1997-2006.

	100%	95%	90%	80%	60%	40%	20%
	$55	$45	$30	$20	$15	N/A	N/A

Last MSR was $66.

✿ *Model 1008SB (Repeatair)* - .177 cal., similar to Model 1008B, except has silver frame. Mfg. 1997-2006.

	100%	95%	90%	80%	60%	40%	20%
	$55	$45	$35	$30	$20	N/A	N/A

Last MSR was $84.

✿ *Model 1008BRD (Repeatair)* - .177 cal., similar to Model 1008B, except has red dot sight. Mfg. 1997-2006.

	100%	95%	90%	80%	60%	40%	20%
	$65	$55	$45	$35	$25	N/A	N/A

Last MSR was $76.

✿ *Model 1008AK/1008SBAK (Repeatair Air Pistol Kit)* - .177 cal., kit includes Model 1008B or 1008SB pistol, red dot sight, shooting glasses, two Powerlet CO_2, 250-ct. package of pellets, and clamshell case. Disc. 2006.

	100%	95%	90%	80%	60%	40%	20%
	$65	$55	$45	$35	$25	N/A	N/A

Last MSR was $77.

Add $2 for Model 1008SBAK kit with Model 1008SB pistol.

✿ *MODEL 1078BG/1078SBG (Repeatair Pistol Kit)* - .177 cal., kit includes Model 1008B or 1008SB pistol, three eight-shot clips, three paper targets, three Powerlet CO_2, 250-ct. package of pellets, and clamshell case. Disc. 2006.

	100%	95%	90%	80%	60%	40%	20%
	$65	$55	$45	$35	$25	N/A	N/A

Last MSR was $77.

Add $2 for Model 1078SBG kit with Model 1008SB pistol.

MODEL 1088BG BB/.175 and .177 cal. pellet, CO_2, one 12g Powerlet, semi-automatic, eight-shot clip, black (Model 1088BG) or silver/black (Model 1088SB) synthetic frame, rifled steel barrel, 435-400 FPS, adj. rear sight, weaver accessory rail under BBR, 7.75 in. OAL, 17 oz. Mfg. 2006-current.

	100%	95%	90%	80%	60%	40%	20%
MSR $95	$80	$70	$60	$40	$25	N/A	N/A

Add 15% for Model 1088AK, kit includes three 12g CO_2, powerlets, 250 pellets, and shooting glasses, mfg. 2006-07. Add 20% for Model 1088BKC, kit includes three 12g CO_2 powerlets, 250 pellets, three official airgun targets, four eight-shot rotary mags., shooting glasses, and hard sided case, mfg. 2007.

GRADING	100%	95%	90%	80%	60%	40%	20%

MODEL 1088SBAK BB/.175 and .177 cal. pellet, CO_2, one 12g Powerlet, semi-automatic, eight-shot clip, silver/black synthetic frame, rifled steel barrel, 430-400 FPS, adj. rear sight, weaver accessory rail under BBR, three 12g CO_2, 250 pellets, and shooting glasses, 7.75 in. OAL, 17 oz. Mfg. 2006-current.

MSR $106	$90	$75	$65	$50	$40	N/A	N/A

MODEL 1300 MEDALIST II - .22 cal., UL (forearm) pneumatic, SS, self-cocking, sliding breech cover, pump handle flared at forward end, 460 FPS, 11.75 in.OAL. Mfg. 1970-1976.

courtesy Robert Lutter

	$80	$70	$65	$60	$50	N/A	N/A

Add 20% for factory box.

MODEL 1322 MEDALIST - .22 cal., UL (forearm) pneumatic, SS, three-ring cocking knob, sliding breech cover, pump handle straight along bottom edge, 13.6 in.overall. First variant: manual cocking, has steel breech and cover. Mfg. 1977-1981. Second variant: has plastic breech and steel cover. Mfg. 1981-1996. Third variant: brass bolt action. Mfg. 1998-2000.

courtesy Robert Lutter

	$65	$55	$45	$40	$30	N/A	N/A

Add 25% for first variant.

MODEL 1357 "SIX" - BB/.175 cal., CO_2, break-open, clip loading (six-shot), one Powerlet, SA/DA, replica of .357 police revolver, 465 FPS, limited distribution may be Michigan only. Mfg. 1988-1996.

	$55	$50	$48	$45	$40	N/A	N/A

MODEL 1377 AMERICAN CLASSIC - .177 cal., similar to Model 1322, pellet only, single shot, brass bolt action, 10.25 in. rifled barrel, 560 FPS, adj. rear sight, 32 oz. First variant: has manual cocking and steel breech. Mfg. 1977-1981. Second variant: has plastic breech. Mfg. 1981-1996. Also sold as Model 1388 "rifle" with shoulder stock. Mfg. 1982-1988.

courtesy Robert Lutter

	$70	$60	$50	$45	$35	N/A	N/A

Add 20% with shoulder stock (Model 1388 "rifle").

○ *Model 1377C* - .177 cal. pellet only, single shot, brass bolt action, 10.25 in. rifled barrel, 600 FPS, adj. rear sight, 32 oz. Mfg. 1998-present.

MSR $91	$80	$70	$60	$40	$25	N/A	N/A

GRADING	100%	95%	90%	80%	60%	40%	20%

MODEL 1600 POWERMATIC - BB/.175 cal., CO_2, one Powerlet, semi-auto replica of Colt Woodsman, seventeen-shot spring-fed magazine, fixed sights, (economy version of Model 454). First variant: flathead gas filler cap screw. Second variant: barrel-shaped filler cap screw. Mfg. 1979-1990.

courtesy Robert Lutter

	$60	$50	$40	$30	$20	N/A	N/A

MODEL 1861 SHILOH - BB/.175, .177 pellet cal., CO_2, one Powerlet, SA revolver, patterned after US Civil War Remington cap and ball revolver, 370 FPS, 1.9 lbs. Mfg. 1981-1983.

courtesy Robert Lutter

	$75	$70	$65	$60	$50	N/A	N/A

Add 20% for factory box.

MODEL 2210SB - .22 cal. pellet, CO_2, one Powerlet, SS, 7.24 in. rifled barrel, 435 FPS, silver-colored finish, adj. rear sight, fiberoptic front sight, 20 oz. Mfg. 1999-2003.

	$50	$42	$35	$25	$20	N/A	N/A

MODEL 2240 - .22 cal. pellet, CO_2, one Powerlet, SS, 7.25 in. rifled barrel, 460 FPS, black finish, adj. rear sight, 29 oz. Mfg. 1999-present.

MSR $92	$80	$60	$45	$35	$25	N/A	N/A

MODEL 2300S - .177 cal., CO_2, one 12g powerlet, BA, SS, 10.1 Lothar-Walther choked match BBL, single stage adj. trigger, adj. hammer spring for 440-520- FPS, Williams adj. rear sight, blue finish, 16 in. OAL, 42.5 oz.

MSR $390	$350	$275	$200	$150	$100	N/A	N/A

MODEL 2300T - .177 cal., CO_2, one 12g powerlet, BA, SS, 10.1 rifled steel BBL, single stage adj. trigger, 520- FPS, LPA adj. rear sight, blue finish, 16 in. OAL, 42.5 oz.

MSR 249	$215	$175	$125	$90	$50	N/A	N/A

MODEL 3357 - .50 cal. version of the Model 357 CO_2 revolver, designed for firing paintballs.

courtesy Robert Lutter

	$80	$65	$50	$40	$30	N/A	N/A

GRADING	100%	95%	90%	80%	60%	40%	20%

MODEL AAII (Auto Air II) - BB/.175 cal. repeater, .177 pellet cal. SS, CO$_2$, one Powerlet, 480FPS (BB), 430 FPS (pellet), black finish, adj. rear sight. Mfg. 1991-1996.

	$25	$20	$15	$10	$8	N/A	N/A

Add 5% for factory box.

❂ *Model AAIIB (Auto Air II)* - BB/.175 cal. repeater, .177 pellet cal. SS, CO$_2$, one Powerlet, smooth barrel, 480 FPS-BB, 430 FPS-pellet, black finish, adj. rear sight, 13 oz. Mfg. 1997-2005.

	$35	$28	$20	$15	$10	N/A	N/A

Last MSR was $45.

❂ *Model AAIIB/AAIIBRD (Auto Air II)* - BB/.175 cal. repeater, .177 pellet cal. SS, CO$_2$, one Powerlet, smooth barrel, 480 FPS (BB), 430 FPS (pellet), black finish, adj. rear sight, red dot sight, 13 oz. Mfg. 1997-2005.

	$50	$40	$30	$20	$15	N/A	N/A

Last MSR was $59.

MODEL C11 - BB/.177 cal., CO$_2$, one 12g Powerlet, semi-automatic, removable fifteen-shot mag., black synthetic frame, metal barrel, 480 FPS, weaver accessory rail under BBR, fixed sights, 6.75 in. OAL, 1.1 lbs. Mfg. 2006-current.

courtesy Crosman

MSR $60	$55	$45	$35	$25	$20	N/A	N/A

The Model C11 was redesigned during 2006, adding a spring-activated BB mag. w/ push button release for 2007.

❂ *Model TACC11* - BB/.177 cal., CO$_2$, one 12g Powerlet, semi-automatic, removable fifteen-shot mag., black synthetic frame, metal barrel, 480 FPS, compensator, weaver accessory rail under BBR, fixed sights, laser, 6.75 in. OAL, 1.1 lbs. Mfg. 2008-current.

MSR $100	$85	$75	$65	$50	$35	N/A	N/A

MODEL C21 - BB/.177 cal., CO$_2$, one 12g Powerlet, semi-automatic, removable fifteen-shot mag., black synthetic frame, metal barrel, 495 FPS, fixed sights, 6.75 in. OAL, 1.1 lbs. Mfg. 2008-current.

MSR $90	$85	$75	$55	$45	$35	N/A	N/A

MODEL C40 (CROSMAN 75TH ANNIVERSARY COMMEMORATIVE) - .177 cal., CO$_2$, eight-shot clip, 4.25 in. rifled barrel, 430 FPS, Zinc alloy frame, silver finish, adj. rear sight, optional laser sight (C40 LS), new 1999, 40 oz. Mfg. 1998-2005.

	$125	$100	$75	$60	$50	N/A	N/A

Last MSR was $138.

Add $45 for Model C40LS Kit with three clips, laser sight, and foam-padded case.

MODEL CB40 (CROSMAN 75TH ANNIVERSARY COMMEMORATIVE) - .177 cal., CO$_2$, eight-shot clip, 4.25 in. rifled barrel, 430 FPS, zinc alloy frame, black finish, adj. rear sight, optional laser sight CB40LS new 1999, 40 oz. Mfg.1998-2003.

	$95	$75	$60	$50	$40	N/A	N/A

Add $30 for CB40LS.

MODEL CK92 - .177 cal., CO$_2$, eight-shot, 435 FPS, rifled steel barrel, solid die-cast zinc (frame, slide action release, safety), adj. rear sight, black or silver finish. Mfg. 2000-03.

	$105	$95	$80	$60	$50	N/A	N/A

Add $20 for silver finish.

MODEL MARK I - .22 cal., CO$_2$, one Powerlet, SS, styled like Ruger .22 semi-auto firearm, rifled 7.25 in. barrel, 43 oz. First variant: adj. power. Mfg. 1966-1980. Second variant: non-adj. power. Mfg. 1981-1983.

courtesy Robert Lutter

	$150	$125	$100	$75	$55	N/A	N/A

Subtract 20% for second variant. Add 10% for factory box.

GRADING	100%	95%	90%	80%	60%	40%	20%

MODEL MARK II - BB/.175 cal., .177 cal. pellet, similar to Model Mark I. First variant: SS Mfg. 1966-1980. Second variant: without adjustable power. Mfg. 1981-1986.

courtesy Robert Lutter

	$135	$105	$85	$70	$50	N/A	N/A

Subtract 20% for second variant. Add 10% for factory box.

MODEL PRO77CS BB/.175 cal., CO_2, one 12g Powerlet, Blowback semi-automatic action, spring-activated seventeen-shot mag., black synthetic frame w/ metal slide, rifled steel barrel, 325 FPS, fixed. sights, weaver accessory rail under BBR, hard sided case, 6.75 in. OAL, 1.3 lbs. Mfg. 2007-current.

courtesy Crosman

MSR $114	$100	$85	$70	$50	$30	N/A	N/A

Add 10% for Model Pro77KT, kit includes two 12g CO_2 powerlets, 1,500 Copperhead BBs, and shooting glasses.

☼ **Model Pro77KT** BB/.175 cal., CO_2, one 12g Powerlet, Blowback semi-automatic action, spring-activated seventeen-shot mag., black synthetic frame w/ metal slide, rifled steel barrel, 325 FPS, fixed. sights, weaver accessory rail under BBR, hard sided case, 6.75 in. OAL, 1.3 lbs. Mfg. 2007-current.

MSR $116	$100	$85	$70	$50	$30	N/A	N/A

Model Pro77KT, kit includes two 12g CO_2 powerlets, 1,500 Copperhead BBs, and shooting glasses.

MODEL SA 6 - .22 cal., CO_2, one Powerlet, SA six-shot, replica of Colt Peacemaker Single Action revolver. Mfg. 1959-1969.

courtesy Robert Lutter

	$120	$105	$85	$70	$55	N/A	N/A

Add 20% for factory box. Add 20% for factory quick draw holster.

MODEL SSP 250 SILHOUETTE PISTOL - .177 cal., CO_2, one Powerlet, SS, dual power settings, interchangeable .20 and .22 cal. rifled steel barrels available. Mfg. 1989-1995.

	$110	$100	$90	$80	$70	$45	$30

Add 25% for each additional caliber barrel. Add 20% for factory box.

GRADING	100%	95%	90%	80%	60%	40%	20%

MODEL T4CS .177 cal. BB and pellet, CO_2, one 12g Powerlet, semi-automatic, eight-shot rotary mag., black synthetic frame, soft ergonomic grip, rifled steel barrel, 430-450 FPS, adj. rear sight, weaver accessory rail under BBR, hard sided case, 8.63 in. OAL, 1.32 lbs. Mfg. 2007-current.

courtesy Crosman

MSR $136	$125	$100	$85	$70	$45	N/A	N/A

Add 10% for Model T4KT, kit includes two 12g CO_2 powerlets, 250 Crosman pellets, 350 Copperhead BB's, and shooting glasses.

⚙ *Model T4KT* .177 cal. BB and pellet, CO_2, one 12g Powerlet, semi-automatic, eight-shot rotary mag., black synthetic frame, soft ergonomic grip, rifled steel barrel, 430-450 FPS, adj. rear sight, weaver accessory rail under BBR, hard sided case, 8.63 in. OAL, 1.32 lbs. Mfg. 2007-current.

MSR $138	$125	$100	$85	$70	$45	N/A	N/A

Model T4KT, kit includes two 12g CO_2 powerlets, 250 Crosman pellets, 350 Copperhead BB's, and shooting glasses.

⚙ *Model T4OPTS* .177 cal. BB and pellet, CO_2, one 12g Powerlet, semi-automatic, eight-shot rotary mag., black synthetic frame, soft ergonomic grip, rifled steel barrel w/ compensator and four weaver accessory rails, 430-450 FPS, Red dot sight, tactical flashlight, hard sided case, 12.88 in. OAL, 2.39 lbs. Mfg. 2007-current.

courtesy Crosman

MSR $279	$245	$195	$150	$115	$75	N/A	N/A

⚙ *Model T4OPTS-CL* .177 cal. BB and pellet, CO_2, one 12g Powerlet, semi-automatic, eight-shot rotary mag., black synthetic frame, soft ergonomic grip, rifled steel barrel w/ compensator and four weaver accessory rails, 430-450 FPS, Red dot sight, tactical flashlight, clamshell, 12.88 in. OAL, 2.39 lbs. Mfg. 2008-current.

MSR $279	$245	$195	$150	$115	$75	N/A	N/A

MODEL V300 - BB/.175 cal., rear grip strap lever cocking, SP, SA, twenty-three-shot spring-fed magazine. Mfg. 1963-1964.

courtesy Robert Lutter

	$175	$150	$125	$100	$75	N/A	N/A

Add 20% for factory box.

GRADING	100%	95%	90%	80%	60%	40%	20%

MODEL Z-77 UZI REPLICA - BB/.175 cal., CO₂, one Powerlet, semi-auto, gravity-fed twenty-shot magazine, with folding stock (but classed as pistol by Crosman). Mfg. 1987-1989.

	100%	95%	90%	80%	60%	40%	20%
	$175	$150	$125	$100	$75	N/A	N/A

Subtract 20% for missing sling.
  Clamshell packaging on new gun.

MODEL C31 - BB/.177 cal., CO₂, one 12g Powerlet, semi-automatic, removable fifteen-shot mag., black synthetic frame, metal barrel, 495 FPS, fixed sights, and holster, 6.75 in. OAL, 1.1 lbs. Mfg. 2008-current.

MSR $76	100%	95%	90%	80%	60%	40%	20%
	$70	$55	$45	$35	N/A	N/A	N/A

RIFLES

FIRST MODEL RIFLE ("1923 MODEL," HI-POWER, OR PLUNGER MODEL) - .22 cal., rifled, bicycle-style plunger rod pump under the barrel, pneumatic, SS. First variant: peep sight mounted in dovetail slot forward of the pellet loading port of receiver; no elevation adjustment, machined steel receiver, steel compression tube. Second variant: peep sight, adjustable for elevation and windage, mounted on bridge-type bracket behind the pellet loading port, steel barrel and compression tube. Third variant: nickel-plated brass compression tube, die-cast receiver with logo: "Crosman Rochester, N.Y. Pat. April 23-23". Mfg. 1923-24.

courtesy Beeman Collection

	100%	95%	90%	80%	60%	40%	20%
	N/A	$2,000	$1,750	$1,600	$1,300	$1,000	$800

Add 50% for first variation. Add 20% for third variation. Subtract 50% for any cocking knob other than short knurled type on First, Second, or Third Model Crosman rifles.
  Watch for refinished specimens and "made-up specimens" recently assembled from parts, usually combined with non-Crosman, recently made receivers – often with sharp edges and somewhat different shape and material (compare with specimen known to be authentic).

SECOND MODEL RIFLE (FIRST LEVER MODEL – "1924 MODEL") - .22 cal., rifled barrel, the first lever-action pump pneumatic, conspicuous "beer barrel" pump-lever handle protrudes under front of gun, single shot, no variations reported, extremely rare. Mfg. 1923-24.

courtesy Beeman Collection

	100%	95%	90%	80%	60%	40%	20%
	N/A	N/A	$2,900	$2,500	$1,900	$1,200	$750

Sometimes refered to as the "1924 Model" but that can be confusing because production began in 1923 and many, much later, models carry the 1924 patent date – which leads collectors to refer them as 1924 Models.

THIRD MODEL RIFLE (SECOND LEVER MODEL) - .22 cal., rifled, first swinging forearm pump pneumatic, SS, produced by both Crosman Rifle Co. (3-4 employees) and Crosman Arms Co. Rarest of the first three Crosman air rifle models. Mfg. 1924-25.

courtesy Beeman Collection

	100%	95%	90%	80%	60%	40%	20%
	N/A	N/A	$2,600	$2,200	$1,600	$950	$600

GRADING	100%	95%	90%	80%	60%	40%	20%

MODEL 1 - .22 cal., swinging forearm pump pneumatic, SS, adj. Williams rear sight, wood stock/forearm, 10 pumps = 635 FPS. First variant: tapered steel barrel housing, mfg. 1981-82. Second variant: straight steel barrel housing, plastic sight sleeve, 5.1 lbs. Mfg.1982-85.

courtesy Robert Lutter

	100%	95%	90%	80%	60%	40%	20%
	$100	$90	$80	$65	$45	$35	$20

Subtract 20% for second variant. Add 20% for factory box.

MODEL 66 POWERMASTER - BB/.175 cal., eighteen-shot mag. (plus 200 round reservoir) or .177 cal. pellet single shot, swinging forearm pump pneumatic. First variant: with zinc receiver. Mfg. 1983-88. Second variant: with plastic receiver, 3.9 lbs. Mfg. began in 1988. Disc.

courtesy Robert Lutter

	100%	95%	90%	80%	60%	40%	20%
	$80	$65	$45	$35	$20	N/A	N/A

Add 20% for first variant. Add 20% for factory box.

⊙ *Model 66RT Powermaster* - similar to Model 66 Powermaster, except has camo stock and forearm. Mfg. 1993-94.

	$100	$80	$65	$45	$35	N/A	N/A

⊙ *Model 66BX Powermaster* - BB/.175 cal. eighteen-shot mag. (plus 200 round reservoir), or .177 cal. five-shot mag. pellet SS, swinging forearm pump pneumatic, bolt action, 680 FPS (BB), 645 FPS (pellet), 20.5 in. rifled steel barrel, black finish, brown checkered synthetic stock and forearm, fiberoptic front and adj. rear sights, 2.9 lbs. Disc. 2005.

	$55	$45	$35	$25	$20	N/A	N/A

Last MSR was $63.

MODEL 70 - .177 cal., pellet, CO_2, BA, copy of Winchester Model 70, 650 FPS, full wood stock and forearm, 41 in. OAL, 5.8 lbs. Mfg. 1973-80.

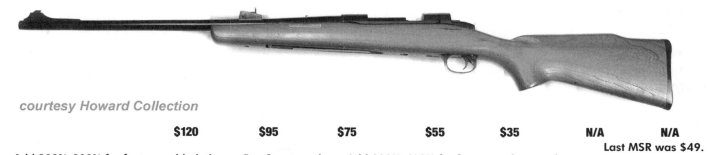

courtesy Howard Collection

	100%	95%	90%	80%	60%	40%	20%
	$120	$95	$75	$55	$35	N/A	N/A

Last MSR was $49.

Add 200%-300% for factory gold plating or Boy Scout versions. Add 300%-400% for factory walnut stock.

GRADING	100%	95%	90%	80%	60%	40%	20%

MODEL 73 SADDLE PAL - .175/BB cal., sixteen-shot repeater or .177 cal. pellet SS; CO_2, one Powerlet, plastic stock, Winchester style lever, 3.2 lbs. First variant: Mfg. 1976-77. Second variant: Mfg. 1977-83.

courtesy Robert Lutter

$50	$45	$40	$35	$25	$20	$20

Add 10% for factory box.

MODEL 84 CHALLENGER - .177 cal., CO_2, match rifle, 720 FPS, fully adj. sights, walnut stock, adj. cheekpiece and buttplate, every Model 84 was "individually hand produced by Crosman model shop," not a "real production gun," 11 lbs. Mfg. 1985-1992.

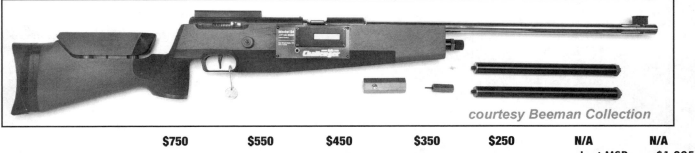

courtesy Beeman Collection

$750	$550	$450	$350	$250	N/A	N/A

Last MSR was $1,295.

The Crosman Model 84 was the first U.S.-made air rifle designed to compete with established European models. Unlike its competitors, it is CO_2, with a digital gauge mounted on the forearm to show remaining pressure. Electronic trigger was a factory option.

MODEL 99 - .22 cal., CO_2, one Powerlet, dual power selection, lever action, resembles Savage lever action big game rifle, 5.8 lbs. Mfg. 1965-1970.

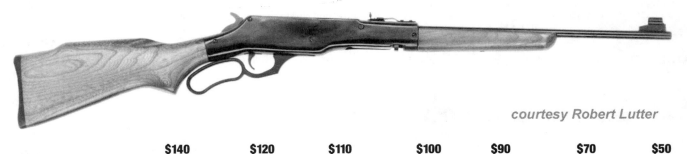

courtesy Robert Lutter

$140	$120	$110	$100	$90	$70	$50

Add 20% for factory box.

MODEL 100 - .177 cal. version of Model 101 (see Model 101). Mfg. 1940-50.

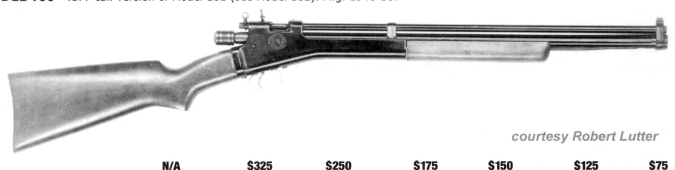

courtesy Robert Lutter

N/A	$325	$250	$175	$150	$125	$75

The Barrel Problem: Some variations have brass barrels and brass body tubes, some have steel barrels with brass tubes, and in others both are steel. Dean Fletcher reports that from about 1925 to early 1927, barrels were rifled steel, probably made by nearby Remington Arms. From about 1927 to 1946, barrels were all bronze. From 1946 to 1947, barrels were either bronze or steel and in 1948 they were all bronze. Crosman preferred bronze for ease of tooling and because condensation which resulted from adiabatic cooling of discharge did not so easily corrode bronze.

GRADING	100%	95%	90%	80%	60%	40%	20%

MODEL 100 "CG" - .177 cal. version of Model 101 "CG" (see Model 101 "CG").

MODEL 101 ("1926 MODEL", SILENT .22 RIFLE) - .22 cal., pneumatic pump, SS, die-cast receiver with logo, pat. Oct. 28, 1924 Crosman Arms Co. Rochester, N.Y. This has been the standard Crosman air rifle for over 25 years. No model number markings, but may show serial numbers, numerous part variations are known: curved vs. straight bolt handles, short vs. medium knurled edge cocking knobs, round stamped aperture discs vs. hexagonal machined discs, various valve details, etc. For identifying post-WWII models see Fletcher`s *The Crosman Arms Library*, Vol. 2 - Crosman Arms Model 101 & 121-GC Engineering Parts Drawings. Mfg. 1925-1950+.

courtesy Robert Lutter

Straight Logo	**Premier Logo**	**Logo Disc**	**Curved Logo**

Short Knurled Knob	**Long Knurled Knob**	**5 Groove Knob**	**Diabolo Knob**

The Barrel Problem: Some variations have brass barrels and brass body tubes, some have steel barrels with brass tubes, and in others both are steel. Dean Fletcher reports that from about 1925 to early 1927, barrels were rifled steel, probably made by nearby Remington Arms. From about 1927 to 1946 barrels were all bronze. From 1946 to 1947 barrels were either bronze or steel and in 1948 they were all bronze. Crosman preferred bronze for ease of tooling and because condensation which resulted from adiabatic cooling of discharge did not so easily corrode bronze.

❁ *Model 101 Period One "Crosman Pneumatic Rifle"* - .22 cal. All variations: receiver area where barrel enters is octagonal, walnut stock and forearm, knurled cocking knob, rare in excellent condition. Mfg. late 1925-29.

courtesy Robert Lutter

	$300	$200	$180	$150	$125	$100	N/A

Add 50% for original factory box. Add 10% for high-comb stock or original checkering. Add 20% for Model 100.

1925-1926 - production models have un-flared trigger and "Famous American manufactured" (Remington?) steel barrel. Circular logo cast into right side of receiver: "PAT. OCT. 28 1924, CROSMAN ARMS CO. ROCHESTER N.Y."

GRADING	100%	95%	90%	80%	60%	40%	20%

1927-1929 - production models have flared trigger, Crosman manufactured bronze barrel, long (1/2 inch) knurled cocking knobs. Disc logo version: on a stamped metal plate impressed into side of receiver - "CROSMAN ARMS COMPANY MADE IN U.S.A. TRADE (PELLET) MARK PATENTED ROCHESTER N.Y."

Note: the presence of a "diabolo pellet" cocking knob is an anomaly. "Diabolo pellet" cocking knobs are for the 121 "CG" series gas rifles (p/n. 121-15) only. However, the presence of this improved cocking knob enhances the look and functionality and, therefore, does not detract from value.

⊙ *Model 101 Premier Brand Version* - logo cast on receiver reads: "PREMIER 22 RIFLE PATENTED OCT 28. 1924". Also known from specimens bearing a lettered disc (probably 1927-29). Not marked Crosman anywhere. Rare.

	$300	$200	$180	$150	$125	N/A	N/A

Add 50% for original factory box. Add 20% for Model 100. Add 10% for high-comb stock or original checkering.

⊙ *Model 101 Period Two "Crosman Silent Rifle"* - .22 cal. All variations: Receiver area is round where barrel enters, walnut stock, long knurled cocking knob, hexagonal rear sight disc., decal applied to forearm. Mfg. 1930-1940.

	$225	$175	$150	$125	$100	N/A	N/A

Add 50% for original factory box. Add 20% for Model 100. Add 10% for high-comb stock or original checkering.

Note: the presence of a "diabolo pellet" cocking knob is an anomaly. "Diabolo pellet" cocking knobs are for the 121 "CG" series gas rifles (p/n. 121-15) only. However, the presence of this improved cocking knob enhances the look and functionality and, therefore, does not detract from value.

◆**Model 101 Period Two "Crosman Silent Rifle" Clickless Variant** - "clickless" (hard rubber) forearm. Mfg. 1938-1939.

	$190	$160	$130	$100	$75	N/A	N/A

Add 50% for original factory box. Add 20% for Model 100. Add 10% for high-comb stock or original checkering.

⊙ *Model 101 Period Three* - .22 cal., all models: five-ring cocking knob, hardwood stock and forearm. Mfg. post- WWII (1946-50+).

courtesy Robert Lutter

	$150	$100	$90	$80	$70	N/A	N/A

Add 50% for original factory box. Add 20% for Model 100. Add 10-15% for high-comb, original checkering, or walnut stock.

Note: the presence of a "diabolo pellet" cocking knob is an anomaly. "Diabolo pellet" cocking knobs are for the 121 "CG" series gas rifles (p/n. 121-15) only. However, the presence of this improved cocking knob enhances the look and functionality and, therefore, does not detract from value.

Extreme rarity precludes accurate pricing on this model.

◆**Model 101 Period Three 1949 Variant** - knurled rear sight, large adjustment knob (same as on Model 107/108).

	$175	$130	$100	$90	$80	N/A	N/A

Add 50% for original factory box. Add 20% for Model 100. Add 10-15% for high-comb, original checkering, or walnut stock.

◆**Model 101 Period Three Sears Variant** - black crinkle finish paint, mfg. 1949-50 and for some time beyond 1950.

	$180	$160	$130	$100	$75	N/A	N/A

Add 50% for original factory box. Add 20% for Model 100. Add 10-15% for high-comb, original checkering, or walnut stock.

⊙ *Model 101 "CG" Variation* - .22 cal., CO_2, 4.5 oz. cylinder vertically attached to gun, same rear sight assembly as found on standard model 101, sold to public, circa 1948-1949, but only through Crosman authorized (ASA) shooting clubs. Typical value $175-$225. Subtract $75 for no CO_2 tank.

	N/A	$350	$250	$175	$150	$125	$75

MODEL 102 - .22 cal., pump-lever pneumatic, ten-round mag., no model number markings, some specimens have pellet logo, others are plain, side of receiver may or may not be marked with "Crosman 22/Patented Oct. 28, 1924/Other patents pending", early versions sometimes have simple checkering on forearm (mfg. 1929-1950) 1929-1940 models are distinguished by knurled cocking knob and walnut stocks, 1945-1950 models have a five-ring cocking knob. Clickless variant: "clickless" hard rubber forearm, mfg. only 1938-39. Mfg. 1929-1950.

courtesy Robert Lutter

	N/A	$250	$200	$175	$150	$120	$80

Add 20% for clickless variant. Add 60% for original factory box. Subtract 25% for 1945-1950 mfg.

GRADING	100%	95%	90%	80%	60%	40%	20%

○ **Model 102 "OSS" Variant** - .22 cal., fifteen-shot pump pneumatic repeater for lead balls, round hole loading port, produced during WWII for the U.S. Office of Special Services.
Rarity precludes accurate pricing.
Crosman states 2000 were delivered. An invoice for 1000 is known from contract #623. 957 specimens were inventoried in a U.S. government warehouse in Calcutta in January of 1945. Over ten specimen are known to exist.

○ **Model 102 "CG" Variant** - .22 cal., CO_2, ten-round magazine repeater, 4.5 oz. cylinder vertically attached to gun.

	N/A	$450	$375	$325	$295	$235	$125

MODEL 104 - .177 cal., pump-lever pneumatic, ten-shot mag., similar to Model 102, except for caliber. Mfg. 1949 only.

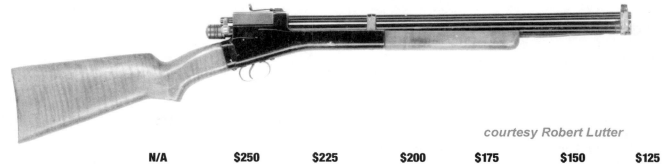

courtesy Robert Lutter

	N/A	$250	$225	$200	$175	$150	$125

Add 60% for original factory box.

○ **Model 102 "Camp Perry" Variant** - first American CO_2 guns, introduced at 1931 Camp Perry matches. Commonly referred to as "hose guns," since CO_2 is supplied via a hose connected to a central tank. Sold only as part of shooting gallery.

courtesy Beeman Collection

Rarity precludes accurate pricing.

MODEL 107 (TOWN & COUNTRY) - .177 cal., pump-lever pneumatic, SS, micro-precision rifling, heavy all wood stock/forearm, instant selection of front sights, 37.8 in. OAL, massive, extremely well built. 6.1 lbs. Mfg. 1949.

courtesy Robert Lutter

	N/A	$1,000	$850	$750	$650	$500	$350

Add 50% for original factory box.

MODEL 108 (TOWN & COUNTRY) - .22 cal., similar to Model 107. Mfg. 1949.

	N/A	$500	$425	$375	$325	$250	$175

Add 50% for original factory box.

MODEL 109 (TOWN & COUNTRY JR.) - .177 cal., pneumatic pump, SS. Mfg. 1949-1951.

courtesy Robert Lutter

	N/A	$195	$165	$120	$95	$60	$45

Add 40% for original factory box.

GRADING	100%	95%	90%	80%	60%	40%	20%

MODEL 110 (TOWN & COUNTRY JR.) - .22 cal., similar to Model 109. Mfg. 1949-1951.

	N/A	$160	$140	$100	$80	$50	$35

Add 40% for original factory box.

MODEL 113 - .177 cal., CO$_2$, 10 oz. charged from separate cylinder, SS, early Models 113 and 114 with fat, straight-line stock, later models with tapered, thin stock. Mfg. 1950-1955.

courtesy Robert Lutter

	$175	$155	$135	$125	$100	$75	$35

Add 30% for original CO$_2$ tank. (Readers are advised not to charge original Crosman CO$_2$ tanks used on Models 113, and 114). Add 20% for straight-line stock. Add 60% for original factory box.

MODEL 114 - .22 cal., CO$_2$, 10 oz. separate cylinder, SS. Mfg. 1950-1955.

	$175	$155	$135	$125	$100	$75	$35

Add 15% for brass barrel. Add 20% for straight-line stock. Add 75% for early production with Crosman Arms logo buttplate as on Models 107-108. Add 30% for original CO$_2$ tank. (Readers are advised not to charge original Crosman CO$_2$ tanks used on Models 113, and 114). Add 60% for original factory box.

MODEL 117 (SHOOT-A-SCORE) - .21 cal., CO$_2$, hose for use with large central gas tank, magazine repeater. Extremely rare. One pc. wood stock like model 118, counter security chain attached at muzzle. Mfg. 1947-1955.

MODEL 118 - .22 cal., CO$_2$, 10 oz. separate cylinder, magazine repeater. Mfg. 1952-54.

courtesy Robert Lutter

	N/A	$450	$375	$325	$295	$235	$125

Add 60% for original factory box. Subtract $50 for no CO$_2$ tank.

MODEL 120 - .22 cal., pneumatic pump, SS. Variant one: brass early. Variant two: steel. Mfg. 1952-1954.

courtesy Robert Lutter

	N/A	$120	$100	$90	$75	$50	$35

Add 20% for variant one. Add 10% for original white bead sight. Add 30% for original factory box.

GRADING	100%	95%	90%	80%	60%	40%	20%

MODEL 121 "CG" (GALLERY RIFLES) - .210 cal., CO_2, repeater, 4.5 oz. cylinder, vertically attached to gun, adj. peep sight. Mfg. 1946-49.

courtesy Robert Lutter

	N/A	$500	$425	$375	$325	$275	$175

Subtract $75 for no CO_2 tank. Add $50-$75 for Slant-Tank variant, a small fitting added (circa 1949) to "CG" models to improve position of CO_2 tank.

Sold to commercial shooting galleries, shooting clubs, hospitals, and industrial companies for employee recreation. Ergonomic variations: various factory-added modifications intended to ease pellet loading, bolt operation, and cocking. Presumably intended for use by VA hospitals and others for rehabilitation. The complex of CG guns still needs study.
Note: .21 caliber intended to restrict supply of pellets to Crosman brand only. Original Crosman .210 pellet container, and some other sources, refer to this model as the Crosman Gas Carbine, Model 200 (caution: do not charge original CO_2 cylinders unless professionally hydro-tested).

MODEL 122 "CG" - .22 cal., CO_2, SS, 4.5 oz. cylinder vertically or 47.5 degree angle attached to gun, adj. peep sights.

	N/A	$450	$375	$325	$295	$195	$100

MODEL 123 (100 CG, SHOOT-A-SCORE) - .177 cal., CO_2, SS, 4.5 oz. cylinder with 47.5 degree angle from stock, SS. Mfg. 1946-1950.

courtesy Beeman Collection

	N/A	$425	$350	$300	$275	$175	$75

Subtract $75 for no CO_2 tank.

MODEL 125 RAWHIDE - BB/.175 cal., single stroke swinging forearm pump pneumatic, repeater with thirty-five-shot magazine, 300 FPS, Crosman´s first BB rifle and first single stroke pump pneumatic, 5 lbs. Mfg. 1973-1974. Recalled by factory.

courtesy Robert Lutter

	$185	$150	$115	$75	$50	N/A	N/A

Add 20% for factory box.

GRADING	100%	95%	90%	80%	60%	40%	20%

MODEL 140 - .22 cal., pneumatic pump, swinging forearm, single shot, 4.8 lbs. First variant: spoon handle breech cover, aluminum breech, fingertip recocking, mfg. 1954. Second variant: spoon handle breech cover, aluminum breech, auto recocking, mfg. 1955-57. Third variant: without spoon handle breech cover, steel breech. Mfg. 1956-62. Fourth variant: die-cast trigger housing, mfg. 1961-68.

courtesy Robert Lutter

	$135	$105	$90	$75	$55	N/A	N/A

Add 10% for first variant. Add 40% for third variant. Add 20% for factory box.

MODEL 147 - .177 cal., similar to Model 140. First variant: with spoon handle breech cover and aluminum breech, and auto recocking, mfg. 1955-56. Second variant: with steel breech and without spoon handle breech cover, mfg. 1956-62.

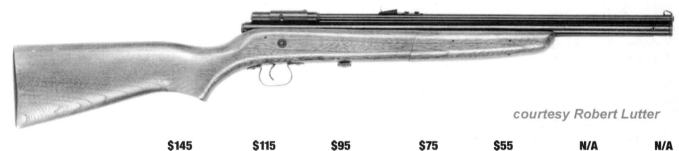

courtesy Robert Lutter

	$145	$115	$95	$75	$55	N/A	N/A

Add 10% for first variant. Add 20% for factory box.

MODEL 147 BP - BB/.175 cal. or .177 cal. pellet version of Model 147, has magnetic bolt tip for steel BBs, rifled barrel. Mfg. 1964-1966.

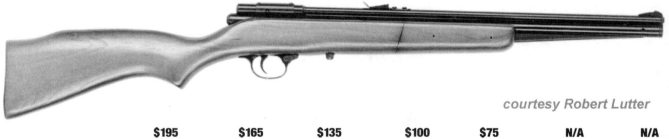

courtesy Robert Lutter

	$195	$165	$135	$100	$75	N/A	N/A

Add 20% for factory box.

MODEL 160 - .22 cal., CO_2, two Powerlets, BA, SS, steel or die cast automatic safety, full wood stock. First variant: steel automatic safety, without barrel band, mfg. 1955-56. Second variant: barrel band, Model 360 peep sight, mfg. 1956-59. Third variant: die cast trigger housing, Model S331 peep sight, mfg. 1960-71.

courtesy Robert Lutter

	$225	$180	$145	$120	$80	N/A	N/A

Add 20% for Model 360 peep sight. Add 40% for Model S331 peep sight. Add 50% for Ted Williams version. Add 25% for "Military" version with sling(Model 160SP). Add 20% for factory box.

See Fletcher (1998) book, *The Crosman Arms Model 160'*, a must-have reference.

GRADING	100%	95%	90%	80%	60%	40%	20%

MODEL 166 (HAHN SUPER BB REPEATER)

BB/.175 cal., CO_2, one Powerlet, Winchester-style lever action repeater, spring-fed thirty-shot magazine. First product of P.Y. Hahn Mfg. Co., Fairport, NY. Mfg.1958-71.

courtesy Robert Lutter

	$125	$95	$75	$60	$45	N/A	N/A

Add 20% for factory box.

MODEL 167

.177 cal., similar to Model 160. First variant: with steel or die cast automatic safety and without barrel band, mfg. 1956. Second variant: with barrel band and Model 360 peep sight, mfg. 1956-59. Third variant: with die-cast trigger housing and Model S331 peep sight, mfg. 1960-66.

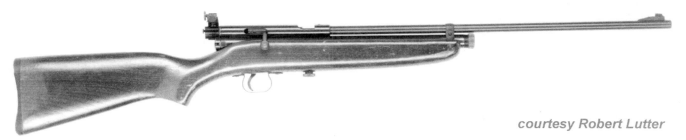

courtesy Robert Lutter

	$250	$225	$185	$150	$100	N/A	N/A

Add 20% for Model 360 peep sight. Add 40% for Model S331 peep sight. Subtract 25% for first and second variants. Add 20% for factory box.

MODEL 180

.22 cal., CO_2, one Powerlet, BA, SS, full wood stock, 4 lbs. First variant: cross bolt safety, mfg. 1956-59. Second variant: die-cast trigger housing. Mfg. 1962-67.

courtesy Robert Lutter

	$130	$120	$100	$80	$75	$65	$55

Subtract 20% for first variant. Add 20% for factory box.

MODEL 187

.177 cal., similar to Model 180. First variant: has cross bolt safety. Mfg. 1956-62. Second variant: with die-cast trigger housing. Mfg. 1962-66.

courtesy Robert Lutter

	$145	$135	$110	$90	$80	$70	$60

Subtract 20% for first variant. Add 20% for factory box.

GRADING	100%	95%	90%	80%	60%	40%	20%

MODEL 197 - 10 oz., CO_2 cylinder (not a gun). Excellent condition = $50 (caution: do not charge original cylinders, for firing use modern steel or aluminum cylinders only). Mfg. 1950-1970.

MODEL 200 - see Model 121 "CG."

MODEL 262 - .177 cal., CO_2, one Powerlet, bolt action, SS, 38.25 in. OAL, 625 FPS, 4.8 lbs. Mfg. 1991-93.

	100%	95%	90%	80%	60%	40%	20%
	$90	$80	$75	$70	$65	N/A	N/A

Add 10% for factory box.

○ *Model 262Y* - youth version of Model 262, 33.75 in. OAL, 610 FPS, 4.7 lbs. Mfg. 1991-93.

	100%	95%	90%	80%	60%	40%	20%
	$90	$80	$75	$70	$65	N/A	N/A

Add 10% for factory box.

MODEL 400 - .22 cal., CO_2, two Powerlets, spring-fed, "swing feed" ten-round mag., full wood stock. First variant: cross bolt safety. Mfg. 1957-62. Second variant: die-cast trigger housing. Mfg. 1962-64.

courtesy Robert Lutter

	100%	95%	90%	80%	60%	40%	20%
	$175	$150	$125	$100	$75	N/A	N/A

Subtract 20% for first variant. Subtract 25% for missing magazine. Add 20% for factory box.

MODEL 500 POWERMATIC - BB/.175 cal., CO_2, one Powerlet, semi-auto fifty-shot, 350 FPS. Mfg. 1970-79.

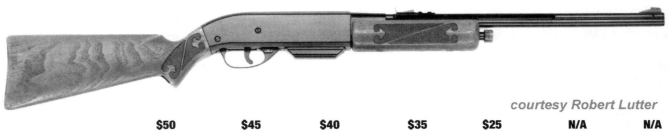

courtesy Robert Lutter

	100%	95%	90%	80%	60%	40%	20%
	$50	$45	$40	$35	$25	N/A	N/A

Add 10% for factory box.

MODEL 622 PELL-CLIP REPEATER - .22 cal., CO_2, one Powerlet, slide action forearm, removable rotating six-shot clip, 450 FPS. Mfg. 1971-78.

courtesy Robert Lutter

	100%	95%	90%	80%	60%	40%	20%
	$110	$100	$90	$80	$60	N/A	N/A

Add 20% for factory box.
   Extended gas tube is an aftermarket addition, not factory original.

MODEL 664X - BB/.175 cal. eighteen-shot mag. (plus 200 round reservoir) or .177 cal. five-shot mag. pellet single shot, swinging forearm pump pneumatic, bolt action, 680 FPS (BB), 645 FPS (pellet), 20.5 in. rifled steel barrel, black finish, brown checkered synthetic stock and forearm, fiberoptic front and adj. rear sights, four-power scope (M-0410) included, 2.9 lbs. Disc. 2004.

	100%	95%	90%	80%	60%	40%	20%
	$50	$40	$30	$20	$15	N/A	N/A

Last MSR was $60.

○ *Model 664GT* - similar to Model 664X, except has black stock and forearm and gold accents. Mfg. 1997-2003.

	100%	95%	90%	80%	60%	40%	20%
	$65	$50	$40	$30	$25	N/A	N/A

○ *Model 664SB* - similar to Model 664X, except has silver barrel and 4x15mm silver scope. Mfg. 1994-present.

MSR $106	100%	95%	90%	80%	60%	40%	20%
	$90	$75	$55	$70	$40	N/A	N/A

MODEL RM650 BB SCOUT - .177 cal., LA, SP, SS, smooth bore steel barrel, 300 FPS, black finish, checkered hardwood stock and forearm, 2.8 lbs. Mfg. 2002-03.

	100%	95%	90%	80%	60%	40%	20%
	$40	$30	$25	$20	$15	N/A	N/A

GRADING	100%	95%	90%	80%	60%	40%	20%

MODEL 700 - .22 cal., CO_2, one Powerlet, SS, rotary tap loading. Mfg. 1967-71.

courtesy Robert Lutter

	$100	$90	$80	$70	$50	N/A	N/A

Add 20% for factory box. Add 100% for Model S331 peep sight.

MODEL 707 - .177 cal., similar to Model 700. Mfg. 1967-71.

	$100	$90	$80	$70	$50	N/A	N/A

Add 20% for factory box. Add 100% for Model S331 peep sight.

MODEL 760 POWERMASTER - combination BB/.175 cal. repeater (180-shot gravity-fed magazine) and .177 cal. pellet SS, 10 pumps = 595 FPS (BB), BA, PP, 17 in. smoothbore steel BBL. The first short-stroke pump pneumatic, developed in Canada as "Canadian Boy" from Model 130 pistol. Large number of variations; key variations listed. Canadian Boy: original 1964 version, continuous wood stock and forearm, mfg. 1964. First variant: wooden stock and forearm. Mfg. 1966-70. Second variant: styrene stock/forearm, scope mount grooves. Mfg. 1971-74. Third variant: self-cocking, styrene stock, wood forearm. Mfg. 1974-75. Fourth variant: ABS stock and forearm. Mfg. 1975-77. Fifth variant: manual cocking. Mfg. 1977-80. Sixth variant: plastic bolt. Mfg. 1980-83. Seventh variant: plastic receiver, welded sights. Mfg. 1983-91. Eighth variant: shortened barrel, pressed on sights. Mfg. began in 1991. Disc.

courtesy Robert Lutter

	$30	$25	$20	$15	$10	N/A	N/A

Subtract 10% for smoothbore (prior to 1981). Add $250 for Canadian Boy. Add 300% for first variant. Add 25% for factory scope. Add 25% for wood stock (except Canadian Boy and first variant). Add 5% for factory box.

○ *Model 760/20 (Model 760 20th Year Commemorative)* - BB/.175 cal. repeater or .177 cal. pellet single-shot pneumatic, similar to Model 760. Mfg. 1985.

courtesy Robert Lutter

	$65	$50	$35	N/A	N/A	N/A	N/A

Variation: Model 760/20-999. Special presentation commemoratives; individually engraved name plates and wall plaques. Special order by Crosman sales rep for key buyers and senior staff. Designed as a wall-mounted item, generally not used. Will bring a premium.

○ *Model 760XL Powermaster* - BB/.175 cal. repeater or .177 cal., deluxe version of Model 760, brass-plated receiver, hooded front sight. Mfg. 1978-80.

courtesy Robert Lutter

	$40	$30	$25	$20	$15	N/A	N/A

GRADING	100%	95%	90%	80%	60%	40%	20%

⊙ *Model 760AB Pumpmaster* - BB/.175 cal. repeater or .177 cal. SS pellet, pneumatic, similar to Model 760 with black stock and forearm. Mfg. began in 1997. Disc.

	$40	$30	$25	$20	$15	N/A	N/A

⊙ *Model 760B Pumpmaster* - BB/.175 cal. eighteen-shot mag. or .177 cal. five-shot mag. pellet, multi-pump pneumatic, 17 in. smooth bore steel barrel, 600 FPS (BB), black finish, brown synthetic stock and forearm, fiberoptic front and adj. rear sights, 2.75 lbs. Mfg. 1997-present.

MSR $64	$55	$45	$35	$25	$20	N/A	N/A

⊙ *Model 760BRD Pumpmaster* - BB/.175 cal. eighteen-shot mag. or .177 cal. five-shot mag. pellet, similar to Model 760B, except red dot sight included. Disc. 2005.

	$55	$48	$40	$35	$25	N/A	N/A

Last MSR was $62.

⊙ *Model 760P Pumpmaster (Classic Pink)* - BB/.175 cal. eighteen-shot mag. or .177 cal. five-shot mag. pellet, multi-pump pneumatic, 17 in. smooth bore steel barrel, 600 FPS (BB), black finish, pink synthetic stock and forearm, fiberoptic front and adj. rear sights, 2.75 lbs. Mfg. 2007-present.

MSR $66	$55	$45	$35	$25	$20	N/A	N/A

⊙ *Model 760SK Pumpmaster Starter Kit* - BB/.175 cal. eighteen-shot mag. or .177 cal. five-shot mag. pellet, Model 760SK kit includes 600 BBs, 250 .177 cal. pellets, red dot sight, shooting glasses and five NRA targets.

MSR $95	$85	$75	$65	$45	$35	N/A	N/A

MODEL 760 40TH ANNIVERSARY EDITION
.177 cal., deluxe version of Model 760, nickel-plated receiver, hooded front sight, hardwood stock and forearm, option for laser engraved name or message on reciever, 1,500 Mfg. 2006.

	$65	$50	$35	N/A	N/A	N/A	N/A

MODEL 760XLS
BB/.175 or .177 pellet cal., SS, multi-stroke pump pneumatic, adj. fiber optic sights, hardwood stock and forearm, rifeled steel BBL, approx. 600 FPS, 33.5 in. OAL, 3.69 lbs. Mfg. 2007-current.

MSR $116	$100	$85	$70	$50	$35	N/A	N/A

MODEL 761XL
- BB/.175 cal. repeater or .177 cal., deluxe version of Model 760, brass-plated receiver, hooded front sight, wood stock. First variant: mfg. 1972-78. Second variant: manual cocking. Mfg. 1978-81.

courtesy Robert Lutter

	$60	$45	$30	N/A	N/A	N/A	N/A

MODEL 764SB
- BB/.175 cal. repeater or .177 cal. SS pellet, pneumatic, similar to Model 760B with silver BBL, black stock and forearm, and 4x15mm scope. Mfg. 1994-present.

MSR $86	$75	$65	$50	$35	$20	N/A	N/A

MODEL 766 AMERICAN CLASSIC
- BB/.175 cal. repeater or .177 cal. pellet SS, multi-stroke pump pneumatic, 10 pumps = 710 FPS (BB), modeled after Remington autoloader firearm. First variant: tapered plastic BBL housing. Mfg. 1975-81. Second variant: tapered steel barrel housing. Mfg. 1977-83. Third variant: straight steel barrel housing. Mfg. 1981-82.

courtesy Robert Lutter

	$60	$50	$45	$40	$30	N/A	N/A

Add 10% for first variant. Add 15% for second variant. Add 10% for original box. Add 50% for wood stock (pre-1983).

MODEL 781
- BB/.175 cal. repeater or .177 cal. pellet SS, single pump pneumatic, smoothbore, 450 FPS (BB), four-shot clip, 195 round reservoir, 2.9 lbs. Mfg. 1983-95.

	$40	$35	$30	$25	$20	N/A	N/A

⊙ *Model 781AK Action Kit* - kit includes Model 7781 rifle, adj. 4 x 15 mm scope, 250-count .177 cal.pellets, 350 BBs, five NRA targets, and shooting glasses. Mfg. 2002-07.

	$75	$65	$55	$40	$30	N/A	N/A

Last MSR was $95.

GRADING	100%	95%	90%	80%	60%	40%	20%

⊚ **Model 7781** - similar to Model 781, except has black stock and forearm. New 2002.

MSR $74	$65	$55	$45	$30	$20	N/A	N/A

MODEL 782 BLACK DIAMOND - BB/.175 cal. repeater or .177 cal. pellet SS, CO_2, one Powerlet, five-shot clip. Mfg. began in 1990. Disc.

	$25	$20	$15	$10	$5	N/A	N/A

⊚ **Model 782B** - .177 cal., CO_2, similar to Model 782 Black Diamond. Disc. 2002.

	$55	$45	$35	$25	$20	N/A	N/A

MODEL 788 BB SCOUT - BB/.175 cal., multi-pump pneumatic, gravity-fed twenty-shot mag., 2.5 lbs., 500 FPS (BB). First variant: short pump stroke. Mfg. 1978-79. Second variant: long pump stroke. Mfg. 1979-90.

courtesy Robert Lutter

	$45	$40	$35	$30	$20	N/A	N/A

Add 20% for short stroke variant. Add 10% for factory box.

⊚ **Model Black Fire** - variation of Model 788, black stock/forearm. Mfg. 1996-97.

	$50	$45	$40	$35	$30	N/A	N/A

Add 20% for short stroke variant. Add 10% for factory box.

MODEL 790 OUTBACKER - BB/.175 cal. repeater or .177 cal. pellet, single pump pneumatic, five-shot pellet clip, plastic stock with hidden canteen, 450 FPS (BB), 2.8 lbs. Mfg. 1990-91.

	$60	$55	$50	$45	$30	N/A	N/A

Subtract 25% for missing canteen.

MODEL 795 SPRINGMASTER - .177 cal., BBC, SP, SS, 500 FPS, rifled steel barrel, hooded front adj. rear sights, black finish, checkered synthetic stock. Mfg. 1995-1997.

	$75	$65	$55	$45	$35	N/A	N/A

⊚ **Model 795 Springmaster** - .177 cal., similar to Model 795 Springmaster, except 600 FPS. Mfg. 1997-2007.

	$65	$55	$45	$35	$25	N/A	N/A

Last MSR was $80.

MODEL 1077 REPEATAIR - .177 cal., CO_2, one Powerlet, twelve-shot mag. repeater, 20.4 in. rifled steel barrel, 625 FPS, black finish, checkered black synthetic stock, fiberoptic front and adj. rear sights, 3.7 lbs. New 1994.

MSR $112	$100	$85	$70	$50	$30	N/A	N/A

⊚ **Model 1077CA Constant Air** - similar to Model 1077 RepeatAir, except bulk fill tank kit. Mfg. 1995.

	$180	$155	$130	$105	$75	N/A	N/A

⊚ **Model 1077LB RepeatAir** - similar to Model 1077 RepeatAir, except black laminated hardwood stock. Mfg. 2002-03.

	$85	$75	$65	$55	$45	N/A	N/A

⊚ **Model 1077LG RepeatAir** - similar to Model 1077 RepeatAir, except green laminated hardwood stock. Mfg. 2002-03.

	$85	$75	$65	$55	$45	N/A	N/A

⊚ **Model 1077RD RepeatAir** - similar to Model 1077 RepeatAir, except red dot sight included. Disc. 2004.

	$85	$75	$65	$55	$45	N/A	N/A

Last MSR was $91.

⊚ **Model 1077SB RepeatAir** - similar to Model 1077 RepeatAir, except has silver barrel. Mfg. 1995.

	$75	$65	$55	$45	$35	N/A	N/A

⊚ **Model 1077W RepeatAir** - similar to Model 1077 RepeatAir, except has walnut stock. Mfg. 1997-2007.

	$100	$90	$80	$70	$60	N/A	N/A

Last MSR was $110.

⊚ **Model 1077KT RepeatAir Action Kit** - .177 cal., CO_2, kit includes Model 1077 rifle, large-lens red dot sight, extra removable mag.,three twelve-shot rotary clips,250-count .177 cal. pellets, three Powerlet CO_2 cartridges, five NRA targets, and shooting glasses. Disc. 2006.

	$90	$80	$70	$60	$50	N/A	N/A

Last MSR was $97.

⊚ **Model AS1077T AirSource** - .177 cal., CO_2, 88g AirSource cylinder, twelve-shot rotary mag. semi-auto repeater, 20.4 in. rifled steel barrel, 625 FPS, black finish, checkered black synthetic stock, fiberoptic front and adj. rear sights, 3.7 lbs. New 2004.

MSR $162	$145	$120	$95	$70	$45	N/A	N/A

Upgrade kit (Model AS1077AD approx. $40) available for Model 1077 RepeatAir rifles manufactured since May 1999.

GRADING	100%	95%	90%	80%	60%	40%	20%

MODEL 1388 - BB/.175 cal. or .177 cal. pellet, pneumatic, SS, BA, 10.25 in. rifled barrel, 560 FPS, adj. rear sight, plastic breech, Model 1377 pistol with shoulder stock. Mfg. 1982-88.

	$85	$70	$60	$50	$45	N/A	N/A

MODEL 1389 BACKPACKER - .177 cal., multi-pump pneumatic, SS, detachable stock, green, 10 pumps = 560 FPS, 3.3 lbs. Mfg. 1989-98.

	$65	$60	$50	$45	$30	N/A	N/A

MODEL 1400 PUMPMASTER - .22 cal., multi-pump pneumatic, SS, 10 pumps = 580 FPS, 5.5 lbs., wood stock/forearm. Highly desired by shooters who have them upgraded and converted for current field use. As with certain other Crosman models sought by shooters, values are determined more by desirability of certain versions for shooting and conversion than rarity. It is increasingly difficult for collectors to locate completely original specimens. First variant: has breech cover. Mfg. 1968-72. Second variant: has bolt handle. Mfg. 1972-73. Third variant: has bolt handle, slim-line stock. Mfg. 1973-78.

courtesy Robert Lutter

	$125	$100	$75	$60	$45	N/A	N/A

Add 30% for second and third variants. Add 10% for factory box.

MODEL 1760 - .177 cal., CO$_2$, one Powerlet, BA, SA, one-piece walnut stock, 24 in. rifled steel barrel, black finish, hardwood stock, adj. rear sight, 600 FPS, 4.8 lbs. Mfg. 1999-2005.

	$80	$65	$50	$40	$35	N/A	N/A

Last MSR was $92.

MODEL 1894 - .177 cal., CO$_2$, LA, two 12 gram Powerlets located in the buttstock, eight-shot rotary mag., 15 (carbine) or 18.9 (rifle) in. barrel, 610 FPS, blue finish, hardwood stock with plastic butt plate and forearm, hooded front and adj. rear sights, crossbolt safety, 7.5 lbs (rifle). Disc. 2002.

	$250	$215	$175	$145	$100	N/A	N/A

MODEL 2000 CHALLENGER - .177 cal., CO$_2$, BA, SS, 19 in. rifled steel BBL, 485 FPS, adj. rear target sight, hooded front sight with removable aperture, matte or gloss black, blue, dark blue, red, silver, or grey composite stock with adj. cheekpiece and buttplate, 36.25 in. OAL, 7 lbs. Mfg. 2000-01.

	$400	$300	$225	$190	$155	$100	N/A

Add 20% for gloss black, blue, dark blue, red, silver, or grey stock.

☉ *Model CH2000 Challenger* - .177 cal., CO$_2$, BA, SS, 485 FPS, rifled barrel, adj. rear target sight, hooded front sight with removable aperture, matte black finish, black composite stock with adj. cheekpiece and buttplate, 36.25 in. OAL, 6.95 lbs. New 2001.

MSR $750	$775	$575	$475	$375	$275	N/A	N/A

MODEL 2100 CLASSIC - BB/.175 cal. repeater or .177 cal. pellet SS, swinging forearm multi-stroke pump pneumatic, 10 pumps = 795 FPS (BB), 4.8 lbs. Similar to Model 766. Mfg. began in 1983. Disc.

courtesy Robert Lutter

	$65	$60	$50	$45	$30	N/A	N/A

☉ *Model 2100B* - similar to Model 2100 Classic, except has fiberoptic front sight. Mfg. 1997-present.

MSR $106	$90	$75	$55	$40	$30	N/A	N/A

☉ *Model 2100SB* - similar to Model 2100 Classic, except has zinc plated barrel. Mfg. 1995-96.

	$70	$65	$60	$50	$45	N/A	N/A

☉ *Model 2100W* - similar to Model 2100 Classic, except has walnut stock and forearm. Mfg. 1997-2003.

	$110	$90	$70	$65	$60	N/A	N/A

MODEL 2104GT - similar to Model 2100, except has gold accents and scope. Mfg. 1997-2003.

	$75	$60	$50	$40	$30	N/A	N/A

GRADING	100%	95%	90%	80%	60%	40%	20%

MODEL 2104X - similar to Model 2100, except with 4x15 mm scope. New 2002.

MSR $119	$100	$85	$70	$55	$40	N/A	N/A

MODEL 2175W 75TH ANNIVERSARY COMMEMORATIVE - .177 cal., handcrafted American walnut stock and forearm with limited edition antique brass 75th anniversary medallion inlaid. Mfg 1998 only.

	$125	$110	$90	N/A	N/A	N/A	N/A

MODEL 2200 MAGNUM - .22 cal., pneumatic, SS, similar to Model 2100, adj. rear sight 4.8 lbs. First variant: with chrome-plated receiver. Mfg. 1978-82. Second variant: with black receiver with silkscreen and straight steel barrel housing with plastic sight sleeve. Mfg. 1982-83. Third variant: with brown stock and forearm. Mfg.1983-89.

courtesy Robert Lutter

	$65	$55	$45	$35	$30	N/A	N/A

Add 25% for first variant. Add 10% for second variant.

○ *Model 2200B* - .22 cal., similar to Model 2200 Magnum, except straight barrel housing. Mfg. 1989-2006.

	$70	$60	$50	$45	$30	N/A	N/A

Last MSR was $84.

○ *Model 2200W* - similar to Model 2200 Magnum, except has walnut stock and forearm. Mfg. 1997-2003.

	$105	$85	$65	$60	$50	N/A	N/A

MODEL 2250B - .22 cal., CO_2, one Powerlet, BA, SS, synthetic detachable skeleton stock, black finish, 14.6 in. rifled steel barrel, fiberoptic front and adj. rear sights, 4X scope, 550 FPS, 3.3 lbs. Mfg. 1998-present.

MSR $134	$125	$100	$75	$60	$45	N/A	N/A

○ *Model AS2250XT AirSource* - .22 cal., CO_2, 88g AirSource cylinder, BA, SS, synthetic detachable skeleton stock, black finish, 14.6 in. rifled steel barrel, fiber optic front and adj. rear sights, 4X32 mm scope, 550 FPS, 5.12 lbs. New 2004.

MSR $234	$210	$175	$135	$95	$70	N/A	N/A

MODEL 2260 - .22 cal., CO_2, one Powerlet, BA, SS, one-piece walnut stock, 24 in. rifled steel barrel, black finish, hardwood stock, adj. rear sight, 600 FPS, 4.8 lbs. New 1999.

MSR $130	$125	$100	$85	$70	$45	N/A	N/A

MODEL 2264X - .22 cal., similar to Model 2260, except 4x32mm scope (M-4032) included. Mfg. 1999-2002.

	$125	$100	$85	$70	$50	N/A	N/A

MODEL 2275W 75TH ANNIVERSARY COMMEMORATIVE - .22 cal., pneumatic pump-up, 595 FPS, handcrafted American walnut stock and forearm. Mfg 1998 only.

	$125	$110	$90	N/A	N/A	N/A	N/A

MODEL 2289G BACKPACKER - .22 cal., swinging forearm pump pneumatic, BA, SS, detachable synthetic skeleton stock and forearm, 14.6 in. rifled steel barrel, black finish, fiberoptic front and adj. rear sights, 525 FPS, 2.9 lbs Mfg. 1998-2002.

	$60	$50	$40	$30	$20	N/A	N/A

MODEL 2576 (MODEL 760 25th YEAR COMMEMORATIVE) - BB/.175 cal., repeater or .177 cal. limited edition, similar to Model 760 original styling, except "Tootsie Roll" pump handle, etc. Mfg. 1991.

	$45	$40	$30	$20	$15	N/A	N/A

MODEL 3100 - .177 cal., BBC, SP, SS, 600 FPS, one-piece hardwood stock, 6 lbs. (imported, Bascaran, Spain), mfg. 1987-90.

	$100	$85	$70	$45	$35	N/A	N/A

MODEL 3500 SLIDEMASTER - BB/.175 cal., push-barrel cocking, SP, twenty-two shot repeater, one-piece hardwood stock, updated version of Model V350. Mfg. 1970-73.

	$120	$110	$100	$95	$75	N/A	N/A

Add 30% for factory box.

GRADING	100%	95%	90%	80%	60%	40%	20%

MODEL 6100 (DIANAWERK MODEL 45) - .177 cal., BBC, SP, 830 FPS, 20.50 in. barrel, 8.4 lbs. Mfg. 1982-88.

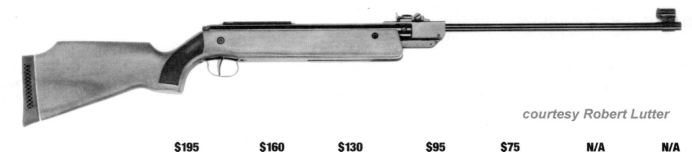

courtesy Robert Lutter

	$195	$160	$130	$95	$75	N/A	N/A

Last MSR was $235.

Basically, a Diana Model 45 with a modified Diana Model 35 stock.

MODEL 6300 (ANSCHÜTZ MODEL 333) - .177 cal., BBC, SP, 700 FPS, 18.50 in. barrel, 6.8 lbs. Mfg. 1986-89.

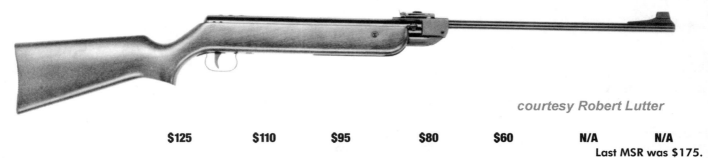

courtesy Robert Lutter

	$125	$110	$95	$80	$60	N/A	N/A

Last MSR was $175.

MODEL 6500 (ANSCHÜTZ MODEL 335) - .177 cal., BBC, SP, 700 FPS, 18.50 in. barrel, 7.7 lbs. Mfg. 1986-88.

courtesy Robert Lutter

	$180	$160	$140	$100	$75	N/A	N/A

Last MSR was $200.

The three German air rifles (M-6100, M-6300, and M-6500) represented Crosman´s 1980s "Challenger Line" excursion into adult precision air rifles. Fletcher´s 1998 book notes that this line "caught between RWS on the low end and Beeman on the high end, never really had a chance."

MODEL 760/20-999 - see Model 760.

MODEL AIR-17 - BB/.175 cal. repeater or .177 cal., swinging forearm pump pneumatic, five-shot pellet clip, twenty-one-round BB magazine, 195 round BB reservoir, replica of Colt AR-15 sporting high-power rifle. Mfg. 1985-90.

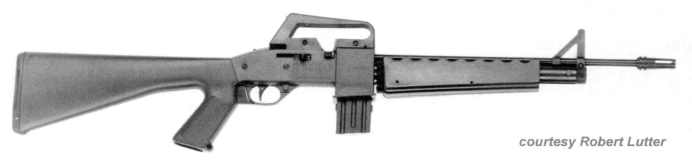

courtesy Robert Lutter

	$150	$125	$100	$85	$65	N/A	N/A

MODEL BLACK FIRE - similar to Model 788, except has black stock and forearm. Mfg. 1996-97.

	$50	$40	$30	$25	$20	N/A	N/A

GRADING	100%	95%	90%	80%	60%	40%	20%

MODEL BLACK LIGHTNING - BB/.175 cal., single stroke pump pneumatic, twenty-shot magazine, 300 round reservoir, replica of Remington Model 1187 shotgun, 350 FPS, 150 round BB container shaped like shotgun shell. Mfg. began in 1997. Disc.

	$30	$25	$20	$15	$10	N/A	N/A

Subtract 10% for missing shotgun style BB container.

MODEL BLACK SERPENT - similar to Model 781, except has black stock and forearm. Mfg. 1996-2002.

	$45	$40	$30	$25	$20	N/A	N/A

QUEST 1000 MODEL C1K77 - .177 cal., BBC, SP, SS, rifled steel (scope stop) barrel, blue finish, 1000 FPS, hardwood Monte Carlo style stock, rubber butt pad, hooded front and adj. rear fiberoptic sights,OAL 45 in., 6 lbs. Mfg..2004-current.

MSR $165	$150	$120	$95	$75	$50	N/A	N/A

⊙ *Quest 1000X Model C1K77X* - .177 cal., similar to Model C1K77, except with 4x32 mm fully adj. scope. Mfg. 2004-current.

courtesy Crosman

MSR $206	$185	$150	$115	$90	$65	N/A	N/A

QUEST MODEL C5M77 - .177 cal., BBC, SP, SS, rifled steel (scope stop) barrel, blue finish, 495 FPS, hardwood Monte Carlo style stock, rubber butt pad, hooded front and adj. rear fiberoptic sights,OAL 41.5 in.,5.5 lbs. Mfg. 2005-07.

	$125	$95	$80	$65	N/A	N/A	N/A

Last MSR was $150.

PHANTOM MODEL CS1K77 - .177 cal., BBC, SP, SS, rifled steel (scope stop) barrel, blue finish, 1000 FPS, ambidextrous black synthetic PG stock, rubber butt pad, hooded front and adj. rear fiberoptic sights,45.5 in. OAL, 6 lbs. New. 2006.

courtesy Crosman

MSR $165	$150	$120	$95	$75	$50	N/A	N/A

⊙ *Phantom X Model CS1K77X* - .177 cal., BBC, SP, SS, rifled steel (scope stop) barrel, blue finish, 1000 FPS, ambidextrous black synthetic PG stock, rubber butt pad, hooded front and adj. rear fiberoptic sights, 4x32mm CenterPoint scope, 45.5 in. OAL, 6 lbs. New. 2006.

courtesy Crosman

MSR $206	$185	$150	$115	$90	$65	N/A	N/A

PHANTOM SHOOTERS KIT MODEL CS1K77KT - .177 cal., BBC, SP, SS, rifled steel (scope stop) barrel, nickel plated, muzzle break, 1000 FPS, ambidextrous black synthetic PG stock, rubber butt pad, hooded front and adj. rear fiber optic sights, CenterPoint Compact 6x32mm scope, 500 Premier pellets, gun sock, 25 official airgun targets, 45.5 in. OAL, 6 lbs. New. 2007.

MSR $309	$275	$235	$185	$145	$100	N/A	N/A

GRADING	100%	95%	90%	80%	60%	40%	20%

MODEL M-1 CARBINE - BB/.175 cal., push-barrel, SP, smoothbore, twenty-two-shot gravity-fed magazine, 180 round reservoir, basically a Model 3500 styled as replica of US M1 .30 cal. carbine. First variant: wood stock, mfg. 1966-67. Second variant: Croswood stock. Mfg. 1968-76.

courtesy Robert Lutter

	100%	95%	90%	80%	60%	40%	20%
	$150	$125	$100	$85	$65	N/A	N/A

Add 60% for wood stock.

MODEL NS1200 NIGHT STALKER - .177 cal., CO_2, semi-automatic blow back action, one 88G Powerlet, twelve-shot rotary mag. repeater, 20.4 in. rifled steel barrel, 580 FPS, black finish, checkered black synthetic thumb hole stock, Mohawk adj. sight system, 30.5 in. OAL, 3.27 lbs. Mfg. 2005-current.

courtesy Crosman

MSR $166	100%	95%	90%	80%	60%	40%	20%
	$145	$120	$95	$70	N/A	N/A	N/A

MODEL NS1204A NIGHT STALKER TK - .177 cal., CO_2, semi-automatic blow back action, one 88G Powerlet, twelve-shot rotary mag. repeater, 20.4 in. rifled steel barrel, 580 FPS, black finish, checkered black synthetic thumb hole stock, Mohawk adj. sight system w/ dual illumination sight, tactical flashlight, collapsible bipod, 30.5 in. OAL, 3.27 lbs. Mfg. 2005-2007.

courtesy Crosman

	100%	95%	90%	80%	60%	40%	20%
	$185	$150	$115	$90	N/A	N/A	N/A

Last MSR was $200.

MODEL RM177 - .177 cal., BBC, SP, SS, rifled steel barrel, blue finish, 825 FPS, checkered hardwood English style stock, rubber butt pad, sling mounts, hooded front and adj. peep rear sights, 7.1 lbs. Mfg. 2002.

	100%	95%	90%	80%	60%	40%	20%
	$110	$90	$75	$60	$45	N/A	N/A

⚙ **Model RM177** - .177 cal., similar to Model RM177, except 4x32 (M-4032) scope included. Mfg. 2002.

	100%	95%	90%	80%	60%	40%	20%
	$125	$95	$80	$65	$50	N/A	N/A

MODEL RM277 - .177 cal., BBC, SP, SS, rifled steel barrel, blue finish, 825 FPS, hardwood Monte carlo style stock, rubber butt pad, hooded front and adj. rear sights, 7.1 lbs. Mfg. 2002-03.

	100%	95%	90%	80%	60%	40%	20%
	$110	$90	$75	$60	$45	N/A	N/A

⚙ **Model RM277X** - .177 cal., similar to Model RM177, except 4x32 (M-4032) scope included. New 2002-03.

	100%	95%	90%	80%	60%	40%	20%
	$125	$95	$80	$65	$50	N/A	N/A

GRADING	100%	95%	90%	80%	60%	40%	20%

MODEL RM422 - .22 cal., BBC, SP, SS, rifled steel barrel, blue finish, 825 FPS, hardwood Monte Carlo style stock, rubber butt pad, hooded front and adj. rear sights, 7.1 lbs. Mfg. 2003-04.

	$115	$95	$75	$60	$45	N/A	N/A

Last MSR was $140.

MODEL RM522 - .22 cal., BBC, SP, SS, rifled steel barrel, blue finish, 825 FPS, hardwood Monte Carlo style stock, rubber butt pad, hooded front and adj. rear sights, 7.9 lbs. Mfg. 2002-03.

	$150	$120	$90	$75	$60	N/A	N/A

MODEL RM577 - .177 cal., BBC, SP, SS, rifled steel barrel, blue finish, 1000 FPS, hardwood Monte Carlo style stock, rubber butt pad, hooded front and adj. rear sights, 7.9 lbs. Mfg. 2002-03.

	$150	$120	$90	$75	$60	N/A	N/A

⊘ *Model RM577X* - .177 cal., similar to Model RM177, except 4x32 (M-4032) scope included. Mfg. 2002-03.

	$175	$150	$120	$90	$75	N/A	N/A

MODEL RM677 - .177 cal., BBC, SP, SS, rifled steel barrel, blue finish, 1000 FPS, checkered hardwood thumbhole stock, rubber butt pad, hooded front and adj. rear peep sights, 7.5 lbs. Mfg. 2002.

	$185	$165	$145	$120	$90	N/A	N/A

MODEL RM877 - .177 cal., BBC, SP, SS, rifled steel barrel, blue finish, 1100 FPS, checkered hardwood Monte Carlo style stock, rubber buttpad, hooded front and adj. rear peep sights, 7.5 lbs. Mfg. 2002.

	$225	$185	$165	$145	$120	N/A	N/A

MODEL V350 - BB/.175 cal., push-barrel, SP, hardwood stock, variation of Quackenbush Model 7. Mfg. 1961-69.

courtesy Robert Lutter

	$120	$90	$70	$45	$30	N/A	N/A

Add 20% for factory box. Add 200% for factory gold-plated version. Add 300-500% for Model V350M Military Trainer.

MODEL 1924 See Second Model and notes about the designation of 1924 Model.

G1 EXTREME MODEL CS1K77KTBX - .177 cal., BBC, SP, SS, rifled steel (scope stop) barrel, black finish, muzzle break, 1000 FPS, checkered ambidextrous black synthetic PG stock, two stage adj. trigger, rubber buttpad, CenterPoint 3-9x32mm Mil-Dot scope, 44.5 in. OAL, 6 lbs. Mfg. 2008-current.

courtesy Crosman

MSR $217	$195	$165	$125	$85	N/A	N/A	N/A

SIERRA PRO MODEL CW1K77XKT - .177 cal., BBC, SP, SS, rifled steel (scope stop) barrel, blue finish, 1000 FPS, checkered hardwood Monte Carlo style stock, rubber buttpad, hooded front and adj. rear fiberoptic sights, 3-9x40mm Mil-Dot scope, OAL 45 in., 7.8 lbs. Mfg. 2008- current.

courtesy Crosman

MSR $309	$285	$250	$195	$145	N/A	N/A	N/A

GRADING	100%	95%	90%	80%	60%	40%	20%

STORM XT MODEL C1K773932 - .177 cal., BBC, SP, SS, rifled steel (scope stop) barrel, blue finish, 1000 FPS, hardwood Monte Carlo style stock, rubber buttpad, adj. rear and bead fiberoptic sights, 3-9x32mm scope, OAL 45 in., 6 lbs. Mfg. 2007- current.

courtesy Crosman

MSR N/A	$100	$80	$65	$50	N/A	N/A	N/A

TAC 1 EXTREME MODEL CST8M22XKT - .22 cal., BBC, SP, SS, rifled steel (scope stop) barrel, nickel plated, muzzle break, 800 FPS, ambidextrous black synthetic PG stock, two stage adj. trigger, rubber buttpad, hooded front and adj. rear fiber optic sights, CenterPoint 3-9x32mm scope, Flashlight, Bipod, Laser 45.5 in. OAL, 6 lbs. Mfg. 2007-current.

courtesy Crosman

MSR $464	$415	$365	$295	$225	$150	N/A	N/A

TAC 77 ELITE MODEL CT1K77XKT - .177 cal., BBC, SP, SS, rifled steel (scope stop) barrel, black finish, muzzle break, 1000FPS, ambidextrous black synthetic PG stock w/ padded adj. cheekpiece, two stage adj. trigger, CenterPoint 3-9x32mm scope, flashlight, Bipod, Laser 45.5 in. OAL, 6 lbs. Mfg. 2008-current.

courtesy Crosman

MSR $400	$365	$295	$250	N/A	N/A	N/A	N/A

GRADING	100%	95%	90%	80%	60%	40%	20%

SHOTGUN

MODEL 1100 TRAPMASTER - .380 bore, CO_2, two Powerlets, SS. Mfg.1968-1971.

courtesy Beeman Collection

	$190	$175	$160	$150	$125	$100	$75

Add 20% for factory box. Add 75% for complete trap set (trap, loading outfit, cases, etc.). Add 200% for factory gold-plated version. Add 75%-200% for high quality conversion to slug firing rifles.

SPECIAL/LIMITED EDITIONS

1760SE SPECIAL EDITION SPORTSMANS MODEL RIFLE - .177 cal., CO_2, one Powerlet, BA, SA, 24 in. rifled steel barrel, 700 FPS, adj. rear blade front sights, CenterPoint 6x32mm scope and rings, black finish, American hardwood PG stock, 39.75 in. OAL, 4.8 lbs. Mfg. 2008-current.

MSR N/A	$166	$135	$100	N/A	N/A	N/A	N/A

Last MSR was $92.

2260SE SPECIAL EDITION SPORTSMANS MODEL RIFLE - .22 cal., CO_2, one Powerlet, BA, SS, 24 in. rifled steel barrel, 600 FPS, adj. rear blade front sights, CenterPoint 6x32mm scope and rings, black finish, American hardwood PG stock, 39.75 in. OAL, 4.8 lbs. Mfg. 2008-current.

MSR N/A	$166	$135	$100	N/A	N/A	N/A	N/A

MODEL 2300SLE LIMITED EDITION PISTOL - .177 cal., CO_2, one 12g powerlet, BA, SS, 10.1 Lothar-Walther choked match rifled BBL, adj. hammer spring for 440-520- FPS, single stage adj. trigger, Williams adj. rear sight, blue finish, pecan hardwood grips w/ fish scale laser etched design, silver muzzel break, silver trigger and silver tigger shoe, 16 in. OAL, 42.5 oz., hand crafted pecan wood case w/ rustic leather appointments, ten Crosman Powerlets, ammo pouch, tin of Crosman Wadcutter pellets, and tube of Pellgunoil. Edition is limited to 100. Mfg. 2008-current.

MSR N/A	$420	$375	$275	N/A	N/A	N/A	N/A

MODEL 2300TLE LIMITED EDITION PISTOL - .177 cal., CO_2, one 12g powerlet, BA, SS, 10.1 Lothar-Walther choked match rifled BBL, adj. hammer spring for 440-520- FPS, single stage adj. trigger, Williams adj. rear sight, blue finish, pecan hardwood grips w/ fish scale laser etched design, silver muzzel break, silver trigger and silver tigger shoe, 16 in. OAL, 42.5 oz., hand crafted pecan wood case w/ rustic leather appointments, ten Crosman Powerlets, ammo pouch, tin of Crosman Wadcutter pellets, and tube of Pellgunoil. Edition is limited to 100. Mfg. 2008-current.

MSR N/A	$360	$335	$300	N/A	N/A	N/A

GRADING	100%	95%	90%	80%	60%	40%	20%

MODEL 2250XE OUTDOORSMAN - .22 cal., CO_2, one Powerlet, BA, SS, long steel breach, 18 in. rifled steel barrel w/ muzzel break, 550 FPS, black finish, CenterPoint 3-9x32mm Mil-Dot scope, hand crafted pecan skeleton stock and forearm, 33 in. OAL, 3.3 lbs. Mfg. 2008-present.

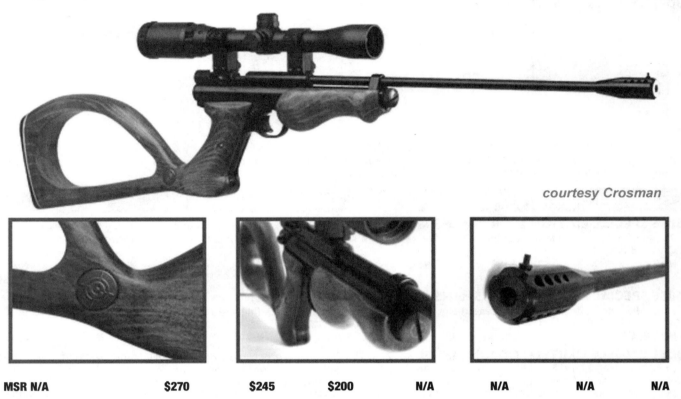

courtesy Crosman

MSR N/A		$270	$245	$200	N/A	N/A	N/A	N/A

CROSS

Previous manufacturer located in Boston, Mass. Circa 1876.

PISTOL

CROSS PATENT PISTOL .21 caliber, SP, SS. Based on U.S. Patent no. 182,899 issued to Wm C. Cross on Oct. 3, 1876. Standard Quackenbush/Bedford Rifle Air Pistol frame, unmarked, probably made by Quackenbush or Bedford. Stationary barrel. Instead of pulling the barrel to cock, a knob under the barrel is pulled to cock the gun. Brass chamber under the barrel which bears the cocking knob also adds. Swinging loading gate similar to that of the Quackenbush Type C air pistol at the rear of the gun. Black Japan enamel finish. Retractable seating pin houses cocking knob return spring. Only one specimen known.

courtesy Stauff Collection

Rarity precludes accurate pricing.

CUB

For information on Cub airguns, see Milbro in the "M" section and Langenhan in the "L" section.

GRADING	100%	95%	90%	80%	60%	40%	20%

CYCLOID/RAPID

Previous trade names previously manufactured by Cycloid Cycle Co. and Rapid Rifle Co., Grand Rapids, MI circa 1889-1900.

The Cycloid and Rapid BB guns are all metal and completely nickel plated. Any boy discovering one of these spectacular and most unusual air rifles under the Christmas tree surely would not be able resist immediately running out with it to show the entire neighborhood! There has been considerable confusion about the maker. Dunathan, in the classic *American BB Gun* book, indicates that A.K. Wheeler founded the Rapid Rifle Company in Grand Rapids, MI in 1898 to produce some version of these air rifles. He reports that they were known under the names Cycloid, Cyclone, and New Rapid. However, at least two versions are known. One version, almost surely the earliest, has a cast iron receiver with cast script letters reading "Cycloid" on the left side and "Cycloid Cycle Co., Grand Rapids, Michigan" on the right. A more streamlined, simplified form, all sheet metal, is stamped, in simple block capitals, as the RAPID made by the RAPID RIFLE CO., GRAND RAPIDS, MICH. USA. It would appear that manufacture began under the name Cycloid as made by the Cycloid Cycle Co. and soon terminated under the name RAPID as made by the Rapid Rifle Co. Perhaps no specimens of the gun are known to be marked Cyclone and there doesn't seem to be any justification for the name "New" Rapid. Dunathan reports that the strange design was invented by Frank Simonds, Chauncey Fisher, and Hugh Ross, and that the company failed before the patent was issued in December 1901.

Aside from the all-metal construction, the most conspicuously strange aspect of the gun's design is an extremely long cocking lever, terminating in a Winchester-style cocking loop *behind* the base of the metal pistol grip. Internally, instead of the mainspring being coiled around or within the piston unit there is a rather long metal piston completely ahead of the forward end of the coiled mainspring. Two long, chain-like links attached to the hooked forward end of the exceptionally long cocking lever pull back the cocking assembly in a manner similar to a break action BB gun. The poor efficiency and high cost of such a design, in the face of considerable emerging competition, probably fated the design to a life of only a year or two, making these guns among the rarest, and most interesting, of American production airguns.

RIFLES

CYCLOID - .180/BB shot cal., muzzle-loading SS, SP, cast iron receiver and cocking lever, balance of parts sheet metal, nickel plated finish, cocking lever pivoted behind the trigger, with a Winchester-style hand loop behind the base of the pistol grip, "Cycloid" is cast in script on LHS of receiver, and "Cycloid Cycle Co, GRAND RAPIDS, MICH. PATD." is cast on RHS of receiver. 31.7 in. OAL, 2.7 lbs. Mfg. circa 1898.

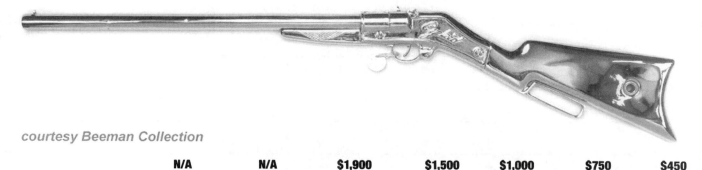

courtesy Beeman Collection

N/A	N/A	$1,900	$1,500	$1,000	$750	$450

RAPID - .180/BB shot cal., muzzle-loading SS, SP, cast iron receiver and cocking lever, balance of parts sheet metal, nickel plated finish, cocking lever, pivoted behind the trigger, with a Winchester-style hand loop behind the base of the pistol grip, stamped in a circular logo on side of receiver "RAPID RIFLE CO. LTD. RAPID. PAT. APP. FOR, GRAND RAPIDS, MICH. USA", 31.5 in. OAL, 2.2 lbs. Mfg. circa 1900.

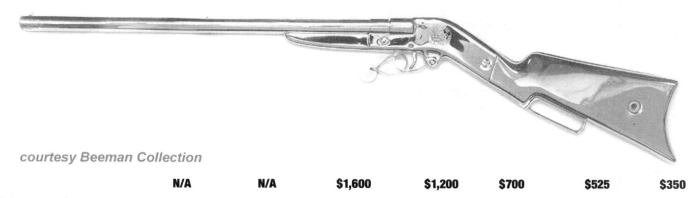

courtesy Beeman Collection

N/A	N/A	$1,600	$1,200	$700	$525	$350

CYCLONE

For information on Cyclone, refer to the Cycloid/Rapid section above.

NOTES

D SECTION

DAISY MANUFACTURING CO., INC.

Current manufacturer and distributor located in Rogers, AR established circa 1895. Previously located in Plymouth, MI 1895-1958. Dealer and consumer direct sales.

Daisy is one of the oldest and largest airgun manufacturers in the world, and for more than a century has produced some of the most coveted air rifles of all time. Vintage Daisy air rifles from the late 1880s can command prices up to $10,000. Daisy is also the maker of the famous Daisy Model 25 and Red Ryder lines. For vast numbers of young boys in the rural America from the 1910s to the 1950s, and then in the developing suburbs of 1950 to about 1979, having an adult show you how to use a Daisy Model 25 slide action BB gun or a Red Ryder lever action BB gun was an integral part of growing up.

Until now there simply had been no "master" guide to Daisy airguns. The pioneering work, Dunathan's 1971 book, *The American BB Gun*, has long been somewhat of a "bible" to American BB gun collectors, but it was only moderately accurate even when it came out. Jim Thomas made a bit of an update of Dunathan's book in 1989, but we still don't have a definitive guide. In 2001, Neal Punchard, a long-time Daisy collector, published *Daisy Air Rifles & BB Guns -The First 100 Years* a wonderfully illustrated general presentation of Daisy products over their first century of production. Finally, *AN ENCYCLOPEDIA OF DAISY PLYMOUTH GUNS* (2007) produced by Gary Garber is a tremendous breakthrough concerning Daisy airgun information, at least for the models produced in Plymouth, MI from the late 1880s to 1958. Daisy airguns are a large and complicated collecting group; this preliminary attempt at a model and value listing cannot be complete. Continual input from collectors and researchers will be necessary for greater and greater completeness and accuracy in future editions.

Unless otherwise noted, all Daisy airguns are spring piston designs in BB/.173 cal. The values quoted generally assume working condition. Many buyers will insist on a significant discount for lack of operation. Commemorative Model Warning: Surplus parts remaining after production of various post-1952 commemorative model airguns have found their way into the market. These parts have sometimes been used to construct or "enhance" regular production models. Sometimes the only way to detect such fraudulent specimens is to ask the Daisy company to compare the stamped registration number against their production records. For information on Daisy airguns manufactured for other trademarks, see the Store Brand Cross-Over List at the back of this text.

For more information and current pricing on both new and used Daisy firearms, please refer to the *Blue Book of Gun Values* by S.P. Fjestad (also available online).

DAISY IS BORN

Clarence Hamilton, known to firearm collectors as the manufacturer of Hamilton .22 caliber boys' firearms, invented the First Model all-metal Daisy air rifle while working at the Plymouth Iron Windmill Company in Plymouth, MI. The Plymouth Iron Windmill Company (founded 1882) became the Daisy company in 1895 and continued operations in Plymouth until their move to their present location in Rogers, AR in 1958. The company has made a variety of products, but most of its production has been oriented towards BB guns and pellet rifles.

THE MODEL 25

The Model 25 slide action BB gun is often considered to be Daisy's most successful model, the model which was mainly responsible for Daisy's outstanding reputation. Made from 1914 to 1979, an amazing span of sixty-five years, the Model 25 is Daisy's longest running model. With approx. fifty-eight variants, total production of the Model 25 was over twenty million by 1979, more than all Ford Model T and Volkswagen "Bug" automobiles combined. The Model 25 probably also was the gun which gave Daisy the reputation of having the hardest hitting BB guns. With a bit of normal dieseling, many specimens could drive a steel BB out at speeds up to 450 FPS. Even that power was well exceeded by several lines of barrel cocking and side-lever air rifles, capable of velocities of 600 to 1000 FPS, which the company sold from the early 1960s to the present. And in the 1980s Daisy introduced a line of Daisy firearms - economical rifles using the potent (about thirty times the energy of a Daisy 880), but inexpensive, .22 long rifle ammunition.

THE POWERLINE AND SAFETY

Well over three decades ago, in 1972, Daisy started its own production of medium-powered pellet guns with the introduction of the "Powerline" Model 880. Contrasting quite completely with the one-cocking-stroke, lever and slide action BB guns, the Model 880 was their first swinging-arm, multiple-pump pneumatic pellet rifle. When fully pumped, these rifles can reach velocities of 680+ FPS. Although basically designed as accurate pellet rifles for field use, even sporting a scope sight or scope base, Daisy made it possible for users to shoot these new pellet rifles economically with BBs by providing them with amazing new rifling – dodecahedral flats in a helical pattern. This special rifling gave a stabilizing spin to even a steel projectile without cutting into the projectile or being injured by a hard steel projectile. The higher velocity of the Powerline guns gave the guns greater utility and greater effective accuracy in outdoor field shooting. The very name "Powerline" is a clear reference to high power, although these guns are by no means as strong as many other airguns now on the market.

While Daisy Powerline airguns were designed for use by shooters at least sixteen years old, Daisy has designated some of its BB guns, designed especially for youth over ten years old with adult supervision, as Youthline models. Mindful of the fact that about 350 FPS is generally accepted as the minimum impact velocity at which a steel BB can perforate the human skin, the Youthline models are all designed to fire below that velocity at the muzzle. In addition to general public sales, these guns have been featured for well over a half-century in Daisy's huge shooting safety and education programs and events (see the Daisy "Take Aim at Safety" program at www.daisy.com).

COMPETITION AIRGUNS

Daisy made limited excursions into the field of high level competition airguns with their introductions of the German Feinwerkbau match airguns in the early 1970s and the Spanish El Gamo match airguns in the early 1990s. Because they were designed as match guns, they produced muzzle speeds in the 550-700 FPS range. Neither line was very strongly marketed and both were dropped rather soon. Much greater success was achieved with match-type guns of their own manufacture: the Model 753 and 853 rifles and the Model 747 and 777 pistols. Daisy now is presenting further expansion of their "Olympic-level" models. They also are marketing the Winchester QP "Quick Power" break-barrel air rifles (made in Turkey), which have the high power produced by the single stroke of barrel cocking airguns, and a popular new lever action Winchester Model 1894 replica.

GRADING	100%	95%	90%	80%	60%	40%	20%

CATEGORY INDEX

This Category Index is provided to help speed the process of locating a Daisy airgun in this text. The categories are in alphabetical order based on the configuration of the Daisy in question (i.e. pistol or rifle, type of action, cocking mechanism,or operating system).

DAISY COMMEMORATIVES

This grouping includes Commemorative airguns issued by Daisy that came in special packaging that dirrectly affects their value. The graphics on these original boxes where specific to the issue and if they are missing can reduce the value by 40%-60%.

Subtract 40%-60% for missing box or any other related issue pieces.

MODEL 111-B AMERICAN YOUTH - BB/.175 cal., wood stock, die-cast cocking lever, stock laser engraved with the logo of a young boy proud to hold his first Daisy air rifle, production number stamped on the butt, gold silk screen words "American Youth" inscribed on the receiver, includes color print of an "American Youth" Bill of Rights. Approx. 1,000 mfg. 1998.

	$200	$160	$125	N/A	N/A	N/A	N/A

This is the lowest number of guns Daisy has ever produced in their collector series. Daisy discovered 1,000 die-cast cocking levers in an old warehouse, and used them to produce this limited edition. Prior to the "American Youth," Daisy had not made an air rifle with a die-cast cocking lever in twenty-five years.

MODEL 95 FIREFIGHTER - BB/.175, .177 cal., similar to Model 95, except buttstock is laser engraved with an image of antique pumper wagon and "The Firefighter" with "going beyond the call" on the forearm, also included is a certificate of authenticity. Mfg. 2003-04.

	$150	$125	$100	N/A	N/A	N/A	N/A

Last MSR was $60.

MODEL 1894 BUFFALO BILL 150TH ANNIVERSARY - BB/.175 cal., Winchester Model 94 style rifle, wood stock, wood forearm, gold style coin in stock. Approx. 2,500 mfg. 1996.

	$195	$150	$150	N/A	N/A	N/A	N/A

MODEL 1894 CARBINE SEARS VARIANT NUMBER 799.19052 - 1894 Commemorative, Winchester-style, octagon barrel, marked "Replica Centennial Rifle, Crafted by Daisy" or "Crafted by Daisy" on the barrel, gold paint finish, Sears. Mfg. 1969-73.

	$250	$200	$150	N/A	N/A	N/A	N/A

MODEL 1894 CARBINE SEARS VARIANT NUMBER 799.19120 - regular 1894 Winchester-style, octagon barrel, gold paint or brass frame, Sears. Mfg. 1969-73.

	$200	$175	$125	N/A	N/A	N/A	N/A

MODEL 3030 WESTERN CARBINE BUFFALO BILL SCOUT - forty-shot, saddle ring on forearm or receiver. Mfg. 1969-73.

	$200	$175	$125	N/A	N/A	N/A	N/A

MODEL 5179 NRA CENTENNIAL COMMEMORATIVE PISTOL/RIFLE SET - two guns, matching serial numbers, value given for pair. Mfg. 1971-72.

	$400	$350	$300	N/A	N/A	N/A	N/A

MODEL 5694 TEXAS RANGERS COMMEMORATIVE RIFLE - mfg. 1973-74.

	$600	$450	$275	N/A	N/A	N/A	N/A

MODEL 5894 NRA CENTENNIAL COMMEMORATIVE CARBINE - mfg. 1971-72.

	$200	$150	$125	N/A	N/A	N/A	N/A

MODEL 5994 WELLS FARGO COMMEMORATIVE RIFLE - mfg. 1974-75.

	$350	$230	$175	N/A	N/A	N/A	N/A

GRADING	100%	95%	90%	80%	60%	40%	20%

MODEL 1938 B CHRISTMAS STORY - BB/.175 cal., Red Ryder model manufactured due to interest in 1984 film *A Christmas Story*, similar to standard "B" Model, but with large compass and sundial on left side of stock. Mfg. 1984.

	$450	$375	$300	N/A	N/A	N/A	N/A

Values equal with small compass.

A Christmas Story author Jean Sheperd invented this model, and Daisy followed his lead. An example in 100% condition must be unopened in original cellophane wrapped display box. To complete *A Christmas Story* set, collectors also need a movie poster, the movie (video tape or DVD), and the small cardboard stand-up display card. Note: Due to the popularity of this model, there unfortunately are a handful of counterfeit Christmas Story BB guns in circulation. (These are made up from regular Red Ryder guns by substituting factory stocks leftover from the production of true Christmas Story models.) Originals have "DAISY" marked in black on a white compass. What no one seems to be able to counterfeit, however, is the original cellophane wrapper! According to a few collectors (who have them and will not part with them at any price), values are still on the conservative side.

MODEL 1938 B - LES KOUBA - BB/.175 cal., standard "B" model Red Ryder, but has extra fancy American walnut stock and forearm, gold forearm band, gold medallion on right side of stock showing a boy with his first Red Ryder. Stamped "Limited Edition", printing filled with gold paint, plastic lever, walnut-look wall rack in box, brass plaque. Includes Les C. Kouba print in cardboard tube marked with the same number as the air rifle. Mfg. 1986.

	$350	$300	$225	N/A	N/A	N/A	N/A

Add 50% for guns with artist's proofed and signed print.

Only 1,100 Les Kouba guns were produced. The print series numbers from 1 to 2500. The first 250 prints are artist proofed and hand signed on lower left side. There are counterfeit Les Kouba posters and guns which were not produced by Daisy. It is advised that you consult with a qualified expert before making a purchase.

NUMBER 1938 B 50TH ANNIVERSARY - Red Ryder, BB/.175 cal., similar to standard Model B, except has walnut stock and forearm, brass medallion on right side of stock, fifty-year warranty. Mfg. 1988.

	$125	$90	$60	N/A	N/A	N/A	N/A

MODEL 1938 B (MFG. 1995) - "It's A Daisy" Red Ryder Limited Edition. Mfg. 1995.

	$150	$100	$75	N/A	N/A	N/A	N/A

CHRISTMAS MORNING - BB/.175, .177 cal., similar to Model 1938 Red Ryder, except gunstock is laser engraved with an image of Santa Claus placing a BB gun under a Christmas tree, also included in the full color package is a laser engraved wooden Christmas ornament (same image).

	$100	$85	$65	N/A	N/A	N/A	N/A

ROY ROGERS/TRIGGER COMMEMORATIVE - BB/.175, .177 cal., similar to Model 1938 Red Ryder, first in series.

	$275	$225	$175	N/A	N/A	N/A	N/A

ROY/DALE LIMITED EDITION COMMEMMORATIVE - BB/.175, .177 cal., similar to Model 1938 Red Ryder, except walnut stock has gold color medallion of Roy Rogers and Dale Evans inserted, forearm is laser engraved with their signatures and the gun's serial number, second rifle in the Roy Rogers Series, 2,500 to be mfg.

	$175	$150	$125	N/A	N/A	N/A	N/A

ROY ROGERS/GABBY HAYES COMMEMORATIVE - BB/.175, .177 cal., similar to Model 1938 Red Ryder, except walnut stock has gold color medallion of Roy Rogers and Gabby Hayes inserted, forearm is laser engraved with Gabby's signature phrase "Yer durn tootin" and gun's serial number, third rifle in the Roy Rogers Series, 2,500 to be mfg.

	$175	$150	$125	N/A	N/A	N/A	N/A

PISTOLS: CO$_2$ POWERED

MODEL 008 - BB/.175 or .177 cal., CO$_2$, semi-auto pistol, eight-shot rotary mag., rifled steel barrel, fixed sights, black finish, molded black checkered grips, rotary hammer block safety, 480 FPS, 7.1 in. OAL, 1 lb. New 2005.

MSR $87	$75	$60	$45	$30	N/A	N/A	N/A

MODEL 15XT - BB/.175 or .177 cal., CO$_2$, semi-auto pistol, fifteen-shot built-in mag., smoothbore steel barrel, fixed sights, black finish, molded black checkered grips, manual trigger block safety, 425 FPS, 1 lb. New 2002.

MSR $51	$40	$30	$25	$20	$15	N/A	N/A

MODEL 15XTP - BB/.175 or 177 cal., similar to Model 15XT, except has Max Speed electronic point sight. New 2002.

MSR $65	$55	$45	$35	$25	$20	N/A	N/A

MODEL 15XK - BB/.175 or .177 cal., CO$_2$, semi-auto pistol, Model 15XT pistol kit including shooting glasses, NRA competition targets, 350 BBs, 12-gram CO$_2$ cylinders. New 2002.

MSR $68	$55	$45	$35	$25	$20	N/A	N/A

MODEL 41 - .22 cal., BA, replica of S&W Model 41, CO$_2$, single shot, chrome plated. Mfg. circa 1984.

	$100	$75	$60	$45	$30	N/A	N/A

MODEL 44 (970) - .177 cal., CO$_2$, replica of S&W 44 Magnum revolver, six-shot swing-out cylinder. Mfg. 1984-2001.

	$100	$75	$60	$50	$40	N/A	N/A

MODEL 45 - .177 cal., CO$_2$, semi-auto pistol, thirteen-shot drop-in mag., rifled steel barrel, fiberoptic fixed sights, black finish, molded black checkered grips, manual lever type trigger block safety, 400 FPS, 1.25 lb. Disc. 2002.

	$65	$60	$55	$40	$30	N/A	N/A

Last MSR was $70.

GRADING	100%	95%	90%	80%	60%	40%	20%

MODEL 45 GI - .177 cal., CO_2, thirteen-shot semi-auto. Colt 45 variant: replica of Colt 1911 .45 auto firearm. Smith & Wesson 45 variant: replica of Smith & Wesson .45 auto firearm. Mfg. 1992-97.

	$60	$50	$35	$30	$25	N/A	N/A

MODEL 45XT - .177 cal., CO_2, semi-auto pistol, thirteen-shot drop-in mag., rifled steel barrel, fiberoptic fixed sights, black finish, molded black checkered grips, manual lever-type trigger block safety, 400 FPS, 1.25 lb.

	$45	$40	$30	$25	$20	N/A	N/A

MODEL 91 - .177 cal., CO_2, SL, SS, wood grips, 10.25 in. barrel, 425 FPS, 2.4 lbs. Imported from Hungary 1991-97.

	$415	$360	$280	$225	$150	N/A	N/A

This was imported by Daisy as an entry level match target pistol.

MODEL 92 - .177 cal., semi-auto, styled like Beretta firearm pistol, ten-shot pellet feed. Mfg. in Japan, 1986-94.

	$75	$60	$50	$40	$30	N/A	N/A

MODEL 93 - BB/.175 or .177 cal., CO_2, semi-auto pistol, fifteen-shot drop-in mag., smooth bore steel barrel, fixed sights, black finish, molded brown checkered grips, manual trigger block safety, 400 FPS, 1.1 lb. Disc. 2004.

	$50	$40	$30	$25	$20	N/A	N/A

Last MSR was $60.

MODEL 100 - BB/.175 cal., CO_2, semi-auto pistol, 200-shot. Mfg. 1962.

	$45	$40	$35	$30	$25	N/A	N/A

MODEL 200 - BB/.175 cal., CO_2, semi-auto, 200-shot. Mfg. 1963-76.

courtesy Beeman Collection

	$40	$35	$30	$25	N/A	N/A	N/A

MODEL 400GX (DESERT EAGLE) - BB/.175 or .177 cal., CO_2, semi-auto pistol, twenty-shot drop-in mag., smooth bore steel barrel, fixed sights, black (1994-97) or gold frame and black slide finish, molded black textured grips, manual lever safety, 420 FPS, 1.4 lb. Disc. 2002.

	$100	$75	$60	$50	$40	N/A	N/A

MODEL 454 - BB/.175 cal., CO_2, semi-auto, twenty-shot. Mfg. 1994-99.

	$45	$35	$30	$30	$25	N/A	N/A

MODEL 500 RAVEN - .177 cal. CO_2, SS, 500 FPS. Mfg. 1994-98.

	$80	$65	$55	$45	$35	N/A	N/A

MODEL 617X - .177 cal. pellet or .177 (4.5mm) BB , CO_2, semi-auto pistol, six-shot rotary magazine holds pellets and BBs simultaneously, rifled steel barrel, fiberoptic fixed sights, black finish, molded black checkered grips, rotary hammer block safety, 485 FPS (BB) 425 FPS (Pellet), 1.3 lb. New 2004.

courtesy Daisy

MSR $82	$75	$60	$45	$30	N/A	N/A	N/A

GRADING	100%	95%	90%	80%	60%	40%	20%

MODEL 622X - .22 cal., CO$_2$, semi-auto pistol, six-shot rotary mag., rifled steel barrel, fiberoptic fixed sights, black finish, molded black checkered grips, rotary hammer block safety, 400 FPS, 1.3 lb. Disc. 2004.

	$75	$65	$50	$40	$30	N/A	N/A

Last MSR was $80.

MODEL 645 - .177 cal., CO$_2$, semi-auto pistol, thirteen-shot drop-in mag., rifled steel barrel, fiberoptic fixed sights, black and nickel finish, molded black checkered grips, manual trigger block safety. Colt 45 variant: styled like a Colt 1911 (1992-97). S&W 45 variant: styled like a S&W .45 auto, 400 FPS, 1.25 lb. Disc. 2004.

	$75	$65	$50	$40	$30	N/A	N/A

Last MSR was $80.

MODEL 693 - BB/.175 or .177 cal., CO$_2$, semi-auto pistol, fifteen-shot drop-in mag., smooth bore steel barrel, fixed sights, black and nickel finish, molded black checkered grips, manual trigger block safety, 400 FPS, 1.1 lb.

MSR $77	$65	$60	$55	$40	$30	N/A	N/A

MODEL 5693 - BB/.175 or .177 cal., CO$_2$, semi-auto pistol, kit including Model 693 pistol, shooting glasses, NRA competition targets, 350 BBs, 12-gram CO$_2$ cylinders, 1.1 lb.

MSR $83	$65	$60	$55	$40	$30	N/A	N/A

MODEL 780 - .22 cal., CO$_2$, BA, SS, replica of S&W Model 41 firearm, blue paint finish, Daisy´s continuation of S&W Model 78G CO$_2$ pistol. Mfg.1982-83.

	$125	$90	$60	$40	N/A	N/A	N/A

MODEL 790 - .177 cal., CO$_2$, BA, SS, replica of S&W Model 41 firearm, blue paint finish, Daisy´s continuation of S&W Model 79G CO$_2$ pistol. Mfg. 1982-88.

	$125	$90	$60	$40	N/A	N/A	N/A

MODEL 807 "CRITTER GITTER" - .38 cal., CO$_2$, BA, SS, 250 FPS, designed to shoot lead shot or patched ball with open ended cylinder as a cartridge (made in Germany by Umarex for Daisy, but Daisy decided not to continue production), very few went into the U.S. market, and some were sold in Germany. No box produced for U.S. market, 12.2 in. OAL, 2.2 lbs. Mfg. 1988 only.

courtesy Beeman Collection

	$750	$700	$650	$550	$450	$350	$325

Add 20% for German box.

MODEL 1200 - BB/.175 cal., CO$_2$, sixty-shot, plastic grips. Mfg. 1977-1989.

	$50	$35	$25	N/A	N/A	N/A	N/A

MODEL 1270 - .177 cal., CO$_2$, sixty-shot pump action repeater, molded polymer forend doubles as pump handle, molded black polymer grip, custom plated finish, 420 FPS, smooth bore steel barrel, adj. rear sight, cross bolt trigger block safety, 1.1 lbs. Disc. 2002.

	$40	$30	$20	$15	$10	N/A	N/A

MODEL 1500 - BB/.175 cal., CO$_2$, similar to Model 1200, except chrome plated. Mfg. 1988 only.

	$35	$30	$25	N/A	N/A	N/A	N/A

MODEL 1700 - .177 cal, CO$_2$, replica of Glock semi-auto firearm, uses Model 1200 valving. Mfg. 1991-96.

courtesy Beeman Collection

	$35	$30	$25	N/A	N/A	N/A	N/A

GRADING	100%	95%	90%	80%	60%	40%	20%

MODEL 2003 - .177 cal., CO_2, thirty-five-shot, helical clip, semi-automatic, plastic grips. Mfg. 1995-2001. Can be converted to full auto, and therefore dropped by Daisy.

	100%	95%	90%	80%	60%	40%	20%
	$120	$100	$80	$60	N/A	N/A	N/A

PISTOLS: PNEUMATIC POWERED

MODEL 717 - .177 cal., side-lever cocking, single-stroke pneumatic, single shot, 360 FPS, rifled steel barrel, adj. rear sight, molded brown checkered grips with right-hand thumb rest, crossbolt trigger block safety, 2.25 lbs.

MSR $221	100%	95%	90%	80%	60%	40%	20%
	$175	$125	$95	$75	$65	N/A	N/A

MODEL 722 - .22 cal., similar to Model 717. Mfg. 1981-96.

	$100	$80	$60	N/A	N/A	N/A	N/A

MODEL 747 TARGET PISTOL - .177 cal., SL, SSP, SS, 360 FPS, Lothar Walther rifled barrel, adj. trigger, left- or right-hand grips available, 3.1 lbs. New 1987.

MSR $265	100%	95%	90%	80%	60%	40%	20%
	$195	$145	$95	$75	$65	N/A	N/A

MODEL 777 TARGET PISTOL - .177 cal., SL, SSP, SS, Lothar Walther rifled barrel, 360 FPS, wood target-style grips, 3.2 lbs. Mfg. 1990-97.

	$215	$175	$155	$130	$100	N/A	N/A

MODEL 1140 - .177 cal. pellet, SSP, SS. Mfg. 1995-2000.

	$60	$55	$50	$45	$40	N/A	N/A

PISTOLS: SPRING POWERED

MODEL 62 TARGET PISTOL - .177 cal., UL, SP, SS. Mfg. by Gamo in Spain 1975-78.

	$90	$75	$50	$35	$25	N/A	N/A

MODEL 118 DAISY TARGETEER - .118 cal., #6 lead or steel shot (Daisy #6 in two sizes of metal tube), SL, SP, indoor shooting gallery air pistol, all-metal construction, fixed rear sight 1937-41, adj. rear sight 1949-52, chrome-plated (1949-52), blue (1937-51) or painted (1937-52) finish. Mfg. 1937-52.

courtesy Beeman Collection

	$150	$125	$90	$70	$50	N/A	N/A

Add 35% for chrome plating on Targeteer pistols separate from shooting gallery sets. Add 10% for non-adjustable rear sight. Add 15% for original box w/ spinners, shot, targets.

⊙ *Model 118 Daisy Targeteer Number 320* - variation: Targeteer shooting gallery set with spinning targets and molded plastic trap, nickel finish gun. Vintage shooting gallery set in good condition is uncommon. Mfg. 1949-52.

	$400	$250	$200	$150	$100	N/A	N/A

MODEL 177 BULLSEYE TARGET PISTOL - BB/.175 cal., target pistol, 150-shot, blue or painted finish, Plymouth or Rogers. Mfg. 1957-78.

	$75	$65	$50	$40	$35	N/A	N/A

Add 30% for Rogers factory box. Add 50% for Plymouth factory box. Add 50% for Family Fun Set with extra tube for shooting corks.

MODEL 179 PEACEMAKER REVOLVER BB/.175 cal., spring catapult action, tubular, 12 shot tubular, spring-fed magazine. Manf. 1960-81.

	$130	$100	$85	$70	$50	N/A	N/A

GRADING	100%	95%	90%	80%	60%	40%	20%

⊙ **Model 179 Peacemaker (Solid Brass Variant)** - BB/.175 cal., variation mfg. of solid cast brass, very heavy, painted gray. Serial numbers to 34 are known, 10.5 in. OAL, No markings except SN stamped on butt, weighs 2.7 lbs!

courtesy Beeman Collection

Rarity precludes accurate pricing.

MODEL 180 PEACEMAKER REVOLVER - BB/.175 cal., similar to Model 179, except boxed set with revolver with holster. Mfg. 1960-81.

	$250	$200	$175	$150	$125	N/A	N/A

MODEL 188 - BB/.175 cal., UL, SP, twenty-four-shot. Mfg. 1979-89.

	$50	$40	$35	$30	$20	N/A	N/A

MODEL 288 - BB/.175 cal., UL, SP, twenty-four-shot. Mfg. 1991-2001.

	$25	$20	$15	N/A	N/A	N/A	N/A

MODEL 579 TEXAS RANGER - BB/.175 cal., Texas Rangers set of two matching guns similar to Model 197, each with grips imbedded with miniature Texas Rangers badges, barrels stamped "1823 - Texas Rangers - 1973", special box, booklet on Texas Ranger history. Mfg.1973-74.

	$500	$400	$300	N/A	N/A	N/A	N/A

MODEL 5179 NRA COMMEMORATIVE - Mfg. 1971-72.

	$150	$125	$100	N/A	N/A	N/A	N/A

RIFLES: BREAK ACTION, PRE-1900 (CAST METAL FRAME)

This grouping includes the early Daisy cast metal lever and break action BB guns, mfg. 1888-1900.

1ST MODEL - large BB/.180 cal., single-shot, muzzle-loading brass tubing barrel and air chamber, cast iron or brass frame, wire skeleton stock without wood, nickel plated, post front sight, V-notch rear sight integral with top cocking lever. Production quantities were very low, but unknown (despite previous claims). Mfg. by Plymouth Iron Windmill Co. 1889-95. Dates on variants unknown.

⊙ **1ST Model Variant One** - cocking lever marked "Pat. Appl. For PIW", cast iron frame.

	N/A	N/A	$4,250	$3,500	$2,500	$1,500	$650

⊙ **1ST Model Variant Two** - similar to variant one, but with brass frame. This may be the rarest of the Daisy First Models.

	N/A	N/A	$7,000	$5,500	$4,000	$2,500	$1,000

⊙ **1ST Model Variant Three** - similar to variant two, brass frame with reinforcing rib where wire stock enters frame.

	N/A	N/A	$4,250	$3,500	$2,500	$1,500	$650

⊙ **1ST Model Variant Four** - cocking lever marked "DAISY PAT. AUG. 1889 PLYMOUTH, MICH.", cast brass frame, no verifiable information on production quantities or mfg. dates.

courtesy Beeman Collection

	N/A	N/A	$3,500	$2,500	$1,500	$850	$450

⊙ **1ST Model Variant Five** - similar to variant four, but with much more prominent, more highly raised cast lettering.

	N/A	N/A	$3,500	$2,500	$1,500	$850	$450

Warning on Daisy First Models: reportedly there are fake specimens of some of the rarest versions of early cast metal Daisy airguns. Sometimes this takes the form of fake cocking levers on legitimate specimens of more common models. Careful measurements may be necessary to detect such fraudulent arrangements. It may be best to consult with a trusted Daisy expert before purchasing some of the most valuable specimens.

Replicas: For collectors who cannot locate some of the rarest models or are not willing to spend the large amounts necessary to obtain them, there are some legitimate replicas available.

GRADING	100%	95%	90%	80%	60%	40%	20%

2ND MODEL - large BB/.180 cal., break-open design, SS, brass tubing barrel and air chamber, cast iron frame, wire skeleton stock, nickel-plated post front sight, V-notch rear sight integral with breech, left frame marked "Daisy Imp´d Pat´ May 6, 90", right frame marked "MFG. BY P.I.W. & CO. PLYMOUTH MICH." Quantities unknown, but far less than 1st Model. 31.5 in. OAL, 2.6 lbs. Mfg. by Plymouth Iron Windmill Co, 1890-91. Extremely rare.

courtesy Beeman Collection

| | N/A | N/A | $7,000 | $5,500 | $4,000 | $2,500 | $1,000 |

3RD MODEL - large BB/.180 cal., break open design, SS, brass tubing barrel and air chamber, cast iron frame, wire skeleton stock with or without wood insert, nickel plated, post front sight, V-notch rear sight, frame marked "Daisy Pat. May 6, 90, July 14, 91", 31.5 in. OAL, 2.3 lbs. Mfg. 1893-94. Rare.
  ⊙ **3RD Model "New Daisy" Variant** - checkered frame, wire stock without wood insert, grip frame marked "NEW DAISY". Mfg. 1892-1895.

| | N/A | N/A | $2,500 | $1,750 | $1,000 | $650 | $350 |

  ⊙ **3RD Model "New Daisy" Variant** - wire stock with wood insert, frame marked "NEW DAISY".

courtesy Beeman Collection

| | N/A | N/A | $2,750 | $2,000 | $1,250 | $800 | $400 |

  ⊙ **3RD Model "Raised Letter" Variant** - wire stock without wood insert, patent dates on left side of grip frame. Garber (2007) recognizes 8 variations of the "RAISED LETTER" variant.

| | N/A | N/A | $2,750 | $2,000 | $1,250 | $800 | $400 |

  ⊙ **3RD Model "Raised Letter" Variant** - wire stock with wood insert, patent dates on left side of grip frame.

| | N/A | N/A | $2,750 | $2,000 | $1,250 | $800 | $400 |

  ⊙ **3RD Model ("Model 96") Variant** - marked "MODEL 96" and "DAISY", all wood stock. Mfg. 1896.

| | N/A | N/A | $2,250 | $1,500 | $950 | $600 | $300 |

  ⊙ **3RD Model "Model" Variant** - marked "MODEL" only on right side of frame, marked "DAISY" on left side (possibly from modified Model 96 mold), all wood stock. Mfg. 1897.

courtesy Beeman Collection

| | N/A | N/A | $2,250 | $1,500 | $950 | $600 | $300 |

RIFLES: BREAK ACTION, POST-1900

This grouping starts with the 20th Century models mfg. beginning circa 1898.

20TH CENTURY CAST IRON FRAME SINGLE SHOT - BB/.180 cal., break action, SS, sheet metal barrel. Removable shot tube. Cast iron trigger, trigger guard, and frame (except as noted below), nickel finish, fixed sights, marked on the right side "20th CENTURY", on the left side marked "DAISY" between bullseyes. Slab-sided stocks. Stocks impressed on left side, "Daisy Mfg. Co., May 6, 90 July 14, 91". Mfg. 1898-1902.
  ⊙ **20th Centery Cast Iron Frame Single Shot First Variant** - wire stock without wood, checkered cast brass below barrel.

| | N/A | N/A | $1,500 | $1,000 | $650 | $400 | $250 |

  ⊙ **20th Centery Cast Iron Frame Single Shot Second Variant** - wood stock, checkered cast brass below barrel.

| | N/A | N/A | $800 | $550 | $400 | $275 | $150 |

GRADING	100%	95%	90%	80%	60%	40%	20%
⊙ *20th Centery Cast Iron Frame Single Shot Third Variant* - wire stock without wood, sheet metal wrap around base of barrel.							
	N/A	N/A	$1,500	$1,000	$650	$400	$250
⊙ *20th Centery Cast Iron Frame Single Shot Fourth Variant* - wood stock, sheet metal wrap around base of barrel.							
	N/A	N/A	$800	$550	$400	$275	$150

20TH CENTURY CAST IRON FRAME REPEATER - BB/.180 cal., break action, forty-shot, marked on right side "REPEATER", left side marked "DAISY". Mfg. 1898-1902.

	100%	95%	90%	80%	60%	40%	20%
⊙ *20th Centery Cast Iron Frame Repeater First Variant* - wood stock, checkered cast brass below barrel.							
	N/A	N/A	$2,000	$1,500	$1,000	$750	$400
⊙ *20th Centery Cast Iron Frame Repeater Second Variant* - wood stock, sheet metal wrap around base of barrel.							
	N/A	N/A	$900	$650	$500	$350	$200

Note: 20th Century models with checkered cast brass below the barrel sometimes are referred to as "Fourth Model" Daisys.

20TH CENTURY SHEET METAL FRAME SINGLE SHOT - BB/.180 cal., break action, sheet metal barrel and frame, cast iron trigger guard and trigger, removable shot tube, nickel finish, peep sight. Mfg.1903-10.

courtesy Beeman Collection

	100%	95%	90%	80%	60%	40%	20%
⊙ *20th Centery Sheet Metal Frame Single Shot First Variant* - two-step body tube (forward end of body tube steps down to barrel diameter in two steps), right side of frame with letters "PATENTED" plus patent numbers in indented rectangle, left side of frame is marked "DAISY" in indented rectangle, cast iron spring anchor (plate inside lower edge of body tube - open action to view). Slab-sided stock.							
	N/A	N/A	$400	$300	$200	$125	$75
⊙ *20th Centery Sheet Metal Frame Single Shot Second Variant* - similar to First Variant, except printing on right side of frame changed to just patent dates, slab-sided stock, most common of Sheet Metal 20th Century air rifles.							
	N/A	N/A	$400	$300	$200	$125	$75
⊙ *20th Centery Sheet Metal Frame Single Shot Third Variant* - similar to second variant, except stock is oval in profile, two-step barrel.							
	N/A	N/A	$400	$300	$200	$125	$75
⊙ *20th Centery Sheet Metal Frame Single Shot Fourth Variant* - one-step body tube, cast iron spring anchor, long body tube (10.7 in.), 7 in. barrel.							
	N/A	N/A	$400	$300	$200	$125	$75
⊙ *20th Centery Sheet Metal Frame Single Shot Fifth Variant* - similar to fourth variant, except shorter body tube (10 in.), 7.4 in. barrel.							
	N/A	N/A	$400	$300	$200	$125	$75
⊙ *20th Centery Sheet Metal Frame Single Shot Sixth Variant* - similar to fourth variant (10.7 in. body tube, 7 in. barrel), except has sheet metal spring anchor.							
	N/A	N/A	$400	$300	$200	$125	$75
⊙ *20th Centery Sheet Metal Frame Single Shot Seventh Variant* - indented rectangle on both side of frame stamped "DAISY" between two bullseyes.							
	N/A	N/A	$600	$450	$300	$200	$125

20TH CENTURY SHEET METAL FRAME REPEATER - BB/.180 cal., break action, sheet metal barrel and frame, cast iron trigger guard and trigger, shot tube and magazine tube remove together as a unit, magazine visible as small removable tube parallel under barrel housing from forward end of one-step body tube to muzzle (not really a repeater; unique forty-shot magazine must be moved to release each BB into firing position), nickel finish, peep sight. Mfg.1903-1910.

	100%	95%	90%	80%	60%	40%	20%
⊙ *20th Centery Sheet Metal Frame Repeater First Variant* - shot tube release is tiny latch behind front sight.							
	N/A	N/A	$700	$600	$500	$450	$400
⊙ *20th Centery Sheet Metal Frame Repeater Second Variant* - shot tube release is a latch under the barrel with a magazine cover.							
	N/A	N/A	$700	$600	$500	$450	$400

GRADING	100%	95%	90%	80%	60%	40%	20%

⊛ *20th Centery Sheet Metal Frame Repeater Third Variant* - shot tube release is a spring-loaded front sight which moves in an L-shaped slot to allow shot tube removal (Hough-style shot tube system).

courtesy Beeman Collection

	N/A	N/A	$750	$650	$550	$500	$450

⊛ *20th Centery Sheet Metal Frame Repeater Fourth Variant* - indented rectangle on both sides of the frame, stamped "DAISY" between two bullseyes.

	N/A	N/A	$800	$550	$400	$275	$150

MODEL A REPEATER - BB/.180 cal., break action, 350-shot loading port behind blade front sight, repeater, nickel. Frame is marked "DAISY" between bullseyes, address and patents are on barrel top. Mfg. 1908-14.

	N/A	N/A	$3,500	$2,750	$2,000	$1,250	$550

MODEL A SINGLE SHOT - BB/.180 cal., break action, SS, marked on barrel: "DAISY SINGLE SHOT MODEL A". Mfg. 1908-14.

	N/A	N/A	$3,500	$2,750	$2,000	$1,250	$550

MODEL C NO. 1 REPEATER - BB/.175 cal., break action, 350-shot. Mfg. 1910-14.

courtesy Beeman Collection

	N/A	N/A	$500	$300	$200	$125	$75

MODEL C NO. 2 SINGLE SHOT - BB/.175 cal., break action, SS, nickel finish. Mfg.1911-14.

	N/A	N/A	$400	$250	$200	$150	$100

MODEL 20 "LITTLE DAISY" - BB/.175 cal., break action, Daisy´s smallest BB rifle.

⊛ *Model 20 "Little Daisy" Variant 1 (Frameless Model)* - nickel finish, no metal around grip. Mfg. 1908-11.

	N/A	N/A	$1,500	$1,000	$650	$400	$250

⊛ *Model 20 "Little Daisy" Variant 2 (Grip Frame Model)* - nickel finish, metal around grip (full grip frame), regular style cast iron trigger in trigger guard. Mfg. 1912-15.

	N/A	N/A	$700	$500	$350	$300	$200

⊛ *Model 20 "Little Daisy" Variant 3 (Ring Trigger Model)* - nickel or blue finish, cast iron ring trigger without guard, full grip frame. Mfg. 1915-37. Garber (2007) recognizes eight variations of this Model 20.

	N/A	N/A	$300	$225	$150	$100	$65

MODEL 21 SIDE BY SIDE - BB/.175 cal., break action, ribbed barrel divider, dark and light brown plastic stock. Mfg. 1968-72.

	N/A	$1,000	$750	$600	$450	$250	$150

Last MSR was approximately $25.

⊛ *Model 21 Sears Side by Side* - BB/.175 cal., break action, checkered barrel divider, wooden stock. Mfg. 1968 only.

	N/A	$1,100	$800	$650	$500	$350	$200

Add 30% for checkered rib. Add 50-100% for the approx. 48 walnut stock sets mfg. by Reinhart Fajen, Inc. and Bishop Stock Co.

GRADING	100%	95%	90%	80%	60%	40%	20%

MODEL 104 SIDE BY SIDE - BB/.175 cal., break action, 96-shot spring-fed repeater, sheet metal, side-by-side barrel tubes with Model 25-type shot tubes, left and right shot tubes marked L and R, dummy sidelocks, blue, walnut stock, stamped designs of game birds, dogs, and scrolls. Approx. 45,000 mfg. 1938-40.

courtesy Beeman Collection

	N/A	$1,100	$800	$650	$500	$350	$200

MODEL 106 - BB/.175 cal., break action, 500-shot, painted finish, Plymouth or Rogers address. Mfg. 1957-58.

	$150	$110	$65	$45	N/A	N/A	N/A

Add 20% for Plymouth address.

MODEL 181 (JUNIOR SHOOTING OUTFIT) - BB/.177 cal., break action, boxed set, special target with gun. Mfg. 1949 only.

	N/A	$1,100	$800	$650	$500	$350	$200

SENTINEL REPEATER - large BB/.180 cal., break action, 303-shot magazine. Sentinel models are not marked Daisy, but are shown in Daisy ads of the time. Mfg. 1900-02. Ref: AR4.

  ✪ *Sentinal Repeater Variant 1* - 20th Century model frame ,marked "SENTINEL" on grip frame. Made for A.F. Chaffee.

	N/A	N/A	$1,200	$850	$600	$400	$250

  ✪ *Sentinal Repeater Variant 2* - marked "SENTINEL" on stock.

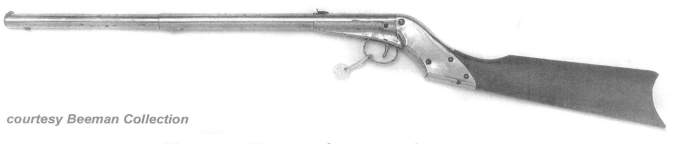

courtesy Beeman Collection

	N/A	N/A	$1,350	$850	$600	$400	$250

SENTINEL SINGLE SHOT - large BB/.180 cal., break action. Mfg. circa 1908.

  ✪ *Sentinal Single Shot Variant 1* - marked "SENTINEL" on grip frame.

	N/A	N/A	$900	$650	$500	$350	$200

  ✪ *Sentinal Single Shot Variant 2* - marked "SENTINEL" on stock.

	N/A	N/A	$900	$650	$500	$350	$200

RIFLES: BREAK BARREL COCKING

MODEL 91 .177 cal., BBC, SS, economy model made in Hungary by FEG.

	$50	$45	$40	$30	$20	N/A	N/A

MODEL 120 - .177 cal. pellet, BBC. Mfg. by El Gamo in Spain, 1984-85.

courtesy Howard Collection

	$75	$50	$40	$30	N/A	N/A	N/A

GRADING	100%	95%	90%	80%	60%	40%	20%

MODEL 130 - .177 cal. pellet, BBC. Mfg. by Milbro in Scotland, 1983-85.

	100%	95%	90%	80%	60%	40%	20%
	$75	$50	$40	$30	N/A	N/A	N/A

MODEL 130 (EL GAMO) - .177 cal. pellet, BBC, auto pellet feed, 800 FPS, adj. micrometer sight, 5.75 lbs. Mfg. by El Gamo in Spain 1986-93.

	100%	95%	90%	80%	60%	40%	20%
	$100	$85	$70	N/A	N/A	N/A	N/A

Last MSR was $150.

MODEL 131 - .177 cal. pellet, BBC, 630 FPS, adj. micrometer sight, 5.4 lbs. Mfg. by El Gamo in Spain.

	100%	95%	90%	80%	60%	40%	20%
	$75	$60	$50	N/A	N/A	N/A	N/A

Last MSR was $120.

MODEL 160 - BB/.175, .177 cal. pellet or dart, blue finish. Mfg. by Milbro in Scotland, 1965-74.

courtesy Beeman Collection

	100%	95%	90%	80%	60%	40%	20%
	$75	$50	$30	N/A	N/A	N/A	N/A

Note: This was a Diana brand airgun made by Milbro in Scotland, not to be confused with Diana brand airguns from Dianawerk in Rastatt, Germany. At the end of WWII, England was given the Diana brand and Dianawerk´s (Mayer and Grammelspacher) factory machinery as war reparations. The defeated Germans had to install all new machinery and temporarily use "Original" as a brand. Milbro, with the old German equipment, went out of business, and the Diana brand was restored to Dianawerk in Germany.

MODEL 220 - .177 cal. pellet, BBC, SP, blue finish. Mfg. by Milbro in Scotland (see note about Diana brand in Model 160 listing), 1965-70.

courtesy Beeman Collection

	100%	95%	90%	80%	60%	40%	20%
	$85	$60	$40	N/A	N/A	N/A	N/A

MODEL 225 - .177 cal. pellet, BBC, SP, blue finish. Mfg. by Milbro in Scotland, 1971-74.

	100%	95%	90%	80%	60%	40%	20%
	$110	$90	$45	N/A	N/A	N/A	N/A

MODEL 230 - .22 cal., BBC, SP, blue finish. Mfg. by Milbro in Scotland, 1965-74.

	100%	95%	90%	80%	60%	40%	20%
	$80	$55	$35	N/A	N/A	N/A	N/A

MODEL 250 - .22 cal., BBC, SP, blue finish. Mfg. by Milbro in Scotland, 1965-74.

	100%	95%	90%	80%	60%	40%	20%
	$130	$100	$65	$50	N/A	N/A	N/A

MODEL 1000 - .177 cal., BBC, 1000 FPS, adj. rear with hooded front sight, hardwood Monte Carlo stock, 6.125 lbs. New 1997. Disc.

	100%	95%	90%	80%	60%	40%	20%
	$135	$115	$90	N/A	N/A	N/A	N/A

Last MSR was $175.

MODEL 1170 - .177 cal., BBC, 800 FPS, adj. micrometer sight, 5 1/2 lbs. Disc.

	100%	95%	90%	80%	60%	40%	20%
	$85	$70	$55	N/A	N/A	N/A	N/A

Last MSR was $110.

NO. 100 MODEL 38 - BB/.175 cal., BBC, SS, blue finish. Mfg. 1938-41, and 1948-52.

	100%	95%	90%	80%	60%	40%	20%
	$250	$150	$100	$80	$60	$40	N/A

GRADING	100%	95%	90%	80%	60%	40%	20%

RIFLES: LEVER ACTION

This grouping includes models with a "Winchester-style" lever under the gun that is also a trigger guard.

MODEL B 1000 SHOT - BB/.175 cal., 1,000 shot. Mfg. 1910.

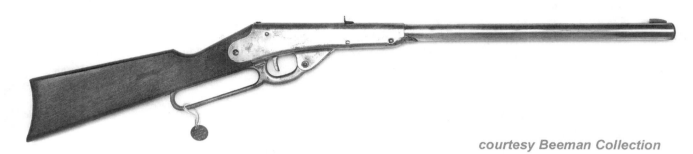

courtesy Beeman Collection

	100%	95%	90%	80%	60%	40%	20%
⊛ *Model B 1000 Shot Variant 1* - nickel finish, cast iron rear sight, brass barrel, steel buttplate.							
	$400	$275	$195	$150	$115	$85	$65
⊛ *Model B 1000 Shot Variant 2* - similar to Variant 1, except w/sheet metal barrel w/o buttplate.							
	$350	$225	$150	$125	$100	$75	$65
⊛ *Model B 1000 Shot Variant 3* - similar to Variant 2, except w/sheet metal rear sight w/o buttplate.							
	$350	$225	$150	$125	$100	$75	$65
⊛ *Model B 1000 Shot Variant 4* - similar to Variant 3, except blue finish.							
	$350	$225	$150	$125	$100	$75	$65

MODEL B 500 SHOT - BB/.175 cal., without steel buttplate. Mfg. 1910-23.

	100%	95%	90%	80%	60%	40%	20%
⊛ *Model B 500 Shot Variant 1* - nickel finish, cast iron rear sight, brass barrel, steel buttplate.							
	$350	$225	$150	$125	$100	$75	$65
⊛ *Model B 500 Shot Variant 2* - similar to Variant 1, except with sheet metal barrel.							
	$350	$225	$150	$125	$100	$75	$65
⊛ *Model B 500 Shot Variant 3* - similar to Variant 2, except with sheet metal rear sight.							
	$350	$225	$150	$125	$100	$75	$65
⊛ *Model B 500 Shot Variant 4* - similar to Variant 3, except has blue finish.							

MODEL H SINGLE SHOT - BB/.175 cal., nickel finish mfg. 1913-20, blue finish mfg. 1921-23.

courtesy Beeman Collection

	100%	95%	90%	80%	60%	40%	20%
	$350	$250	$150	$125	$115	$75	$60

Add 20% for nickel finish.

Historical Note: This specimen, and several other illustrated BB rifles, engraved W.R.A. with date, were formerly in the Winchester Repeating Arm collection.

MODEL H REPEATER - BB/.175 cal., 500-shot nickel finish mfg. 1914-17, 350-shot nickel finish mfg. 1921-32, 350-shot blue finish mfg. 1918-20.

	100%	95%	90%	80%	60%	40%	20%
	$300	$250	$200	$150	$100	$65	$40

MODEL 3 SERIES B "DAISY SPECIAL" - BB/.175 cal., 1000-shot, black nickel finish, in lithograph box. Mfg. 1904-08.

	100%	95%	90%	80%	60%	40%	20%
	$1,500	$800	$500	$350	$250	N/A	N/A

Add 10% for poor original box. Add 20% for restored original box. Add 100% or more for excellent original box.

MODEL 27 (500 SHOT) - BB/.175 cal., 500-shot, blue finish. Mfg. 1927-32.

	100%	95%	90%	80%	60%	40%	20%
	$225	$150	$125	$100	N/A	N/A	N/A

MODEL 27 (1000 SHOT) - BB/.175 cal., 1000-shot, nickel finish. Mfg. 1927-32.

	100%	95%	90%	80%	60%	40%	20%
	$300	$200	$175	$150	$125	N/A	N/A

GRADING	100%	95%	90%	80%	60%	40%	20%

MODEL 50 GOLDEN EAGLE - BB/.175 cal., commemorates 50th anniversary of Daisy, special copper-plated model, similar to No. 195 Buzz Barton, pistol grip stock and curved lever, easily identified by black painted stock with red, white, and blue federal eagle decal, and sight tube mounted on top of gun, hooded front sight. Mfg. 1936-1940. Very scarce.

	100%	95%	90%	80%	60%	40%	20%
	$400	$300	$200	$150	$100	N/A	N/A

Originally sold for $2.34 by Sears Roebuck & Co. in 1937.

MODEL 75 SCOUT RIFLE - BB/.175 cal., 500-shot, painted finish. Mfg. 1954-58.

	$110	$75	$40	N/A	N/A	N/A	N/A

MODEL 80 - BB/.175 cal., 1000-shot repeater, with scope and canteen, painted. Mfg. 1954-57.

	$300	$250	$200	$150	$100	$50	N/A

⊙ **MODEL 80/155** - over stamp. Mfg. 1955.

	$150	$125	$100	$75	$50	N/A	N/A

MODEL 83 - BB/.175 cal., 350-shot, scope. Mfg. 1961-63.

	$300	$250	$200	$150	$100	$50	N/A

MODEL 86 SERIES 70 SAFARI MARK 1 - BB/.175 cal., 240-shot repeater. Mfg. 1970-76.

	$130	$85	$50	N/A	N/A	N/A	N/A

Add 20% for factory box with large game poster.

MODEL 88 HUNTER - BB/.175 cal., 1000-shot, 2X scope, plastic stock, painted finish. Mfg. 1959-60.

	$100	$85	$75	$65	$50	N/A	N/A

⊙ **Sears Variant** - BB/.175 cal., Sears number 799.19920, Golden Hunter - J.C. Higgins. Mfg. 1957-58.

	$125	$75	$50	N/A	N/A	N/A	N/A

MODEL 90 SPORTSTER - BB/.175 cal., 700-shot, safety, plastic stock, painted finish. Mfg. 1973-78.

	$75	$50	$45	N/A	N/A	N/A	N/A

MODEL 95 - BB/.175 cal., 700-shot, early versions: wood stock, plastic forearm; later version: wood/wood, painted finish. Mfg. 1962-76.

	$50	$45	$40	$35	N/A	N/A	N/A

Quick Kill version - see Model 2299 Quick Kill listing.

⊙ **Model 95A** - BB/.175 cal., 700-shot, plastic stock, painted finish. Mfg. 1979-80.

	$50	$45	$40	$35	N/A	N/A	N/A

⊙ **Model 95 Timberwolf** - BB/.175, .177 cal., LA, spring air, 325 FPS, 700-shot, black finish, stained wood stock, crossbolt trigger block safety, adj. rear sight, 2.4 lbs. Mfg. 2002-04.

	$39	$32	$25	$20	N/A	N/A	N/A

⊙ **Model 95 Pony Express** - similar to Timberwolf. Mfg. 1999.

	$150	$125	$100	$75	$50	N/A	N/A

⊙ **Model 95 Gold Rush** - similar to Pony Express. Mfg. 1999.

	$150	$125	$100	$75	$50	N/A	N/A

MODEL 96 - BB/.175 cal., LA, 700-shot, painted finish. Mfg. 1963-73.

	$85	$55	$45	$40	N/A	N/A	N/A

MODEL 97 SADDLE GUN - BB/.175 cal., LA, 650-shot, ricochet sound device, painted finish, plastic stock. Mfg. 1961 only.

	$180	$140	$100	$85	$65	$50	N/A

MODEL 98 - BB/.175 cal., 700-shot, plastic or wood stock. Mfg. 1974 only.

	$85	$70	$60	N/A	N/A	N/A	N/A

Add 20% for wood stock.

MODEL 98 DAISY EAGLE - BB/.175 cal., 2X scope, plastic stock, painted finish, leather sling, Plymouth or Rogers addresses. Mfg. 1955-60.

	$300	$250	$200	$175	$125	$60	N/A

Add 20% for Plymouth address.

⊙ **Model 98 Golden Eagle** - similar to Model 98 Daisy Eagle, with scope. 1957.

	$300	$250	$200	$175	$125	$60	N/A

⊙ **Model 98 Golden Hunter** - similar to Model 98 Daisy Eagle, with scope. 1958.

	$300	$250	$200	$175	$125	$60	N/A

MODEL 99 TARGET SPECIAL - BB/.175 cal., painted finish, web sling.

⊙ **Model 99 Target Special Variant 1** - gravity-fed magazine. Mfg. only 1959.

	$135	$90	$60	$50	N/A	N/A	N/A

⊙ **Model 99 Target Special Variant 2** - spring-fed magazine. Mfg. 1960-1979.

	$100	$70	$50	$40	N/A	N/A	N/A

MODEL 99 CHAMPION - mfg. 1967.

	$100	$75	$50	N/A	N/A	N/A	N/A

Add 10% for peep sight.

GRADING	100%	95%	90%	80%	60%	40%	20%

MODEL 99 LUCKY MCDANIELS INSTINCT SHOOTER - BB/.175 cal., no sights. Mfg. 1960 only.

	$350	$225	$125	$100	N/A	N/A	N/A

MODEL 102 CUB - BB/.175 cal., 350-shot, blue finish, wooden stock. Mfg. 1952-78.

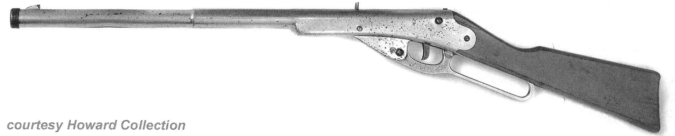

courtesy Howard Collection

	$85	$65	$50	N/A	N/A	N/A	N/A

MODEL 103 SCOUT - BB/.175 cal., plastic stock, painted finish. Mfg. 1964-65 (disc. circa 1990).

	$75	$50	$30	N/A	N/A	N/A	N/A

MODEL 104 GOLDEN EAGLE - BB/.175 cal., 500-shot, plastic stock, peep sight, gold or black paint. Mfg. 1966-74.

	$125	$90	$75	$65	$50	N/A	N/A

MODEL 105 BUCK - BB/.175, .177 cal., LA, SP, 275 FPS, 400-shot, black finish, stained wood stock, crossbolt trigger block safety, fiberoptic fixed sights, 1.6 lbs.

MSR $40	$35	$25	$20	N/A	N/A	N/A	N/A

MODEL 105 CUB - BB/.175 cal., 350-shot, painted finish. Mfg. 1979-81, 1982-90.

courtesy Beeman Collection

	$45	$30	$25	N/A	N/A	N/A	N/A

MODEL 108 SERIES 39 LONE SCOUT - BB/.175 cal., lightning loader, blue finish. Mfg. 1939 only.

	$500	$400	$250	N/A	N/A	N/A	N/A

✪ *Model 108 Series 39* - BB/.175 cal., lightning loader, adj. or fixed rear sight, blue finish. Mfg. 1939-42 and 1945.

	$200	$125	$65	N/A	N/A	N/A	N/A

MODEL 110 AIR FORCE ROCKET COMMAND - BB/.175 cal., LA. Mfg. 1959 only.

	$300	$225	$175	$150	$125	N/A	N/A

MODEL 111 WESTERN CARBINE - BB/.175 cal., 700-shot, plastic stock, curved cocking lever. Mfg. 1963-78.

courtesy Howard Collection

	$125	$90	$60	$50	$40	$30	N/A

MODEL 155 - BB/.175 cal., repeater, blue finish (painted finish 1953), stamped "1000 shot", cast iron cocking lever 1946, aluminum lever 1947-49. Mfg. 1931. Reintroduced 1952-53.

	$180	$125	$95	N/A	N/A	N/A	N/A

MODEL 299 - BB/.175 cal., 1000-shot, peep sight. Gravity-fed version of Model 99. Mfg. 1975-76.

	$100	$65	$50	N/A	N/A	N/A	N/A

GRADING	100%	95%	90%	80%	60%	40%	20%

MODEL 400 - BB/.175 cal., five-shot Roto-clip, .177 cal. pellet. Mfg. 1971-72.

	100%	95%	90%	80%	60%	40%	20%
	$100	$75	$55	N/A	N/A	N/A	N/A

MODEL 403 - BB/.175 cal., five-shot Roto-clip, .177 cal. pellet. Status of this model not clear. Mfg. 1973-76.

	$125	$85	$60	N/A	N/A	N/A	N/A

MODEL 404 - BB/.175 cal., five-shot Roto-clip, .177 cal. pellet. Mfg. 1974-76.

	$125	$85	$60	N/A	N/A	N/A	N/A

MODEL 450 - BB/.175 cal., five-shot Roto-clip, .177 cal. pellet. Mfg. 1972-73.

	$75	$65	$50	N/A	N/A	N/A	N/A

MODEL 452 - BB/.175 cal., five-shot Roto-clip, .177 cal. pellet. Mfg. 1973 only.

	$125	$85	$60	N/A	N/A	N/A	N/A

MODEL 453 - BB/.175 cal., five-shot Roto-clip, .177 cal. pellet. Mfg. 1974-76.

	$75	$65	$50	N/A	N/A	N/A	N/A

MODEL 454 - BB/.175 cal., five-shot Roto-clip, .177 cal. pellet. Mfg. 1974-76.

	$110	$75	$55	N/A	N/A	N/A	N/A

MODEL 499 - BB/.175 cal., target single shot, plastic or wood stock. Mfg. 1976-79.

	$125	$85	$60	N/A	N/A	N/A	N/A

AVANTI MODEL 499 CHAMPION - BB or .177 (4.5 mm steel shot) cal., SP, SS muzzle loading, lever action smoothbore steel BBL, 240 FPS, hooded front with aperture inserts and adj. rear peep sights, Monte Carlo stained hardwood stock and forearm with weight compartments, 36.25 in. OAL, 3.1 lbs. New 2003.

MSR $179	$150	$125	$100	$75	$50	N/A	N/A

MODEL 770 SUPER - .177 cal. pellet, UL, SP, single-stroke cocking. Mfg. 1978-80.

	$115	$85	$55	N/A	N/A	N/A	N/A

MODEL 1000 - BB/.175 cal., Western Auto. Mfg. 1957-58.

	$90	$75	$50	N/A	N/A	N/A	N/A

MODEL 1105 - BB/.175 cal., 500-shot, safety. Mfg. 1975-79.

	$50	$40	$25	N/A	N/A	N/A	N/A

MODEL 1201 - BB/.175 cal., gold finish, blond stock, Western Auto. Mfg. 1976-77.

	$125	$75	$50	N/A	N/A	N/A	N/A

MODEL 1205 - BB/.175 cal., economy version of Model 1200, sixty-shot. Mfg. 1979-81.

	$100	$60	$40	N/A	N/A	N/A	N/A

MODEL 1776 GOLDEN EAGLE - BB/.175 cal., 500-shot, peep sight, gold paint finish. Mfg. 1968-72.

	$200	$125	$75	N/A	N/A	N/A	N/A

MODEL 1894 WESTERN CARBINE - BB/.175 cal., forty-shot, grey painted finish, metal buttplate, plastic stock. Mfg. 1961-86.

	$125	$90	$50	N/A	N/A	N/A	N/A

   Subtract 40% for missing factory box.

◎ *Model 1894 Western Carbine And Pistol Set* - BB/.175 cal., valued as a set. Mfg. 1970-80.

	$250	$125	$75	N/A	N/A	N/A	N/A

   Subtract 40% for missing factory box.

◎ *Model 1894 Buffalo Bill 150th Anniversary Model* - see Daisy Commemorative section.

◎ *Model 1894 Carbine Sears Variant Number 799.19052* - see Daisy Commemorative section.

◎ *Model 1894 Carbine Sears Variant Number 799.19120* - see Daisy Commemorative section.

◎ *Model 1894 Commemorative Wells Fargo Limited Edition* - BB/.175 cal. Mfg. 1975-76.

	$300	$200	$125	N/A	N/A	N/A	N/A

   Subtract 40% for missing factory box.

◎ *Model 1894 Commemorative 1894-1994 Limited Edition* - BB/.175 cal., octagon barrel. Mfg. 1994.

	$140	$100	$70	N/A	N/A	N/A	N/A

   Subtract 40% for missing factory box.

◎ *Model 1894 Cactus Carbine Sears Number 799.19210* - J.C. Higgins. Mfg. 1960-70.

	$100	$50	$25	N/A	N/A	N/A	N/A

◎ *Daisy 1894 Carbine Sears Varian Number 799.19250* - BB/.175 cal., J.C. Higgins. Mfg. 1952-55.

	$100	$50	$25	N/A	N/A	N/A	N/A

MODEL 2299 QUICK SKILL - civilian version of the U.S. Govt. Quick Kill, no sights, in box with safety glasses, aerial targets. Mfg. 1968-72.

	$200	$150	$125	$100	$90	$50	N/A

   Subtract 35% for missing box.

GRADING	100%	95%	90%	80%	60%	40%	20%

MODEL 2299 QUICK KILL U.S. GOVERNMENT ISSUE - no sights, used with fluorescent BBs to teach instinct shooting to troops in the Vietnam war, U.S. Govt. marking stamped into, or stenciled onto, stock. Mfg. 1968-70.

courtesy Beeman Collection

	100%	95%	90%	80%	60%	40%	20%
	N/A	N/A	$275	$225	$150	N/A	N/A

NO. 3 MODEL 24 - BB/.175 cal., thousand-shot, nickel plated. Mfg. 1924-26.

	100%	95%	90%	80%	60%	40%	20%
	$1,000	$800	$500	$350	$250	$200	$150

NO. 11 MODEL 24 - BB/.175 cal., 350-shot, nickel finish. Mfg. 1924-28.

	100%	95%	90%	80%	60%	40%	20%
	$225	$150	$125	$100	N/A	N/A	N/A

NO. 11 MODEL 29 - BB/.175 cal., 350-shot, nickel finish. Mfg. 1929-32.

	100%	95%	90%	80%	60%	40%	20%
	$225	$150	$125	$100	$75	N/A	N/A

NO. 12 MODEL 24 - BB/.175 cal., single-shot, blue finish. Mfg. 1924-28.

	100%	95%	90%	80%	60%	40%	20%
	$225	$150	$125	$100	N/A	N/A	N/A

NO. 12 MODEL 29 - BB/.175 cal., single-shot, blue finish. Mfg. 1929-32.

	100%	95%	90%	80%	60%	40%	20%
	$225	$150	$125	$100	$75	N/A	N/A

NO. 24 MODEL 30 - BB/.175 cal., 500-shot, blue finish. Mfg. 1924-26.

	100%	95%	90%	80%	60%	40%	20%
	$1,000	$700	$400	$250	$175	N/A	N/A

NO. 30 MODEL 24 - BB/.175 cal., 500-shot, blue finish. Mfg. 1924-26.

	100%	95%	90%	80%	60%	40%	20%
	$250	$175	$150	$125	$100	N/A	N/A

NO. 101 MODEL 33 - BB/.175 cal., "Daisy for a Buck," SS, blue finish. Mfg. 1933-35.

	100%	95%	90%	80%	60%	40%	20%
	$130	$100	$75	N/A	N/A	N/A	N/A

NO. 102 MODEL 33 - BB/.175 cal., 500-shot, nickel finish, wooden stock. Mfg. 1933-35.

	100%	95%	90%	80%	60%	40%	20%
	$175	$125	$100	$75	$50	N/A	N/A

NO. 101 MODEL 36 - BB/.175 cal., SS, blue finish. Mfg. 1936-42.

	100%	95%	90%	80%	60%	40%	20%
	$150	$125	$90	$80	$70	N/A	N/A

NO. 102 MODEL 36 - BB/.175 cal., 500-shot, nickel (1936-40), blue (1941-42 and 1945-47), or painted (1953) finish, wood stock (plastic stock 1954), aluminum lever 1950 (none mfg. 1947-49).

	100%	95%	90%	80%	60%	40%	20%
	$150	$125	$100	$100	$75	N/A	N/A

NO. 111 WESTERN CARBINE - BB/.175 cal., 700-shot, plastic stock, straight, uncurved cocking lever. Mfg.1963-78.

	100%	95%	90%	80%	60%	40%	20%
	$150	$125	$100	$100	$75	N/A	N/A

BENNETT 1000 SHOT - BB/.175 cal., thousand-shot, nickel. Mfg. 1903-09.

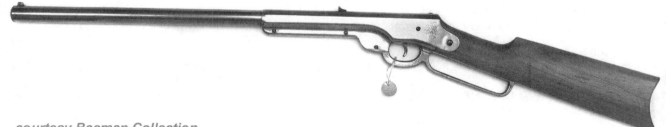

courtesy Beeman Collection

	100%	95%	90%	80%	60%	40%	20%
	$1,250	$850	$650	$500	$350	$300	$250

BENNETT 500 SHOT - 500-shot. Mfg. 1905-09.

	100%	95%	90%	80%	60%	40%	20%
	$1,800	$1,200	$750	$600	$450	$400	$350

MODEL 111-B AMERICAN YOUTH - see Daisy Commemorative section.

GRADING	100%	95%	90%	80%	60%	40%	20%

RIFLES: LEVER ACTION, BUZZ BARTON SERIES

NUMBER 103 MODEL 33 SUPER BUZZ BARTON SPECIAL - BB/.175 cal., thousand-shot LA on Model 27 frame, easy to recognize Buzz Barton series by rear sight tube, bright nickel plate and star-shaped "Buzz Barton" brand in stock. Mfg. 1933-37.

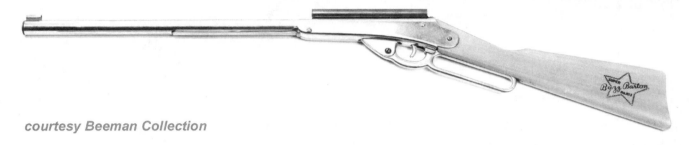

courtesy Beeman Collection

	100%	95%	90%	80%	60%	40%	20%
	$575	$425	$350	$275	$200	$150	$100

Add 10% for mahogany stock.

NO. 195 MODEL 32 BUZZ BARTON SPECIAL - BB/.175 cal., LA, thousand-shot, straight barrel and plunger housing with a patch shoulder underneath, blue, cast iron lever, rear sight tube, walnut stock with brand "Buzz Barton Special No. 195" inside lariat with two cowboys. Paper label 1932.

	$450	$300	$250	$200	$150	$100	$75

Add 50% for paper label.

This is a Markham/King design based upon the King No. 55.

✪ **No.195 Model 33** - BB/.175 cal., similar to Model 32 except has brand on stock, mfg. 1933-35.

	$450	$300	$250	$200	$150	$100	$75

Add 50% for paper label.

This is a Markham/King design based upon the King No. 55.

✪ **No. 195 Model 36** - BB/.175 cal., similar to Model 36 except has larger frame, mfg. 1936-41.

	$450	$300	$250	$200	$150	$100	$75

Add 50% for paper label.

This is a Markham/King design based upon the King No. 55.

RIFLES: LEVER ACTION, DEFENDER SERIES

NO. 40 MILITARY MODEL (WWI MILITARY MODEL) - full-length, one-piece wood stock, no bolt handle, 10 in. rubber-tipped metal bayonet, web sling.

✪ **No. 40 Military Model (WWI Military Model) Variant 1** - adj. front sight, extended shot tube with knurled end extends about .25 in. beyond muzzle. Mfg. 1916-18.

courtesy Beeman Collection

	N/A	N/A	$500	$400	$300	$200	N/A

Add $300-$500 for bayonet. Add $100 for sling.

✪ **No. 40 Military Model (WWI Military Model) Variant 2** - fixed front sight, standard no. 25 shot tube. Mfg. 1919-32.

	N/A	N/A	$400	$300	$200	$100	N/A

Add $300-$500 for bayonet. Add $100 for sling.

The metal bayonets were often taken away from children, and subsequently either lost or thrown away. Bayonet alone may sell for $300-$400.

NO. 140 DEFENDER ("WWII DEFENDER") - BB/.175 cal., military-style two-piece wooden stock with extended forearm, blue finish, bolt handle (acts as auto safety), gravity-fed, web sling, no bayonet. Very rare. Mfg. 1942 only.

	N/A	N/A	$375	$275	$175	$75	N/A

NO. 141 DEFENDER ("KOREAN WAR DEFENDER") - similar to No. 140, except with plastic stock and forearm, web sling, blue or painted finish, fifty-shot spring-fed repeater. Mfg. 1951-53.

	N/A	$150	$100	$65	$50	$40	N/A

Add 50% for variation with wood stock.

NO. 142 DEFENDER MODEL - same military style, thousand-shot, gravity-fed, blue or painted finish. Mfg.1954, painted, blue, mfg. 1957.

	$250	$125	$95	N/A	N/A	N/A	N/A

GRADING	100%	95%	90%	80%	60%	40%	20%

RIFLES: LEVER ACTION, DEMOULIN INITIATION SERIES

MODEL B - first DeMoulin initiation guns have external water tubing on Daisy Bennett model and no markings on stock, rifles (pair). Mfg.1910-18.

	$1,500	$1,250	$1,000	$800	$700	$600	N/A

Special Daisy BB gun adapted to shoot water. Used as part of the Rough Masonic Initiation ceremony. Usually sold in pairs; one of the pair shot water forward; the other shot water backwards into the face and eyes of the shooter. (Contrary to previous reports, these guns were also sold individually). Stocks are stamped "DeMoulin Bros. & Co, Greenville, Illinois".

MODEL 3 SERIES 24 - (pair) mfg. 1924-26.

	$2,000	$1,500	$1,000	$900	$800	$700	N/A

Special Daisy BB gun adapted to shoot water. Used as part of the Rough Masonic Initiation ceremony. Usually sold in pairs; one of the pair shot water forward; the other shot water backwards into the face and eyes of the shooter. (Contrary to previous reports, these guns were also sold individually). Stocks are stamped "DeMoulin Bros. & Co, Greenville, Illinois".

MODEL 27 (WATER SHOOTER) - (pair) mfg. 1926-35.

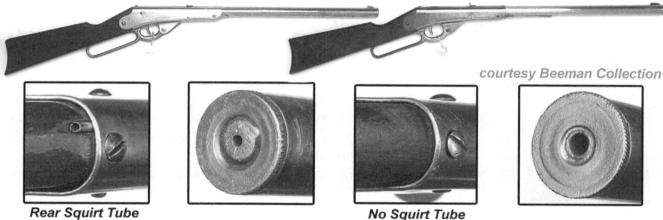

courtesy Beeman Collection

Rear Squirt Tube   **No Squirt Tube**

	$2,000	$1,750	$1,250	$1,100	$1,000	$900	N/A

Special Daisy BB gun adapted to shoot water. Used as part of the Rough Masonic Initiation ceremony. Usually sold in pairs; one of the pair shot water forward; the other shot water backwards into the face and eyes of the shooter. (Contrary to previous reports, these guns were also sold individually.) "Stocks are stamped: DeMoulin Bros. & Co, Greenville, Illinois".

RIFLES: LEVER ACTION, RED RYDER SERIES

This grouping contains the Red Ryder models manufactured beginning 1939-1940.

MODEL 1938 - BB/.175 cal., Red Ryder similar to Number 111 Model 40, wood stock and forearm, logo stamped on left side of stock, narrow barrel bands, saddle ring staple does not go completely through side of receiver, blue paint finish, screws are slotted. Mfg. 1972-78.

	$150	$115	$90	$75	N/A	N/A	N/A

Survival rate on these later models is very slim due to excessive use. Examples in 100% condition are extremely rare.

MODEL 1938 B DUCKS UNLIMITED - BB/.175 cal., special Red Ryder edition for Ducks Unlimited, walnut stock, right side of receiver stamped "Limited Edition", stamping lines filled with gold paint, walnut look rack with brass plaque. Mfg. 1975.

	$175	$150	$125	$100	N/A	N/A	N/A

MODEL 1938 A-B - BB/.175 cal., Red Ryder, marked "1938 A-B" in gold paint on right side of receiver, loading gate on left side of barrel near muzzle, no muzzle band, plastic saddle ring staple, fake loading tube, plastic front sight and muzzle plug, trigger safety, hole in left side of receiver. Mfg. 1978.

	$150	$100	$90	N/A	N/A	N/A	N/A

MODEL 1938 B - BB/.175 cal., Red Ryder similar to Model 1938 A-B but with no hole on left side of receiver, stamped "1938-B". New 1979.

	$40	$35	$30	$25	N/A	N/A	N/A

MODEL 1938 B BUFFALO BILL - export model, plastic loading port, plain Red Ryder stock, gold stencil. Mfg. 1980-85.

	$125	$90	$80	$65	N/A	N/A	N/A

MODEL 1938 "LAND OF BUFFALO BILL" RED RYDER MODEL - styled by Bill Cody, sold only from William Cody Museum, plastic stock. Mfg. about 1977.

	$150	$100	$60	N/A	N/A	N/A	N/A

GRADING	100%	95%	90%	80%	60%	40%	20%

MODEL 1938 "DIAMOND ANNIVERSARY" COMMEMORATIVE - BB/.175 cal., commemorates the 60th anniversary of the introduction of the Red Ryder BB gun, limited edition white scroll on the receiver, burnished forearm band, and special lariat logo in the stock. Mfg. 1998.

	$85	$65	$50	N/A	N/A	N/A	N/A

MODEL 1938 GOLD RUSH COMMEMORATIVE - BB/.175 cal., commemorates the 150th anniversary of the California Gold Rush, "Gold Rush" stamped on the top of the gold-painted barrel, natural finish walnut stock and forearm, countersunk in the stock is a 1-in. gold-colored medallion with a prospector panning for gold, forearm is laser engraved with the gun´s production number. Approx. 2,500 mfg.

	$125	$100	$85	N/A	N/A	N/A	N/A

MODEL 1938 MILLINEUM EDITION COMMEMORATIVE - BB/.175 cal., commemorates the year 2000 with engraving on stock, natural finish walnut stock and forearm, barrels were numbered. Manufactured for one year in 2000.

	$65	$35	$25	N/A	N/A	N/A	N/A

MODEL 1938 RED RYDER - BB/.175, .177 cal., LA, SP, 280 FPS, 650-shot, black finish, stained wood stock/forearm with lariat logo and burnished forearm band, crossbolt trigger block safety, adj. rear sight, saddle ring with leather thong, 2.2 lbs.

MSR $56	$45	$35	$25	N/A	N/A	N/A	N/A

MODEL 9938 RED RYDER KIT - BB/.175, .177 cal., LA, SP, kit includes Model 1938 Red Ryder rifle, shooting glasses, two Shatter-Blast stakes, eight ShatterBlast targets, PrecisionMax BBs, Red Ryder tin of BBs, and Daisy gun case.

MSR $75	$65	$55	$50	$40	$30	N/A	N/A

MODEL 1938 (MFG. 1978) - BB/.175 cal., Red Ryder similar to Model 1938 but with logo on right side of stock, screws are Phillips type. Mfg. 1978.

	$150	$100	$90	$80	$60	N/A	N/A

MODEL 94 CARBINE - BB/.175 cal., 850-shot, plastic stock and forearm, gold (paint) embossed long horn and logo on left side of stock, dummy hammer on stock with leather boot, bright finish forearm band, high front sight, combo peep or open rear sight, blue paint finish, Plymouth and Rogers addresses. Mfg. 1955-62.

	$250	$150	$100	$60	N/A	N/A	N/A

Subtract 50% for missing boot or barrel band.   **Add 20% for Plymouth address.**

NO. 111 MODEL 40 RED RYDER VARIANT 1 - BB/.175 cal., thousand-shot, LA, copper plated forearm and barrel bands, front barrel band pinched into place, wood stock and forearm, saddle ring with leather thong, Red Ryder brand burned into left side of stock, cast iron lever, small screw through top of stock, adj. rear sight. Mfg. 1940-41.

	N/A	$600	$450	$300	$200	N/A	N/A

NO. 111 MODEL 40 ("1942" MODEL) VARIANT 2 - BB/.175 cal., barrel bands either prick-pinched or welded into place, wood stock and forearm, logo burned into left side of stock, cast iron lever (blue), small original size screw through the top of stock, fixed rear sight. Steel shortage due to WWII caused production to stop in early 1942. Mfg. 1941-42.

	N/A	$400	$275	$200	$150	N/A	N/A

Extreme rarity precludes accurate pricing on this model.

NO. 111 MODEL 40 VARIANT 3 - BB/.175 cal., blue barrel bands, wood stock and forearm, Red Ryder logo silk screened onto stock with black paint on red background (because of temporary breakdown of regular stock marking equipment), fixed sights. About 1,000 mfg. The very rarest of all Red Ryder Models. Mfg. 1941.

Extreme rarity precludes accurate pricing on this model.

NO. 111 MODEL 40 VARIANT 4 - BB/.175 cal., large screw through top of stock. Mfg. 1946.

	N/A	$375	$200	$150	$125	N/A	N/A

NO. 111 MODEL 40 VARIANT 5 - BB/.175 cal., wood stock, plastic forearm, logo stamped on left side of stock, black painted cast aluminum lever, fixed sights. Mfg. 1947.

	N/A	$350	$175	$150	$100	N/A	N/A

Note: Steel shortage of 1947 forced use of aluminum in cocking lever.

NO. 111 MODEL 40 VARIANT 6 - BB/.175 cal., wood stock, plastic forearm, logo stamped on left side of stock, black painted cast aluminum lever, fixed sights, plastic forearms. Mfg. 1952.

	N/A	$350	$175	$150	$100	N/A	N/A

Plastic forearms on pre-1966 models had a tendency to warp.

NO. 111 MODEL 40 VARIANT 7 - BB/.175 cal., plastic stock and forearm, logo molded into left side of stock, blue painted finish, painted aluminum lever, fixed or adj. rear sight.

	N/A	$150	$125	$100	$75	N/A	N/A

First use of batch registration numbers in 1952.

NO. 111 MODEL 40 VARIANT 8 - BB/.175 cal., plastic stock, painted finish, white filled checkering on stock.

	$200	$175	$150	$125	$100	N/A	N/A

NO. 311 - Red Ryder set, gun similar to Number 111, except set with scope, bell target, cork firing tube, corks, etc., in large box. Mfg.1947-50.

	$650	$55	$450	$3675	$250	N/A	N/A

GRADING	100%	95%	90%	80%	60%	40%	20%

RIFLES: PNEUMATIC & CO₂ POWERED

This grouping contains models powered by CO_2 or compressed air.

MODEL 22SG - .22 cal., multi-pump pneumatic, UL, SS, 550 FPS, die-cast metal receiver, rifled steel barrel, black finish, hardwood stock and forearm, fiber optic front and adj. rear sights, 4.5 lbs. Mfg. 2002-2007.

	100%	95%	90%	80%	60%	40%	20%
	$105	$90	$80	$60	$50	N/A	N/A

Last MSR was $110.

MODEL 22X - .22 cal., multi-pump pnuematic, UL, SS, 550 FPS, die-cast metal receiver, rifled steel barrel, black finish, hardwood stock and forearm, fiberoptic front and adj. rear sights, dovetail mount and 4x32 scope, 4.5 lbs. Disc. 2002.

	$95	$75	$65	$50	$40	N/A	N/A

MODEL 126 EL GAMO - .177 cal., SSP, match style. Mfg. in Spain by El Gamo, 1984.

	$75	$50	$40	N/A	N/A	N/A	N/A

MODEL 126 EL GAMO SUPER MATCH TARGET RIFLE - .177 cal., SSP, 590 FPS, adj. sights, hardwood stock, match style. 10.6 lbs. Mfg. in Spain by El Gamo. Disc. 1994.

	$470	$400	$300	N/A	N/A	N/A	N/A

Last MSR was $765.

MODEL 128 GAMO OLYMPIC - .177 cal., similar to El Gamo 126 Super Match Target, except has adj. cheekpiece and buttplate, high quality European diopter sight. Mfg. in Spain by El Gamo.

	$440	$375	$300	N/A	N/A	N/A	N/A

Last MSR was $735.

MODEL 177X - .177 cal., multi-pump, ULP, SS, 550 FPS, die-cast metal receiver, rifled steel barrel, black finish, hardwood stock and forearm, fiberoptic front and adj. rear sights, 4.5 lbs. Mfg. 2003-06.

	$75	$60	$50	$40	N/A	N/A	N/A

Last MSR was $80.

MODEL 300 - BB/.175 cal., CO₂ semi-auto, futuristic styling, plastic stock, five-shot repeater. Mfg. 1968-75.

	$85	$75	$70	$45	N/A	N/A	N/A

✪ *Model 300 Sears Variant* - Sears number 799.19062 - similar to Model 300 except gold painted receiver and buttplate.

	$95	$85	$80	$55	N/A	N/A	N/A

MODEL 822 - .22 cal., pneumatic, rifled barrel. Mfg. 1976-78.

	$75	$60	$40	N/A	N/A	N/A	N/A

MODEL 836 POWERLINE - BB/.175, or .177 cal. Mfg. 1984-85.

	$75	$60	$40	N/A	N/A	N/A	N/A

MODEL 840 - BB/.175, or .177 cal., SSP. Mfg. 1978-89.

	$75	$60	$40	N/A	N/A	N/A	N/A

MODEL 840 GRIZZLY/MODEL 840B GRIZZLY - BB/.175, or .177 cal., SSP, 320 FPS (BB/.175 cal.), smooth bore steel barrel, 350-shot (BB/.175 cal.) or SS (.177 cal.), black finish, adj. rear sight, molded woodgrain with checkering stock and forearm, cross-bolt trigger block safety, 2.25 lbs.

MSR $61	$50	$45	$35	$25	$20	N/A	N/A

✪ *Model 840C Grizzly* - BB/.175, or .177 cal., similar to Model 840 Grizzly, except has Mossy Oak Break Up camouflage stock and forearm.

MSR $65	$50	$45	$35	$25	$20	N/A	N/A

Add $15 for kit (Model 5840).

✪ *Model 3840 Grizzly* - BB/.175, or .177 cal., kit includesModel 840C Grizzly rifle, safety glasses, Truglo fiberoptic sights, 350 BBs, 250 pellets, pad of targets, and Daisy's Right Start to Shooting Sports video. Disc. 2006.

	$65	$60	$50	$40	N/A	N/A	N/A

Last MSR was $70.

Add $15 for kit (Model 5840).

✪ *Model 4841 Grizzly* - BB/.175, or .177 cal., includes Model 840C Grizzly rifle, shooting glasses, 4x15 scope, two ShaterBlast stakes with eight ShaterBlast targets, PrecisionMax pellets and BBs.

MSR $70	$55	$45	$35	N/A	N/A	N/A	N/A

Add $15 for kit (Model 5840).

MODEL 845 TARGET - similar to Model 840, except has peep sights. Mfg. 1980-89.

	$75	$60	$40	N/A	N/A	N/A	N/A

GRADING	100%	95%	90%	80%	60%	40%	20%

MODEL 850 POWERLINE - BB/.175, or .177 cal., SSP, rifled barrel, black die-cast metal, adj. rear sight, hand-wiped checkered woodgrain finished stock, buttplate, BB 520 FPS, 4.3 lbs. Mfg. 1982-84.

courtesy Howard Collection

	100%	95%	90%	80%	60%	40%	20%
	$75	$60	$40	N/A	N/A	N/A	N/A

MODEL 851 POWERLINE - BB/.175, or .177 cal., similar to Model 850 Powerline, except has select hardwood stock. Mfg. 1982-84.

	$110	$60	$40	N/A	N/A	N/A	N/A

MODEL 853 TARGET - .177 cal., SSP. Mfg. 1984.

	$250	$180	$140	N/A	N/A	N/A	N/A

MODEL 856 POWERLINE - .177 cal. (early versions .177 pellet SS/BB repeater combination), multi-pump pneumatic, SS, 670 FPS, rifled steel barrel, black finish, molded wood grain sporter style stock and forearm, crossbolt trigger block safety, adj. rear sight, 2.7 lbs.

courtesy Beeman Collection

	$40	$30	$20	N/A	N/A	N/A	N/A

Add 25% for combination pellet and BB gun.

☼ *Model 856F Powerline* - .177 cal., similar to Model 856 Powerline, except has fiberoptic sights. Disc. 2004.

	$45	$35	$25	N/A	N/A	N/A	N/A

Last MSR was $50.

Add 25% for Model 808 4x15 scope (Model 7856).

☼ *Model 856C Powerline* - .177 cal., similar to Model 856 Powerline, except has fiberoptic sights and Mossy Oak Break Up Camo stock and forearm. Disc. 2004.

	$55	$40	$30	$20	$15	N/A	N/A

Last MSR was $60.

MODEL 860 POWERLINE - BB/.175, or .177 cal. Mfg. 1984-85.

	$75	$60	$40	N/A	N/A	N/A	N/A

MODEL 880 POWERLINE - BB/.175, or .177 cal., pellet, multi-stroke pump pneumatic. Mfg. 1972-89.

courtesy Beeman Collection

	$65	$40	$30	N/A	N/A	N/A	N/A

Add 100% for early models with metal receiver, metal pumping arm, no warnings printed on the guns – the "pure" original version. Add 50% for metal receiver.

MODEL 880 POWERLINE (CURRENT) - BB/.175, or .177 cal., UL, multi-pump pneumatic, 685 FPS (BB), 75-125 (BB) or SS (pellet), dodecahedral rifling suited to pellet or steel BBs, steel barrel, black finish, molded Monte Carlo-style stock and forearm, adj. rear sight, crossbolt trigger block safety, 3.7 lbs. New 1990.

MSR $72	$55	$40	$30	$20	$15	N/A	N/A

Add $5 for fiberoptic front sight. Add $15 for Model 808 4x15 scope (Model 1880).

GRADING	100%	95%	90%	80%	60%	40%	20%
MODEL 5880 POWERLINE - BB/.175, or .177 cal., UL, multi-pump pneumatic, kit includes shooting glasses, 4x15 scope, targets and ammo. New 2004.							
MSR $89	$65	$55	$40	$30	$20	$15	N/A
Add $5 for fiberoptic front sight. Add $15 for Model 808 4x15 scope (Model 1880).							
MODEL 881 POWERLINE - similar to Model 880, rifled barrel. Mfg. 1973-83.							
	$75	$60	$40	N/A	N/A	N/A	N/A
MODEL 882 CENTENNIAL - similar to Model 880, rifled barrel. Mfg. 1975-76.							
	$75	$60	$40	N/A	N/A	N/A	N/A
MODLE 900 SNAP SHOT - .177 cal., auto-fed, clip. Mfg. 1986.							
	$95	$70	$50	N/A	N/A	N/A	N/A
MODEL 901 - BB/.175, or .177 cal., UL, multi-pump pneumatic, 750 FPS (BB), 50 (BB) or SS (pellet), rifled steel barrel, black finish, molded composite stock and forearm, fiberoptic front and adj. rear sight, crossbolt trigger block safety, 37.5 in. OAL, 3.7 lbs. New 2005.							
MSR $84	$65	$55	$45	$30	N/A	N/A	N/A
Add $5 for fiberoptic front sight. Add $15 for Model 808 4x15 scope (Model 1880). Add $15 for shooting kit (Modle 5901).							
MODEL 917 - .177 cal., multi-stroke pneumatic, five-shot clip. Mfg. 1979-82.							
	$95	$70	$50	N/A	N/A	N/A	N/A
MODEL 920 - multi-stroke pump pneumatic, similar to Model 922 except has wood stock and forearm, five-shot clip. Mfg. 1978-89.							
	$130	$105	$80	$65	N/A	N/A	N/A
MODEL 922 - pneumatic, multi-stroke, five-shot clip. Mfg. 1978-89.							
	$95	$70	$50	N/A	N/A	N/A	N/A
MODEL 953 TARGETPRO - .177 cal., SSP, ULP, SS, 560 FPS, die-cast metal receiver, rifled steel barrel, black finish, black composite stock and forearm, fiberoptic front and adj. rear sights, 39 3/4 in. OAL, 6.4 lbs. New 2004.							
MSR $119	$90	$75	$60	$40	N/A	N/A	N/A
MODEL 953 U.S. SHOOTING TEAM - .177 cal., single-stroke pneumatic. Mfg. 1984-85.							
	$195	$150	$100	N/A	N/A	N/A	N/A
MODEL 9953 TARGETPRO - .177 cal., SSP, ULP, SS, kit includes shooting glasses, ShatterBlast targets and stakes, Shoot-N-C targets, and pellets. New 2004.							
MSR $155	$135	$105	$70	$50	N/A	N/A	N/A
MODEL 977 - similar to Model 880, except has rifled barrel, peep sight. Mfg. 1980-83.							
	$100	$75	$50	N/A	N/A	N/A	N/A
MODEL 990 BB/.175 or .177 cal., 100 shot gravity feed BB magazine, SS pellet, combination multi-pump pneumatic and CO_2, rifled bbl, manual cross-bolt safety, vel. 630 fps, 37.4 in. OAL, 4.1 lbs. Manf. 1993-96 (listed until 2000).							
	$150	$110	$100	$75	$50	N/A	N/A
MODEL 1880 - similar to Model 880, except with scope. Mfg.1978-80.							
	$100	$75	$60	N/A	N/A	N/A	N/A
MODEL 1881 POWERLINE - BB/.175 or .177 cal., pneumatic pump. Mfg. 1978-80.							
	$115	$90	$65	N/A	N/A	N/A	N/A
MODEL 1917 POWERLINE - .177 cal., five-shot clip, scope. Mfg. 1978-80.							
	$115	$90	$65	N/A	N/A	N/A	N/A
MODEL 1922 POWERLINE - .22 cal., pneumatic, multi-stroke. Mfg. 1978-80.							
	$75	$50	$40	N/A	N/A	N/A	N/A
MODEL 7840 BUCKMASTER - BB/.175, or .177 cal., SSP, 320 FPS (BB/.175 cal.), smooth bore steel barrel, 350 (BB/.175 cal.) or SS (.177 cal.), black finish, adj. rear sightand electronic point sight, molded woodgrain with checkering stock and forearm, crossbolt trigger block safety, 2.25 lbs. Mfg. 2003-06.							
	$50	$40	$33	$25	$20	N/A	N/A
							Last MSR was $55.
AMERICAN SPIRIT - BB/.175, or .177 cal., CO_2 similar to Model 840 Grizzly, except stock and forearm are finished in stars and stripes design. Mfg. 2002.							
	$50	$40	$33	$25	$20	N/A	N/A
AVANTI MODEL 753 ELITE - .177 cal., SSP, 480 FPS, competition sights, hardwood stock, high cheekpiece, adj. trigger, Lothar Walther rifled barrel, 6 lbs. 8 oz.							
MSR $558	$385	$325	$265	$215	$170	N/A	N/A
AVANTI MODEL 853 LEGEND - .177 cal., SSP, 480 FPS, Lothar Walther barrel, adj. sights, 5 lbs. 8 oz.							
MSR $432	$315	$265	$215	$165	$125	N/A	N/A
AVANTI MODEL 853C LEGEND EX - .177 cal., similar to Model 853 Target, except has five-shot mag.							
MSR $432	$315	$265	$215	$165	$125	N/A	N/A

GRADING	100%	95%	90%	80%	60%	40%	20%

AVANTI MODEL 888 MEDALIST - .177 cal., CO₂ 2.5 oz. cylinder, 500 FPS, SS bolt action, Lothar Walther rifled steel target barrel, hooded front sight with changeable aperture inserts, micrometer adj. rear sight, multi-color laminate three-position sporter style hardwood stock, adj. trigger, 6.9 lbs. New 2001.

	100%	95%	90%	80%	60%	40%	20%
MSR $525	$395	$295	$250	$200	$150	N/A	N/A

AVANTI PREMIO PRECISION MODEL XP 30 - .177 cal., CO₂, 580-600 FPS, built-in gauge in the cylinder, 19.8 in. Lothar Walther rifled steel barrel, Hämmerli precision target sights, hardwood laminate stock with adj. cheek piece and buttplate, fully adj. trigger, 8.5 lbs. Mfg. 2001-2002.

	100%	95%	90%	80%	60%	40%	20%
	$799	$720	$610	$490	N/A	N/A	N/A

AVANTI TROFEO PRECISION MODEL XT 10 - .177 cal., compressed air, 580-600 FPS, built-in gauge in the cylinder, 23.54-in. Lothar Walther rifled steel barrel, Anschütz precision target sights, hardwood laminate stock with carbon fiber finish, fully adj. cheek piece and buttplate, fully adj. trigger, 11.42 lbs. Mfg. 2001-2002.

	100%	95%	90%	80%	60%	40%	20%
	$1,600	$1,440	$1,225	$980	N/A	N/A	N/A

AVANTI VALIANT MODEL XS 40 - .177 cal., compressed air, 580-590 FPS, built-in gauge in the cylinder, 19 in. rifled steel target barrel, front globe sight with changeable aperture inserts, rear diopter sight with micrometer click adjustments for windage and elevation, hardwood stock with adj. cheek piece and buttplate, adj. trigger, 7 lbs. Mfg. 2001-06.

	100%	95%	90%	80%	60%	40%	20%
	$550	$450	$400	$350	N/A	N/A	N/A

Last MSR was $881.

AVANTI VITTORIA PRECISION MODEL XV 20 - .177 cal., compressed air, 580-600 FPS, built-in gauge in the cylinder, 23.54-in. Lothar Walther rifled steel barrel, Anschütz precision target sights, fully adj. target stock with adj. cheek piece and buttplate, fully adj. trigger, 11.42 lbs. New 2001-2002.

	100%	95%	90%	80%	60%	40%	20%
	$1,200	$1,080	$915	$730	N/A	N/A	N/A

⊚ **Model 9840** - BB/.175, or .177 cal., kit includesModel 840C Grizzly rifle, safety glasses, Truglo fiberoptic sights, 350 BBs, 250 pellets, pad of targets, and Daisy's Right Start to Shooting Sports video. Mfg. 2008-current.

	100%	95%	90%	80%	60%	40%	20%
MSR $87	$65	$60	$50	$40	N/A	N/A	N/A

Last MSR was $70.

Add $15 for kit (Model 5840).

RIFLES: PUMP/SLIDE ACTION

This grouping contains models that use a mechanical pump/slide action to cock the spring.

MODEL 25 SERIES - BB/.175 cal. elbow-slide pump action cocking, large takedown knurled-head bolt, MV to 450 FPS, internal spring-fed magazine, about 45 rounds, no safety. About 58 variants, 1914 to 1979.

⊚ **Model 25 Variant 1 ("1914")** - short lever, slide handle with five grooves, straight stock, solder patch, adj. front sight (slides from side to side), black over nickel finish (never sold in bright nickel). Mfg. 1914 only.

	100%	95%	90%	80%	60%	40%	20%
	N/A	$500	$400	$300	$250	N/A	N/A

⊚ **Model 25 Variant 2 ("1916")** - similar to variation 1 except blue, adj. sights.

	100%	95%	90%	80%	60%	40%	20%
	N/A	$350	$250	$200	$150	N/A	N/A

⊚ **Model 25 Variant 3** - short lever, straight stock, fixed front sight. Mfg. date unknown.

courtesy Beeman Collection

	100%	95%	90%	80%	60%	40%	20%
	N/A	$250	$200	$150	$125	N/A	N/A

⊚ **Model 25 Variant 4** - long lever, five-grooved slide handle, straight stock, fixed front sight.

courtesy Beeman Collection

	100%	95%	90%	80%	60%	40%	20%
	$300	$200	$150	$125	$100	N/A	N/A

⊚ **Model 25 Variant 5** - pistol grip stock, small takedown screw.

	100%	95%	90%	80%	60%	40%	20%
	$300	$200	$150	$125	$100	N/A	N/A

GRADING	100%	95%	90%	80%	60%	40%	20%
⊕ **Model 25 Variant 6 ("1932")** - pistol grip stock, six-groove slide handle.							
	$300	$200	$150	$125	$100	N/A	N/A

⊕ **Model 25 Variant 7 ("1936")** - pistol grip stock, stamped "engraving" with gold paint. Mfg. 1936-42 and 1945-51.

courtesy Beeman Collection

	100%	95%	90%	80%	60%	40%	20%
	$350	$250	$200	$175	$125	$100	$65
⊕ **Model 25 Variant 8 ("1952")** - pistol grip stock, factory Model 40 Daisy scope. Mfg. 1952 only.							
	$600	$500	$475	$400	$350	N/A	N/A
⊕ **Model 25 Variant 9** - plastic stock, stamped engraving, electrostatic painted receiver. Mfg. 1952-55.							
	$175	$150	$125	N/A	N/A	N/A	N/A
⊕ **Model 25 Variant 10 ("1954")** - combination rear sight, mfg. 1954.							
	$150	$125	$100	$90	$80	N/A	N/A
⊕ **Model 25 Variant 11 ("1955")** - added scope mounting holes and oil hole. Mfg. 1955.							
	$150	$125	$100	$90	$80	N/A	N/A
⊕ **Model 25 Variant 12 ("1956")** - plastic PG, stenciled "engraving," Plymouth address. Mfg. 1956-57.							
	$150	$125	$100	$90	$80	N/A	N/A
⊕ **Model 25 Variant 12 Jr. NRA Commemorative Model** - Plymouth, MI. Mfg. 1956 only.							
	$300	$250	$200	$150	N/A	N/A	N/A
⊕ **Model 25 Variant 13 ("1958")** - plastic PG, stenciled engraving, Rogers address. Mfg. 1958-76.							
	$150	$125	$100	$90	$80	N/A	N/A
Add 20% for Preston Ontario-marked guns							
⊕ **Model 25 Variant 14 ("Bronze Blond")** - bronze finish, blond plastic stock. Mfg. 1958.							
	$150	$125	$100	$90	$80	N/A	N/A
⊕ **Model 25 Sears Variant** - PG, plastic stock, marked Sears. Mfg. 1970-72.							
	$150	$125	$100	$90	$80	N/A	N/A
⊕ **Model 25 Wards Variant** - PG, plastic stock, Montgomery Wards, Hawthorne brand. Mfg. 1970-72.							
	$150	$125	$100	$90	$80	N/A	N/A
⊕ **Model 25 Variant 15 ("1977")** - plastic Monte Carlo stock. Mfg. 1977-79.							
	$150	$125	$100	$90	$80	N/A	N/A
⊕ **Model 25 Centennial** - replica, straight wood stock. Mfg. 1986 only.							
	$275	$150	$125	$75	N/A	N/A	N/A
MODEL 26 FIELD MASTER - slide action, forty-five-shot. Mfg. 1964-67.							
	$125	$90	$80	$70	N/A	N/A	N/A
MODEL 105 JUNIOR - slide action, blue finish. Mfg. 1932-34.							
	$1,000	$750	$500	$300	$200	$150	$100
MODEL 105 RANGER - slide action, made for Sears & Roebuck. Mfg. 1932-34.							
	$2,800	$2,000	$1,500	$750	$500	$400	$350

MODEL 107 BUCK JONES SPECIAL - slide action, blue finish, sundial markings on wooden stock, needle or floating compass, Daisy marked on compass dial, sixty-shot gravity-fed magazine. Mfg. 1934-42.

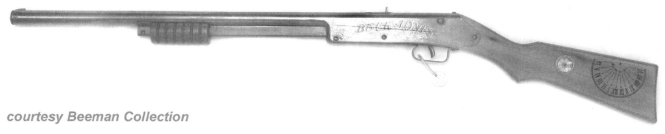

courtesy Beeman Collection

	100%	95%	90%	80%	60%	40%	20%
	N/A	$650	$450	$300	$200	N/A	N/A

GRADING	100%	95%	90%	80%	60%	40%	20%

MODEL 107 - trombone action, 500-shot, plastic stock, Plymouth. Mfg. 1957-58.

	100%	95%	90%	80%	60%	40%	20%
	$125	$90	$80	$70	$50	N/A	N/A

MODEL 225 - pump action, plastic Monte Carlo stock, plastic barrel cap. Mfg. 1991-93.

	$90	$50	$40	N/A	N/A	N/A	N/A

MODEL 325 - Model 25 rifle with scope set, target, and extra cork ball barrel. Mfg. 1936-37.

	$650	$575	$500	$450	$350	N/A	N/A

MODEL 572 FIELD MASTER - slide action, forty-five-shot. Mfg. 1968-72.

	$125	$90	$80	$70	N/A	N/A	N/A

MODEL 799 There really aren´t any "Model 799" guns. Rather, 799 is the prefix that Sears uses for all its Daisy airguns. Some of the Sears guns are listed as variations in the appropriate Daisy sections (i.e. 799.10275 is a Sears variation of the Daisy Model 25). A crossover listing (see "Storebrand Cross-Over List") has been provided in the back of this text .

RIFLES: VL SERIES

MODEL VL - .22 cal., combination airgun/firearm rifle designed to use special Daisy VL caseless ammunition. Mfg. 1968-69.

Clearly an underlever, spring-piston airgun, which will fire as just an airgun, but which is designed to have its typical airgun action supplemented by the ignition of a propellant mass molded on the base of special 29-grain bullets, i.e., caseless cartridges. Ignition is due to the high temperature normally developed by spring-piston airguns at the moment of firing (adiabatic compression)– not friction in the barrel as usually reported. MV is 1150 FPS.

Developed at Daisy by Jules van Langenhoven (= VL), but apparently the unique valve system, which seals the gun against the back pressure of ignition, was invented by M.R. Kovarik, and some other German engineers. Richard Daniel, former president of Daisy, reported that 25,000 guns had been made and were ready for a promotional launch just as U.S. Senator Robert Kennedy was assassinated. The public backlash against firearms was seen as a threat to Daisy´s excellent public image, so the project was immediately dropped. When considering the question of whether this gun is an airgun or not, remember that power augmentation is not new in the airgun world. The Weihrauch Barakuda used ether to boost its power, and many airgunners, most notably the Brits, have been jacking up airgun power by dripping low flashpoint oil into their spring-piston guns for over a century.

The resulting diesel explosion can add real zest to the shot -- and real strain to the gun. This is why so many originally beautiful, originally tight, BSA and Webley airguns sound like a bag of bolts when you shake them. (Collectors and shooters beware.) In final analysis, the VL does not fit cleanly into any group; it definitely is both a firearm and an airgun!

⊙ **V/L Standard Rifle** - .22 V/L cal. (caseless air-ignited cartridge), UL, SP airgun action, 1150 FPS, 18 in. barrel, plastic stock, not particularly accurate. Approx. 19,000 mfg. 1968-69.

courtesy Beeman Collection

	N/A	$225	$195	$145	$95	N/A	N/A

Add 50% for early version shown with checkered underlever, cheekpiece, Monte Carlo stock.

⊙ **V/L Collector´s Kit** - V/L Rifle comes with case, gun cradle, 300 rounds of ammo, walnut stock w/ brass plate with owner´s name and serial number of gun. Approx. 4,000 mfg., available only by direct factory order.

	N/A	$500	$425	$350	$275	N/A	N/A

Last MSR was $125.

⊙ **V/L Presentation** - similar to Collector´s Kit, except does not have owner´s name inscribed on buttplate, walnut stock. 4,000 mfg. for dealers.

courtesy Beeman Collection

	N/A	$500	$425	$350	$275	N/A	N/A

Last MSR was $125.

GRADING	100%	95%	90%	80%	60%	40%	20%

DAYSTATE LTD

Current manufacturer located in Stone, Staffordshire, England. Imported/distributed exclusively by Precision Airgun Distribution/Airguns of Arizona Gilbert, AZ. Dealer and consumer sales. Founded 1973.

Although often reported as starting with captive bolt cattle killers, the company made only three specimens of such guns. Initially concentrating on tranquilizer guns, Daystate generally is now recognized as the founder of modern PCP airguns, producing PCP air rifles by 1973. By 1987, high precision PCP rifles had become their main line. The publisher and authors of the *Blue Book of Airguns* wish to thank Tony Belas, Sales Manager at Daystate, for assistance with this section.

PISTOLS

FIRST MODEL - PCP, SS, single stage trigger, no trigger guard, approx. 20 made to order circa 1980. Specs may vary as all were made to order, but these are not prototypes.

Value of well-worn specimens from animal control companies about $700.

COMPETA - .177 or .22 cal., PCP, SS, based on Huntsman PCP rifle, breech loading, 8.0 in. barrel, 425 fps in .177 cal., sliding 2-stage trigger, no safety, 14 in. OAL, 2.9 lbs. Mfg. 1980-1995.

	100%	95%	90%	80%	60%	40%	20%
	$750	$625	$525	$425	$350	N/A	N/A

Last MSR was $730.

Add 20% for Midas Brass Model.

Most hand made, w/ serial numbers standard after 1993.

RIFLES

CR 94 - all steel action, specialized Field Target rifle, no safety, 60 guns mfg. 1994-1996.

Current values not yet determined.

Successor to Model 2000.

CR 97 - similar to CR 94 except has improved and restyled breech block, cocking bolt and lighter alloy cylinder, improved regulator, no safety. Mfg. 1996-1998.

Last MSR was $1,750.

Current values not yet determined.

☻ **CR 97 Special Edition** - special Silver gun production with improved regulator and new, highly adjustable match trigger, no safety. 50 mfg. 1998-1999.

Last MSR was $1,900.

Current values not yet determined.

CR-X - .177, .20, or .22 cal., PCP, BA, SS, 20.5 in. barrel, blue-black matte finish, two-stage adj. trigger, improved breechblock and other refinements, field target competition wood stock with adj. cheek piece and butt, no safety, 43 in. OAL, 9.6 lbs. Mfg. 1999-2003.

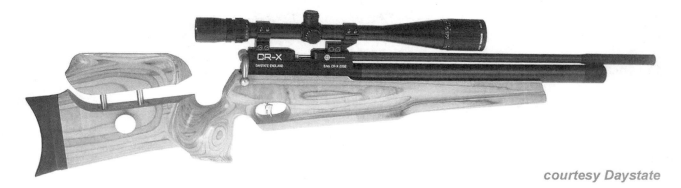

courtesy Daystate

	100%	95%	90%	80%	60%	40%	20%
	$1,795	$1,600	$1,295	$850	$650	N/A	N/A

Last MSR was $2,055.

Add 10% for .20 or .25 cal.

Several stock options available. Harrier-style blue-black matte finish (last ten rifles with gloss finish).

☻ **CR-MM** an special version of the CR-X. Made of pure titanium. May be the most expensive sporter/FT air rifle made in the 20th century.

CR-X ST - .177, .20, or .22 cal., PCP, BA, SS, similar to CR-X, except all steel action, improved breechblock and other refinements, no safety 9.6 lbs. Mfg. 1999-2003.

	100%	95%	90%	80%	60%	40%	20%
	$2,150	$1,895	$1,600	$1,295	$850	N/A	N/A

Last MSR was $2,055.

Add 10% for .20 or .25 cal.

All-steel action version of Model CR-X manufactured for USA only.

GRADING	100%	95%	90%	80%	60%	40%	20%

LR90 (LIGHT RIFLE 1990) - .177 cal., PCP, SS, BA, 930 FPS, similar to Huntsman except has one-inch diameter body tube, smooth or hand checkered stock, adj. trigger, manual safety, 7.3 lbs., 38.5 in. OAL. Mfg. 1995-99.

	100%	95%	90%	80%	60%	40%	20%
	$825	$700	$550	$450	$325	N/A	N/A

Last MSR was $900.

Add 50% for FT model with checkered thumbhole stock.
  Same as Beeman Mako.

MK3 FT-R - .177 or .22, PCP, BA, ten-shot rotary mag., 16.25 in. fully shrouded and rifled BBL w/ threaded end, MFC, matt black finish, Harper patent CDT electronic firing system, adj. trigger with electronic lock and MK3 CDT electronic rotary safety, keyed power switch in trigger guard, pneumatic regulator, checkered walnut thumbhole with adj. cheek piece and buttplate stock, 37.5 in. OAL, 8 lbs. New 2003.

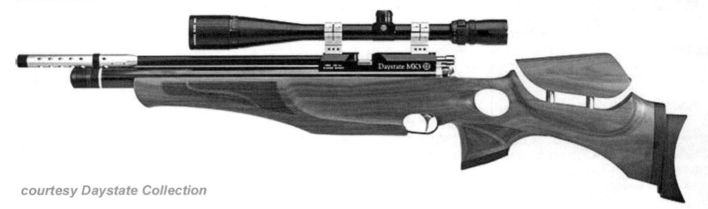

courtesy Daystate Collection

MSR N/A	$2,195	$1,869	$1,590	$1,350	$1,000	N/A	N/A

Early A type: "on" light in stock behind action, brass trigger blade, UK only. Current B type: "on" light in the action, alloy trigger blade.

MK3 S (SPORT) - .177 or .22, PCP, BA, ten-shot rotary mag., 16.25 in. shrouded and rifled BBL w/ threaded end, matt black finish, Harper patent CDT electronic firing system, adj. trigger with electronic lock and MK3 CDT electronic rotary safety, keyed power switch in trigger guard, pneumatic regulator, checkered pistol grip walnut stock, 37.5 in. OAL, 8 lbs. New 2003.

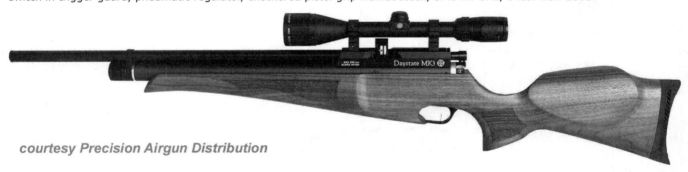

courtesy Precision Airgun Distribution

MSR N/A	$1,695	$1,395	$1,150	$895	N/A	N/A	N/A

Early A type: "on" light in stock behind action, brass trigger blade, UK only. Current B type: "on" light in the action, alloy trigger blade.

MK3 ST (SPORT THUMBHOLE) - .177 or .22, PCP, BA, ten-shot rotary mag., 16.25 in. shrouded and rifled BBL w/ threaded end, matt black finish, Harper patent CDT electronic firing system, adj. trigger with electronic lock and MK3 CDT electronic rotary safety, keyed power switch in trigger guard, pneumatic regulator, checkered thumbhole walnut stock, 37.5 in. OAL, 8 lbs. New 2003.

courtesy Precision Airgun Distribution

MSR N/A	$1,895	$1,595	$1,350	$1,095	N/A	N/A	N/A

Early A type: "on" light in stock behind action, brass trigger blade, UK only. Current B type: "on" light in the action, alloy trigger blade.

QC (QUICK CHANGE) - .22 cal., PCP with removable 16-in. air cylinder. Mfg. 1997-1998.
Current values not yet determined.

GRADING	100%	95%	90%	80%	60%	40%	20%

✪ **QC 2** - improved version of QC w/ alloy air cylinder. Mfg. 1992-1996.

Current values not yet determined.

Last MSR was $875.

X2 AMBI/X2 SPORTS/X2 PRESTIGE - .177 or .22 cal., PCP, BA, SS, 15.75 in. fully shrouded and rifled BBL w/ threaded end (New 2008), alloy breech block, satin finish, adj. trigger, ambidextrous beech (X2 Ambi Disc. 2006), RH or LH synthetic (Disc. 2006) or walnut (New 2006) (X2 Sports), or thumbhole extra grade American walnut (X2 Prestige Disc. 2006) stock, manual rocker safety, 38 in. OAL, 7.5 lbs. Mfg. 2004-current.

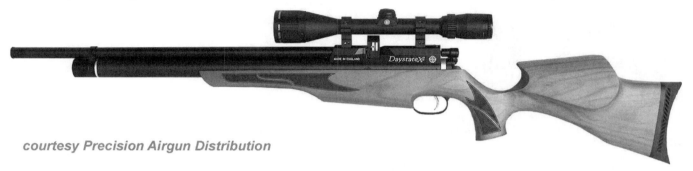

courtesy Precision Airgun Distribution

MSR N/A	$1,395	$1,095	$825	$600	N/A	N/A	N/A

Add 20% for regulated versions, less desirable in USA. Add 35% for Prestige variant with Gary Cane stock (Disc. 2006).
Most are marked "Daystate X2", a few early guns are marked "Harrier X2". Sports Variant: black synthetic stock, black bolt handle (also, in British market regulated version, chrome bolt handle, limited to 25 ft./lb. ME).

X2 MERLYN - .177 or .22 cal., PCP, BA, SS, 15.75 in. fully shrouded and rifled BBL w/ threaded end (New 2008), MFC, alloy breech block, regulator, satin finish, adj. trigger, walnut thumbhole stock w/ rosewood cap, manual rocker safety, 38 in. OAL, 7.5 lbs. New 2006.

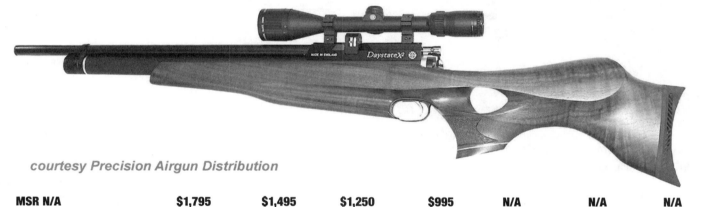

courtesy Precision Airgun Distribution

MSR N/A	$1,795	$1,495	$1,250	$995	N/A	N/A	N/A

X2 SPORTS REGULATED - .177 or .22 cal., PCP, BA, SS, 15.75 in. BBL, alloy breech block, regulator, satin finish, adj. trigger, walnut PG stock, manual rocker safety,, 36 in. OAL, 7.5 lbs. New 2006.

MSR N/A	$1,595	$1,295	$1,025	$795	N/A	N/A	N/A

AIR RANGER .177 or .22 cal., PCP, BA, 400cc or 500cc bottle, ten-shot rotary mag., 16.8 in. fully shrouded and rifled BBL, factory tuned to 35 or 50 fp/lbs, matt black finish, adj. trigger, manual rotary safety, checkered thumbhole walnut stock, 35.5 in. OAL, approx. 7.8 lbs. New 2006.

courtesy Precision Airgun Distribution

MSR N/A	$1,895	$1,595	$1,350	$1,095	N/A	N/A	N/A

GRADING	100%	95%	90%	80%	60%	40%	20%

✪ *Air Ranger (80 Ft/Lbs)* .177 or .22 cal., PCP, BA, 400cc or 500cc bottle, ten-shot rotary mag., 24.25 in. rifled BBL, factory tuned to 80 fp/lbs, matt black finish, adj. trigger, manual rotary safety, checkered thumbhole walnut stock, 42.75 in. OAL, approx. 9 lbs. New 2008.

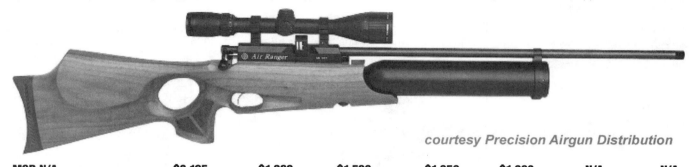

courtesy Precision Airgun Distribution

MSR N/A	$2,195	$1,869	$1,590	$1,350	$1,000	N/A	N/A

AIR WOLF .177 or .22 cal., PCP, BA, 400cc or 500cc bottle, ten-shot rotary mag., 16.8 in. rifled BBL, matt black finish, Harper patent CDT electronic firing system, adj. trigger with electronic lock and MK3 CDT electronic rotary safety, keyed power switch in trigger guard, checkered thumbhole walnut stock, 41 in. OAL, approx. 8.1-8.6 lbs. New 2006.

courtesy Daystate Collection

MSR N/A	$2,195	$1,869	$1,590	$1,350	$1,000	N/A	N/A

FIRST PELLET RIFLE - .22 cal., SS, PCP, no safety, SN 1-42. Mfg. 1975-78.

Current values not yet determined.

These were Daystate's first pellet rifles, made while "still on the farm" by applying 42 surplus .22 cal. barrels which had been removed from Brno .22 rifles when they modified those firearms to 13 mm tranquilizer firearms.

FIREFLY - similar to Mirage except 36 in. OAL, 6 lbs., manual rocker safety. 50 rifles mfg. March to Dec. 2002.

Last MSR was $930.

Current values not yet determined.

HARRIER - .177, .20, .22, or .25 cal., PCP, BA, SS, 16 in. barrel, alloy breech block, matt black finish, adj. trigger, ambidextrous beech or walnut stock, manual rocker safety, Extra Short (XS) variant (for Spanish market where most tanks will be hand filled), silencer, 35 in. OAL, 7 lbs. Mfg. 1997-2002.

courtesy Daystate

	$625	$550	$475	$395	$325	N/A	N/A

Last MSR was $855.

Add 10% for .20 or .25 cal. Add 5% for walnut stock. Add 15% for XS variant. Add 10% for thumbhole walnut stock.

Basically a Huntsman shortened by two inches with a new alloy breech block.

GRADING	100%	95%	90%	80%	60%	40%	20%

○ **Harrier SE** - .177, .20, .22, or .25 cal., PCP, similar to Harrier, except has satin chrome finish on steel parts, Gary Cane handmade walnut stock, manual rocker safety, 38 in. OAL, 8.6 lbs. Mfg. 1997-2002.

	100%	95%	90%	80%	60%	40%	20%
	$890	$815	$725	$600	$495	N/A	N/A

Last MSR was $900.

Add 10% for .20 or .25 cal.

○ **Harrier PH6** - .177, .20, .22, or .25 cal., PCP, similar to Harrier, except has stainless steel six-shot rotary mag., Muzzle Flip Compensator (MFC), cylinder rotates counter-clockwise away from loading point, manual rocker safety. 38 in OAL. 8.4 lbs. Mfg. 1998-2002.

	100%	95%	90%	80%	60%	40%	20%
	$1,015	$895	$750	$625	$525	$425	$350

Last MSR was $1,050.

Add 10% for .20 or .25 cal. Add 50% for SE version. (like Harrier SE).
 Designed with Paul Hogarth. Several stock and finish options were available.

○ **Harrier PH6 SE** - .177, .20, .22, or .25 cal., PCP, similar to Harrier SE, except has stainless steel six-shot rotary mag. and is fitted with MFC. 8.6 lbs. Mfg. 2003.

	100%	95%	90%	80%	60%	40%	20%
	$1,150	$950	$715	$625	$500	N/A	N/A

Last MSR was $1,260.

○ **Harrier X** -.177 or .22 cal., PCP, BA, ten-shot rotary mag. 15.8 in. BBL, MFC, matte black finish, adj. two-stage trigger, rotary manual safety, 35 in. OAL, 7.5 lbs. Mfg. 2003-2004.

courtesy Daystate

	100%	95%	90%	80%	60%	40%	20%
	$835	$625	$550	$475	$395	N/A	N/A

Last MSR was $835.

Add 10% for walnut stock. Add 25% for thumbhole walnut stock.

HUNTSMAN MIDAS
- .22 cal., PCP, SS, two-piece cylinder, square breechblock, pressed steel, single- or two-stage trigger designed by Barry McGraw, manual cross-bolt safety, Midas Mk2 variant -- HM prefix on SN and rocker safety. Mfg. 1983-1992.

	100%	95%	90%	80%	60%	40%	20%
	$890	$815	$725	$600	$495	N/A	N/A

Last MSR was $900.

Add 5% for brass body tube or two-stage trigger. Add 15% for stainless steel body tube. Add 10% for Huntsman Midas Mk2 variant. Very early guns made for animal control companies have stainless steel body tube. Later versions with brass body tube gave rise to the Midas name which is still used for blued models. High power versions prefix SN with HH (Huntsman High) prefix, low power version with HL prefix.

HUNTSMAN MK I
- .22 cal., PCP, SS, round tubular breechblock - early versions with loading port as scallop on right side, later versions with loading port cut completely across, higher pressure valve intro. April 1994. Final version with square breechblock, single stage trigger, manual rocker safety, barrels by BSA. Mfg. 1988-1995.

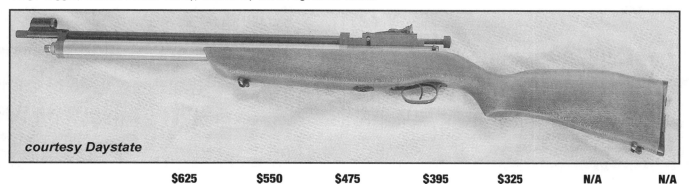

courtesy Daystate

	100%	95%	90%	80%	60%	40%	20%
	$625	$550	$475	$395	$325	N/A	N/A

Less expensive version of Midas, designed by Rob Thompson.

GRADING	100%	95%	90%	80%	60%	40%	20%

HUNTSMAN MK II - .177, .20, .22, or .25 cal., PCP, bolt action, SS, new version of Mk I, MK II engraved on breech, lighter body tube reduced wt. 2 lbs., adj. two-stage trigger, beech or walnut stock, several finish options, manual rocker safety. Three versions: 1. Heavy Air Tube Variant - used Mk 1 air tube, figure of dart protrudes from engraved logo. 2. BSA Barrel Variant - deeply concave muzzle crown, unchoked, early. 3. Walther Barrel Variant - Lothar Walther choked barrel - later. 8.4 lbs. Mfg.1995 -2002.

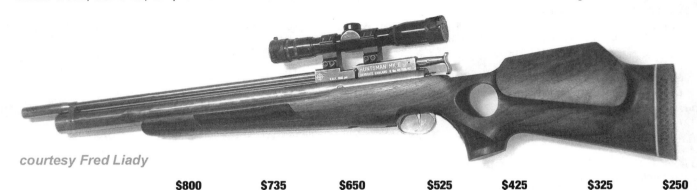

courtesy Fred Liady

	100%	95%	90%	80%	60%	40%	20%
	$800	$735	$650	$525	$425	$325	$250

Last MSR was $810.

Add 10% for walnut stock. Add 10% for "TH" (thumbhole version). Add 10% for .20 or .25 cal. Add 250% for solid brass construction, two manufactured in .22 cal., 10.3 lbs.

⊙ *Huntsman MK II PH6* - .177, .20, .22, or .25 cal., similar to Huntsman MK II, except has stainless steel six-shot rotary mag., 8.4 lbs. Disc. 2003.

	100%	95%	90%	80%	60%	40%	20%
	$1,015	$895	$750	$625	$525	N/A	N/A

Last MSR was $1,040.

Add 10% for .20 or .25 cal.
   Several stock and finish options available.

MIRAGE XLR (EXTRA LIGHT RIFLE) - .177, .20, .22, or .25 cal., PCP, bolt action, SS, 16 in. BBL, aircraft aluminum cylinder, matte blue finish, adj. trigger, beech or walnut stock, 36 in. OAL, 4.2 lbs. Mfg. 1999-2002.

courtesy Daystate

	100%	95%	90%	80%	60%	40%	20%
	$850	$765	$675	$550	$445	N/A	N/A

Last MSR was $895.

Add 5% for walnut stock. Add 10% for .20 or .25 cal.
   Several stock and finish options available.

MIRAGE MK2 - .177 or .22 cal., PCP, SS, BA, improved version of Mirage with steel LR90 air cylinder, more robust breech block, new valve design, scope grooves, no sights, manual rocker safety, 1000/860 FPS, 37 in. OAL, 5.5 lbs. Mfg. 2002-2004.

	100%	95%	90%	80%	60%	40%	20%
	$825	$700	$550	$450	$325	N/A	N/A

Last MSR was $895.

   Same as Beeman Mako 2.

MODEL 2000 - .177 or .22 cal., PCP, SS. Similar to Huntsman with added regulator, manual rocker safety. 41 in. OAL, 9 3/4 lbs. Mfg. 1990-1994.

Last MSR was $1,400.

Current values not yet determined.
   Regulators for 12 ft./lb. British versions did not work, but rifle could fire at a reduced force. Most specimens now have an aftermarket regulator or have removed the regulator.

SPORTSMAN - .22 cal., SS, UL, multi-pump pneumatic, Monte Carlo stock w/o cheekpiece, manual safety. FAC models fire to 855 FPS on 9-10 pumps. Non-FAC multi-pump models require six strokes. 38.5 in. OAL, 7.9 lbs. Mfg. 1980-86.

	100%	95%	90%	80%	60%	40%	20%
	$1,000	$900	$800	$700	$600	$500	$400

Last MSR was $375.

SPORTSMAN MK II - .22 cal. SS, side-lever SSP for British market, two-stroke pneumatic for unrestricted markets, no safety. Mfg. 1996-98.

Last MSR was $570.

Current values not yet determined.

GRADING	100%	95%	90%	80%	60%	40%	20%

TRANQUILIZER AIRGUN .50 in. (13 mm) cal., SS, PCP, Daystate's first airguns,. PCP tranquilizer gun. 1973-78.
Current values not yet determined.

SHOTGUNS

SHOTGUN - .38 or .50 (?) caliber smoothbore, SS, PCP, 24.3 in.BBL, designed for controlling pests, such as small birdsand rats in grain storage, without lead or powder. Fired hard, silver-colored, BB-shaped, candy cake decorations (in UK = "Dragees" or "Rainbow Pearls") from tubular brass case. Basically a tranquillizer barrel built onto a Huntsman air rifle, 45 in. OAL, 8.3 lbs. Approx. 17 mfg. 1987.

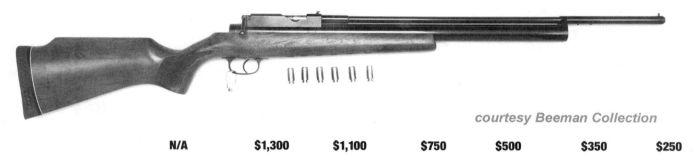

courtesy Beeman Collection

N/A	$1,300	$1,100	$750	$500	$350	$250

DECKER

Previous trademark of Decker Manufacturing Company located inDetroit, Michigan from about 1898 to 1991.

Decker Manufacturing Company, formerly produced sheet metal BB guns. Decker produced some cast iron guns under the Decker name around 1898. Charles Decker and his brother, Frederick Decker, and associate Frank Trowbridge, formed the Hexagon Air Rifle Company which produced the Hexagon air rifles about 1900-1901. These BB guns featured a hexagon shaped barrel cover and an unusual BB reservoir (not properly called a magazine) in the buttstock. Despite a cast iron grip, the Hexagon rifles did not stand up and are rarely found. Prices of the Hexagon airguns now may run from about $300 to over $1000 depending on model and condition. Additional details about the guns and their values are subject to further study and information for future editions of the Blue Book of Airguns. Ref. Dunathan (1957).

DIANAWERK GmbH & CO. KG, MAYER & GRAMMELSPACHER

Current manufacturer located in Rastatt, Germany. Currently imported exclusively by Umarex USA located in Fort Smith, AR begging 2006. Previosly imported by Dynamit Nobel RWS Inc., located in Closter, NJ. Dynamit Nobel RWS Inc. is a division of RUAG AmmoTec GmbH, located in Furth, Germany. Dealer and consumer direct sales.

Dynamit Nobel RWS, Inc. also imports airguns manufactured by Air Arms, BSA, Gamo, and Shinsung/Career. Please refer to their respective listings for pricing.

The authors and publisher wish to thank Ulrich Eichstädt, Mike Driskill, and John Atkins, for their valuable assistance with the following information in this edition of the *Blue Book of Airguns*. Because of the destruction of records in two World Wars, it was not possible to verify all information. Additional information and corrections will be made in future editions. Such information is actively solicted. Please send inputs directly to BlueBookEdit@Beemans.net.

This section covers only the real Dianawerk airguns, made by Mayer & Grammelspacher of Rastatt, Germany. It DOES NOT INCLUDE British "Diana" airguns. For British made "Diana" airguns, see the Millard Brothers section.

DIANAWERK BACKGROUND

Despite the company´s 110 year history, the trademark with the hunting goddess Diana has become more famous than the official name of its company: "Mayer & Grammelspacher Dianawerk GmbH & Co. KG." One of the founders, Jakob Mayer, born in 1866, worked as a toolmaker at the Eisenwerke ("Ironworks") Gaggenau, in Gaggenau, Germany before he left to start his new company in 1890 in nearby Rastatt on the German/French border.

Mayer was the technical director of the new company; his friend, Josef Grammelspacher, financed it. Almost nothing is known of Josef Grammelspacher. He seems to have left the company by 1901 and the Grammelspacher family died out about 70 years ago. All documents concerning the family were lost during the two World Wars.

DIANAWERK 1892-1932: BIRTH OF THE TRADEMARK

Around 1892, Mayer presented his first air pistol, which showed a great resemblance to a Gaggenau patent taken on the Haviland & Gunn patent design of 1872. Composed chiefly of a single piece of cast iron, it housed its mainspring in the grip and was marked only with the cast letters "MGR". The MGR trademark, representing Mayer & Grammelspacher in Rastatt, apparently was first used with the MG over the R and later was combined, at least in printed materials, with a target and a smiling boy´s face. It is not known exactly when the famous Diana trademark, showing the hunting goddess Diana holding her air rifle aloft while standing on her discarded bow and arrows, was first used.

One of Mayer´s many patents was issued in 1901 for a spring-loaded wedge mechanism to serve as a detent lock on barrel-cocking airguns. This mechanism, which has appeared on millions of airguns, is still in common use. Production of a number of models of airguns and toy guns developed rapidly during the 1890 to 1910 period, but, again, wars have destroyed most of the records. The toy guns, shooting corks and suction cup darts, were produced under the trademark "Eureka."

Trying to look back through the mists of time, what we do seem to see of the period around the start of the 20th century is a company that did not seem to have a focus. Like so many other airgun makers, they were adding, without particular distinction, to the seemingly endless flow of GEM airguns and toy guns. The advent of the solid MGR "First Model" pistols and rifles, both incorporating superb patent features of Jakob

Mayer, seems to been the developmental and economic base, for the future of the company. However, the rapidly growing success of Dianawerk probably was due, as with contemporary Daisy, and even recent airgun company success stories, to aggressive marketing efforts and skills of a visionary, in this case, Jakob Mayer. The creation of the Diana name and logo was the first major step in this marketing.

In the "roaring twenties" the demand of military air rifle trainers was replaced by airgun shooting as a new family game and leisure-time sport. The quality and performance of these first Diana "adult air rifles," like the models 25 and 27, was increased. In 1930, a Model 25 was offered for 25 Marks, while the extra high quality LG 58 was available for 90 Marks. A tin of the newly invented "diabolo" pellets sold for 3.40 Marks. Unfortunately, the catalogs of that period did not mention velocities of the airguns and most of the specimens in collections are not capable of their original power, so we don´t know the potential of those "adult airguns."

DIANAWERK 1933-1949: LOSS OF THE TRADEMARK

By 1933, the emerging NAZI government had had a bad effect on DIANAWERK. Decreasing sales forced withdrawal from the Leipzig trade fair and export to 28 countries was forbidden for political reasons. By 1936, Rastatt had become a center for housing troops and in 1940 all civilian production was halted when the company was forced to produce gun parts for the Mauser factory in Oberndorf (Dianawerk´s military production was marked with the secret code "lxr"). This military activity resulted in extremely heavy bombing of Rastatt by the British. In 1945, the French occupied the area and DIANAWERK was completely dismantled. As production of air rifles was then subject to a death penalty, the French were glad, to sell, at a donative price (in the spirit of war reparations), all of the company, including its machinery, old parts, and Diana trademark, to London-based Millard Bros. Ltd. With the abbreviated name "Milbro," the operation was moved to Motherwell in Scotland. The first Scottish "Dianas" were produced in 1949.

DIANAWERK 1950-1984: REGAINING THE TRADEMARK

The Allied Control Council again allowed production of airguns in 1950. By September, the Mayers began production of airguns in their old factory in Rastatt. The loss of their world-famous "Diana" trademark hit them very hard. Within Germany the air rifles were sold as "Original." To commonwealth countries Diana exported "GECADO" models; "Condor," "Firebird," or "Original Diana" was used for Dianawerk guns in England. Many large foreign companies contracted for Diana models, or special variations including different cosmetics and features, under the names of Winchester, Hy-Score, Beeman, Peerless, etc. By 1982, despite the advantage of the trademark, Milbro, using Dianawerk´s old machinery and materials, had gone out of business. Dianawerk repurchased their trademark in 1984.

DIANAWERK MATCH AIRGUNS AND RESTRICTIONS

Although DIANAWERK never became a major force in the growing market of match airgun production like Walther and Feinwerkbau, they had a major effect on that market. Kurt Giss, the chief designer in Rastatt, invented the double piston system at the end of 1950s. This design used two pistons, connected and synchronized by a gear rod. The forward piston compressed the air for pellet propulsion. The second piston moved backward and eliminated recoil. The Giss System resulted in the production of the first recoilless match-guns: the LP 6 air pistol in 1960 and then in 1963 the LG 60 air rifle. The introduction of recoilless airguns caused a revolution in the design of match airguns and established Germany as the leader in this field.

A complete family of airguns with the double piston system followed. However, production of the numerous parts was very expensive and maintenance was very difficult. In the mid-1960s, Dianawerk, like many gun companies, began to simplify the construction and materials of their guns. By the mid-1970s competitors Feinwerkbau, Anschütz, and Walther had eclipsed Dianawerk. Dianawerk continued to concentrate on the production of economy-level, leisure-time models and on reducing production and material costs. A few attempts to get back into the "match market," with the LG 100 (a single-stroke pneumatic rifle), and match grade smallbore rifles, failed. A 1972 German gun law severely restricted air rifles with power over 7.5 joules; only about 5.5 ft./lb. or 575 FPS in .177 caliber! The British limit is 12 ft./lb. This led to a deepening crisis within the company. The 1979 to 1982 discontinuance of key Diana airgun models by Beeman Precision Airguns in the USA, one of their largest potential markets, may also have had a further disastrous effect. However, as of April 1, 2002, the German airgunners have a new lease on life: they now can have air rifles (over 60 cm) up to 16.3 joules (12 ft./lb.) for field target competition and even more powerful ones on a hunting license permit.

DIANAWERK TODAY

So at the beginning of the 1990s, directors Peter Mayer, the last descendant of the Diana founder, and Hans-Günther Frey faced serious decisions. More than five hundred employees had worked in the huge halls at Karlstraße, but now the halls were empty, and rumors went out that M & G desperately needed a buyer to keep the last hundred employees. No competitor, who was interested in the still successful Diana line, wanted to take the high risk of also buying the buildings. So Dianawerk began to rescue itself. Several production processes were outsourced. Retiring employees were no longer replaced. Models were slightly altered to use standard, plastic, and interchangeable parts. Stock making was discontinued. And a large browning/blueing machine was purchased, which, by drawing work from other companies, could profitably be used to full capacity.

German airgun shooting received a huge boost from the introduction of field target shooting. Firms like Diana, Weihrauch, Dynamit Nobel, and Haendler & Natermann cooperated to help form the first clubs and establish rules which considered the special German situations. Development of separate classes for air rifles above and below the 7.5 joule limit and also for precharged and spring-piston air rifles helped the shooters who had to document a need for high power air rifles. Now many different kinds of airguns and shooters could find shooting opportunities ranging from local fun to serious international competition.

Despite rumors to the contrary, the firm entered 2003 owned 100% by the Frey family (with relatives left from the Mayer and Dorf clans). Now with ninety employees and seven apprentices, Dianawerk was back in the black, beginning its 111th year without old headaches, looking forward to what the future might bring.

DIANAWERK COLLECTING

At the current time, Dianawerk airguns present a usually good collecting opportunity and challenge. These guns generally are under appreciated and under valued. There is a great deal yet to be learned about Dianawerk airguns. Certainly a major matter is how to designate the many different guns which bear the same factory model number!

Numbering of Diana models is somewhat confusing. Not only were model numbers not issued in chronological order, but sometimes the same

GRADING	100%	95%	90%	80%	60%	40%	20%

model number has been issued to very different guns at different historical periods. Letters shown ahead of and after the model numbers generally do not appear on the guns themselves. Production dates may be stamped on gun in very small type - the date may be the key to the model variation.

DIANAWERK COMPARABLE MODEL NUMBERS

For information onDiana airguns manufactured for other trademarks, see the Dianawerk Comparable Model Numbers chart in the Store Brand Cross-Over Listat the back of this text.

Important note:Comparable models often have very different values due to different demand by collectors, different levels of rarity, and because distributors of private label guns often specified different power levels (for different markets, and not just mainspring differences), stock design, stock material and quality, calibers, sights, trigger mechanisms, etc., which may be different from the basic manufacturer's model. Beeman and pre-1970 Winchester-marked guns generally sell for a premium. Early models of the same number may differ from more recent models.

HANDGUNS

MGR FIRST MODEL - .177 cal., SP, slugs, pellets, or darts, 6.7 in.BBL, frame, sights, barrel, and grip of single piece are cast iron, spring piston in grip cocked by attaching intergrated "T" bar handel to pull action bar, loaded via screw-in breech plug with leather seal, adjustable trigger, no trigger guard, black lacquer or completely nickel-plated finish, integrally cast floral design on sides of frame with cast letters MG over R, for Mayer & Grammelspacher in Rastatt, the company's early trademark, smoothbore barrel, later versions with brass liner, 1.3 lbs., 7.9in. OAL, Mfg.circa 1892-1914. Ref: Gilbart, Guns Review, Nov. 1988, Atkins, Airgunner, July 1976.

courtesy Beeman Collection

NA	$1,000	$800	$600	$450	$325	$200

Add 20% for nickel-plated version. Add 20% for early version with original separate cocking tool. Add 30% for original wood box with papers and accessories.

Probably Dianawerk's first air pistols. Sold as the Tahiti by A.W. Gamage Ltd. of England, but this name should not be applied to this model in general. Evidently Dianawerk also provided Gamage, circa 1909/11, with a large BC, SP air pistol, like a cut-down Diana 20 air rifle, under the private label of Holborn.

MODEL 1 - .177 cal., 5 3/4in. barrel, similar to MGR First Model, except economy version with pressed sheet metal, tubular brass barrel in sheet metal housing, spring piston in grip, several minor variations. Mfg. 1924-1935.

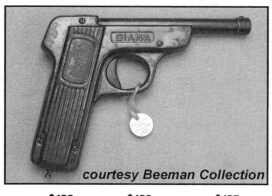

courtesy Beeman Collection

$200	$180	$160	$135	$110	$85	$60

GRADING	100%	95%	90%	80%	60%	40%	20%

MODEL 2 (PRE-WWII MODEL) - .177 cal., push-barrel cocking, with shaped sheet steel frame, nickel finish, 7.9 in. smoothbore telescopic two-part steel barrel, removable knurled knob at back end of receiver for loading pellets or darts, marked "DIANA" on grip (1930-33), "Model 2" marked on barrel, post 1933 w/ huntress on top of cylinder (not on grips) fixed sight, 10.6 oz. Pre-WWII variant, approx. 100,000 mfg. 1933-1940.

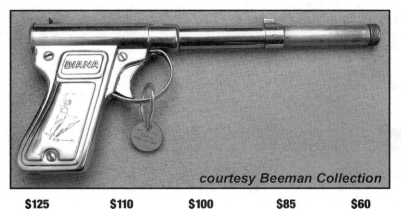

courtesy Beeman Collection

	$125	$110	$100	$85	$60	$50	$40

✪ *Model 2 Improved* - similar to Model 2, except has adj. sights and riveted wooden grips. Mfg. 1955-1985.

courtesy Beeman Collection

	$85	$75	$65	$55	$45	$35	$25

MODEL 3 - .177 cal., BBC, 7.1 in. rifled barrel, blue finish, plastic grips, adj. rear sight, 325 FPS, 2.4 lbs. New 1991- disc.

courtesy Diana

	$95	$85	$75	$65	$55	$45	$35

Last MSR was $97.

MODEL 5 ("V") - .177 cal., BBC, SP, rifled or smoothbore 7.5 in. barrel, hand checkered wood grip, 13.3 in. OAL. Mfg. 1931-1940.

	$200	$170	$135	$100	$70	N/A	N/A

Probably the only Dianawerk airgun with circle "D" trademark. Not related to post-WWII Model 5 listed below.

GRADING	100%	95%	90%	80%	60%	40%	20%

MODEL 5 - .177 or .22 cal., BBC, 7.3 in. tapered barrel, 450/300 FPS, metal trigger guard, adj. rear sight, hooded front sight, adj. trigger and wood grip until 1960, light gray plastic grip in early 1970s, later dark brown, safety, 15.75 in.OAL, 2.4 lbs. Mfg. 1958-1978.

courtesy Beeman Collection

	100%	95%	90%	80%	60%	40%	20%
	$110	$95	$85	$75	$65	$55	$45

Add 40% for wooden grip versions with tapered barrel. Add 5% for gray grips. Add 10% for "Beeman´s Original" markings -- the rarest version.

⊙ *Model 5FO* - fiberoptic sight inserts.

	100%	95%	90%	80%	60%	40%	20%
	$145	$115	$95	$85	$75	$65	$55

⊙ *Model 5G/GS* - .177 or .22 cal., BBC, 450/300 FPS, 7 in. barrel, improved version of Model 5, precision-cast alloy frame, smaller plastic grip (right/left-handed) with grip angle of 125°, receiver with plastic end cap, two-stage adj. trigger, GS Model equipped with factory scope, 16.5 in. OAL, 2.5 lbs. Mfg. beginning in 1978. Disc.

courtesy Diana

	100%	95%	90%	80%	60%	40%	20%
	$170	$135	$100	$70	$50	N/A	N/A

Last MSR was $260.

Add 20% for GS. Add 20% for GN with matte nickel plating.

⊙ *Model 5GM (Magnum)* - .177 cal., BBC, SP, SS, 700 FPS, blue finish, molded black grips, adj. rear sight, adj. trigger. Marked Umarex USA beginning 2006. New 2003.

courtesy Diana

	100%	95%	90%	80%	60%	40%	20%
MSR $246	$200	$170	$135	$100	$70	N/A	N/A

⊙ *Model P5 Magnum* - .177 or .22 cal., BBC, SP, SS, 568/422 FPS, 9 in. BBL, blue finish, molded black grip, fiberoptic adj. rear sight, 2.64 lbs. Mfg. 2001-03.

	100%	95%	90%	80%	60%	40%	20%
	$200	$170	$135	$100	$70	N/A	N/A

Last MSR was $250.

GRADING	100%	95%	90%	80%	60%	40%	20%

MODEL 6 - .177 cal., BBC, similar to Model 5, recoilless Giss double contra-piston system, 7.1 in. tapered barrel, wood grip, adj. trigger, 16.5 in. OAL, 2.9 lbs. Mfg. 1960-1978.

courtesy Beeman Collection

	100%	95%	90%	80%	60%	40%	20%
	$200	$170	$135	$100	$70	N/A	N/A

Sometimes misread as "Model 8."

○ *Model 6G* - .177 cal., BBC, 450 FPS, 7 in. barrel (professional target), alloy frame, separate plastic grip similar to Model 5. Mfg. 1978-2000.

	$300	$275	$230	$195	$150	N/A	N/A

Add 5% for gray grips. Add 20% for "Beeman's Original" markings - the rarest version.

○ **MODEL 6GS** - .177 cal., BBC, 450 FPS, 7 in. barrel (professional target), equipped with factory scope and scope rail, muzzle weight, plastic sport or wooden palm rest grip, 3 lbs. Importation disc. 1995.

	$360	$315	$275	$230	$195	N/A	N/A

Last MSR was $445.

Add 15% for palm rest grips.

○ *Model 6M* - .177 cal., BBC, 450 FPS, 7 in. barrel (professional target), match style, plastic sport or wooden palm rest grip, rotating barrel-shroud from Model 10 without sight hood. Mfg. 1978-1999.

	$400	$350	$300	$250	$210	N/A	N/A

Last MSR was $620.

Add 15% for palm rest grips.

MODEL 8 .177 in. cal., SS, SP, BC. 20 in OAL, 2.4 lbs. Walnut 1 pc. grip and forearm. Mfg. 1907-14.

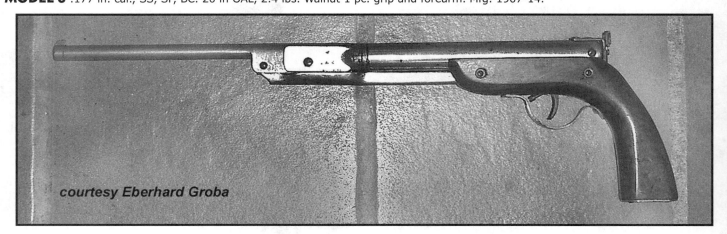

courtesy Eberhard Groba

Values TBD.

GRADING	100%	95%	90%	80%	60%	40%	20%

MODEL 10 - .177 cal., BBC, recoilless Giss double contra-piston system, 7.1 in. barrel, 450 FPS, adj. trigger and rear sight, open front sight with adj. width 0.1 in. to 0.2 in., rotating barrel shroud covered front sight during cocking and carried a special designed additional weight, matte phosphate finish, adj. wooden grip, eccentric rotating plastic sleeve around rear of receiver to secure shooting hand on early variant, 7 in. barrel, 16.1 in. OAL, 2.5 lbs. Mfg. 1974-1989.

courtesy Beeman Collection

	100%	95%	90%	80%	60%	40%	20%
	$500	$425	$375	$275	$195	N/A	N/A

Last MSR was $670.

Add 15% for cased model.   Add 10% for left-hand variation.   Add 10% for eccentric rotating plastic sleeve.

RIFLES

MGR FIRST MODEL - These airguns are Dianawerk's first airguns. They are marked M&G over R, for Mayer & Grammelspacher, Rastatt, instead of Diana. All are very rare. Ref: Larry Hannusch, *US Airgun* Oct. 1995, or in *Pneumatic Reflections* by Larry Hannusch, 2001.

courtesy Beeman Collection

⊚ **MGR First Model 1901 Variant** - .177 cal., BC, SP, 19 in. smoothbore octagonal blued barrel, rest of gun is nickel plated, complex cast spring cylinder projects straight ahead of trigger, guard, fixed rear sight, side-barrel latch, quarter length straight grip buttstock with cheekpiece, 41.3 in. OAL, 5.3 lbs. M&G German Sept. 1901 patent no. 135599. Mfg. 1901-1904/05.

			80%	60%	40%	20%
N/A	N/A	N/A	$1,500	$1,400	$1,300	$900

⊚ **MGR First Model 1904 Variant** - .177 cal., BC, SP, 18.9 in. rifled octagonal blued barrel, rest of gun is nickel plated, complex cast spring cylinder projects straight ahead of trigger, guard, side-mounted barrel latch, wedge-shaped detent, quarter length straight grip buttstock with cheekpiece, 42.6 in. OAL, 7.1 lbs. M&G German Aug. 1904 patent no. 163094. Mfg. 1904/05.

			80%	60%	40%	20%
N/A	N/A	N/A	$1,250	$1,100	$900	$700

GEM MODELS - from about 1895 Mayer and Grammelspacher produced many Gem-style air rifles (copied from Haviland and Gunn designs), reportedly including a "Ladies" model and MGR "Patent Repeating Air Gun," capable of 100 shots per loading, around end of 19th century. (See Gem in the "G" section.)

MODEL 10DL - .177 cal., SL, SP, blue finish, revmovable smoothbore barrel for darts, balls, and pellets, fires corks with barrel removed, wood halfstock, fixed sights, 29.5 in.OAL, 1.5 lbs. Mfg. 1950-52.

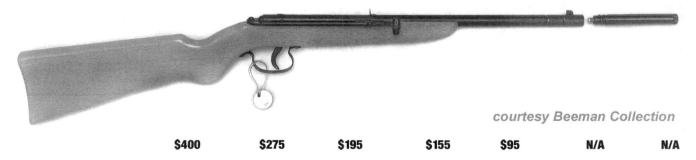

courtesy Beeman Collection

100%	95%	90%	80%	60%	40%	20%
$400	$275	$195	$155	$95	N/A	N/A

GRADING	100%	95%	90%	80%	60%	40%	20%

MODEL 1 (JUNIOR) - .177 cal., BBC, SP, blue finish, tinplate construction, wooden buttstock, Diana goddess trademark above the trigger, fixed sights, loaded via removable rifled barrel (darts or balls), 31.5 in. OAL, 2 lbs. Mfg. 1913-1940.

courtesy Beeman Collection

	$75	$65	$55	$45	$35	$25	N/A

✿ *Model LG 1 Improved* - .177 cal., BBC, SP, blue finish, an unspecified major improvement was made, per factory newsletter, after March 1, 1933. Readers determining the improvement should advise *Blue Book of Airguns*. Reported about 60,000 made per year from Nov. 1952 to 1960s, often with various private brand marks.

	$50	$45	$35	$25	$20	$15	N/A

MODEL 2 - .177 cal., UL, SP, nickel finish, fixed sights, rotating loading tap. Mfg. circa 1910-1940.

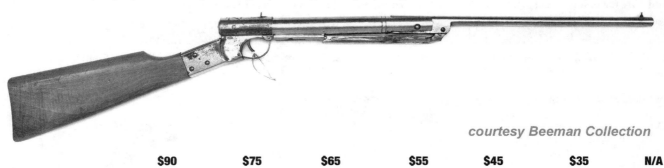

courtesy Beeman Collection

	$90	$75	$65	$55	$45	$35	N/A

MODEL 3 - .177 cal. blue finish, gallery-type trigger-guard cocking lever ("Bügelspanner"), break barrel to load, fixed sights, 35.4 in.OAL, 5.3 lbs. Mfg. 1913-1940.

courtesy Beeman Collection

	$135	$115	$90	$75	$65	$55	N/A

✿ *Model 3L* - .177 cal., blue finish, 34.6 in. OAL, 4.4 lbs.

	$135	$115	$90	$75	$65	$55	N/A

MODEL 3 (MFG. 1927-1940) - .177 or .22 cal., BBC, SP, blue finish, smoothbore or rifled barrel, developed as training rifle for smallbore rifle shooters, two-stage trigger (special order: set trigger), beech stock with pistol grip, finger grooves in forearm, screw-in rear sight, bead front sight. 43.3 in. OAL, 6.6 lbs. Mfg. 1927-1940.

	$225	$185	$150	$105	$75	N/A	N/A

MODEL 6 - .177 cal., BBC, SP, blue finish, less powerful version of Model 3, fixed sights, octagon steel barrel, cylinder and trigger guard nickel plated, walnut stock, 33.5 in. OAL, 4 lbs.

	$110	$85	$65	$55	$45	$35	N/A

GRADING	100%	95%	90%	80%	60%	40%	20%

MODEL 10 - .177 cal., BBC, SP, blue finish, 29.9 in. OAL, 2 lbs. Mfg. 1950-52.

courtesy Beeman Collection

	$125	$100	$75	$60	$50	$40	N/A

MODEL 14 - .177 cal., bolt-action-style cocking, SP, blue finish, fixed sights, 38.2 in. OAL, 3.5 lbs. Mfg. 1913-1940.

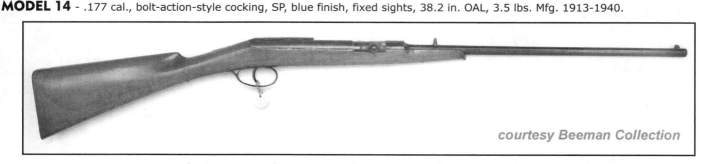

courtesy Beeman Collection

	$150	$115	$85	$65	$55	$45	N/A

✪ *Model 14A* - .177 cal., military style full stock, contained a cleaning rod which looks like a bayonet.

	$300	$225	$175	$125	$80	$50	N/A

MODEL 15 (MFG. 1930-1940) - .177 cal., BBC, SP, smoothbore, blue finish, tinplate design, lighter and shorter child´s version of Model 16, without forestock. Mfg. circa 1930-1940.

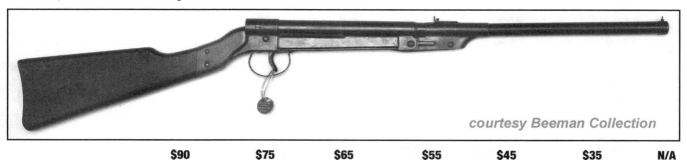

courtesy Beeman Collection

	$90	$75	$65	$55	$45	$35	N/A

MODEL 15 (MFG. 1951-1980) - .177 cal., BBC, SP, blue finish, tinplate, stamped construction, beech buttstock, 12 in. rifled barrel inside sheet steel body tube, two-stage trigger, bead front sight, adj. rear sight, 32.5 in. OAL, 2.4 lbs. Mfg. 1951-1980.

	$50	$45	$35	$25	$20	$15	N/A

MODEL 16 (MFG. 1922-1940) - .177 cal., BBC, SP, smoothbore blue finish octagon barrel, all other metal parts nickel plated, beech buttstock and forearm, rear sight adj. for elevation, no safety, 37.8 in. OAL, 4.4 lbs. Approx. 25,000 per year mfg. 1922-1940.

	$90	$75	$65	$55	$45	$35	N/A

✪ *Model 16 Special Order Variation* - completely blued, matte oiled stock.

	$145	$115	$90	$75	$65	$55	N/A

✪ *Model 16 (Mfg. 1950-1985)* - .177 cal., BBC, SP, blue finish, similar to pre-WWII Model 16, stamped until 1984 with "Original Diana 16", 33 in. OAL, 2.7 lbs. Mfg. 1950-1985.

	$45	$35	$25	$20	$15	$10	N/A

MODEL 17 - .177 cal., BBC, SP, blue finish, similar to Model 16, except 41 in. OAL, 5.5 lbs. Mfg. 1922-1940.

	$75	$60	$50	$40	$30	$20	N/A

✪ *Model 17P* - .177 cal., BBC, SP, blue finish, similar to Model 17, except has pistol grip.

	$110	$90	$75	$65	$55	$45	N/A

MODEL 18 - .177 cal., BBC, SP, blue finish, similar to Model 16, except 41.3 in. OAL, 6.6 lbs. Mfg. 1922-1940.

	$75	$60	$50	$40	$30	$25	N/A

GRADING	100%	95%	90%	80%	60%	40%	20%

✪ Model 18P - .177 cal., BBC, SP, blue finish, similar to Model 18, except has pistol grip.

	100%	95%	90%	80%	60%	40%	20%
	$95	$80	$70	$60	$50	$40	N/A

MODEL 19 - .177 cal., BBC, SP, blue finish octagon barrel, all other metal parts nickel plated, beech buttstock, adj. rear sight, 37.4 in. OAL, 6.6 lbs. Mfg. 1922-1940.

	100%	95%	90%	80%	60%	40%	20%
	$95	$80	$70	$60	$50	$40	N/A

✪ Model 19 Special Order Variation - similar to Model 19, except completely blued, matte oiled walnut stock.

	100%	95%	90%	80%	60%	40%	20%
	$125	$100	$85	$75	$65	$55	N/A

✪ Model 19P - similar to Model 19, except with pistol grip.

	100%	95%	90%	80%	60%	40%	20%
	$110	$90	$75	$65	$55	$45	N/A

✪ Model 19S - similar to Model 19, except with safety.

	100%	95%	90%	80%	60%	40%	20%
	$110	$90	$75	$65	$55	$45	N/A

✪ Model 19PS - .177 or .22 cal., BBC, SP, blue finish, 14 in. barrel, 36 in. OAL, 3.75 lbs. Mfg. 1953-1985. Similar to Model 19, except with both pistol grip and safety.

	100%	95%	90%	80%	60%	40%	20%
	$120	$95	$80	$70	$60	$50	N/A

MODEL 20 (MFG. 1907-1911) - .177 cal., UL, tinplate construction, 12.6 in. smoothbore brass barrel, all metal parts nickel plated, beech buttstock, 20 in. OAL, 2.7 lbs. Mfg. circa 1907-11.

	100%	95%	90%	80%	60%	40%	20%
	$170	$145	$115	$90	$75	$65	N/A

NOTE: The 1907-1911 Model 20, Model 20 Youth, and Model 20 Adult are not related to each other.

MODEL 20 YOUTH - .177 cal., BBC, SP, youth model, all-metal parts are nickel plated, walnut buttstock, date of mfg. stamped on heel, 35 in. OAL, 2.7 lbs. Tens of thousands mfg. 1912-1940.

courtesy Beeman Collection

	100%	95%	90%	80%	60%	40%	20%
	$100	$85	$70	$60	$50	$40	N/A

Add 10% for early versions with simple rear sight mounted on receiver tube. Add 20% for stamping "Foreign" instead of "Made in Germany" (just prior to WWII). Add 20% for specimens w/o model markings but marked "Diana Luft-Gewehr Schutzenmarke". Add 50% for original box.

NOTE: The 1910-1911 Model 20, Model 20 Youth, and Model 20 Adult are not related to each other. Circa 1930 the rear sight was moved to the barrel block and changed to adjustable.

MODEL 20 ADULT - .177 cal., BBC, SP, 480 FPS, 17 in. barrel, black finish, hardwood stock, hooded front and adj. rear sights, 5.5 lbs. Mfg. 1991-2003.

courtesy Diana

	100%	95%	90%	80%	60%	40%	20%
	$95	$75	$55	$45	$35	N/A	N/A

Last MSR was $120.

NOTE: The 1910-1911 Model 20, Model 20 Youth, and Model 20 Adult are not related to each other.

MODEL 21 - .177 cal., BBC, 460 FPS, 16.5 in. barrel, black finish, black composit stock, Truglo adj. sights, 5.8 lbs. Mfg. 2005-06.

	100%	95%	90%	80%	60%	40%	20%
	$130	$105	$85	$65	$45	N/A	N/A

GRADING	100%	95%	90%	80%	60%	40%	20%

MODEL 22 (MFG. 1927-1940) - .177 cal., BBC, SP, blue finish, youth model, walnut stock, brass barrel either smooth or rifled in sheet steel body tube, adj. rear sight, 35.8 in. OAL. Mfg. 1927-1940.

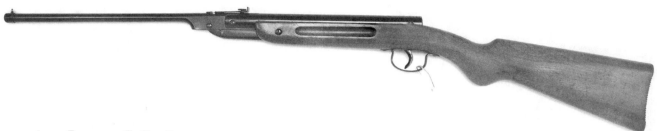

courtesy Beeman Collection

	$115	$90	$75	$65	$55	$45	N/A

NOTE: The 1927-1940 and 1953-1985 Model 22 air rifles appear somewhat similar, but they are completely unrelated with virtually no common parts.

MODEL 22 (MFG. 1953-1985)

	$65	$55	$45	$35	$25	$15	N/A

NOTE: The 1927-1940 and 1953-1985 Model 22 air rifles appear somewhat similar, but they are completely unrelated with virtually no common parts.

MODEL 23 (DISC. 1940) - .177 cal., BBC, SP, blue finish, smoothbore or rifled barrel, 35.8 in. OAL. 4.2 lbs. Disc. 1940.

	$115	$90	$75	$65	$55	$45	N/A

NOTE: The Disc. 1940 and 1951-1983 Model 23 air rifles appear somewhat similar, but they are completely unrelated with virtually no common parts.

MODEL 23 (MFG. 1951-1983) - .177 or .22 cal., BBC, SP, blue finish, 14 in. smoothbore or rifled barrel, bead front and adj. spring-leaf rear sights, 36 in. OAL, 4.25 lbs. Mfg. 1951-1983.

	$65	$55	$45	$35	$25	$15	N/A

Subtract 20% for post-1965 versions with thicker stocks without forearm grooves, with stamped checkering, shallow cheekpieces, front sights as screwed-on ramps or clamped-on tunnels, plastic rear sights.

NOTE: The Disc. 1940 and 1951-1983 Model 23 air rifles appear somewhat similar, but they are completely unrelated with virtually no common parts.

MODEL 24/24C - .177 or .22 cal., BBC, 700/400 FPS, 13.5 (Model LG 24C) or 17 in. barrel, black finish, hardwood stock, hooded front and adj. rear sights 5.6 lbs. Mfg. 1984-2007.

courtesy Diana

	$160	$135	$95	$75	$55	N/A	N/A

Last MSR was $187.

⊙ **Model 24 TO1** - similar to LG 24 except with metal trigger, no safety.

	$170	$145	$115	$90	$75	$65	N/A

⊙ **Model 24 TO2 "Diana Star"** - similar to Model 24, except has colored stocks without model number.

	$120	$95	$80	$70	$60	$50	N/A

MODEL 25A - .177 cal., BBC, SP, blue finish, solid steel parts, walnut stock with finger grooves in forearm, adj. rear sight, no safety, 38.5 in. OAL. Mfg. 1925-1934.

	$115	$90	$75	$65	$55	$45	N/A

NOTE: The Model 25A, 25 Improved, 25D, and 25DS air rifles appear somewhat similar, but they are completely unrelated with virtually no common parts.

⊙ **Model 25 Improved** - .177 or .22 cal., BBC, SP, blue finish, smoothbore or rifled barrel, slightly longer forestock, metal rear sight, 39.7 in. OAL, Mfg. 1933-1940 and 1950-1986.

	$65	$55	$45	$35	$25	$15	N/A

Add 30% for pre-WWII version. Subtract 20% for post-1965 versions with thicker stocks without forearm grooves, with stamped checkering, shallow cheekpieces, front sights as screwed-on ramps or clamped-on tunnels, plastic rear sights.

NOTE: The Model 25A, 25 Improved, 25D, and 25DS air rifles appear somewhat similar, but they are completely unrelated with virtually no common parts.

GRADING	100%	95%	90%	80%	60%	40%	20%

MODEL 25D - .177 or .22 cal., BBC, ball trigger sear 525/380 FPS, 15.75 in. smooth or rifled barrel, 5.75 lbs. Disc. 1986.

courtesy Beeman Collection

	100%	95%	90%	80%	60%	40%	20%
	$120	$95	$70	$55	$40	N/A	N/A

Last MSR was $120.

NOTE: The Model 25A, 25 Improved, 25D, and 25DS air rifles appear somewhat similar, but they are completely unrelated with virtually no common parts.

✪ **Model 25DS** - .177 or .22 cal., similar to Model 25D, except has two-piece cocking lever, trigger block manual safety, angular stock styling. Disc. 1986.

	$150	$120	$90	$70	$50	N/A	N/A

Subtract 20% for post-1965 versions with thicker stocks without forearm grooves, with stamped checkering, shallow cheekpieces, front sights as screwed-on ramps or clamped-on tunnels, plastic rear sights.

Approx. ten million Model LG 25 have been sold; this model group is one of the world´s most successful air rifles.

NOTE: The Model 25A, 25 Improved, 25D, and 25DS air rifles appear somewhat similar, but they are completely unrelated with virtually no common parts.

MODEL 26 YOUTH - .177 cal., BBC, SP, blue finish, youth model, no safety. Mfg. 1913-1933.

courtesy Beeman Collection

	$350	$275	$215	$185	$145	N/A	N/A

NOTE: The Model 26 Youth, 26U, and 26 air rifles are not related to each other.

MODEL 26U - similar to Model 26 Youth, except UL cocking and loading tap, 38.2 in. OAL, 5 lbs. Mfg. 1933-1940.

	$300	$225	$165	$135	$95	N/A	N/A

NOTE: The Model 26 Youth, 26U, and 26 air rifles are not related to each other.

MODEL 26 - .177 or .22 cal., BBC, SP, 750/500 FPS, 17.25 in. barrel, 6 lbs. Importation 1984-1992.

	$150	$125	$95	$75	$55	N/A	N/A

Last MSR was $195.

NOTE: The Model 26 Youth, 26U, and 26 air rifles are not related to each other.

MODEL 27L - .177 cal., BBC, SP, blue finish, 18.5 in. smoothbore or rifled barrel, "Millita"-style, beech stock with metal buttplate, adj. trigger, no safety, 42.5 in.OAL, tens of thousands mfg. 1910-1936.

	$110	$90	$75	$65	$55	$45	N/A

Add 20% for pre-1923 version with octagonal to round barrel.

One of the most successful barrel cocking adult air rifles of all time.

NOTE: The Model 27L, 27A, 27E, 27S, and 27 air rifles appear somewhat similar, but they are completely unrelated with virtually no common parts.

MODEL 27A - .177 or .22 cal., BBC, SP, blue finish, 17.5 in. smoothbore or rifled barrel, two-stage trigger, adj. rear sight, triangular front sight, wooden half stock, 41.3 in. OAL, 6.2 lbs. Mfg. 1936-1940.

	$135	$115	$90	$75	$65	$55	N/A

Add 20% for smoothbore.

NOTE: The Model 27L, 27A, 27E, 27S, and 27 air rifles appear somewhat similar, but they are completely unrelated with virtually no common parts.

MODEL 27E - .177 or .22 cal., BBC, SP, blue finish, checkered beech stock with pistol grip.

	$245	$195	$145	$105	$75	$65	N/A

NOTE: The Model 27L, 27A, 27E, 27S, and 27 air rifles appear somewhat similar, but they are completely unrelated with virtually no common parts.

GRADING	100%	95%	90%	80%	60%	40%	20%

MODEL 27S - .177 or .22 cal., BBC, SP, blue finish, two-piece cocking lever, trigger block safety, angular stock styling.

	100%	95%	90%	80%	60%	40%	20%
	$190	$160	$125	$95	$65	$55	N/A

NOTE: The Model 27L, 27A, 27E, 27S, and 27 air rifles appear somewhat similar, but they are completely unrelated with virtually no common parts.

MODEL 27 - .177 or .22 cal., BBC, SP, 550/415 FPS, 17.25 in. smoothbore or rifled barrel, pre-1965 version with ball trigger sear, 6 lbs. Disc. 1987.

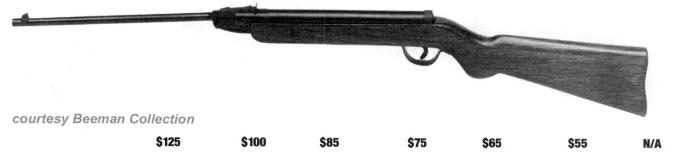

courtesy Beeman Collection

	100%	95%	90%	80%	60%	40%	20%
	$125	$100	$85	$75	$65	$55	N/A

Last MSR was $150.

Subtract 20% for post-1965 versions with thicker stocks without forearm grooves, with stamped checkering, shallow cheekpieces, front sights as screwed-on ramps or clamped-on tunnels, plastic rear sights.

NOTE: The Model 27L, 27A, 27E, 27S, and 27 air rifles appear somewhat similar, but they are completely unrelated with virtually no common parts.

MODEL 28 (MFG. 1913-1940) - .177 cal., BBC, SP, blue finish, adj. rear sight, smoothbore or rifled barrel, no safety, 46.5 in. OAL, 7 lbs. Mfg. 1913-1940.

courtesy Diana

	100%	95%	90%	80%	60%	40%	20%
	$225	$185	$150	$105	$75	N/A	N/A

✪ **Model 28 Improved** - .177 cal., BBC, SP, blue finish, improved version after 1923, sight moved to base of barrel and made adjustable.

	100%	95%	90%	80%	60%	40%	20%
	$185	$150	$100	$75	$55	N/A	N/A

✪ **Model 28 (Mfg. 1985-1992)** - .177 or .22 cal., BBC, SP, 15.75 in. barrel, 750/500 FPS, automatic safety, 6.75 lbs. Importation 1985-1992.

	100%	95%	90%	80%	60%	40%	20%
	$185	$150	$100	$75	$55	N/A	N/A

Last MSR was $205.

MODEL 30B (BUGELSPANNER) - .25 cal., gallery-type with trigger-guard cocking system ("Bügelspanner"), beech buttstock with cheekpiece, octagon blued barrel, nickel finish, adj. rear sight, no safety, 41.7 in. OAL, 6.2 lbs. Mfg. 1913-1935.

	100%	95%	90%	80%	60%	40%	20%
	$850	$750	$600	$450	$350	N/A	N/A

Note: The Model 30B, 30M, and 30R air rifles are not related to each other. The suffix letters have been added to distinguish these models; these letters donot appear on the guns.

MODEL 30M (MILITARY) - .177 cal., UL, cocking lever hidden in forearm, military-style full stock with top hand guard, fixed barrel with loading tap, two-stage trigger, wing safety, front and rear sights similar to the Mauser 98k carbine, 41.7 in. OAL, 5.5 lbs. Mfg. 1935-1940.

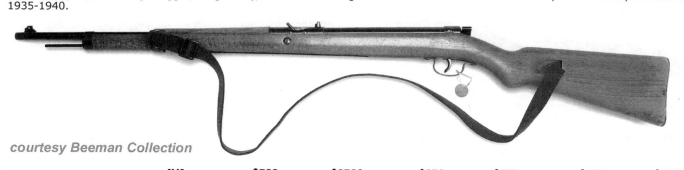

courtesy Beeman Collection

	100%	95%	90%	80%	60%	40%	20%
	N/A	$500	$3500	$250	$175	$125	$100

Note: The Model 30B, 30M, and 30R air rifles are not related to each other. The suffix letters have been added to distinguish these models; these letters donot appear on the guns.

GRADING	100%	95%	90%	80%	60%	40%	20%

MODEL 30R (REPEATER) - 4.4mm (RWS #7) round ball cal., bolt-action cocking system, ball shot repeater, fixed barrel, 16.9 in., mechanical shot-counter in left side of forearm for gallery use, capacity 125 balls, beech stock with rubber buttplate, two-stage trigger, manual safety, adj. rear sight, triangular front sight, 43.3 in. OAL. 7.25 lbs. Limited mfg. 1972-2000.

courtesy Beeman Collection

	N/A	$450	$325	$225	$150	$100	N/A

Last MSR was $1,025.

Special orders were still possible through 2003.

Note: The Model 30B, 30M, and 30R air rifles are not related to each other. The suffix letters have been added to distinguish these models; these letters donot appear on the guns.

MODEL 32 - .177 cal., BBC, SP, blue finish, similar to Model LG 27, except with more power, 42.5 in. OAL, 6.6 lbs. Mfg. 1936-1940.

	$225	$185	$150	$105	$75	N/A	N/A

MODEL 33 - .177 cal., BBC, SP, blue finish, checkered wood stock with pistol grip, 42.9 in. OAL, 6.6 lbs. Mfg. 1928-1940.

	$250	$215	$165	$135	$80	N/A	N/A

MODEL 34 (MFG. 1928-1940) - .177 cal., BBC, SP, blue finish, similar to LG 33, except with British market style stock and pistol grip. Mfg. 1928-1940.

	$250	$215	$165	$135	$80	N/A	N/A

NOTE: The 1928-1940 Model 34 and later Model 34 air rifles are not related to each other.

MODEL 34/34BC/34C/34N - .177, .20 (Disc.) or .22 cal., BBC, blue, matte nickel (Model 34N), or matte black finish, hardwood stock or black epoxy finish stock (Model 34BC), 920/ 690 FPS, 15.5 (carbine, Model 34C) or 19 in. barrel, approx. 7 lbs. New 1984.

courtesy Diana

MSR $254	$215	$180	$150	$105	$75	N/A	N/A

Add 5% for the hundred-year Diana Commemorative Model (new 1990). Add 25% for .20 cal. model (Disc.). Add 15% for Model 34N matte nickel finish. Add $51 for compact w/ 4x32 airgun scope and C-Mount. Add 100% for black epoxy finish stock and 4x32 airgun scope. Add 15% for "Sport Mfg." without model number.

NOTE: The 1928-1940 Model 34 and later Model 34 air rifles are not related to each other.

⊙ **Model 34 Panther** - .177 or .22 cal., BBC, 1000-800 FPS, 19.75 in. BBL, black finish, black composit stock, Truglo adj. sights, 46 in. OAL, 7.7 lbs. Mfg. 2007-current.

courtesy Umarex USA Collection

MSR $239	$205	$175	$135	$95	$65	$55	N/A

Add $40 for Combo w/ 4x32 compact scope and mount.

GRADING	100%	95%	90%	80%	60%	40%	20%

⊘ **Model 34 Panther Pro** - .177 cal., BBC, SP, SS, 1000 FPS, 19.75 in. rifled BBLw/ weight, black finish, ambidextrous black composit stock w/ rubber recoil pad, two-stage adj. trigger, 3-9x40mm scope, 46 in. OAL, 8.5 lbs. Mfg. 2008-current.

courtesy Umarex USA

MSR $312	$275	$225	$185	$145	$100	N/A	N/A

⊘ **Model 34 Panther Pro Compact** - .177 cal., BBC, SP, SS, 1000 FPS, 19.75 in. rifled BBLw/ weight, black finish, ambidextrous black composit stock w/ rubber recoil pad, two-stage adj. trigger, 3-9x40mm scope, 42.12 in. OAL, 8 lbs. Mfg. 2008-current.

courtesy Umarex USA

MSR $326	$285	$235	$195	$155	$110	N/A	N/A

MODEL 34 MEISTERSCHÜTZE PRO - .177 cal., BBC, SP, SS, riffled 19 in. BBL w/ weight, 1000 FPS, matte black finish, classic ambidextrous hardwood streight stock w/ PG and rubber recoil pad, two-stage adj. trigger, auto-safety, 3-9x40mm w/ "C" mount, 46.12 in. OAL, 8 lbs. Mfg. 2008-current.

courtesy Umarex USA

MSR $358	$325	$275	$225	$175	$125	N/A	N/A

MODEL 34 MEISTERSCHÜTZE PRO COMPACT - .177 cal., BBC, SP, SS, riffled 15.75 in. BBL w/ weight, 1000 FPS, matte black finish, classic ambidextrous hardwood streight stock w/ PG and rubber recoil pad, two-stage adj. trigger, auto-safety, 3-9x40mm w/ "C" mount, 42.25 in. OAL, 7.75 lbs. Mfg. 2008-current.

courtesy Umarex USA

MSR $376	$345	$295	$245	$195	$145	N/A	N/A

GRADING	100%	95%	90%	80%	60%	40%	20%

MODEL 35 (MFG. 1953-1964)

.177 or .22 cal., BBC, SP, 665/540 FPS, 19 in. barrel, Monte Carlo stock with shallow cheekpiece, stamped checkering, globe front sight, plastic or metal click adj. rear sight with four-notch insert, plastic or stamped trigger blade, ball sear, 8 lbs. Mfg. circa 1953-1964.

courtesy Beeman Collection

⊙ **Model 35 Standard Variant 1** - sporting stock, alloy trigger blade, fixed post front sight, simple rear sight in transverse dovetail.

	$225	$185	$150	$105	$75	N/A	N/A

⊙ **Model 35A Variant 2** - like Model 35 Standard except hashooded front sight withfour posts on rotating star, click adj. rear sight with four-notch insert, extra dovetail on rear of receiver.

	$250	$215	$165	$135	$80	N/A	N/A

⊙ **Model 35B Variant 3** - like 35A except aperture attachment replaces rear sight notch assembly, allowing rear sight to mount on receiver dovetail for match shooting.

	$275	$225	$175	$145	$90	N/A	N/A

⊙ **Model 35M Variant 4** - like 35B except has match stock with cut checkering.

	$275	$225	$175	$145	$90	N/A	N/A

About 1964 these were replaced with a simpler version with three variations in addition to standard model.

MODEL 35 (MFG. 1965-1987)

.177 or .22 cal., BBC, SP, 665/540 FPS, 19 in. barrel, 8 lbs. Mfg. 1965-1987.

	$120	$95	$80	$60	$40	N/A	N/A

Last MSR was $160.

Add 10% for metal rear sight or solid alloy trigger blade. Subtract 20% for post-1965 versions with thicker stocks without forearm grooves, with stamped checkering, shallow cheekpieces, front sights as screwed-on ramps or clamped-on tunnels, plastic rear sights.

⊙ **Model 35 Centennial** - commemorative model.

	$160	$135	$105	$85	$65	N/A	N/A

⊙ **Model 35M** - target stocked version. Mfg. 1958-1964.

	$150	$125	$95	$75	$55	N/A	N/A

Add 10% for metal rear sight or solid alloy trigger blade. Subtract 20% for post-1965 versions with thicker stocks without forearm grooves, with stamped checkering, shallow cheekpieces, front sights as screwed-on ramps or clamped-on tunnels, plastic rear sights.

⊙ **Model 35S** - two-piece cocking lever, trigger block safety, angular stock styling.

	$150	$125	$95	$75	$55	N/A	N/A

Add 10% for metal rear sight or solid alloy trigger blade. Subtract 20% for post-1965 versions with thicker stocks without forearm grooves, with stamped checkering, shallow cheekpieces, front sights as screwed-on ramps or clamped-on tunnels, plastic rear sights.

MODEL 36/36C/36S

.177 or .22 cal., BBC, SP, 1000/800 FPS, 15.5 (Model 36C) or 19.5 in. barrel, 8 lbs.

courtesy Diana

	$300	$245	$215	$185	$145	N/A	N/A

Last MSR was $350.

Add $40 for 36S Model with scope. Subtract $10 for muzzle brake model without factory sights.

MODEL 37

.177 cal., BBC, SP, blue finish, beech buttstock without forearm, simple rear sight, bead front sight, no safety, 42.9 in. OAL, 6 lbs. Mfg. 1922-1940.

	$250	$215	$165	$135	$80	N/A	N/A

⊙ **Model LG 37E** - British market-style stock.

	$300	$225	$165	$135	$95	N/A	N/A

GRADING	100%	95%	90%	80%	60%	40%	20%

MODEL 38 (MFG. 1922-1940) - .177 cal., BBC, SP, Deluxe version of the Model 36, similar to Model 37, except 7 lbs. Mfg. 1922-1940.

	$200	$175	$150	$125	$80	$50	N/A

NOTE: The 1922-1940, 38E, and disc. 1998 Model 38 air rifles are not related to each other.

MODEL 38E - British market-style stock.

	$250	$215	$165	$135	$80	N/A	N/A

NOTE: The 1922-1940, 38E, and disc. 1998 Model 38 air rifles are not related to each other.

MODEL 38 (MFG. DISC. 1998) - .177 or .22 cal., BBC, 919/689 FPS, 19.5 in. barrel, beech stock, 345.3 in. OAL, 8 lbs. Importation Disc. 1998.

courtesy Diana

	$275	$225	$175	$145	$90	N/A	N/A

Last MSR was $345.

NOTE: The 1922-1940, 38E, and disc. 1998 Model 38 air rifles are not related to each other.

MODEL 40 - .177 or .22 cal., BBC, SP, 950/780 FPS, 19 in. rifled barrel with muzzle brake, blue finish, hardwood stock with buttpad, adj. trigger, 7.5 lbs. New 2002.

MSR $282	$245	$195	$145	$105	$75	N/A	N/A

MODEL 42 - .177 or .22 cal., UL, SP, blue finish, similar to Model 27, except 19.1 in. fixed barrel, adj. rear sight, bead front sight, adj. trigger, 40.9 in. OAL, 6.8 lbs. Mfg. 1927-1940.

	$250	$215	$165	$135	$80	N/A	N/A

⊙ *Model 42E* - British market-style stock.

	$275	$225	$175	$145	$90	N/A	N/A

MODEL 43 - .177 or .22 cal., UL, SP, blue finish, similar to Model 42, except has additional checkering, pistol grip, and manual safety. Mfg. 1928-1940.

	$275	$225	$175	$145	$90	N/A	N/A

MODEL 44 - .177 or .22 cal., UL, SP, blue finish, similar to Model 48, except 43.7 in. OAL, 7 lbs. Mfg. 1928-1940.

	$235	$195	$160	$115	$75	N/A	N/A

MODEL 45U - .177 or .22 cal., UL, SP, blue finish, loading tap, similar to Model 26 (and simpler version of the later Model LG 58), 40.2 in. OAL, 7 lbs. Mfg. 1927-1940.

	$295	$235	$185	$155	$105	N/A	N/A

MODEL 45/45S DELUXE (MFG. 1978-1988) - .177, .20, or .22 cal., BBC, SP, 790/550 FPS, 19. in. barrel, blue finish, two-stage adj. trigger, adj. rear sight, front sight with inserts, hardwood stock with rubber butt pad, 8 lbs. Mfg. 1978-1988.

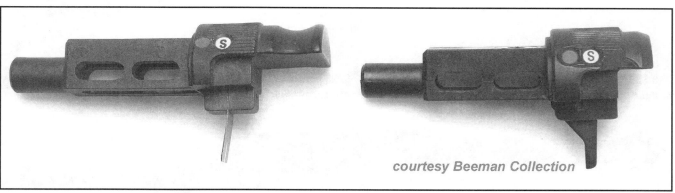

courtesy Beeman Collection

	$220	$185	$145	$100	$65	N/A	N/A

Add 15% for Deluxe version. Add 25% for .20 caliber. Add 20% for LG 45S Model with scope and sling. Add 10% for original long safety (recalled), within metal flap below, not marked (use guns with original safety with caution). Subtract 20% for RWS 45 or Crosman Challenger 6100 markings, less desirable sight and stock systems; inferior handling to standard Diana 45. Ref: Walther, *The Airgun Book.*

GRADING	100%	95%	90%	80%	60%	40%	20%

⊙ **Model 45 Jubilaums Modell** - commemorative model with special Rastatt factory plates in stock.

	100%	95%	90%	80%	60%	40%	20%
	$295	$235	$185	$155	$105	N/A	N/A

MODEL 45/45S DELUXE/45 TO1 (RECENT MFG.) - .177, .20, or .22 cal., BBC, SP, basically a restocked Model 34, 1000/800 FPS, 19. in. barrel, blue finish, two-stage adj. trigger, adj. rear sight, front sight with inserts, hardwood stock with rubber butt pad, 8 lbs. Mfg. 1988-2004.

courtesy Diana

	100%	95%	90%	80%	60%	40%	20%
	$220	$185	$145	$100	$65	N/A	N/A

Last MSR was $350.

Add 20% for Deluxe version. Add 35% for Model 45S with scope and sling.
  The post-WWII Model 45 is not related to the pre-WWII Model 45 and the post-WWII model 45 was replaced, still using the Model 45 designation, about 1988 with a restocked Model 34!

MODEL 46 - .177 or .22 cal., UL, SP, 950/780 FPS, 18 in. barrel, blue finish, auto-safety, adj. trigger, extended scope rail, Monte Carlo stock with checkered forearm and grip (Model 46), recoil pad, 8.2 lbs. New 1998.

courtesy Diana

	100%	95%	90%	80%	60%	40%	20%
	$345	$305	$265	$215	$165	N/A	N/A

Last MSR was $387.

⊙ **Model 46C** - .177 or .22 cal., UL, SP, similar to Model 46, except shorter. New 1998.

courtesy Diana

MSR $387	$345	$295	$225	$175	$125	N/A	N/A

⊙ **Model 46 Stutzen** - .177 or .22 cal., UL, SP, similar to Model 46, except full length Mannlicher-style stock. New 1998.

courtesy Diana

MSR $611	$565	$515	$450	$375	N/A	N/A	N/A

GRADING	100%	95%	90%	80%	60%	40%	20%

⚙ **Model 46 Stutzen Luxus** - .177 or .22 cal., UL, SP, similar to Model 46 Stutzen, except has deluxe stock. New 1998.

courtesy Diana

	100%	95%	90%	80%	60%	40%	20%
	$895	$815	$685	$625	$565	N/A	N/A

Last MSR was $975.

⚙ **Model 46 Stutzen Prestige** - .177 or .22 cal., UL, SP, similar to Model 46, except engraved. New 1998.

courtesy Diana

	100%	95%	90%	80%	60%	40%	20%
	$1,750	$1,450	$1,250	$995	$795	N/A	N/A

Last MSR was $2,000.

The Model 46 combines under-lever cocking with a flip-up loading port that provides easy loading, and allows the pellet to be inserted directly into the rifled barrel for pinpoint accuracy.

MODEL 48U - 177 or .22 cal., UL, SP, unlicensed copy of the British Jeffries pattern air rifle, adj. rear sight, 46 in. OAL, 7.5 lbs. Mfg. circa 1920-1940.

	100%	95%	90%	80%	60%	40%	20%
	$350	$275	$215	$185	$145	N/A	N/A

⚙ **Model 48E** - English-style stock.

	100%	95%	90%	80%	60%	40%	20%
	$350	$275	$215	$185	$145	N/A	N/A

MODEL 48/48A/48B/48SL - .177, .20 (disc. 2006), .22, or .25 (mfg. 1994-2006) cal., SL, SP, SS, 950/575 FPS, rifled 17 in. barrel, adj. cheekpiece (Model 48SL), 42.5 in. OAL, 8.5 lbs.Disc. 2007.

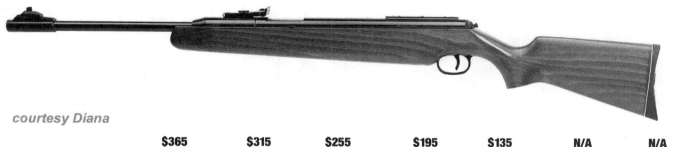

courtesy Diana

	100%	95%	90%	80%	60%	40%	20%
	$365	$315	$255	$195	$135	N/A	N/A

Last MSR was $410.

Add 10% for .25 cal. Add 15% for .20 cal. Add 5% for Model 48B with black matte finish stock (new 1995). Add 20% for Model 48A. Add 10% for combo w/ 4x32 compact scope and mount (new 2006).

⚙ **Model 48 (New 2008)** - .177 or .22, cal., SL, SP, sliding-breech SS, rifled 17 in. BBL, 1000/900 FPS, adj. rear and front sights, classic ambidextrous wood stock w/ contoured rubber recoil pad, two-stage adj. trigger, auto-safety, 42.5 in. OAL, 9 lbs. Mfg. 2008-current.

courtesy Umarex USA

MSR $442	100%	95%	90%	80%	60%	40%	20%
	$395	$350	$275	$205	$165	N/A	N/A

Add $44 for combo w/ 4x32 compact scope and mount.

GRADING	100%	95%	90%	80%	60%	40%	20%

MODEL 50 - .177, or .22 cal., UL, SP, two-piece cocking lever, angular stock styling, trigger block safety about two years after the introduction of angular stock styling. 1952-65.

courtesy Beeman Collection

⊕ **Model 50 Standard Variant 1** - sporting stock, alloy trigger blade, fixed post front sight, simple rear sight in transverse dovetail.

	$200	$175	$150	$125	$80	N/A	N/A

⊕ **Model 50A Variant 2** - similar to Model 50 Standard, except hooded front sight with four posts on rotating star, click adj. rear sight with four-notch insert, extra dovetail on rear of receiver.

	$220	$195	$170	$145	$100	N/A	N/A

⊕ **Model 50B Variant 3** - similar to Model 50A, except with match aperture sight mounted on receiver dovetail for match shooting, 45.3 in. OAL, 8.38 lbs.

	$245	$220	$195	$170	$145	N/A	N/A

⊕ **Model 50M Variant 4** - similar to Model 50B, except multi-purpose rear sight, match stock with cheekpiece and deep rubber butt-plate 45.3 in. OAL, 10.6 lbs.

	$255	$230	$205	$180	$155	N/A	N/A

MODEL 50S - replaced regular Model 50 about 1965 with a simplified version without the ball sear trigger.

	$175	$150	$120	$95	$80	$70	N/A

MODEL 50T/T01 - .177, .22, or .25 cal., UL, SP, 745/600 FPS, 18.5 in. barrel, ball trigger sear, 8 lbs. Mfg. 1952-1987.

⊕ **Model 50T/T01 Variant 1** - standard with sporting stock, blued finish, sporting front sight with interchangeable posts.

	$285	$235	$185	$155	$110	N/A	N/A

Add 10% for .25 cal. Add 25% for T01 Model. Subtract 20% for post-1965 versions with thicker stocks without forearm grooves, with stamped checkering, shallow cheekpieces, front sights as screwed-on ramps or clamped-on tunnels, plastic rear sights.

⊕ **Model 50T/T01 Variant 2** - military with parkerized finish, military front sight with fixed post and protective wings.

	$260	$210	$165	$135	$95	N/A	N/A

Last MSR was $210.

Add 10% for .25 cal. Add 25% for T01 Model. Subtract 20% for post-1965 versions with thicker stocks without forearm grooves, with stamped checkering, shallow cheekpieces, front sights as screwed-on ramps or clamped-on tunnels, plastic rear sights.

MODEL 52/52 DELUXE - .177, .22, or .25 (disc. 2006) cal., SL, SP, 950/550 FPS, 17 in. barrel, walnut-stained beech Monte Carlo stock, checkering on forend and pistol grip, ventilated rubber butt pad, 43.75 in. OAL, 8.5 lbs. Disc. 2007.

courtesy Diana

	$450	$395	$335	$270	$205	N/A	N/A

Last MSR was $481.

Add 10% for .25 cal. Add 55% for Deluxe version with handcrafted walnut stock, patterned checkering on forend and pistol grip, ornamental black wood insert in forend and base of pistol grip. Add 8% for combo w/ 4x32 scope and mount (new 2006).

⊕ **Model 52 (New 2008)** - .177 or .22 cal., SL, SP, sliding breech loading SS, rifled 17 in. BBL, adj. rear and front sights, two-stage adj. trigger, checkered hardwood Monte Carlo stock w/ contoured rubber butt pad, 43.75 in. OAL, 9 lbs. Mfg. 2008-current.

MSR $520	$485	$415	$365	$295	$250	N/A	N/A

Add $43 for combo w/ 4x32 scope and mount.

GRADING	100%	95%	90%	80%	60%	40%	20%

⊙ *Model 52 Luxus (New 2008)* - .177 or .22 cal., SL, SP, sliding breech loading SS, rifled 17.5 in. BBL, 1000/900 FPS, adj. rear and front sights, two-stage adj. trigger, checkered Walnut Monte Carlo stock w/ ventilated rubber butt pad and Ebony forend tip/PG cap, 44.12 in. OAL, 8.75 lbs. Mfg. 2008-current.

courtesy Umarex USA

	100%	95%	90%	80%	60%	40%	20%
MSR $677	$600	$495	$425	$350	N/A	N/A	N/A

MODEL 54 - .177 or .22 cal., SL, SP, recoilless action, 950/780 FPS or 1100-900 FPS (New 2008), 17 in. barrel, match type trigger safety catch with additional cocking guard, adj. front and rear sights, beechwood Monte Carlo stock with rubber butt pad, hand-checkered forend and pistol grip, 44 in. OAL, 9-10 lbs.

courtesy Diana

	100%	95%	90%	80%	60%	40%	20%
MSR $737	$685	$625	$550	$450	$375	N/A	N/A

Add $44 for combo w/ 4x32 scope and mount (new 2006).

MODEL 58 - .177 or .22 cal., UL, SP, three main variations, "Dianawerk's pre-WWII flagship." Mfg. 1915-1940.

courtesy Beeman Collection

⊙ *Model 58/1915 First Variant* - .177 or .22, cal., UL, SP, 625/500 FPS, set trigger, steel turn bolt, walnut buttstock with PG, steel buttplate. 45.25 in. OAL, 8.25 lbs. Mfg. 1915-16.

		95%	90%	80%	60%	40%	20%
	N/A	$1,400	$1,150	$795	$550	$425	$300

⊙ *Model 58/2 Second Variant* - .177 or .22, cal., UL, SP, 641 FPS (.177), different design: turn bolt replaced by knurled knob at the end of the receiver, checkered pistol grip stock with finger groove forearm, $70 in Stoeger´s 1937 catalog, when the Winchester Model 12 shotgun was $42.50, 47.25 in. OAL, 8.8 lbs. Mfg. early 1920s-1935.

		95%	90%	80%	60%	40%	20%
	N/A	$1,300	$1,150	$875	$675	$475	$275

⊙ *Model 58/3 Third Variant* - .177 or .22, cal., UL, SP, adj. trigger, no outer trigger cocking device, 45.25 in. OAL, 7.9 lbs. Mfg. circa 1936-1940.

		95%	90%	80%	60%	40%	20%
	N/A	$900	$750	$550	$350	$250	$125

MODEL 60/60T - .177 cal., Giss double contra-SP system, 17.9 in. barrel, beech, Tyrolean (Model LG 60T) or walnut stock with rubber buttplate, match diopter rear and tunnel front sight with inserts, adj. trigger, optional barrel weight (tube), 42.7 in. OAL, 9.9 lbs. Mfg. 1963 to circa 1982 (Tyrolean stocks were discontinued by 1980).

courtesy Beeman Collection

	100%	95%	90%	80%	60%	40%	20%
	$550	$455	$385	$295	$235	$185	$145

Add 30% for Model 60T.

GRADING	100%	95%	90%	80%	60%	40%	20%

MODEL 64 - .177 cal., records not yet clear about this model - if it existed, it probably was only a restocked Model 34. Mfg. circa 1986-89.

MODEL 65/65T - .177 cal., BBC, Giss double contra-SP system with radial lock lever, beech, Tyrolean (Model 65T), or walnut stock with rounded forearm, rubber butt pad, automatic safety, match diopter rear and tunnel front sight with inserts, adj. trigger, 43.3 in. OAL, 10.6 lbs. Mfg. 1968-1989 (Tyrolean stocks gone by 1980).

courtesy Beeman Collection

	100%	95%	90%	80%	60%	40%	20%
	$500	$405	$325	$255	$205	$145	$105

Add 35% for Model 65T.

MODEL 66/66M - .177 cal., BBC, similar to Model 65, except squared and deeper forestock, modified pistol grip and vertically adjustable rubber buttplate. Mfg. 1974-1983.

	100%	95%	90%	80%	60%	40%	20%
	$425	$365	$295	$235	$185	N/A	N/A

MODEL LG 68 - variant of Models 34/36/38 action with different stock.
    Values TBD

MODEL 70 - .177 cal., BBC, 450 FPS, 13.5 in. barrel, youth dimensions. Mfg. 1979-1994.

	100%	95%	90%	80%	60%	40%	20%
	$130	$105	$85	$65	$45	N/A	N/A

Last MSR was $190.

MODEL 72 - .177 cal., similar to Model 70, except with Giss recoilless action. A rifle version of Model 6 pistol. Mfg. 1979-1993.

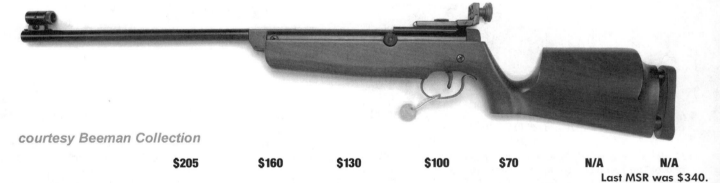

courtesy Beeman Collection

	100%	95%	90%	80%	60%	40%	20%
	$205	$160	$130	$100	$70	N/A	N/A

Last MSR was $340.

MODEL 75/75HV/75K/75S/75U/75TO1 MATCH MODEL - .177 cal., SL, 580 FPS, 19 in. barrel, micrometer-adj. rear sights, adj. cheekpiece, adj. recoil pad, 43.3 in. OAL, 11 lbs.

courtesy Howard Collection

	100%	95%	90%	80%	60%	40%	20%
	$850	$750	$600	$450	$350	N/A	N/A

Last MSR was $1,745.

Subtract 10% for left-hand version.
    Premiums may exist for variations Model 75 mfg. 1977-1983, Model 75B mfg. 1988-1994, Model 75HV and Model 75TO1 mfg. 1983-88, Model 75K was disc. in 1990, Model 75S mfg. beginning in 1999, now disc., Model 75U mfg. 1982-86.

GRADING	100%	95%	90%	80%	60%	40%	20%

MODEL 100 - .177 cal., SSP, 580 FPS, 18.9 in. barrel, adj. cheekpiece, target model, 42.9 in. OAL, 11 lbs. Mfg. 1989-1998.

	100%	95%	90%	80%	60%	40%	20%
	$995	$800	$640	$480	$395	N/A	N/A

Last MSR was $1,950.

MODEL 300 - .177 or .22 cal., UL, SP, 900/700 FPS, 11 in. barrel, blue finish, adj. rear sight, auto-safety, Monte Carlo stock with checkered forearm and grip (Model 46), recoil pad, 45.31 in. OAL, 7.9 lbs. New 2005.

courtesy Diana

	100%	95%	90%	80%	60%	40%	20%
	$485	$425	$365	$315	$265	N/A	N/A

Last MSR was $537.

MODEL 350 MAGNUM - .177 or .22 cal., BBC, SP, SS, 1200/1000 FPS, 19.5 in. barrel, hooded front sight, adj. rear sight, checkered Monte Carlo beech stock with cheekpiece, 48 in. OAL, 8.5 lbs. New 2001.

courtesy Diana

MSR $458	$415	$365	$295	$235	N/A	N/A	N/A

Add $45 for combo w/ 4x32 scope and mount.

MODEL 350 FEUERKRAFT - .177 or .22, cal., SL, SP, sliding-breech SS, rifled 19.62 in. BBL, 1250/1000 FPS, adj. rear and front fiber optic sights, classic ambidextrous wood stock w/ rubber recoil pad, two-stage adj. trigger, auto-safety, 48.37 in. OAL, 8 lbs. Mfg. 2008-current.

MSR $423	$375	$330	$250	$195	$150	N/A	N/A

Add $40 for combo w/ 4x32 compact scope and mount.

⊙ *Model 350 Feuerkraft Pro Compact* - .177 or .22, cal., SL, SP, sliding-breech SS, rifled 15.75 in. BBL w/ weight, 1250/1000 FPS, 3-9x40mm scope, classic ambidextrous wood stock w/ rubber recoil pad, two-stage adj. trigger, auto-safety, 44.62 in. OAL, 8.5 lbs. Mfg. 2008-current.

courtesy Umarex USA

MSR $504	$450	$395	$350	$295	$250	N/A	N/A

MODEL 1000 - .177 cal., BBC, colored plastic stocks (black, red, blue, white, and yellow). Disc. 1991.

	100%	95%	90%	80%	60%	40%	20%
	$150	$125	$100	$75	$50	N/A	N/A

Last MSR was $215.

Model 1000 was the sport model of the standard Model 34.

GRADING	100%	95%	90%	80%	60%	40%	20%

MODEL 460 MAGNUM - .177 or .22 cal., ULC, SP, 1350/1150 FPS, 18.5 in. barrel, adj. rear sight, checkered Monte Carlo stock with cheekpiece, vent. rubber butt pad, 45 in. OAL, 8.3 lbs. New 2007.

courtesy Umarex USA Collection

MSR $611	$565	$515	$450	$375	N/A	N/A	N/A

Add $72 for combo w/ 4x32 scope and mount.

MODEL SCHÜTZE (YOUTH) - .177 cal., BBC, SP, SS, rifled 16.5 in. BBL, 580 FPS, black finish, classic streight hardwood PG stock w/ rubber recoil pad, Truglo adj. sights, auto-safety, 41 in. OAL, 5 lbs. Mfg. 2008-current.

courtesy Umarex USA

MSR $215	$185	$150	$125	$95	$65	N/A	N/A

DOLLA

The Dolla name appeared about 1927 as a general designation for a number of push barrel air pistols with a cast one-piece grip and frame of distinctive shape but typically with no maker's name.

Most apparently were produced in Germany between WWI and WWII and may have been produced by several makers. They were especially promoted by Darlow of Bedford, England and Midland Gun Company of Birmingham, England. All are very solid and have very low power. The name came from the fact that the guns were priced at about the equivalent of an American dollar at the time of their introduction (SP, SS, .l77 cal.).

Noted European airgun historian, John Atkins, indicates that the term Dolla, strictly speaking, should be applied only to models produced after 1927. Earlier, similar appearing pistols, perhaps first produced about the 1895 by the Langenhan and Eisenwerke Gaggenau factories in Zella Mehlis, Germany, never had this name applied to them while they were in production. The recent Dolla pistols typically have a trigger guard with a completely rounded opening while the similar, older, pre-Dolla versions typically had the upper rear area of the trigger guard opening with a distinct right angle profile. The pre-Dolla versions are worth significantly more.

Push barrel air pistols with sheet metal trigger guards, as made by Anschütz, and perhaps others, as early as 1930, had graduated to the designation of Dolla Mark II.

Dolla values range from about $100 to $500 depending on model, condition, and case. Ref: AG Jan. 2005.

courtesy Beeman Collection

GRADING	100%	95%	90%	80%	60%	40%	20%

DONG KI

Current manufacturing/marketing group in Seoul, Korea whose products include airguns.

RIFLES

M1 CARBINE MODEL 106 - .177 cal., SP, SL, full-scale replica air rifle of the U.S. Model M1 Carbine complete with military sling stock slots and bayonet base.

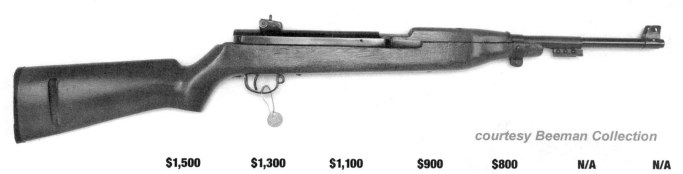

courtesy Beeman Collection

	$1,500	$1,300	$1,100	$900	$800	N/A	N/A

DREIBUND

For information on Dreibund airguns, see Philippines Airguns in the "P" section.

DRULOV

Current manufacturer located in Litomysl, Czech Republic. Currently imported and distributed by Top Gun Air Guns Inc. located in Scottsdale, AZ.

PISTOLS

DRULOV DU-10 CONDOR - .177 cal., CO_2, five-shot mag., adj. sights, blue finish, wood grip.

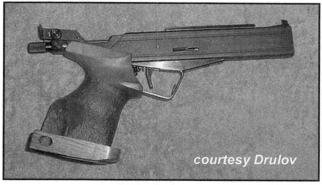

courtesy Drulov

MSR $405	$375	$300	$250	$150	N/A	N/A	N/A

DRULOV LOV-21 - .177 cal., CO_2, SS, black plastic frame, 6 in. rifled steel BBL, 420 FPS, adj. sights, 11.3 in. OAL. New 2004.

courtesy Drulov

MSR $119	$110	$95	$75	$50	N/A	N/A	N/A

GRADING	100%	95%	90%	80%	60%	40%	20%

DRULOV RADA PISTOL - 9mm cal., CO_2, SS, adj. sights, rifled steel BBL, 210 FPS, blue finish, wood grip and forend, detachable wire shoulder stock. New 2004.

	100%	95%	90%	80%	60%	40%	20%
MSR $430	$395	$325	$250	$150	N/A	N/A	N/A

Add 10% for Rada Convertible with longer BBL.

RIFLES

DRULOV 10 EAGLE - .177 cal., CO_2, five-shot mag., 525 FPS, 15.75 or 19.7 in. barrel, adj. sights, blue finish, wood stock.

	100%	95%	90%	80%	60%	40%	20%
MSR $418	$400	$350	$300	$250	N/A	N/A	N/A

DRULOV 10 SOKOL - .375 or 9mm cal., CO_2, SS, adj. sights, blue finish, wood stock.

courtesy Howard Collection

	100%	95%	90%	80%	60%	40%	20%
MSR $430	$430	$360	$310	$260	N/A	N/A	N/A

DUK IL

Current manufacturing group currently located in Pusan, South Korea, previously located in Seoul, Korea. Products include pre-charged pneumatic airguns. Previously imported/distributed in USA by Air Rifle Specialists.

For information on Duk Il airguns, see ARS in the "A" section.

E SECTION

EM-GE

Previous trademark manufactured by Moritz & Gerstenberger located in Zella-Mehlis, Thüringen, Germany circa 1922-1940, for airguns, starting pistols, blank-firing guns, and flare pistols. Re-established as Gerstensberger & Eberwein located in Gerstetten-Gussenstadt, Germany about 1950. Company seems to have vanished circa 1997.

Moritz & Gerstenberger apparently produced products for the German military program during WWII under the code "ghk". Now known mainly for rather low grade airpistols and teargas and blank-firing pistols; some of their pre-WWII products, such as the very interesting top-lever Zenit air pistol (SP) were quite good. Among their older products is a BBC, SP pistol, without model markings, which is very similar to a pre-WWII Diana Model 5 (probably an early version of the EmGe LP3A).

Research is ongoing with this trademark, and more information will be included both in future editions and online. Ref: AR2: 16-20.

GRADING	100%	95%	90%	80%	60%	40%	20%

PISTOLS

MODEL 3 - .22 cal., BC, SS, fixed sights, 7.4 in. stepped, rifled steel BBL, all steel receiver, blue finish, checkered wood grips, no safety, 15.5 in. OAL, 2.6 lbs. Mfg. pre-WWII.

	100%	95%	90%	80%	60%	40%	20%
	$250	$225	$200	$150	$100	$65	N/A

Rear sight at back end of receiver.

MODEL LP 3 - .177 or .22 cal. BC, SS, 5.8 in. rifled steel BBL, adj. trigger, adj. sights, no safety, checkered brown plastic, grips, anodized blue finish on zinc barrel cover, receiver, and other zinc die-cast metal parts, 12.4 in. OAL, 2.7 lbs. Mfg. circa 1957-1975.

	100%	95%	90%	80%	60%	40%	20%
	$150	$125	$100	$65	$40	N/A	N/A

Subtract 25% for LP3A (top of receiver and BBL ribbed). Ref: GR, Aug. 76. Ca. 1975-1980.
Branded as HyScore 822T in USA. Ref: GR Dec. 74.

MODEL 100 Specs and values TBD.

HERKULES - .177 cal, BC, SS, fixed sights, 325 FPS, fixed sights, blue finish, wood grips, no safety. Mfg. 1933-1940.

EM-GE LP3A
courtesy Beeman Collection

100%	95%	90%	80%	60%	40%	20%
$275	$225	$175	$125	$85	N/A	N/A

ZENIT - .177 cal., TL, SS or 10-shot repeater, fixed sights, smoothbore or rifled steel BBL, 325 FPS, blue finish, wood grip, (marked "gez") translates to rifled, no safety. Ref: AR2:16-20. Mfg. circa 1936-1940.

EM-GE Zenit
courtesy Beeman Collection

100%	95%	90%	80%	60%	40%	20%
$325	$250	$200	$150	$100	N/A	N/A

Add 300% for ten-shot repeater (if with mag.). Add 40% for black backalight grip.

GRADING	100%	95%	90%	80%	60%	40%	20%

RIFLES

EM-GE KRONE - 4.5mm cal., BBC, SS or 15-shot repeater, 15.75 in. rifled steel BBL, 560 FPS, adj. rear and blade front sights, walnut stock w/ PG, 38.5 in. OAL, 5.1 lbs.

	100%	95%	90%	80%	60%	40%	20%
	N/A	N/A	$350	$275	$195	$125	$70

Add 300% for 15-shot repeater, marked "KRONE M" w/ original mag.

EASTERN ENGINEERING CO.

Previous manufacturer located in Syracuse, NY.

PISTOLS

GAMESTER - .177 or .25 cal., SP, SS, push-barrel action similar to the Hubertus air pistol of Germany. Bronze frame, blued steel body tube, silver colored thin barrel. No marks on gun but fitted cardboard factory box with illustrated information inside cover, 5.5 in. BBL, 11 in. OAL, 2.1 lbs. four known specimen as of November 2005, with two sales durring 2007. 1. at $550. 2. at $1,400.

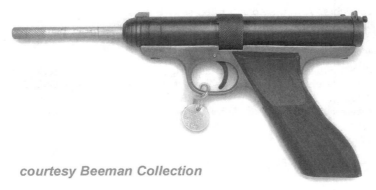

courtesy Beeman Collection

Rarity precludes accurate pricing.
Factory information indicates that .177 barrel and supplied mainspring was for "semi-harmless use" while an optional .25 cal. barrel and stronger mainspring was available for pest control.

EDISON GENERAL ELECTRIC

Previously manufactured by Edison General Electric Appliance Co., Chicago, IL.

These are large airguns which simulated heavy machine guns for training gunners during WWII. Used in simulated combat with back projected images of enemy planes flying at different speeds and angles. Edison General Electric Appliance became General Electric after WWII. "Hotpoint" was their appliance brand. Mfg. circa 1943-45. Ref. Behling (2006).

TRAINER MACHINE GUNS

Gunnery trainer machine guns -- fully automatic, powered via hose from air compressor. .375 cal. bakelite ball ammo, magazine tube above and parallel to shorter true barrel, magazine loaded by unscrewing cap at muzzle end and attaching loader which mates with projectile exit opening below. 100 rouond loader filled from separate projectile hopper. 115v/60 cycle firing mechanism, painted black. There are three known models.

ANTI-AIRCRAFT MACHINE GUN MODEL M9 - .375 cal., ground to air gunnery trainer, 500 rpm., dual hand grips, massive steel plate pivoting/swiveling base, barrel sleeve about 4 3/4 in.diameter to simulate water-cooled barrel jacket of .50 cal. machine gun; marked with Edison General Electric Appliance Company name but without Hotpoint brand marking, 67 in. OAL, 78 lbs.

courtesy Beeman Collection

	100%	95%	90%	80%	60%	40%	20%
	N/A	N/A	N/A	$4,000	$3,500	$3,000	$2,500

Add 10% for loading funnel, hopper.
Original shipping box, operating manual, and bags of ammo typically have retail values are in the $25-$50 range for each item.

GRADING	100%	95%	90%	80%	60%	40%	20%

AERIAL GUNNERY MACHINE GUN MODEL E11 - .375 cal., side gunner version for training gunners in U.S. bombers, dual hand grips; barrel sleeve simulates barrel sleeve of air-cooled machine guns, small steel pin support base, marked with Hotpoint brand and Edison General Electric Appliance Company name 57.5 in. OAL, 41 lbs.

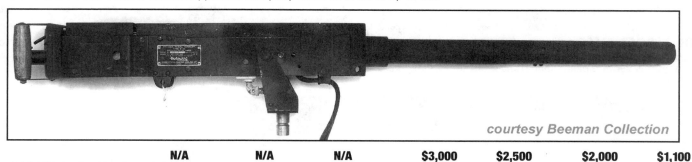

courtesy Beeman Collection

	N/A	N/A	N/A	$3,000	$2,500	$2,000	$1,100

Add 10% for loading funnel, hopper.

AERIAL GUNNERY MACHINE GUN MODEL E10 - .375 cal., remote control version of E10, no hand grips; probably mounted in pairs in remote gun turrets, marked with Hotpoint brand and Edison General Electric Appliance Company name, 48 in. OAL, 24 lbs.

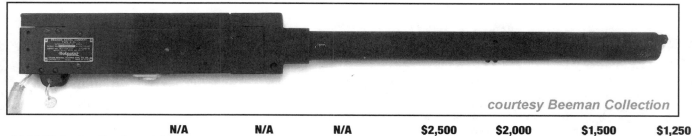

courtesy Beeman Collection

	N/A	N/A	N/A	$2,500	$2,000	$1,500	$1,250

Add 10% for loading funnel, hopper.

EISENWERKE GAGGENAU (GAGGENAU IRONWORKS)

See Gaggenau Ironworks in the "G" section.

As noted in the Gaggenau Ironworks listing, there is NO such brand as "Eisenwerk". That word simply means "iron works" or "factory".

EL GAMO

For information on El Gamo airguns, see Gamo in the "G" section.

ELMEK

Previously unknown maker, presumed Danish, mid-twentieth century.

RIFLES

ELMEK RIFLE - .25 cal., smoothbore, SP, UL, SS, 21.5 in. BBL, blue/nickel finish, iron cocking lever behind trigger with unique attached wooden pistol grip, downswing of underlever causes breech block, which contains the mainspring and piston, to move back as a unit – exposing barrel breech for direct loading – upswing causes compression chamber tube only to move forward, leaving piston cocked, and closing breech – similar to the complex, fully opening breech system in the Feinwerkbau 300 and 65 airguns, receiver body is brass with nickel plating, hexagon containing the word "ELMEK" is stamped on lower edge of receiver.

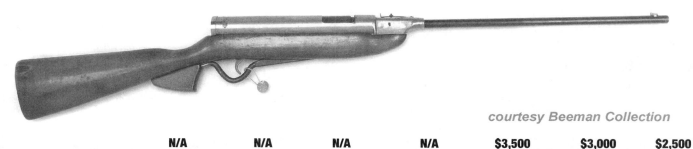

courtesy Beeman Collection

	N/A	N/A	N/A	N/A	$3,500	$3,000	$2,500

ENSIGN ARMS CO., LTD.

Previous international distributors for Saxby Palmer Airguns located in Newbury, England. Previously imported until 1988 by Marksman Products, located in Huntington Beach, CA.

Ensign Arms previously distributed the Saxby Palmer line of airguns into the U.S. Please refer to the Saxby Palmer section for these guns. Ensign-designated models were trademarked by Ensign Arms Co., Ltd.

GRADING	100%	95%	90%	80%	60%	40%	20%

ERIE IRON WORKS

Previous manufacturer orig. located in St. Thomas, Ontario, Canada, later moved to Toronto, Canada. Manf. ca. 1940 - 1955.

RIFLE

ERIE TARGET RIFLE BB/.174 cal., trigger gd UL, SP. 1000 shot. Flat sided hardwood stock. Manual safety at rear of receiver. Unique trigger guard cocking lever w/no metal on inner side. Early versions w/hooded front sight and cast iron levers. Later versions w/ aluminum lever and plain blade front sight. 36 in. OAL, ca. 3 lbs. Diamond shape yellow and black decal on LHS forearm.

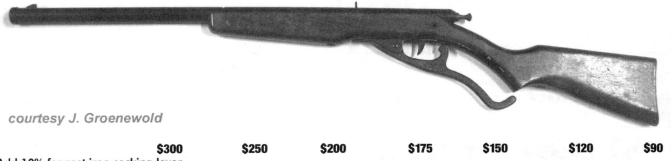

courtesy J. Groenewold

	100%	95%	90%	80%	60%	40%	20%
	$300	$250	$200	$175	$150	$120	$90

Add 10% for cast iron cocking lever.

ERMA

Previously manufactured by Erma-Werke GmbH, located in München-Dachau, Germany.

Erma produced their only airgun, the ELG 10, in 1981, which was discontinued in the 1990s. Apparently related to pre-WWII Erfurter Maschinenfabrik. Erma (= ER-Furter MA-Schinenfabrik) was relocated from Erfurt to Bavaria after WWII like the other companies (which mostly went to the Baden-Wurtemmberg region, Ulm, etc.). Having the same origin in the 1990s, Erma went back to Suhl (after near insolvency and a management buyout). In 1998, the company was officially closed. Some models and spare parts were bought and distributed by Frankonia Jagd, Würzburg (wholesaler).

Makers of blowback copies of the Luger-style firearms, such as the Beeman P-08 and MP-08 in .22 LR and .380 ACP, respectively, and copies of the U.S. M1 carbine in .22 LR (and in .22 WMR, famous as the "Jungle Carbine" in banana republics). They also produced some very little-known electro-optical shooting guns, including a version of the ELG 10, known as the EG 80 Ermatronic, and an Ermatronic copy of a Colt revolver. For more information and current values on Erma-Werke firearms, please refer to the *Blue Book of Gun Values* by S.P. Fjestad (also available online).

RIFLES

ELG 10 - .177 in. cal., SP, SS, LA, manual safety, copy of the Winchester 1894, 38 in. OAL, 6.4 lbs.

courtesy Beeman Collection

	100%	95%	90%	80%	60%	40%	20%
	$550	$450	$350	$295	$250	N/A	N/A

Add 10% for Webley "Ranger" marking.

EUSTA

Previous trademark used by Alpina-Werk M&M Vorwerk GmbH & Co., KG,8950 Kaufbeuren, Germany on inexpensive sheet metal air pistols.

The authors and publisher wish to thank Dr. Trevor Adams for his valuable assistance with the following information in this edition of the *Blue Book of Airguns*. Trademark registered in Germany on October 13, 1965. Gun design was invented by Walter Ussfeller, A. Weber, and H. Witteler. Most notable for the concentric piston design. Distributed by Eckhard G. Damaschke, Weickartshain, Germany,1968-76.

PISTOLS

LP 100 - .177 cal., SP, TL, SS, sheet metal frame with plastic grips, concentric piston, 6.3 in rifled steel barrel, 8 in. OAL, 1.5 lbs. Mfg. 1965-68.

	100%	95%	90%	80%	60%	40%	20%
	$350	$300	$250	$200	$150	$100	$50

Add 20% for factory box and papers.
Patented in Germany by Walter Ussfeller on Sept. 24, 1969.

GRADING	100%	95%	90%	80%	60%	40%	20%

LP 210 - .177 cal., SP, TL, SS, similar to LP 100, except for a modified top lever catch, breech-end of cylinder sloped forward, and two-piece trigger. Mfg. 1968-1971.

courtesy Trevor Adams

	N/A	$175	$125	$75	$50	$30	$20

Add 20% for factory box and papers.
Based on Alpina Werk patent of Nov. 5, 1970.

EXCELLENT

Previous manufacturer, Exellent Geväret AB of Stockholm, Sweden and several different makers and owners circa 1905-1974. The authors and publisher wish to thank Kenth Friberg for his valuable assistance with the following information in this edition of the *Blue Book of Airguns*.

Note that C1 and CI, etc. are different models! The models with Roman numerals have heavier stocks with pistol grips. Additional research is underway concerning this group, and any updates will be available through online subscriptions and in future editions. The 5.5mm caliber models have paragon rifles barrels and are to shoot 5.4mm balls only. The values below are more indicative of the low survival rate than the age of these models.

PISTOLS

MODEL 1950 CONCENTRIC PISTON PISTOL - .177 (4.5mm pellet) cal., TL, SP, SS, concentric piston. Marked "EXCELLENT" but without model marking. 8.1 in. rifled BBL, no safety. 8.5 in. OAL, 2.0 lbs. Approx. 4,800 mfg. 1946-58. Ref: AGNR Apr. 1989.

courtesy Beeman Collection

$650	$550	$450	$350	$300	N/A	N/A

Add 20% for factory box.

PHANTOM "REPETER" PISTOL - .173 (4.4 mm) lead balls cal., SP, repeater, UL, zinc metal cast frame, "Phantom" cast into LHS frame. Cocking lever consists of front of grip and trigger guard. No safety. 7.1 in. OAL, 1.5 lbs. Approx. 4,572 mfg. 1953-59, but rare due to the common breakage resulting from defective design in the muzzle area.

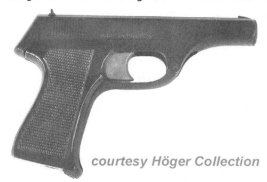

courtesy Höger Collection

N/A	$650	$550	$400	$250	$150	N/A

Add 30% for factory box.

GRADING	100%	95%	90%	80%	60%	40%	20%

RIFLES

MODEL AE - .22 cal., smoothbore folded/rolled metal barrel jacket w/ insert, pump pneumatic, 35.4-39.4 in. OAL, 3.5-4.4 lbs. Two versions mfg. 1904-12.
Current values not yet determined.

MODEL C1 (Slim Stock) - 5.5mm (for 5.4mm lead balls only)cal., smoothbore, pump pneumatic, slim stock with no pistol grip, 39.4 in. OAL, 4.4 lbs. 1905-1939.
Values approximate Model C2.

MODEL C2 - 5.5mm (for 5.4mm lead balls only) cal., rifled, SS, trombone-style pump pneumatic with metal pump handle, breech block swings to left to load, rifled 22.5 in. round BBL, blue and nickel finish, slim stock with no pistol grip, no safety, 39.4 in OAL, 4.4 lbs. Mfg. 1905-39.

courtesy Beeman Collection

	N/A	N/A	$650	$550	$450	N/A	N/A

Add 20% for early version with checkered metal slide handle.
See also Bahco in the "B" section of this guide.

MODEL CI (Large Stock) - 5.5mm (for 5.4mm lead balls only) cal., smoothbore, pump pneumatic w/ wood pump handle, large stock with pistol grip, 38.2 in. OAL, 5.1 lbs. 1945-52.

	N/A	N/A	$650	$550	$450	N/A	N/A

MODEL CII - 5.5mm (for 5.4mm lead balls only) cal., trombone-style pumppneumatic, swinging breech block, various sight versions, large buttstock with pistol grip, 38.2 in. OAL, 5.1 lbs. mfg. 1945-52.

courtesy Beeman Collection

	N/A	N/A	$650	$550	$450	N/A	N/A

MODEL CIIK - similar to Model C2, except .22 in. cal, trombone-style pump pneumatic, with faucet tap loading breech, similar to Model C2, large buttstock with pistol grip,22.3 in. rifled round BBL, no safety, 38.2 in. OAL, 4.6 lbs. Mfg. 1953-67.

	$650	$500	$400	$300	$225	N/A	N/A

MODEL CIII - 5.5mm (for 5.4mm lead balls only) cal., pump pneumatic, Mauser mechanism, rifled or smoothbore, 39.8 in. OAL, 5.5 lbs. No specimens known. Mfg. 1907-?
Current values not yet determined.

MODEL CIV - 6 1/3mm cal., CO_2, 39.8 in. OAL, 5.5 lbs. No known specimens, mfg. circa 1912-?
Current values not yet determined.

MODEL C5 - 5.5mm (for 5.4mm lead balls only) cal., CO_2, charge from separate tank, slim stock with no pistol grip, 39.8 in. OAL, 5.5 lbs. one specimen known, mfg. 1907-?
Current values not yet determined.

MODEL CVI - 5.5mm (for 5.4mm lead balls only) cal., CO_2, rifled or smoothbore, 39.8 in. OAL, 5.5 lbs. no known specimens, 1907-?
Current values not yet determined.

MODEL CF - 4.5mm cal., SP, SS, BBC, rifled BBL, slim stock with very small pistol grip, 39.4 in. OAL, 4.4 lbs., 1933-48.

	N/A	N/A	$995	$750	$600	N/A	N/A

Add 25% for earlier version with straight grip stock.

GRADING	100%	95%	90%	80%	60%	40%	20%

MODEL F1 - 4.5mm cal., SS, TL, SP, smoothbore, 39.8 in., 4.4 lbs. mfg. c. 1919-?
   Current values not yet determined.

MODEL F2 - 4.5mm cal., smoothbore, SS, TL, SP, checkered metal pad on each side of receiver, forward bolt slides to open breech for loading, similar to F1, no safety. Very early model. 38.2 in. OAL, 4.1 lbs. Mfg. c. 1919-?

courtesy Beeman Collection

	100%	95%	90%	80%	60%	40%	20%
	N/A	N/A	N/A	$1,850	$1,700	$1,400	$1,000

MODEL F3 - 4.5mmcal, SS, SP, TL, tap loading, 39.4 in OAL, 4.4 lbs. Mfg. 1925-?
   Current values not yet determined.

MODEL MATCH - 5.5mm (for 5.4mm lead balls only) cal., lead balls, short tubular, gravity-fed magazine loads tap loading breech block, trigger guard swings to cock the action, trombone-style pump pneumatic, pistol grip, wooden slide handle, no safety. 38.6 in. OAL, 5.9 lbs., 1967-71.

courtesy Beeman Collection

	100%	95%	90%	80%	60%	40%	20%
	N/A	N/A	$700	$600	$500	$400	$300

NOTES

F SECTION

FARAC (FABRICA ARGENTINA DE RIFLER DE AIR COMPRIMIDO)

Previous manufacturer of spring piston airguns located in Buenos Aires, Argentina circa 1990s.

GRADING	100%	95%	90%	80%	60%	40%	20%

RIFLES

SUPER VALIANT - .22 lead ball cal., SP, UL, vertical loading tap with tubular magazine, blue finish, hardwood stock, 42.6 in. OAL, 9.6 lbs.

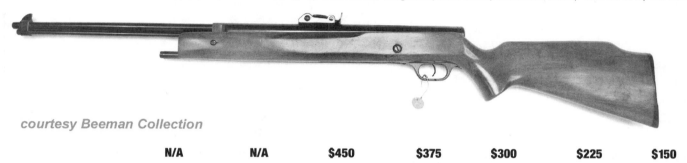

courtesy Beeman Collection

	100%	95%	90%	80%	60%	40%	20%
	N/A	N/A	$450	$375	$300	$225	$150

FAS

Current manufacturer located in Milan, Italy. Previously imported by Airguns of Arizona, located in Mesa, AZ, by Beeman, then located in Santa Rosa, CA, by Nygord Products, located in Prescott, AZ, and Top Gun Air Guns Inc., located in Scottsdale, AZ.

Research is ongoing with this trademark, and more information may be included both in future editions and online.

For more information and current pricing on both new and used FAS firearms, please refer to the *Blue Book of Gun Values* by S.P. Fjestad (also available online).

PISTOLS

FAS 400 - .177 cal., TL, SSP, similar to Model 604, except without dry fire feature.

	100%	95%	90%	80%	60%	40%	20%
	$195	$150	$100	$80	$60	N/A	N/A

FAS 604 - .177 cal., TL, SSP, adj. trigger, adj. sights, target model.

courtesy Beeman Collection

	100%	95%	90%	80%	60%	40%	20%
MSR N/A	$300	$265	$195	$150	$100	N/A	N/A

FAS 606 - .177 cal., TL, SSP, 7.5 in. barrel, adj. trigger, adj. sights, UIT target model, walnut grips, 2 lbs. 3 oz. Disc. 1994.

	100%	95%	90%	80%	60%	40%	20%
MSR N/A	$395	$325	$295	$225	$150	N/A	N/A

FAS 609 - .177 cal., PCP, 7.5 in. barrel, adj. trigger, adj. sights, UIT target model, adj. walnut grips. New 1997.

	100%	95%	90%	80%	60%	40%	20%
MSR N/A	$550	$425	$345	$250	$175	N/A	N/A

FB RECORD (BARTHELMS, FRITZ)

Current manufacturer located in Heidenheim-Oggenhausen, Germany.

Founded by Fritz Barthelms in 1948 and now owned by his son, Martin Barthelmes. Production of airguns began in the late 1960s. The specialty of the company is producing economical air pistols using alloy and plastic casting methods that have minimal labor involvement. Annual production in the mid-1980s was about 40,000 air pistols, produced by only twenty workers.

In the 1980s, the Record brand began to include more substantial and interesting air pistols. The little, strangely named Jumbo features one of the most interesting mechanisms in the airgun field, a very compact concentric piston design. The extremely unexpected oval profile of the piston forces perfect piston alignment.

GRADING	100%	95%	90%	80%	60%	40%	20%

PISTOLS

FB RECORD LP 1 - .177 cal., smoothbore, SP, BBC, SS, fixed sights, brown plastic grips with RH thumbrest, no safety, 10.9 in. OAL, 1.6 lbs.

	$40	$35	$30	$25	$20	$15	$10

FB RECORD LP 2 - .177 cal., rifled, SP, BBC, SS, adj. sights, white plastic grips with RH thumbrest, no safety, 11.5 in. OAL, 1.7 lbs.

courtesy Beeman Collection

	$50	$45	$40	$35	$30	$25	$20

FB RECORD LP 3 - .177 cal., rifled, SP, BBC, SS, adj. sights, brown plastic grips with RH thumbrest, no safety, 11.5 in. OAL, 1.9 lbs.

	$60	$55	$45	$40	$35	$30	$25

FB RECORD 68 - .177 cal., rifled, SP, BBC, SS, adj. sights, brown plastic grips with RH thumbrest, no safety, 14.6 in. OAL, 3.1 lbs.

	$90	$80	$70	$55	$50	$30	$25

FB RECORD 77 - .177 cal., rifled, SP, BBC, SS, adj. sights, tan plastic grip with RH thumbrest, trigger guard and bar molded in front of grip, ventilated rib on barrel, anti-bear trap, no safety, 12.4 in. OAL, 2.1 lbs.

courtesy Beeman Collection

	$65	$60	$50	$45	$40	$30	$25

FB RECORD CHAMPION - .177, SP, TL, SS, styling like Beeman P1 or BSA 240, blue finish, hardwood grips, 6 in. round barrel. Mfg. 2001-Disc.

courtesy Beeman Collection

	N/A	$200	$150	$95	$65	$55	$45

GRADING	100%	95%	90%	80%	60%	40%	20%

FB RECORD JUMBO - .177, 260 FPS, rifled, TL, SS, oval-shaped concentric piston, fixed sights, contoured walnut grips, may be marked with "Mauser U90/U91", 7.3 in. OAL, 1.9 lbs. Mfg. 1982-1997.

courtesy Beeman Collection

	100%	95%	90%	80%	60%	40%	20%
	$150	$125	$100	$75	$60	$50	$35

Add 10% for Target model, adj. sights (intro. 1983). Add 10% for Deluxe model, oakleaf carving on walnut grips.
This air pistol is very compact, well balanced, may be marked with "Mauser U90/U91" (not made by Mauser). Previously imported by Beeman Precision Airguns, then located in San Rafael, CA.

FEG

Current manufacturer located in Hungary (FEG stands for Fegyver es Gepgyar) since circa 1900. Previously imported by K.B.I. Inc. (formerly Kassnar Imports). Dealer sales.

Research is ongoing with this trademark, and more information will be included both in future editions and online.
For more information and current pricing on both new and used FEG firearms, please refer to the *Blue Book of Gun Values* by S.P. Fjestad (also available online).

PISTOLS

MODEL GPM-01 - .177 cal., CO_2 cartridge or bulk fill, 425 FPS, 10.25 in. barrel, 2 lbs. 7 oz.

MSR $525	$425	$360	$315	$235	$165	N/A	N/A

The Model GPM-01 has been imported as the Daisy Model 91.

RIFLES

CLG-62 - .177 cal., match rifle. Disc.

courtesy Beeman Collection

	$425	$360	$315	$235	$165	N/A	N/A

CLG-462 - .177 or .22 cal., CO_2 cartridge or cylinder charge, 490-410 FPS, 16.5 or 24 (.22 cal. only) in. barrel, 5 lbs. 8 oz.

	$400	$350	$270	$215	$145	N/A	N/A

Last MSR was $550.

CLG-468 - .177 or .22 cal., CO_2 cartridge or cylinder charge, 705-525 FPS, 26.75 in. barrel, 5 lbs. 12 oz.

	$450	$380	$300	$225	$150	N/A	N/A

Last MSR was $600.

F.I.E.

Previous importer (F.I.E. is the acronym for Firearms Import & Export) located in Hialeah, FL until 1990.
For more information and current pricing on F.I.E. firearms, please refer to the *Blue Book of Gun Values* by S.P. Fjestad (also available online).

GRADING	100%	95%	90%	80%	60%	40%	20%

PISTOLS

TIGER - .177 cal., BBC, SP, SS, black enamel finish, black plastic grip frame, marked "Made in Italy" (by Gun Toys?), 12.6 in. OAL, 1.7 lbs.

courtesy Beeman Collection

	$50	$45	$40	$35	$30	N/A	N/A

Add 10% for factory box with new targets.

Factory box bears the letters "MAM" in raised foam, thus probably eliminating Mondial as the maker, as their initials are MMM.

FLZ

For information on FLZ air pistols, see Langenhan in the "L" section.

FX AIRGUNS

Current manufacturer located in Hova, Sweden. Currently imported and distributed by Airguns of Arizona/Precision Airgun Distribution, located in Mesa, AZ. Dealer and consumer direct sales.

PISTOLS

RANCHERO .177 or .22 cal., PCP, biathlon style BA, eight-shot rotary mag., 8.5 in. Lothar Walther match grade barrel, blue finish, two-stage adj. trigger, walnut grip, grooved receiver for scope mounting, adj. power, built-in pressure gauge, removable air cylinder, 18 in. OAL, 3.3 lbs. Mfg. 2006-current.

courtesy Precision Airgun Distribution

MSR N/A	$1,095	$950	$875	$700	$625	N/A	N/A

RIFLES

CYCLONE - .177 or .22 cal., PCP, biathlon style BA, eight-shot rotary mag., 19.7 in. Lothar Walther match grade barrel, blue finish, two-stage adj. trigger, synthetic stock with rubberized PG, grooved receiver for scope mounting, adj. power, built-in pressure gauge, removable air cylinder, 6.6 lbs.

courtesy Precision Airgun Distribution

MSR N/A	$1,295	$995	$895	$775	$675	N/A	N/A

Add 15% for walnut stock.

GRADING	100%	95%	90%	80%	60%	40%	20%

GLADIATOR - .22 cal., PCP, dual air cylinders (butt stock and forearm) self-closing Biathlon style action, eight-shot rotary mag., 19.7 in. Lothar Walther match grade barrel, adj. power level, blue finish, two-stage adj. trigger, black thumbhole synthetic stock, grooved receiver for scope mounting, external power adjuster, built-in pressure gauge, 41.5 in. OAL, 7.8 lbs. Mfg. 2006-current.

courtesy Precision Airgun Distribution

MSR N/A	$1,395	$1,150	$950	$785	$695	N/A	N/A

MONSOON - .177 or .22 cal., PCP, semi-auto repeater, 12 shot mag., 19.7 in. Lothar-Walther Match grade fully shrouded barrel, blue finish, black synthetic thumb hole stock, adj. ventilated recoil pad, grooved receiver for scope mounting, disabling safety catch, 43 in OAL, 6.6 lbs. Mfg 2006-current.

courtesy Precision Airgun Distribution

MSR N/A	$1,449	$1,250	$995	$875	$725	N/A	N/A

Add 20% for walnut stock.

REVOLUTION - .22 cal., PCP, semi-auto repeater, 12 shot mag., 19.25 in. barrel, blue finish, black ambidextous synthetic stock, grooved receiver for scope mounting, disabling safety catch, 39.75 in OAL, 7.7 lbs. Mfg 2006-current.

MSR N/A	$1,795	$1,550	$1,395	$1,250	$995	N/A	N/A

Add 20% for walnut stock.

SUPER SWIFT - .177 or .22 cal., PCP, self-closing Biathlon style action, eight-shot rotary mag., 19.7 in. Lothar Walther match grade barrel, blue finish, two-stage adj. trigger, black thumbhole synthetic stock, grooved receiver for scope mounting, external power adjuster, built-in pressure gauge, 40.5 in. OAL, 5.3 lbs. New 2004.

courtesy Precision Airgun Distribution

MSR N/A	$1,295	$995	$895	$775	$675	N/A	N/A

TARANTULA - .177, or .22 cal., PCP, BA, eight-shot rotary mag., 19.7 in. Lothar Walther match grade barrel with threaded muzzle weight, blue finish, two-stage adj. trigger, checkered gradethree hand rubbed oil finished Turkish Circassian walnut (Tarantula) stock, ventilated recoil pad, grooved receiver for scope mounting, adj. power, built-in pressure gauge, 6 lbs., 39.5 OAL. Disc. 2007.

	$925	$850	$750	$665	$580	N/A	N/A

Last MSR was $946.

Add 15% for grade four walnut stock.

GRADING	100%	95%	90%	80%	60%	40%	20%

TARANTULA SPORT - .177, or .22 cal., PCP, BA, similar to Tarantula, except gradetwo English walnut stock, 6 lbs., 39.5 in. OAL. Disc. 2006.

courtesy Precision Airgun Distribution

	$795	$695	$515	$450	$375	N/A	N/A

Last MSR was $815.

TIMBERWOLF - .22 cal., PCP, bolt action, two-shot mag., 19.7 in. Lothar Walther match grade barrel, blue finish, two-stage adj. trigger, checkered beech or grade two walnut stock, ventilated recoil pad, grooved receiver for scope mounting, adj. power, built-in pressure gauge, 6.5 lbs. Disc. 2005.

	$515	$425	$350	$275	$225	N/A	N/A

Last MSR was $578.

Add $42 for walnut stock.

TYPHOON - .177 or .22 cal., PCP, BA, SS, 19.7 in. fully shrouded barrel, blue finish, synthetic sporter or ambidextrous walnut stock, ventilated recoil pad, grooved receiver for scope mounting, 41 in OAL, 6.1-7.1 (walnut stock) lbs. Mfg 2006-current.

courtesy Precision Airgun Distribution

MSR N/A	$795	$625	$550	$450	$350	N/A	N/A

Add 20% for walnut stock.

TYPHOON 12 - .177 or .22 cal., PCP, BA, 12 shot mag., 19.7 in.Lothar-Walther Match grade fully shrouded barrel, blue finish, synthetic sporter or ambidextrous walnut stock, adj. ventilated recoil pad, grooved receiver for scope mounting, two-stage adj. match trigger, 41 in OAL, 6.1-7.1 (walnut stock) lbs. Mfg 2006-current.

MSR N/A	$869	$750	$665	$580	$475	N/A	N/A

Add 20% for walnut stock.

ULTIMATE - .177 or .22 cal., PCP, pistol grip pump action, eight-shot rotary mag., 19.7 in. Lothar Walther match grade barrel, blue finish, two-stage adj. trigger, synthetic stock, grooved receiver for scope mounting, built-in pressure gauge, 6.6 lbs. Disc. 2007.

	$650	$575	$495	$415	$345	N/A	N/A

Last MSR was $729.

XTERMINATOR - .177 or .22 cal., PCP, forearm pump action, eight-shot rotary mag., 19.7 in. Lothar Walther match grade barrel, blue finish, two-stage adj. trigger, synthetic stock, grooved receiver for scope mounting, built-in pressure gauge, 4.4 lbs. Disc. 2007.

courtesy Precision Airgun Distribution

	$1,250	$1,050	$950	$795	$635	N/A	N/A

Last MSR was $1,397.

GRADING	100%	95%	90%	80%	60%	40%	20%

FALCON

Current trademark manufactured by Falcon Pneumatic Systems Limited located in Birmingham, England. Falcon Pneumatic Systems has been manufacturing air guns since 1993, when it took over air gun production from Titan Enterprises. Currently imported and distributed by Airhog Inc. located in Dallas, TX. Dealer and consumer direct sales.

Falcon name also used by Beeman for economy-level Spanish air rifles. See Beeman in the "B" section.

PISTOLS

SINGLE SHOT PISTOL MODELS (FN6-PG, FN6-WG, FN8-PG, FN8-WG)
- .177, .20, or .22 cal., PCP, SS, 6 (FN6, disc. 2004) or 8 (FN8) in. Walther rifled barrel, grooved receiver for adj. rear sight or scope, high gloss blue finish, checkered hardwood (PG) or walnut with stippled palm swell (WG) grip, 2.7 lbs., 12-13.5 in. OAL.

MSR $554	$525	$465	$415	$375	$295	N/A	N/A

Add 5% for left-hand variation. Add 10% for open front and adj. rear sights. Add 20% for walnut grip with stippled palm swell (WG).

HAWK PISTOL MODELS (FN6-PGH, FN6-WGH, FN8-PGH, FN8-WGH)
- .177, or .22 cal., PCP, eight-shot mag., 6 (FN6, disc. 2004) or 8 (FN8) in. Walther rifled barrel, grooved receiver for adj. rear sight or scope, high gloss blue finish, checkered hardwood (PGH) or walnut with stippled palm swell (WGH) grip, 2.9 lbs., 12-15 in. OAL.

MSR $650	$625	$550	$495	$425	$375	N/A	N/A

Add 5% for left-hand variation. Add 10% for open front and adj. rear sights. Add 20% for walnut grip with stippled palm swell (WGH).

RAPTOR PISTOL MODELS (FN6-PGR, FN6-WGR, FN8-PGR, FN8-WGR)
- .177, or .22 cal., PCP, similar to Hawk Pistol, eight-shot mag., 6 (FN6, disc. 2004) or 8 (FN8) in. Walther rifled barrel, grooved receiver for adj. rear sight or scope, high gloss blue finish, checkered hardwood (PGR) or walnut with stippled palm swell (WGR) grip, 2.9 lbs., 12-15 in. OAL.

MSR $654	$625	$560	$515	$495	$405	N/A	N/A

Add 5% for left-hand variation. Add 10% for open front and adj. rear sights. Add 20% for walnut grip with stippled palm swell (WGR).

RIFLES

CLASSIC FALCON SINGLE SHOT RIFLE MODELS (FN19-SB, FN19-SW, FN19-TW, FN19-WS, FN19-SL)
- .177, .20, .22, or .25 cal., PCP, SS, 19 in. Walther rifled barrel, grooved receiver for adj. rear sight or scope, high gloss blue finish, checkered beech pistol grip sporter (SB), checkered walnut pistol grip sporter (SW), walnut thumb hole with stippled palm swell and forend (TW), walnut skeleton (WS), or laminate skeleton (SL) stock, ventilated (SB, SW) or adj. (TW, WS, SL) butt pad, 5.8-6.5 lbs., approx. 37.5 in. OAL.

MSR $665	$615	$545	$465	$395	$325	N/A	N/A

Add 5% for left-hand variation. Add 10% for open front and adj. rear sights. Add 15% for walnut sporter stock (SW). Add 25% for walnut thumbhole stock (TW). Add 20% for walnut skeleton stock (WS). Add 30% for laminate skeleton stock (SL).

CLASSIC FALCON SINGLE SHOT CARBINE MODELS (FN12-SB, FN12-SW, FN12-TW, LIGHTHUNTER 12W, LIGHTHUNTER 8W, LIGHTHUNTER 12L, LIGHTHUNTER 8L)
- .177, .20, .22, or .25 cal., PCP, SS, 8 or 12 in. Walther rifled barrel, grooved receiver for adj. rear sight or scope, high gloss blue finish, checkered beech pistol grip sporter (SB), checkered walnut pistol grip sporter (SW), walnut thumb hole with stippled palm swell and forend (TW), walnut skeleton (Lighthunter W), or laminate skeleton (Lighthunter L) stock, ventilated (SB, SW) or adj. (TW, Lighthunter W, Lighthunter L) butt pad, 4.75-5.9 lbs., 26.5-30.5 in. OAL.

MSR $665	$615	$545	$465	$395	$325	N/A	N/A

Add 5% for left-hand variation. Add 10% for open front and adj. rear sights. Add 15% for walnut sporter stock (SW). Add 25% for walnut thumbhole stock (TW). Add 20% for walnut skeleton stock (Lighthunter W). Add 30% for laminate skeleton stock (Lighthunter L).

HAWK RIFLE MODELS (FN19-HB, FN19-HW, FN19-HT, FN19-HS, FN19-HL)
- .177, .20, .22, or .25 cal., PCP, similar to Single Shot Rifle, except has eight-shot mag., 5.8-6.6 lbs., 37.5 in. OAL.

MSR $786	$745	$625	$550	$475	$395	N/A	N/A

Add 5% for left-hand variation. Add 5% for open front and adj. rear sights. Add 10% for walnut sporter stock (HW). Add 20% for walnut thumbhole stock (HW). Add 15% for walnut skeleton stock (HS). Add 25% for laminate skeleton stock (HL).

HAWK CARBINE MODELS (FN12-HB, FN12-HW, FN12-HT, FN12-HS, FN12-HL)
- .177, .20, .22, or .25 cal., PCP, similar to Single Shot Carbine, except has eight-shot mag., 5.5-6.3 lbs., 30.5 in. OAL.

MSR $786	$745	$625	$550	$475	$395	N/A	N/A

Add 5% for left-hand variation. Add 5% for open front and adj. rear sights. Add 10% for walnut sporter stock (HW). Add 20% for walnut thumbhole stock (HW). Add 15% for walnut skeleton stock (HS). Add 25% for laminate skeleton stock (HL).

GRADING	100%	95%	90%	80%	60%	40%	20%

PRAIRIE FALCON MULTI-SHOT CARBINE MODELS (PF18-MB, PF18-MW, PF18-MP) - .177 or .22, cal., PCP, 8 or 16

shot mag., 18 in. Walther rifled barrel, similar to Classic Falcon Model except, larger air cylinder, pressure gauge, quikfill system, and moderator, checkered beech pistol grip sporter (SB), checkered walnut pistol grip sporter (SW), walnut profile thumb hole with checkered palm swell and forend (SP) stock, ventilated butt pad, approx. 37.75 in OAL, approx. 6.1 lbs. Mfg. 2006-current.

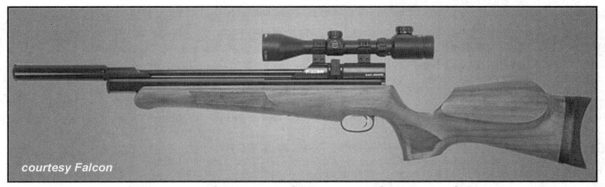

courtesy Falcon

MSR $858	$825	$775	$675	$575	$475	N/A	N/A

Add 20% for walnut sporter stock (SW). Add 35% for walnut profile thumbhole stock (SP).

PRAIRIE FALCON MULTI-SHOT RIFLE MODELS (PF25-MB, PF25-MW, PF25-MP) - .177 or .22, cal., PCP, 8 or 16 shot

mag., 18 in. Walther rifled barrel, similar to Classic Falcon Model except, larger air cylinder, pressure gauge, quikfill system, and moderator, checkered beech pistol grip sporter (SB), checkered walnut pistol grip sporter (SW), walnut profile thumb hole with checkered palm swell and forend (SP) stock, ventilated butt pad, approx. 44.75 in OAL, approx. 6.5 lbs. Mfg. 2006-current.

MSR $880	$845	$795	$695	$595	$495	N/A	N/A

Add 20% for walnut sporter stock (SW). Add 35% for walnut profile thumbhole stock (SP).

PRAIRIE FALCON SINGLE SHOT CARBINE MODELS (PF18-SB, PF18-SW, PF18-SP) - .177 or .22, cal., PCP, SS, 18 in.

Walther rifled barrel, similar to Classic Falcon Model except, larger air cylinder, pressure gauge, quikfill system, and moderator, checkered beech pistol grip sporter (SB), checkered walnut pistol grip sporter (SW), walnut profile thumb hole with checkered palm swell and forend (SP) stock, ventilated butt pad, approx. 37.75 in OAL, approx. 6.25 lbs. Mfg. 2006-current.

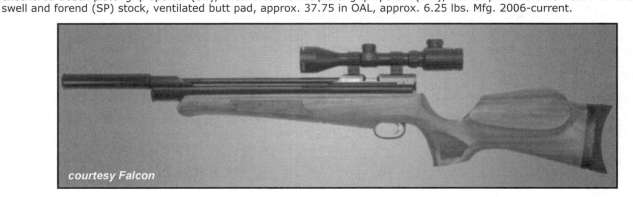

courtesy Falcon

MSR $739	$695	$625	$575	$475	$375	N/A	N/A

Add 20% for walnut sporter stock (SW). Add 35% for walnut profile thumbhole stock (SP).

PRAIRIE FALCON SINGLE SHOT RIFLE MODELS (PF25-SB, PF25-SW, PF25-SP) - .177 or .22, cal., PCP, SS, 25 in.

Walther rifled barrel, similar to Classic Falcon Model except, larger air cylinder, pressure gauge, quikfill system, and moderator, checkered beech pistol grip sporter (SB), checkered walnut pistol grip sporter (SW), walnut profile thumb hole with checkered palm swell and forend (SP) stock, ventilated butt pad, approx. 44.5 in OAL, approx. 6.25 lbs. Mfg. 2006-current.

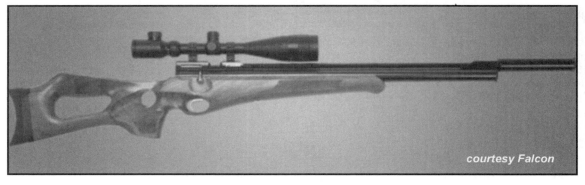

courtesy Falcon

MSR $771	$745	$625	$550	$475	$395	N/A	N/A

Add 20% for walnut sporter stock (SW). Add 35% for walnut profile thumbhole stock (SP).

GRADING	100%	95%	90%	80%	60%	40%	20%

PRAIRIE FALCON B (BULL BARREL) MULTI-SHOT CARBINE MODELS (PF18B-MW,PF18B-MP) - .177 or .22, cal.,
PCP, 8 or 16 shot mag., 18 in. Walther rifled barrel, similar to Prairie Falcon Model except, full shrouded barrel, checkered walnut pistol grip sporter (SW), walnut profile thumb hole with checkered palm swell and forend (SP) stock, ventilated butt pad, approx. 35.5 in OAL, approx. 7.5 lbs. Mfg. 2006-current.

courtesy Falcon

MSR $1,021	$975	$825	$775	$675	$575	N/A	N/A

Add 15% for walnut profile thumbhole stock (SP).

PRAIRIE FALCON B (BULL BARREL) MULTI-SHOT RIFLE MODELS (PF25B-MW,PF25B-MP) - .177 or .22, cal., PCP, 8
or 16 shot mag., 25 in. Walther rifled barrel, similar to Prairie Falcon Model except, full shrouded barrel, checkered walnut pistol grip sporter (SW) or walnut profile thumb hole with checkered palm swell and forend (SP) stock, ventilated butt pad, approx. 42.5 in OAL, approx. 7.75 lbs. Mfg. 2006-current.

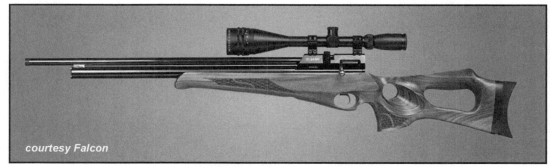

courtesy Falcon

MSR $1,045	$995	$845	$795	$695	$595	N/A	N/A

Add 15% for walnut profile thumbhole stock (SP).

RAPTOR RIFLE MODELS (FN19-RB, FN19-RW, FN19-RT, FN19-RS, FN19-RL) - .177, .20, .22, or .25 cal., PCP, similar to
Hawk Rifle, eight-shot mag., 5.8-6.6 lbs., 37.5 in. OAL.

MSR $806	$785	$695	$595	$495	$395	N/A	N/A

Add 5% for left-hand variation. Add 5% for open front and adj. rear sights. Add 10% for walnut sporter stock (RW). Add 20% for walnut thumbhole stock (RW). Add 15% for walnut skeleton stock (RS). Add 25% for laminate skeleton stock (RL).

RAPTOR CARBINES MODELS (FN12-RB, FN12-RW, FN12-RT, FN12-RS, FN12-RL) - .177, .20, .22, or .25 cal., PCP,
similar to Hawk Carbine, eight-shot mag., 5.5-6.3 lbs., 30.5 in. OAL.

MSR $806	$785	$695	$595	$495	$395	N/A	N/A

Add 5% for left-hand variation. Add 5% for open front and adj. rear sights. Add 10% for walnut sporter stock (RW). Add 20% for walnut thumbhole stock (RW). Add 15% for walnut skeleton stock (RS). Add 25% for laminate skeleton stock (RL).

TARGET RIFLE MODELS (FN19-FSJ, FN19-FSP, FN19-FSPL, FN19-TR, FN19-TRL, FN19-PTB, FN19-PTL) - .177, or,
.22, cal., PCP, SS, 19 in. Walther rifled barrel, grooved receiver for adj. rear sight or scope, high gloss blue finish, beech (FSJ or PTB), walnut (FSP or TR), or laminated (FSPL, TRL, or PTL) target stock with adj. cheek piece and butt pad, adj. match trigger, 6.3-8.7 lbs., 35.5-38 in. OAL.

MSR $819	$795	$705	$605	$505	$405	N/A	N/A

Add5% for left-hand variation. Add5% for open front and adj. rear sights. Add25% for walnut stock Field Star Pro-Target Rifle (FN19-FSP). Add35% for laminated stock Field Star Pro-Target Rifle (FN19-FSPL). Add25% for walnut stock Field Target Rifle (FN19-TR). Add35% for laminated stock Field Target Rifle (FN19-TRL). Add35% for beech stock 10 Meter Target Rifle (FN19-PTB). Add45% for laminated stock 10 Meter Target Rifle (FN19-PTL).

FALKE AIRGUN

Previous manufacturer located in Wennigsen, Germany 1951-1958.

The authors and publisher wish to thank Mr. Trevor Adams for assistance with the following information in this edition of the *Blue Book of Airguns*.

In February 1949, Albert Föhrenbach founded the engineering firm of Falkewerke in Wennigsen near Hanover, Germany. It provided maintenance for conveyer belt machines, a service vital to the industrial recovery of post-WWII Germany. Very soon their conveyer belt expertise was extended to making shooting arcade games. By mid-1951 they started production of a variety of air rifles and one air pistol under the brand of Falke (German for Falcon). The rifles were superior copies of guns made by Dianawerk, Haenel, BSA, and Will. The one air

GRADING	100%	95%	90%	80%	60%	40%	20%

pistol, the Falke 33, apparently was a Falke original. Despite the excellence of Falke products, the firm failed to prosper. The advertising and marketing strengths of larger manufacturers such as Mayer & Grammelspacher, BSA, and Webley prevented Falke from becoming a well-known brand. Financial difficulties led to cessation of production in 1958, and in 1961 Falkewerke went into airgun history. Due to their very limited production run during only seven years and their special quality of manufacture, Falke airguns now are of considerable interest to both collectors and shooters.

The production period of each model isn´t known. An early 1953 catalog describes all models and *Smith´s Encyclopaedia of Air Gas & Spring Guns*, published in 1957, notes the full range of models as available – just one year before the end of production. Special Reference: *John Walter, Guns Review* April 1988.

PISTOLS

MODEL 33 - .177 cal., trigger guard swings forward to cock, SP, rifled barrel, beech grip with Falcon badge on each side, 11.25 in. OAL, 1.75 lbs. Mfg. 1951-58.

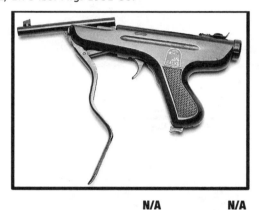 

courtesy Beeman Collection

	100%	95%	90%	80%	60%	40%	20%
	N/A	N/A	$250	$200	$175	$150	$100

RIFLES

MODEL 10 - .177 cal., BBC, SP, tinplate, smoothbore, wood buttstock, 30.5 in. OAL.

	100%	95%	90%	80%	60%	40%	20%
	N/A	N/A	N/A	$60	$50	$40	$30

MODEL 20 - .177 cal., BBC, SP, similar to model 10, except has checkered wood forearm.

	N/A	N/A	N/A	$100	$80	$60	$50

MODEL 30 - .177 cal., BBC, SP, tinplate, smoothbore, 32 in. OAL.

	N/A	N/A	N/A	$70	$60	$50	$40

MODEL 40 - .177 cal., BBC, SP, tinplate, smoothbore, simple post front sight, 35 in. OAL.

	N/A	N/A	N/A	$70	$60	$50	$40

MODEL 50 - similar to Model 40, except has seamless tube steel smooth or rifled barrel, ramp rear and blade front sight, 36 in. OAL.

	N/A	N/A	N/A	$100	$80	$60	$50

MODEL 60 - .177 or .22 cal., BBC, SP, solid steel, rifled, adj. trigger, some mfg. with breech lock, 38 in. OAL.

courtesy Beeman Collection

	N/A	N/A	N/A	$100	$80	$60	$50

MODEL 70 - .177 or .22 cal., BBC, SP, adj. trigger, breech lock device, 42.5 in. OAL, 6.6 lbs.

	N/A	N/A	N/A	$140	$115	$90	$70

This is the most frequently encountered Falke rifle.

MODEL 80 - .177 or .22 cal., UL, SP, auto. opening loading tap, micrometer rear sight, interchangeable insert front sight, elm stock, 44.5 in. OAL, 8.25 lbs. approx. 400 mfg.

	N/A	N/A	N/A	$425	$350	$275	$200

Add 10% for diopter sight.

GRADING	100%	95%	90%	80%	60%	40%	20%

MODEL 90 - .177 or .22 cal., UL, SP, similar to Model 80, except has walnut stock, micrometer and diopter rear and interchangeable insert front sight, sling swivels, 44.5 in. OAL, 9.5 lbs., approx. 200 mfg.

courtesy Howard Collection

	N/A	N/A	N/A	$550	$425	$350	$275

MODEL 100 - .177, .22, or .25 cal., trigger guard cocking gallery gun, blue finish with nickel action, barrel drops for loading, 42 in. OAL, 7 lbs.

	N/A	N/A	N/A	$350	$275	$200	$150

FAMAS

Currently imported by Century International Arms, Inc., located in St. Albans, VT.

RIFLES

FAMAS MODEL - .177 cal., CO_2, semi-auto, copy of French-made MAS .223, used for military training, clip-fed.

No MSR	$395	$350	$285	$195	$125	N/A	N/A

FARCO

Current manufacturer located in the Philippines. Previously imported by ARS located in Pine City, NY. Dealer or consumer direct sales. Ref: AR 2:10.

RIFLES

FARCO FP SURVIVAL - .22 or .25 cal., footpump action multi-pump pneumatic, SS, 22.75 in. barrel, nickel finish, hardwood stock, fixed sights, 5.75 lbs. Disc. 2001.

courtesy Beeman Collection

$260	$220	$175	$125	$85	N/A	N/A

Last MSR was $295.

LONG CYLINDER RIFLE - .22 or .25 cal., CO_2, similar to Short Cylinder Rifle except gas cylinder extends to end of barrel. Approx. 25 mfg. Disc. 2001.

courtesy Beeman Collection

$475	$425	$375	$275	$175	N/A	N/A

Last MSR was $460.

GRADING	100%	95%	90%	80%	60%	40%	20%

FARCO SHORT CYLINDER RIFLE - .22 or .25 cal., CO_2, charged from bulk fill 10 oz. cylinder, stainless steel, adj. rear sight, Monte Carlo hardwood stock, hard rubber buttplate, approx. 7 lbs. Disc. 2001.

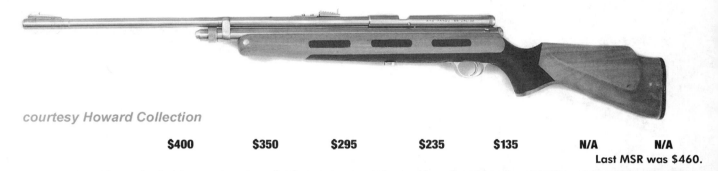

courtesy Howard Collection

	$400	$350	$295	$235	$135	N/A	N/A

Last MSR was $460.

SHOTGUNS

FARCO SHOTGUN - 28 ga., CO_2, 30 in. barrel, charged from bulk fill 10 oz. cylinder, hardwood stock, 7 lbs. Importation 1988-2001.

courtesy Howard Collection

	$400	$350	$295	$235	$135	N/A	N/A

Last MSR was $460.

Add $20 for extra CO_2 cylinder. (Caution, use only recently mfg. stainless steel cylinders!) Add $1 for extra brass shells (12 included with gun).

FEINWERKBAU WESTINGER & ALTENBURGER GmbH

Current manufacturer established circa 1951, and located in Oberndorf, Germany. Currently imported and distributed by Marksman (marked Beeman), located in Huntington Beach, CA, and Brenzovich Firearms & Training Center located in Ft. Hancock, TX, also distributed by Pilkington Competition Equipment LLC located in Monteagle, TN. Dealer and consumer direct sales.

FWB COMPANY OVERVIEW

The authors and publisher wish to thank Mr. Ulrich Eichstädt for his valuable assistance with the following information in this edition of the Blue Book of Airguns.

Feinwerkbau, an airgun industry leader, has been responsible for developing many of the current technical innovations used in fabricating target air pistols and rifles. In 1992, Feinwerkbau swept the Olympic competition. Feinwerkbau guns are prized by both match shooters and those who just enjoy fine guns - especially ones that they can shoot indoors!

"Feinwerkbau" means "fine work factory" and was just a brand name. For many years it was only a prefix to the actual company name (named for its founders): Westinger & Altenburger. Gradually, the word Feinwerkbau (and the abbreviation FWB) came to be an equivalent term for this airgun maker and their products. So, you find this text under "F" instead of "W" in this book.

Although the Westinger & Altenburger company never used big advertising campaigns or sponsored top shooters, their products are on top: the first recoilless match air rifle with a fixed barrel was the Feinwerkbau Model 150. Introduced in 1961, it soon forced the UIT (Union Internationale de Tir, now known as the International Shooting Sports Federation or ISSF) to reduce the size of their targets. This success was repeated in 1965 with the introduction of the FWB model 65 match air pistol. This pistol was in production and pretty much ruled air pistol competition for more than three decades. The Feinwerkbau 600 series have simply owned this title since 1984. The pre-charged successor to the FWB 600 series, the FWB P 70, wins one title after another (including the world record with the maximum score of 600 out of 600 points).

The firm was founded by two engineers, Ernst Altenburger and Karl Westinger. They both worked in the famous Mauser factory in Oberndorf/Neckar, which has been the leading gun manufacturing city in Germany since 1870. After WWII, the factory fell into the French occupation zone. The French authorities ordered the disassembly of all Mauser´s machines. Metal processing was forbidden, and the two engineers desperately sought a new way to use their technical knowledge. In 1948, they were allowed to establish a small workshop in Dettingen. It was not far away, but because the French military authority had poor maps, they did not realize that they had allowed the establishment of a shop across the line in the adjoining Hohenzollern territory, which was not under French control.

With the help of a small punch machine they produced wooden wheels for children´s scooters, wooden casings for pencils, and even wooden spoons. Stealthily, in the attic of what is now Oberndorf College, they designed their first prototype of an electro-mechanical calculator. In 1948, after the Allies again allowed metal processing companies in that region, Feinwerkbau Westinger & Altenburger became a registered company. Their new calculator went into production at the Olympia-Werke in Wilhelmshaven, Germany. Thousands of their machines were sold internationally. Later they produced textile mandrels, counters, and, for IBM, a small device to cut letters out of paper punchcards. Today, a part of the company manufactures vital, but undisclosed, parts for "Formula-One" race cars.

The Feinwerkbau Westinger & Altenburger factory is still located in Oberndorf at the headwaters of the Neckar River in Germany´s Black Forest, and has about two hundred employees. The company is managed by two sons of the founders: Jörg Altenburger and Rolf Westinger, while two other sons, Reiner Altenburger and Gerhard Westinger, respectively, oversee the sales and purchasing departments. Note: Do not depend on dates in importer catalogs for model production dates.

FWB HISTORY 1951-1979

In 1951, the German Shooting Federation was re-established. Starting in 1952, the production of rifled barrels was again allowed. The 1950s was the decade of the Carl Walther Company in Ulm. Their barrel-cocking air rifles Model 53 and, later, Model 55, were used by almost every competitive European air rifle shooter. However, many of the top marksmen believed that wear at the hinge point in these barrel-cocking guns caused reduced accuracy.

In 1961, Walter Gehmann, one of the top marksmen in Germany before WWII and also a famous inventor, came to visit his old friend Ernst Altenburger, with whom he had worked in the legendary Mauser R & D department. (Together they had invented the Mauser "Olympia" smallbore rifle, which was the predecessor of all modern .22 match rifles.) Soon the company started to design air rifles with the barrel rigidly fixed to the receiver.

Anschütz also presented a fixed barrel air rifle, their side-lever Model 220. Feinwerkbau replied with their Model 100. It was immediately successful. Helmut Schlenker, the reigning German shooting champion, took the German championship with this gun in 1961 - this is especially significant because that was the year of the German Shooting Federation´s centennial.

Feinwerkbau exceeded that success with the Model 150. This gun featured an elegantly simple, very effective recoil-elimination device which made Feinwerkbau rifles almost unbeatable during the next decade: When the trigger was released, the entire rigid, upper action and barrel was released to ride on concealed steel rails and thus absorb the recoil. The basic mechanism was based on a recoil control mechanism that Westinger and Altenburger had developed, when working for Mauser, for controlling machine gun recoil. All the succeeding FWB spring-piston match airguns used this mechanism. It was covered by patent 1,140 489, awarded in February of 1961 to Westinger and Altenburger and their chief engineer, Edwin Wöhrstein. Walter Gehmann was honored for his input with a gift of the Model 150 with serial number "000001."

The 1966 World Shooting Championship in Wiesbaden, Germany was a turning point for air rifle shooting. Here the world was introduced to precision match air rifles. While the first world championship was won by Gerd Kuemmet with a non-production, prototype Anschütz Model 250, Feinwerkbau would come into its glory with world championships by Gottfried Kustermann (1970), Oswald Schlipf (1978), Walter Hillenbrand (1979), Hans Riederer (1986 and 1990), and Sonja Pfeilschifter (1994).

Feinwerkbau extended their very successful recoilless sledge mechanism to an air pistol in 1965; the FWB Model LP 65. It had special arrangements to block the recoil compensating mechanism and to switch the trigger pull from 500 to 1360 grams. This allowed this air pistol to be used for simulated firearm pistol training. It was produced in several minor variations until 1998. Although other models, such as the LP 80 and the LP 90 (the first air pistol with an electronic trigger), were introduced during that period, the Model 65 reigned supreme. Air pistol shooting became an official international sport in 1969 and Feinwerkbau had come to virtually "own" that field of competition. Model 65 air pistols also had become very popular with non-match shooters, especially in the USA.

FWB HISTORY 1980 CURRENT

At the beginning of the 1980s, two Austrian technicians, Emil Senfter and Viktor Idl revived the century-old French patent by Paul Giffard for a CO_2 pistol with a tubular gas tank under the barrel. The first "Senfter" pistols were very successful in competition and could be shot like a free pistol. Their advantage over the spring-piston air pistols was a lack of movement from a piston during firing and a quicker shot release. When Senfter and Idl parted company, Senfter offered the system to Walther and Idl went to Feinwerkbau. As a result, the first two CO_2 pistols of both companies, the Walther CP 1 and FWB Model 2, respectively, appear to be almost identical. (Some years later a lawsuit awarded the patent and system to Senfter.)

Feinwerkbau took an excursion into producing sporting air rifles in the early 1970s. This was the "Sport" series under the model numbers 120 to 127. These were slim, highly efficient barrel-cocking, spring-piston air rifles. The primary market was the United States where the high power versions were known the Model 124 in 4.5 mm (.177) caliber and the much less popular Model 127 in 5.5 m (.22) caliber. A lower powered version of the 5.5mm caliber model was fairly popular in Great Britain. Limited numbers of the lowest powered version, the Model 121, were made for countries like Germany where there were very strict airgun power limits. Feinwerkbau began a joint effort with Beeman Precision Airguns to develop a 5mm version, with a special stock to Beeman specifications, to be known as the Beeman R5. Regular production was not possible because Feinwerkbau was not able to find suitable 5 mm barrels in the numbers projected for first sales. The Model R5 is now one of the rarest of collectors´ items. Production of the Sport series was halted in the 1980s because Feinwerkbau´s technicians were so tuned to produce limited quantities of match guns with extremely close fitting and quality control that they could not seem to produce such production level items at reasonable cost! Now much sought after by both shooters and collectors, its slender profile and trigger placement make it a favorite for restocking with premium quality custom stocks.

In the USA, Beeman Precision Airguns, Feinwerkbau´s American partner, had taken an unusual step. They created a larger market for match air rifles among America´s quality conscious non-match gun buyers than had existed for America´s much lower concentration of match shooters. So, in America, the sales of FWB match guns continued to exceed those of all other match airguns combined.

In 1973, Walther introduced a new type of recoilless air rifle, the Walther LGR, a single-stroke pneumatic. It had a shorter shot release time than the spring-piston air rifles and was soon adopted, at least in Europe, by most of the top competitive air rifle shooters.

In 1984, Feinwerkbau struck back, from its factory deep in the German Black Forest, with their own single stroke pneumatic rifle, the FWB 600 (named after the 600-point maximum possible score in the new 60-shot international competitions). This rifle featured a reverse cocking lever which closed towards the body, a much easier motion, and had a shorter barrel of only 420mm (16.5 in.), which reduced the shot release time even more. Feinwerkbau again dominated the world of match air rifles. Scores of 600 became so common that the international shooting authorities again had to reduce the size of the ten ring, from one to one/half millimeter (2/100") diameter! However, the FWB 600 shooters soon began to crowd even that incredibly small bullseye with all of their shots. The models FWB 601, 602, and 603, introduced during the 1990s, were only slight modifications of FWB´s basic single-stroke pneumatic system.

In air pistol competitions, only a few shooters preferred pneumatic pistols instead of CO_2 models (and later PCP), but the air rifle shooters were more reluctant in choosing the easy-to-shoot carbon dioxide systems: They didn´t want to rely on uncertain CO_2 supplies during competitions in foreign countries and therefore had to tolerate the heavier cocking effort of the single-stroke pneumatic rifles.

That changed again in 1997, when the key manufacturers of precision airguns introduced their pre-charged pneumatic (PCP) match air rifles. These guns did not depend on local supplies of CO_2 and did not have the physical limitations of CO_2 guns. They simply were charged from

GRADING	100%	95%	90%	80%	60%	40%	20%

easily portable tanks of compressed air. Despite the keen competition of Anschütz, Walther, Steyr-Mannlicher, and Hämmerli, the FWB Model P70 PCP match air rifle has maintained the lead in air rifle competition. Using the FWB P70, Gaby Bühlmann from Switzerland fired the first ever maximum of 400, followed by the first 600 score by Tavarit Majchacheep from Thailand.

Today´s leading airguns are the Feinwerkbau P34 PCP air pistol and the Model 603 single-stroke pneumatic and P70 PCP air rifles. These models use a special "Absorber" feature which reduces even the tiny recoil produced by the pellet itself during its acceleration. A five-shot version of the PCP air pistol, known as the P55, was developed for the new ISSF "Falling Targets" event. And, a five-shot PCP rifle, the Model P75, is used in the summer biathlon competitions. Several smaller and lighter versions of these models are designed for young shooters and smaller adults.

Feinwerkbau now also produces some very successful match firearms: The FWB smallbore rifle earned the Olympic gold medal in 1992, the FWB semi-auto .22 caliber pistol, and the AW 93 (based on a Russian patent).

PISTOLS

MODEL 2 - .177 cal., CO_2, 425-525 FPS, adj. trigger, adj. sights, UIT target model, 2.5 lbs. Disc. 1989.

courtesy Beeman Collection

	$650	$550	$450	$350	N/A	N/A	N/A

Last MSR was $780.

Add $50 for mini. Subtract $50 for left-hand version.
Feinwerkbau manufactured three helical barrel (twisted around gas cylinder), and yes, it shoots accurately.

MODEL C5 - .177 cal., CO_2, five-shot, 7.33 in. barrel, 510 FPS, 2.4 lbs. Disc. approx. 1993.

	$650	$500	$400	$300	N/A	N/A	N/A

Last MSR was $1,350.

Subtract 7% for left-hand variation.

MODEL C10 - .177 cal., CO_2, 510 FPS, adj. trigger, adj. sights, UIT target model, 2.5 lbs. Disc. 1990.

courtesy Beeman Collection

	$600	$500	$450	$400	N/A	N/A	N/A

Last MSR was $965.

Subtract 5% for left-hand model.

MODEL C20 - .177 cal., CO_2, 510 FPS, adj. trigger, adj. sights, UIT target model, 2.5 lbs. Mfg. 1991-95.

	$695	$650	$600	$550	$475	N/A	N/A

Last MSR was $1,160.

Subtract 10% for left-hand model.
This model was intended as a replacement for the Model C2 and the Model C10.

MODEL C25 - .177 cal., CO_2, 510 FPS, CO_2 flask placed directly below action, adj. trigger, adj. sights, UIT target model, 2.5 lbs.

	$650	$500	$400	$300	N/A	N/A	N/A

Last MSR was $1,325.

Subtract 10% for left-hand model.

GRADING	100%	95%	90%	80%	60%	40%	20%

MODEL C55 - .177 cal., CO_2, SS or five-shot, 510 FPS, CO_2 flask placed directly below action for vertical CO_2 feed, up to 225 shots/fill, 2.5 lbs. Mfg. 1994-2001.

	$800	$750	$700	$675	N/A	N/A	N/A

Last MSR was $1,460.

Subtract 10% for left-hand model.

☼ *Model C55P* - .177 cal., compressed air, five-shot, 8.75 in. barrel, 510 FPS, adj. rear and interchangeable front sights, adj. trigger, swiveling anatomical grip, compressed air cylinder is fitted with integrated manometer, 2.4 lbs. Mfg.2001-04.

	$1,425	$1,300	$1,100	$900	$700	N/A	N/A

Last MSR was $1,570.

Subtract 5% for left-hand model.

MODEL P30 - .177 cal., PCP, 515 FPS, adj. match trigger, adj. sights, UIT target model, stippled walnut match grip, 2.4 lbs. Disc.

	$1,095	$1,000	$900	$800	$695	N/A	N/A

Last MSR was $1,275.

Subtract 10% for left-hand model.

MODEL P34 - .177 cal., PCP, 515 FPS, adj. match trigger, adj. sights, UIT target model, 7.2 and 9.2 in. (standard) barrel, blue or red air cylinder, stippled walnut match grip, revised version of the P30 with contoured barrel shroud, sliding barrel weight system, valve housing reduced in size, and removable trigger guard, 2.4 lbs. Mfg. 1999-2004.

courtesy Beeman Collection

	$1,000	$900	$800	$750	N/A	N/A	N/A

Last MSR was $1,640.

Add 5% for left-hand model. Add 10% for Morini walnut grip and interchangeable trigger unit.

MODEL P40 - .177 cal., PCP, 515 FPS, adj. match trigger, adj. sights, UIT target model,5.9 in. barrel,two air cylinders with integrated manometer, fully adj. multi-color Morini laminated grip,sliding barrel weight system,16.1 in. OAL, 2.5 lbs., cased. Mfg. 2004-07.

	$1,550	$1,350	$1,050	$750	$550	N/A	N/A

Last MSR was $1,574.

Add 5% for left-hand model.

☼ *Model P40 Basic* - .177 cal., PCP, similar to Model P40 except hasanatomical adj. Morini walnut grip, no weight system, 16.1 in. OAL, 2.3 lbs. Mfg. 2004-07.

	$1,300	$1,100	$900	$700	$495	N/A	N/A

Last MSR was $1,314.

Add 5% for left-hand model.

MODEL P44 - .177 cal., PCP, 515 FPS, adj. match trigger, adj. sights, UIT target model,5.9 in. barrel,two air cylinders with integrated manometer, fully adj. multi-color Morini laminated grip,sliding barrel weight system,16.1 in. OAL, 2.5 lbs., cased. Mfg. 2008- current.

MSR $1,476	$1,450	$1,350	$1,050	$750	$550	N/A	N/A

Last MSR was $1,574.

Add 5% for left-hand model.

MODEL P56 - .177 cal., compressed air, five-shot, 8.75 in. barrel, 510 FPS, adj. rear and interchangeable front sights, adj. trigger, swiveling anatomical grip, compressed air cylinder is fitted with integrated manometer, 2.4 lbs. New 2006.

MSR $1,890	$1,825	$1,600	$1,300	$900	$700	N/A	N/A

Last MSR was $1,570.

Subtract 5% for left-hand model.

MODEL 65 MK I AND II - .177 cal., SL, SP, 525 FPS, recoil compensating mechanism may be locked, adj. trigger pull may be instantly switched from 500 to 1360 grams, adj. sights, UIT target model, 2.6-2.9 lbs., MKII Model has shorter barrel. M-65 MK I. Approx. 145,000 mfg. 1965-1998.

	$695	$650	$600	$550	$475	N/A	N/A

Last MSR was $1,070.

Subtract 10% for left-hand model. Add 7% for adj. grips.

GRADING	100%	95%	90%	80%	60%	40%	20%

MODEL 80 - .177 cal., SL, SP, 475-525 FPS, similar to Model 65, except has stacking barrel weights and fine mechanical trigger, adj. sights, UIT target model, 2.8-3.2 lbs. Approx. 48,000 mfg. 1977-1983.

	100%	95%	90%	80%	60%	40%	20%
	$695	$650	$600	$550	$475	N/A	N/A

Last MSR was $625.

Add 100% for factory gold plating.

MODEL 90 - similar to Model 80, except has electronic trigger. Approx. 20,000 mfg. 1982-1992.

	$695	$650	$600	$550	$475	N/A	N/A

Last MSR was $1,155.

Add 5% for short barrel. Subtract 10% for left-hand model.

MODEL 100 - .177 cal., pneumatic action, adj. trigger, adj. sights, UIT target model, 460 FPS, 2.5 lbs. Disc. 1992.

	$695	$650	$600	$550	$475	N/A	N/A

Last MSR was $1,100.

Subtract 10% for left-hand variation.

MODEL 102 - similar to Model 100, except has two cocking levers. Mfg. 1992.

	$1,095	$1,000	$900	$800	$695	N/A	N/A

Last MSR was $1,555.

Subtract 10% for left-hand variation.

MODEL 103 - .177 cal., detachable UL, pneumatic, 6.38 in. BBL, 475/508 FPS, adj. trigger, adj. sights, adj. Morini grip (new 2005), 10.5 in. OAL, 3 lbs.

courtesy Beeman Collection

MSR $1,555	$1,550	$1,350	$1,050	$750	$550	N/A	N/A

Add 5% for left-hand variation.

RIFLES

MODEL 110 - .177 cal., SP, SL, SS, similar to Model 150 but no recoil-compensating mechanism, less than 200 made March 1962-March 1964. Extremely rare, esp. in good condition.

	$1,800	$1,400	$1,000	$800	$600	N/A	N/A

Most existing specimens heavily used by individuals or shooting club members.

MODEL 121 - .177 or .22 cal., basic European low power version of the Models 124 and 127, 465 mm barrel, plain beechwood stock without buttplate or high comb. 7.2 lbs.

courtesy Beeman Collection

	$350	$295	$250	$195	$150	N/A	N/A

Add 30% for Deluxe version with checkered beechwood stock, buttplate, high comb.
This low-velocity model was not distributed in the USA.

GRADING	100%	95%	90%	80%	60%	40%	20%

MODEL 124 - .177 cal., BBC, SP, 780-830 FPS, early version w/ plastic trigger, rear sight marked 50m, 7.2 lbs. Disc. 1989. Ref: AR3: 61-62.

courtesy Beeman Collection

	$495	$450	$395	$295	$195	N/A	N/A

Last MSR was $490.

Add15% for deluxe.Add 5% for San Rafael address. Add 40% for factory deluxe with walnut stock. Add 10% for left-hand deluxe-version (rare). Add 100% for custom select. Add 100% for custom fancy. Add 110% for custom extra fancy. Deduct 10% for no Wundhammer palm swell on Deluxe models.

MODEL 127 - .22 cal., BBC, SP, 620-680 FPS, rear sight marked 40m, 6 lbs./7 lbs. 1 oz. Disc. 1989.

	$495	$450	$395	$295	$195	N/A	N/A

Last MSR was $490.

Add 15% for deluxe version. Add 35% for factory deluxe with walnut stock. Add 10% for left-hand deluxe variation (rare). Add100% for custom select. Add 100% for custom fancy. Add 120% for custom extra fancy.

MODEL 150 - .177 cal., SL, SP, first FWB airgun with the patented recoil-compensation sledge system, 20 in. (510 mm) barrel, 450FPS. Mfg. 1961-68.

	$800	$600	$500	$475	$300	N/A	N/A

Add 60% for Tyrolean stock.
   Most existing specimens heavily used by individuals or shooting club members.

MODEL 200 - similar to Model 300 but without recoil-compensation mechanism.
   Current values not yet determined.

MODEL 300 - .177 cal., SP long SL, recoil-compensation system, 460 FPS, rubber buttplate, rounded forearm, match aperture sight. Disc. 1972.

	$650	$600	$500	$400	$250	N/A	N/A

⊙ *Model 300S* - .177 cal., SP, SL, 640 FPS, 8.8/10.8 lbs. Disc. circa 1996.

courtesy Beeman Collection

	N/A	$650	$550	$450	$350	N/A	N/A

Last MSR was $1,235.

Add 50% for Tyrolean stock. Add 10% for Running Boar stock configuration or Universal Model w/ adj. cheek piece. Add 20% for Match L Model, similar to Universal Model w/o adj. cheek piece. Add 10% for figured walnut. Subtract 10% for left-hand variation (all styles). Add 10% for junior stock.

MODEL 600 - .177 cal., SL, SSP, recoilless top-of-the-line match rifle with aperture sights, unique hardwood laminate stock, 585 FPS, 10.5 lbs. Disc. 1988.

	$800	$600	$500	$450	$300	N/A	N/A

Last MSR was $900.

Subtract 10% for left-hand variation.
   This model was also available in a Running Boar variation with an extra-long barrel cover that unscrewed for transporting.

MODEL 601 - .177 cal., SL, SSP, 10.5 lbs.

	$850	$750	$650	$600	$400	N/A	N/A

Last MSR was $1,750.

Add 5% for 5454 diopter sight. Subtract 10% for left-hand variation.
   This model replaced the Model 600, and a Running Target Model was also available (add 25%).

GRADING	100%	95%	90%	80%	60%	40%	20%

MODEL 602 - .177 cal., SL, SSP.

	100%	95%	90%	80%	60%	40%	20%
	$900	$800	$700	$650	$450	N/A	N/A

Last MSR was $1,875.

Subtract 10% for left-hand variation.
This model replaced the Model 601.

MODEL 603/603 JUNIOR - .177 cal., SL, SSP, recoilless top-of-the-line match rifle with aperture sights, unique hardwood laminate stock, 570 FPS, 43 in. OAL,10. lbs.

courtesy Beeman Collection

MSR $2,445	$2,150	$1,500	$1,300	$900	$795	N/A	N/A

Add 5% for left-hand variation. Add 10% for multicolored laminated stock. Add 15% for left-hand multicolored laminated stock. Subtract 20% for FWB 603 Junior.
This model replaced the Model 602.

MODEL C60 - .177 cal., CO$_2$, 570 FPS, similar to Model 600, 9.2-10.6 lbs.

	100%	95%	90%	80%	60%	40%	20%
	$600	$525	$475	$375	NA	N/A	N/A

Last MSR was $1,675.

A Running Target Model was also available.

MODEL C60 MINI - .177 cal., CO$_2$, quick change cylinder (bottle), mini version of C60 Match Rifle, 7.75 lbs. Mfg. beginning in 1991. Disc.

	100%	95%	90%	80%	60%	40%	20%
	$650	$550	$475	$375	N/A	N/A	N/A

Last MSR was $1,675.

MODEL C62 - .177 cal., CO$_2$, similar to Model C60.

	100%	95%	90%	80%	60%	40%	20%
	$650	$550	$475	$375	N/A	N/A	N/A

Last MSR was $1,750.

MODEL P70 - .177 cal., PCP, lever cocking, match model, 17 in. barrel, adj. trigger, 570 FPS, laminated wood or multicolor stock with fully adj. cheekpiece and buttplate, 10.6 lbs. New 1998.

courtesy Beeman Collection

MSR $2,060	$1,850	$1,650	$1,250	N/A	N/A	N/A	N/A

Add 5% for left-hand variation. Add 10% for multicolored stock. Add 45% for right-hand P70 variation with aluminum stock (Field Target). Add 50% for left-hand P70 variation with aluminum stock. Subtract 10% for right-hand Running Target model with laminated wood stock. Add 1% for left-hand Running Target model with laminated wood stock.

✿ *Model P70 Junior* - .177 cal., similar to Model P70, except has youth dimensions. Mfg. 1998-2006.

	100%	95%	90%	80%	60%	40%	20%
	$1,150	$1,000	$895	$750	$650	N/A	N/A

Last MSR was $1,595.

GRADING	100%	95%	90%	80%	60%	40%	20%

MODEL P75 BIATHLON - .177 cal., PCP, five-shot mag., match model, 17 in. barrel, repeat lever trigger system cocks trigger and transports magazine simultaneously, 570 FPS, laminated wood stock with fully adj. cheekpiece and buttplate. New 2000.

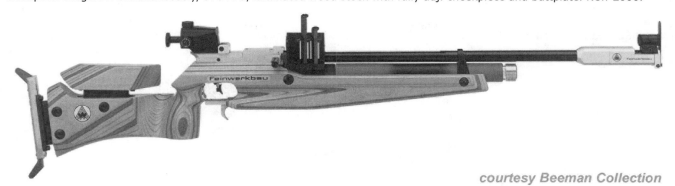

courtesy Beeman Collection

MSR $2,623	$2,575	$2,295	$2,000	$1,595	$1,195	N/A	N/A

MODEL P700 ALUMINUM - .177 cal., PCP, SS, match model, 10.8 in. barrel, interior vibration absorber, 570 FPS, aluminum stock with fully adj. cheekpiece, grip, and buttplate, adj. match trigger, 43.3-46.25 in. OAL, 10.8 lbs. New 2004.

MSR $2,480	$2,350	$2,195	$1,850	$1,550	$1,250	N/A	N/A

✪ *Model 700 Aluminum Junior* - .177 cal., PCP, SS, match model, 10.8 in. barrel, interior vibration absorber, 570 FPS, aluminum stock with fully adj. cheekpiece, grip, and buttplate, adj. match trigger, 39.4-43.3 in. OAL, 9.7 lbs. New 2004.

MSR $2,385	$2,250	$2,095	$1,750	$1,450	$1,150	N/A	N/A

MODEL P700 UNIVERSAL - .177 cal., PCP, SS, match model, 10.8 in. barrel, interior vibration absorber, 570 FPS, laminated wood stock with fully adj. cheekpiece, grip, and buttplate, adj. match trigger, 43.7 in. OAL, 9.9 lbs. New 2004.

MSR $2,065	$1,850	$1,650	$1,350	$1,150	$950	N/A	N/A

✪ *Model 700 Junior* - .177 cal., PCP, SS, match model, 10.8 in. barrel, interior vibration absorber, 570 FPS, laminated wood stock with fully adj. cheekpiece, grip, and buttplate, adj. match trigger, 39.4-43.3 in. OAL, 7.5 lbs. New 2004.

MSR $1,840	$1,695	$1,495	$1,250	$1,050	$750	N/A	N/A

FELTMAN PRODUCTS

Previous manufacturer of arcade and military training air machine guns. Founded by Chas. Feltman in Coney Island, N.Y. in 1939. Sold to Wm. Meinch in early 1960s - for a short time Meinch added his name to the Feltman nameplates. Moved to Scotch Pines, N.J. in 1978 and then to Center Moriches, N.Y. in 1986. Sold to Vintage Pneumatics in Sheboygan, WI in 1994 and then to Air Force Airguns in Fort Worth, Texas in 2003- where the last 50 Vintage Starfire guns were sold.

Fred Andreae Jr., former factory head of Feltmans, opened Shooting Star Inc. in N.J. in 1986 to make high quality near-clones of the original Feltman Tommyguns (NOT available to collectors) under the Shooting Star brand and to repair the originals. Ref. Behling (2006).

MILITARY TRAINERS AND GALLERY AUTOMATICS

FELTMAN "CONEY ISLAND" PNEUMATIC MACHINE GUN Feltman's first product. .174 in. cal. steel BBs. Hose pneumatic, 110 AC, full auto 600 rpm @ 300 fps, 200 shot convoluted tubular magazine. Very similar appearance to Browning Water-Cooled Machine Gun. "Water Jacket" painted orange, receiver painted blue-black or blue. Very sturdy, heavy construction of cast aluminum, steel, copper, and brass. Heavy metal spade handles and massive swiveling tripod. Patent 2,238,384 issued June 1, 1939, improved w/ Patent 2,312,244 issued April 15, 1941. Used at Coney Island Amusement Park in N.Y. and 1939 World's Fair in San Francisco. 22 in smoothbore bbl, 35 in. OAL, 24 lbs. Highest known SN is 97; 10 specimens known.

courtesy Beeman Collection

N/A	N/A	$3,500	$2,750	$2,000	$1,250	$750

Add 20% for original tripod. Add 5% for use counter in window under "water jacket" barrel shroud.

GRADING		100%	95%	90%	80%	60%	40%	20%

FELTMAN "AIR-COOLED" PNEUMATIC MACHINE GUN

.160 in. cal. (No. 1 lead shot), full auto 1200 rpm @ 280 fps, (Feltman Second Model) 101 shot convoluted tubular magazine. Hose pneumatic. Very similar appearance to Browning Air-Cooled .30 cal. Machine Gun. Metal spade grips, ball-bearing 2 axis mount. Ring rear sight w/ cross-wires, front post. Same int. mechanism as Feltman Tommygun. About 1945-50s.

⊙ *Feltman Second Model First Variation* Welded steel plate receiver, 21 in smoothbore bbl, 38.8 in OAL, 16.1 lbs. 5 known.

courtesy Beeman Collection

		N/A	N/A	$3,500	$2,750	$2,000	$1,250	$750

⊙ *Feltman Second Model Second Variation* Cast aluminum receiver. 20 in. smoothbore bbl., 37.1 in. OAL, 14.9 lbs. 1 specimen known.

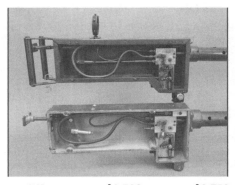

courtesy Beeman Collection

		N/A	N/A	$3,500	$2,750	$2,000	$1,250	$750

Subtract 10% for missing mount.

FELTMAN "TOMMYGUN" PNEUMATIC MACHINE GUN

.160 in. cal. (No. 1 lead shot). Hose pneumatic, full auto 1200 rpm @ 280 fps, 101 shot convoluted tubular magazine. Very similar appearance to Thompson Sub-Machine Gun w/ double grip handles, distinctive buttstock. Walnut grip plates and stock. The infamous "Shoot Out the Star" target, designed by Wm. Meinch, was all the harder to shoot out because some operators reused the lead shot! Point of impact adj. internally by moving the bbl. 12 in smoothbore bbl., 35.5 in OAL, 6.4 lbs. 5700 manf. 1941-1994.

		N/A	N/A	$750	$600	$450	$350	$250

SHOOTING STAR COMMERCIAL GALLERY MACHINE GUNS

Excellent current copies of Feltman Tommyguns sold by unrelated Shooting Star Inc. (See Feltman introduction) in kits of 2-6 guns for amusement parks only - so all are used. Regular Shooting Star (800+ made as of Jan. 2006) and Shooting Star Combat (3000+ made as of Jan. 2006) - both sell used for about $750 per gun. Ref. Behling (2006).

VINTAGE PNEUMATICS STARFIRE

.160 in. cal. (No. 1 lead shot). Hose pneumatic, 125 psi, full auto 800 rpm @ 280 fps, 113 shot loading tube. Basically a very high quality copy of the Feltman Tommygun. 12 in smoothbore bbl, 36 in. OAL, 6 lbs. 1994-2003.

courtesy Beeman Collection

		N/A	N/A	$850	$750	$600	$450	$350

Add 30% for deluxe kit set from Air Force Airguns.

MSR $575 (1995) w/ 5 loading tubes, glasses, 25 Starfire targets, oil, rod. Production under 200, last 50 sold by Air Force Airguns in deluxe kits for $1000 each w/ above items plus 25 lbs. #1 shot and a walnut display plaque made by Tom Gaylord. 2003 only.

GRADING	100%	95%	90%	80%	60%	40%	20%

FIONDA

Trademark of previous line of CO_2 guns from Ind. Brasileira of Brazil. Production closed about 1990 due to governmental suppression of civilian arms.

RIFLES

FIONDA MODEL 63 .177 in. balls, CO_2 filled from bulk tank, semi-automatic, began in Europe as the Italian ArmiGas Olimpic or the Austrian Tyrol C-O-Matic CO_2 rifle, then copied as the Venturini Golondrina C-O-Matic rifle and pistol in Argentina. Key feature is the removeable, spring-fed 80 shot 21.3 in. tubular magazine along the RHS of barrel. Marked LHS: MOD. 63, PAT. PROV. NO. 129,028. RHS: FIONDA, IND. BRASILEIRA. One pc. hardwood buttstock and forearm. Cross bolt manual safety. Metal black or black and silver. 22.2 rifled barrel, 39.4 in. OAL, 4.5 lbs. Now rare in Brazil due to ban by Brazilian government; only a few outside of Brazil.

courtesy Beeman Collection

	$750	$650	$500	$450	$400	N/A	N/A

Add 10% for original bulk fill CO_2 tank.

FIRE BALL (FIREBALL)

For information on Fire Ball (Fireball) airguns, see Apache in the "A" section.

FIREFLY

For information on Firefly air pistols, see Anson, E. & Co. in the "A" section.

FLÜRSCHEIM

For information on Flürscheim, see Gaggenau.

FOOTE, H.S.

Previous manufacturer of unknown location, probably U.S.A. 1904.

PISTOL

TROMBONE PISTOL .21 in. cal., SS, SP., 6 in. cocked by using two fingers of off hand on lateral prongs to pull cocking tube back, brass cover slides open to breech load thin, brass, smoothbore 6 in. barrel, brass frame and receiver, walnut inset grips. Marked on top of receiver: H.S. FOOTE, MAKER, 1904. 14.3 in OAL, 1.4 lbs.

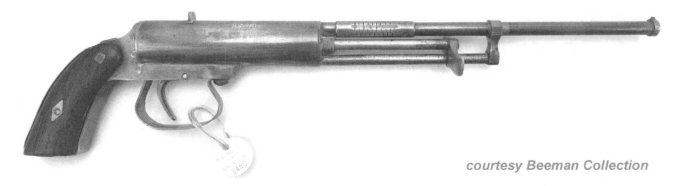

courtesy Beeman Collection

Rarity precludes accurate pricing.

NOTES

G SECTION

GAGGENAU IRONWORKS (EISENWERKE GAGGENAU)

Previous airgun manufacturer located in Gaggenau, Germany circa 1879-1900. (See also Dianawerk, Gem, Haviland & Gunn and Lincoln sections in this text.)

The authors and publisher wish to thank Mr. Ulrich Eichstädt for much of the following information in this edition of the *Blue Book of Airguns*. The Gaggenau Ironworks (Eisenwerke Gaggenau) was noted as a "very old company" in a letter dated 1680. Gaggenau is a small town near Rastatt in the middle of the German Black Forest, an area traditionally famous for gunmaking (Feinwerkbau, Dianawerk, Heckler & Koch, and Mauser). The ironworks were not very successful during the 17th century. Although they had cheap power from the nearby Murg-creek, the distance to iron ore forced them to use scrap metal as raw material. Their fortunes were changed in the mid-1800s with the addition of a new casting furnace and especially by their connection, via the Murgtal railroad, to Rastatt and the modern rail system spreading across Europe. By the end of the century, they were producing structural steel, bridges, railings, gas regulators, crushing and paint mills, enamel advertising signs, and bicycles. In 1873, Michael Flürscheim (1844-1912) purchased the works with its forty workers. Flürscheim added a joiners' shop, a tool shop, metal-plating equipment, and a wood processing division to produce rifle stocks. The staff grew to 390 in 1882 and 1041 in 1889.

Theodor Bergmann (later famous with Louis Schmeisser as a designer of self-loading cartridge pistols) joined Flürscheim as managing partner in 1879. One year earlier Flürscheim had been granted a patent for an air pistol, and in 1879, he patented two air pistol improvements. Thus, the company's first air pistol, sometimes known as the Bergmann Air Pistol is more properly the Flürscheim air pistol. The Flürscheim air pistol may be Germany's oldest production air pistol. Actually, this pistol, right down to the detail of its disassembly/cocking tool, seems to be a clear copy of the Haviland and Gunn pistol patented in the USA in 1872. At that time, companies outside of the USA were more interested in local monopoly than they were worried about overseas lawsuits.

Jakob Mayer worked in the Gaggenau Ironworks before he founded Dianawerk in nearby Rastatt in 1890. It comes as no surprise that he used the same basic design for his first MGR air pistol (see Dianawerk section). Around 1905, the same design again appeared in Belgium, marked "Brevet" (French for Patent!). Possibly the same unknown maker also made the virtually identical "Dare Devil Dinkum" air pistol which later appeared on the British market based on George Gunn's 1872 invention in far-off Ilion, New York. As noted in the Lincoln section of this book, the same design led to the Lincoln air pistols and the famous Walther LP 53.

By 1891, the "gun division" in Gaggenau produced hunting and military rifles, air rifles and air pistols, gun barrels, reloading tools, and clay-target traps. Production of airguns had become significant, especially of Gem-style air rifles. Pellets and darts were made by automatic machines at about 20,000 pellets per hour.

From 1885 to 1898, the official brand of Gaggenau was two crossed Flürscheim air pistols, usually with the letter "E" above and "G" below. Apparently, many guns made by Gaggenau were not marked, probably so that they could be sold under other trade names.

Two other Flürscheim patents for airguns are known: Patent no. 399962 covers a combination air rifle/.22 firearm apparently derived from George Gunn's combination airgun/rimfire rifle or its derivatives, the Quackenbush Model 5 and Gem air rifles. The second patent, no. 42091 from June 5, 1887, covers a repeating air rifle with a spring-fed magazine for pointed pellets.

Production of Gaggenau airguns apparently ceased about 1900. (However, some airguns bearing the Bergmann name or Th.B. may date from 1880 to as late as 1920.) Today the Gaggenau company is one of the largest manufacturers of built-in kitchen appliances in Germany and sells to fifty countries on all five continents. The former question as to whether the company should be called Eisenwerke, which simply means Iron Works in German (no more descriptive than Manufacturing Works or just Factory), or Gaggenau, has been resolved by the company which calls itself Gaggenau. With a name like Gaggenau, it has to be good. Refs: Atkins, AG July 1990; Hannusch, AAG Jan-May 1992.

GRADING	100%	95%	90%	80%	60%	40%	20%

PISTOLS

FLUERSCHEIM - several calibers including .181 cal., smooth bore for darts, SP, mainspring in grip, barrel and grip of gray cast iron, outer parts nickel plated, deeper parts of raised floral patterns and checkering painted black, separate cocking device has two small hooks which grip protruding piston shaft knob during cocking, two prongs at other end of this tool serve as a spanner wrench for removing mainspring retainer ring, later version of the pistol has large T-shaped handle at the end of the piston shaft to allow cocking without a separate tool, fitted wooden cases. Mfg. circa 1881- early 1900s.

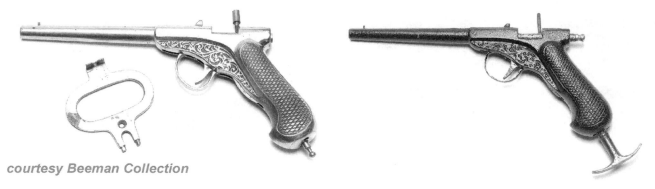

courtesy Beeman Collection

$1,500	$1,400	$1,250	$1,100	$1,000	$800	$600

The wooden cases almost surely were also made by Gaggenau; the company had a box factory producing nearly 300,000 special wooden boxes per year for tools, guns, cigars, etc.
Reference: Dr. Bruno Brukner

GRADING	100%	95%	90%	80%	60%	40%	20%

PEERLESS - .21 cal., SP, rear cocking "T"-shaped handle, one-piece wood grip and forearm, nickel plated.

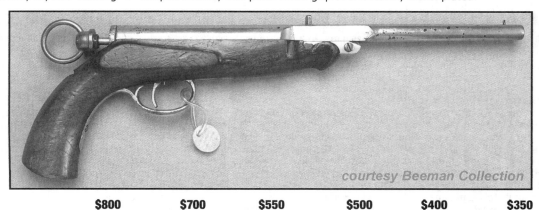

courtesy Beeman Collection

	$800	$700	$550	$500	$400	$350	$300

Ring appears to be a replacement.

CONTRACT MODELS - evidently a large variety of air pistols, esp. push-barrel models as illustrated, were made under other brands or without brand markings. Values generally run from about $50 to $300.

PP TARGET PISTOL ("PATENT-PRÄCISIONS") - .180 cal., SP, BBC, SS, small, LHS "push-lever" lock barrel release lever assembly, one-piece hardwood grip and forearm, carved flutes on grip, Schnabel forearm, complex cocking leverage system, cocking plunger exposed under barrel, marked "PATENT" and with Gaggenau crossed-pistols logo on barrel, almost identical mechanism and styling as Gaggenau rifles marked "COLUMBIA". Nickel-plated/blued. 8.7 in. smoothbore, octagonal BBL, 18.3 in. OAL, 2.8 lbs. Mfg. circa 1890s.

courtesy Beeman Collection

	N/A	N/A	$2,750	$2,000	$1,500	$995	$500

RIFLES

MODEL 1 GALLERY RIFLE - .25 in. cal., SP, UL, SS, 23.5 in. smoothbore blued BBL, nickel-plated metal work, the forward end of the cocking lever has a very distinctive, trigger-guard-like loop just behind the real trigger guard loop. 42.5 in. OAL, 6 lbs. circa 1881-87. Values TBD. Ref: AAG - Jan. 1992.
Ref: Hannusch AAG Jan-March 1992.

MODEL 2 COLUMBIA - .21 cal., SP, BBC, SS, rear sight slides as barrel release, smoothbore octagonal barrel, one-piece hardwood buttstock, sweeping cheekpiece, and Schnabel forearm, complex cocking leverage system, cocking plunger exposed under barrel, marked "PATENT" and with Gaggenau crossed-pistols logo and "COLUMBIA" on barrel (some not marked "COLUMBIA"). Nickel-plated/blued. 8.7 in. smoothbore, octagonal BBL. Circa 1860s.

courtesy Beeman Collection

	N/A	N/A	$2,500	$2,000	$1,500	$1,000	$500

Subtract 10% if not marked "COLUMBIA" (U.S. market name).

GRADING	100%	95%	90%	80%	60%	40%	20%

MODEL 3 GEM - (see Gem section) especially the distinction between combo rimfire firearm/airgun and airgun-only models (see figures here and in the Gem section).

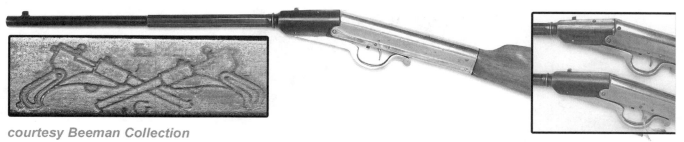

courtesy Beeman Collection

LH insert shows Gaggenau logo stamped on the barrel. It depicts a crossed pair of Flürscheim air pistols.
Upper gun in RH insert is a combination rimfire and air gun. Note the side wings of the cartridge case extractor.

GALWAY

Previous trademark of Galway Arms Co. located in Leicestershire, England, founded in 1964.

The Galway Arms Co. manufactured high grade firearm silencers and introduced the first airgun silencers (requiring a $200 transfer tax in USA). In 1983 they developed and produced in limited numbers the Fieldmaster Mark 2 PCP rifle with adjustable power levels and easily interchanged barrels in .177, .20, or .22 cal. Excellent condition specimens sell in the $2,000 range.

GAMO PRECISION AIRGUNS

Current trademark manufactured by Industrias El Gamo, located in Barcelona, Spain. Currently imported by Gamo USA, Corp., located in Ft. Lauderdale, FL. Previously imported by Stoeger Industries, located in Wayne, NJ, and by Dynamit Nobel, RWS, Inc., located in Closter, NJ. Some models were also sold by Daisy (see Daisy El Gamo 126 and Daisy Model 128 Gamo Olympic). Dealer sales.

One of the oldest manufacturers of lead products in Europe, Gamo was founded during the late 1880s in Barcelona, Spain, as Antonio Casas, S.A. Sixty years ago, the company changed its name to Industrias El Gamo, and expanded into the manufacturing of high-quality airgun pellets and precision airguns. Today, Gamo is one of the largest airgun manufacturers in Europe.

HANDGUNS

AF-10 - .177 cal., pneumatic, 430 FPS, 7 in. barrel, 1 1/4 lbs. Importation disc. 1993.

	$90	$75	$55	$45	$35	N/A	N/A

Last MSR was $115.

AUTO 45 - .177 cal., CO_2, DA, 12 BB magazine or SS with pellets, 410 FPS, 4.3 in. rifled steel BBL, 1.1 lbs., manual safety. Mfg. 1999-2004.

	$75	$65	$55	$45	$35	N/A	N/A

Last MSR was $100.

CENTER - .177 cal., UL, SP, 400-435 FPS, 14 in. barrel, 2 lbs. 8 oz. Mfg. 1973-1994.

courtesy Tim Saunders

$105	$85	$65	$50	$35	N/A	N/A

GRADING	100%	95%	90%	80%	60%	40%	20%

COMPACT TARGET - .177 cal., SSP, 400 FPS, 9 1/4 in. rifled steel barrel, adj. match trigger, fully adj. rear sight, anatomical walnut grip with heavy stippling and adj. palm shelf, 1.94 lbs.

courtesy Gamo Collection

	100%	95%	90%	80%	60%	40%	20%
MSR $290	$245	$205	$180	$155	$110	N/A	N/A

FALCON - .177 cal., UL, SP, 430 FPS, 7 in. barrel. ABS plastic grips, 2 7/8 lbs. Importation disc. 1993.

	$80	$65	$55	$45	$35	N/A	N/A

Last MSR was $105.

P-23 - .177 cal., CO_2, DA, 12 BB magazine or SS with pellets, 410 FPS, 4.25 in. rifled steel barrel, manual safety, 1.0 lbs.

courtesy Gamo Collection

	100%	95%	90%	80%	60%	40%	20%
MSR $90	$65	$55	$45	$35	$25	N/A	N/A

P-23 COMBO LASER - .177 cal., CO_2, DA, 12 BB magazine or SS with pellets, 410 FPS, 4.25 in. rifled steel barrel, 650Nm laser sight mounted under frame, manual safety, 1.1 lbs.

courtesy Gamo Collection

	100%	95%	90%	80%	60%	40%	20%
MSR $140	$105	$85	$65	$50	$35	N/A	N/A

PR-45 - .177 cal., pneumatic, 9 1/4 in. barrel, 1 lb. 9 oz.

	$115	$95	$75	$55	$35	N/A	N/A

Last MSR was $135.

PT-80 - .177 cal., CO_2, semi-auto, SA or DA, tilt-up barrel for quick loading of the eight-shot rotary magazine, 4.25 in. rifled steel barrel, 410 FPS, manual safety, adj. three-dot sights, 1.2 lbs. New 2001.

courtesy Gamo Collection

	100%	95%	90%	80%	60%	40%	20%
MSR $110	$85	$65	$55	$45	$35	N/A	N/A

Add $10 for wood grips (new 2002).

GRADING	100%	95%	90%	80%	60%	40%	20%

PT-80 LASER - .177 cal., CO_2, semi-auto, SA or DA, tilt-up barrel for quick loading of the eight-shot rotary magazine, 4.25 in. rifled steel barrel, 410 FPS, manual safety, adj. three-dot sights, 650Nm laser sight mounted under frame, 1.2 lbs. Mfg. 2001-06.

courtesy Gamo Collection

MSR $160	$135	$95	$75	$55	$45	N/A	N/A

PT-80 TACTICAL - .177 cal., CO_2, semi-auto, SA or DA, tilt-up barrel for quick loading of the eight-shot rotary magazine, 4.25 in. rifled steel barrel, 410 FPS, manual safety, adj. three-dot sights, tactical sc ope rail w/ Quick Shot illuminated red point scope, and tactical 35 lumens flashlight. New 2006.

courtesy Gamo Precision Airguns

MSR $150	$130	$95	$75	$55	$45	N/A	N/A

Add $10 for wood grips (new 2002).

PT-90 - .177 cal., CO_2, semi-auto, SA or DA, tilt-up barrel for quick loading of the eight-shot rotary magazine, 4.25 in. rifled steel BBL, 410 FPS, blue or chrome finish, manual safety, adj. three-dot sights, 1.2 lbs. Mfg. 2002-06.

	$80	$65	$55	$45	$35	N/A	N/A

Last MSR was $115.

Add $5 for chrome finish.

PX-107 - .177 cal., CO_2, semi-auto, fifteen-shot BB magazine also holds CO_2 cylinder in grip, 425 FPS, rifled steel BBL, black or chrome finish, adj. rear three-dot sight, manual safety, 7.9 in. OAL , 0.8 lbs. New 2005.

courtesy Gamo Precision Airguns

MSR $90	$70	$55	$45	$35	$25	N/A	N/A

Add $10 for chrome finish.

GRADING	100%	95%	90%	80%	60%	40%	20%

PX-107 LASER - .177 cal., CO_2, semi-auto, fifteen-shot BB magazine also holds CO_2 cylinder in grip, 425 FPS, rifled steel barrel, black or chrome finish, adj. rear three-dot sight, 650Nm laser sight mounted under frame, manual safety, 7.9 in. OAL, 0.8 lbs. Mfg. 2005-07.

courtesy Gamo Collection

	$125	$95	$75	$55	$35	N/A	N/A

Last MSR was $140.

Add $10 for chrome finish.

R 357 - .177 cal., CO_2, SA or DA revolver, 5.7 in. Lothar Walther barrel, target-style front sight adj. rear sight, plastic grips. Mfg. 1997-2001.

	$115	$95	$75	$55	$35	N/A	N/A

Last MSR was $130.

R-77 CLASSIC/COMBAT 2.5/COMBAT 4 - .177 cal., SA or DA revolver, CO_2 (12-gram cartridge in grip housing), checkered walnut (Classic) or Santoprene (Combat) grips, swing-out cylinder holdseight pellets, 2.5 (R-77 2.5), 4 (Combat) or 6 in. rifled steel barrel, 400 FPS, adj. rear sights, cross-bolt hammer block safety, 1.5 lbs., 8-11.6 in. OAL. Disc. 2006.

	$70	$55	$45	$35	$25	N/A	N/A

Last MSR was $100.

Add $20 for R-77 Classic.

R-77 COMBAT LASER - .177 cal., SA or DA revolver, CO_2 (12-gram cartridge in grip housing), checkered walnut (Classic) or Santoprene (Combat) grips, swing-out cylinder holdseight pellets, 2.5 (R-77 2.5), 4 (Combat) or 6 in. rifled steel BBL, 400 FPS, adj. rear sights, cross-bolt hammer block safety, R77 Laser has built-in grip-pressure activated 650 Nm laser mounted in barrel shroud. Disc. 2006.

	$125	$100	$85	$65	$50	N/A	N/A

Last MSR was $200.

V-3 - .177 cal., CO_2, semi-auto, fifteen-shot BB magazine also holds CO_2 cylinder in grip, 425 FPS, rifled steel barrel, black or chrome finish, adj. rear three-dot sight, manual safety, skeletonized trigger, 7.6 in. OAL, 1.1 lbs.

courtesy Gamo Collection

MSR $100	$70	$55	$45	$35	$25	N/A	N/A

Add $10 for chrome finish.

GRADING	100%	95%	90%	80%	60%	40%	20%

V-3 LASER - .177 cal., CO_2, semi-auto, fifteen-shot BB magazine also holds CO_2 cylinder in grip, 425 FPS, rifled steel barrel, black or chrome finish, adj. rear three-dot sight, 650Nm laser sight mounted under frame, manual safety, skeletonized trigger, 7.6 in. OAL, 1.1 lbs.

courtesy Gamo Collection

	100%	95%	90%	80%	60%	40%	20%
MSR $150	$125	$95	$75	$55	$35	N/A	N/A

Add $10 for chrome finish.

RIFLES

RECALL NOTICE: December 6, 2006 GAMO USA Corp., of Fort Lauderdale, Fla. issued a recall for the following GAMO models: Hunter Pro, Hunter Sport, Shadow Sport, and F1200. These models bear the serial numbers 04-IC-415577-06 through 04-IC-579918-06. The model and serial numbers can be found on the left side of the barrel just above the front left side of the stock. Models Shadow Sport and F1200 look identical. Sold by: Sporting goods stores and gun shops nationwide from June 2006 to September 2006. Contact GAMO USA Corp. directly or on their website (see Trademark Index) for additional information.

Note: Integrated dampener (built in noise reduction device) see Silencer in the Glossary.

Antonio Casas BB Gun - .173/BB cal., SP, Winchester-style lever action, decal on RHS has Casas' initials around a deer and an ad for El Gamo lead "Diabolo" pellets, 6.2 in. BBL. Mfg. circa 1930.

courtesy Beeman Collection

	100%	95%	90%	80%	60%	40%	20%
	N/A	N/A	N/A	$400	$350	$300	$200

CF 20 - .177 or .22 cal., UL, SP, 790-625 FPS, 17.75 in. barrel, checkered stock, 6 lbs. 6 oz. Importation disc. 1993.

	100%	95%	90%	80%	60%	40%	20%
	$155	$125	$100	$65	$50	N/A	N/A

Last MSR was $190.

CF-30 - .177 cal., UL, SP, 950 FPS, rifled steel barrel with scope mount rail, micrometer rear sight with four-position interchangeable windage plate, two-stage trigger, manual cocking and trigger safeties, Monte Carlo-style walnut stained beech stock with checkered grip, ventilated rubber butt pad, 6.4 lbs. Disc. 2001.

	100%	95%	90%	80%	60%	40%	20%
	$215	$180	$145	$105	$75	N/A	N/A

Last MSR was $270.

CFX - .177 cal., UL, SP, 1000/1200 (w/ PDA ammo) FPS, rifled steel barrel with scope mount rail, Truglo adj. rear sight, two-stage trigger, manual cocking and trigger safeties, synthetic stock, ventilated rubber butt pad, 44 in. OAL, 6.6 lbs. New 2003.

	100%	95%	90%	80%	60%	40%	20%
MSR $250	$25	$175	$140	$105	$75	N/A	N/A

GRADING	100%	95%	90%	80%	60%	40%	20%

CFX COMBO - .177 cal., UL, SP, 1000/1200 (w/ PDA ammo) FPS, similar to CFX except, with BSA 2-7x32mm or 4x32mm scope. New 2004.

courtesy Gamo Collection

MSR $270	$245	$180	$135	$95	$75	N/A	N/A

CFX ROYAL - .177 cal., UL, SP, 1000 FPS, similar to CFX except with deluxe wood stock. Mfg. 2004-06.

courtesy Gamo Collection

	$250	$210	$175	$125	$95	N/A	N/A

Last MSR was $300.

CADET - .177 cal., BBC, SP, 570 FPS, beechwood stock, 5 lbs.

	$70	$55	$45	$35	$25	N/A	N/A

CARBINE SPORT - .177 cal., BBC, SP, 640/880 (w/ PDA ammo) FPS, rifled steel BBL, adj. trigger, cocking and trigger safeties, 4x32 scope, Monte Carlo-style synthetic stock w/ soft forearm insert, ventilated rubber butt pad, 41.75 in. OAL, 5.3 lbs. Mfg. 2006- current.

courtesy Gamo Collection

MSR $170	$150	$120	$95	$80	N/A	N/A	N/A

CONTEST - .177 cal., SL, SP, 543 FPS, beechwood stock, 10.1 lbs.

	$100	$80	$60	$45	$35	N/A	N/A

CUSTOM 600 - .177 or .22 cal., BBC, SP, 690 FPS, 17.75 in. barrel, two-stage adj. trigger, checkered stock, 6 lbs. 3 oz.

	$130	$105	$80	$65	$45	N/A	N/A

Last MSR was $170.

DELTA - .177 cal., BBC, SP, 525 FPS, 15.75 in. barrel, two-stage trigger, automatic safety, adj. sights, plastic stock, 5 lbs. 5 oz. Disc. 2006.

	$65	$50	$40	$30	$20	N/A	N/A

Last MSR was $90.

Add $25 for 4x15 scope, rings, and 1000 rounds ammo (Delta Combo).

EUROPIA - .177 cal., SL, SP, 625 FPS, adj. sights, Monte Carlo stock.

	$165	$145	$115	$90	$60	N/A	N/A

EXPO - .177 or .22 cal., BBC, SP, 625 FPS, adj. trigger, special sights, 5 lbs. 8 oz. Disc. 1994.

	$80	$65	$50	$40	$30	N/A	N/A

Last MSR was $130.

GRADING	100%	95%	90%	80%	60%	40%	20%

EXPO 24 - .177 cal., BBC, SP, 560 FPS, 15.7 in. rifled steel BBL with non-glare polymer coating, two-stage trigger, automatic anti-beartrap safety, manual trigger safety, adj. rear sight, hardwood beech stock with black ABS buttplate, 4.2 lbs.

courtesy Gamo Precision Airguns

	100%	95%	90%	80%	60%	40%	20%
	$70	$55	$45	$35	$25	N/A	N/A

Last MSR was $120.

EXPOMATIC - .177 cal., BBC, SP, repeater, 575 FPS, adj. trigger, 5 lbs. 5 oz. Disc. 1997.

	$120	$100	$80	$60	$40	N/A	N/A

Last MSR was $170.

EXPO 2000 - .177 cal., BBC, SP, 625 FPS, 17 in. barrel, Monte Carlo-style stock, 5 1/2 lbs. Mfg. 1992-1994.

	$90	$75	$55	$45	$35	N/A	N/A

Last MSR was $135.

EXTREME CO$_2$ - .22 cal., CO$_2$, pump action repeater, 10-shot rotary mag., 88g. cylinder, fluted and rifled steel bull BBL, adj. fiber optic sights, manual trigger safeties, 3-9x40 scope w/ one-piece mount, Monte Carlo-style synthetic stock w/ ventilated rubber butt pad, 8 lbs. Mfg. 2008-current.

MSR $330	$300	$265	$225	$195	N/A	N/A	N/A

GAMO 68 - .177 or .22 cal., BBC, SP, 600 FPS, 6 lbs. 8 oz.

	$80	$65	$50	$40	$30	N/A	N/A

GAMATIC 85 - .177 cal., BBC, SP, 560 FPS, 17.75 in. BBL, two-stage trigger, pistol grip stock, 6 lbs. 3 oz.

	$75	$65	$55	$45	$35	N/A	N/A

Last MSR was $160.

G-1200 - .177 cal., CO$_2$ cylinder, 560 FPS, 17.75 in. barrel, 6 lbs. 6 oz.

courtesy Gamo Precision Airguns

	$165	$145	$115	$90	$60	N/A	N/A

Last MSR was $185.

HUNTER 220/220 COMBO - .177 cal. or .22 cal., BBC, SP, 1000 FPS, rifled steel BBL, adj. barrel-mounted rear sight or BSA 4x32 scope (Hunter 220 Combo), hooded front sight, manual cocking and trigger safeties, matte finish beechwood stock, black buttplate, 6.2 lbs. Disc. 2006.

	$140	$110	$90	$65	$40	N/A	N/A

Last MSR was $190.

Add $20 for Hunter 220 Combo.

HUNTER 440/440 COMBO - .177or .22 cal., BBC, SP, 1000/750 FPS, 18 in. rifled steel BBL, two-stage adj. trigger, fully adj. rear sight or BSA 4x32 scope (Hunter 440 Combo), wood Monte Carlo-style stock with checkered grip, rubber ventilated butt pad, 6.6 lbs. Disc. 2006.

courtesy Gamo Precision Airguns

	$185	$140	$105	$75	$55	N/A	N/A

Last MSR was $230.

Add $20 for .22 cal. Add $50 for Hunter 440 Combo.

GRADING	100%	95%	90%	80%	60%	40%	20%

HUNTER REALTREE/REALTREE COMBO - .177 cal., BBC, SP, 1000 FPS, 18 in. rifled steel barrel, two-stage adj. trigger, fully adj. rear sight or BSA 4x32 scope (Hunter Realtree Combo), Realtree impregnated wood Monte Carlo-style stock with checkered grip, rubber ventilated butt pad, 6.6 lbs. Disc. 2004.

	$225	$175	$140	$105	$75	N/A	N/A

Last MSR was $250.

Add $30 for Hunter Realtree Combo.

HUNTER 890S - .177 cal. or .22 cal., BBC, SP, 1000/750 FPS, 18 in. rifled steelBBL with muzzle brake, two-stage adj. trigger, manual safety and automatic anti-beartrap safety, walnut-stained beech Monte Carlo-style stock with checkered grip, rubber ventilated butt pad, includes BSA 3-12x44 mm air rifle scope, 7.5 lbs. Disc. 2006.

courtesy Gamo Precision Airguns

	$275	$245	$205	$175	$125	N/A	N/A

Last MSR was $300.

HUNTER 1250 HURRICANE - .177 cal., BBC, SP, 1250 FPS, rifled steelBBL with muzzle brake, two-stage adj. trigger, hand-finished walnut stained beech Monte Carlo-style stock, checkered grip, ventilated rubber butt pad, 7.5 lbs. Mfg. 1999-2006.

	$320	$275	$220	$165	$125	N/A	N/A

Last MSR was $400.

HUNTER ELITE - .177 cal., BBC, SP, 1000/1200 (w/ PDA ammo) FPS, polymer and rifled steel bull BBL, adj. trigger, cocking and trigger safeties, 3-9x50 OIR scope, checkered Monte Carlo-style hardwood stock, ventilated rubber butt pad, 43.25 in. OAL, 8 lbs. Mfg. 2006- current.

courtesy Gamo Collection

MSR $320	$295	$245	$205	$175	N/A	N/A	N/A

HUNTER EXTREME - .177 cal., BBC, SP, 1250/1600 (w/ PBA ammo) FPS, polymer and rifled steel bull BBL, adj. trigger, cocking and trigger safeties, 3-9x50 OIR scope, full size checkered Monte Carlo-style select beech stock, ventilated rubber butt pad, 48.5 in. OAL, 10.5 lbs. Mfg. 2006- current.

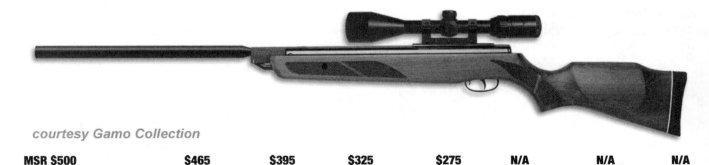

courtesy Gamo Collection

MSR $500	$465	$395	$325	$275	N/A	N/A	N/A

GRADING	100%	95%	90%	80%	60%	40%	20%

HUNTER PRO - .177 cal., BBC, SP, 1000 /1200 (w/ PDA ammo) FPS, fluted polymer and rifled steel BBL, adj. trigger, cocking and trigger safeties, 3-9x40 OIR scope, checkered Monte Carlo-style hardwood stock, ventilated rubber butt pad, 43.25 in. OAL, 7 lbs. Mfg. 2006- current.

courtesy Gamo Collection

	100%	95%	90%	80%	60%	40%	20%
MSR $300	$275	$225	$195	$165	N/A	N/A	N/A

See recall notice.

HUNTER SPORT - .177 cal., BBC, SP, 1000/1200 (w/ PDA ammo) FPS, fluted polymer and rifled steel BBL, adj. trigger, cocking and trigger safeties, 3-9x40 scope, Monte Carlo-style hardwood stock, ventilated rubber butt pad, 43.25 in. OAL, 6.5 lbs. Mfg. 2006-current.

courtesy Gamo Collection

	100%	95%	90%	80%	60%	40%	20%
MSR $230	$210	$195	$175	$155	N/A	N/A	N/A

See recall notice.

MAGNUM 2000 - .177 or .22 cal., BBC, SP, 820-660 FPS, 17.75 in. barrel, adj. two-stage trigger, checkered stock, 7 lbs. 2 oz.

	100%	95%	90%	80%	60%	40%	20%
	$165	$145	$115	$90	$60	N/A	N/A

Last MSR was $200.

MAXIMA - .177 cal., BBC, SP, 1000 FPS, rifled steelBBL with muzzle brake, manual safety and automatic anti-beartrap safety, walnut-stained beech Monte Carlo-style stock with checkered grip, rubber ventilated butt pad, includes BSA 3-12x40 mm air rifle scope, 46.3 in. OAL,6.8 lbs. Mfg. 2005-06.

courtesy Gamo Collection

	100%	95%	90%	80%	60%	40%	20%
	$255	$225	$185	$155	$115	N/A	N/A

Last MSR was $280.

MAXIMA COMBO - .177 cal., BBC, SP, 1000 FPS,similar to Maxima exceptincludes BSA 3-12x40 mm air rifle scope, 46.3 in. OAL,6.8 lbs. Mfg. 2005-06..

	100%	95%	90%	80%	60%	40%	20%
	$295	$265	$225	$185	$135	N/A	N/A

Last MSR was $320.

GRADING	100%	95%	90%	80%	60%	40%	20%

MODEL F1200 (BIG CAT) - .177 cal., BBC, SP, 1000/1200 (w/ PDA ammo) FPS, fluted polymer and rifled steel BBL, adj. trigger, cocking and trigger safeties, 3-9x40 scope, Monte Carlo-style synthetic stock, ventilated rubber butt pad, 43.5 in. OAL, 6.25 lbs.

courtesy Gamo Precision Airguns

	MSR N/A	$195	$150	$115	$85	N/A	N/A	N/A

See recall notice. The Model F1200 looks identical to the Shadow Sport and was sold exclusively at Wal-Mart stores.

MULTISHOT - .177 cal., BBC, SP, eight-shot rotary mag., 750 FPS, rifled steel BBL with polymer-coated finish, adj. rear sight, hooded front sight, dovetail grooves for scope, adj. trigger, cocking and trigger safeties, beech stock, hard rubber butt pad, 6.4 lbs. Mfg. 2001-04.

	$170	$145	$115	$80	$60	N/A	N/A

Last MSR was $190.

NITRO 17 - .177 cal., BBC, SP, 850/1050 (w/ PBA ammo) FPS, fluted polymer and rifled steel BBL, adj. trigger, cocking and trigger safeties, 3-9x40 scope, Monte Carlo-style synthetic stock w/ soft forearm insert, ventilated rubber butt pad, 43.5 in. OAL, 6.25 lbs. Mfg. 2006-current.

courtesy Gamo Collection

	MSR $190	$175	$155	$120	$95	N/A	N/A	N/A

RECON - .177 cal., BBC, SP, 525 FPS, rifled polymer and steel barrel with 4x20 scope, two-stage trigger, manual cocking and trigger safeties, synthetic thumb-hole stock, ventilated rubber butt pad, 37.2 in. OAL, 4 lbs. New 2006.

courtesy Gamo Collection

	MSR $120	$99	$85	$65	$50	$40	N/A	N/A

Add 70% for CF-X Royal with Deluxe hardwood stock (new 2004).

SHADOW 1000/HUNTER BLACK/SILVER/SILVER SUPREME/COMBO - .177 or .22 cal., BBC, SP, SS, 1000/722 FPS, rifled steelBBL with black polymer-coated or nickel (Silver/Silver Supreme) finish, adj. rear fiberoptic sight, BSA 4x32 scope (Shadow/Silver Combo) BSA 30mm red dot scope (Hunter Black), or BSA 3-12x50 scope (Silver Supreme), dovetail grooves for scope, adj. trigger, cocking and trigger safeties, synthetic stock, hard rubber butt pad, 6.6 lbs. Mfg. 2002-06.

	$170	$145	$115	$80	$60	N/A	N/A

Last MSR was $190.

Add $40 for Silver Shadow (new 2003). Add $30 for Shadow Combo (new 2003). Add $60 for Silver Shadow Combo (new 2003). Add $150 for Silver Shadow Supreme (new 2003). Add $50 for Shadow Hunter Black (new 2003).

GRADING	100%	95%	90%	80%	60%	40%	20%

SHADOW 640 - .177 cal., BBC, SP, 640 FPS, rifled barrel, two-stage trigger, automatic safety, Truglo adj. sights, synthetic stock, 41 in. OAL, 5.3 lbs. Mfg. 2003-04.

courtesy Gamo Precision Airguns

	100%	95%	90%	80%	60%	40%	20%
	$115	$90	$65	$50	$40	N/A	N/A

Last MSR was $140.

SHADOW FOX - .177 cal., BBC, SP, 1200 FPS w/ PBA ammo, fluted and rifled steel bull barrel w/ 3-9x40mm scope and one-piece mount, two-stage trigger, manual cocking and trigger safeties, synthetic thumb-hole stock, ventilated rubber recoil pad, 43.5 in. OAL, 5.28 lbs. Mfg. 2008- current.

MSR $280	$245	$180	$135	$95	$75	N/A	N/A

Add 70% for CF-X Royal with Deluxe hardwood stock (new 2004).

SHADOW SPORT - .177 cal., BBC, SP, 1000/1200 (w/ PDA ammo) FPS, fluted polymer and rifled steel BBL, adj. trigger, cocking and trigger safeties, 3-9x40 scope, Monte Carlo-style synthetic stock, ventilated rubber butt pad, 43.5 in. OAL, 6.25 lbs. Mfg. 2006-current.

courtesy Gamo Collection

MSR $230	$195	$150	$115	$85	N/A	N/A	N/A

See recall notice.

SPORTER - .177 cal., BBC, SP, 760 FPS, rifled steel BBL with polymer coated finish, adj. rear sight, hooded front sight, adj. trigger, cocking and trigger safeties, Monte Carlo-style beech stock, ventilated rubber butt pad, 5.5 lbs. Disc. 2004.

	$120	$95	$80	$65	$50	N/A	N/A

Last MSR was $160.

STINGER - .177 cal., BBC, SP, eight-shot mag., 750 FPS, rifled steel barrel, fully adj. rear sight, cocking and trigger safeties, Monte Carlo-style beech stock, hard rubber butt pad, 6.4 lbs. Disc. 2001.

	$145	$115	$90	$60	$45	N/A	N/A

Last MSR was $190.

STUTZEN - .177 cal., UL, SP, 950 FPS, micrometer rear sight with a four-position interchangeable windage plate, rifled steel BBL, one-piece, full-length hardwood Mannlicher stock, hand-carved cheekpiece, and ventilated rubber butt pad. New 2000.

courtesy Gamo Collection

MSR $400	$365	$315	$265	$225	N/A	N/A	N/A

SUPER - .177 cal., SL, SP, 593 FPS, 10 lbs. 8 oz.

	$145	$115	$90	$60	$45	N/A	N/A

TROOPER RD CARBINE - .177 cal., BBC, SP, 560 FPS, rifled steel BBL with polymer coated finish, muzzle brake, two-stage trigger, manual safety, automatic anti-beartrap safety, Gamo red dot sight, black synthetic stock with cheekpiece and checkered grip, 5.3 lbs.

	$90	$65	$55	$45	$35	N/A	N/A

Last MSR was $120.

GRADING	100%	95%	90%	80%	60%	40%	20%

TWIN - .177 or .22 cal., BBC, SP, 675 FPS. adj. sights, barrel insert tubes to change from .177 to .22 cal., hardwood stock.

	100%	95%	90%	80%	60%	40%	20%
	$140	$110	$85	$70	$45	N/A	N/A

Last MSR was $165.

VARMINT HUNTER - .177 cal., BBC, SP, SS, 1000/1200 (w/ PBA ammo) FPS, rifled steelBBL with black polymer coated finish, 4x32 scope, laser, flashlight, dovetail grooves for ounting all three on special bracket, cocking and trigger safeties, ambidextrous synthetic stock, deluxe recoil pad, 43.8 in. OAL, 6.2 lbs. New 2005.

courtesy Gamo Collection

MSR $250	100%	95%	90%	80%	60%	40%	20%
	$225	$175	$135	$95	$75	N/A	N/A

YOUNG HUNTER/COMBO - .177 cal., BBC, SP, 640 FPS, 17.7 in. rifled steel BBL, adj. rear sight, hooded front sight, two-stage adj. trigger, manual trigger safety, automatic anti-beartrap safety, Monte Carlo-style beech stock, ventilated rubber butt pad. Disc. 2005.

courtesy Gamo Precision Airguns

	100%	95%	90%	80%	60%	40%	20%
	$85	$75	$60	$45	$30	N/A	N/A

Last MSR was $130.

Add $40 for Young Hunter Combo with 4x32 scope.

560 CARBINE - .177 cal., BBC, SP, 560 FPS,rifled steelbarrel with muzzle brake, blue finish, ambidextrous black synthetic stock, two-stage trigger, automatic safety, 4x20 scope with mounts, 42.1 in. OAL, 5.2 lbs. Mfg. 2005-06.

	100%	95%	90%	80%	60%	40%	20%
	$65	$50	$40	$30	$20	N/A	N/A

Last MSR was $90.

640 CARBINE - .177 cal., BBC, SP, 640 FPS,rifled steelbarrel with muzzle brake, blue finish, ambidextrous black synthetic stock, two-stage trigger, automatic safety, 4x28 scope with mounts, 42.1 in. OAL, 5.3 lbs. Mfg. 2005-06.

	100%	95%	90%	80%	60%	40%	20%
	$95	$65	$50	$40	$30	N/A	N/A

Last MSR was $100.

850 CARBINE - .177 cal., BBC, SP, 850 FPS,rifled steelbarrel with muzzle brake, blue finish, ambidextrous black synthetic stock, two-stage trigger, automatic safety, 4x32 scope with mounts, 43.1 in. OAL, 5.3 lbs. Mfg. 2005-06.

	100%	95%	90%	80%	60%	40%	20%
	$99	$85	$65	$50	$40	N/A	N/A

Last MSR was $120.

VIPER - .177 cal., BBC, SP, 1000/1200 (w/ PBA ammo) FPS, polymer and steel rifled bull BBL, adj. trigger, cocking and trigger safeties, 3-9x40 OIR scope, abidextrous Monte Carlo-style synthetic stock w/ soft forearm and pistol grip inserts, ventilated rubber butt pad, 43.5 in. OAL, 7.25 lbs. Mfg. 2006- current.

courtesy Gamo Collection

MSR $320	100%	95%	90%	80%	60%	40%	20%
	$295	$245	$205	$175	N/A	N/A	N/A

GRADING	100%	95%	90%	80%	60%	40%	20%

WHISPER - .177 cal., BBC, SP, 1200 (w/ PBA ammo) FPS, 18 in. fluted and rifled steel bull BBL w/ non-removable noise dampener, adj. fiber optic sights, adj. trigger, cocking and trigger safeties, 3-9x40 scope w/ one-piece mount, Monte Carlo-style synthetic stock w/ ventilated rubber recoil pad, 43.5 in. OAL, 5.28 lbs. Mfg. 2008-current.

courtesy Gamo Precision Airguns

MSR $280	$240	$215	$175	$155	N/A	N/A	N/A

❂ **Wisper Deluxe** - .177 cal., BBC, SP, 1200 (w/ PBA ammo) FPS, 18 in. fluted and rifled steel bull BBL w/ non-removable noise dampener, adj. fiber optic sights, adj. trigger, cocking and trigger safeties, 3-9x40 scope w/ one-piece mount, Deluxe Monte Carlo-style synthetic stock w/ ventilated rubber recoil pad, 43.5 in. OAL, 5.28 lbs. Mfg. 2008-current.

courtesy Gamo Precision Airguns

MSR $330	$300	$260	$235	$195	$165	N/A	N/A

❂ **Wisper VH** - .177 cal., BBC, SP, 1200 (w/ PBA ammo) FPS, 18 in. fluted and rifled steel bull BBL w/ non-removable noise dampener, adj. fiber optic sights, adj. trigger, cocking and trigger safeties, 4x32 scope w/ one-piece mount, flashlight and laser, thumb-hole Monte Carlo-style synthetic stock w/ ventilated rubber recoil pad, 43.5 in. OAL, 5.28 lbs. Mfg. 2008-current.

MSR $330	$300	$260	$235	$195	$165	N/A	N/A

SHOTGUNS

SHADOW EXPRESS .22 cal. shotshell or .22 cal. pellet w/ chamber adapter, BBC, SP, ventilated rib steel rifled BBL, adj. trigger, cocking and trigger safeties, bead front sight, abidextrous Monte Carlo-style synthetic stock, ventilated rubber butt pad, 43.3 in. OAL, 5.5 lbs. Mfg. 2008- current.

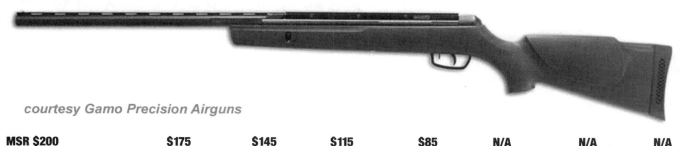

courtesy Gamo Precision Airguns

MSR $200	$175	$145	$115	$85	N/A	N/A	N/A

VIPER EXPRESS .22 cal. shotshell or .22 cal. pellet w/ chamber adapter, BBC, SP, ventilated rib steel rifled BBL, adj. trigger, cocking and trigger safeties, bead front sight, abidextrous Monte Carlo-style synthetic stock w/ soft forearm and pistol grip inserts, ventilated rubber butt pad, 43.5 in. OAL, 5.5 lbs. Mfg. 2006- current.

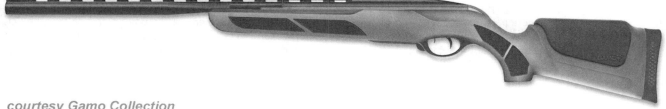

courtesy Gamo Collection

MSR $250	$235	$205	$165	$115	N/A	N/A	N/A

GAMESTER

For information on Gamester, see Eastern Engineering Co. in the "E" section.

GARCO

For information on Garco airguns, see Philippines Airguns in the "P" section.

GAT

Previous trademark of T. J. Harrington & Son located in Walton, Surrey, England.

For information on GAT airguns, see Harrington in the "H" section.

GECADO

Previous tradename used on sporting goods made by Mayer and Grammelspacher (Dianawerk).

Gecado was used by G.C. Dornheim of Suhl, Germany until 1940 and was used in certain German and other markets for guns made by Mayer and Grammelspacher. For more information see Dianawerk in the "D" section of this book.

GECO

Previous tradename used on sporting goods by Gustav Genschow & Co. located in Berlin prior to 1959.

This company was purchased by Dynamit Nobel in 1959, the present owners of Mayer and Grammelspacher. For more information see Dianawerk in the "D" section of this book.

GEM

A general term sometimes used like a brand name. See also Haviland & Gunn, Gaggenau Ironworks, and Dianawerk (Mayer & Grammelspacher).

The term "Gem" has been used torefer to an enormous number of spring piston air rifles. Although a great variety of airguns fall into this category, they have a general similarity in appearance characterized by having the compression chamber in the slanted wrist of the gun rather than ahead of the trigger, and a one-piece wooden buttstock behind the compression chamber. Apparently all are derived from a USA patent issued to George Gunn on April 18, 1871 as modified by a USA patent issued to Asa Pettengill on May 28, 1878. The original Gunn patent is the basis for the drop-barrel cocking mechanism so popular among spring piston airguns throughout the world for over a century. George Peck Gunn combined the wrist-cylinder with the drop-barrel mechanism in his USA patent of March 9, 1886.

Patents properly licensed to Henry Quackenbush in the United States were further licensed to Eisenwerke Gaggenau in Europe, where production of European Gems began in the 1880s. Other early makers, eager for monopoly control of their own markets and simply ignoring prior foreign patents, often copied the basic Gunn and Pettengill patterns or added minor features. Most guns so produced are airguns, but some are combination firearm/airgun designs derived from the Haviland & Gunn designs which became the Quackenbush Model 5.

Gem-type guns were made by many manufacturers from circa 1885 until the 1930s and were at least distributed from many countries and companies, esp. Eisenwerke Gaggenau, Langenham, and Mayer & Grammelspacher (Dianawerk) in Germany, Jean Marck, a Belgian gunmaker (using an encircled "M" as a mark), Arbebz, Sugg, Lane Bros, Baker & Marsh in England, and Coirier of France. They range from crude to excellent in quality and often are "notoriously difficult to classify." Ref: GR March 1974.

Most Gems are small to medium size with octagonal, smoothbore barrels ranging from .177/4.5mm to .25/6.35mm caliber. Current values typically run from about $50 to $100 with few exceeding $250.

Gem Air Rifle. Typical shape and design with angled body tube which serves as mainspring/piston housing and pistol grip. This Jewel Model by Lane of England is special for its "Lane-style" barrel latch and because it is a .177 cal. smoothbore shotgun, designed to fire Lane´s Patent Shot Cartridges, filled with No. 7 or No. 9 lead birdshot.

courtesy Beeman Collection

GIFFARD

Previous trade name of airguns manufactured in succession, by Rivolier & Fils and Sociéte d´Stephanoise d´Armes, and Manufacture Française d´Armes et Cycles located in St. Étienne, France. Paul Giffard (1837-1897) was the designer of pump pneumatic and CO$_2$ air rifles and pistols.

Giffard´s 1862 patent for a pump pneumatic with an in-line pump built under the barrel is often credited with being the basis of virtually all pump pneumatics of the present time. The basic design quickly appeared (1869) in far-off America as Hawley´s Kalamazoo air pistol.

The first production CO$_2$ guns were patented by Giffard in 1873. Giffard, and many military experts of the time, predicted that the CO$_2$ guns would produce a major revolution in warfare; perhaps even lead to an end of warfare! Very small quantities of a hammerless CO$_2$ rifle were made by International Giffard Gun Company Ltd. in London. Giffard also patented (1872) and produced an air cartridge rifle which is similar to the Saxby-Palmer air cartridge system introduced in England in the 1980s.

GRADING	100%	95%	90%	80%	60%	40%	20%

PISTOLS

PNEUMATIC PISTOL - .177 cal., in-line pneumatic pump along underside of 8 in. barrel, Faucet loading tap with RH oval turning tab, walnut forearm and grip continuous, grip fluted, floral craving on forearm, moderate engraving on all metal parts except barrel and pump, blue finish, no safety, 16.3 in. OAL, 1.8 lbs. 1860s.

courtesy Beeman Collection

		N/A	N/A	$4,000	$3,000	$2,000	$1,400	$800

Add 150% for matched pairs of pistols.

GAS PISTOL - .177 cal., CO$_2$ with removable gas cylinder affixed horizontally under the 10 in. round barrel of single diameter or stepped midway to smaller diameter, SS, BA tap-loading, exposed hammer rests on power adjustment wheel, arched walnut grip with fine checkering and ornate blued steel grip cap, deep blue finish, no safety. 17.9 in. OAL, 3.0 lbs. Mfg. late 1870s.

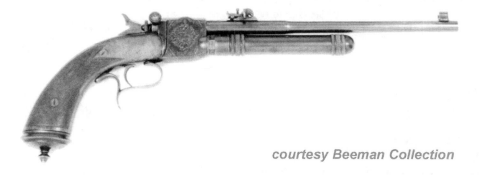

courtesy Beeman Collection

		N/A	N/A	$3,250	$2,500	$1,750	$1,150	$650

Add 25% for hand guards, reportedly designed to reduce injuries during "dueling practice" with wax projectiles.

RIFLES

PUMP PNEUMATIC RIFLE - 4.5mm, 6mm or 8mm cal., in-line pneumatic pump along underside of 19.3-20.3 in. barrel, SS, faucet-loading tap with RH folding or rigid bi-lobed turning tab, external hammer, walnut forearm with deep floral engraving or smooth raised panels and English grip finely checkered or smooth, plain or deeply engraved on all metal parts except barrel and pump, blue or blue with German Silver on receiver and steel buttplate finish, "Giffard-style" guard. No safety, 36.3-38.0 in. OAL, 4.1-4.6 lbs. Mfg. 1870s.

courtesy Beeman Collection

		N/A	N/A	$3,250	$2,500	$1,750	$1,150	$650

Add 50% to 100% for engraving, German silver, stock carving, etc.

GRADING	100%	95%	90%	80%	60%	40%	20%

GAS RIFLE (EXTERNAL HAMMER MODEL) - 4.5mm, 6mm or 8mm cal., CO_2 removable and rechargeable gas cylinder with decorative knurled rings affixed horizontally under the 24.4-24.9 in. round barrel, SS, exposed hammer rests on power wheel, rotating loading tap, operated by bolt or small lever on surface of receiver which exposes rectangular or round loading port, simple or complex rear sight, slim walnut stock, English grip with fine checkering and ornate blued steel grip cap, Giffard name and maker's name may be stamped or inlaid in gold, deep blue finish, simple or ornate "Giffard style" trigger guard, no safety, 41.6-42.6 in. OAL, 5.4 lbs. Mfg. late 1870s.

courtesy Beeman Collection

		N/A	N/A	$2,250	$1,750	$1,250	$800	$450

Add 30% for 4.5mm cal. Add 50% to 100% for highly engraved. Add 50% for first CO_2 models w/ transverse loading tap.

Also known in a pneumatic version with hand pump – may not be original.

GAS RIFLE (HAMMERLESS MODEL) - 8mm cal. conical lead projectile, CO_2 with removable, 10.2 in. rechargeable gas cylinder affixed horizontally under the round barrel, SS, gas cylinder with flats for removal, top-loading tap operated by trigger guard acting as a cocking lever, LHS receiver marked "The Giffard Gun Company Limited London", advertised by maker as "A gun shooting three hundred shots without reloading," with or w/o white-face shot counter (to 200), English-style walnut stock with fine checkering, tang manual safety, light engraving, blue steel parts. Mfg. late 1880s to early 1890s.

courtesy Beeman Collection

	N/A	N/A	$2,250	$1,750	$1,250	$800	$450

Add 5% for shot counter.

Again showing the confusion in describing the number of projectiles held within a repeater and the number of shots which a single shot airgun can produce from a single charge of air or gas.

SHOTGUNS

GAS SHOTGUN - 8mm cal., CO_2, similar to Gas Rifle except, small brass pin front sight, double flip up "V" rear sight, rectangle loading port.

	N/A	N/A	$2,250	$1,750	$1,250	$800	$450

GLOBE

Trade name of BB rifles previously manufactured by J.A. Dubuar Manufacturing Company of Northville, MI circa 1890-1908.

The Globe airguns were invented by Merritt F. Stanley, a former Markham Air Rifle Company employee. Stanley set up a small machine shop in the second story of the Ely Dowell Manufacturing Company in Northville, MI. Apparently unable to make a go of machine work by himself, he moved into a larger shop in the J.A. Dubuar Manufacturing Company and apparently began making the first Globe air rifles in 1890. Stanley had three BB gun patents issued to him; one for a lever action gun which evidently was never produced. Stanley's patents went to Daisy Manufacturing Company in 1908 as Daisy closed down the production of another competitor.

courtesy Beeman Collection

GRADING	100%	95%	90%	80%	60%	40%	20%

RIFLES

All have smoothbore barrels and are without safeties.

FIRST MODEL – (IRON LATTICE MODEL) - .180 large BB cal., BO, SP, SS, frame and diamond lattice pattern stock of cast iron. Nickel finish. Brass smoothbore barrel. Globe design at body hinge. Circa 1890-91.

	N/A	N/A	N/A	$1,200	$1,100	$1,000	$900

SECOND MODEL - .180 large BB cal., BO, SP, SS, similar to first model, except has wood stock with metal parts marked "GLOBE, Pats. Jan. 28, 1890" on both sides. Nickel finish. Brass smoothbore barrel. Globe design at body hinge. Peep sight, post front sight. Circa 1892-97.

	N/A	N/A	N/A	$1,050	$950	$875	$800

THIRD MODEL ("G" MODEL) - .180 large BB cal., BO, SP, SS. Similar to first model. Cast iron frame, more ornate than first model. Pine wood stock with oval containing "J.A. Dubuar" and address. Nickel finish. Sheetmetal smoothbore barrel with full length external patch. Grip frame marked "GLOBE" and large "G". Circa 1894.

	N/A	N/A	N/A	$1,000	$900	$825	$750

GENERAL CUSTER - no known specimens.

MICHIGAN - no known specimens.

SPECIAL (PUSH BARREL MODEL) - .180 large BB cal., SP, SS. Push-barrel cocking. Cast iron frame, sheet metal plunger housing. Plunger housing marked "GLOBE SPECIAL". Wood stock with oval containing "J.A. Dubuar" and address, deep crescent butt. Nickel finish. Brass tube smoothbore barrel. Grip frame with checkered pattern. Circa 1897-99.

	N/A	N/A	N/A	$1,000	$900	$825	$750

WARRIOR - .180 large BB cal., BO, SP, SS. Sheet metal frame, barrel shroud, sights. Pine wood stock without stamping. Nickel finish. Sheetmetal smoothbore barrel. Grip frame marked "GLOBE" and J.A. Dubuar address. Circa 1900-08.

	N/A	N/A	N/A	$600	$500	$450	$400

◈ *Warrior Repeater Version* - .180 cal., similar to Warrior, except repeater. Mfg. circa 1908.

	N/A	N/A	N/A	$750	$625	$550	$475

Subtract 25% if not complete.
These are usually missing parts.

◈ *Warrior Barrel Lug Version* - .180 cal., similar to Warrior, except with lug under barrel near muzzle. Circa 1908.

	N/A	N/A	N/A	$550	$450	$400	$350

◈ *Warrior Embossed Version* - .180 cal., similar to Warrior, except sides with embossed design. Dubuar stock stamp. Circa 1901.

	N/A	N/A	N/A	$575	$475	$425	$375

◈ *Warrior Buster Brown Version* - .180 cal., similar to Warrior, except has Dubuar oval logo on buttstock with "BUSTER BROWN SHOES". Spring loaded shot cup under barrel. Circa 1908.

	N/A	N/A	N/A	$650	$550	$500	$450

MODEL 99 - .180 large BB cal., BO, SP, SS. Similar to Third Model w/ cast iron frame, no "J.A. Dubuar" marking, 16.75 in. SB BBL, nickel finish grip frame marked "99 GLOBE", 31.3 in. OAL..

	N/A	N/A	$1,500	$1,000	$700	$525	$350

GOLONDRINA

For information on Golondrina airguns, see Venturini in the "V" section.

GREENER, W.W., LIMITED

Previous manufacturer located in Birmingham, England, since 1829. No current U.S. importation.

Producers of many guns from sub-machine guns to fine shotguns and a unique spring piston air rifle. The rifle was based on British patent 411,520, issued 8 June 1934, to Charles Edward Greener, for a cam mechanism to tightly seal the breech area.

For more information and current pricing Greener firearms, please refer to the *Blue Book of Gun Values* by S. P. Fjestad (also available online).

RIFLES

GREENER - .177 or .22 cal., BBC, SP, SS, usually distinguished by a large cam lever on the left forward end of the compression tube, this lever swings forward to cause the barrel to move forward of the breech block for opening and loading the breech, moving it back cams the barrel tightly shut, buttstock similar to BSA designs with top ridge for the shooting hand´s web, no wood forward of trigger, 43 in. OAL, 7.5 lbs. Mfg. 1934 to 1960s.

courtesy Beeman Collection

$995	$850	$700	$550	$450	$350	$250

GRADING	100%	95%	90%	80%	60%	40%	20%

GUN POWER STEALTH

Previous trademark manufactured by AirForce Airguns, located in Ft. Worth, TX.

See listing for AirForce Airguns in the "A" section.

GUN TOYS SRL

Current manufacturer of inexpensive barrel cocking air pistols and pistol/carbines located in Miliano, Italy beginning about early 1970.

Gun Toys SRL also privately labeled airguns to Scalemead and Sussex Armory of Britain.

PISTOLS/CARBINES

RO-71 - .177 cal., SP, BBC, SS, die-cast metal and plastic parts, black plastic buttstock, about 250 FPS, 13.3 in. OAL, 2.1 lbs. Mfg. circa 1973.

courtesy Beeman Collection

$50	$40	$35	$30	$20	$10	N/A

Sold as Scalemead Hotshot Standard, Sussex Armory Panther, Classic, IGI202, and Bullseye. Also known as IGI 202 (IGI became FAS about 1980). Ref: AW Dec. 2004.

RO-72 - .177 cal., SP, BBC, SS, similar to RO71, except has one-piece black plastic buttstock, 300 FPS, 14.2 in. OAL, 2.3 lbs.

$55	$45	$40	$35	$25	$15	N/A

Also sold as Scalemead Hotshot Deluxe, Sussex Armory Panther Deluxe, Classic Deluxe, and IGI203.

RO-76 - .177 cal., SP, BBC, SS, similar to RO-72, except has hardwood buttstock and separate pistol grip.

$55	$45	$40	$35	$25	$15	N/A

RO-77 - .177 cal., SP, BBC, SS, similar to RO-76, except has longer barrel and shoulder stock rod screwed directly into end cap of receiver.

$55	$45	$40	$35	$25	$15	N/A

RO-80 - .177 cal., SP, BBC, SS, similar to RO-72, except has plain receiver end cap and grey buttstock.

$55	$45	$40	$35	$25	$15	N/A

H SECTION

HS (HERBERT SCHMIDT)

Previous trademark of Herbert Schmidt located in Ostheim an der Röhn, Germany. Manufacturers of cartridge and blank firing pistols and air pistols including the HS 71A, a side lever BB repeater, and the HS 9A, a push barrel model of the type known to the British as a "Gat."

GRADING	100%	95%	90%	80%	60%	40%	20%

PISTOLS

HS 9A - .177 cal., push-barrel cocking, SP, screw-in breech plug for loading, smoothbore barrel, port in right side of frame to allow lubrication of mainspring and piston seal, hard plastic coated frame, approx. 250 FPS, no safety, 5-7.8 in. OAL, 0.5 lbs. Mfg. 1975-1995.

courtesy Beeman Collection

	$40	$35	$30	$25	$20	N/A	N/A

Earlier versions are known.

HS 71A - .177 cal. lead balls, SL, SP, spring-fedhundred-shot magazine, composition or wood grips, 6 in. BBL. Mfg. 1971-1990s.

courtesy Beeman Collection

	$250	$200	$175	$150	$125	$100	N/A

Add 20% for factory box and accessories.

HAENEL

Previous manufacturer located in Suhl, Germany. Previously imported by Pilkington Competition Equipment LLC located in Monteagle, TN, Cape Outfitters, located in Cape Girardeau, MO, and G.S.I., located in Trussvile, AL.

The Haenel Company was founded in 1840 by Carl Gottlieb Haenel. The company originally produced military weapons, then sporting guns and later airguns. The company was sold around 1890 and the Haenel brand name has changed hands many times since then. Haenel airguns were most recently made by Suhler Jagd-und Sportwaffen GmbH, Suhl, Germany. Waffentechnik in Suhl currently has control. Identity of the company itself and all of the records were lost when the firm was integrated into the communist state-run firearms industry in the late 1940s. Therefore, accurately dating and identifying every Haenel airgun is not always possible.

Haenel guns are all stamped with the Haenel name and model number. The 1926 catalog only lists the models I, II, III, and IV air rifles and no air pistols. The 1937 catalog lists the model 10 and IV ER and VR, and four air pistols including the 28R and 50.

The Luger-style Model 28 air pistol and the Model 33 air rifle are Haenel´s most famous models. Designed by Hugo Schmeisser, of submachine gun fame, the model 33 was the basis for the later Haenel 49, 310,400, 510, LP55R and the Anschütz 275. The Schmiesser brothers worked at the factory for about twenty years.

Haenel had been noted for exceptionally high quality, but standards seemed to almost vanish under the state-owned operation. Quality improved some after the unification of Germany.

The key reference on post-WWII Haenel airguns was compiled by Ernst Dieter (a pseudonym) (2002), a former top engineer at Haenel: *Luftgewehre und Luftpistolen nach 1945 aus Suhl und Zella-Mehlis*.

Spare parts and repairs for some discontinued Haenel air rifles may be available at:

WTS Waffentechnik in Suhl GmbH, Lauter 40, 98528 Suhl, Germany

GRADING	100%	95%	90%	80%	60%	40%	20%

phone: + 49 (0) 36 81 / 46 15 21, fax: + 49 (0) 36 81 / 80 57 66, e-Mail: wts@trimm.de
http://www.gunmaker.org/englisch/index_e.htm
For more information and current pricing on used Haenel firearms, please refer to the *Blue Book of Gun Values* by S.P. Fjestad (also available online).

PISTOLS

MODEL 26 - .177 cal. pellets, SP, SS, smoothbore or rifled barrel, GC cocks by lifting receiver tube up from trigger guard and grip frame, loaded by tipping breech open, black enamel finish, ribbed black plastic or hardwood grips with straight line checkering, no safety, 10 in. OAL, 1.5 lbs. Circa 1926-late l930s.

courtesy Beeman Collection

N/A	$225	$175	$145	$105	$85	$50

Add 30% for factory box.

MODEL 28 - .177 or .22 cal pellets, SP, SS, smoothbore or rifled barrel (rifled barrel indicated by asterisk after caliber marking), GC cocks by lifting receiver tube up from trigger guard and grip frame, loaded by tipping breech open, blue finish, synthetic or wood grips with brass Haenel or Super medallion, no safety, 10 in. OAL, 2.5 lbs. Pistols marked "Heanel Air Pistol" mfg. 1928.1930, marked "Haenel Model 28" mfg. 1930-1940.

courtesy Beeman Collection

N/A	$185	$150	$!25	$100	$75	$50

Add 30% for factory box. Add 30% for Super 28 markings.

MODEL 28R - .177 or .22 cal. pellets, GC, SP, similar to Model 28, except repeating mechanism,twenty rounds of .177 orfifty rounds of .22, rifled barrel, manual safety, 10.5 in. OAL, 2.6 lbs. Magazine knob projection from rear of receiver immediately identifies this gun. Mfg. 1930-1940s.

courtesy Beeman Collection

N/A	$300	$235	$185	$135	$100	$75

Add 30% for factory box.

GRADING	100%	95%	90%	80%	60%	40%	20%

MODEL 50/51 - .174 cal. (4.4 mm lead balls), SP, repeater, fifty-shot gravity-fed magazine (Model 51 - lighter, SS), smoothbore barrel, nickel finish, hardwood grips with or without Haenel brass medallion, no safety, 8.8 in. OAL, 2.6 lbs. Shorter version was also available. Mfg. 1930-1934.

courtesy Beeman Collection

	N/A	$300	$275	$225	$185	$145	$110

Add 30% for factory box.

MODEL 100 - .174 cal. (4.4 mm lead balls), SP, cocked by pulling ring on base of grip to release grip-backstrap cocking lever, fifty-shot gravity-fed magazine, smoothbore barrel, nickel or blued finish, no safety. Mfg. 1932-1940.

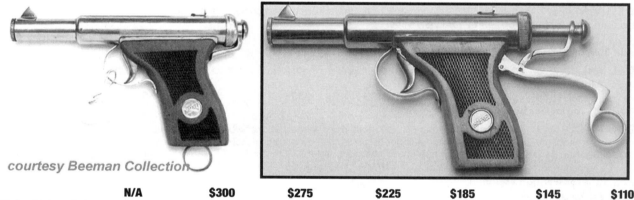

courtesy Beeman Collection

	N/A	$300	$275	$225	$185	$145	$110

Add 30% for factory box.

RIFLES

MODEL 1 - .177 or .22 cal., SS, BBC, SP, smoothbore or rifled barrel, beech stock, small pistol grip, blue finish, no safety, 38.3 in. OAL, 4.6 lbs. Mfg. 1925-1939. (Listed in 1939 Stoeger Catalog as their Model 3100).

courtesy Beeman Collection

$130	$100	$85	$65	$45	N/A	N/A

Add 30% for factory box. Add 20% for Stoeger markings.

MODEL 1-53 - .177 in. cal., SS, BBC, SP, rifled barrel with lock similar to Haenel II and III, beech stock, small pistol grip, manual safety, blue finish, 38.3 in. OAL, 4.6 lbs. 1949-1969.

$150	$125	$100	$80	$60	N/A	N/A

Add 30% for factory box.

GRADING	100%	95%	90%	80%	60%	40%	20%

MODEL II/MODEL III - .177 or .22 cal. pellets, rifled (eight grooves) or smoothbore, SS, BBC, SP, barrel release lever LHS of breech. 43.3 in. OAL, sight radius 17.7 in., 6.6 lbs. Numbers stamped under barrel may be manufacturing date and serial number. Model II with only wood buttstock. Model III with full stock with integral finger-grooved forearm. Circa 1925 to 1939.

courtesy Beeman Collection

	N/A	$225	$200	$160	$120	$80	$40

Add 30% for factory box.

MODEL III-53/III-56/III-60/III-284/3.014 - .177 or .22 cal. pellets, SS, BBC, SP. Five variations of Model III made from 1950 to 1993. 568 FPS (173 MPS) for .177, 400 FPS (122 MPS) for .22, 43.3-44.3 in. OAL, 19 in. barrels with 12-groove rifling. Walnut finish beech or laminated stocks. Open or micrometer sights. 6.8 to 7.7 lbs. East German quality problems and very limited distribution outside of East Germany preclude determination of market values at this time (estimated $50 to $150).

MODEL IV - .177 or .22 cal. pellet, SS, SP, UL, wood buttstock behind trigger guard (Millita-style), 43.3 in. OAL, sight radius 17.7 inches, 6.6 lbs. Model IV-E - repeater, drum magazine on top of breech. Ca. 1927-39.

	N/A	$300	$250	$225	$190	$140	N/A

Add 30% for factory box. Add 100% for Repeater.

MODEL IV/M - .177 cal. pellet, SP,SS, TL, match rifle, characteristic top cocking bolt pivots at rear sight. Available in 1958 and 1959; became the IV/M in 1960. 43 in. OAL, 6.75 lbs.

	N/A	$275	$250	$225	$200	$170	N/A

Add 30% for factory box. Add 100% for Repeater.

MODEL VIII - .177 or .22 cal. pellets, UL, SP, smoothbore or rifled, wood buttstock behind grip. Blued. 42.9 in. OAL, sight radius 17.3 in., 5.7 lbs.Mfg. ca. 1925-39.

	$130	$100	$85	$65	$45	N/A	N/A

Add 30% for factory box.

MODEL 10 (X) - .177 cal. smoothbore, SP, SS, BO, slab-sided wood buttstock behind grip area, sheetmetal "tinplate construction" (may have been made by Dianawerk; this model is not listed in Dieter's book), nickel-plated, 1.3 lbs., 31 in. OAL, date stamp on under edge of stock. German variation: stamped rippling on air chamber, stamped 'MADE IN GERMANY", blued finish. Mfg. ca. mid-1930s-1939.

	N/A	N/A	$180	$135	$105	$80	$55

Add 50 % for German variation.

MODEL 15 (XV) - .177 cal., BBC, SP, SS, smoothbore barrel, loaded by removing brass inner barrel from sheetmetal barrel shroud, sheetmetal/tinplate construction, beech buttstock behind grip area, blued or nickel. 32.5 in. OAL, 2 lbs. 7 oz. Model XV (Model VA) similar but with wood forearm side slabs, more complex barrel lock, 2.75 lbs. 1929 to late 1930s.

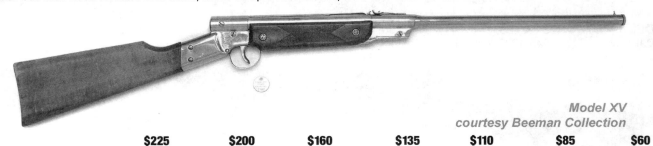

Model XV
courtesy Beeman Collection

	$225	$200	$160	$135	$110	$85	$60

Add 30% for factory box. Add 30% for Model XV/VA.

MODEL 20 (XX) - .177 cal. smoothbore, similar to Model 15, except direct breech loading, thin inner barrel within sheetmetal barrel shroud, early versions with round Haenel logo; later with typical Haenel arrow logo, late 1930s rear sight moved from body tube to barrel, nickel or blued finish, 34.5 in. OAL, 3.2 lbs. Mfg. ca. mid-1920s-1930s.

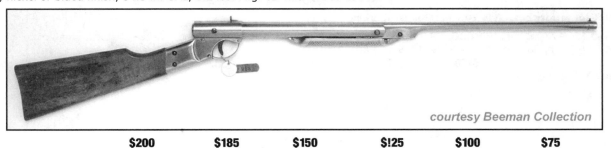

courtesy Beeman Collection

	$200	$185	$150	$!25	$100	$75	$50

Add 20% for round Haenel logo. Subtract 10% for rear sight on barrel. Add 30% for factory box.

GRADING	100%	95%	90%	80%	60%	40%	20%

MODEL 30 (XXX) - .177 cal., similar to Model 20, except rifled or smoothbore, full stock with pistol grip and grooved forearm, no buttplate, no safety, 34.5 in. OAL, 3.1 lbs.

	$200	$185	$150	$125	$100	$75	$50

MODEL 33/33 JUNIOR - .174 cal. (4.45 mm lead balls), SP, bolt lever cocking, paramilitary-style with bayonet lug and stock slot for sling, detachable spring-fed 8 or 12 (Model 33) or 6 or 12 (Model 33 Junior) round box magazines, Mauser type wing manual safety, 44 in. OAL, 7.5 lbs. (Model 33), 40 in. OAL, 5.3 lbs (Model 33 Junior). Model 33 sling on side of stock. 33 Junior sling on bottom of stock. Ca. 1933-early 1940s. Production may have been resumed in 1950s. Schmeisser's Patent.

courtesy Beeman Collection

	N/A	$375	$350	$300	$250	$200	$150

Add 30% for factory box.

MODEL 40 - .177 cal., SP, BBC, SS, similar to Model 30 (XXX) except solid 14.8 in. barrel, pistol grip stock with finger grooved forearm, no buttplate, no safety, 35.5 in. OAL, 3.75 lbs. Mfg. 1930s to 1939.

	$150	$130	$110	$100	$80	$60	$40

MODEL 45 - .177 cal. only, SP, BBC, SS, solid steel rifled or smoothbore barrel, straight grip stock with no forearm, 35 in. OAL, 3.6 lbs. Mfg.1930s to 1939.

	$150	$130	$110	$100	$80	$60	$40

MODEL 49/MODEL 49a - .174 cal. (4.4 mm lead balls), SP, rocking-bolt lever cocking, Sporter version of Model 33, detachable spring-fed six-, eight-, or twelve-shot round ball box magazines, Mauser-type wing manual safety, date stamp on steel buttplate. OAL Model 49 41.5 in., Model 49a 41.75 in., 5.9 lbs. Model 49 sight radius: 16.2 in., Model 49a sight radius:18.5 in. Mfg. ca. 1949-1960.

courtesy Beeman Collection

	N/A	N/A	$350	$300	$250	$200	$150

Add 30% for factory box.

MODEL 85 (KI 1) - .177 cal. Importation disc. 1993.

	$100	$80	$70	$50	$40	N/A	N/A

Last MSR was $130.

MODEL B96 BIATHLON TRAINER - .177 cal., PCP, SS or five-shot repeater using one-round and five-round magazines, Fortner-type action, adj. match trigger, adj. sights, competition stock with adj. cheekpiece, 39.4 in. OAL, 9.6 lbs.

	$1,435	$1,290	$1,050	$800	$600	N/A	N/A

Last MSR was $1,595.

Add 10% for semi-auto conversion.

This model is designed as a trainer for Biathlon rifle disciplines.

MODEL 100/MODEL 510 - .177 cal., SS, BBC, small pistol grip, blue finish, 38.3 in. OAL, 4.6 lbs. Model. 510: 1989-1991; Model 100: 1991-1993.

	$150	$125	$100	$80	$60	N/A	N/A

Number change for Model 300.

MODEL 110/MODEL 520 - .177 cal. pellets, Model 110:1992-1993. Model 520:1991-1993.

	$125	$100	$85	$65	$45	N/A	N/A

Improved deluxe versions of Model 303.

MODEL 300 - .177 cal., SS, BBC, small pistol grip, blue finish, 38.3 in. OAL, 4.6 lbs. Mfg. 1969-1989.

	$150	$125	$100	$80	$60	N/A	N/A

Became Model 510 in 1989. Became Model 100 in 1991.

MODEL 302 - .177 or .22 cal., SS, BBC, larger version of Model 300, several versions with minor changes. Production began in 1966.

	$150	$100	$85	$80	$60	N/A	N/A

GRADING	100%	95%	90%	80%	60%	40%	20%

MODEL 303 (KI)/MODEL 303-8 SUPER - .177 or .22 cal., similar to Model 302 with minor improvements. Production began 1969. Presumably replaced Model 302. USA importation discontinued ca. 1993. Unusual variation: Model 303-8 Super with target stock and aperture sights.

	$125	$100	$85	$65	$45	N/A	N/A

Last MSR was $190.

Add 75% for 303-8 Super.

MODEL 304 - similar to Model 303, except with plastic stock. Mfg. after 1976.

	$125	$100	$85	$65	$45	N/A	N/A

MODEL 308-8 - .177 cal., SP, SS. Importation disc. 1993.

	$225	$175	$145	$125	$95	N/A	N/A

Last MSR was $300.

Not well known outside of former iron curtain countries.

MODEL 310 (KI 104) - 4.4 mm round lead ball. SP, rocking-bolt lever cocking, sportier version of Model 49/49a, detachable, spring-fed six-, eight-, or twelve-shot round ball box magazines. Push pull safety at rear of compression tube. Numerous versions differ mainly in sights and stock. Fifth version (4.5 [.177] cal) has horizontal seven-shot drum repeating mechanism mounted horizontally over top of breech. Mfg. 1960-1989.

	$175	$140	$110	$85	$50	N/A	N/A

Last MSR was $200.

Add 100% for repeater version 310-5.

MODEL 311 (KI 102) - .177 cal. pellets, SS, SP, top action bolt cocking handle, tap loader. Open or aperture sight. 43.75 in. OAL, 7.2 lbs. Mfg. 1964-1992.

	N/A	$225	$175	$125	$95	N/A	N/A

Last MSR was $395.

Numerous variations mainly are minor stock changes.

MODEL 312 - .177 cal., SL, SP, multiple spring/rubber buffer recoil-reduction system, tap-loading. 42.5 in. OAL, 10.8 lbs. Mfg. early 1970s-1990s.

courtesy Beeman Collection

	N/A	$200	$175	$150	$125	$100	$50

MODEL 400/MODEL 570 - upgrades of model 310. Model 570 is 1989 model number change for Model 310. Model 400 is 1991 model number change for Model 570. Detachable spring-fed six-, eight-, or twelve-round box magazines for 4.4 mm round lead balls.

	$175	$140	$110	$85	$50	N/A	N/A

MODEL 410/MODEL 580 - 4.4 mm lead balls, SP, unique lever action repeater. Same magazine system as Models 400 and 570. Dummy in-line magazine below barrel resembles tubular .22 in cal. rimfire magazine.

	$175	$140	$110	$85	$50	N/A	N/A

MODEL 600 - .177 or .22 cal., SP. SS. SL, Match rifle, open or aperture sights, adj. buttplate, 42.13 in. OAL, 8.8 lbs.

	$250	$225	$200	$175	$150	$125	$50

Replaced Model 312.

MLG 550 (KI 101) - .177 cal, SP, SS, tap-loading, SS top lever mechanism, 25.6 in. BBL, recoilless match rifle, the MLG (Meister-schafts-Luftgewehr) approx. 500 FPS, match trigger. 42.8 in OAL, 10.8 lbs. USA importation disc. 1993.

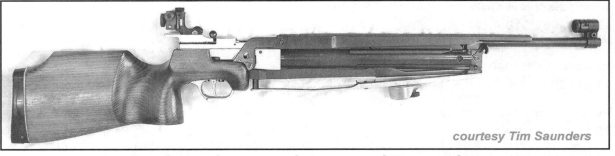

courtesy Tim Saunders

	$550	$450	$375	$275	$225	N/A	N/A

Last MSR was $695.

Small numbers made for Soviet bloc international match competitors.

GRADING	100%	95%	90%	80%	60%	40%	20%

MODEL 800 - .177 cal. SS, SP, match rifle, characteristic top-cocking bolt pivots at rear sight. Mfg. ca. 1990-1992.

	$450	$400	$350	$250	$200	N/A	N/A

Replaced Model 550-1.

HAKIM

For information on this Egyptian military training air rifle, please refer to Anschütz in the "A" section of this text.

HÄMMERLI AG

Current manufacturer located in Lenzburg, Switzerland, with most manufacturing actually done in Schaffhausen in the old SIG factory. They are now separate from SIG, but owned by San Swiss AG which also owns J.P. Sauer und Sohn, Blaser, B. Rizzini, and SIG. Current match/ target airguns imported by Larry´s Guns, located in Portland, ME and George Brenzovich located in Fort Hancock, TX. Current sport airguns imported by Umarex USA located in Fort Smith, AR beginning 2006. Previously imported until 1995 by Champion´s Choice, located in LaVergne, TN, Gunsmithing, Inc., located in Colorado Springs, CO., 10 Ring Service Inc. located in Jacksonville, FL, and Wade Anderson (Hämmerli Pistols USA), located in Groveland, CA. Dealer and consumer direct sales.

The Hämmerli CO_2 rifles and pistols were the first true precision CO_2 guns in the world. This is only a partial listing of models, with preliminary information. Additional research is underway and more information will be presented about Hämmerli airguns in future editions of this guide. A devastating fire in 1977 destroyed the production lines for precision CO_2 guns. Some recent airguns bearing the Hämmerli name have been built to much more economical standards than the pre-1977 models. Hämmerli recently has served as a distributor of BSA and El Gamo airguns, but the claims that any of the Hämmerli brand airguns were made by other companies evidently is not true.

Beginning 2007, Umarex USA took over the importation and marketing of a new Hämmerli sport airgun product line with some models not manufactured in Switzerland. These sport airguns will be marked Umarex USA. As of 2007, all Hämmerli match/ target airguns are still being manufactured in Switzerland.

For more information and current pricing on both new and used Hämmerli AG firearms, please refer to the *Blue Book of Gun Values* by S.P. Fjestad (also available online).

PISTOLS

Add 20% for original factory box. Add 30% for factory fitted case.

DUELL - .177 cal., CO_2 cylinder, five-shot manual, spring-fed magazine horizontal on top of receiver feeds pop-up loading block, black crinkle and blued finish, composition checkered RH thumbrest grip. 16.1 in. OAL, 2.6 lbs. Mfg. 1967-70.

courtesy Beeman Collection

$1,000	$950	$900	$700	$500	$350	$250

MASTER - .177 cal., CO_2 (bulk fill or capsules), adj. sights and trigger, UIT target model, no safety, 15 9 in. OAL, 2.4 lbs. Mfg. 1964-1979.

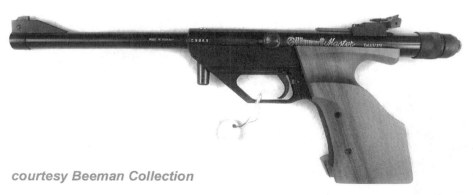

courtesy Beeman Collection

$475	$450	$350	$300	$250	$200	$150

Add 15 % for wood grips.

This model won the German National Championships in 1965, 1966, and 1967.
Additional information and values were not available at time of printing.

GRADING	100%	95%	90%	80%	60%	40%	20%

PRINZ - .177 cal., CO_2 cylinder, five-shot manual, spring-fed, vertical magazine replaces pop-up loading block, black crinkle and blued finish, composition checkered RH thumbrest grip. Not marked Hammerli (identified by box), the only marking is "MOD 5/1". 11.8 in. OAL, 2.2 lbs. Mfg. 1967-70.

courtesy Beeman Collection

	100%	95%	90%	80%	60%	40%	20%
	$850	$800	$650	$500	$300	$225	$200

RAPID - .174/BB lead ball cal., CO_2, five-shot semiautomatic, adj. sights and trigger, training pistol for UIT rapid fire, 13 in. OAL, 3.4 lbs. Mfg. 1966-69.

courtesy Beeman Collection

	100%	95%	90%	80%	60%	40%	20%
	$750	$650	$550	$450	$350	N/A	N/A

Add 10% for wood grips.

SINGLE - .177 cal., CO_2, (bulk fill or capsules), adj. sights and trigger, pop-up breech loading plug. no safety, 13.8 in. OAL, 2.2 lbs. Junior target model. Mfg. 1961-1970s.2nd Variant has the same grip frame and trigger as Master Model so that 12 gm CO_2 cylinders may be used.

courtesy Beeman Collection

	100%	95%	90%	80%	60%	40%	20%
	N/A	N/A	$395	$350	$300	N/A	N/A

Add 10 % for wood grips.

Declining velocity is prevented by two measures: 1. Constant pressure metering sytem. 2. Pressure vented to atmosphere when a set low pressure level is reached.

GRADING	100%	95%	90%	80%	60%	40%	20%

SPARKLER - .175/BB and .177 cal., CO_2 "Sparkler" cartridge, manual repeaterfive-shot magazine. Two versions: R and RD. The RD can fire lead balls as a repeater and pellets as a SS, 13.7 in. OAL, 2.7 lbs. Mfg. 1958-1960.

courtesy Beeman Collection

	100%	95%	90%	80%	60%	40%	20%
	N/A	N/A	$295	$250	$200	$150	$100

Add 10 % for wood grips. Add 25% for RD version. Add 15% for fitted factory case.

MODEL 480 - .177 cal., CO_2 or PCP, fixed cylinder, adj. grips, UIT target model, adj. sights, adj. trigger, adj. grip, up to 320 shots per full compressed air tank, approx. 2.25 lbs. Mfg. 1994-99.

	100%	95%	90%	80%	60%	40%	20%
	$500	$400	$350	$300	$250	N/A	N/A

Last MSR was $1,355.

Add $145 for walnut grips.

MODEL 480K - .177 cal., CO_2 or PCP, similar to Model 480, except has detachable cylinders.

	100%	95%	90%	80%	60%	40%	20%
	$650	$550	$475	$400	$350	N/A	N/A

Add $145 for walnut grips.

MODEL 480K2 - .177 cal., CO_2 or PCP, similar to Model 480, except has detachable cylinders. Mfg. 1998-2000.

	100%	95%	90%	80%	60%	40%	20%
	$800	$680	$550	$475	$400	N/A	N/A

Add $145 for walnut grips.

MODEL AP 40 MATCH - .177 cal., PCP (tank with integral pressure gauge), adj. rear target sights, integral front sight with three different sight widths, fully adj. trigger system, optional adj. "Hi-Grip," blue or gold breech and cylinder, 9.85 in. aluminum barrel, includes case and replacement tank, 2.2 lbs. Mfg. in Switzerland. New 2001.

	100%	95%	90%	80%	60%	40%	20%
MSR N/A	$1,150	$995	$795	$650	N/A	N/A	N/A

Add 6% for ported steel BBL (Model AP40 Pro new 2005).

☉ *Model AP 40 Junior* - .177 cal., PCP (tank with integral pressure gauge), adj. rear target sights, integral front sight with three different sight widths, fully adj. trigger system, optional adj. "Hi-Grip," blue breech and cylinder, includes case and replacement tank, 14.82 in. OAL, 1.9 lbs. Mfg. in Switzerland.

	100%	95%	90%	80%	60%	40%	20%
MSR N/A	$975	$895	$725	$595	N/A	N/A	N/A

Add 5% for adj. "Hi-Grip".

RIFLES

AIR GUN TRAINER - 4.4 mm cal. precision lead balls, SP, SS, SL, A side-lever, spring piston powered insert designed to instantly replace the bolt in the Swiss Kar. 31 service rifle, with its own barrel which fits into the firearm barrel. Uses the frame, stock, trigger mechanism, and sights of the host rifle; its cocking action mimics that of this straight pull bolt action rifle. Developed in the late 1950s; machined and bluedRef.: Smith (1957, pp. 155-166, 168). 28 in. OAL (fits into K31 rifle w/ OAL of 43 in.), 1.0 lbs., ca. 250 fps. Marked Hammerli Trainer, SN, and model of host firearm. A 6 shot, gravity fed, CO_2 version definitely was also patented and developed for the German Kar. 98 service rifle, but actual production may not have been commenced; SN 10 is the highest number reported to Blue Book as of March 2005. A number of experimental and prototype versions apparently were made for other rifles and even pistols such as the German P38. Evidently actually produced only for the Mauser 98 and the Swiss Kar. 31 firearms. Extremely rare, most specimens surviving WWII reportedly were lost in a fire. Estimated value, about $1500. Ref: W.H.B Smith (1957).

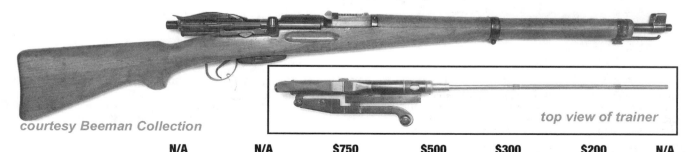

courtesy Beeman Collection   *top view of trainer*

	100%	95%	90%	80%	60%	40%	20%
	N/A	N/A	$750	$500	$300	$200	N/A

Subtract 20% for trainer w/o equal or better condition K31 rifle. (Note that the rifle w/ airgun trainer insert still is subject to USA firearm regulations because the firearm receiver is intact.) Values of versions other than K31: TBD.

GRADING	100%	95%	90%	80%	60%	40%	20%

CADET REPEATER (MEHRLADER) - .174/BB cal., CO$_2$ cylinder, BA, spring-fed eighty-shot magazine, derived from a previous SS Cadet Model, no safety, 41.5 in. OAL, 6 lbs. Mfg. 1968-69.

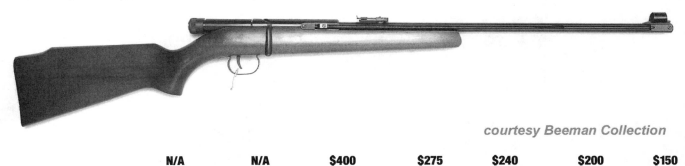

courtesy Beeman Collection

	N/A	N/A	$400	$275	$240	$200	$150

Add 20% for older Cadet SS model.

JUNIOR - similar to the Match, except uses disposable CO$_2$ cartridges, does not have a rubber buttplate or barrel sleeve, and is scaled down in size, no safety, aperture sight/base swing forward for charging. 41.5 in. OAL, 6 lbs. Mfg. 1962-1970.

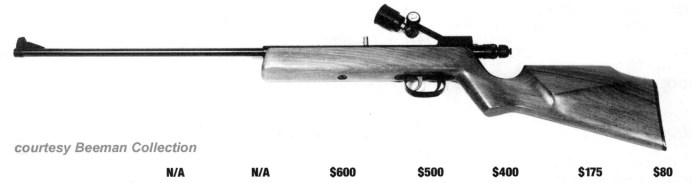

courtesy Beeman Collection

	N/A	N/A	$600	$500	$400	$175	$80

MATCH - .177 cal., CO$_2$ filled from storage tank, SS, cocking the gun by pushing the cocking knob forward automatically pops up the loading block, heavy barrel sleeve, extremely angular stock lines and cheekpiece, no safety. 41.5 in. OAL, 9.6 lbs. Mfg.1962-67.

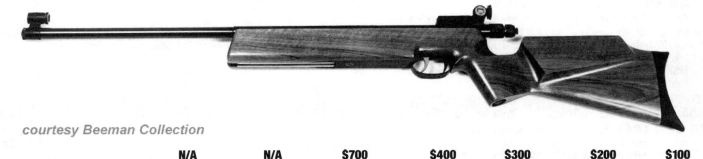

courtesy Beeman Collection

	N/A	N/A	$700	$400	$300	$200	$100

MODEL 3 (OR PUMA 496) - .177, SL, SP, SS, rotary tap, intended for match shooting, but provided with fixed sights, barrel-like weight under barrel, no safety, w/o barrel wgt., 44.3 in. OAL, 7.5 lbs. Mfg. 1971-74

courtesy Beeman Collection

	$200	$185	$150	$125	$100	$75	$50

Side lever may be very dangerous as it has sharp edges and no anti-beartrap mechanism (Models 1, 2,4, and 10 are similar rifles in the Puma 490 series with different sights, barrel wgts., etc.), all the 490 series were replaced by a 400 series circa 1974 which has an anti-bear trap mechanism and manual safety. The 490 series included Models 401, 402, 403 and the strange military-style 420 with a greenish plastic stock with pistol grip handle and dummy cartridge magazine.

MODEL 403 - .177 cal., SL, SP, 700 FPS, adj. sight target model, 9.25 lbs.

	$325	$275	$225	$175	$100	N/A	N/A

Last MSR was $400.

GRADING	100%	95%	90%	80%	60%	40%	20%

MODEL 420 - .177 cal., SL, SP, 700 FPS, plastic stock, 7.5 lbs.

	100%	95%	90%	80%	60%	40%	20%
	$225	$195	$155	$115	$75	N/A	N/A

Last MSR was $300.

MODEL 450 - .177 cal., TL, SP, adj. target sight and cheekpiece, target model. Imported 1994-2001.

	100%	95%	90%	80%	60%	40%	20%
	$1,230	$1,020	$795	$595	$425	N/A	N/A

Last MSR was $1,400.

Add $40 for walnut stock.

MODEL AR 30 - .177 cal., PCP, fully adj. rear precision peep sight, hooded front sight, polygon rifling, adj. trigger system, aluminum adj. stock in silver finish, interchangeable pistol grips, 8.6 lbs. New 2005.

	100%	95%	90%	80%	60%	40%	20%
MSR N/A	$925	$825	$695	$500	N/A	N/A	N/A

Add 30% forModel AP 30 Pro w/ Hämmerli Prec sight and MEC buttplate and weights (new 2006).

MODEL AR 50 - .177 cal., PCP, fully adj. rear precision peep sight, hooded front sight, 19.5 in. polygon rifling, adj. trigger system, laminated wood or four-piece all aluminum fully adj. (Model AR 50 Alum Pro) stock in blue or silver finish, interchangeable pistol grips (aluminum stock), adj. pistol grip and cheek piece, 10.5 lbs. New 2001.

	100%	95%	90%	80%	60%	40%	20%
MSR N/A	$1,075	$895	$750	$600	N/A	N/A	N/A

Add 40% for AR 50 Alu. Add 50% for AR 50 Alu Pro w/ IRC (new 2006). Add 60% for AR 50 Alu Bench Rest w/ IRC (new 2006). Subtract 10% for AR 50 Junior w/ beech stock and curved rubber butt plate.

MODEL 490C - .177 cal., BBC, SP, less than 500 FPS, adj. rear sight, automatic safety, Monti Carlo wood stock w/ butt pad. Mfg. 2007-current.

courtesy Umarex USA Collection

MSR $95	100%	95%	90%	80%	60%	40%	20%
	$85	$70	$55	$45	N/A	N/A	N/A

Add 20% for combo w/ 4x32 scope.

MODEL 850 AIR MAGNUM - .177 or .22 cal., CO_2, 88g cylinder, BA repeater w/ 8-shot mag., 23.5 in. BBL, 760-655 FPS, adj. rear fiber optic sights, automatic safety, checkered black polymer ambidextrous Montew Carlo stock, butt pad, 41 in. OAL, 5.8 lbs. Mfg. 2007-current.

courtesy Umarex USA Collection

MSR $274	100%	95%	90%	80%	60%	40%	20%
	$235	$185	$140	$95	N/A	N/A	N/A

Add 15% for combo w/ 4x32 scope.

MODEL X2 - .177 and .22 cal., BBC, SP, interchangable two-barrel system, 1000-900 FPS, adj. rear and fiber optic front sights, automatic safety, Monti Carlo wood stock w/ butt pad. Mfg. 2007-current.

courtesy Umarex USA Collection

MSR $258	100%	95%	90%	80%	60%	40%	20%
	$225	$195	$135	$95	N/A	N/A	N/A

Add 20% for X2 Combo.

GRADING	100%	95%	90%	80%	60%	40%	20%

NOVA - .177 cal., UL, SS, 18 in. BBL, 1000 FPS, adj. rear fiber optic sights, automatic safety, checkered vaporized beech wood competition stock, butt pad, 45.5 in. OAL, 7.8 lbs. Mfg. 2007-current.

courtesy Umarex USA Collection

MSR $342	$305	$275	$235	$190	N/A	N/A	N/A

QUICK - .177 cal., BBC, SP, 18.25 BBL, 623 FPS, adj. rear sight, automatic safety, black synthetic stock w/ butt pad, 41 in. OAL, 5.5 lbs. Mfg. 2007.

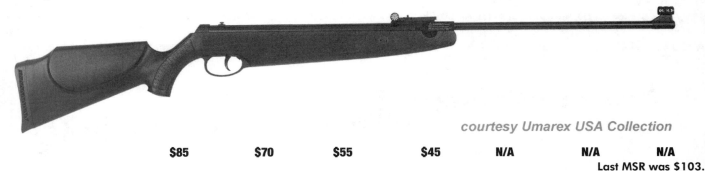

courtesy Umarex USA Collection

	$85	$70	$55	$45	N/A	N/A	N/A

Last MSR was $103.

Add 40% for combo w/ 4x32 compact scope.

RAZOR - .177 or .22 cal., BBC, SS, 19 in. BBL, 1000-820FPS, adj. rear fiber optic sights, automatic safety, checkered vaporized beech wood Monte Carlo stock, butt pad, 45.5 in. OAL, 7.5 lbs. Mfg. 2007.

courtesy Umarex USA Collection

	$285	$235	$195	$150	N/A	N/A	N/A

Last MSR was $310.

STORM - .177 or .22 cal., BBC, SS, 19.5 in. BBL, 1000-820FPS, adj. rear fiber optic sights, automatic safety, checkered black polymer ambidextrous Monte Carlo stock, butt pad, 45.5 in. OAL, 6.5 lbs. Mfg. 2007.

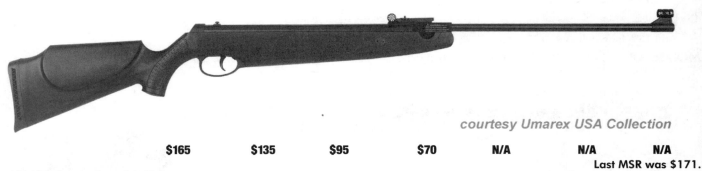

courtesy Umarex USA Collection

	$165	$135	$95	$70	N/A	N/A	N/A

Last MSR was $171.

Add 15% for combo w/ 4x32 scope.

GRADING	100%	95%	90%	80%	60%	40%	20%

STORM ELITE - .177 cal., BBC, SS, 19.5 in. nickel plated BBL, 1000-820FPS, adj. rear fiber optic sights, automatic safety, checkered burled wood look polymer ambidextrous Monte Carlo stock, butt pad, 45.5 in. OAL, 6. lbs. Mfg. 2007.

courtesy Umarex USA Collection

	$195	$165	$125	$95	N/A	N/A	N/A

Last MSR was $223.

STUTZEN Hämmerli marked Stutzen-style long forearm SP air rifle. Apparently a private brand production by BSA of their Stutzen model.

For more information on this air rifle see BSA in the "B" section of this text.

TITAN - .177 cal., BBC, SP, 1000 FPS, adj. rear sight and 4x32 scope, automatic safety, Monti Carlo wood stock w/ butt pad. Mfg. 2007-current.

courtesy Umarex USA Collection

MSR $145	• $125	$95	$65	$45	N/A	N/A	N/A

HAMMOND, KEN

Current custom airgun maker located in Ontario, Canada. Direct sales only.

Ken Hammond makes custom airguns with a military look, even using military spec M-16 parts to mimic the firearm. His airguns feature a spool valve of his own design which doubles as the intermediate air reservoir. The back of the valve is at atmospheric pressure and thus requires very little force to open. This allows for a simple trigger design with a low trigger release pressure.

RIFLES

HAMMOND WASP - 9 mm cal., PCP or CO_2 up to 3000 PSI. 850 FPS, SS with interchangeable barrels of any caliber. Uses a "cartridge" which holds a standard bullet and acts as connector between valve and barrel. 44 in. OAL, 10 lbs.

courtesy Fred Liady

$2,500	$2,250	N/A	N/A	N/A	N/A	N/A

HARLIE

For information on Harlie airguns, see Philippines Airguns in the "P" section.

HARPER CLASSIC GUNS

Previous manufacturer located in Buckingham, England. Previously imported by Beeman Precision Airguns, Santa Rosa, CA. Introduced circa 1985.

Products include air canes and pistols. Some Harper pneumatics, based on the Saxby-Palmer rechargeable air cartridges. More recent airguns, including electronic trigger guns, will be considered in future editions of this guide. See Brocock introduction in the "B" section of this guide for information on the 2004 ban on production and sale of air cartridge airguns.

GRADING	100%	95%	90%	80%	60%	40%	20%

PISTOLS

CLASSIC MICRO PISTOL - .177 cal., air cartridge forms the body of the gun, SS, manual firing block, includes separate 9.6 in. air pump, which uses a special chamber to fill the air cartridge without connecting to the cartridge, 2.3 in. OAL, 0.8 oz.

courtesy Beeman Collection

	100%	95%	90%	80%	60%	40%	20%
	$350	$295	N/A	N/A	N/A	N/A	N/A

Subtract 40% for missing pump.

This model was created to be the world´s smallest air pistol and, unlike true miniatures, it is a full size caliber. Brass collection ID tag in illustration is 7/8 inches in diameter. Under their anti-airgun-cartridge law, this gun is now illegal in England as a dangerous weapon!

CLASSIC PISTOL - .22 or .25 cal., Harper Air Cane rifle action, walnut handle, brass barrel, concealed fold-out trigger, 300 FPS, 6.5 OAL, 4 oz. Mfg. 1989 only.

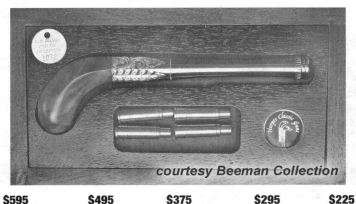

courtesy Beeman Collection

	100%	95%	90%	80%	60%	40%	20%
	$595	$495	$375	$295	$225	N/A	N/A

Last MSR for a cased pair was $700.

Add 50% if cased. Add 10% for .25 cal. Add 10% for deluxe. Add 50%-75% for rare specimens of air pistols in the form of smoking pipes, ball-point pens, etc.

Only six were imported into U.S. Under their anti-airgun-cartridge law, this gun is now illegal in England as a dangerous weapon!

CLASSIC PEPPERBOX - .22 cal., PCP, similar to Beeman/Harper Classic Pistol, 9.8 oz. Mfg. 1989 only.

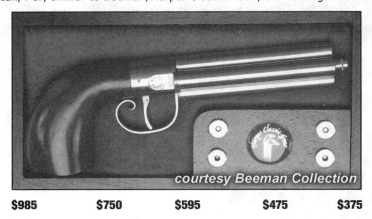

courtesy Beeman Collection

	100%	95%	90%	80%	60%	40%	20%
	$985	$750	$595	$475	$375	N/A	N/A

Last MSR was $575.

Only three were imported into the U.S. Under their anti-airgun-cartridge law, this gun is now illegal in England as a dangerous weapon!

GRADING	100%	95%	90%	80%	60%	40%	20%

AIR CANES

CLASSIC AIR CANE - .22 or .25 cal., pneumatic (reusable gas cartridge), 650 FPS, reproduction of 19th century Walking Cane Gun, 1 lb. Mfg. circa 1980s.

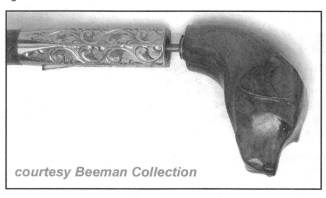

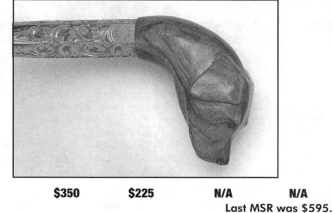

courtesy Beeman Collection

$795	$695	$495	$350	$225	N/A	N/A

Last MSR was $595.

Add $55 for decorative head piece.

Only ten of these models were imported into the U.S. Under their anti-airgun-cartridge law, this gun is now illegal in England as a dangerous weapon!

HARRINGTON

Current Trade name of T.J. Harrington & Sons Ltd. of Walton, Surrey, England. Made about one million spring-piston, push-barrel airguns (based on the 1877 H.M. Quackenbush patent) from 1937 to 1940 and 1947 to 2000. Sold to Marksman Products of Huntington Beach, CA about 2000 with production continuing.

The GAT is a low cost, mostly cast alloy, pop-out type pistol. This gun enjoyed enormous popularity for decades. In fact, most airgunners outside of the USA probably cut their teeth on a GAT. It was first introduced in 1937, production ceased during the war but recommenced postwar and still carries on. The design of the GAT drew heavily upon an H. M. Quackenbush patent of 1877. All GATs have a smoothbore .177 barrel. Many are also fitted with a muzzle device that enables corks, as well as pellets and darts, to be fired.

The GAT design has undergone few variations; the most significant one would be the addition of a safety catch in 1982, to make the gun acceptable on the U.S. market.

In 1987 a smoothbore long gun version of the GAT was produced and marketed with little success.

The authors and publisher wish to thank Trevor Adams and John Atkins for their valuable assistance with the following information in this edition of the *Blue Book of Airguns*.

PISTOLS

GAT - .177 darts, slugs, waisted pellets, or corks, SP, SS, push-barrel cocking, cast alloy and (later) plastic, smoothbore barrel. Muzzle nut for shooting corks. Safety added in 1982 for USA market. Initially black or bright chrome finish, then black paint or polished (buffed bare metal) and finally black paint only.

courtesy Beeman Collection

$40	$30	$20	$10	N/A	N/A	N/A

Add 25% for bright nickel finish. Add 50% for original green factory box. Add 20% for other factory boxes.

RIFLES

GAT RIFLE - .177 cal. darts, balls, or pellets, SP, SS, push-barrel cocking similar to Gat Pistol, except long gun version. Current retail values in the $50 to $75 range depending on condition. Mfg. 1987.

HATSAN ARMS CO.
Current manufacturer located in Izmir, Turkey. No current importation.

HAVILAND AND GUNN (G.P. GUNN COMPANY)
Previous airgun designers and manufacturers located in Ilion, NY circa 1871-1882. Then the company was purchased by H.M. Quackenbush. (See also Gem and Quackenbush sections).
The authors and publisher wish to thank Mr. John Groenwold for the following information in this edition of the *Blue Book of Airguns*.

GEORGE GUNN

The airgun designs of George Gunn have had enormous impact on the development of modern airguns. Patent number 113766, dated April 18, 1871, registered to Benjamin Haviland and George Gunn, was the basis for not only the Haviland & Gunn barrel-cocking air rifles and the resulting, wonderful H.M. Quackenbush Model 5 rifles, but led to the great variety of air rifles known as the Gem airguns in Europe and indeed most of the amazing number and variety of barrel-cocking air rifles and pistols which have been developed since then! Patent number 126954, dated May 21, 1872, also registered to Haviland and Gunn, for an air pistol with the mainspring within the grip, is the basis for another more than century-long parade of airguns, including some early Gaggenau air pistols, the MGR air pistols, the Lincoln air pistols, and even the Walther LP 53 made famous by James Bond!
George P. Gunn was born in Tioga County,PA in 1827. He was a gunsmith in North Ilion, NY. He first he marketed an airgun under his own name while working for Remington Arms Company and then another after leaving their employ. These guns, based on his first patents, were marked "G. P. GUNN, ILION, NY, PAT. APR. 18, 1871".

BENJAMIN HAVILAND JOINS GEORGE GUNN

About the time of Gunn´s first patent, he joined with Benjamin Haviland to form the firm of Haviland and Gunn. Benjamin Haviland (1823-1920) had been involved with the grocery, commission, and freighting fields. His position as senior partner in the new firm evidently resulted from bringing essential marketing skills and financial backing. Throughout the 1870s the firm of Haviland and Gunn was engaged in the manufacture of airguns at the Ilion Depot, on the New York Central Railroad, in Ilion, NY.

HAVILAND AND GUNN HISTORY

Most of the rifles produced by Gunn or Haviland & Gunn were combination guns which could function as either an air rifle or as a .22 rimfire firearm. Some models were strictly air rifles and some may have been strictly rimfire. A "patch box" in the buttstock of the combination guns stored the firing pin and/or breech seal. When used as a rimfire gun, the firing pin was installed in the air transfer port on the front of the cylinder face. When the trigger was pulled, the piston moved forward, without significant air compression, and struck the firing pin which in turn crushed and detonated the primer of the rimfire cartridge. The patch box on the Haviland and Gunn rifles underwent several changes in shape, style, lid type and functioning, and location, finally ending up as round on the right side of the stock.
A traditional "tee bar" breech latch is found on most Haviland and Gunn air rifles and combination rifles. A side swinging breech latch on smooth bore air rifles probably was an earlier design.
Haviland & Gunn developed numerous "improved" modifications of their various models during the 1870s. They produced their last catalog in 1881. In 1882, H.M. Quackenbush purchased at least part of the Haviland and Gunn Company, including patent rights, machinery, existing stock, and equipment related to gun and slug manufacture. George Gunn agreed to work for H.M. Quackenbush but Benjamin Haviland did not.

QUACKENBUSH TAKES OVER

In 1884, Quackenbush offered exactly the same gun as the Haviland and Gunn "Improved 1880" as the Quackenbush Model 5. The parts were the same but not all were interchangeable. Quackenbush soon began offering it with an increased number of options. The stronger marketing by Quackenbush contributed to a much increased success of the Number 5 Rifle.
While working for H. M. Quackenbush, George Gunn considered a repeating version of the combination rifle known as the Hurricane. Apparently it exists only in the papers of patent number 337,395 of March 9, 1886. That Henry Marcus Quackenbush´s name does not appear on this patent, filed August 12, 1885, may be related to George Gunn leaving the Quackenbush firm in that year.
A mechanical target, as produced by Haviland and Gunn for many years, was improved with several Quackenbush patents and became an important item in the Quackenbush line. A reversible "iron face" plate with a hole in the center created the "bullseye." When the shooter struck the bullseye, a figure popped up on the top of the target and/or a bell sounded. These targets are known only unmarked or with Quackenbush markings.
George Gunn also invented the felted airgun slug, patenting the process for manufacturing them on December 18, 1883. Quackenbush was granted United States patent 358,984, on March 8, 1887, for improvements in their manufacturing process. The felted slug was so superior to the burred slug that its sales immediately surpassed those of the burred slug, but Quackenbush continued selling the burred slugs until 1947.
Entries in H.M Quackenbush´s personal diary indicate that George Gunn was ill, on and off, for quite some time after joining the Quackenbush Company. The last record of his employment by Quackenbush was August 12, 1885, at which time he was working on the Quackenbush Safety Rifle.

ATLAS GUN CO.

After leaving Quackenbush, George Gunn invented another airgun and started the Atlas Gun Company, in Ilion, NY to market it. He died on March 2, 1906 when he was hit by a train while walking home from the Central Depot in Ilion, NY.

GRADING	100%	95%	90%	80%	60%	40%	20%

PISTOLS

1872 MODEL - .177 cal., SP, SS, breech loading, mainspring within grip. It is cocked by inserting the breech block hook into a hole in the piston rod projecting from the base of the grip, has cast iron body with smooth surface or cast checkered grip, stamped metal trigger blade with round wire trigger guard, smoothbore, unmarked except for patent date of May 21, 1872 stamped onto surface of mainspring ring retainer. This design was also apparently licensed for Morse patent improved air pistol.

courtesy Beeman Collection

	N/A	N/a	$2,250	$1,750	$1,250	$850	$500

Subtract 20% for missing breech block with cocking hook.

RIFLES

All models are breech-loading airguns with walnut buttstocks and no forearms unless otherwise noted. Smoothbore models had a brass-lined barrel to fire darts, slugs, or shot. Rifled barrels were designed for burred or felted slugs. A tee bar breech latch is found on most guns; a side swinging latch is less common, presumably an earlier style. Except for the Parlor rifle, the H&G guns were finished in nickel plating or browning.

STRAIGHT LINE MODEL - .22 cal., BBC, SP, SS, receiver/spring chamber in straight line with barrel, metal stock wrist does not contain mainspring, receiver nickel plated, barrel brown finish.

	N/A	N/A	$3,500	$3,000	$2,200	$1,000	$500

NEW MODEL - combination air rifle/.22 rimfire gun, "patch box" of various shapes in buttplate holds firing pin or breech seal when other is in use, spring chamber angled down from barrel to form wrist of stock above trigger.

courtesy Beeman Collection

	N/A	N/A	$3,000	$2,500	$1,800	$1,000	$500

Add 10% for browned finish. Add 25% for side swinging breech latch.

NEW IMPROVED 1880 MODEL - combination air rifle/.22 caliber rimfire rifled gun (rare version: smoothbore air rifle only), predecessor to the Quackenbush Model 5, spring chamber angled down from barrel to form wrist of stock above trigger, patch box for firing pin only in lower edge of buttstock, serial number stamped on rear of barrel, under barrel latch, trigger. Barrel base only under lower half of barrel.

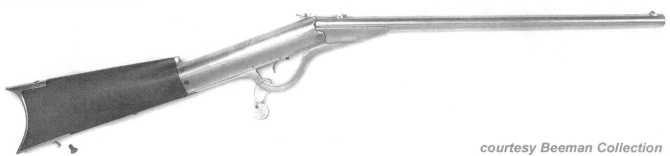

courtesy Beeman Collection

	N/A	N/A	$3,500	$3,000	$2,500	$1,500	$1,000

Add 10% for browned finish. Add 20% for nickel finish. Add 25% for smoothbore airgun only.

GRADING	100%	95%	90%	80%	60%	40%	20%

IMPROVED JUNIOR MODEL - .22 cal., BBC, SP, SS, spring chamber angled down from barrel to form wrist of stock above trigger, rifled or smoothbore barrel. Minor differences in barrel lengths and patch box locations, airgun action only so "patch box" served no real purpose.

		N/A	N/A	$3,000	$2,500	$1,800	$1,000	$500

Add 10% for browned finish. Add 25% for smoothbore airgun only.

PARLOR MODEL - .22 cal., piston cocked by pulling plunger ring within wire skeleton stock, 17.8 in. smoothbore barrel, heavy cast iron receiver, black and gilt (Japan black enamel and bright nickel) finish, other colors are known but have no factory documentation.

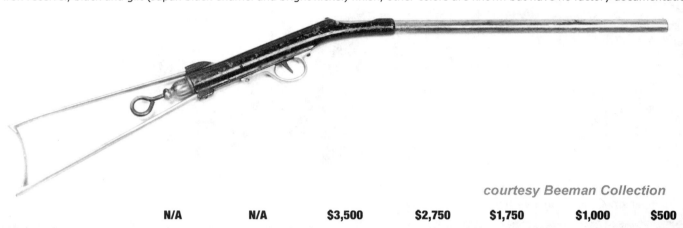

courtesy Beeman Collection

N/A	N/A	$3,500	$2,750	$1,750	$1,000	$500

HAWLEY

Previous maker of the "Kalamazoo" air pistol, located in Kalamazoo, MI about 1870.

Probably should be called the "Hawley" after Edwin H. Hawley, its inventor and maker, but it has been affectionally known by the delightfully sounding name of "Kalamazoo". That refers to the location of manufacture, but actually neither name, nor any other markings, appear on the pistol itself! In addition to being delightful both in name and design, this gun has special historical significance: Evidently this is America's first commercial pneumatic pistol. (Lukens and Kunz made pneumatic rifles in Philadelphia area ca. 1800-15 but evidently did not make pistols.). Based on patent #90,749, issued June 1, 1869 to Hawley but built to design advertised in 1870, covered by improved patent #118,886, issued to Edwin Hawley and George Snow on Sept. 12, 1871. A butt-reservoir pneumatic with straight pump affixed under barrel. Hammer suggestive of flintlock hammer with sear mechanism fully visible on bottom curve.

Improved patent including making front sight by merely turning up section of front barrel band. Sight arrangement strikingly strange: valve release pin protrudes from top center of receiver, thus rear sight groove has been displaced to right. To sight gun one must tip it about 45 degrees to left (this may be half-way precursor to flat-on-its-side "gangsta" firing stance of 20th century!).

Cast iron receiver contains air reservoir in the butt and firing mechanism in forward part. Three large casting holes sealed by pewter/lead or brass plugs. Plug just ahead of trigger allows access to install and repair exhaust valve.

PISTOLS

HAWLEY KALAMAZOO .25,.32, possibly other cals., smoothbore bbls. about 4.5 - 5 in, one known to 10.5 in., SS, PP, breech-loading, Japan black enamel finish on grip; nickel finish on bbl. and pump. Longitudinal pump with forward ring may have used a simple rod as pumping handle. Ref. AW (Nov. 1979), USA (July 1995), Hannusch (2001). Two variants:

✪ ***Lead Plug Version*** Receiver holes closed w/ large, somewhat crude, pewter/lead plugs with odd-shaped groove prob. to allow access only w/ special tool. Sliding loading cover w/ knurling. Hammer may have flat sided or grooved exterior side (flat side hammer and knurled loading cover illustrated in June 1970 Scientific American ad and in 1871 patent drawing.) Specimens w/ 1 or 2 brass plugs probably are not transitional forms but represent repairs - even the maker would find it difficult to replace removed lead plug, or would want to substitute new and improved brass plug. Forward access hole most likely to have substitute brass plug.

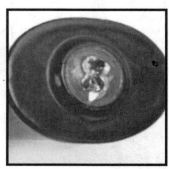

courtesy Beeman Collection

N/A	$2,250	$1,650	$1,400	$1,050	$825	$550

Add 15% for nickel finish. Add 30% for unusual purple original box. Add 30% for original instruction sheet and target.

GRADING	100%	95%	90%	80%	60%	40%	20%

◊ **Brass Plug Version** similar to earlier lead plug version except receiver plugs neatly machined from brass w/ standard groove for typical tools. Sliding loading cover longer and smooth.

courtesy Beeman Collection

	N/A	$1,800	$1,500	$1,250	$950	$750	$500

Add 15% for nickel finish. Add 30% for unusual purple original box. Add 30% for original instruction sheet and target.

HAWTHORNE

Previous Store Brand name used by Montgomery Wards.

For the original manufacturer and model name/number of Hawthorne Brand airguns see the Store Brand Cross-Over List at the back of this text.

HEALTHWAYS, INC.

Previous trademark manufactured and distributed by Healthways, Inc., Compton, CA into the 1970s. Healthways purchased Baron Mfg. Co. in 1947 and discontinued Baron air p[istols. CO_2 versions designed by Richard Kline and Kenneth Pitcher in 1955-56; patented in late 1950s. Healthways was purchased by Marksman.

For additional information on Plainsman Model airguns, see Challenger Arms Corp. in the "C" section.

PISTOLS

PLAINSMAN MODEL 9400 - BB/.175 cal. steel only, CO_2 (8 gm. CO_2 cylinders inserted in grip) semi-auto with coin-slotted, three-position power screw, hundred-shot gravity-fed mag., manual thumb safety, black plastic (later Marksman production had simulated woodgrain) grips, black epoxy finish, 5.9 in. rifled barrel, 350 FPS. 1.72 lbs.

	$90	$75	$65	$55	$45	$35	$25

1977 retail was approx. $30.

Add 25% for box, accessories, and factory papers.

PLAINSMAN MODEL 9401 - BB/.175 cal., similar to Model 9400, except smoothbore.

	$90	$75	$65	$55	$45	$35	$25

1977 retail was approx $30.

Add 25% for box, accessories, and factory papers.

PLAINSMAN MODEL 9404 "SHORTY" - .22 cal. for lead-coated steel round balls, CO_2 (8 gm. or 12 gm), forty-shot magazine, similar to Model 9400, except 3.9 in. barrel, 1.65 lbs.

courtesy Beeman Collection

	N/A	$100	$85	$75	$55	$45	$35

1977 retail was approx $35.

Add 30% for box, accessories, and factory papers.

GRADING	100%	95%	90%	80%	60%	40%	20%

PLAINSMASTER MODEL 9405 - BB/.175 cal., CO_2, 9.4 in. rifled barrel, black epoxy finish, detachable walnut wood-grain plastic thumbrest grip and forend, adj. rear sight, thumb safety, three-position power switch, hundred-round capacity, approx. 2.54 lbs.

	$90	$75	$65	$55	$45	$35	$25

1977 retail was approx $45.

Add 25% for box, accessories, and factory papers. Subtract 75% for missing forearm and hand grip.

PLAINSMASTER MODEL 9406 - .22 cal. for lead-coated steel round balls, similar to Model 9405, except smoothbore.

courtesy Beeman Collection

	N/A	$90	$75	$65	$55	$45	$35

1977 retail was approx $45.

Add 25% for box, accessories, and factory papers. Subtract 75% for missing forearm and hand grip.

PLAINSMAN MODEL MA 22 - .22 cal. lead covered steel balls, CO_2, approx. 350 FPS, gravity-fed fifty-shot mag., manual safety, styled like Colt Woodsman. Mfg. 1969-1980.

courtesy Beeman Collection

	$135	$100	$85	$65	$45	N/A	N/A

PLAINSMAN MODEL ML 175 - .175/BB cal., CO_2, approx. 350 FPS, gravity-fed fifty-shot mag., manual safety, metal grips, styled like Colt Woodsman, black finish, plastic grips, 6 in. BBL, 9.3 in. OAL, 1.9 lbs. Mfg.1969-1980.

courtesy Beeman Collection

	$80	$65	$55	$45	$35	N/A	N/A

Add 25% for chrome finish.

GRADING	100%	95%	90%	80%	60%	40%	20%

PLAINSMAN WESTERN - .175/BB cal., CO_2 or SP, spring-fed magazine (approx. fifteen shots), no safety, styled like Colt Peacemaker SA revolver. 11.5 in. OAL, 2.1 lbs.

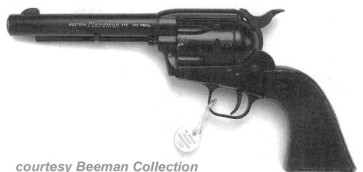

courtesy Beeman Collection

	$95	$80	$70	$55	$45	$35	$25

Add 20% for spring version, barrel sleeve will rove to shoot corks or darts.

TOPSCORE MODEL 9100 - BB/.175 cal., lifting-barrel spring air action, 6.5 in. smoothbore barrel, approx. 200 FPS, fifty-shot gravity-fed mag., manual thumb safety, die-cast one-piece grip/frame, 1.7 lbs.

	$75	$60	$50	$45	$40	$30	$25

1977 retail was approx $20.

Add 25% for box, accessories, and factory papers.

PLAINSMAN TOPSCORE 175 - .177 BB cal., CO_2, repeater, 10.5 in. OAL, 2.2 lbs.

	$75	$60	$50	$45	$40	$30	$25

PLAINSMAN SHARP SHOOTER 175 - .177 BB cal., CO_2, repeater.
Values and dates not available at the time of publication.

RIFLES

PLAINSMAN MODEL MX175 - BB/.175 cal., CO_2 12 gm., 20 in. barrel, scope rail cast in top, low power, beech stock. 4 lbs.

courtesy Beeman Collection

	$65	$55	$50	$40	$35	$30	$20

Add 20% for box, accessories, and factory papers.

PLAINSMAN MODEL MC22 - .22 cal., lead coated steel round balls, similar to Model MX175.

	$75	$65	$55	$50	$40	$35	$30

Add 20% for box, accessories, and factory papers.

HEGMANS, THEO

Current craftsman located in Kerken, Germany.

Theo Hegmans is a German who can only be described as a craftsman genius - although he is a graduate economist and computer specialist, he retreats to an old-fashioned shop in his barn to make too many things to describe, but all wonderful. These creations include the most unusual firearms and astonishing airguns. His inventions include a version of the old large bore German airguns, or Windbüchsen. This Windbüchse is most unusual in that it uses a percussion cap to open the air valve to a charge of stored air and push a 200-grain, .45 caliber lead bullet out at great velocity. Ref: VISIER, March 2005.

PISTOLS

HEGMANS MCAIRROW CLASSIC - soda straw cal, the only Hegmans airgun ever made in quantity. The straw projectiles are fitted with a rubber tip and some fins cut from other straws. The projectile is shoved over the concealed barrel - the missile is around the barrel rather than in it! Two to twelve pumps power the gun. On full power it fires up to 230 FPS to a range of 30 or 40 yards! Original retail price equaled about $125. Rarity precludes accurate pricing.

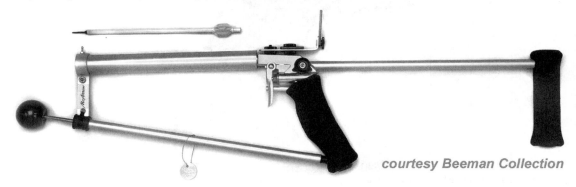

courtesy Beeman Collection

In 1999, this started out as a toy for his then nine-year-old nephew, made from a bicycle tire pump, a grease gun, and garden soaker hose! As projectiles, he used plastic drinking straws from an international fast food firm whose name may be suggested by the name of this gun. The fast food firm was not pleased and he was pressured to stop production after only exactly fifty specimens had been made over three years.

RIFLES

AIR TWIN - .177 or .22 cal., SxS double-barrel, SP, SS, mainsprings around the barrels, 18.5/33.4 ft./lb. ME, 41.3 in. OAL, 8.8 lbs. Rarity precludes accurate pricing.

courtesy Theo Hegmans

Each BBL holds 10mm group ctc at 25 yds, together 20 mm ctc.

CHIP MUNK - .22 cal., SS, PCP, realBBL hidden under false barrel air reservoir, 25 shots per charge, 52 ft./lb. ME, 41.3 in OAL, 7.0 lbs. Rarity precludes accurate pricing.

courtesy Theo Hegmans

GRADING	100%	95%	90%	80%	60%	40%	20%

GO WEST - .177 cal., PCP, real BBL hidden under false barrel air reservoir, eight-shot repeater with lever activated cylinder, 32 shots @ 14.8 ft./lb. ME, 16 shots @ 11.4 ft./lb. ME, 40.6 in. OAL, 9.3 lbs. Rarity precludes accurate pricing.

courtesy Theo Hegmans

GRANDPA - .45 cal., PCP, muzzle loader, walnut stock, 297 ft./lb. ME at 3000 PSI with 250 gr. bullet, 900 PSI, 89 ft./lb. ME, 47.2 in. OAL, 9.7 lbs. Rarity precludes accurate pricing.

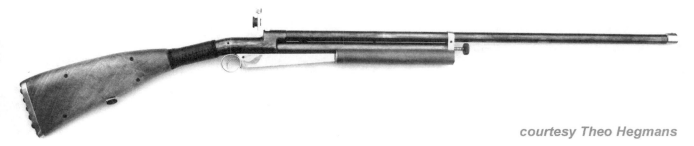

courtesy Theo Hegmans

HOW STUFF WORKS - .177 cal., BBC, SP, SS, butt reservoir, all operating elements on the outside of the gun, 40 shots per charge @ 18 ft./lb. ME. 43.3 in. OAL, 6.2 lbs. Rarity precludes accurate pricing.

HEILPRIN MANUFACTURING CO.

For information on Heilprin Manufacturing Co. airguns, see Columbian in the "C" section.

HEIRINKAN

Previous trade name of Heirinkan Co. located in Tokyo, Japan.

Heirinkan airguns were designed by the company's founder, the late Ueda Shoji (1918-81). Former producer of high power, pneumatic air rifles. These rifles were made only in small numbers and for a very short time in the 1970s. Reportedly most of the rifles remaining in Japan were destroyed by the government and ownership is forbidden without a special need – such as professional pest control. Collection as such is not allowed. Much sought by collectors and shooters because of their high power, accuracy, and high quality. Reportedly in production 1953-81, information not confirmed. Research is ongoing with this trademark, and more information will be included both in future editions and online.

RIFLES

MODEL A .177 cal., swinging arm, multi-pump pneumatic, sporter model, 6.6 lbs, 36.6 in. OAL. Rarity precludes exact pricing.

courtesy Beeman Collection

	100%	95%	90%	80%	60%	40%	20%
	N/A	N/A	N/A	$650	$450	$300	$150

MODEL SS Apparently similar to Model A with telescopic sight.
Rarity precludes accurate pricing.

MODEL Z no information at this time.
Rarity precludes accurate pricing.

MODEL 120 Apparently similar to Model A but w/ thumbhole stock.
Rarity precludes accurate pricing.

BREAK BARREL MODEL - NO ADDITIONAL INFORMATION AT THIS TIME.

HEXAGON

For information on Hexagon airguns, see Decker in the "D" section.

HEYM WAFFENFABRIK GmbH

Current manufacturer established in 1865 and located in Gleichamberg, Germany since 1995. Made airguns from 1949-52.

Currently firearms are imported beginning 1999 by New England Custom Gun Service, Ltd., located in Plainfield, NH. During 1998, Heym underwent a management change. Previously manufactured in Muennerstadt, Germany circa 1952-1995 and Suhl, Germany between 1865 and 1945. Originally founded in 1865 by F.W. Heym. Previously imported by JagerSport, Ltd. located in Cranston, RI 1993-94 only, Heckler & Koch, Inc. (until 1993) located in Sterling, VA, Heym America, Inc. (subsidiary of F.W. Heym of W. Germany) located in Fort Wayne, IN, and originally by Paul Jaeger, Inc. 1970-1986.

For more information and current pricing on both new and used Heym firearms, please refer to the *Blue Book of Gun Values* by S.P. Fjestad (also available online).

PISTOLS

LP 103 - .177 cal., SP, SS, push-barrel Gat-style air pistol, white plastic checkered grips, 7.8 in. OAL, 12 oz. Estimated value in average condition about $35.

courtesy Beeman Collection

RIFLES

Research is ongoing for this rifles section, and more information will be included both in future editions and online. Three models are known: LG 100 (about 3000 produced), LG 101 (repeater version of LG 100), and LG 103 (junior version of LG 100).

HILL & WILLIAMS

Previous manufacturer located in Staffordshire, England, circa 1905-1911.

The Hill & Williams air rifle, in .22 cal., is a barrel-cocking, spring-piston design cocked by pushing forward a barrel latch at the breech and then pivoting the barrel downward. British patent number 25222/´05 was issued to Arthur Henry Hill and Walter F. Williams on 16 July 1908 for the design. Hill´s address was 28 Leyton Road, Handsworth, Staffordshire, England. Walter notes that the gun may not have been made by Hill and Williams until about 1908. It was probably too complicated and expensive to compete with the Lincoln Jeffries design underlever rifles from BSA. Production ended by 1911. Apparently abouttwo hundredguns were produced.

This gun evidently was one of the pioneer production designs, along with the somewhat similar MGR First Model Rifle, developed at the very beginning of the 20th century. Specimens in good condition should have a retail value in the $2,600 range. Refs: *Airgunner* April 1986, Dec. 1986, and *Guns Review*, Aug. 1978.

courtesy Beeman Collection

HOLBORN

For information on Holborn airguns, see Dianawerk in the "D" section.

HORNET

For information on Hornet airguns, see Plymouth Air Rifle Company in the "P" section.

GRADING	100%	95%	90%	80%	60%	40%	20%

HOTSHOT

For information on Hotshot airguns, see Gun Toys SRL in the "G" section.

HOWA

Current manufacturer located in Tokyo, Japan, and previously located in Nagoya, Japan. No current importation.

Howa Machinery Limited, formerly manufacturers of Japanese defense force assault rifles, Weatherby Vanguard rifle actions, and rifles and shotguns for Smith & Wesson. Also produced small numbers of extremely high grade CO_2 rifles (styled like the Weatherby Mark V semi-auto rifle, reportedly to induce Weatherby to distribute them in the USA) in the mid-1970s.

For more information and current pricing on both new and used Howa firearms, please refer to the *Blue Book of Gun Values* by S.P. Fjestad (also available online).

RIFLES

MODEL 55G - .177 cal., two CO_2 cylinders back-to-back, BA feedsfive pellets from spring-fed magazine, blue finish, highly polished steel parts with highly finished and detailed hardwood or synthetic stocks, 38.7 in. OAL, 6.0 lbs. Mfg. 1975- current.

courtesy Beeman Collection

MSR $1,200	$1,200	$900	$700	$450	$300	N/A	N/A

This model is very rarely seen anywhere in the world, esp. outside of Japan.
User´s note and warning: bolt will not close after magazine delivers its last pellet until the charging rod is retracted.

HUBERTUS

Previously manufactured by Jagdwaffenfabrik, in Suhl, Germany. (Other addresses may include Molin, Germany.)

PISTOLS

HUBERTUS - .177 or .22 cal., push-barrel, spring-piston action, single shot (barrel must be pulled back out before loading and firing), blue steel receiver, plain barrel, both front and rear sights on receiver, marked "D.R.G.M. Deutsches Reichs-Gebrauch-Muster" (a low level patent notice). Small frame variant: smoothbore, 8.5 in. OAL, early production. Large frame variant: rifled, forward breech ring ribbed, 10.5 in.OAL, about 1.5 lbs., patented 1925, mfg. 1925-1935. See *Guns Review*, May, 1973 and Dec. 1975.

small frame *large frame*

courtesy Beeman Collection

N/A	$250	$175	$135	$100	$75	$50

Add 40% for factory box and papers. Add 40% for cocking aid and pellet tin. Add 40% for spare barrel. Add 60% for small frame version. Add 25% for .22 caliber.

The large version was distributed as the Snider Air Pistol for a short time in the USA by E.K. Tryon & Co, Philadelphia, PA.

RIFLES

MODEL 53 .177 in. cal. (may be for shot cartridges), BB, SS, SP, breech-opening lever. Marked DRGM for "Deutsches Reich Gebrauchs Muster" (German Government Registered Design - a weak patent level.) Details and values TBD.

GRADING	100%	95%	90%	80%	60%	40%	20%

HYDE

Previous trademark manufactured by Floyd Hyde located in South California.

PISTOLS

HYDE PISTOL - BB/.174 cal., CO_2, semi-auto repeater, similar to Daisy Model 100. April 1959.

	N/A	N/A	$150	$125	$100	$65	$40

HY-SCORE ARMS CORPORATION

Previous distributor and importer located in Brooklyn, NY.

The American Hy-Score CP (Concentric Piston) air pistols are well-made airguns by a unique American company. As spring piston airguns, especially with their unusual concentric piston design, they stand in bold contrast to the pump and CO_2 guns that were the standard in the USA. Steven E. Laszlo founded the S.E. LaszloHouse of Imports of Brooklyn,NY in 1933. The company imported many items, including airguns, ammunition, black powder firearms, binoculars, telescopes, magnetic compasses, and movie camera lenses. The S.E. Laszlo House of Imports served as the umbrella company for the Hy-Score Arms Corporation, whose main claim to fame was their development and manufacture of a unique series of concentric piston spring air pistols. The company originally was located at 25 Lafayette St. in Brooklyn, NY. In October 1965, the firm moved to 200 Tillary Street, Brooklyn, NY, where it remained until Steve Laszlo´s death in 1980.

In 1970, Hy-Score discontinued marketing of the Hy-Score CP air pistols, perhaps due to increased legal and political pressure for a safety mechanism. The cost and effort of converting the design to appease these pressures may not have been of interest to Steve Laszlo in that stage of his life. He had started to import other airguns as early as 1950. From 1970 until his death in 1980, he concentrated on selling airguns made by overseas factories.

The American Hy-Score CP air pistols were produced for only about twenty-five years, but they form one of the most interesting groups of airguns for collectors who appreciate their unique nature.

In 1989, the Hy-Score concentric-piston design returned full circle to England when the Hy-Score brand became British. Richard Marriot-Smith purchased the trademark, plans, and what remained of the long idle Hy-Score factory machinery and Hy-Score pistol parts. Operating under the name of the Phoenix Arms Co., in Kent, England, he began production of the "New Hy-Score" Single-Shot pistol using original Hy-Score machinery and many original American parts. The general appearance was that of the Model 803 Sportster with the muzzle threaded for a moderator. It was a rather expensive, unfamiliar style for the English market and regular exports to the USA were precluded by the lack of a safety mechanism. Production was extremely limited; almost as soon as Phoenix Arms had arisen from the ashes of Marriot-Smith´s other gun enterprises, it disappeared, having created instant collectibles.

HY-SCORE PISTOL DESIGN

Steve Laszlo was an expert marketer, but he was not a designer. About 1940, he asked his brother, Andrew Lawrence (nee Laszlo), an engineer in applied mechanics, to develop a compact, modern high-powered air pistol. See Ref: Lawrence (1969).

Andrew designed the gun to be produced without the forgings and leather seals typical of contemporary air pistols, to have a light, good trigger action, and to look like a firearm. A desire for easy cocking, no pumping, and reliability dictated a spring piston powerplant. His Stanford University research paper, which outlined the development of this pistol, discussed the pros and cons of the Zenit, Webley, Diana, and Haenel spring piston airguns. He settled on the concentric piston design found in the English Acvoke, Warrior, Westley Richards, and Abas-Major air pistols. These pistols are conspicuous by their lack of any mention in Andrew´s paper and he dismissed consideration of English patents as "too costly."

Concentric piston airguns use the barrel as a guide for a piston snugly fitted around it. The concentric powerplant allowed for a very long, powerful mainspring and a long barrel, conducive to both high power and accuracy, in a rather compact pistol. World War II delayed production until about 1946. Hy-Score advertised their new pistols as the world´s most powerful airguns, with the accuracy of an air rifle, and the looks and feel of a Luger.

Andrew was skilled in automotive engineering; so instead of the conventional leather seals, the first Hy-Score CP pistols used automotive-type steel piston rings made by the Perfect Circle Co., expected to be good for a lifetime of normal use. (The seals were later changed to o-rings when the steel piston rings proved to be a maintenance problem.) The solid, durable grips were made of Tenite, a new plastic from General Electric. Steel blocks cast into the grip provided excellent heft and balance.

The trigger system is unique and deserves special mention. Rather than having the full pressure of the mainspring bear on the sear, Lawrence designed a special "servo-mechanism" to enable the shooter to apply relatively little pressure to very smoothly release the shot. A "dry practice" feature allowed the shooter to slightly open the gun, without cocking the mainspring, to set the trigger for practice trigger pulls.

Lawrence´s genius is revealed by the loading mechanism. The loading gate is a very ingenious camera-shutter system, which, in the repeater version, is coupled with one of the cleverest projectile feeding mechanisms in the world of gun design. When the breech cap is turned by the shooter, six little steel cylinders cam their way around, like bumper cars at a carnival, to each feed their contained pellet into the firing chamber. This mechanism apparently has never been duplicated in any other gun.

The body tube is a very sturdy, drawn steel tube which, in the later models, is smoothly tapered down to form the barrel profile. The frame is a smooth stamping. Engraving-style, stamped scroll markings were added to the frame at approximately serial number 850,000. An excellent blue finish was standard. Chrome plating was an extra cost option and is rarely seen.

The various Hy-Score CP air pistol models all used the same basic mechanism and frame. The key differences were in single vs. repeater mechanism, finish, grip color, barrel style, and barrel length. The 700 and 800 model series appear to be fixed long-barrel single-shots, although what appears to be the visible barrel in the Model 700 is just a large-bore tube extending forward from the frame which contains a short barrel. The 802 is a fixed long-barrel repeater. The 803 Sportster is a short interchangeable-barrel single-shot. The 804 is a short fixed-barrel repeater. An "R" on the repeaters or an "S" on the Sportster models precedes serial numbers in the 800,000 range. Serial numbers over 900,000 are without the prefixes.

HY-SCORE COMPARATIVE MODEL NUMBERS

Most of Hy-Score´s airgun imports were made by Dianawerk of Rastatt, Germany. (See the comparative model chart in the Dianawerk section.) Various other airguns were made for Hy-Score by BSF, Hämmerli, Anschütz, Baikal, Em-Ge, Slavia, and FN. Important note: Compara-

GRADING	100%	95%	90%	80%	60%	40%	20%

ble models often have different values due to varying degrees of rarity, different demand by collectors, and because distributors of private label guns often specified different power levels (for different markets, not just mainspring differences), stocks, calibers, sights, trigger mechanisms, etc. from the basic manufacturer´s model. Early models of the same number may differ from more recent models.

Hy-Score imports not made by Dianawerk:

Hy-Score 822T Pistol - Made by Em-Ge in Germany.

Hy-Score 821, 833SM, 894 sidelever rifle - Made by Hämmerli of Germany.

Hy-Score 824M Pistol - Hämmerli "Master" CO_2.

Hy-Score 823M Pistol - Hämmerli "Single" CO_2.

Hy-Score 817M Pistol - BSF (Wischo) CM w/o front sight hood.

Hy-Score 818 Pistol - toy-like pistol from Anschütz, etc. (8¾ ounces).

Hy-Score 833 - Hämmerli Model 10 (Puma Model 497).

Hy-Score 870 Mark III - Izhevsk Vostok IZh022 (Baikal).

Hy-Score 894 or 894 Sport - Hämmerli Model 4 (Puma Model 490).

PISTOLS

All models feature no safety.

MODEL 700 TARGET SINGLE SHOT - .177 or .22 cal., GC, rifled short barrel within the frame, what appears to be the visible barrel is only a tube for cosmetic purposes, angular step where false barrel base is pinned to the separate compression tube, rear sight attached with screw, Tenite grips (walnut, petrified wood, ivory, or onyx), blue finish. Not marked with model number but all Model 700 serial numbers begin with a seven. Approx. 2500 mfg 1947 only.

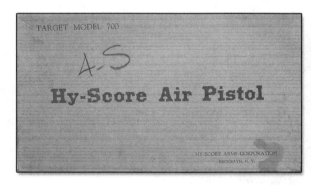

courtesy Beeman Collection

$350	$275	$240	$200	$150	$125	$90

Add 10% for grip colors other than walnut. Add 50%-60% for box and instruction sheet (box must say "700" on it). Subtract 5% for missing rear sight riser.

MODEL 800 TARGET SINGLE SHOT - BB/.175 smoothbore, .177 or .22 rifled cal., GC, 10.25 in. barrel, barrel cover and compression chamber a single smoothly tapered unit, dovetailed rear sight, Tenite grips (walnut, petrified wood, ivory, or onyx), blue or chrome finish. Mfg. 1948-1970.

courtesy Beeman Collection

$180	$130	$100	$90	$80	$60	$40

Add 75% for chrome finish ("C"). Add 10% for grip colors other than walnut. Add 30%-50% for box and instruction sheet. Add 10% for BB smoothbore barrel (model 800BB). Add 5%-10% for Hy-Score holster. Subtract 5% for missing rear sight riser.

GRADING	100%	95%	90%	80%	60%	40%	20%

MODEL 802 TARGET REPEATER - BB/.175 smoothbore, .177 or .22 rifled cal., GC, 10.25 in.barrel, six-shot, cammed rotation magazine, barrel cover and compression chamber a single smoothly tapered unit, dovetailed rear sight, Tenite grips (walnut, petrified wood, ivory, or onyx), blue or chrome finish. Mfg. 1949-1970.

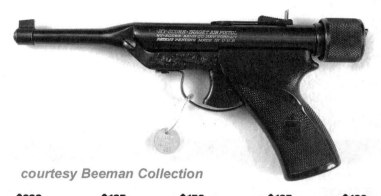

courtesy Beeman Collection

	$230	$195	$150	$135	$120	$90	$60

Add 80% for chrome finish ("C"). Add 10% for grip colors other than walnut. Add 30%-50% for box and instruction sheet. Add 10 % for BB smoothbore barrel (model 802BB). Add 5%-10% for Hy-Score holster. Subtract 5% for missing rear sight riser.

MODEL 803 SPORTSTER SINGLE SHOT - BB/.175 smoothbore, .177 and .22 rifled cal., GC, interchangeable 7.75 in.barrels, short design, dovetailed rear sight, blue or chrome finish. Mfg. 1952-1954.

courtesy Beeman Collection

	$250	$190	$170	$150	$125	$90	$75

Add 60% for chrome finish ("C"). Add 25%-40% for box and instruction sheet. Add 10%-15% for each extra barrel. Add 70% for five-in-one gun kit, blue, two extra barrels, ammo, and accessory tin (Model 803 SB). Add 100% for five-in-one gun kit, chromed, two extra barrels, ammo, and accessory tin (Model 803 SC). Subtract 5% for missing rear sight riser.

MODEL 804 SPORTSTER REPEATER - BB/.175 smoothbore, .177 or .22 rifled cal., GC, fixed 7.75 in.barrel, short design,six-shot cammed rotation magazine, dovetailed rear sight, blue or chrome finish. Mfg.1953-1954.

courtesy Beeman Collection

	$325	$305	$285	$255	$230	$210	$190

Add 35% for chrome finish ("C"). Add 30%-50% for box and instruction sheet. Add 10% for BB only smoothbore barrel. Subtract 5% for missing rear sight riser.

GRADING	100%	95%	90%	80%	60%	40%	20%

MODEL 805 SPORTSTER SINGLE SHOT .177 cal, GC, SP, SS, 7.75 in. rifled barrel,, similar to Model 803 except, the barrel is fixed by a steel pin.

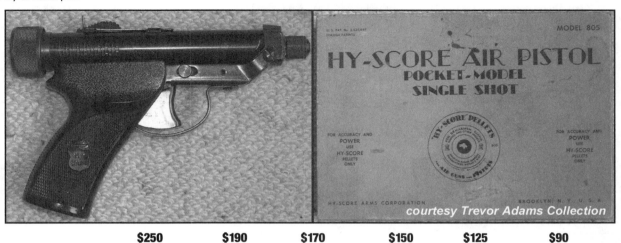

courtesy Trevor Adams Collection

	$250	$190	$170	$150	$125	$90	$75

Add 25%-40% for box and instruction sheet.

MODEL 814 JUNIOR SINGLE SHOT - .177 cal., push-barrel cocking, with shaped sheet steel frame, nickel finish, 7.9 in. smoothbore telescopic two-part steel barrel, removable knurled knob at back end of receiver for loading pellets or darts, adj. sights and riveted wooden grips, 10.6 oz.

courtesy Beeman Collection

	$45	$40	$35	$25	$15	N/A	N/A

NEW HY-SCORE SPORTER SINGLE SHOT - .177 cal., SP, GC, SS or repeater (intro. 1991), rifled barrel, semi-compact design with flat sided fixed barrel, threaded at the muzzle for moderator, rear sight adjustable for windage only or fully adjustable, blue finish. Made by Phoenix Arms Co., England. 1989-1994.

courtesy Beeman Collection

	N/A	$350	$300	$275	$250	$175	$125

Add 10% for fully adjustable rear sight (Mk II Model). Add 20% for factory box and literature. Add 10% for extra interchangeable barrel (modified original Hy-Score 803 barrels). Add 25% for repeater. Add 50% for chrome finish and white grips. Add 20% for Fake Moderator (apparently a non-functional expansion chamber). Add 100% or more for functional silencer/moderator with transferable $200 federal permit (required in U.S.).

NOTES

I SECTION

IAR, INC.

Current importer and distributor located in San Juan Capistrano, CA.
Previously imported of Chinese air rifles.

GRADING	100%	95%	90%	80%	60%	40%	20%

RIFLES

MODEL B-19 - .177 cal., BBC, SP, SS, rifled steel barrel, 900 FPS, blue finish, hardwood Monte Carlo-style stock with recoil pad, hooded front and adj. rear sight, push/pull safety, 5.5 lbs.

	100%	95%	90%	80%	60%	40%	20%
No MSR	$90	$65	$50	$40	$30	N/A	N/A

MODEL B-21 - .177 cal., SL, SP, SS, rifled steel barrel, 1000 FPS, blue finish, hardwood Monte Carlo-style stock with recoil pad, hooded front and adj. rear sight, dovetail scope base, push/pull safety, 9.9 lbs.

	100%	95%	90%	80%	60%	40%	20%
No MSR	$150	$115	$80	$65	$50	N/A	N/A

MODEL B-22 - .22 cal., SL, SP, SS, rifled steel barrel, 800 FPS, blue finish, hardwood Monte Carlo-style stock with recoil pad, hooded front and adj. rear sight, dovetail scope base, push/pull safety, 9.9 lbs.

	100%	95%	90%	80%	60%	40%	20%
No MSR	$150	$115	$80	$65	$50	N/A	N/A

IGA

For information on IGA airguns, see Anschütz in the "A" section.

IGI

For information on IGI airguns, see Gun Toys SRL in the "G" section.

IMPERIAL AIR RIFLE CO.

Previous manufacturer of the Double Express, a double barrel airgun manufactured by Mike Childs in the UK, who subsequently produced the Skan airguns.

Many components produced by Helston Gunsmiths in Helston, Cornwall, England.

RIFLES

DOUBLE EXPRESS - .177, .22, or .25 cal., DB, multiple-pump pneumatic DT, flip-open breech block loading, blue finish, walnut stocks, 10 ft./lb. ME, no sights, scope rail on valve housing, 40.5 in. OAL, 7.4 lbs. Mfg. 1987.

courtesy Vic Thompson

100%	95%	90%	80%	60%	40%	20%
$1,500	$1,250	$1,000	N/A	N/A	N/A	N/A

Add 10% for mixed calibers.
Seventeens guns produced with approximately fourteen sold, most were .22 cal.

IN KWANG

Previous manufacturing or marketing group in Seoul, Korea whose products included pre-charged pneumatic airguns.

RIFLES

MIRACLE GLS - .22 cal., PCP, six-shot revolving cylinder, 42.4 in. OAL, 8.3 lbs. Disc.

courtesy Beeman Collection

100%	95%	90%	80%	60%	40%	20%
$1,000	$850	$700	$600	$450	$300	N/A

INDUSTRY BRAND

Current trademark manufactured by Shanghai located in Shanghai, China. Currently imported by Compasseco, located in Bardstown, KY, and Air Gun Inc. located in Houston, TX.

See Compasseco listing.

ISAAC

For information on Isaac airguns, see Philippines Airguns in the "P" section.

ISW

Previous maker of air rifles and pistols in Calcutta, India. Generally produced copies of other airguns. About 1980s.

PISTOLS

SENIOR - .22 cal., SP, SS, barrel-lift cocking, copy of Webley Senior air pistol. Details and values TBD.

courtesy UK collector

IZH

Please refer to the Baikal section in this text.

J SECTION

JBC
For information on JBC airguns, see Philippine Airguns in the "P" section.

JAGUAR ARMS
Previous trademark manufactured in the mid-1970s by Jaguar Arms of Batavia N.Y.
Tiny, compact CO_2 pistols, produced as "the smallest CO_2 gun ever made." Very low power, inaccurate, and the finish was not durable. Thus, only a small number were sold and survived.

GRADING	100%	95%	90%	80%	60%	40%	20%

PISTOLS

CUB - .177 or .22 cal., use 8-gram CO_2 cylinders, black painted finish, brown or white grips.

courtesy Beeman Collection

	100%	95%	90%	80%	60%	40%	20%
	$225	$150	$125	$100	$75	$55	$45

Add 30% for box and papers. Add 60% for .22 cal.

BICENTENNIAL CUB - .177 or .22 cal., similar to Cub, except has chrome-plated finish, brown or white grips.

courtesy Beeman Collection

	100%	95%	90%	80%	60%	40%	20%
	$300	$225	$185	$150	$100	$80	$65

Add 30% for box and papers. Add 60% for .22 cal.

JAPANESE MILITARY TRAINER
Previously produced by unknown maker or makers in Osaka, Japan during WWII.
SS, air powered version of Japanese service rifles. Muzzle 193 in, original ammo not known, but fires .177 pellets well. Straight-pull bolt action cocks on pull, spring piston completely built into bolt. Well machined bolt, trigger guard, bbl bands, and heavy, nickeled buttplate. Functional bayonet lug; fake cleaning rod. Marked w/ various Japanese characters (inc. Osaka address), JAPAN OSAKA, bomb symbol containing letters HA, and stamped with large AFC under sunburst on forward receiver ring. SN of specimen shown: L93497. 19.8 in. smoothbore bbl., 38.2 in. OAL, 13.1 in. stock pull, ca. 8 lb. trigger pull, wgt. 4.8 lbs. Very rare; Japanese wartime production efforts desperately had to turn to production of only actual firearms. Very heavy wear is to be expected of military trainers, – average specimens valued about $1,100.

courtesy Beeman Collection

GRADING	100%	95%	90%	80%	60%	40%	20%

JELLY

For information about the Jelly mark on airguns, see Relum Limited in the "R" section.

JIFRA

Current manufacturer located in Guadalajara, Jalisco, Mexico beginning about 1980.

RIFLES

MODEL 700 - BB/.174 cal., SP, LA, repeating BB gun of classic Daisy styling, finished in bright color paints or nickel plated, may have fake telescope tube, riveted tinplate construction, 32.8 in. OAL.

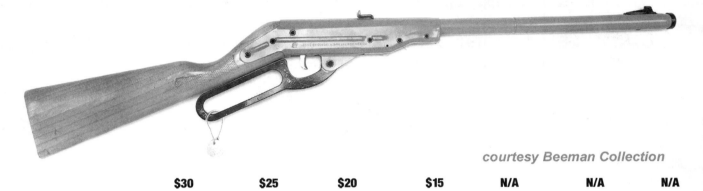

courtesy Beeman Collection

$30	$25	$20	$15	N/A	N/A	N/A

JOHNSON & BYE

Previous trade name of the Johnson & Bye Co. located in Worchester, MA.

Iver Johnson was the co-patentee, with Martin Bye, on U.S. patents 176,003 and 176,004 of April 11, 1876. These two Norwegian immigrants had developed an air pistol in which the barrel rotates to form a T-shaped cocking handle. Iver Johnson started his small gunsmithing shop about 1867 and then joined with Bye to form Johnson and Bye about 1875. In 1883 the company became Iver Johnson & Company and soon changed to Iver Johnson Arms & Cycle Works which became famous for inexpensive revolvers.

As noted elsewhere, Johnson, Bye, Bedford, Walker, and Quackenbush all were close associates. Their production, distribution, and ownership is confusing at times: H.M. Quackenbush recorded selling 69 Champion air pistols in 1884. It is not clear who made those 69, or how the total production of Champion air pistols was divided. And Albert Pope of Boston apparently was the main seller of Champion air pistols and also marketed air pistols, made by Quackenbush, under the Pope name. The Bedford & Walker air pistol production started in the Pope plant, then went to the Bedford & Walker plant, and finally transferred to the H.M. Quackenbush factory.

For more information and current pricing on Iver Johnson firearms, please refer to the *Blue Book of Gun Values* by S.P. Fjestad (also available online).

PISTOLS/RIFLES

CHAMPION - .21 cal., SP, SS, barrel turns to form cocking handle, 8.3 in. smoothbore barrel, Japan black lacquer, nickel plated, or nickel plated with rosewood grips finish, a standard, or perhaps optional, feature, was a fitted wooden case with a wire shoulder stock, 100 slugs, six targets, a dart pulling claw, and a wrench, Only markings: PAT. MAR, 7. APR. 11. 76 ENG. JULY 1, 75, MAY 20, 76,15.5 in. OAL, 1.6 lbs. Mfg. 1875-1883, w/ advertising untill 1893.

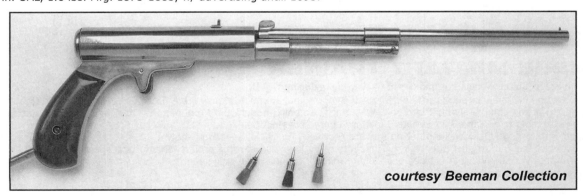

courtesy Beeman Collection

N/A	N/A	$750	$550	$400	$250	$100

Add 10% for nickel plating. Add 10% for wire shoulder stock. Add 20% for deluxe model with nickel plating and rosewood grip plates. Add 20% for original fitted wood case with some accessories.

GRADING	100%	95%	90%	80%	60%	40%	20%

JOHNSON AUTOMATICS, INC.

Previous manufacturer located in Providence, RI. Johnson Automatics, Inc. moved many times during its history, often with slight name changes. M.M. Johnson, Jr. died in 1965, and the company continued production at 104 Audubon Street in New Haven, CT as Johnson Arms, Inc. mostly specializing in sporter semi-auto rifles in .270 Win. or 30-06. For more information and current pricing on both new and used firearms, please refer to the Blue Book of Gun Values by S.P. Fjestad (also available online).

Evidently also produced the Johnson Indoor Target Gun circa 1945.

RIFLES

INDOOR TARGET GUN - BB/.174 cal., catapult rifle, hundred-shot, spring-fed magazine, 100 FPS, brown bakelite stock, 28.7 in. OAL.

courtesy Beeman Collection

N/A	$80	$60	$50	$40	N/A	N/A

Add 20% for original factory shooting range box.

Originally available with shooting gallery setup in factory cardboard box retailing for $15.

Johnson "Micro-Match Pellets" were precision made BB sized, ground ball bearings.

JONES, TIM

Current custom airgun maker located in Hawley, PA.

Designs typically include modern sporting rifles with Monte Carlo or thumb hole stocks or eighteenth century traditional ball reservoir guns. These Tim Jones rifles will usually retail in the $3,000-$6,000 range. Tim Jones air rifles are stamped "ETJ" on back of the action under the stock.

RIFLES

395 LONG RIFLE - .395 cal., 850 FPS, SS, PCP (3000 PSI), tiger maple Kentucky-styled stock, steel barrel and cylinder, cast brass furniture, 7.2 lbs. New circa 2000.

courtesy Fred Liady

.22 SPORTER .22 cal., PCP, SS.

.357 SPORTER .357 cal., PCP, SS.

.44 BALL RESEVOIR .44 cal., ball reservoir, SS, octagon BBL, fixed sights, full stock, left hand action.

courtesy Don R.

JONISKEIT

Current manufacturer Detlef Joniskeit located in Allmersbach im Tal, near Stuttgart.
Developed the Waffentechnik Joniskeit sidelever match air pistol in 1983.

PISTOLS

WAFFENTECHNIK JONISKEIT - .177 cal., SP, SL, SS, match grips, left-hand cocking lever lifts barrel for loading. A slightly improved version; the "Joniskeit Hurrican" was introduced in 1990. Special international distribution included Beeman Precision Airguns in USA ceased in the 1980s, but the pistol is still made to order. Experiments with the very low 120 m/s velocity of this pistol revealed that differences in lock time between low and high velocity pistols are far below the human reaction time, which is around 15 milliseconds.
Value is about $2000.

JONISKEIT FINALE - .177 cal., SS, PCP and/or CO_2, modified and vented version of the Tau 7 air pistol from Aeron, a daughter company of CZ in Czechia introduced in 1991. Many variations: Finale PCP, Finale CO_2, and Finale Super (hybrid) in variousbarrel lengths, compensators, etc. Works at 300 bar pressure.
Value from about $500 to $650, plus shipping and duty.
Test review in 1991 VISIER.

K SECTION

KAFEMA

Previous trademark of Industria Argentina, Buenos Aires, Argentina circa pre-WWII.
Research is ongoing with this trademark, and more information will be included both online and in future editions.

GRADING	100%	95%	90%	80%	60%	40%	20%

RIFLES

KAFEMA - .177 cal., BBC, SS, SP, hardwood stock with fluted forearm, no buttplate.

courtesy Beeman Collection

	100%	95%	90%	80%	60%	40%	20%
	$200	$175	$150	$115	$85	$50	N/A

KALAMAZOO

For information on Kalamazoo airguns, Hawley see in the "H" section.

KEENFIRE

For information on Keenfire airguns, see Anschütz in the "A" section.

KESSLER

Previous trade name of Kessler Rifle Company, located in Buffalo, Rochester, and Silver Creek, NY, circa 1948-50. Ref: AR 1: pp 18-21.

RIFLES

ONE-PIECE STOCK MODEL .22 cal, swinging arm pump pneumatic, BA, SS, distinctive ball exhaust valve apparently descended from the Rochester airgun which in turn apparently derived from the Sheridan Super Grade, 36 in. OAL.

courtesy Beeman Collection

	100%	95%	90%	80%	60%	40%	20%
	N/A	$235	$200	$175	$150	$125	$95

Variation 1: Small Stock Version - black barrel, body tube, and cocking knob.
Variation 2: Large Stock Version - chromed barrel, body tube, and cocking knob. Large walnut stock with checkpiece; stock styled like Sheridan Super Grade.

TWO-PIECE STOCK MODEL .177 cal,. swinging arm pump pneumatic, BA, SS, same as Rochester air rifle with two piece stock (see Rochester in the "R" section of this guide), except stamped "KESSLER" on the barrel.

courtesy Beeman Collection

	100%	95%	90%	80%	60%	40%	20%
	N/A	$200	$175	$150	$100	$75	$50

Airgun smith and historian John Groenewold investigated the Rochester/Kessler arrangement in his local New York area. He reports that the Rochester Airgun Company was formed by a few ex-Crosman employees. The Rochester company and all of its assets, including parts

GRADING	100%	95%	90%	80%	60%	40%	20%

and patent rights, were purchased by Kessler Gun Co. Kessler proceeded to use up the Rochester parts making Rochester-style airguns and marking some of the barrels with the Kessler name. Some of these guns have the Rochester name on a hidden part of the barrel, and the name Kessler, evidently stamped later, on the exposed part. There are legitimate Rochester airguns and legitimate Kessler airguns of identical design and appearance. Numrich Arms purchased Kessler when they went out of business and still have some parts for sale (including some of the earlier Rochester parts).

KOFFMANZ

For information on Koffmanz airguns, see Philippine Airguns in the "P" section.

KRICO

Current trademark manufactured by Kriegeskorte Handels GmbH Co, located in Pyrbaum, Germany. Previously located in Stuttgart-Hedelfingen, Germany.

Manufacturers of spring piston air rifles after WWII and quality firearms since the mid-1950s. Krico firearms previously were imported by Beeman Precision Arms Inc., Santa Rosa, CA in the 1980s. Only one basic model of airgun was made circa 1946-1953.

For more information and current pricing on both new and used Krico firearms, please refer to the *Blue Book of Gun Values* by S.P. Fjestad (also available online).

RIFLES

MODEL LG 1 - .177 or .22 cal., BBC, SP, SS, rifled barrel, grooved forearm, no buttplate.

courtesy Beeman Collection

	100%	95%	90%	80%	60%	40%	20%
	$350	$300	$250	$200	$150	$100	$75

MODEL LG 1S - .177 or .22 cal., BBC, SP, SS, similar to Model LG 1, except has buttplate, checkered pistol grip and grooved forearm.

	100%	95%	90%	80%	60%	40%	20%
	$400	$350	$300	$250	$200	$150	$100

MODEL LG 1 LUXUS - .177 cal. only, similar to LG 1S, except heavier stock, better sights, and heavy checkered forearm.

	100%	95%	90%	80%	60%	40%	20%
	$450	$400	$350	$300	$250	$200	$150

KÜNG (KUENG) AIRGUNS

Current tradename of Dan Küng (Kueng) located in Basel, Switzerland.

Working in Switzerland, Dan Kueng builds high-end, side-lever, spring-piston, recoilless magnum air rifles and is in the final stages of developing a spring piston air pistol that will produce over 10 ft./lb. ME. His website, at http://www.blueline-studios.com/kuengairguns.com, gives a great deal of technical airgun information and illustrates the products. Productionisbased almost entirely on components made in-house, thus production is still very limited. Costs up to $6000 for guns like those illustratedon the websiteare expected to be considerably reduced.

KYNOCH LIMITED

Current ammunition manufacturer located in Witton, Brimingham, Warwickshire England, founded in 1862.

Manufacturers of sporting rifle and shotgun cartridges, previously produced the Swift air rifle. Also produced the Mitre airgun slug and the Lion, Match, and Witton diabolo airgun pellets.

RIFLE

SWIFT - .177 or .25 cal., BBC, SP, SS, BBC, SP, snap hook on each side of the breech, plain walnut buttstock, based on the 1906 patents of George Hookham and Edward Jones. Circa 1908.

courtesy Beeman Collection

	100%	95%	90%	80%	60%	40%	20%
	N/A	N/A	$950	$750	$550	$400	$250

L SECTION

LD AIRGUNS

Previous manufacturer located in Mandaluyong City, Manila, Philippines 1968-2001.

As discussed in the *Philippine Airguns* section of this guide, the unexpected development of powerful, bulk-fill CO_2 guns for hunting primarily was due to one man, president/dictator Ferdinand Edralin Marcos, who declared martial law and outlawed civilian firearms in the Philippines in 1972.

There had been a few airgun makers around before martial law hit, but one soon came to the foreground. That was the shop of Eldyfonso Cardoniga which had opened
in 1968 in Mandaluyong City, a part of metropolitan Manila.

Values have yet to be established for many LD airguns, but in the Philippines it is said that excellent specimens sell for about triple their original cost. Good specimens are about double and poor specimens go for about their original cost.

I felt that it was important to chronicle this amazing line of airguns before the information faded away. Having jumped in and made this first listing, I recognize that much of this information needs improvement and augmentation. This must not be considered as a complete nor final list. We actively solicit your positive input at BlueBookedit@Beemans.net or at Blue Book Publications.

The authors and the publisher wish to thank Guillermo Sylianteng Jr. and Mandy Cardoniga for their assistance with this section.

LD HISTORY

Eldyfonso Cardoniga (or "Eldy" or just "LD") was born in 1930 in Navotas, Rizal, then a fishing port north of Manila. Reportedly, he made his first airgun at eight years of age by welding together various worn out guns. He studied architecture at the excellent Mapua University in Manila and worked as an architectural assistant for a while, and then as a skilled mechanic and welder. He started the LD airgun factory in 1968 from a design that he had developed. This was the LD 380, a combo rifle/shotgun. The key features were the multi-caliber barrel system, a breech block that swings to the side for loading, and an external hammer for releasing the exhaust valve. This breech system, now known as the "hammer swing action," has been basic to perhaps most of the Philippine airguns. To overcome the power limits of the Crosman hammer-valve system, the LD designs used a larger valve and valve stem activated by a stronger and heavier hammer arrangement. The result was exactly what the market needed: a dependable airgun that was economical to produce and use and of unprecedented POWER! [1]

Of the Philippine airguns, those made by LD certainly are the best known and among the very best quality. The innovation represented by the LD airguns is well demonstrated by the "Rancher" version of the LD 380S. This .50 caliber air rifle is provided with insert barrels of several calibers for pellets, balls, darts, arrows, spears, and shot charges. Some versions of this model were equipped with spinning reels, from the fishing equipment trade, to provide for retrieval of arrows and spears. The .50 caliber barrel could fire large tranquilizer syringes or even fearful "torpedoes" consisting of finned brass projectiles containing a shaped charge of TNT! When Eldy visited the Beemans in California in the 1980s he told us that these torpedoes were very effective, but presented the problem of sometimes "blowing away one quarter of the water buffalo!" (Times have changed - note: he had some of these loaded torpedoes with him, carried on the plane in his coat pocket!)

The factory grew rapidly and Eldy brought in his son Mandy as an apprentice and then as a partner. As his skill grew, Mandy developed the MC TOPGUN line of precision match guns and moved to a nearby separate shop to concentrate on these models. However, this market was too limited due to the high cost of the guns and the diminished ranks of match shooters. He returned to work with his father on the powerful hunting guns and inherited the shop when Eldy passed away in September 1998. During those thirty years, Eldy is credited with at least thirty airgun designs, including several full auto ball shooters. The LD airguns developed and maintained a reputation as dependable, innovative, and powerful. The quality of the rifling in LD guns is believed to be due to the barrels being imported from a precision barrel manufacturer in Japan.

Mandy Cardoniga, now a master gunmaker in his own right, continued to produce LD airguns until sometime in 2001 when the tooling was changed to produce stainless steel industrial accessories, especially equipment for the baking industry. The LD airguns became history.

[1] Eldy reported that one tuned specimen fired a single charge of three .380 cal. steel balls, combined wgt 180+ grains of 800 FPS MV. Three groups of three balls all punched through both sides of a 55 gallon steel drum (18 ga.) at 5 meters. Used with #4 or #6 lead shot for duck hunting.

AIRGUN PRODUCTION

All Philippine hunting airguns are relatively scarce. Production ran from an average of less than one hundred guns per month for LD, evidently the largest maker, down to a few guns a month from a custom maker such as JBC. Perhaps 70 to 99% of most production runs stayed in the Philippines. Most American and European airgun factories, and large importers, figure on several thousand or tens of thousands of guns per month.

GRADING	100%	95%	90%	80%	60%	40%	20%

PISTOLS

LD M45 - .22 cal., CO_2 bulk fill, SS, close replica of M1911A1 Colt U.S. military pistol, slide action and manual safety like original firearm, 4.3 in. rifled brass BBL, Narra wood grips, black nickel or satin nickel finish, adj. sights, 8 in. OAL, 2.5 lbs. Mfg.1987.

courtesy Beeman Collection

	100%	95%	90%	80%	60%	40%	20%
	$295	$250	$225	$200	$150	$100	N/A

Add 20% for Colt 80 Mark V markings.

GRADING	100%	95%	90%	80%	60%	40%	20%

LD M45 REPEATER - .25 cal., CO_2 bulk fill, close replica of M1911A1 Colt U.S. military pistol, slide action and manual safety like original firearm, spring-fed magazine in slide for 6-8 .25 in. ball bearings or #3 lead buck shot balls, manual repeating action, 4.3 in. rifled brass BBL, Narra wood grips, black nickel or satin nickel finish, adj. sights, 8 in. OAL, 2.5 lbs. Mfg. circa 1990s.

| | $395 | $350 | $315 | $280 | $225 | N/A | N/A |

LD BERETTA 9M - .22 cal., CO_2 bulk fill, SS, close replica of Beretta 92SB-F U.S. military pistol, slide action and manual safety like original firearm, 4.3 in. rifled brass BBL, Narra wood grips, black nickel or satin nickel finish, adj. sights, 8 in. OAL, 2.7 lbs. Mfg.circa 1990s.Approx. 200 units mfg.

courtesy Beeman Collection

| | $350 | $325 | $300 | $250 | $225 | $200 | $150 |

LD GLOCK - .22 cal., CO_2 bulk fill, SS, close replica of Glock Model 19 semi-auto pistol, slide action like original firearm, blued steel slide, polymer frame, rifled brass BBL, exact copy of Glock logo on LHS grip, shipped in actual Glock plastic case, 7.4 in. OAL, 2.2 lbs. Mfg.circa 1990s. Approx. 30 units mfg.

courtesy Howard Collection

| | $295 | $250 | $200 | $180 | $160 | $140 | $100 |

Subtract 15% for "politically correct" specimens with Glock logo not legible.

LD LONG PISTOL (REPEATER) - .22/.380 cal. combo, CO_2 bulk fill, hammer swing action, adj. trigger, deluxe Narra grip with forearm, dark wood grip cap, black nickel finish, smoothbore .380 shot barrel with rifled brass barrel .22 cal. insert, (fires pellets, lead or steel balls, shot cartridges, short arrows, and spears, etc.), threaded muzzle ring for suppressor and/or barrel retaining insert, spring-fed tubular magazine LHS for about ten .22 cal. lead balls, see-through scope mounts, 21.1 in. OAL, 3.6 lbs.

courtesy Beeman Collection

| | N/A | $350 | $300 | $250 | $200 | $150 | N/A |

GRADING		100%	95%	90%	80%	60%	40%	20%

LD LONG PISTOL (SINGLE SHOT) - .177/.380 cal. combo, CO_2 bulk fill, hammer swing action, SS, adj. trigger, deluxe Narra grip with forearm, dark grip cap, black nickel finish, smoothbore .380 shot barrel rifled brass barrel .177 cal. insert, (fires pellets, lead or steel balls, shot cartridges, short arrows, and spears, etc.), threaded muzzle ring for suppressor and/or barrel retaining insert, regular scope base, 20 in. OAL, 2.7 lbs.

courtesy Beeman Collection

		N/A	$300	$250	$175	$135	$95	N/A

LD M100 - .22/.380 cal. combo, CO_2 bulk fill, hammer swing action, SS, adj. trigger, deluxe Narra grip with forearm, dark grip cap, black nickel finish, smoothbore .380 shot barrel rifled brass barrel .22 cal. friction-fit insert (fires pellets, lead or steel balls, shot cartridges, short arrows, and spears, etc.), no scope base, extended gas tube under barrel gives over/under appearance, heavy aluminum trigger guard, nickel satin finish, 17.1 in. OAL, 2.6 lbs.

courtesy Beeman Collection

		N/A	$275	$225	$175	$125	$75	N/A

LD MC 87 - target pistol, info. not available at time of printing. 700 units.
Values TBD.

RIFLES

Note: Some of the guns listed below may be combination (combo) calibers, but this could not be determined at time of writing. Degrees of metal engraving, stock shaping, stock decorations, and special features will affect pricing from 10% to 100%.

LD LC 3000 - .22 cal., CO_2 bulk fill, SS, hammer swing action, two-stage trigger, double cock hammer, deluxe Narra Monte Carlo stock, ambidextrous cheekpieces,rubber buttplate, black nickel or satin nickel finish, 27 in. rifled brass barrel, 42 in. OAL.
Values TBD.

LD M 300 M - .22/,380 cal. combo, CO_2 bulk fill, SS, hammer swing action, two-stage trigger, double cock hammer, gas tube extended to end of barrel, deluxe Narra Monte Carlo stock, thumbhole grip (for RH only), ambidextrous cheekpieces, rubber buttplate, smoothbore .380 shot barrel rifled brass barrel .22 cal. insert(fires pellets, lead or steel balls, shot cartridges, short arrows and spears, etc.), threaded muzzle ring for suppressor and/or barrel retaining insert, black nickel or satin nickel finish, 42.8 in. OAL, 5.8 lbs.

		N/A	$1,000	$750	$600	$450	$375	N/A

LD 500 - hunting rifle. Info not available at time of printing.
Values TBD.

LD STINGER - .22 cal., CO_2 bulk fill, SS, SL action, adj. power, exotic carbine-style Narra stock like a pistol with shoulder stock, separate Narra forearm, adj. open sights and scope grooves, 19 in. rifled brass barrel, gold, black nickel, or satin nickel finish, 42 in. OAL, 11 lbs. 300 units.
Values TBD.

LD MATCH - .177 cal., CO_2 bulk fill, SS, hammer swing or SL action, micrometer aperture sights, Narra match stock with adj. high cheekpiece and buttplate, 27 in. rifled brass barrel, 42 in. OAL, 11 lbs.
Values TBD.

GRADING	100%	95%	90%	80%	60%	40%	20%

LD 600 SPORTER - .177 or .22 cal., CO_2 bulk fill, SS, hammer swing action, adj. two-stage trigger, adj. power, deluxe Narra Monte Carlo stock, rubber buttplate, black nickel or satin nickel finish, 27 in. rifled brass barrel, 44 in. OAL.
Values TBD.

LD SPORTER - .22 cal., CO_2 bulk fill, SS, hammer swing or SL action, adj. trigger, deluxe Narra Monte Carlo stock, rubber buttplate, black nickel finish, 24 in. rifled brass barrel, 42 in. OAL, 5.5 lbs.
Values TBD.

LD 380/380S (SPECIAL) - evidently all variations had these features in common: multiple caliber barrel inserts, CO_2 bulk fill, SS, hammer swing action, two-stage trigger, double cock hammer, deluxe Narra Monte Carlo stock with rubber buttplate and sling swivels, black nickel or satin nickel finish, rifled brass barrel insert, threaded muzzle ring for suppressor and/or barrel retaining insert. Two of the many variations suggest the range of features, calibers, size, and weights possible.

courtesy Beeman Collection

This was Eldy's first and highest production model. During the thirty years of production from 1966 to 1996, 17,500 guns were produced. They probably had more variations and custom features than any other model.

✪ **LD 380/380S (Special) Rancher** - four caliber combo: .50smoothbore, .380 smoothbore insert, .22rifled insert, .177 rifled insert cal. Laminated two-tone Narra stock with RH cheekpiece and RH Wundhammer swell grip, standard scope mount base. 44.6 in. OAL, 9.0 lbs.

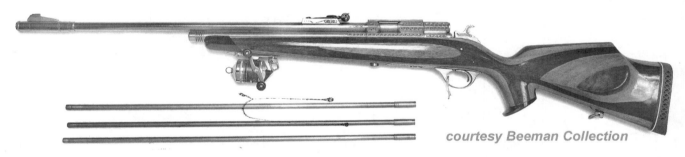

courtesy Beeman Collection

	N/A	$1,150	$900	$750	$600	$450	N/A

Add 20% for thumbhole stock. Subtract 20% if stock is not laminated Add 50% for .50 caliber (less than one hundred were made).
This caliber range gave the Rancher amazing flexibility: it could project .177 or .22 cal. pellets, .38 cal. shot charges, .38 cal. bullets or lead or steel balls, arrows without fletching, expanding tip spears, multi-prong spears, .50 in. tranquilizer darts, and even shaped TNT charges in brass "torpedoes." A spinning reel mounted under the forearm enhanced fishing and frog hunting. (Perhaps less than five hundred of this Special variation were produced. Many were elaborately engraved and given special stock checkering and treatment.)

✪ **LD 380/380S (Special) Barbarella** - three caliber combo: .380 smoothbore, .22 cal. rifled insert, .177 cal. rifled insert. Could fire: .177 or .22 cal. pellets, .38 cal. shot charges, .38 cal. bullets or lead balls, arrows w/o fletching, expanding tip spears, and multi-prong spears. SS, ambidextrous checkered Narra stock with both cheekpieces and thumbhole grip (top of the stock has a saddle-like appearance), metal engraving, blackened design areas on the stock, see-through scope mount base. 41.5 in. OAL, 6.8 lbs.

courtesy Beeman Collection

	N/A	$700	$600	$450	$300	$175	N/A

Subtract 30% for single caliber (.22, .25, or .380). Subtract 20% for no thumbhole. Add 30% for retractable wire stock.

LD 300 SS PHANTOM - hunting rifle. Info not available at time of printing. 2,500 units.
Values TBD.

GRADING	100%	95%	90%	80%	60%	40%	20%

LD 380 SS PHANTOM - .22 cal., CO_2 bulk fill, SS, hammer swing, action, two-stage trigger, double cock hammer, Narra cruiser-style stock ends at pistol grip, retractable stainless steel folding wire shoulder stock, sling swivels, black nickel or satin nickel finish, 22 in. rifled barrel, see-through scope base, muzzle ring covers suppressor threads, 27 in. OAL, retracted. 5,000 units.

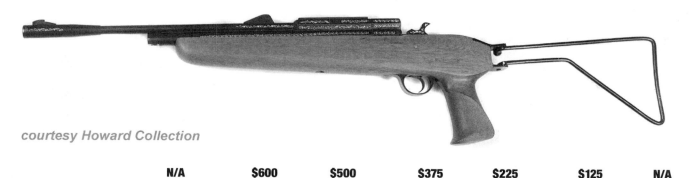

courtesy Howard Collection

	N/A	$600	$500	$375	$225	$125	N/A

LD 700 - .32 or .40 (10 mm) cal., CO_2 bulk fill, bolt action, styled after Remington Model 700 big bore rifle. SS, rifled. Deluxe Narra stock with semi-ambidextrous cheekpiece. Threaded for suppressor, satin nickel finish. Manual safety. 39.3 in. OAL, 6.6 lbs. 24 units made (17 RH 10mm, 4 LH 10mm, 1 RH .32, 2 LH .32) – all to order, may not be marked LD.

courtesy Beeman Collection

	N/A	$500	$400	$300	$200	$100	N/A

Add 25% for highly engraved. Add 50% for PCP (only one was made).
Suppressor requires $200 Federal Transfer Tax in USA.

LD MC 2400 - bolt action sporter rifle. Info not available at time of printing. 320 units.
Values TBD.

LD MC 2800 - lever action sporter rifle. Info not available at time of printing. 180 units.
Values TBD.

LD HOME DEFENSE REPEATER - .380/.22 cal. combo., CO_2 bulk fill, SS, 24 in. barrel with .22 cal. rifled insert, .380 steel ball smoothbore manual repeater, probably seven-shot, spring-fed, tubular magazine attached along left side of barrel. Not marked. Hammer swing action. Cruiser-style stock with pistol grip and extendable heavy wire shoulder stock. Machined trigger guard. Threaded muzzle cap. Light engraving plus recessed panels of unique engraving designs. Open sights, no scope grooves, 41.1 in. OAL (32.8 in. retracted), 6.7 lbs. Costs 45% more than standard LD 380.

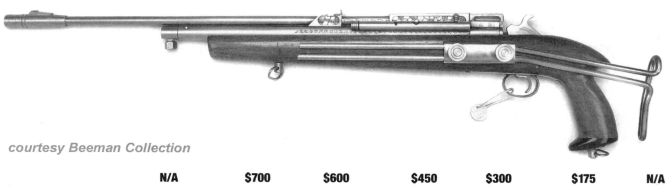

courtesy Beeman Collection

	N/A	$700	$600	$450	$300	$175	N/A

Confirmed by Mandy Cardoniga as work of Eldy Cardoniga.

GRADING	100%	95%	90%	80%	60%	40%	20%

LD SLIDE ACTION REPEATER - .22 (and .25 and .380?) cal. ball repeater, CO_2 bulk fill, slide action; spring-fed, fixed tubular magazine ca. 10 balls; two-stage trigger, double cock hammer, Narra Monte Carlo stock with ambidextrous cheekpieces, rubber buttplate, sling swivels on Narra wood buttstock and separate wood cocking slide, satin nickel finish, scope grooves, cast aluminum trigger guard. Light engraving plus recessed panels of unique engraving designs. 22.5 in. BBL, 39.5 in. OAL, 6.1 lbs. Circa 1980s, rare, less than 1500 total; most stayed in the Philippines.

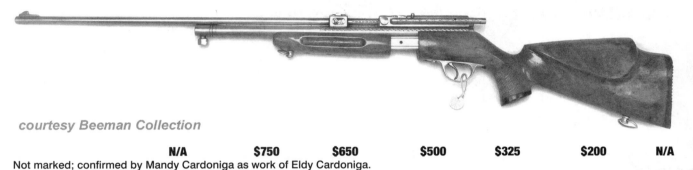

courtesy Beeman Collection

	100%	95%	90%	80%	60%	40%	20%
	N/A	$750	$650	$500	$325	$200	N/A

Not marked; confirmed by Mandy Cardoniga as work of Eldy Cardoniga.

SHOTGUNS

See also Rifles – the .380 and .50 cal. models served as both shotguns and rifles.

LD 20 GAUGE - 20 ga., CO_2 bulk fill, SB shotgun, block hammer action, scope rails, nickel black finish, uses 1.8 in. aluminum tubes with wad in each end to hold shot, Narra stock with skip checkering, Wundhammer swell RHS pistol grip, 46.1 in. OAL, 6.9 lbs. Only 18 made, plus four double barrel specimens. All special order, therefore not marked with LD mark. 29.8 in. BBL, 46 in. OAL, 7.1 lbs.

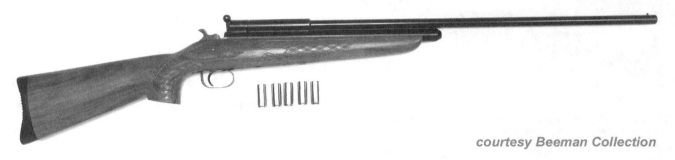

courtesy Beeman Collection

100%	95%	90%	80%	60%	40%	20%
$850	$800	$750	$650	$600	$550	$500

Add 50% for double barrels (only four were made). Add 10% for rifled barrel inserts (.22, .32, .38, and .40 cal.).

LANGENHAN

Previous manufacturer of firearms and airguns. Founded by Valentin Friedrich Langenhan in Zella Mehlis, Germany in 1842. Moved to adjacent Zella St. Blasii in 1855.

About 1900, they started production of airguns, apparently making huge numbers of them under a wide variety of their own and private labels. The most definitive mark is FLZ (i.e. Friedrich Langenhan in Zella-Mehlis) with the letters in a three-segmented circle. Other labels include Ace, Favorit, and FL. Among the most commonly encountered Langenhan airguns are the militia-style air rifles (commonly imported into England from Germany by Martin Pulverman & Company of London circa 1900) and the rifle-like break-barrel, spring-piston FLZ pistols, made MFG. 1927-1940, 2nd variation (pictured) 1937-1940. Langenhan finally succumbed to competition from Mayer und Grammelspacher, Weihrauch, Haenel, etc.

The FLZ pistols generally sell in the $200 range; more for excellent specimens. (The FLZ air pistols range from about 1.6 to 1.9 lbs, and from about 16.7-18.0 in. OAL). The British Cub, which may have been made by another maker for Langenhan, will have a retail value in the $125 range for very good specimens. Ref: AGNR - Oct. 1985.

courtesy Beeman Collection

GRADING	100%	95%	90%	80%	60%	40%	20%

LARC

Previous trade name of LARC International located in Miami, FL.
Previous manufacturer of freon-charged, fully automatic BB sub-machine guns designed by LARC president Russell Clifford circa 1974-80.

RIFLES

MODEL 19A - .174/BB cal., powered from removable can of freon gas, fully automatic, 3000-round gravity-fed magazine, rate of fire approx. 2500 RPM. 350 FPS, approx. range 120 yards, plastic body, aluminum smoothbore barrel black with white or red/brown insert plates, early models may have heavy wire shoulder stock; fake suppressor, later models with plastic shoulder stock bar, 23.5-33 in. OAL, 1.0 lbs - 0.8 lbs.

courtesy Beeman Collection

$70	$60	$50	$40	$30	N/A	N/A

Add 150% for early Model 19 with pressure hose and hose for BB magazine. Add 100% for metal body. Add 20% for fitted case.

LINCOLN JEFFRIES

Previous designer and gunmaker located in Birmingham, England circa 1873-1930s.
The authors and publisher wish to thank Mr. John Groenwold and John Atkins for valuable
assistance with the following information in this edition of the *Blue Book of Airguns*. Lincoln Jeffries was born in Norfolk, England in 1847. By 1873 he had established a well regarded gun business in Birmingham producing shotguns and breech loading and muzzle loading air canes. The firm also put their name on a variety of imported break barrel, smoothbore air rifles – generally Gem-style copies of Haviland & Gunn designs and rifled militia-style (not military!) airguns. In 1904, he patented a fixed-barrel, under-lever, tap-loading, rifled air rifle which was the forerunner of the enormously successful BSA underlever air rifles. These rifles were manufactured for Jeffries by the Birmingham Small Arms factory. They were branded Lincoln Jeffries and later as BSA. These airguns are discussed and listed in the BSA section.

The Lincoln Jeffries firm continued to market the Lincoln Jeffries air rifles until the line of models came completely under the BSA label. By 1921, Lincoln Jeffries, Jr. had been issued a patent for a Lincoln air pistol with the mainspring housed in the gun's grip. Two versions of this unusual, all-metal air pistol were produced in very small numbers during the 1920s, with a few special pistols being individually made by Lincoln Jeffries, Jr. until circa 1927. The first version had a lever in the back of the grip which was pulled down to compress the mainspring and cock the gun. The second type was a barrel cocking air pistol which used the forward part of the trigger guard as a link to compress the mainspring. This was based on the American Haviland and Gunn patent. The Walther LP52 and LP53 air pistols were clearly derived from this gun. The all-metal Lincoln differed from the Walther mainly by not having grip plates and in having an exposed slot in the forward part of the grip which could take flesh samples from a shooter unlucky enough to have his fingertips in that groove when the piston head rushed upward during firing.

The grandsons of Lincoln Jeffries, Messrs. A.H. Jeffries, and L.G. Jeffries were still operating the company in the 1990s, but now only to produce Marksman brand airgun pellets. Ref: *Guns Review*, Dec. 87.

PISTOLS

BISLEY BACKSTRAP COCKING MODEL - .177 cal., SP, SS, all-metal construction, fixed trigger guard, lever along backstrap of grip for cocking mainspring in the grip, blued finish, rotary or side latch for locking cocking lever. approx. 150 mfg. 1911 to theearly 1920s. Ref: AG. Small and Large size variants.

courtesy Beeman Collection

N/A	N/A	$3,500	$3,000	$2,500	$1,500	$1,000

Add 20% for rotary lock variant.
A handful of other variations exist. These may be experimental, special order, or prototypes. SN 3 has grip safety on forward side of grip and dull nickel finish. A larger specimen based on the 1910-11 patents, with top loading tap, brass frame, and walnut grip plates, is known. Values of these special forms cannot be estimated at this time.

GRADING	100%	95%	90%	80%	60%	40%	20%

BARREL-COCKING MODEL - .177 cal. (one known in .22 cal.), BBC, SP, SS, all-metal construction, trigger guard is cocking link between barrel and piston assembly in grip. Standard version: .177 cal., large knurled screw head on take-down screw linking barrel block and cocking arm, receiver steps up in thickness just above trigger, spring chamber cap top at angle to barrel, thick trigger, crowded trigger guard area, point on inside of trigger guard ahead of trigger. Grip cylinder typically about 5.5 in., but several specimens with extended cylinders known. Rare. Large version: .177 cal., receiver uniform in thickness, spring chamber cap top in line with axis of barrel, thin trigger, uncrowded trigger guard area, trigger guard/cocking lever with only smooth curves, grip cylinder over 5.5 in. long, max. (diagonal) OAL about 14.9 in. Small head on takedown screw. Very rare. Giant version: .177 and .22 cal., larger diameter grip cylinder, 15.5 in. max. OAL. Extremely rare, only two known in .22 cal. approx. 1500 mfg.circa 1921-1930. Ref: AG.

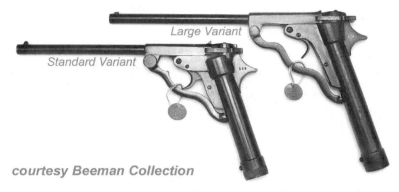

Large Variant

Standard Variant

courtesy Beeman Collection

	N/A	N/A	$2,500	$1,950	$1,250	$750	$400

Add 30% for standard versions with extended grip cylinder. Add 30% for large version.
Other experimental and special order versions known. Values not estimated yet.

RIFLES

All rifles sold by Lincoln Jeffries were rifled and stamped "H THE AIR RIFLE" or "L THE LINCOLN AIR RIFLE". The meaning of the "H" and "L" letters has yet to be clearly determined. The guns stamped "H" are larger than the guns stamped "L", but the theory that these letters refer to "Heavy" and "Light" is not strong. All single shot.

GEM STYLE - H THE AIR RIFLE/L THE LINCOLN AIR RIFLE - various cals., SS, BBC, SP, mainspring in grip similar to Haviland and Gunn air rifle design, from various European makers, sizes varied. Mfg. late 1800s-very early 1900s.

$300	$250	$200	$160	$120	$90	$60

MILITIA STYLE - H THE AIR RIFLE/L THE LINCOLN AIR RIFLE - various cals., BBC, SS, SP, from various European makers (although Militia actually was a Langenhan/Pulvermann air rifle brand or model, "Militia" is commonly used to represent a barrel cocking type of air rifle that does not have wood forward of the grip area), sizes varied. Mfg. late 1800s and first few years of 1900s.

courtesy Beeman Collection

$300	$250	$200	$160	$120	$90	$50

UNDERLEVERS - H THE AIR RIFLE/L THE LINCOLN AIR RIFLE - various cals., SS, SP, UL (bayonet style), made on the Lincoln Jeffries 1904 Patent by BSA and sold as Lincoln Jeffries air rifles (as sold by BSA as The BSA Air Rifle - see BSA in the "B" section), faucet tap loading. The bayonet type underlever was the original Lincoln Jeffries design. The front end of this lever bears a small handle, or "bayonet" dropping down from, but parallel to the barrel. Original bayonet underlevers just had a bend where they engaged the latch mechanism. Variation H: The Air Rifle model, marked "H", 43.5 in. OAL. Mfg. 1904-1908. Variation L: The Lincoln Air Rifle, 39 in. OAL, marked "L", sometimes referred to as the "Ladies" or "Light" version. Mfg. 1906-1908.

courtesy Beeman Collection

$500	$450	$400	$325	$275	$200	$100

GRADING	100%	95%	90%	80%	60%	40%	20%

LINDNER

Previous manufacturer of unique American air pistol, probably Lindner & Molo, New York, N.Y. Based on U.S Patent No. 37,173 issued to E. Lindner on Dec. 16, 1862.

PISTOL

LINDNER - .23 cal., SS, SP, system cocked by a unique, internally hinged cocking lever which wraps all around the back, bottom, and front of the pistol grip, brass receiver, tip up smoothbore brass 5.4 in. octagonal BBL, fine wood grips, 13 in OAL, 2.2 lbs. No markings.

courtesy Beeman Collection

Rarity precludes exact valuation, estimated about $6500.

LOGUN

Current manufacturer located in Willenhall, West Midlands, UKbeginning 1998. Currently distributed by Pyramyd Air Inc. located in Cleveland, OH, Straight Shooters Precision Airguns located in St. Cloud, MN and Crosman Corporation located in East Bloomfield, NY.

RIFLES

AXSOR - .177 or .22 cal., PCP, Supa Glide BA, eight-shot rotary magazine, equipped for scope mounts, two-stage adj. trigger, 19.5 in. rifled steel barrel, blue finish, 1000 FPS, English gloss walnut Monte Carlo stock, checkered grip and forearm (with pressure gauge), rubber recoil pad, 40 in. OAL, 6.8 lbs. New 2004.

N/A	$850	$695	$550	N/A	N/A	N/A	N/A

While first advertised during 2001, this model was first imported into the USA during 2004.

DOMIN8OR .177 or .22 cal., PCP, Side Speed side lever action, eight-shot rotary mag., two-stage adj. trigger, equipped for scope mounts,19.7in. rifled steel barrel, blue finish, checkered synthetic thumbhole stock, rubber recoil pad, 490 cc Buddy Bottle encased in butt stock,40.5in. OAL,5.3 lbs. New 2004.

courtesy Logun

N/A	$800	$700	$495	N/A	N/A	N/A	N/A

EAGLE - .177 or .22 cal., PCP, ambidextrous Versa Glide action, SS or eight-shot manual mag., two-stage adj. trigger, equipped for scope mounts, 17.5 in. rifled steel barrel, blue finish, molded synthetic thumbhole PG stock, rubber recoil pad, 36 in. OAL, 5.6 lbs. New 2005.

courtesy Logun

$800	$700	$495	N/A	N/A	N/A	N/A

As this edition went to press, retail pricing had yet to be established.

GRADING	100%	95%	90%	80%	60%	40%	20%

GEMINI - .177 or .22 cal., PCP, BA, multi-shot magazine (two shots: .177 or .22), equipped for scope mounts, English gloss walnut Monte Carlo stock, checkered grip and forearm, rubber recoil pad, 37.75 in. OAL, 7.1 lbs.

N/A	$695	$595	$495	N/A	N/A	N/A	N/A

GLADI8OR - .177 or .22 cal., PCP, Side Speed side lever action, eight-shot rotary mag., two-stage adj. trigger, equipped for scope mounts, 19.7 in. rifled steel barrel, blue finish, checkered pistol grip, rubber recoil pad, 490 cc Buddy Bottle, 41.5 in. OAL, 7.8 lbs. New 2004.

N/A	$950	$850	$595	N/A	N/A	N/A	N/A

LG-MKII PROFESSIONAL - .177 or .22 cal., PCP, Supa Glide BA, nine-shot inline magazine, equipped for scope mounts, 21 1/4 in. rifled steel barrel, blue finish, 1050 FPS, English gloss walnut Monte Carlo stock, checkered grip and forearm (with pressure gauge), rubber recoil pad, 45 in. OAL, 8.25 lbs. New 2004.

courtesy Logun

N/A	$1,425	$1,225	$995	N/A	N/A	N/A	N/A

While first advertised during 2001, this model was first imported into the USA during 2004.

S-16s (SWEET SIXTEEN) - .22 cal., PCP, Supa-Speed BA, 400cc buddy bottle, sixteen-shot (two eight-shot rotary) mag., equipped for scope mounts, two-stage adj. trigger, 14.5 in. rifled steel shrouded BBL, blue finish, checkered synthetic grip and forearm (with pressure gauge), cross over safety, 34.5-38 in. OAL, 8.5 lbs. New 2004.

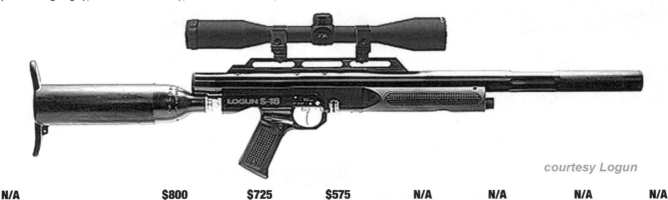

courtesy Logun

N/A	$800	$725	$575	N/A	N/A	N/A	N/A

SOLO - .177 or .22 cal., SS or eight-shot manual mag., PCP, BA, equipped for scope mounts, checkered English gloss walnut Monte Carlo stock, rubber recoil pad, 41 in. OAL, 6.1 lbs.

N/A	$575	$495	$395	N/A	N/A	N/A	N/A

LUCZNIK

Previous tradename probably used by the Polish state firearms company, Zaklady Metalowe Lucznik.

As with most Iron Curtain guns, the construction is more sturdy than precise. The guns are infamous for unavailability of parts. Formerly imported into UK by Viking Arms Company. Dates not known.

PISTOLS

PREDOM-LUCZNIK 170 - .177 cal., BBC, SP, SS, a copy of the Walther LP 53, 12.2 in. OAL, 2.6 lbs. Mfg. circa 1975-1985.

N/A	N/A	$200	$145	$95	$50	N/A

Add 10% for factory box w/ test target.

GRADING	100%	95%	90%	80%	60%	40%	20%

RIFLES

MODEL 87 - .177 in. cal., BBC, SP, SS, simple hardwood stock with fluted forearm.

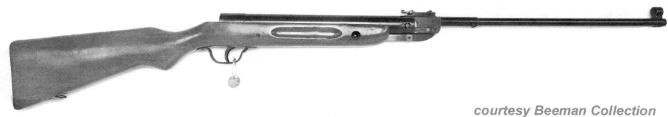

courtesy Beeman Collection

	$100	$75	$50	$35	$25	$15	N/A

MODEL 141 - .177 in. cal., BBC, SP, SS, 14.5 rifled steel barrel, adj. rear sight, hardwood stock with fluted forearm, 36.5 in. OAL. Mfg. 1970s.

	$80	$60	$50	$40	$30	$20	$10

MODEL 188 - .177 in. cal., BBC, SP, SS, similar to Model 87 except, larger stock w/ cheekpiece and grooved forearm.

	$220	$200	$180	$150	$120	N/A	N/A

NOTES

M SECTION

MC

For information on MC airguns, see Philippine Airguns in the "P" section.

MGR

For information on MGR, see Dianawerk in the "D" section.

MMM - MONDIAL

Previous tradename of Modesto Molgora located in Milano, Italy circa 1950s to 1990s.

Most Molgora products are toys and blank-firing guns, but there are several youth/adult airguns. Research is ongoing with this trademark, and more information will be included both online and in future editions.

GRADING	100%	95%	90%	80%	60%	40%	20%

PISTOLS

OKLAHOMA - .177 cal., BBC, SP, SS, 6.3 in. rifled BBL, 200 FPS, fixed sights, with only minor variations, resembles the Steiner air pistol, black or nickel finish, plastic or hardwood grips, no safety, 12.3 in. OAL, 1.9 lbs. Mfg. 1960s-1988.

	100%	95%	90%	80%	60%	40%	20%
	$45	$40	$35	$30	$25	$20	$15

ROGER - .173/BB cal., CO_2, semi-auto, styled after Colt Woodsman, smoothbore BBL, adj. sights, DA trigger, hundred-shot gravity-fed magazine, manual safety, black finish, die-cast parts, 10.9 in. OAL, 2.3 lbs.

courtesy Beeman Collection

	100%	95%	90%	80%	60%	40%	20%
	$50	$45	$40	$30	$25	$20	$15

Add 100% for gun in factory shooting kit.

MACGLASHAN AIR MACHINE GUN CO.

Previous manufacturer in Long Beach, CA.

The MacGlashan Air Machine Gun Company began production in early 1937 with a single shot BB air rifle. During WWII, they produced two models of the now famous air machine gun trainer, used to train gunners in U.S. bombers. In 1945, they returned to making airguns for arcades with a pump action .24 cal rifle. In 1947, they produced a .24 cal. semi-automatic carbine, followed by an improved and lighter version in 1951.

RIFLES: SEMI-AUTO

SEMI-AUTOMATIC CARBINE ARCADE GUN - .24 cal. round lead shot, twenty-five-shot semi-auto, magazine parallel to barrel, wood stock, cross-bolt feed, 600 FPS at 1500 PSI. First Model: fiber fore grip, 35.75 in. overall, 6 lbs. Improved Model: wood fore grip, 37.5 in. OAL, 5 lbs.

courtesy Beeman Collection

	100%	95%	90%	80%	60%	40%	20%
	N/A	N/A	$350	$275	$200	$150	$100

Add 10% for First Model.

GRADING	100%	95%	90%	80%	60%	40%	20%

RIFLES: SLIDE ACTION

"DRICE" SLIDE ACTION RIFLE - .24 cal. round lead shot, pump action twenty-five-shot magazine parallel to barrel, 750FPS at 1500PSI (can operate at CO_2 pressures also), rifled barrel, blue finish, walnut stockand "tootsie roll" slide, designed to compete with .22 cal firearms in arcades, 40.5 in.OAL, 6.6 lbs.

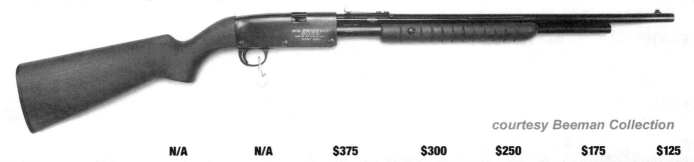

courtesy Beeman Collection

	100%	95%	90%	80%	60%	40%	20%
	N/A	N/A	$375	$300	$250	$175	$125

RIFLES: TRAINER/ARCADE AUTOMATIC

MODEL E-3 AERIAL GUNNERY TRAINER .174 cal. steel BB cal, 15 in. smoothbore barrel full automatic 300-500 rpm @ 500-600 fps, simulates .30 cal. Browning M1919A4 machine gun w/ dual wood spade grips, button trigger, steel cylinder parallel to top is a 1100 round magazine concentric w/ an inner cavity for a E-5 telescope sight (no telescope sight specimens known). Traditional blued steel finish. Requires hose fed compressed air (or CO_2) @ 180-200 psi and 24 volts DC, solenoid operated air valve, racheted BB feed disc. Used in WWII to train gunners with Model 2000N target carrier w/ pivoting arms on top of 18 ft. high spinner shaft, carrying 10" airplane models in target plane circle of 30 ft. Gun is 30.75 in. OAL, l6 lbs. About 1941-45. Ref. Behling (2006).

⦿ **Model E-3: Army Air Force Variant** may have post front sight but generally without ring rear sight w/ cross wires and without ventilated barrel shroud. Approx. 50+ known specimens.

courtesy Beeman Collection

	100%	95%	90%	80%	60%	40%	20%
	N/A	N/A	$2,250	$1,700	$1,400	$1,200	$900

Add 15% for Ring rear sight with cross wires. (as illustrated). Add 5% for USAAF inspection tag.

⦿ **Model E-3N: Navy Variant** ring rear sight w/ cross wires, ventilated barrel shroud, different arrangement of internal trigger and breech block travel assembly switches. Perhaps 10+ known specimens.

	100%	95%	90%	80%	60%	40%	20%
	N/A	N/A	N/A	$2,200	$2,000	N/A	N/A

GRADING	100%	95%	90%	80%	60%	40%	20%

MODEL E-13 REMOTE CONTROL AERIAL GUNNERY TRAINER Same specifications as E-3 models but designed to be used in pairs in remote control machine gun turrets. No sights. Magazine is a 6 in. tall vertical cylinder w/ rubber top plug. 15 in. smooth-bore barrel. 30 in. OAL, 14 lbs. Approx. 50 known specimens.

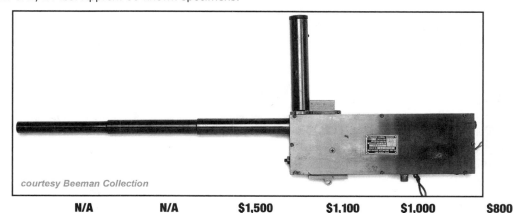

courtesy Beeman Collection

		90%	80%	60%	40%	20%
N/A	N/A	$1,500	$1,100	$1,000	$800	$250

Various modified versions of the above models are known. Deductions are appropriate in proportion to lack of authentic original condition.

MACGLASHAN "TOMMYGUN" - SUB-MACHINE ARCADE GUN 174 in. steel BB cal., full automatic, version of E-3 solenoid air valve system, requires compressed air (or CO_2) probably @ 180-200 psi and 24 volts DC. Spring-loaded 100 shot tubular magazine under barrel. Dual grips and buttstock of hardwood. Heavily built. Cooling louvers on receiver sides. Cast aluminum buttplate with stamped serial number and in raised print: MACGLASHAN AIR MACHINE GUN CO. LONG BEACH CALIF PAT PEND (No MacGlashan patents are known.) Installed in Frontierland Shooting Gallery at original Disneyland in California from opening in 1955 until mid-1960s. Smoothbore16 in. barrel w/ traditional cooling ribs, OAL 40.6 in., 9.6 lbs. Seven specimens known. Ref. Behling (2006).

courtesy Beeman Collection

Rarity precludes accurate pricing.

MAC-1 AIRGUN DISTRIBUTORS

Current manufacturer and importer located in Gardena, CA. Dealers and consumer direct sales. Started in 1932 as Les McMurray's Fin Fur & Feather. Name changed to McMurray and Son in 1959, then to Custom Airguns by McMurray & Son in 1978, and is now known as Mac1 Airgun Distributors.

Mac-1 is celebrating their 75th anniversary in the airgun business in 2007. Present owner Tim McMurray has spent a lifetime challenging himself, and others, to find the last bit of accuracy and power from standard production airguns. In 2004 he and associate, Larry Durham, conceived the idea that became the first purpose-built field target gun to be manufactured in the United States. In 2005 Mac1 started shipping their United States Field Target (US FT) Model rifle and in 2006 produced and shipped the US FT "Hunter Model" configuration of the gun. Tim McMurray is continuing the practice of small-shop produced, high quality airguns in the tradition of makers going back centuries. Mac1 can be reached at www.mac1airgun.com.

RIFLES

US FT (UNITED STATES FIELD TARGET) MODEL .177 cal., PCP, SS, 25 in. rifled bbl., color or clear anodizing per customer choice. Machined Aluminum and steel construction throughout with pistol grip. Mac1 markings on breech. Standard equipment includes: Weirauch barrel, Walnut thigh rest, forearm and cheekpiece; butt hook; Weaver scope base, Colt Model 1911A style grip panels, pressure gau, no sights, 40 in. OAL, 12 lbs. New 2005.

MSR $1,800	$1,800	N/A	N/A	N/A	N/A	N/A	N/A

Available options include: Left hand, carbine length, lightweight, upright (non-canted scope position), .22 cal. barrels. Contact Mac1 directly (see Trademark Index) for details.

US FT HUNTER MODEL .22 cal., PCP, SS, 20 in. rifled bbl., 800 fps., similar to US FT Model except, standard with upright (non-canted scope position), No butt hook, no thigh rest, black and clear anodized only, 36 in. OAL, 10 lbs.

MSR $1,500	$1,500	N/A	N/A	N/A	N/A	N/A	N/A

Similar options as US TF Model. Contact Mac1 (see Trademark Index) directly for details.

MAGIC

For information onMagic airguns, see Plymouth Air Rifle Company in the "P" section.

GRADING	100%	95%	90%	80%	60%	40%	20%

MAGNUM RESEARCH, INC.

Current trademark of pistols and rifles with company headquarters located in Minneapolis, MN. Currently imported and distributed by Umarex USA located in Fort Smith, AR begining 2006.

Centerfire pistols (Desert Eagle Series) are manufactured beginning 1998 by IMI, located in Israel. Previously mfg. by Saco Defense located in Saco, ME during 1995-1998, and by TAAS/IMI (Israeli Military Industries) 1986-1995. .22 Rimfire semi-auto pistols (Mountain Eagle) were previously manufactured by Ram-Line. Single shot pistols (Lone Eagle) were manufactured by Magnum Research sub-contractors. Distributed by Magnum Research, Inc., in Minneapolis, MN. Dealer and distributor sales. For more information and current pricing on both new and used Magnum Research, Inc. firearms, please refer to the *Blue Book of Gun Values* by S.P. Fjestad (also available online).

PISTOLS

DESERT EAGLE .177 cal., CO$_2$, SA or DA, blow-back action, eight-shot cylinder mag., 5.7 in. rifled steel barrel, 425 FPS, fixed sights, Picatinny rails (top and bottom), ambidextrous safety, plastic grips, black finish,11 in. OAL, 2.5 lbs. Mfg. 2007-current.

	100%	95%	90%	80%	60%	40%	20%
MSR $181	$159	$125	$95	N/A	N/A	N/A	N/A

BABY DESERT EAGLE .177 cal., CO$_2$, DA, blow back action, fifteen-shot mag., 4 in. rifled steel barrel, 420 FPS, fixed sights, Picatinny rail bottom (opptional top), ambidextrous safety, plastic grips, black or silver finish,8.25 in. OAL, 1 lbs. Mfg. 2007-current.

	100%	95%	90%	80%	60%	40%	20%
MSR $36	$30	$25	$20	N/A	N/A	N/A	N/A

MAHELY

Previous trademark of Giachetti Gonzales & Cia., located in Buenos Aires, Argentina. Not regularly exported. About 1950s-1990s.

PISTOLS

MAHELY 51 - .177 cal., SP, SS, BBC, 8.2 in. rifled barrel, plastic or wooden vertically grooved grips. 2.3 lbs. Mfg. 1950s. Ref: Hiller (1993).

100%	95%	90%	80%	60%	40%	20%
N/A	N/A	$375	$250	$175	$125	$100

RIFLES

MAHELY 1951 - .177 cal., SP, UL, SS, wood handle on underlever looks like a pump action handle, 39.4 in. OAL, 7.2 lbs. Disc. about 1950s.

courtesy Beeman Collection

100%	95%	90%	80%	60%	40%	20%
$450	$400	$350	$300	$250	$200	$150

MAHELY R 0.1 - .177, SP, BBC, SS, thumbhole stock. Disc. late 1990s.

courtesy Beeman Collection

100%	95%	90%	80%	60%	40%	20%
$375	$325	$300	$250	$200	$150	$100

MANU-ARMS

Previous French trademark of confusing origin and association. ManuArm is a French company formed in 2000, but both of the airguns below are from the 1980s. An association with Manufacture Française d'Armes et de Cycles de Saint Etienne, a.k.a. Manufrance, has been suggested. The original company was the producer of Paul Giffard's famous CO$_2$ guns in the 1880s and Manufrance was a household name in France, selling almost every form of consumer hard goods until the firm closed in 1986.

GRADING	100%	95%	90%	80%	60%	40%	20%

PISTOLS

MANU-ARMS AIR PISTOL - .177, BBC, SP, SS, very similar to the Dianawerk Model 5, black or brightly colored paint finish, receiver is marked "MANU ARMS", 14.3 in. OAL, 2.7 lbs.

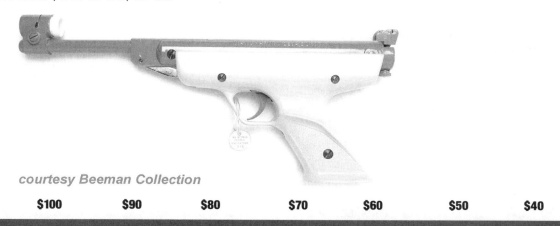

courtesy Beeman Collection

	$100	$90	$80	$70	$60	$50	$40

RIFLES

MANU-ARMS AIR RIFLE - .177., BBC, SP, SS, wood stock, beavertail forearm.

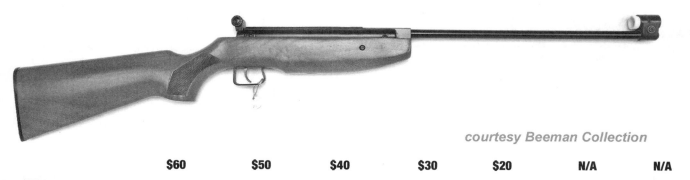

courtesy Beeman Collection

	$60	$50	$40	$30	$20	N/A	N/A

MARKHAM-KING

Previous manufacturer located in Plymouth, MI. Circa 1887-1941. Owned and operated by Daisy Manufacturing Company from 1916.

The Markham Air Rifle Company has been credited with the development of the first commercially successful toy BB airgun. Dunathan's *American BB Gun* (1971) reported two BB rifles with the Challenger name as the first models made by Markham. However, the gun listed there as an 1886 Challenger actually represents only a single patent model without any markings and almost surely not made by Markham. The second gun, listed as an 1887 Challenger, actually was marked "Challenge" and was made in small numbers, but, again, probably not by Markham. There seems to be no justification for referring to either one under the Challenger name or as Markhams. The Chicago model, which appeared about 1887, made mainly of wood, probably was Markham's first real model.

The story of how the company grew to producing over 3,000 guns per day in 1916 is one of the great stories of airgun development and production. However, the company did little promotion and eventually was absorbed into the emerging airgun giant, Daisy. The history and models of Markham-King and Daisy became inseparably intertwined for a quarter of a century. Although Daisy ownership began in 1916, the Markham King models continued for decades and the sub-company gradually became known as King. In 1928, Daisy officially changed the company name to King. The advent of WWII probably caused Daisy to issue the last King price list on Jan. 1, 1942. Much of the model information in Dunathan's book has now been superseded, but this pioneering work absolutely is still required reading.

There are many variations of the early Markham air rifles. All minor variations cannot be covered in this guide. Variations may include changes in type or location of sights, location and text of markings, muzzle cap design, etc.

The authors and publishers wish to thank Robert Spielvogel and Dennis Baker for assistance with this section of the *Blue Book of Airguns*.

RIFLES: NO ALPHA-NUMERIC MARKINGS

All models have smoothbore barrels and are without safety.

GRADING	100%	95%	90%	80%	60%	40%	20%

CHICAGO - .180 large BB cal., darts, BC, SP, SS, exterior all maple wood with rosewood stain, double cocking rods pass through the stock. Stock stamped: "Chicago Air Rifle – Markham's Patent" on two lines. 9.8 in. brass barrel liner. 32 in. OA, circa 1887-1910. Patch Box Variation: Wooden "Patch Box" (dart storage?), 2.4 in. diameter, on LH side of stock. Stock stamped on left side with logo printed "Markham Air Company, Plymouth, Michigan, Chicago, patented" or "CHICAGO AIR RIFLE, MARKHAM'S PATENT". Considered by some to be the oldest version. Circle Logo Variation: slight change in stock shape, stock stamped "Markham Air Rifle Co. – Plymouth Mich." and "CHICAGO – Patented" in circle.

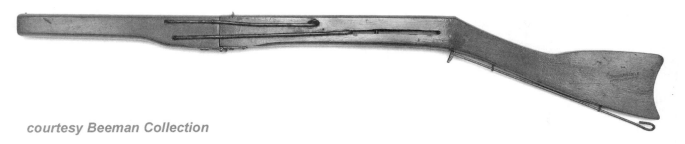

courtesy Beeman Collection

	N/A	N/A	$600	$450	$350	$250	$150

Add 10% for BB clearing rod. Add 15% for patch box variation. Subtract 10% for circle logo variation. Subtract 15% for cracked stock (common fault).

1890 KING - .180 large BB cal., darts, BC, SP, SS, cast iron frame, brass barrel, screw-on muzzle cap, button barrel release on side of receiver, nickel finish. "KING" cast in grip frame. 31 in. OAL. Mfg. circa 1890-1893.

	N/A	N/A	$2,500	$1,700	$1,000	$600	$400

1892 KING - .180 large BB cal., darts, BC, SP, SS, sheet metal frame, brass barrel, screw-on muzzle cap, barrel release button on side of receiver, flat sided stock with oval King logo, 31 in. OAL. Mfg. circa 1892.

	N/A	N/A	$1,500	$1,000	$750	$500	$300

1896 NEW KING SINGLE SHOT - .180 large BB cal., darts, BC, SP, SS, sheet metal frame, sheet metal barrel shroud, metal patch soldered over seam under shroud, muzzle cap over barrel shroud. Red stained stock stamped: "New King Patent Number 483159" in oval logo on slab sided stock. 31 in. OAL. Mfg. circa 1896-1905.

courtesy Beeman Collection

	N/A	N/A	N/A	$1,000	$700	$450	$250

1896 NEW KING REPEATER -.180 large BB cal., BC, SP, sheet metal frame, 150-shot magazine, domed muzzle cap lever allows BBs to be fed one by one from magazine to shot tube. Barrel release button on top of frame. Soldered patch under full length of barrel shroud. Shaped stock (oval in cross section) with logo. Later versions with flush muzzle cap and slab-sided stock. Variation: foreign patent numbers on stock. 31 in. OAL. Mfg. circa 1896-1904.

	N/A	N/A	N/A	$1,200	$900	$600	$300

Add 20% for shaped stock. Subtract 10% for flush muzzle cap.

1900 NEW KING SINGLE SHOT - .180 large BB cal., darts, BC, SP, SS, first use of "friction latch barrel": a section of rear frame snaps over raised part of trigger guard part of frame – holding gun together by friction; this replaced barrel release button of previous King air rifles. Fixed muzzle cap over outside of barrel shroud. (Variations: rounded muzzle cap.) Slab-sided stock stamped "New King" on one side and patent dates on other side. Nickel plated. 31 in. OAL. Mfg. circa 1900-1904.

	N/A	N/A	N/A	$750	$550	$350	$200

There may have been a repeater version.

1900 PRINCE SINGLE SHOT - .180 large BB cal., darts, BC, SP, SS, sheet metal frame, sheet metal barrel shroud, friction barrel latch. Marked "Prince". Nickel finish. No trigger guard. Walnut stock with oval profile, crescent butt. Ref: AR4. (Sears Roebuck advertised a New Rival version, but no specimens are known.) Mfg. circa 1900-07. Variation: "Dandy," made by Markham for private label sales, marked "DANDY" with Markham patent dates (not marked "Markham"), not sold directly by Markham.

	N/A	N/A	N/A	$1,000	$800	$400	$250

Add 100% for Dandy variation.

1900 PRINCE REPEATER - similar to Prince Single Shot but with 150-shot magazine, BB release button on muzzle cap. Not a true repeater. Mfg. circa 1900-07.

	N/A	N/A	N/A	$1,200	$900	$600	$350

1900 PRINCE (TRIGGER GUARD MODEL) - .180 large BB cal., darts, BC, SP, SS, sheet metal frame wraps completely around wrist, sheet metal barrel shroud, separate sheet metal trigger guard. Variant: Marked "Boy's Own", premium gun. Mfg. circa 1900-07.
Values TBD.

GRADING	100%	95%	90%	80%	60%	40%	20%

1900 QUEEN - .180 large BB cal., darts, BBC, SP, SS, removable pins were substituted for rivets to allow gun to be taken down to three pieces, no trigger guard, similar to 1900 Prince Single Shot. Circular markings on wrist: "Markham Air Rifle Co. Plymouth, Mich" plus two patent numbers, advertised as the "Queen Take Down," but not marked "Queen", nickel finish, 33 in. OAL. Mfg. 1900-07.

	N/A	N/A	N/A	$450	$375	$335	$225

1903 NEW KING SINGLE SHOT - .180 large BB cal., darts, BC, SP, SS, friction barrel latch. Fixed muzzle cap within barrel shroud. Stamped "New King" on one side and patent dates on other of slab sided stock. Nickel plated. 31 in. OAL. Mfg. circa 1903-1904.

	N/A	N/A	N/A	$750	$550	$350	$200

1904 SINGLE SHOT - .180 in large BB cal., BBC, SP, SS, friction barrel latch, domed muzzle cap with sight. Patch under barrel shroud. Slab sided stock marked "King Markham Air Rifle Co." Later versions with oval shaped stocks, without markings. Early versions had name stamping on small area on top of receiver; later name stamping was on barrel shroud. Mfg. circa 1904.

courtesy Beeman Collection

	N/A	N/A	$600	$500	$400	$300	$150

1904 REPEATER - 180 large BB cal., BBC, SP, friction barrel latch, spring release at muzzle like 1896 New King Repeater. Later versions had oval-shaped stocks without markings. Mfg. circa 1904.

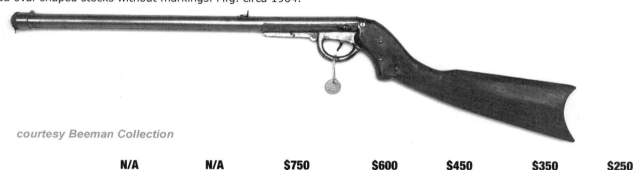

courtesy Beeman Collection

	N/A	N/A	$750	$600	$450	$350	$250

RIFLES: WITH ALPHA-NUMERIC MARKINGS

MODEL C (SINGLE SHOT) - .180 BB or .177 lead air rifle shot cal., SP, BC, SS. Smooth contour Polley patent sheet metal frame wraps around wrist, barrel shroud with step, nickel finish, walnut stock with oval profile and deep crescent butt. Domed muzzle cap allows a BB to be shaken from BBs stored in barrel shroud into the shot tube (true barrel). Not a true repeater. Oval stock. 32 in. OAL. Mfg. 1905-09.

	N/A	N/A	$600	$500	$400	$350	$250

MODEL C (REPEATER) - .180 BB or .177 in. lead air rifle shot cal., SP, BC, gravity-fed 500-shot storage. Smooth contour Polley patent sheet metal frame wraps around wrist, barrel shroud with step, nickel finish, walnut stock with oval profile and deep crescent butt, stock stamped "King 500 Shot Repeater". Not a true repeater. 33 in. OAL. Mfg. circa 1906-09.

	N/A	N/A	$700	$550	$450	$350	$300

MODEL D (SINGLE SHOT) - .180 BB caliber or .177 in. lead air rifle shot cal., SP, BC, muzzle loading SS, barrel tube retained by spring clip, muzzle cap not removable. Smooth contour Polley patent sheet metal frame wraps around wrist, barrel shroud with step, marked "KING MODEL D, THE MARKHAM AIR RIFLE CO., PLYMOUTH, MICH., U.S.A.", nickel finish, walnut stock with oval profile and deep crescent butt. 9.5 in barrel, 31 in. OAL. Mfg. circa 1907-09.

courtesy Beeman Collection

	N/A	N/A	$600	$500	$400	$350	$300

GRADING	100%	95%	90%	80%	60%	40%	20%

MODEL D (REPEATER) - .180 BB or .177 in. lead air rifle shot cal., SP, BC, 350-shot gravity-fed magazine, barrel tube removes to load, shot tube with oval cap. Smooth contour Polley patent sheet metal frame wraps around wrist, barrel shroud with step, marked "KING MODEL D, THE MARKHAM AIR RIFLE CO., PLYMOUTH, MICH., U.S.A.", nickel finish, walnut stock with oval profile and deep crescent butt. 9.5 in barrel, 31 in. OAL. Mfg. circa 1907-09.

	N/A	N/A	$700	$550	$450	$350	$300

MODEL E (REPEATER) - .180 large BB cal., darts, BC, SP, Model D frame with straight (no step down) Prince type barrel, muzzle lever repeater, gravity-fed, smooth profile (Polley Patent) sheet metal frame, sheet metal barrel shroud, full length solder patch, walnut stock with oval profile, deep crescent butt. Nickel finish. 32 in. OAL. Dates not known.

	N/A	N/A	N/A	$600	$500	$400	$350

NUMBER 1 -.180 large BB cal., darts, BC, SP, SS, similar to Model D, removable shot tube, barrel marked "KING NO. 1", 31 in. OAL. Mfg. 1910-14.

	N/A	N/A	$500	$400	$350	$250	$200

NUMBER 2 - .180 large BB cal., darts, BC, SP, 350-shot repeater, loading port below front sight, side of grip stamped "KING 350 SHOT NO. 2", 31 in. OAL. Mfg. 1910-14.

	N/A	N/A	$750	$600	4500	$400	$300

NUMBER 4 - 177 lead air rifle shot cal., SP, lever action, gravity-fed 500-shot magazine, one-piece sheet metal frame and half-round, half-octagonal barrel shroud, frame with scroll stamping "King 500 Shot" with Markham address and patent dates, nickel finish, walnut stock with deep crescent butt, 34 in. OAL. Mfg. circa 1908-15. Smooth variation: no scroll stamping on frame. Mfg. 1910-14. Blued finish mfg. 1914-22.

courtesy Beeman Collection

	N/A	N/A	$700	$600	$500	$400	$300

Add 5% for smooth variation. Subtract 15% for blued finish.
Markham's first lever action repeater.

NUMBER 5 LEVER ACTION - .177 lead air rifle shot cal., SP, LA, gravity-fed 1000-shot magazine, one-piece sheet metal frame and half-round, half-octagonal barrel shroud, blue or nickel finish, walnut stock with deep crescent butt, 36 in. OAL, 2.5 lbs. Mfg circa 1908-22.

	N/A	N/A	$700	$600	$500	$400	$300

⊙ *Number 5 Lever Action Scroll Side Variant* - frame with scroll stamping "King 1000 Shot" with Markham address and patent dates, nickel finish, walnut stock with deep crescent butt. Mfg. circa 1908-22.

courtesy Beeman Collection

	N/A	N/A	$800	$675	$550	$450	$350

⊙ *Number 5 Lever Action Plain Side Variant* - markings on top, no scroll stampings on side, nickel finish, mfg. 1910-14.

	N/A	N/A	$850	$700	$600	$500	$400

⊙ *Number 5 Lever Action Blued Variant* - blue finish, mfg. 1914-22.

	N/A	N/A	$675	$575	$475	$375	$275

NUMBER 5B SPECIAL LEVER ACTION - .177 lead air rifle shot cal., SP, lever action, gravity-fed magazine, one-piece sheet metal frame and half-round, half-octagonal barrel shroud. Frame with scroll stamping "King 1000 Shot" with Markham address and patent dates, special black nickel finish on metal, special finish on walnut stock with deep crescent butt. Hinged gift box with color lithographing. 36 in. OAL. Mfg. circa 1908-16.

	N/A	N/A	$950	$800	$700	$550	$400

Deduct 25% for missing gift box.

GRADING	100%	95%	90%	80%	60%	40%	20%

NUMBER 5 SLIDE ACTION - .177 lead air rifle shot cal., SP, sixty-shot gravity-fed magazine, six-groove wooden cocking slide, pistol grip stock, 36 in. OAL (same design used by Daisy for Daisy No. 105 Junior Pump Gun and Daisy No. 107 Buck Jones Special). Mfg. 1932-36.

	N/A	N/A	$450	$400	$300	$250	$200

NUMBER 10 JUNIOR - .177 air rifle shot cal., SP, BC, SS. Sheet metal frame. Flat sided walnut stock with crescent butt. Cast iron trigger guard (E.S. Roe patent) extends into wrist and provides cocking action fulcrum. Nickel or blued finish. 29 in. OAL. Variation 1: cast iron trigger guard and conventional trigger. One-piece barrel. Nickel finish. Variation 2: cast iron trigger guard and conventional trigger. Stepped barrel. Blued finish. Variation 3: ring trigger, one-piece barrel, blue finish. Variation 4: stepped barrel, blue finish. Mfg. 1909-41.

courtesy Beeman Collection

	$350	$300	$250	$225	$200	$175	$150

Subtract 25% for variation two. Subtract 50% for variations three and four.

NUMBER 11 JUNIOR (THREE IN ONE GUN) - .177 air rifle shot or darts cal., or corks fired with shot tube removed, SP, BC, SS. Sheet metal frame and straight one-piece barrel shroud. Flat-sided walnut stock with crescent butt. Cast iron trigger guard (E.S. Roe patent) extends into wrist and provides cocking action fulcrum. Nickel finish. 29 in. OAL. Mfg. 1910-16.

	N/A	N/A	$450	$400	$350	$300	$250

NUMBER 17 BREECH LOADER - .177 lead air rifle shot or darts cal., SP, SS, sheet metal frame and barrel shroud, blued finish, BC action with two external cocking rods similar to Chicago Model. 12 in. BBL, 31 in. OAL. Mfg. circa 1917-32.

	N/A	N/A	$350	$300	$250	$175	$150

Add 20% for ammo box variant.

Ammo box variant – small ammo storage chamber below barrel pivot. Bears June 13, 1922 patent date.

NUMBER 21 SINGLE SHOT - .177 lead air rifle shot or darts cal., SP, SS, removable shot tube, lever action, cast iron lever, sheet metal frame and barrel shroud, blue or nickel finish. "NO. 21, KING MANUFACTURING Co., PLYMOUTH, MICH., SINGLE SHOT" plus patent dates marked on gun. 31 in. OAL. Mfg. circa 1913-32. Variation one: earlier production with scroll stamped receiver marked "KING SINGLE SHOT No. 21, THE MARKHAM AIR RIFLE CO." with 1907 to 1913 patent dates. Variation two: blued finish, plain receiver. Variation Three: nickel finish, plain receiver.

	N/A	N/A	$200	$175	$150	$125	$100

Add 50% for variation one.

Note: The dash in the following four-digit model numbers does not appear on the guns themselves – but is added here to highlight the two-digit date of introduction which is added to the basic two-digit model number (i.e. Number 2123 is shown as Number 21-33 to indicate that it is a variation of No. 21 introduced in 1933).

MODEL 21-33 SINGLE SHOT - .177 lead air rifle shot or darts cal., SP, SS, removable shot tube, lever action, cast iron lever, sheet metal frame and barrel shroud, blue finish. Barrel marked "KING MFG. CO" and with Markham address. 31 in. OAL. Mfg. circa 1933-35.

	N/A	N/A	$200	$175	$150	$100	$75

NUMBER 21-36 SINGLE SHOT - .177 air rifle shot cal., SP, SS, cast iron cocking lever, sheet metal frame and barrel shroud, removable shot tube, blued finish. Straight grip stock. 32 in. OAL. Mfg. circa 1936-41.

courtesy Beeman Collection

	N/A	N/A	$200	$175	$150	$100	$75

GRADING	100%	95%	90%	80%	60%	40%	20%

NUMBER 22 REPEATER - .177 inch air rifle shot, SP, same as Number 21 gun but with 500-shot gravity-fed magazine repeater. Lever action, cast iron lever, sheet metal frame and barrel shroud, blue or nickel finish. Markham address on barrel. Loading port below front sight. 31 in. OAL. Mfg. circa 1916-1932.

	N/A	N/A	$220	$195	$170	$140	$115

NUMBER 22-33 REPEATER - .177 air rifle shot, SP, 500-shot gravity-fed magazine repeater, lever action, cast iron lever, sheet metal frame and barrel shroud, blue finish. Marked "King". Markham address on barrel. Loading port on RH side. 32 in. OAL. Mfg. circa 1933-35.

	N/A	N/A	$175	$150	$125	$100	$80

NUMBER 22-36 500 SHOT REPEATER - .177 lead air rifle shot cal., SP, lever action, gravity-fed magazine, one-piece sheet metal frame and barrel shroud, cast iron lever, blued finish, straight grip wood stock. Daisy design influence, replaced King Number 22-33. 32 in. OAL. Mfg. circa 1936-1941.

	$125	$100	$75	$65	$50	$35	$25

NUMBER 23 KADET ARMY - .177 air rifle shot cal., SP, gravity-fed 500-shot magazine repeater, lever action, cast iron lever, sheet metal frame and barrel shroud, nickel finish. Frame marked "King Kadet". Markham address on barrel. Military type rear sight, rubber tipped bayonet. Web sling. 31 in. OAL (38 in. with bayonet). Mfg. circa 1915-16.

	N/A	N/A	$650	$550	$450	$350	$250

Subtract 30% for missing bayonet. Subtract 10% for missing sling.

NUMBER 24 NEW CHICAGO - .177 lead air rifle shot or darts cal., SP, SS, BC. Barrel marked "New Chicago Number 24" and Markham address. Bolt action locking device. Blued finish. 36 in. OAL. Mfg. 1917 only. Ref: AR 2.

courtesy Beeman Collection

	N/A	N/A	$600	$500	$400	$300	$250

NUMBER 55 REPEATER - .177 lead air rifle shot or .174 in. steel BB cal., SP, lever action, gravity-fed 1000-shot magazine, one-piece sheet metal frame and barrel shroud, cast iron lever, blued finish. Markham address on top of barrel. Variation one: straight walnut stock. Variation two: pistol grip model with curved lever. 35 in. OAL. Mfg. 1923-1931.

	N/A	N/A	$180	$160	$140	$120	$100

Add 30% for variation two.

NUMBER 55-32 SINGLE SHOT - .177 lead air rifle shot or 174 in. steel BB cal., SP, lever action, one piece sheet metal frame and barrel shroud, cast iron lever, blued finish, pistol grip wood stock. Used Number 55 frame. Loading port LH side. 35 in.OAL. Mfg. 1932 only.

	$100	$85	$65	$50	$35	$25	$20

NUMBER 55-33 1000 SHOT REPEATER - .174 steel BB cal., SP, lever action, 1,000 shot gravity feed magazine, new frame with Daisy-type spring anchor and rear sight, straight grip stock, blued finish. 35 in. OAL. Mfg. 1933-35.

courtesy Beeman Collection

	$100	$85	$65	$50	$35	$25	$20

Add 5% for peep sight.
Also available with peep sight.

NUMBER 55-36 1000 SHOT REPEATER - .174 BB cal., SP, lever action gravity-fed magazine, one-piece sheet metal frame and barrel shroud, cast iron lever, blued finish, pistol grip wood stock. Daisy design influence, similar to Daisy Red Ryder and Number 155. 36 in. OAL. Mfg. circa 1936-41.

	$125	$100	$75	$65	$50	$35	$25

Add 5% for peep sight.

GRADING	100%	95%	90%	80%	60%	40%	20%

MARKSMAN PRODUCTS

Current manufacturer and importer located in Huntington Beach, CA. Marksman is a division of S/R Industries. Dealers and consumer direct sales.

Morton Harris, operating as Morton H. Harris Inc. in Beverly Hills and then Los Angeles, CA, developed a simple spring piston pistol during 1955-57. The firm continued as Marksman Products in Torrance, CA with airguns and expanded to slingshots and accessories. They later acquired Healthways, the manufacturer of some of the airguns sold under the Plainsman label. They also formerly imported Milbro Diana from Scotland, BSA from England, and Weihrauch/BSF, and Anschütz spring piston air rifles from Germany. Most of these imports were not special Marksman models and many were not marked with the Marksman name and thus generally are not covered here. Marksman produced the Model 1010 air pistol under private labeling via Milbro of Scotland. Today Marksman Products operates in Huntington Beach, CA as a division of S/R Industries of Maryland.

PISTOLS

MODEL MP (MARKSMAN PISTOL) - .175/ BB or .177 cal. pellet or dart. SS, SP, one-stroke cocking by sliding top of receiver, 2.5 in. smoothbore BBL, black paint or chrome finish, die-cast body. Morton Harris markings. Variation one: rotating cover in left grip over an ammunition storage area; marked "Beverly Hills, Calif." Apparently produced only in 1955 in very limited numbers. Variation two: without ammunition storage area; marked "Los Angeles, Calif." 1.5 lbs., 8.75 in. OAL. Mfg. 1955-57.

courtesy Beeman Collection

	$75	$60	$45	$30	N/A	N/A	N/A

Add 100% for factory box, ammo samples, and literature. Subtract 50% for variation two. Add 100% for chrome finish. Add 200% for Dillingham Industries, Los Angeles, Calif. markings.

MSR was $6.95 for black finish, $8.95 for chrome finish.

MODEL MPR (MARKSMAN PISTOL REPEATER) - .175/ BB or .177 cal. pellet or dart, SP-slide cocking, smoothbore 2.5 in. BBL, die-cast, twenty-shot spring-fed BB magazine, forerunner of nearly identical Model 1010, black paint or chrome finish, early production marked "Los Angeles 25", later ones may be marked "Torrance, Calif." Sears Model 1914 with "Sears" cast into sideplate instead of "Marksman". Styrofoam box base appeared in 1967. 1.7 lbs, 8.75 in. OAL. Mfg. 1958-1977.

	$15	$10	N/A	N/A	N/A	N/A	N/A

Add 10% for Los Angeles address. Add 50% for box, ammo samples, and paperwork. Add 35% for chrome finish. Add 100% for Sears markings.

MSR was $8.95 for black, $12.95 for chrome.

MODEL 1010/1010C/1010H/1010HC - .175/ BB or .177 cal. pellet or dart, slide action cocking, SP, smoothbore, 200 FPS, die-cast, twenty-shot spring-fed BB magazine, black paint, brass, or chrome finish (Model 1010C), fixed sights, and holster (Model 1010H). Mfg. 1977-present.

MSR $20	$20	$17	$13	N/A	N/A	N/A	N/A

Add 20% for models other than basic 1010. Add 50% for box and literature (later versions clamshell packaging, no premium). Add 50% for chrome. Add 200% for gold color plating, presentation box. Add 100% for original presentation case.

Model 1015 Special Edition - "combat" styling. Model 1300 with "Shootin' Darts" set. Model 1320 "Shootin' Triangles" with self-contained target box.

MODEL 1010X - similar to Model 1010, except has full nickel plating and black plastic grip panels with inlaid silver colored Marksman logos.

	$22	$18	$15	N/A	N/A	N/A	N/A

MODEL 1015 - similar to Model 1010, except has full nickel plating and brown plastic grip panels with inlaid silver colored Marksman logos.

	$18	$13	$10	N/A	N/A	N/A	N/A

MODEL 1020 - BB/.175 cal., slide action, SP, black finish, eighteen-shot reservoir (BB), 200 FPS, fixed sights.

	$18	$13	$8	N/A	N/A	N/A	N/A

Last MSR was $21.

MODEL 1049 (PLAINSMAN) - BB/.174 cal., CO_2 (12 gram), repeater, hundred-shot BB gravity-fed reservoir, adj. 300-400 FPS.

	$40	$30	$25	$15	N/A	N/A	N/A

Discontinued in 1990s. See Healthways in the "H" section of this guide.

GRADING	100%	95%	90%	80%	60%	40%	20%

MODEL 1399 - BB/.175 cal. and .177 pellet, darts, or bolts, slide action, SP, silver chrome finish, gravity-fed twenty-four-shot BB reservoir, 230 FPS, fiberoptic front sight, extended barrel, includes dartboard and twelve darts.

MSR $26	$23	$18	$13	N/A	N/A	N/A	N/A

MODEL 2000 - BB/.175 cal., slide action, SP, 200 FPS similar to Model 1010C, except has silver chrome finish and squared trigger guard.

MSR $35	$32	$25	$17	$12	N/A	N/A	N/A

Add 25% for Model 2000K, kit includes safety glasses, speed loader, and BB/pellet/dart samples.

MODEL 2004 DELUXE - .177 pellet, SSP, over-cocking, polymer frame with finger grooves and cast aluminum slide, black finish, 410 FPS, adj. rear sight, squared trigger guard, automatic trigger safety, 9.5 in. OAL, 1.7 lbs. Mfg. 2005-06.

	$40	$35	$30	N/A	N/A	N/A	N/A

Last MSR was $45.

MODEL 2005 - BB/.175 cal. and .177 pellet, darts, or ballistic bolt, slide action, SP, silver chrome finish, twenty-four-shot BB reservoir, 260 FPS, "Laserhawk" fiberoptic front sight, extended barrel, squared trigger guard.

	$23	$17	$13	N/A	N/A	N/A	N/A

Last MSR was $26.

MODEL 2010 - BB/.175 cal., slide action, SP, 230 FPS, black composite frame and silver chrome finish slide. New 2006.

MSR $25	$25	$17	$12	N/A	N/A	N/A	N/A

RIFLES

JUNIOR MODEL 28 - .177 cal., BBC, SP, 600 FPS, 16.75 in. barrel, blue finish, 6 lbs. Mfg. for Marksman by Weihrauch.

	$135	$120	$95	$75	$50	N/A	N/A

Last MSR was $225.

MODEL 29/30 - .177 or .22 cal., BBC, SP, 800/625 FPS, 18.5 in. barrel, blue finish, 6 lbs. Mfg. for Marksman by BSA. Disc. 1991.

	$135	$120	$95	$75	$50	N/A	N/A

Last MSR was $200.

MODEL 40 - .177 cal., BBC, SP, 720 FPS, 18.4 in. barrel, blue finish, 7 lbs. 5 oz.

	$145	$125	$105	$85	$55	N/A	N/A

Last MSR was $250.

MODEL 45 - .177 cal., BBC, SP, 900-930 FPS, 19.2 in. barrel, blue finish, 7.15 lbs. New 1993.

	$125	$110	$80	$60	$40	N/A	N/A

Last MSR was $195.

MODEL 55 (RIFLE) & 59 CARBINE - .177 cal., BBC, SP, 925 FPS, 19.75 (rifle) or 14 (carbine) in. barrel, blue finish, 7.5 lbs. Mfg. for Marksman by Weihrauch, using B.S.F. tooling.

	$195	$160	$125	$80	$60	N/A	N/A

Last MSR was $300.

MODEL 56/56K - .177 cal., BBC, SP, 925 FPS, 19.6 in. barrel, blue finish, adj. cheekpiece and trigger, 8.7 lbs.

	$300	$250	$225	$165	$115	N/A	N/A

Add 50% for 56K Model with Marksman Model 6941 scope.
The Model 56/56K is manufactured for Marksman by Weihrauch, using B.S.F. tooling.

MODEL 58/58K - .177 cal., BBC, SP, 925 FPS, 16 in. heavy bull barrel, blue finish, adj. trigger, designed for silhouette shooting, 8 lbs. 8 oz. Importation disc. 1993.

	$250	$205	$165	$125	$85	N/A	N/A

Last MSR was $390.

Add 50% for 58K Model with Marksman Model 6941 scope.
Manufactured for Marksman by Weihrauch, using B.S.F. tooling.

MODEL 60/61 CARBINE - .177 cal., UL, SP, blue finish, 810-840 FPS, 8 lbs. 12 oz.

	$300	$250	$225	$165	$115	N/A	N/A

Last MSR was $490.

This model is a modified version of HW77 by Weihrauch manufactured for Marksman using B.S.F. tooling.

MODEL 70 - .177, .20, or .22 cal., BBC, SP, 19.75 in. barrel, blue finish, 925/760 FPS, 8 lbs.

	$235	$185	$145	$105	$65	N/A	N/A

Last MSR was $355.

Add 10% for .20 cal.
Mfg. for Marksman by Weihrauch using B.S.F. tooling.

MODEL 72 - .177, .20, or .22 cal., BBC, SP, similar to Model 70.

	$235	$185	$145	$105	$65	N/A	N/A

Last MSR was $355.

Add 10% for .20 cal.
Mfg. for Marksman by Weihrauch using B.S.F. tooling.

GRADING	100%	95%	90%	80%	60%	40%	20%

MODEL 746 - .177 cal., BBC, SP, SS, rifled barrel, 580 FPS, 42 in. OAL.

	$125	$85	$60	$45	$30	N/A	N/A

Marksman private branding of Diana Milbro G79 from Scotland.

MODEL 1700 - .177/BB cal., pump action cocking, SP, 275 FPS, twenty-shot spring-fed mag., blue finish.

	N/A	$18	$13	$10	N/A	N/A	N/A

MODEL 1702 - .177/BB cal., pump action cocking, SP, 275 FPS, twenty-shot spring-fed mag., blue finish, adj. rear and fiberoptic front sights.

	$23	$18	$13	N/A	N/A	N/A	N/A

Last MSR was $26.

MODEL 1705 - .177/BB cal., similar to Model 1702, except has three-position length adj. stock.

	$27	$22	$17	N/A	N/A	N/A	N/A

Last MSR was $30.

MODEL 1710 (PLAINSMAN) - .177/BB cal., pump action cocking, SP, 275 FPS, twenty-shot spring-fed mag., blue finish.

	$20	$15	$10	N/A	N/A	N/A	N/A

MODEL 1740 - .177/BB cal., BBC, SP, 450 FPS, eighteen-shot reservoir, blued finish.

	N/A	$35	$25	$15	N/A	N/A	N/A

MODEL 1745 - .177/BB cal., BBC, SP, 450 FPS, eighteen-shot reservoir, blued finish, ambidextrous Monte Carlo plastic stock.

	N/A	$27	$22	$17	N/A	N/A	N/A

Add 20% for Model 1745S with factory installed Marksman 1804 scope.

MODEL 1750 - .177/BB cal., BBC, SP, similar to Model 1740, except skeletonized.

	N/A	$30	$20	$10	N/A	N/A	N/A

MODEL 1780 - .177/BB cal., BBC, SP, 450 FPS, single shot version of Model 1740.

	N/A	$30	$20	$10	N/A	N/A	N/A

MODEL 1790 (BIATHLON TRAINER) - .177/BB cal., BBC, SP, 450 FPS, plastic stock.

	N/A	$60	$50	$40	N/A	N/A	N/A

MODEL 1792 - .177 cal., BBC, SP, 450 FPS, similar to Model 1790.

	N/A	$45	$35	$25	N/A	N/A	N/A

MODEL 1795 - .177/BB cal., UL, SP, bolt action loading, 450/500 FPS, ten-round spring-fed magazine.

	N/A	$50	$40	$30	N/A	N/A	N/A

Add 10% for Model 1795S with factory installed Marksman 1804 scope.

MODEL 1798 - .177 cal., BBC, SP, similar to Model 1790 Biathlon Trainer, except has "Laserhawk" sighting system.

	N/A	$50	$40	$30	N/A	N/A	N/A

MODEL 2015/2015K - .177/BB cal., similar to Model 1705, except has "Laserhawk" sighting system, BB speed loader, and targets (Model 2015K only).

	$39	$33	$27	N/A	N/A	N/A	N/A

Last MSR was $42.

Add 10% for Model 2015K with all accessories.

MODEL 2020 - .177/BB cal., single-stroke pump action cocking, 300 fps, 20 shot mag., fiber optic front sight, adj. rear sight, black composite stock and finish, automatic safety, 33.5 in. OAL, 2. lbs. New 2005.

MSR $25	$22	$17	$10	N/A	N/A	N/A	N/A

MODEL 2025 - .177/BB cal., single-stroke pump action cocking, 300 fps, 20 shot mag., fiber optic front sight, adj. rear sight, 4 x 20 scope, black composite stock and finish, automatic safety, 33.5 in. OAL, 2.5 lbs. New 2005.

MSR $35	$32	$25	$17	N/A	N/A	N/A	N/A

MODEL 2030 - .177/BB cal., single-stroke pump action cocking, 300 fps, 20 shot mag., fiber optic front sight, adj. rear sight, black composite stock, zink finish, automatic safety, 33.5 in. OAL, 2.5 lbs. New 2007.

MSR $40	$37	$30	$24	N/A	N/A	N/A	N/A

MODEL 2040 - .177/BB cal., single-stroke pump action cocking, 300 fps, 20 shot mag., fiber optic front sight, adj. rear sight, 4 X 20 scope, black composite stock, zink finish, automatic safety, 33.5 in. OAL, 2.5 lbs. New 2007.

MSR $45	$39	$33	$27	N/A	N/A	N/A	N/A

MARS

Previous trade mark manufactured by Venus Waffenfabrik located in Thüringen, Germany.

The Mars military-style air rifles were listed with many models of Tell airguns in old Venus Waffenfabrik factory catalogs. It presently is assumed that VWF were the makers. For more information on Mars airguns, see Tell in the "T" section.

GRADING	100%	95%	90%	80%	60%	40%	20%

MATCHGUNS srl

Current manufacturer located in Parma, Italy. Previously imported and distributed by Nygord Precision Products, located in Prescott, AZ.

For more information and current pricing on Matchguns srl firearms, please refer to the *Blue Book of Gun Values* by S.P. Fjestad (also available online).

PISTOLS

MODEL MG I - .177 cal., PCP, SS, 9.36 in. barrel, black finish, 625 FPS, adj. anatomical wood grip, adj. electronic trigger, fully adj. sights, adj. stabilizer, 10.7 in. OAL, 2.42 lbs.

No MSR	$825	$750	$695	N/A	N/A	N/A	N/A

MODEL MG I LIGHT - .177 cal., PCP, SS, similar to Model MG 1 except, standard grip and no stabilizers, 10.7 in. OAL, 2.42 lbs.

courtesy Matchguns srl

As this edition went to press, retail pricing had yet to be established.

MATCHLESS

Previous trade name of BB rifles manufactured by Henry C. Hart Company located in Detroit, MI, circa 1890 to 1900.

These were spring piston BB rifles using a top lever for cocking; similar in this function to the First Model Daisy introduced in 1889. Cast iron parts made them more substantial and heavier than contemporary BB rifles. Promoted as the only repeating BB guns on the market, they actually were single shots, which, like some of the early Daisy "repeaters," could be fed BBs one at a time from a built-in magazine.

RIFLES

FIRST MODEL - .180/large BB cal., SP, TL, sixty-five-shot gravity-fed magazine, cast iron frame with black paint finish, blued steel barrel, marked "MATCHLESS" in a curving line on the side of the grip frame, top cocking lever w/o knob, no safety, 35.5 in. OAL, 2.5 lbs. Mfg. 1890-95.

courtesy Beeman Collection

		N/A	N/A	$2,000	$1,650	$1,300	$995	$600

Commonly the rear sight, magazine latch, and/or loading gate at the muzzle have been lost.

SECOND MODEL - similar to First Model, except "MATCHLESS" name is much smaller and in a straight line on the side of the breech area of the receiver, seamless brass nickel-plated barrel, top cocking lever with false-hammer knob. Mfg. 1895-1900.

courtesy Beeman Collection

		N/A	N/A	$2,000	$1,650	$1,300	$995	$600

GRADING	100%	95%	90%	80%	60%	40%	20%

MAUSER

Current trademark manufactured in Europe by various subcontractors. No current U.S. importation. Mauser airguns are not manufactured by Mauser-Werke. Previously imported and distributed by Beeman Precision Airguns located in San Rafael, CA, and Marksman, located in Huntington Beach, CA.

For more information and current pricing on both new and used Mauser firearms, please refer to the *Blue Book of Gun Values* by S.P. Fjestad (also available online).

PISTOLS

U90/U91 JUMBO AIR PISTOLS - for information on this model, see FB Record (Fritz Barthelms) in the "F" section.

RIFLES

MATCH 300SL/SLC - .177 cal., UL, SP, 550/450 FPS, adj. sights and hardwood stock, 8 lbs. 8 oz.

	100%	95%	90%	80%	60%	40%	20%
	$200	$165	$120	$85	$55	N/A	N/A

Last MSR was $330.

> Add 25% for SLC Model with diopter sights.
> This model was mfg. in Hungary.

MAYER AND GRAMMELSPACHER

For information on Mayer and Grammelspacher, see Dianawerk.

MEIER

Previously produced by Jeff Meier of Miami, FL.

PISTOLS

MEIER SLUG/SHOT PISTOL - .38 cal. smoothbore, fires .375 slugs or .38 shot shells built on Crosman 2240 frame, 18.5 in OAL. Circa 1990. Estimated value in 90% condition about $275.

courtesy Beeman Collection

MENALDI

Current tradename of Menaldi Armas Neumaticas located in Cordoba, Argentina.

In 2004 Luis Mendaldi started development of a line of CO_2 rifles of high end quality for both target and hunting. At time of printing only a few handmade samples had been made and digital illustrations were not available. Additional information on this line will be provided in future issues of this guide. Best current source of information is the Menaldi website at www.menaldi.com.ar.

MENDOZA S.A. de C.V.

Current manufacturer Productas Mendoza, S.A. located in Xochimilco, Mexico. Currently imported and distributed under the Benjamin and Crosman names by Crosman Corp., located in East Bloomfield, Pyramyd Air locqated in Cleveland, OH, Previously distributed by Airgun Express, Inc. located in Montezuma, IA. Compasseco located in Bardstown, KY, and by Airgun Express located in Montezuma, IA.

For information on Models RM622 and RM777, see Benjamin Air Rifle Co. in the "B" section. For information on Models RM177, RM277, RM522, RM577, RM677, RM877, and RM 650 BB Scout, see Crosman Corp. in the "C" section.

The Mendoza brand has an exotic history, beginning in 1911 when engineer Rafael Mendoza established the company to develop a unique 7 mm two-barrel machine gun and then an improved Mauser-type bolt action rifle. Mendoza produced machine guns and hand grenades, 35 and 37 mm field artillery cannons, and field heliographs for General Francisco Villa (Pancho Villa) during the Mexican Revolution. In 1934, the Mendoza 1934 C model rifle/machine gun was selected as standard ordnance for the Mexican Army and Navy.

In the 1950s, Mendoza began production of an interesting variety of BB guns including the Model 50 double barrel BB gun – a gun considerably rarer than the Daisy double barrel BB guns. In 1971, still owned by the family, the Mendoza Company moved from exclusive production of guns to six different product lines, including sophisticated pellet guns such as the RM 2003 with its quick change calibers and dual component safety trigger (RM, in case you hadn't guessed, stands for Rafael Mendoza).

A wide variety of airguns has been produced by Mendoza. This is a first, preliminary model list. There presently is confusion regarding the designation, specifications, and dates for several models. Additional research is being done on this brand and results will appear in future editions of this guide and on the web. Information is actively solicited from Mendoza collectors. Please contact Blue Book Publications or send

GRADING	100%	95%	90%	80%	60%	40%	20%

inputs to BlueBookedit@Beemans.net.

The authors and publisher of *Blue Book of Airguns* wish to express their appreciation to Ralph Heize Flamand of the Mendoza Company for his assistance with this section in this edition.

PISTOLS

MODEL M-56 - tinplate copy of Colt Single Action Army revolver. No additional info at this time; please submit info. to BBAinput@Beemans.net.

Values TBD.

RIFLES

MODEL 4 - .177 or .22 cal., SP, UL, SS, mahogany or habillo wood stock, rubber buttplate.

courtesy Mendoza

Values TBD.

MODEL 5 - deluxe version of Model 4.

courtesy Mendoza

Values TBD.

MODEL 25 - .177/BB cal., BBC, tinplate construction, nickel plated. Mfg. circa 1950.

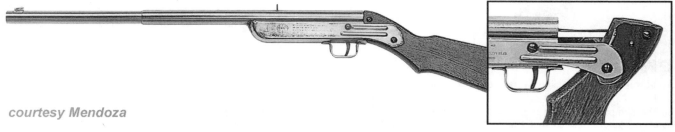

courtesy Mendoza

Values TBD.

Mendoza's first airgun.

MODEL 50 DOUBLE BARREL BB GUN - double barrel version of Model 25; extremely rare. Mfg. circa 1954.

courtesy Beeman Collection

	N/A	N/A	N/A	$1,500	$1,400	$1,300	$1,000

GRADING	100%	95%	90%	80%	60%	40%	20%

MODEL 50 LEVER ACTION BB GUN - .174/BB cal., SP, Winchester-style cocking lever, tinplate BB gun-type construction. Separate wood buttstock and forearm.
Values TBD.
No other information or values available at time of printing.

MODEL 85 LEVER ACTION BB GUN - .174/BB cal., SP, Winchester-style cocking lever, tinplate BB gun-type construction. Separate wood buttstock and forearm.
Values TBD.
No other information or values available at time of printing.

MODEL COMPETITION - BB, SP, SS, mahogany or habillo wood Monte Carlo stock, checkered grip and forearm, buttplate with white line spacer, sling swivels, rear body tube cap styled like Webley Airsporter, blued finish, pellet holder at base of BBL. Circa 1980s.
Values TBD.
No other information or values available at time of printing.

MODEL HM-3 - .177 BB, SP, UL, thirty-five-shot spring-fed magazine, folding metal stock, nickel plated. Mfg. 1957-60.

 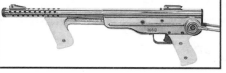 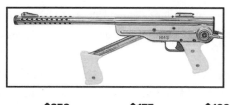

courtesy Mendoza

N/A	$350	$300	$275	$250	$175	$100

MODEL LARGO Values TBD.
No other information or values available at time of printing.

MODEL MAGNUM - BB, SP, SS, "high velocity," mahogany or habillo wood Monte Carlo stock, checkered grip and forearm, buttplate with white line spacer, sling swivels, rear body tube cap styled like Webley Airsporter, blued finish, pellet holder at base of BBL. Circa 1980s.
Values TBD.
No other information or values available at time of printing.

MODEL RM 10 - .22 cal., SP, BBC, SS, 14.2 in. BBL, 450 FPS, mahogany or habillo wood Monte Carlo stock, sling, 35.4 in. OAL, 5.94 lbs. New 1986.

courtesy Mendoza

N/A	$127	$100	$75	$50	N/A	N/A	N/A

MODEL RM 65 - .174/BB cal., SP, Winchester-style cocking lever, 11.8 in. BBL, 250 FPS, tinplate BB gun-type construction, separate Monte Carlo-style wood buttstock and forearm, blue finish, 35.83 in. OAL, 3.08 lbs. New 1986.

courtesy Mendoza

Values TBD.
No other information or values available at time of printing.

⊙ *Model RM 650* - similar to RM 65, except with 500-shot magazine.
Values TBD.
Note No other information or value available at time of printing.

GRADING	100%	95%	90%	80%	60%	40%	20%

MODEL RM 100 - .177 or .22 cal., SP, BBC, SS, 19 in. BBL, 750/675 FPS, mahogany or habillo wood Monte Carlo stock, sling, 41 in.OAL, 6.6 lbs. New 1986.

courtesy Mendoza

Values TBD.
No other information or values available at time of printing.

MODEL RM 200 - .177 or .22 cal., BBC, SP, SS, 19 in. BBL, mahogany or habillo wood Monte Carlo stock, RH cheekpiece, swivels and sling, 41 in. OAL, 6.6 lbs.

N/A	$162	$130	$100	$70	N/A	N/A	N/A

Add $51 for Model RM-200 Combo with 4x32mm scope.

MODEL RM 450C/450L - .177 cal., BBC, SP, SS, 18.5 in. BBL, 600 FPS, mahogany or habillo wood Monte Carlo stock, RH cheekpiece, deep belly forearm, swivels and sling. 40.16-42.5 in. OAL, 6.82 lbs.

Values TBD.
No other information available at time of printing.

MODEL RN 600 - .22 cal., BBC, SP, SS, 18.5 in. BBL, 900 FPS, mahogany or habillo wood Monte Carlo stock, RH cheekpiece, swivels and sling, 45.28 in. OAL, 7.7 lbs.

N/A	$200	$165	$125	$85	N/A	N/A	N/A

Add $49 for Model RM-600 Combo with 4x32mm scope. Add $75 for Model RM-600 Combo with 3-9x32mm scope.

MODEL RM 800 - .177 or .22 cal., SP, BBC, SS, 18.5 in. BBL, 1050/900 FPS, laminated wood, thumbhole stock, nylon sling, rubber pellet holder on barrel, manual safety, blue finish, 20.5 in. round barrel, 45.28 in. OAL, 7.92 lbs. New 1986.

	$350	$325	$300	$250	$225	$200	$175

MODEL RM 1000 - .22 cal., SP, BBC, seven-shot repeater, 19 in. BBL, 650 FPS, mahogany or habillo wood Monte Carlo stock, 45.28 in. OAL, 7.7 lbs. New 1986.

Values TBD.
No other information or values available at time of printing.

MODEL RM 2000 - .22 cal., BBC, SP, SS, 18.5 in. BBL, 850 FPS, mahogany or habillo wood Monte Carlo stock, RH cheekpiece, swivels and sling, 45.28 in. OAL, 7.7 lbs.

N/A	$241	$205	$175	$135	N/A	N/A	N/A

Add $47 for Model RM-2000 Combo with 4x32mm scope.

MODEL RM 2003 ADVANCE - .177 or .22 cal., SP, BBC, SS, 18.5 in. BBL, 1200/1000 FPS, mahogany or habillo wood Monte Carlo stock, instant change barrels with dual caliber muzzle brake, double blade safety trigger. 45 in. OAL, 7.7 lbs. New 2003.

courtesy Mendoza

N/A	$271	$230	$185	$145	N/A	N/A	N/A

Add $45 for Model RM-600 Combo with 4x32mm scope. Add $86 for Model RM-600 Combo with 3-9x32mm scope.

MODEL 2800 - .22 CAL., BBC, SP, SS, 18.5 in. BBL, 1150/950 FPS, mahogany or habillo wood Monte Carlo thumbhole stock, RH cheekpiece, swivels and sling, 45.28 in. OAL, 7.7 lbs.

Values TBD.
No other information or values available at time of printing.

MODEL SHORT M6 - BB, SP, SS, mahogany or habillo wood Monte Carlo stock, buttplate with white line spacer, sling swivels, rear body tube cap styled like Webley Airsporter, blued finish, pellet holder at base of BBL. Mfg. circa 1980s.

Values TBD.
No other information available at time of printing.

GRADING	100%	95%	90%	80%	60%	40%	20%

MODEL SUPER V-57 - .177/BB cal., gravity-fed magazine, Daisy-style lever action cocking, tinplate construction, nickel plated.

courtesy Mendoza

Values TBD.
No other information or values available at time of printing.

MODEL TI MEN - .177/BB cal., gravity-fed magazine, Daisy-style lever action cocking, tinplate construction, blued.

courtesy Mendoza

Values TBD.
No other information or values available at time of printing.

MODEL VAQUERO - appears to be a copy of Beeman C1 hunting carbine, BB, SP, SS, mahogany or habillo wood straight shotgun-style stock without pistol grip, buttplate with white line spacer, rear body tube cap styled like Webley Airsporter, blued finish. Mfg. circa 1980s.

Values TBD.
No other information available at time of printing.

MILBRO

Previous trade name of Millard Brothers located in Motherwell, Lanarkshire, Scotland

The name Milbro is derived from "Millard Brothers," a family owned business founded in 1887; apparently the senior figure was David W. Millard.

Milbro began producing airguns in 1949, using machinery and equipment taken as WW2 war reparations from the Mayer and Grammelspacher Company (DIANAWERK) in Rastatt, Germany in 1945. Milbro also received the brand name DIANA and even the Diana logo showing the goddess of hunting, Diana, discarding her bow and arrow in favor of an airgun, held high above her head. This resulted in today's collectors having both German and British airguns bearing the Diana name and logo! In 1950, DIANAWERK again began the production of airguns. in their old factory in Rastatt. They were forced to use names other than "Diana." Within Germany the Dianawerk airguns were sold as "Original." The brand "Original Diana" was used for Dianawerk guns in England. Dianawerk repurchased their trademark in 1984 after Milbro ceased airgun production. After 1984 all Diana airguns were again made in Rastatt, Germany (see Dianawerk section). For greater detail on this aspect, see DIANAWERK in the D section of this book.

Milbro produced airguns under both their own name and the acquired Diana brand. Most of these guns were close copies of the German pre-war models; many bore the same model number as their German pre-war siblings. This even while Dianawerk in Germany had resumed production of some of the same models under the same model numbers (but under the Original or Original Diana labels); some with modifications or improvements! Milbro made airguns for other firms in the shooting trade including Umarex in Germany, Daisy in the USA, and Webley & Scott and Phoenix Arms in England. The Webley Jaguar was manufactured by Milbro and the virtually identical Webley Junior may also have been a Milbro product. Some of the Milbro airguns did not bear the Diana name, but were marked "Milbro Foreign" which indicates that they may have been made for Milbro of Scotland by Dianawerk in Germany in the pre-WW2 period when German markings were not in favor in England.

Milbro was sold in 1970 to Grampian Holdings who also owned businesses making fishing tackle, golf clubs, and other items. During the mid-1970s Milbro sold airguns to mail order catalog retailers. By 1982, despite the advantage of the famous old Diana trademark, Milbro, using Dianawerk´s old machinery and materials, had ceased making airguns. The machinery was sold to El Gamo. Some remaining guns were sold to a Swiss firm for mail order sales.

Milbro began making airgun pellets in 1950. The pellet business was sold to former Milbro employee Jim Mark. Milbro pellets, under the names of Caledonian, Jet, Rhino, Clipper, Match and TR are still made in Motherwell, Scotland.

The authors and publisher wish to thank Tim Saunders and Jim Markfor their valuable assistance with the following information in this edition of the *Blue Book of Airguns*. Ref.: Dennis Hiller´s British based "The Collectors´ Guide to Air Rifles" and The Collectors' Guide to Air Pistols. Much of the following is based on those books. Additional information is actively sought from readers; direct info to BBAinfo@Beemans.net.

GRADING	100%	95%	90%	80%	60%	40%	20%

PISTOLS

DIANA G2 .177 cal., pellets or darts. SP, SS, derived from German Diana Model 2 except, black or nickel finish, 2 pc. black plastic grips. "Gat" style push-barrel cocking. Mfg. 1965-1982.

courtesy Beeman Collection

	$55	$45	$35	$25	$20	N/A	N/A

Add 50% for factory box. Add 20% for nickel finish.

DIANA MODEL 2 .177 cal., pellets or darts, SP, SS, "Gat" style push-barrel cocking, black or nickel finish, similar to German Diana Model 2 push-barrel pistol except, w/ wood grips. Mfg. l1949-1965.

courtesy Beeman Collection

	$55	$45	$35	$25	$20	N/A	N/A

Add 50% for factory box. Add 20% for nickel finish.

MILBRO MK II .177 cal., SP, TL, SS, based on 1937 patent of German Em-Ge Zenit, single stage trigger, one piece wooden stock, 11 in. OAL, 1.5 lbs.

	$160	$125	$110	$90	$80	$60	$40

Add 60% for original six sided box. Add 30% for original four sided box.

DIANA MK II (G4) .177 cal., SP, TL, SS, based on 1937 patent of German Em-Ge Zenit, single stage trigger, one piece wooden stock w/ medallion of Diana logo or Diana name, 11 in. OAL, 1.5 lbs.

	$150	$120	$105	$85	$75	$55	$35

Add 25% for factory box.

MILBRO CUB 2.41 mm lead balls (No.7 lead birdshot) caL., fired by a quick squeeze on the rubber bulb in the grip, gravity feed 500 shot magazine, one piece cast alloy construction; no moving parts, purple anodized finish or polished zinc alloy. Mfg.began during late 1940s.

courtesy Beeman Collection

	$300	$250	$175	$125	$75	$50	N/A

Add 50% for factory box.

"World's Weakest Air Pistol". Shot sold by Milbro in packets marked "Spare charges". Patented in France 1948 and also produced in France in all plastic version.

GRADING	100%	95%	90%	80%	60%	40%	20%

MILBRO G10 .177 cal., SP, slide pulls to load and cock, 20 shot repeater w/ BBs, SS w/ pellets or darts, may be various finishes, markings, and accessories. Mfg. 1952-1982.

	$35	$30	$25	$20	$20	N/A	N/A

    A private branding of Marksman 1010 air pistol from California.

DIANA SP50 .177cal., SP, SS, push barrel design, 400 fps., styled like an automatic pistol, cast alloy frame, darts or pellets loaded at the rear, sold in polystyrene cartons complete with packets of .177 darts and pellets. Mfg. 1970s -1982. OAL 7 in., weight 1.6 lbs.

courtesy Beeman Collection

	$55	$45	$35	$25	$15	N/A	N/A

    Add 5% for factory box.

    Identical pistol marketed by Phoenix Arms Company, Eastbourne, East Sussex, England as G50 until at least 1989. Also sold as Perfecta SP50.

MILBRO COUGAR .177 or .22 cal., SP, BBC, SS, similar to BSA Scorpion, grips and barrel pivot cover plates of simulated wood, blue steel body tube and barrel, black finished cast metal receiver, 18.5 in. OAL. Mfg. 1978-1982.

	$175	$150	$125	$95	$75	N/A	N/A

    Add 20% for box with shoulder stock, sight blades, scope ramp, and pellets.

MILBRO BLACK MAJOR .177 or .22 cal., SP, BBC, SS, similar to Milbro Cougar except, skeletal shoulder stock, reflector sight system. Mfg. 1981-82.

	$200	$165	$135	$100	$70	N/A	N/A

MILBRO TYPHOON .177 cal., push-barrel, aluminum pistol, similar to Harrington "GAT", beech grip, 6.8 in OAL. Mfg.1950s.

    Current values not yet determined.

    Name conflict w/ Webley Typhoon air pistol and Relum Typhoon air rifle.

RIFLES

Early models may have date stamp on the lower edge of the stock.

DIANA MODEL 1 .177 in., BBC, SP, SS, similar to pre-WW2 German Diana Model 1, removable smoothbore barrel, tinplate construction. Mfg. circa 1949-1959.

	$75	$50	$35	$25	$15	N/A	N/A

DIANA MODEL 15 .177 cal., BBC, SP, SS, similar to pre-WW2 German Diana Model 1, tinplate construction, smoothbore barrel. Mfg. 1950s–1980.

	$90	$75	$60	$45	$30	N/A	N/A

DIANA MODEL 16 177 cal., BBC, SP, SS, similar to pre-WW2 German Diana Model 16, tinplate construction, smoothbore barrel, later models w/ scope ramp spot welded to body.cylinder. Mfg. late 1940s -1974.

courtesy Beeman Collection

	$110	$90	$75	$60	$45	N/A	N/A

    Also sold in USA as Winchester 416, HyScore 805, Daisy 160.

GRADING	100%	95%	90%	80%	60%	40%	20%

DIANA MODEL 22 177 cal., BBC, SP, SS, similar to pre-WW2 German Diana Model 22, tinplate construction, smoothbore barrel. Mfg. late1940s- early 1970s.

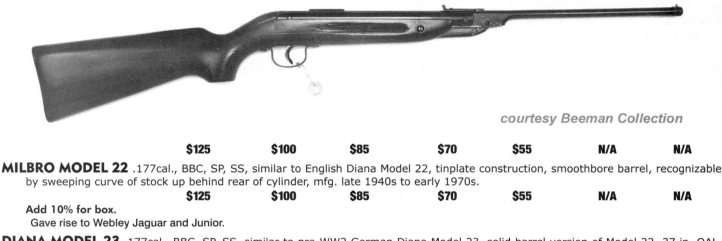

courtesy Beeman Collection

	$125	$100	$85	$70	$55	N/A	N/A

MILBRO MODEL 22 .177cal., BBC, SP, SS, similar to English Diana Model 22, tinplate construction, smoothbore barrel, recognizable by sweeping curve of stock up behind rear of cylinder, mfg. late 1940s to early 1970s.

	$125	$100	$85	$70	$55	N/A	N/A

Add 10% for box.
> Gave rise to Webley Jaguar and Junior.

DIANA MODEL 23 .177cal., BBC, SP, SS, similar to pre-WW2 German Diana Model 23, solid barrel version of Model 22, 37 in. OAL. Mfg. late 1940s to approx. 1960.

	$150	$125	$95	$75	$50	N/A	N/A

> Became Milbro G23.

MILBRO G23 .177 cal., BBC, SP, SS, similar to English Diana Model 23, 37 in OAL, 3.5 lbs. Mfg. circa 1970s.

	$150	$125	$100	$85	$70	N/A	N/A

DIANA 25 .177 or .22 cal., BBC, SP, SS, similar to pre-WW2 German Diana Model 25, rifled or smoothbore., 38.3 in. OAL, 5 lbs.

	$120	$95	$75	$55	$40	N/A	N/A

DIANA COMET .177 or .22 cal., BBC, SP, SS, kit version, similar to pre-WW2 German Diana Model 25. Mfg.early 1960s-1963.

	$250	$215	$185	$150	$125	N/A	N/A

DIANA G25 177 or .22 cal., BBC, SP, SS, similar to English Diana Model 25, 38 in. OAL, 5 lbs. Mfg. 1963-66.

	$130	$115	$95	$80	$65	N/A	N/A

DIANA 27 - .177 or .22 cal., BBC, SP, SS, similar to pre-WWII German Diana Model 27, smoothbore or rifled BBL, 5.8 lbs. Mfg. circa 1950s-1963.

	$120	$95	$80	$65	$50	N/A	N/A

DIANA G27 .177 cal., smoothbore/rifled BBL, .22 rifled cal., similar to English Diana 27 except, with manual safety (early production may lack safety), 41.5 in. OAL, 5.9 lbs. Mfg. circa 1963-67.

	$125	$95	$80	$65	$50	N/A	N/A

DIANA G36 .177 or .22 cal. BBC, SP, SS, manual safety, 41.5 in OAL, Mfg. 1966-early 1970s.

	$120	$95	$80	$65	$50	N/A	N/A

DIANA G44 (TARGETMASTER) .177 or .22 cal., BBC, SP, SS, similar to British Diana Model 25, rifled or smoothbore, manual safety, aperture sight, 42 in. OAL, 6.3 lbs. Mfg.circa 1967-early 1970s.

	$250	$215	$185	$155	$115	N/A	N/A

DIANA G46 (TARGETMASTER) .177 or .22 cal., BBC, SP, SS, similar to British Diana Model 27, rifled or smoothbore in .177; rifled only in .22, aperture sight, manual safety. Mfg. circa 1967-early 1970s.

	$250	$115	$85	$65	$50	N/A	N/A

DIANA 55/G55 .177 or .22 cal., UL, SP, SS, similar to German Original Model 50, faucet tap loading, 42 in. OAL, 7.2 lbs. Mfg. circa late 1950s-early 1960s.

	$375	$325	$265	$215	$165	N/A	N/A

DIANA SERIES 70 .177 or .22 cal., BBC, SP, SS. Mfg. circa 1971-1980s.

⊛ *Model 71* .177 cal., BBC, SP, SS, rear manual safety, deluxe Monte Carlo stock w/ white line buttpad, checkering, BBL w/ outer sleeve, 42.8 in. OAL. MFG. Ca. 1971-1982.

	$225	$185	$155	$115	$85	N/A	N/A

⊛ *Model 74 (G74)* .177 cal. BBC, SP, SS,similar to German Original Model 16 except improved stock, tinplate construction, smoothbore barrel, 32.5 in. OAL, 3 lbs.Mfg. early 1970s-late 1970s.

	$50	$40	$30	$20	N/A	N/A	N/A

⊛ *Model 75* .177cal., BBC, SP, SS, similar to Diana Series 70, Model 74 exceptrifled barrel, tinplate construction, 32.5 in. OAL, 3 lbs. Mfg. circa 1980-1982.

	$60	$50	$40	$30	N/A	N/A	N/A

GRADING	100%	95%	90%	80%	60%	40%	20%

✪ *Model 76* 177 or .22 cal., BBC, SP, SS, semi- tinplate construction, rifled barrel, 400/300 fps., 37 in. OAL, 5.3 lbs. Mfg. Ca. 1972-1980s.

	$120	$95	$70	$55	$40	N/A	N/A

✪ *Model 77* .177 or .22 cal., BBC, SP, SS, rifled barrel. 400/300 fps, 38.5 in. OAL, 6 lbs. Mfg. circa 1972-1980s.

	$120	$95	$70	$55	$40	N/A	N/A

✪ *Model 78 (Standard)/Model 79 (Deluxe)* .177 in. cal. BBC, SP, SS, manual safety on side, 38.5 in. OAL. Mfg. circa 1978-1980s.

	$120	$95	$70	$55	$40	N/A	N/A

DIANA G80 .177 or .22 cal., BBC, SP, SS, 625/500 FPS, sloping forearm as of 1980, 42 in. OAL, 6.8 lbs. Mfg. early 1977-82.

	$150	$115	$95	$70	$45	N/A	N/A

DIANA G85 (BOBCAT) .177 cal., BBC, SP, SS, smoothbore barrel. 33 in. OAL, 3.8 lbs. Mfg. circa 1978-82.

	$120	$95	$75	$55	$40	N/A	N/A

Similar to DIANA Series 70, Model 74 (G74), an updated version of Model 16.

MILBRO SCOUT .177cal., BBC, SP, SS, similar to pre-WW2 German Diana Model 1 except 2 ball detents to hold barrel shut.

	$35	$30	$25	$20	$15	N/A	N/A

MILLARD BROTHERS

For information on Millard Brothers airguns, see Milbro in this section.

MONDIAL

For information on Mondial airguns, see MMM - Mondial in this section.

MONOGRAM

For information on Monogram, see Accles & Shelvoke Ltd. in the "A" section.

MONTGOMERY WARD

Catalog sales/retailer which subcontracted various domestic and international manufacturers to private label various brand names under the Montgomery Ward conglomerate.

Montgomery Ward airguns have appeared under various labels and endorsers, including Western Field and others. Most of these models were manufactured through subcontracts with both domestic and international firms. Typically, they were "spec." airguns made to sell at a specific price to undersell the competition. Most of these models were derivatives of existing factory models with less expensive wood and perhaps missing the features found on those models from which they were derived. Please refer to the Store Brand Crossover Section in the back of this book under Montgomery Ward for converting models to the respective manufacturer.

To date, there has been limited interest in collecting Montgomery Ward airguns, regardless of rarity. Rather than list Montgomery Ward models, a general guideline is that values generally are under those of their "first generation relatives." As a result, prices are ascertained by the shooting value of the airgun, rather than its collector value.

MORINI COMPETITION ARM SA

Current manufacturer located in Bedano, Switzerland. Currently imported and distributed Pilkington Competition Equipment, located in Monteagle, TN, and by Champion's Choice, located in LaVergne, TN. Previously imported 1993-2004 by Nygord Precision Products, located in Prescott, AZ. For more information and current pricing on both new and used Morini Competition Arm SA firearms, please refer to the *Blue Book of Gun Values* by S.P. Fjestad (also available online).

PISTOLS

MODEL 162E - .177 cal., PCP, UIT pistol with fixed cylinder, electronic trigger, adj. sights, adj. grips.

	$795	$600	$450	$300	$225	N/A	N/A
							Last MSR was $1,000.

MODEL 162EI/162EI SHORT - .177 cal., PCP, SS, match pistol, 7.41 (Short) or 9.36 in. Lothar Walther barrel, two detachable cylinders, black finish, Morini anatomical adj. wood grip, adj. electronic trigger, adj. sights, 2.2 lbs.

courtesy Morini

MSR $1,368	$1,250	$1,100	$850	$750	$650	N/A	N/A

MODEL 162MI/162MI SHORT - .177 cal., similar to Model 162EI, except has mechanical trigger.

courtesy Morini

| MSR $1,368 | $1,250 | $1,100 | $850 | $750 | $650 | N/A | N/A |

N-O SECTION

NATIONAL (KOREA)

Current status not known. Beeman Precision Airguns imported examples of one model in the mid-1970s.

GRADING	100%	95%	90%	80%	60%	40%	20%

RIFLES

NATIONAL VOLCANIC - .25 cal., SS, swinging lever pump pneumatic, with sliding loading port system identical to Yewha 3B air shotguns, requires same plastic shot tube, rifled barrel, nomarkings. Blued barrel and body tube, parkerized trigger guard. 37 in.OAL, 6.6 lbs. Extremely rare in USA. Ref: AA Oct. 1987 (reprinted as Hannusch, 2001).

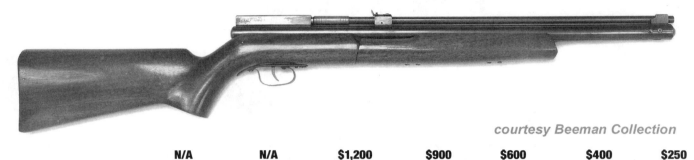

courtesy Beeman Collection

		N/A	N/A	$1,200	$900	$600	$400	$250

NATIONAL RIFLES LTD. (INDIA)

Current maker located in Ahmedabad, India. Distributed by Indian Hume Pipe Co. Ltd., Bombay, India.

India's leading airgun manufacturer; production based on German machinery and airgun designs. Walter (1984) reported that National produced a National Cadet CO_2 bulb rifle version of the Hammerli Cadet CO_2 rifle under a 1968 license from Hammerli and the National 25, as a simpler version of the Dianawerk Model 25.

NORICA FARMI S.A.L.

Current trademark manufactured by Norica-Farmi, S.A.L., located in Eibar, Spain. No current U.S. importation. Previously imported by American Arms, Inc., located in North Kansas City, MO, K.B.I., located in Harrisburg, PA, and by S.A.E., located in Miami, FL.

Norica produces several economy level, private label airguns. Norica airguns imported by American Arms, Inc. will appear under the American Arms, Inc. heading in this text.

RIFLES

MODEL 47 - .177 cal., SL, SP, 600 FPS, black pistol grip, 5.5 lbs.

	$120	$90	$65	$45	$35	N/A	N/A

MODEL 61C - .177 cal., BBC, SP, 600 FPS, 5.5 lbs.

	$85	$70	$50	$35	$25	N/A	N/A

MODEL 73 - .177 or .22 cal., BBC, SP, 580/525 FPS, 6 lbs. 4 oz.

	$110	$85	$60	$45	$30	N/A	N/A

MODEL 80G - .177 or .22 cal., BBC, SP, 635/570 FPS, 7 lbs. 2 oz.

	$140	$120	$80	$60	$40	N/A	N/A

MODEL 90 - .177 cal., BBC, SP, 650 FPS, includes scope.

	$130	$100	$75	$55	$40	N/A	N/A

MODEL 92 - .177 cal., SL, SP, 650 FPS, 5.75 lbs.

	$125	$95	$70	$55	$40	N/A	N/A

NORICA YOUNG - .177 cal., BBC, SP, 600 FPS, colored stock.

	$85	$70	$50	$35	$25	N/A	N/A

BLACK WIDOW - .177 or .22 cal., BBC, SP, 500/450 FPS, black plastic stock, 5 lbs.

	$120	$90	$65	$45	$35	N/A	N/A

NELSON PAINT COMPANY

Paint company located in Iron Mountain, MI, previous manufacturers of paintball markers founded in 1940.

Marketed the first paintball guns (invented by James C. Hale of Daisy, U.S. patent 3,788,298, Jan 29, 1974). Originally marketed to ranchers and foresters for marking cattle and trees. Undoubtedly, one day, a cowboy or ranger was holding a Nelson marking gun when he saw his partner, not too far away, bend over to pick something up. At that moment, the paintball combat game market was born! The first organized paintball game in 1981 used Nelson 007 pistols. The first paintball game gun was the Splatmaster (U.S. patent 4,531,503, Robert G Shepherd,

GRADING	100%	95%	90%	80%	60%	40%	20%

July 30, 1985), also rather collectible, values $25 to $40.

Paintball markers are now a huge specialized field onto themselves (http://apg.cfw2.com/article.asp?content_id=7282) and thus will not be covered in this guide except where the models have historical connections with the regular airgun field.

Nelson tree markers today are specialized paint spraying devices, but the company continues to produce paintballs.

PISTOLS

NEL-SPOT 007 - .68 cal. paintball, 12 gm. CO_2 cylinder, eight- (ten with threaded ball tube) shot gravity-fed, bolt action, steel and brass construction, black paint finish, 3 lbs., 11 in. OAL. Mfg. by Daisy beginning 1974. Disc.

courtesy Beeman Collection

	100%	95%	90%	80%	60%	40%	20%
	$200	$150	$100	$75	$50	N/A	N/A

Add 5% for holster. Add 100% for early versions without removable barrel sleeve, magazine tube threaded inside to accept threaded aluminum paint ball tubes. Plastic pellet stop snapped into magazine center holes.

NEL-SPOT 707 - .68 cal. paintball, CO_2, six-ball gravity-fed magazine along LHS of receiver, blue finish, 11.6 in. OAL, 3.2 lbs. unloaded. Disc.

courtesy Beeman Collection

	100%	95%	90%	80%	60%	40%	20%
	$400	$325	$250	$175	$100	N/A	N/A

Add 5% for holster.

Briefly made by Crosman, apparently before the 007.

O'CONNELL GAS RIFLE

Previous trade name manufactured by the George Robinson Co. located in Rochester, NY circa 1947-49. See George Robinson Co. in the "R" section.

courtesy Beeman Collection

OKLAHOMA

For information on Oklahoma airguns, see MMM – Mondial in the "M" section.

P SECTION

PAFF

Previous tradename used by the merchant Henry Schuermans located in Liege, Belgium.

In 1890, Henry Schuermans registered the bow and arrow trademark, with the letters "PAFF", found on the airgun discussed here. Schuermans was the producer and/or distributor for the Paff air rifle patented by L. Poilvache of Leige under Belgian patents– number 76743 (March 1887), 79663 (November, 1887), and 84461 (December, 1888). This most unusual barrel-cocking, spring piston, .177 cal. air rifle has a 3.5 in. long air chamber which resembles the cylinder on a Colt revolving rifle. This chamber contains three concentric mainsprings which power a hollow piston. 37.7 in. OAL, 5.1 lbs. Retail values will be in the $1,000-$2,000+ range. Ref: John Atkins, AG, Feb. 2003.

courtesy Beeman Collection

PAINTBALL

For information on Paintball, see Nelson in the "N" section.

PALMER

Previous trade name used by Frank D. Palmer Inc., Chicago, IL.

Frank D. Palmer Inc., Chicago, IL, maker of carnival machine guns. Research on this brand is ongoing and additional material will be published in this guide series and on the web as available.

MACHINE GUN

PALMER MACHINE GUN - .174 BB cal., not known if steel or lead, or both, 9 in. smoothbore BBL, electrically driven horizontally rotating feeding disc which is gravity fed from top 2000 BB hopper, approximately one hundred balls, dual spade handle grips with RH trigger built in. 69 in. tall, 20 in. wide, 1/6 HP AC motor for built in compressor, about 300 pounds on original steel stand, black paint finish, marked with eagle shaped logo plate bearing the Palmer name.

courtesy Beeman Collection

Value in good condition about $3,000.

PALMER CHEMICAL AND EQUIPMENT CO.

Current manufacturer of tranquilizer guns located in Douglasville, GA.

Manufacturers of Palmer CapChur tranquilizer guns, generally based on CO_2 models of Crosman airguns. Generally use a small explosive charge in the syringe dart to force out the contents into the target, but the guns themselves are not firearms. Please contact the company directly for more information and prices of current products (see Trademark Index listing).

GRADING	100%	95%	90%	80%	60%	40%	20%

PISTOLS

STANDARD CAPCHUR PISTOL - .50 cal. tranquilizer darts, SS, CO_2, bolt action, small explosive charge for injecting the contents of the syringe dart into the animal to be subdued.

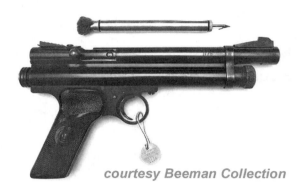

courtesy Beeman Collection

	100%	95%	90%	80%	60%	40%	20%
	$250	$200	$150	$100	$75	N/A	N/A

VEWT 4X CHAPCHUR PISTOL - more recent version of Standard CapChur pistol.

courtesy Beeman Collection

	100%	95%	90%	80%	60%	40%	20%
	$200	$150	$100	$85	$65	N/A	N/A

RIFLES

RED'S SPECIAL - .50 cal. tranquilizer darts, SS, CO_2, bolt action, small explosive charge for injecting the contents of the syringe dart into the animal to be subdued.

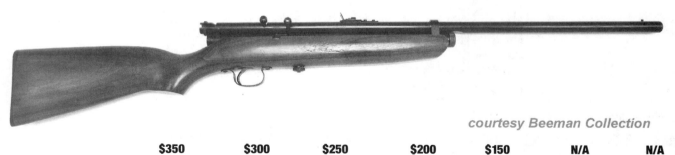

courtesy Beeman Collection

	100%	95%	90%	80%	60%	40%	20%
	$350	$300	$250	$200	$150	N/A	N/A

PAMPANGA

For information on Pampanga airguns, see Philippine Airguns in this "P" section.

PANTHER

For information on Panther airguns, see Gun Toys SRL in the "G" section.

PARDINI, ARMI S.r.l.

Current manufacturer located in Lido di Camaiore, Italy. Currently imported by Larry's Guns, located in Portland, ME. Previously imported by Nygord Precision Products, located in Prescott, AZ, by MCS, Inc.

For more information and current pricing on both new and used Pardini firearms, please refer to the *Blue Book of Gun Values* by S.P. Fjestad (also available online).

GRADING	100%	95%	90%	80%	60%	40%	20%

PISTOLS

MODEL K-2 - .177 cal., CO_2, (250-shot capacity), UIT model, 9.1 in. barrel, adj. trigger, adj. walnut grip, 16 in. OAL, 2.6 lbs.

	100%	95%	90%	80%	60%	40%	20%
MSR $919	$919	$750	$650	$550	N/A	N/A	N/A

MODEL K-2 JUNIOR - .177 cal., CO_2, (250-shot capacity), UIT model, similar to Model K-2 except, 7.6 in. barrel.

	100%	95%	90%	80%	60%	40%	20%
MSR $919	$919	$750	$650	$550	N/A	N/A	N/A

MODEL K-2 LIGHT - .177 cal., CO_2, (250-shot capacity), UIT model, similar to Model K-2 except, 2.3 lbs.

	100%	95%	90%	80%	60%	40%	20%
MSR $919	$919	$750	$650	$550	N/A	N/A	N/A

MODEL K-2S .177 cal., PCP, (250-shot capacity), UIT model, 9.1 in. barrel, adj. trigger, adj. walnut grip, 16 in. OAL, 2.6 lbs.

	100%	95%	90%	80%	60%	40%	20%
MSR $999	$950	$775	$675	$575	$475	N/A	N/A

MODEL K-2S JUNIOR .177 cal., PCP, (250-shot capacity), UIT model, similar to Model K-2S except, 7.6 in. barrel.

	100%	95%	90%	80%	60%	40%	20%
MSR $999	$950	$775	$675	$575	$475	N/A	N/A

MODEL K-2S LIGHT .177 cal., PCP, (250-shot capacity), UIT model, similar to Model K-2S except, 2.3 lbs.

	100%	95%	90%	80%	60%	40%	20%
MSR $999	$950	$775	$675	$575	$475	N/A	N/A

MODEL K58 - .177 cal., UL, 9 in. barrel, UIT model, 2 lbs. 6 oz.

	100%	95%	90%	80%	60%	40%	20%
MSR $819	$775	$650	$575	$450	$350	N/A	N/A

MODEL K60 - .177 cal., CO_2, 9.5 in. barrel, 2 lbs. 4 oz. Disc. 1997.

	100%	95%	90%	80%	60%	40%	20%
	$500	$450	$400	$325	$250	N/A	N/A

Last MSR was $795.

Add 20% for pre-charged pneumatic.

MODEL K90 - .177 cal. CO_2, youth model, 7.25 in. barrel, 1.85 lbs.

	100%	95%	90%	80%	60%	40%	20%
	$450	$375	$300	$250	$175	N/A	N/A

Last MSR was $580.

MODEL P10 - .177 cal., UL, 7.75 in. barrel, 2 lbs. 3 oz. Disc. 1990.

	100%	95%	90%	80%	60%	40%	20%
	$400	$350	$300	$250	$175	N/A	N/A

Last MSR was $560.

PARK RIFLE COMPANY

Current manufacturer located in Kent, England. No current U.S. importation.

RIFLES

RH93/93W/93-800 - .177 or .22 cal., UL, 12ft./lb. energy, 37 or 38 (Model 93-800) in. barrel. 9 lbs. 10 oz.

	100%	95%	90%	80%	60%	40%	20%
MSR $500	$400	$350	$275	$200	$135	N/A	N/A

Add $100 for thumbhole walnut stock.

PARKER-HALE

Parker was the previous tradename of the A.G. Parker Company located in Birmingham, England, which was formed from a gun-making business founded in 1890 by Alfred Gray Parker. The company became the Parker-Hale company in 1936. Purchased by John Rothery Wholesale about 2000. This firm made an air pistol designed by Alfred Hale and Ernest Harris and Lee-Enfield sporter firearm rifles. For more information and current pricing on Parker-Hale firearms, please refer to the *Blue Book of Gun Values* by S.P. Fjestad (also available online).

PISTOLS

These guns are often referred to as the "Parker-Hale" air pistols. However, this is not correct, as these pistols were made about 1921 and the Parker-Hale Company did not come into existence until 1936.

GRADING	100%	95%	90%	80%	60%	40%	20%

PARKER PATENT PRECISION AIR PISTOL - .177 cal,. SP, SS, fixed rifled 9.6 in. BBL, piston moves rearward during firing. Cocked by turning a large crank on the RHS 3.5 turns; crank remains attached to gun at all times but disengages internally for firing; blued finish. Loaded by unscrewing a large knurled screw on the breech block and swinging the loading gate downward. A built-in pellet seater could help swage the pellet into place. Later production had a two-diameter compression cylinder/body tube, there was a larger diameter area between the barrel support and about the middle of the wooden grip. Serial numbers known to 215. 10.6 in. OAL, 3.3 lbs. Ref: John Atkins, AG, April 1992: 65.

courtesy Beeman Collection

		N/A	N/A	$1,950	$1,500	$1,000	$750	$500

Add 10% for first version with single-diameter body tube.

RIFLES

PHOENIX MK 1 - .177 or .22 cal., PCP, detachable air cylinder in buttstock, ten-shot BSA Superten magazine, lever action cocking, beech stock. Mfg.circa 1998-99.
Current values not yet determined.
Designed by Graham Bluck.

PHOENIX MK 2 - .22 cal., PCP, detachable air cylinder in buttstock, new repeater magazine, other design improvements, deluxe walnut stock. Intro. 2004.

courtesy Tim Saunders

Current values not yet determined.

DRAGON - .177 or .22 cal., SSP, SS, walnut sporter stock (about twelve with large FT stocks). Mk1 and Mk 2 variants: identical except for hardened valve in Mk 2, 40 in. OAL. Made about 1995.

	$400	$350	$275	$195	$150	N/A	N/A

Designed by Graham Bluck.

PARRIS MANUFACTURING COMPANY

Previous manufacturer located in Savannah, TN.

Company began in Iowa in 1943 making toy guns (pop guns, cork guns, Kadet training rifles, etc). Made a few bolt action military training firearm rifles during WWII. Moved to Savannah, TN circa 1953. BB guns manufactured circa 1960 - 1970 when the company became a Division of Gayla Industries. All BB rifles with decal, on RHS buttstock, usually marked Kadet or Trainer but w/o model number. Additional research is underway on this complex group. Information given here must be considered as tentative. The authors and publisher wish to thank John Groenewold for his valuable assistance with the following information in this edition of the Blue Book of Airguns.

PISTOLS

KADET 507 .174 cal., SP, SS, BB or Cork, 11 in. OAL.

	$150	$140	$120	$100	$80	$60	$40

GRADING	100%	95%	90%	80%	60%	40%	20%

RIFLES

KADET 500 .l74 cal., SP, LA, "Selector Loader" mechanism at muzzle holds 50 BBs; twisting it releases 1 to 6 BBs to be fired together at one time, magnetic shot retainer holds BBs until fired, one piece wood stock, 30 in. OAL, 2.6 lbs.

courtesy Beeman Collection

	$150	$140	$120	$100	$80	$60	$40

KADET 501 .174 cal. BB or cork., SS, SP, LA, 32 in. OAL, 2.6 lbs.

	$150	$140	$120	$100	$80	$60	$40

Add 40% for shooting kit model 501WT.

KADET 502 .l74 cal., SP, LA, "Selector Loader" mechanism at muzzle holds 50 BBs; twisting it releases 1 to 6 BBs to be fired together at one time, magnetic shot retainer holds BBs until fired, one piece wood stock, 37.5 in. OAL, 3.2 lbs.

courtesy Beeman Collection

	$150	$140	$120	$100	$80	$60	$40

Add 40% for shooting kit model 502WT.

KADET 504 similar to Kadet 502 except army style stock and 1 inch sling.

	$200	$175	$150	$125	$100	$75	$50

Add 40% for shooting kit model 504WT.

KADET "X" (MODEL NO. UNKOWN) .174 cal., SP, LA, plastic muzzle piece and rectangular assembly under the barrel near muzzle houses safety, 37 in. OAL, 2.9 lbs. Mfg. circa 1969-1970.

courtesy Beeman Collection

	$250	$225	$200	$175	$150	$125	$100

Probably the last BB gun configuration made by Parris Manufacturing Company.

PAUL

Previous trademark manufactured by William Paul locatred in Beecher, IL.
Pump pneumatic SS shotgun with bicycle-type pump under barrel. To charge, fold out the foot pedal on the forward end of pump rod held to ground, and gun moved up and down for about seventy strong strokes. Additional strokes needed between shots. See *Airgun Journal* 4(1) - 1983, AGNR - Apr. 1987.

SHOTGUNS

MODEL 420 - .410 cal smoothbore barrel slides forward for breech loading, nickel plated brass receiver, barrel, and pump; cast aluminum buttplate and trigger guard; 43 in. overall, walnut stock, shotshells are brass tubes with wad at each end, cardboard shotshells illustrated on cover of cartridge box not known, each shell contains about 32 pellets number 6 birdshot (1/6 oz.). Jan. 1924 patent shows cocking rod in pistol grip (apparently never produced). Production followed Sept. 1924 patent with cocking rod projecting from forearm. Two variants (with small variations within each type): 6.5 lbs., approx. 1,000 mfg. mid-1920s to mid-1930s.

GRADING	100%	95%	90%	80%	60%	40%	20%

⊙ *Model 400 Ringed Variant* - barrel and pump tube connected by soldered rings, barrel flat spring soldered to body tube.

courtesy Beeman Collection

	N/A	$1,250	$995	$895	$795	$650	$400

Add 25% for original shotshell loading kit.

⊙ *Model 400 Banded Variant* - barrel and pump tube connected by soldered bands, barrel flat spring clamped to body tube.

courtesy Beeman Collection

	N/A	$1,000	$900	$850	$750	$700	$600

Add 25% for original shotshell loading kit.

MODEL 420 REPLICA See Dennis Quackenbush in the "Q" section of this book.

PEERLESS

Previous tradename used pre-WWII by Stoeger Arms of New York for airguns imported from Germany, probably all from Dianawerk, using original Dianawerk model numbers. See Dianawerk in the D section of this book for more information.

PENNEY'S, J.C.

Catalog sales/retailer that has subcontracted manufacturers to private label airguns.

To date, there has been limited interest in collecting J.C. Penney's airguns, regardless of rarity. Rather than list models, a general guideline is that values generally are under those of their "first generation relatives." As a result, priceshave beenascertained by the shooting value of the airgun, rather than its collector value. See "Store Brand Crossover List" located in the back of this text.

PERFECTA

Apparently a private brand name used for at least a copy of the Milbro Diana SP50 air pistol.

Perfecta was a brand name for spring piston airguns made by Oskar Will of Zella Mehlis, Germany in the 1920s for the Midland Gun Company of Birmingham, England, so it may have been resurrected by Midland Gun Company, or another company, for use on this pistol which was made in the British Diana form from the mid-1970s to 1982.

PISTOL

PERFECTA SP50 - .177 cal., darts or pellets, push barrel SP, SS, die-cast body, black paint finish.

courtesy Beeman Collection

	$25	$20	$15	$10	N/A	N/A	N/A

Same as the Milbro Diana SP50.

PHILIPPINE AIRGUNS

Previous and current producers.

There has been a thriving production of airguns in the Philippines since the 1970s. The reason for this and why the spring piston airgun revolution largely bypassed the Philippines basically was due to one man: President/Dictator Ferdinand Edralin Marcos. In 1972 [1], Marco declared martial law and all gun importations were stopped, including importation of airguns. All firearms were confiscated except for those belonging to people who were able to get a special license only for pistols under 9mm, .22 rimfire rifles, and shotguns. Even those guns became hard to get because of the ban on importation. Local supplies of American airguns, like the popular Crosman 114 and 160, and precision European airguns, quickly dried up. The Squires Bingham Company tried to resurrect the Crosman 160, but this failed and, in any case, that gun was not up to the hunting standards of Philippine shooters. Airgun clubs dedicated to the precision shooting sports closed because of the halt in the importation of precision airguns; there were no precision airguns produced locally. Philippine shooters suddenly needed airguns, but mainly they wanted power for hunting. Spring piston airguns and guns using soda pop cartridges were not up to their needs, and PCP guns were not a viable choice due to the difficult filling requirements. Bulk fill CO_2 was the answer for this new hunter-driven market. Bulk fill CO_2 guns were light and easy to fill from a 10 oz. tank on the shooter's belt and the cylinders could be filled easily and cheaply at many places. So the Philippines became a hunter's airgun market, not a precision airgun market!

The most interesting things about Philippine airguns are their power, freewheeling designs, and their variety. Separate sections of this guide now give an introduction to some of the main Philippine brands found in the USA: Some of the best known makers are LD, Farco, MC Topgun, Valesquez, Valiente, Rogunz, Koffmanz, JBC, Harlie, Isaac, Garco, Centerpoint, Trident, Dreibund, Armscor (SB), and Spitfire. Some especially interesting guns are the beautifully made side lever Pampanga-type CO_2 guns.

It is reported that the majority of the Philippine airguns that have come into the USA were brought via service men who purchased them in the Philippines. This was especially true of the LD airguns; apparently about 20% to 25% of their production came in via that route. Several models of Philippine airguns also have been imported into the USA by Air Rifle Specialties in New York and Bryan and Associates in South Carolina. (Dave Schwesinger, owner of Air Rifle Specialties in New York, used to live in the Philippines and spent a lot of time in the LD airgun shop.) All Philippine hunting airguns are relatively scarce. Production ran from an average of less than one hundred guns per month for LD, evidently the largest maker, down to a few guns a month from a custom maker such as JBC. Perhaps 70% to 99% of most production runs stayed in the Philippines. Most American and European airgun factories, and large importers, figure on several thousand or tens of thousands of guns per month. Thus Philippine hunting airguns are very desirable from an airgun hunter's or collector's standpoint.

[1] By interesting coincidence, this was just about the time that the adult airgun market in the USA got its first significant commercial start, based primarily on spring-piston airguns. (See www.beemans.net/adult_airguns_in_america.htm.)

A sampling of Philippine airguns is given below. See the "L" section for LD airguns and the "F" section for Farco airguns.

JBC/LD/PAMPANGA/ROGUNZ/VALESQUEZ/UNKNOWN MAKERS

Selected brands (all are CO_2 bulk fill and in calibers .177 to .25 as specified by buyer):

JBC - High end, small maker. Valve body and stem aluminum or brass. 12-groove rifling. Expansion chambers.

⊙ **MONKEY GUN** - .22 cal., SS, BA rifle, thumbhole stock, 33.9 in. OAL, 6.3 lbs, approx. 725 FPS. Serial numbers up to 3 are known. 1987.

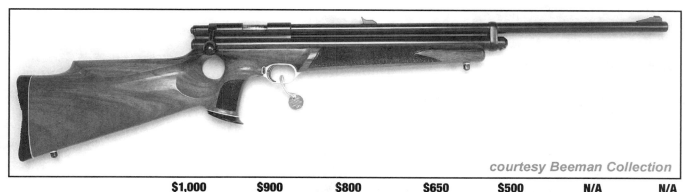

courtesy Beeman Collection

| $1,000 | $900 | $800 | $650 | $500 | N/A | N/A |

LD - For more info and other LD models, see LD Airguns in the "L" section of this guide.

⊙ **LD 380 (RANCHER)** - four caliber combo: .50 in. smoothbore, .380 smoothbore insert, .22 cal. rifled insert, .177 cal. rifled insert. This caliber range gave the Rancher amazing flexibility: it could project .177 or .22 cal. pellets, .38 cal. shot charges, .38 cal. bullets or lead balls, arrows w/o fletching, expanding tip spears, multi-prong spears, .50 in. tranquilizer darts, and even shaped TNT charges in brass "torpedoes." A spinning reel mounted under the forearm enhanced fishing and frog hunting. Laminated two-tone Narra stock.

PAMPANGA This is not a brand, but a geographical group of guns made in the central Luzon section of the Philippines in the region of the former U.S. Clark Air Force Base. This area was turned into hundreds of square miles of desert by the massive Pinatubo volcanic explosion. The Pampanga guns are especially designed for hunting the wild dogs and ducks which now abound there. The identifying characteristics are: 1) extensive use of red Narra wood (very decorative, but too heavy according to some); 2) finely made stainless steel parts; brass or stainless steel valve parts; 3) removable CO_2 reservoirs extended under the barrel; 4) straight-pull bolt action or a modified LD-type hammer swing action. 5) unusually good fitting of parts; 6) lack of an expansion chamber so that these guns may dump CO_2 as fast as possible for maximum power; 7) twelve-groove rifling. There are very few shops in the Pampanga area, especially in the City of San Fernando, that specialize in acquiring these guns from very small makers (two- or three-man operations) who do not produce more than five or six guns a month. Pampanga airguns are the most expensive airguns in the Philippines, but generally are the finest and most desired of all Philippine airguns. Values begin circa $1250.

Not all Pampanga guns have the above features. Some are high end copies of LD, JBC, Rogunz, and other brands. The best way to identify unmarked Philippine bulk fill CO_2 guns is to count the rifling grooves; the Pampanga guns almost always have twelve grooves while most of the main line Philippine guns have seven- or eight-groove rifling. Also, Pampanga guns have brass or stainless steel valves, while others have only brass valve bodies (or brass or aluminum, in the case of JBC guns) with Teflon valve stems (white for LD, colored for Rogunz). Because they are made for the retailers, they generally do not bear any conspicuous sign of the maker. However, close examination of the reservoir and areas hidden by the stock often reveals small identification marks of the actual maker.

⊙ **PAMPANGA RIFLE** - .22 cal., 47.3 in. OAL, straight pull bolt action.

courtesy Beeman Collection

⊙ **PAMPANGA SHOTGUN** - 20 ga., 57.4 in. OAL, straight pull bolt action, almost entirely stainless steel.

courtesy Beeman Collection

ROGUNZ Major maker. Seven- or eight-groove rifling, valve body of Tiger brass; value stem of Teflon, lock ring (bolt retaining ring) is always knurled. Expansion chambers.

⊙ **FALCON 1-132** - SS, hammer swing match rifle. Value about $750.

courtesy Beeman Collection

⊙ **MATCH MODEL** - .22 cal., turning bolt, robust match stock with decorative panels cut in forearm, lateral easy-feed magazine on RHS. Expansion chamber.

UNKNOWN MAKERS Perhaps as a result of subcontracting gun construction, many of the Philippine airguns are not marked. An example is this well made, bulk fill, long range pistol, made in .22 and .25 calibers, hand checkered black ebony wood grips, no maker's name, two specimens marked only "1" and "2" on hidden grip frame area. 14.6 OAL.

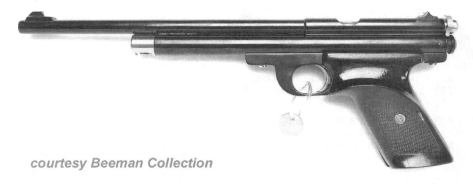

courtesy Beeman Collection

Value estimated at $295 in 90% condition.

VALESQUEZ - seven- or eight-groove rifling, valve body of Tiger brass; valve stem of Teflon. Expansion chambers.

GRADING	100%	95%	90%	80%	60%	40%	20%

✪ Brass Beauty - .22 in. cal., SS, bolt action, barrel and most metal parts are brass. Value about $850.

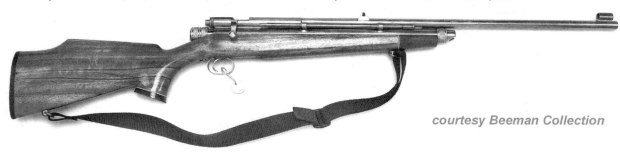

courtesy Beeman Collection

✪ Bolt Action match Rifle - value about $700.

courtesy Beeman Collection

PIPER

Current manufacturer located in Lampasas, Texas. Founded by Paul Piper; manf. started 1999. Huge variety of air machine guns. Most are high end products designed around rotating barrel Gatling Gun design of the American Civil War - a system adopted for ultra-high rate of fire U.S. military air borne weapons. Most air machine guns run out of ammo very quickly; Piper's designs have projectile capacities from 1200 to 24,000 BBs! Models operate on standard screw-on CO_2 bottles, high pressure compressed air (HPA), or 80 to 150 psi pressure from shop-type air compressors. Distributed by Xcaliber Tactical www.xcalibertactical.com. The great, wonderful variety of high and middle cost guns cannot be covered here. See www.piper-sprecisionproducts.com and excellent coverage and illustrations in Behling (2006).

Research is ongoing with this trademark, and more information will be included both online and in future editions.

RIFLES: AUTOMATIC

MINI-VULCAN - .174/steel BB cal., CO_2, portable 12 oz. tank mounted in center axis of six rotating barrels, laser sight, powered by onboard DC motor, 1200 rounds per minute, portable gun fired from arm sling, machined aluminum and steel, some optional features. 24 in. OAL, 22 lbs. 20 mfg. Ref: AR4: 75-76, Behling (2006).

courtesy Beeman Collection

$3,500	$2,900	$2,500	$2,200	N/A	N/A	N/A

Last MSR was $2,800.

PLYMOUTH AIR RIFLE COMPANY

Previous manufacturer of iron and wooden BB guns, located in Plymouth, Michigan, 1888-1894.

Daisy was not the first to produce BB rifles for boys! Markham produced an all-wood BB rifle in 1886, but the Plymouth Air Rifle Company produced the first conventional BB rifle (invented by Clarence Hamilton in 1887) with an iron barrel and wooden stock. (The Daisy all-metal BB rifle was introduced in 1889.) Founded by Cyrus Pinckney and Clarence Hamilton (who founded the Plymouth Iron Windmill Company in 1882 and invented the Daisy BB gun and a line of .22 rimfire rifles for boys). Previous references have confused the history of the Plymouth Air Rifle Company with that of the Decker Air Rifle Company. To clear up the confusion: The Plymouth Air Rifle Company produced the Plymouth, Challenge, Bijou, and Magic airguns. Ref.: Wesley Powers, American Rifleman (Feb. '88) and U.S. Airgun (May/June 1998).

GRADING	100%	95%	90%	80%	60%	40%	20%

RIFLES

PLYMOUTH - .180 large BB cal., SS, SP, cocking lever snaps under screw in stock on lower edge of buttstock, breech loading, barrel slides fwd to receive BB on underside, s/b bbl angles up to muzzle, blue or nickel finish, flat walnut buttstock; invented 1887, patn'd 2 October 1888, intro. 1888. No markings except pat. date on 2nd, 3rd, and 4th models; Extreme rarity and great historical significance precludes pricing, but knowledgeable collectors suggest $2,500 and up for any model in fair condition.

courtesy Beeman Collection

1888 MSR was $2.35.

First Version - straight, blued bbl, no markings.
Second Version - nickel plated, brass bbl w/ step, date OCT 2, 88 on left side of anchor casting.
Third Version - trigger gd part of 2-pc frame, screw holding anchor casting to stock is perpendicular, pat.date OCT 2, 88 stamped on anchor frame
Fourth Version - 2 step bbl, nickeled, sep. 1-pc trigger guard, frame straddles stock w/screw on each side, pat.date OCT 2, 88 straddling left ear of frame, 32 in. OAL, s/b bbl 9.25 in. (Copied exactly in Australia as the Hornet air rifle.)

CHALLENGE - .180 large BB cal., SP, almost all wood gun produced to compete w/ Markham CHICAGO. Iron cocking lever fwd of trgr gd, sheet metal trgr gd, , "CHALLENGE" recess cast into iron spring anchor, solid 1 pc. yellow maple stock w/o center hinge.. (Listed as unmarked Challenger under Markham-King brand by Dunathan's American BB Gun book.) Extreme rarity precludes pricing, est. values over $2,500, more for repeater.

1890 MSR was $1.

Single Shot Version (Pat.#390,311 Oct. 2, 1888).
Repeater Version (Pat. # 477,385, June 21, 1892, George Sage).

MAGIC - .180 large BB cal., SP, LA under bbl, cast iron frame, receiver, and lever, all metal nickeled. Walnut stock. Ring on fwd. end of cocking lever. Marked MAGIC on grip frame. Rare.Ca. 1891.
First Version - SS, BC, black painted frame, "MAGIC" recess cast in cartouche.
Second Version - same as 1st but repeater, black painted frame.
Third Version - same as 2nd, nickel plated.
Fourth Version - same as 3rd, w/ round tang on half of frame for improved stock connection.

BIJOU - .180 large BB cal., SS, SP, BC, nickel plated metal. Ca. 1893-1895.
First Version - 10.25 in. frame, "BIJOU" recess cast in grip frame, wooden stock.
Second Version - 9 in. sheet metal frame, area of BIJOU casting as a plaque w/ rays and dots. Wooden stock.
Third Version - cast iron skeleton stk, action w/ spring-loaded detent. (Perhaps actually the 1st model?)

PNEUDART, INC.

Current marketers of tranquilizer guns located in Williamsport, PA.

Manufacturers of tranquilizer guns Models 176 (CO_2) and 178 (pneumatic) single shot rifles plus the models 179 and 190 CO_2 pistols. They also supply firearm dart projectors and tranquilizer supplies. Guns and parts made by Benjamin/Crosman. Crosman parts diagrams and Crosman parts numbers. Evidently, repeating air projectors are no longer available. Please contact the company directly for more information and prices of their products (see Trademark Index listing).

RIFLES

MODEL 167 - .50 cal., three-shot sliding magazine repeater, CO_2 charged. Blue steel, hardwood stock, 37.2 in. OAL, 6.6 lbs.

courtesy Beeman Collection

	$350	$300	$250	$200	$150	N/A	N/A

GRADING	100%	95%	90%	80%	60%	40%	20%

PODIUM

Previous trademark of Sportil S.A. Portal De Gamarra, Vitoria, Spain.

From 1983 to 1987, Sportil manufactured and distributed three CO_2 powered guns. Each bore an uncanny resemblance to an obsolete Crosman model, but this firm says that Sportil did not manufacture under license. Although they were well made and very reliable, Podium gas guns had a very limited international distribution. The authors and publisher wish to thank Trevor Adams for his valuable assistance with the following information in this edition of the *Blue Book of Airguns*.

PISTOLS

MODEL 284 - BB cal., CO_2, repeating pistol and a clone of the Crosman Model 454.

	100%	95%	90%	80%	60%	40%	20%
	$80	$55	$40	$30	N/A	N/A	N/A

RIFLES

MODEL 186 - BB cal., CO_2, BA, fires a single pellet or BBs from a magazine, outwardly resembling the Crosman 766 pneumatic rifle, powerlet concealed beneath the forearm.

	100%	95%	90%	80%	60%	40%	20%
	$100	$80	$65	$50	$35	N/A	N/A

MODEL 286 - BB cal., CO_2, BA, similar to Crosman Model 70, fires either a single lead pellet or BBs from an eight-shot mag., powerlet lies in the forearm, knurled ring, halfway along the plastic barrel shroud, helps prevent barrel warp in the noonday sun (maybe).

	100%	95%	90%	80%	60%	40%	20%
	$120	$95	$80	$65	$50	N/A	N/A

POPE

Previous tradename of Pope Brothers located in Boston, MA.

At least part-time producers and sellers of a spring piston air pistol invented by H.M. Quackenbush. Patented in 1874, this was not Quackenbush´s first air pistol, as sometimes reported, but it was the basis for the Bedford, Bedford & Walker, Johnson and Bye, and later Quackenbush air pistols and other airguns. Produced from at least 1871. Pope received the rights to the gun in 1874, but abandoned the original Quackenbush design later, allowing Quackenbush to have the patent reissued to him. Quackenbush reported sales of seventy-four Eureka air pistols in 1884. Some of the never-to-be-completely-unraveled features of the relationship of Pope and other makers of this time and place in America are summarized in the Johnson & Bye listing in the "J" section of this guide.

PISTOLS/RIFLES

POPE AIR PISTOL - .210 cal., SP, SS, pull-barrel cocking and loading, Japan black enamel or nickel finish, hole in base of "Birds Head" grip for wire shoulder stock, 12 in. OAL. Mfg. circa 1874-1878.

courtesy Beeman Collection

	100%	95%	90%	80%	60%	40%	20%
	N/A	$750	$600	$450	$300	$200	$100

Add 10% for H.M. Quackenbush name stamped on gun, with patent dates. Add 10% for nickel finish. Add 10% for wire shoulder stock. Add 10%-40% for factory fitted wooden case w/ accessories.

POWERLINE

For information on Powerline, see Daisy in the "D" section.

PRECHARGE AB

Current manufacturer located in Hova, Sweden.

During 2002 PRECharge AB changed its name to FX Airguns AB. PRECharge AB are the manufacturers of FX trademark airguns imported and/or distributed by ARS, Airguns of Arizona, RWS, and Webley & Scott. See FX Airguns AB listing in the "F" section.

RIFLES

FX EXCALIBRE - .177 or .22 cal., PCP, bolt action, eight-shot rotary mag., 21 in. choked Lothar Walther rifled barrel, high gloss blue finish, checkered walnut Monte-Carlo style stock with Schnabel forend and recoil pad, adj. trigger, receiver grooved for scope, 7 lbs.

No MSR	$995	$800	$700	$575	N/A	N/A	N/A

Add 20% for deluxe Turkish walnut stock.

GRADING	100%	95%	90%	80%	60%	40%	20%

PREDOM

For information on Predom airguns, see Lucznik in the "L" section.

PRODUSIT

Previous manufacturer located in Birmingham, England.

Produsit Ltd., previous makers of a concentric piston air pistol very similar to the Tell II in design, but somewhat larger.

PISTOLS

THUNDERBOLT JUNIOR - .177 cal, SP, SS, concentric piston design, cocked with lever which includes the backstrap, rear loading cover, brown plastic grips marked with "THUNDERBOLT JUNIOR", a lightning bolt, and "MADE IN ENGLAND", 6.7 in. OAL. Approx. 8,000 mfg. circa 1947-49.

courtesy Beeman Collection

$300	$275	$250	$175	$135	$100	$75

Also marked "Big Chief".

RIFLES

BIG CHIEF - .174/BB cal., SS, SP, break action, folded metal construction, slab sided hardwood stock with colored decal: "BIG CHIEF AIR GUN BRITISH MADE". No other markings. Patented Feb.13, 1952, blue steel finish, 31.7 in. OAL, 2.5 lbs.Ref: Trevor Adams, Dec. 1991, New Zealand Guns Magazine. (Also known with Abbey Alert decal on stock and "Prov Pat 33207" on frame. May have been a premium gun and may appear with other labels.) Circa 1950s.

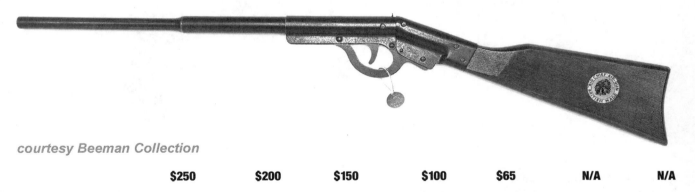

courtesy Beeman Collection

$250	$200	$150	$100	$65	N/A	N/A

PULSE-MATIC

Previous trade mark manufactured by Pulse Manufacturing Inc., Pittsburg, Pennsylvania. Produced three production models of full automatic CO_2 rifles based on pat. no. 5,054,464, issued Oct. 8. 1991 to William Young. Manufactured 1987-1992. William Young died Oct. 2005. Ref. Behling (2006).

Pulse-Matic model rifles do not show any markings of any kind! The authors and publisher wish to thank Mr. Will Hartlep for his assistance in the introduction in this edition of Blue Book of Airguns.

GRADING	100%	95%	90%	80%	60%	40%	20%

RIFLES

MODEL A - .22 in. cal., pellet or round lead ball. Operates off three 12 gm CO_2 cylinders. Rifled bbl. 6, 7.5, or 12 in., 36.5 in. OAL, 10 lbs, flat walnut, 2 pc. stock, tubular 30-50 round magazine, loaded from muzzle. 1800-2000 rpm, 550 fps, bursts will saw a pop can in half. Manual bolt safety. Large CO_2 chamber looks like the barrel. Actual muzzle far back from muzzle, thus shooter may inadvertently place his hand over the muzzle during firing. Approx. 60 Mfg.

courtesy Beeman Collection

	100%	95%	90%	80%	60%	40%	20%
	$1,250	$1,000	$750	$550	$350	N/A	N/A

Last MSR was $500.

MODEL B - basically same as Model A except with longer bbl for safety and with rear wooden stock replaced w/ skeleton stock. Tubular 75 round magazine. Bbl. 13 in, 42 in OAL, 9.5 lbs. Approx. 25 Mfg.

courtesy Beeman Collection

	100%	95%	90%	80%	60%	40%	20%
	$1,750	$1,350	$1,000	$750	$500	N/A	N/A

Last MSR was $600.

MODEL C - basically same as Model B with large CO_2 chamber for 3 CO_2 Powerlets replaced with large on-board bulk CO_2 bottle held in sleeve under center of gun. Bbl. 12 in. rifled, 36 in. OAL, 9 lbs. w/ CO_2 bottle. Tubular 75 round magazine. Approx. 15 mfg.

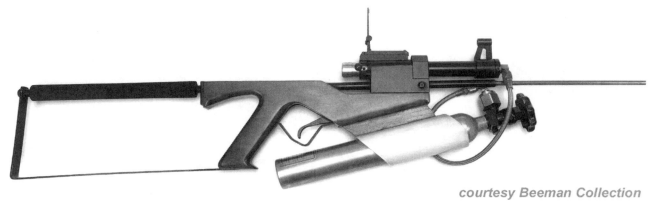

courtesy Beeman Collection

	100%	95%	90%	80%	60%	40%	20%
	$2,150	$1,850	$1,500	$1,000	$650	N/A	N/A

Prototype of Model C also known.

GRADING	100%	95%	90%	80%	60%	40%	20%

PYRAMYD AIR INTERNATIONAL

Current importer and distributor located in Pepper Pike, OH.

Pyramyd Air International imports and markets the largest caliber air rifle in mass production, the Big Bore 909, manufactured in Korea by Sam Yang.

Pyramyd Air International also imports Air Arms, China Shanghai, Umarex, Gamo, IZH-Baikal, Rutten, Tau Brno, Walther, Webley & Scott Ltd./Venom, and Weihrauch airguns. Please refer to these individual listings in this text

RIFLES

MODEL 909 BIG BORE 44 - .45 cal., PCP, 550-775 FPS (670 FPS with cast .454 190 gr. SWC), 670 FPS, 22.25 in. rifled barrel, carved and checkered walnut stock, 7.5 lbs. Mfg. 2000-04.

	100%	95%	90%	80%	60%	40%	20%
	$525	$450	$350	$300	$150	N/A	N/A

Last MSR was $585.

MODEL 909S BIG BORE 45 - .45 cal., PCP, 550-775 FPS (670 FPS with cast .454 190 gr. SWC), 670 FPS, 21.65 in. rifled barrel, carved and checkered walnut stock, 42.1 in. OAL, 7.15 lbs. New 2005.

MSR $600	$500	$425	$350	$300	$150	N/A	N/A

DRAGON MODEL - .50 cal., PCP, SS, BA, 22. in. rifled barrel, adj. trigger, checkered hardwood stock, rubber butt pad. New 2004.

MSR $650	$575	$495	$450	$350	$250	N/A	N/A

Q SECTION

QUACKENBUSH, DENNIS

Current manufacturer located in Urbana, MO beginning in 1992.

In addition to the listed models, Dennis Quackenbush has also produced a wide variety of single order items and some excellent replicas of antique airguns, such as External Lock (Liege Lock) Air Rifles and Paul Air Shotguns (see Paul in the "Q" section of this guide). See a wider range and notice of current products at www.quackenbushairguns.com.

GRADING	100%	95%	90%	80%	60%	40%	20%

PISTOLS

These pistols were custom manufactured action and barrel conversions for the Crosman Models SSP 250 and 2240 pistols. Production through 2006 of complete pistols is as follows: Crosman 250 frame: .375 smoothbore cal., 144 mfg., .375 rifled round ball cal., 36 mfg., 9mm cal., 4 mfg.. Crosman 2240 frame .25 cal., round breach 144 mfg., square breech 327 mfg., 9mm 90 mfg. Crosman 2440 steel breech 850 mfg.

PISTOL - .25, 9mm, or .375 cal., CO_2 or PCP, SS, BA, 8-11 in. rifled barrel, blue finish, adj. rear sight. Approx. 450 mfg. Disc.

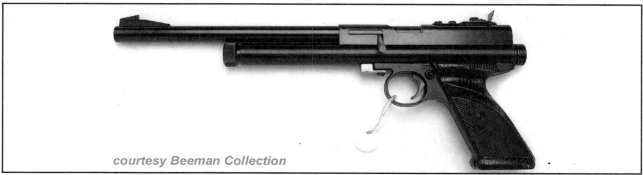

courtesy Beeman Collection

N/A	$250	$200	$125	$75	$50	N/A

Subtract 50% for guns built from a top-end kits (conversion units). Add 100% for 9mm with "A", "B", "C", and "D" serialization. Add 50% for rifled .375 and .25 cal. pistols sold by the maker as completed guns (not kits).

Manufactured as a custom barreled action conversion for the Crosman SSP 250 and 2240 pistols. The .375 CO_2 smoothbore shot version (utilizing Crosman 1100 shotshells as ammunition and breech seal). Early guns have round breeches (sold as complete guns), later versions are square-section (many sold as kits meant to use a customer's existing gun).

OUTLAW - .25, .308, 9mm, .45, or .50 (limited) cal., PCP, SS, BA, 10-14 in. rifled barrel, approx. 1000/500 FPS (depending on caliber), blue finish, no sights. mfg. beginning 2004.

N/A	$650	$550	$475	$350	$200	N/A

Subtract 20% .25 cal. Add 5% for carbine buttstock

RIFLES: OUTLAW SERIES

Production of Outlaw rifles through 2006: Brigand .375 cal., CO_2 84 mfg., Brigand .375 cal., PCP 9, Rogue .44 cal., 28, Knave .25 cal., 10, Bandit .50 cal., 341 mfg., Exile .308 cal., 228 mfg.

50%-150% (depending on condition) premiums are being paid for current production and used rifles by individuals that can not wait for production to catch up to demand.

AMARANTH (LEIGE LOCK) .375 or .43 cal. (optional .445 barrel available), PCP (20 mfg. 1995-1999), SS, removable reservoir, tap-loading 24-36 in. rifled steel barrel, 600-800 FPS, blue finish, leather covered butt-reservoir, 41 in. OAL. Mfg. 1996-1999.

N/A	$1,000	$900	$775	$600	N/A	N/A

Subtract 25% for smoothbore muzzle-loading versions.

BANDIT - .50 cal., PCP, SS, fixed reservoir, 26 in. rifled steel barrel, 780 (.50 cal.) FPS, blue finish, American walnut stock, 43 in. OAL, 7.25 lbs. Mfg. 2000-04.

courtesy Beeman Collection

N/A	$600	$550	$47	$400	N/A	N/A

Last MSR was $535.

Add 5% for Standard grade with deluxe blue. Add 10% for Select grade with deluxe blue and select stock. Add 15% for Superior grade with deluxe stock or master blue.

GRADING	100%	95%	90%	80%	60%	40%	20%

BRIGAND - .375 cal., CO_2 or PCP, SS, fixed reservoir, rifled steel barrel, 600-800 FPS, blue finish, walnut stock, 41 in. OAL, 7.25 lbs. Mfg. 1996-99.

courtesy Beeman Collection

	N/A	$500	$450	$375	3225	N/A	N/A

Add 20% for PCP.

EXILE - .308 cal., PCP, SS, fixed reservoir, 26 in. rifled steel barrel, 780 (.50 cal.) FPS, blue finish, American walnut stock, 43 in. OAL, 7.25 lbs. New 2000.

	N/A	$600	$550	$47	$400	N/A	N/A

Last MSR was $495.

Add 5% for Standard grade with deluxe blue. Add 10% for Select grade with deluxe blue and select stock. Add 15% for superior grade with deluxe stock or master blue.

LIADY SPECIAL - .22 cal., uses Brocock-type air cartridges (large style, about size of 20 ga. Shotgun cartridge), BA, SS. No open sights, grooved for scope. No markings. 41.8 in OAL, 5.3 lbs. with scope. One specimen known, about 1997.

courtesy Beeman Collection

Rarity precludes accurate pricing.

LIGHT SPORTER - .22 or .25 cal., CO_2 or PCP, SS, fixed reservoir, Lothar Walther barrel, 650-850 FPS, blue finish, walnut stock, 35 in. OAL, 6.75-7 lbs. Mfg. circa 1995-96.

	N/A	$425	$350	$285	$225	$175	N/A

LA (LONG ACTION) OUTLAW .457 cal., PCP, SS, fixed reservoir, 25 in. rifled steel barrel (30 in. optional), 730 FPS, blue finish, Walnut stock, 44 in. OAL, 8.25 lbs. Mfg. 2005-Present.

MSR $660	N/A	$660	$550	N/A	N/A	N/A	N/A

Add 5% for Standard grade with deluxe blue. Add 10% for Select grade with deluxe blue and select stock. Add 15% for superior grade with deluxe stock or master blue.

ROGUE - .44 cal., PCP, SS, fixed reservoir, rifled steel barrel, 800 FPS, blue finish, walnut stock, 41 in. OAL, 7.25 lbs. Approx. 40 mfg. in 1999 only.

	N/A	$550	$485	$385	$325	$275	N/A

XL - .22 cal., CO_2 or PCP, SS, removable bottle, Lothar Walther barrel, 650-850 FPS, blue finish, walnut stock, 35 in. OAL, 6.75-7 lbs. Mfg. beginning in 1994. Disc.

	N/A	$425	$350	$285	$225	$175	N/A

QUACKENBUSH, H.M.

Previous manufacturer located in Herkimer, NY from 1871 to 1943.

The first airguns made by Henry. M. Quackenbush were air pistols. (See Bedford & Walker, Johnson & Bye, and Pope sections of this guide.) The authors and publisher wish to thank Mr. John Groenewold for his valuable assistance with the following information in this edition of *Blue Book of Airguns*.

The H.M. Quackenbush factory began air rifle production in 1876. The airguns sold from 1929 to 1943 were assembled from parts on hand. During that time no parts manufacturing occurred, only airgun assembly. Some airguns made after 1903 had two-part serial numbers, separated by a hyphen. The number to the left of the hyphen is the model number. These guns were available in several different types of boxes. The Model 1 came with a combination wrench and a cast iron dart removal tool. The other airguns came with a steel dart removal tool. Airguns with these accessories will command significantly more than the listed prices.

H.M. Quackenbush also produced airgun ammunition, rimfire rifles, and targets. For precise identification of all models and more information on the guns and accessories manufactured by H.M. Quackenbush, see the book *Quackenbush Guns*, by John Groenewold. Price adjustments for "original bluing" below mean factory bluing or browning applied instead of nickel plating before the gun left the factory. Reblued or replated guns are substantially lower in value.

For more information and current pricing on used Quackenbush firearms, please refer to the *Blue Book of Gun Values* by S.P. Fjestad (also available online).

Square loading port detail

Spoon shape loading port detail

Round loading port detail

Model 9/10 muzzle cap detail
courtesy Beeman Collection

PISTOLS

Made from 1871 to about the late 1890s. Identifying QB air pistols is a special problem. They are covered here in hope of unearthing additional specimens. Henry Quackenbush, Iver Johnson, Martin Bye, Albert Pope, Augustus Bedford, and George Walker were close associates; there seems to have been a great deal of sharing of designs, production (with QB doing most of it), and even sales. Evidently huge numbers of QB design guns, and related designs, were produced without the maker's name on the gun and/or were made under private labels. There must be many old specimens of QB pistols that we presently cannot identify as having been made by QB. Overuse of punctuation by Henry QB may be a clue to his production of guns stamped with other makers' names. Pistols which may have been made by QB, but which were made to patents issued to others, such as Pope, Johnson & Bye, Bedford, Bedford & Walker, Cross, and others are listed under the company name which held the patent for that design, even if QB may have retailed such models or listed them in QB ads. QB records reveal that QB sold 74 "Eureka" brand pistols and 69 "Champion" air pistols in 1871.

SIX TYPES OF QB AIR PISTOLS The types are lettered to avoid confusion with QB air rifle models and because each type may contain several models and variations of the same basic design. Some of these types and sub-models apparently were made only as prototypes. Henry QB's grandson, Bronson QB, who worked in the QB firm from before 1928 to 1986 and was President from 1968, had a collection of the full range of air pistols using Henry's various QB patented and unpatented ideas. Bronson, and Henry QB's scrapbooks, are the source of many of the details of this QB chapter. When Bronson died in 1996, he left a collection of prototype air pistols, all marked H.M. Quackenbush. For additional information, patent details and illustrations see Groenewold (2000). The patent numbers given below are only those granted to Henry Quackenbush. Values will be established as specimens are located and sold.

○ *Type A – Target Air Pistol* .22 cal., darts, SS, SP. Cast iron body and grip, saw handle grip w/ embossed coarse checkering, frame hexagonal for rear half, forward frame cylindrical, cocking knob around muzzle, cocked by pulling muzzle knob forward, loaded by pushing barrel back for loading at rear of gun, side-swinging gate to close rear end of barrel after loading, rear-firing piston, blade trigger w/o guard, trigger sear mid-gun, projectile storage compartment w/ sliding door at bottom of grip, 5 in. barrel concentric around piston, 12 oz. Patent 115,638 granted June 6, 1871. Combined features from patent number 122,193, granted Dec. 26, 1871. Sometimes compared to the "Gat" air pistols, but Gats have a forward firing piston, their trigger sear is at the very rear, and lack many of the Target Air Pistol features.

This was H.M. QB's first gun. It was featured in his two page circular of 1872 which Bronson QB said was "laboriously composed after a great deal of mental effort while sitting under an apple tree adjacent to his first factory". Specimens beyond the prototypes have not been identified, but must exist as unmarked pistols. The above distinctive features should enable collectors to locate strong suspects.

○ *Type B – Improved Target Pistol* basically the same as the Target Pistol, but with an improved device to receive the dart when the gun is loaded from behind, combined with a groove, to align the barrel and close its rear end when the barrel is moved forward as to be flush with the back of the gun, ready for firing. QB's flyer for 1872 may illustrate this patent's design, leading us to wonder if the basic Target Pistol was ever produced in quantity for sale. Patent 122,193 issued Dec. 26, 1871.

○ *Type C- Transitional Pistol* Barrel is above compression tube and no longer concentric with piston - as in Type D- Rifle Air Pistols. Basically still based on Patent 115,638 with a flip-to-the-right side-swinging loading gate as shown in that patent. Major change was a cocking knob that pulled out to cock the gun's mainspring. The knob and its plunger stayed out until firing caused it to travel into the gun as the piston rushed to the rear compressing air to force the projectile out of the barrel. This is so similar to the 1876 Cross patent (see the "C" section of this guide) that the two designs may be related.

○ *Type D – Rifle Air Pistol* .22 in. cal, s/b, SS, SP, cast iron frame nickel-plated or Japan black, 12.75 in. OAL, 1.5 pounds. Barrel above compression tube. Cocked by pulling barrel forward. Loaded w/ dart when barrel is moved forward for cocking. Saw handle grip w/ embossed checkering. Blued, browned, or nickel finish. Marked H.M. Quackenbush on LHS upper panel of frame. Based on patent 156,890 issued Nov. 17, 1874, earlier patents, and others into 1876. Quackenbush's most successful air pistol.

GRADING	100%	95%	90%	80%	60%	40%	20%

◆Type D – Rifle Air Pistol Variant 1 PATCH BOX PISTOL -functions only as a pistol; stamped: MFGD. BY H.M. QUACKENBUSH. HERKIMER. N.Y. PATD. JUNE.6.DEC.26.1871. No provision for shoulder stock wire, base of grip w/ sliding brass door which opens to store projectiles inside hollow grip, head of brass screw or dimple which secures door not visible from side. Approx. 2mm dia. hole in upper rear edge of grip. Non-adj. trigger, no safety.

courtesy Beeman Collection

	N/A	N/A	N/A	$4,000	$3,000	$2,500	$2,000

Add 25% for original box and literature. Subtract 10% if wire shoulder stock is missing.

◆Type D – Rifle Air Pistol Variant 2 rifle air pistol - early version. Marked: MFGD. BY H.M. QUACKENBUSH. HERKIMER. N.Y. PATD. JUNE.6.DEC.26.1871; grip w/ small screw holes in butt for attaching wire shoulder stock, (This version shown in QB flyers and stationary).

Add 30% for proper wire shoulder stock with flattened forward end with holes for screw attachment to gun.

◆Type D – Rifle Air Pistol Variant 3 rifle air pistol- Late version. Marked: MFGD. BY H.M. QUACKENBUSH. HERKIMER. N.Y. PATD. JUNE.6.DEC.26.1871. Iron screw runs up from butt to secure wire shoulder stock in 5/16 in. hole in rear edge of grip; screw head visible from side. Non-adj. trigger, no safety.

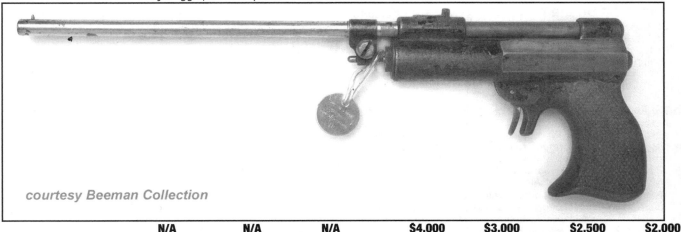

courtesy Beeman Collection

	N/A	N/A	N/A	$4,000	$3,000	$2,500	$2,000

Add 25% for original box and literature. Subtract 10% if wire shoulder stock is missing. Add 10% for proper wire shoulder stock (20% for early versions with flat on lower side of angled front end - to receive securement screw pressure).

This version gave rise to the Bedford Rifle Air Pistols, with saw-handle grip and the Pope air pistols which all have a "bird's head" cast iron grip. This "saw handle" version may have been the one sold by H.M. QB after he took back this design from Pope, due to non-payment, after Pat. No. 158,890 was reissued to him as re-issue patent no. 6973 on March 7, 1876. A saw handle version was also sold under the name Creedmoor by Peck & Synder in New York. (Note that the "Eureka" name, a generic term at that time, has been applied to both the QB "Rifle Air Pistol" and to Bedford and Walker's push plunger air pistol - probably it should best be restricted to the Bedford and Walker design, just as QB apparently did.)

☺ *Type E- Push Barrel Pistol* .22 cal., SS, SP. Pushing in barrel cocks forward-firing piston. Barrel, concentric w/ piston, must be pulled forward before firing. Pat. no. 178,327 issued June 6, 1876. No specimens known, but this design was basic to the QB Rifle No. 1 which revolutionized the air rifle market.

☺ *Type F – Gat Style Pistol* .22 cal., SS, SP. Very simple, inexpensive design. At rest the mainspring is visible wrapped around fwd part of bbl. Pushing in barrel cocks piston. Barrel is attached to piston; both move forward at firing. Simple sear hook retains cocked piston at very rear of pistol. QB marked pistols of this design were made w/ frames of cast alloy or iron. Patent No. 188,028 (issued March 6, 1877) drawings show a birds-head shaped grip. While not very successful for QB, this design has been made by others in enormous numbers for well over a century.

GRADING	100%	95%	90%	80%	60%	40%	20%

RIFLES

MODEL EXCELSIOR - .21 cal., spring powered, SS, smooth bore, nickel-plated, walnut stock, action is very similar to the Johnson and Bye Champion pistol (see the Johnson and Bye section of this book), very low powered, sequential serial number is usually found on the bottom rear of the compression tube, some not serial numbered, 35 in. OAL, 3.5 lbs. Approx. less than 1,000 mfg. circa 1887-1891.

	N/A	N/A	$4,000	$3,500	$3,000	$2,500	$2,000

Many parts are interchangeable with the Champion and other Quackenbush air guns.

MODEL 0 (LIGHTNING) - .21 cal., smooth bore rubber band powered SS, nickel-plated, walnut stock, 32 in. OAL, weight 4 pounds. The only rubber band powered air rifle made by H.M. Quackenbush. Only made in 1884.

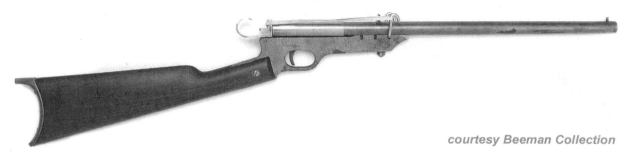

courtesy Beeman Collection

	N/A	N/A	$4,000	$3,500	$3,000	$2,500	$2,000

Add 50% for original box and literature.

MODEL 1 - .21 cal., push-barrel, SP, SS, smooth bore, nickel finish, walnut stock. Designed to shoot round shot, felted slugs, burred slugs, or darts. Loads through rectangular loading port in front part of receiver. Easily identified by the two-part receiver and simple, single loop trigger guard. Eleven variations of the Model 1 are distinguished by various features. The serial number can be used to approximate these variations. Later versions not listed below can be valued by listed prices unless special circumstances exist. Mfg. 1876-1938.

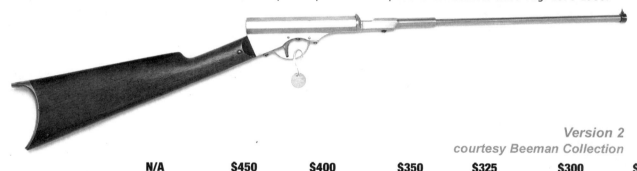

Version 2
courtesy Beeman Collection

	N/A	$450	$400	$350	$325	$300	$250

Add 10% for original bluing. Add 50% for original wood box and literature. Add 25% for original cardboard box and literature. Add 100% for Version 1, no serial number, round receiver, and no name. Add 60% for Version 2, serial number 1 to 300 or w/o number, octagon receiver. Add 40% for Version 3, serial number 301 to 1000. Add 20% for Version 4, serial number 1001 to 7500. Add 10 % for Version 5, serial number 7501 to 12484.

Versions 6 to 11, serial number 12485 to 36850 – use prices listed above.

MODEL 2 - .21 cal., push-barrel, SP, SS, smooth bore, nickel finish, walnut stock. Distinguished from Model 1 by much heavier, one-piece receiver. Versions 1 and 2 with rectangular loading port ahead of rear sight; other versions with spoon shaped loading port behind rear sight. Version 1 with single loop, simple trigger guard; later versions with forward end of trigger guard much extended and with another loop. Designed to shoot round shot, felted slugs, burred slugs, or darts. Five versions distinguished by various features. The serial number can be used to approximate these variations. Mfg. 1879-1918.

Version 2
courtesy Beeman Collection

	N/A	$650	$575	$500	$365	N/A	N/A

Add 10% for original bluing. Add 35% for original cardboard box and literature. Add 35% for Version 1, serial number 1 to 5500. Add 30% for Version 2, serial number 5501 to 20000. Add 25% for Version 3, Model 83, serial number 1 to 8000 (number sequence started over). Add 10% for Version 4, serial number 1 to 8000 (number sequence started over).

Version 5 serial number 8001 to 16823.

GRADING	100%	95%	90%	80%	60%	40%	20%

MODEL 3 - .21 cal., round ball, push-barrel, SP, SS, smooth bore, nickel finish, walnut stock. Round loading port/hole in top of receiver behind rear sight. Five versions are distinguishable by various features. The serial number can be used to approximate these variations. Values for Version 5 are listed. Mfg. 1881-1919.

	N/A	$750	$625	$500	$450	N/A	N/A

Add 10% for original bluing. Add 50% for original box and literature. Add 35% for Version 1, serial number 1 to 1300. Add 30% for Version 2, serial number 1300 to 2600. Add 25% for Version 3, serial number 2600 to 8000. Add 10% for Version 4, serial number 8000 to 88700.

MODEL 4 - .21 cal., round ball, push-barrel, SP, smooth bore, nickel finish, walnut stock, gravity-fed in-line magazine repeater. Three variations distinguished by various features. The serial number can be used to approximate these variations. Version 3 values are listed. Mfg. 1882-1910.

Version 2
courtesy Beeman Collection

	N/A	$900	$700	$625	$435	N/A	N/A

Add 10% for original bluing. Add 50% for original box and literature. Add 10% for Version 1, serial number 1 to 1000. Add 5% for Version 2, serial number 1001 to 1425.

MODEL 5 (COMBINATION GUN) - .22 cal., BBC, SP, smooth bore, blue or nickel finish, walnut stock. The smooth bore version did not have an extractor and operated only as an airgun. Designed to shoot round shot, felted slugs, burred slugs, or darts. Another version, rifled and with an extractor, could operate as an air rifle or fire .22 caliber rimfire ammunition. A removable firing pin was stored in a "patch box" on the right side of the buttstock. To function as a firearm, the firing pin was installed in place of the breech seal. (Replacement firing pins are available from John Groenewold.) Four variations are distinguished by various features. The serial number can be used to approximate these variations. Prices below are for the 22-inch barrel version. Mfg. 1884-1913.

Version 3
courtesy Beeman Collection

	N/A	$1,125	$950	$800	$550	N/A	N/A

Subtract 20% for rifled barrel. Subtract $50.00 for missing firing pin. Add 10% for 18-inch barrel. Add 20% for original bluing. Add 20% for optional hooded front sight and flip-up rear aperture sight. Add 35% for original cardboard box and literature. Add 50% for original wood box and literature. Add 15% for Version 1, serial number 1 to 100. Add 10% for Version 2, serial number 101 to 1350. Add 5% for Version 3, serial number 1351 to 2850.

MODEL 6 - BB/.175 cal., push-barrel, SP, smooth bore, blue finish, one-piece walnut buttstock/forearm, breech loading SS, sheet metal barrel housing, almost same general appearance as Number 7 except for round cocking stud in "2" slot under barrel instead of flat rectangular lug. Early versions with Z-shaped slot for cocking stud. Later versions with J shaped slot. No serial numbers. Mfg. 1907 to approximately 1911.

courtesy Beeman Collection

	N/A	N/A	$1,600	$1,300	$1,000	N/A	N/A

Add 50% for original box and literature.

GRADING	100%	95%	90%	80%	60%	40%	20%

MODEL 7 - BB/.175 cal., push-barrel, SP, breech loading SS, smooth bore, blue finish, one-piece walnut buttstock/forearm, sheet metal barrel housing, flat, rectangular cockinglug in slot running almost full length of underside of barrel shroud (housing). No serial numbers. Mfg. 1912-1936.

courtesy Beeman Collection

	N/A	$400	$325	$250	$200	N/A	N/A

Add 35% for original box and literature.

MODEL 8 - BB/.175 cal., push-barrel, SP, SS, muzzle loader, smooth bore, blue finish, walnut stock, similar to Models 6 and 7, except no cocking lug/stud or open slot on underside of barrel housing. Sheet metal barrel housing. No serial numbers. Mfg. 1918-1920.

	N/A	N/A	$2,200	$1,750	$1,400	N/A	N/A

Add 50% for original box and literature.
 Beware of recently assembled Model 8 from Model 7 parts be sold as originals.

MODEL 9 - BB/.175 caliber, push-barrel, spring piston, smooth bore, felted slugs and darts, nickel-plated finish, walnut stock. Similar to Model 2 (with spoon shaped loading port), except for .175 caliber and a sheet metal barrel shroud with knurled muzzle piece to support shot tube at muzzle. Two-part serial numbers, e.g., 9-16620. Sold from 1920-1941.

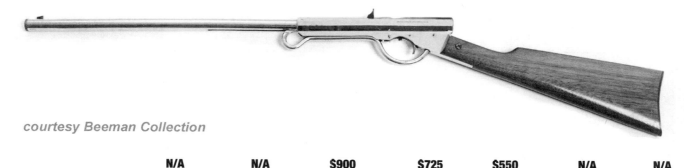

courtesy Beeman Collection

	N/A	N/A	$900	$725	$550	N/A	N/A

Add 10% for original factory blue finish. Add 35% for original box and literature.

MODEL 10 - BB/.175 cal., push-barrel, spring piston, smooth bore, nickel planted finish, walnut stock. Similar to Model 3 (with round loading port), except for .175 caliber and sheet metal barrel shroud with knurled muzzle piece to support shot tube at muzzle. Two-part serial numbers, e.g., 10-16000. Sold from 1919-1943.

	N/A	N/A	N/A	$1,825	$1,500	$1,100	N/A

Add 10% for original factory blue finish. Add 35% for original box and literature.

MODEL 83 - see Model 2, version 3.

NOTES

R SECTION

RWS PRECISION PRODUCTS

Current trademark currently imported and distributed by Umarex USA located in Fort Smith, AR beginning 2006. Previosly imported and distributed by Dynamit Nobel-RWS (Rheinisch Westfalische Spregstoff-Fabriken) Inc. located in Closter, NJ. RWS is a division of RUAG AmmoTec GmbH, located in Furth, Germany. Dealer sales only.

The RWS trademark appears on airguns manufactured by Dianawerk, Mayer and Grammelspacher, these models are listed in the "D" section of this book.

For more information and current pricing on both new and used RWS firearms, please refer to the *Blue Book of Gun Values by* S.P. Fjestad (also available online).

GRADING	100%	95%	90%	80%	60%	40%	20%

PISTOLS

MODEL 9B/9N - .177 cal., SL, SP, SS, 550 FPS, black or nickel finish, molded black grips, adj. rear sight. Mfg. 2002-2004.

	$115	$80	$65	$50	$35	N/A	N/A

Last MSR was $157.

MODEL C-225 - .177 cal., CO_2, semi-auto, SA or DA, 385 FPS., 4 or 6 in. barrel, eight-shot rotary clip, styled after a modern handgun, interchangeable 4 or 6 in. barrels, adj. rear sight, black or nickel finish. Disc. 2001.

	$175	$150	$125	$95	$65	N/A	N/A

Last MSR was $210.

Add $10 for nickel finish. Add $10 for 6 in. barrel, $25 for nickel model.

MODEL C-357 - .177 ca., CO_2 revolver, 380 FPS, eight-shot cylinder, 6 in. rifled barrel. Mfg. 1998-99.

	$150	$115	$90	$65	$45	N/A	N/A

Last MSR was $170.

MODEL CP-7 - .177 cal., match/sport SS, CO_2 refillable from tank or 12-gram capsule, 425 FPS, adj. rear sight, adj. trigger, adj. counter weight, 8.27 in. barrel, includes hard case and accessories, 2.23 lbs. Mfg. 1999-2001.

	$345	$295	$235	$165	$115	N/A	N/A

Last MSR was $450.

Subtract $50 for left-hand model.

MODEL CP95 - .177 and .22 cal. match grade SS, CO_2 refillable from tank or 12-gram capsule, 425 FPS, adj. rear sight, adj. trigger, adj. barrel weight, adj. pistol grip, 10.24 in. Lothar Walther barrel, 2.31 lbs. Disc. 2001.

	$405	$345	$275	$205	$145	N/A	N/A

Last MSR was $525.

This model includes UIT regulations for international match shooting.

MODEL CP96 - .177 cal. match grade five-shot, CO_2 refillable from tank or 12-gram capsule, 425 FPS, adj. rear sight, adj. trigger, adj. barrel weight, adj. pistol grip, 10.24 in. Lothar Walther barrel, 2.23 lbs. Mfg. 1999-2001.

	$490	$415	$335	$255	$175	N/A	N/A

Last MSR was $635.

Subtract $100 for left-hand model.
This model includes UIT regulations for international match shooting.

RIFLES

MODEL 92 - .177 cal., BBC, SP, SS, 700 FPS, black finish, beech stock, grooved receiver for scope, rifled barrel, adj. rear sight, automatic safety. Mfg. in Spain. Mfg. 2002-04.

	$95	$75	$55	$45	$35	N/A	N/A

Last MSR was $122.

MODEL 93 - .177 or .22 cal., BBC, 850 FPS (.177 cal.), beech stock, adj. trigger, grooved receiver for scope, rifled barrel, adj. rear sight, hooded front sight, manual safety. Mfg. in Spain. Mfg. 2001-04.

	$160	$135	$110	$85	$55	N/A	N/A

Last MSR was $172.

MODEL 94 - .177 or .22 cal., BBC, SP 1000 FPS (.177 cal.), beech stock, adj. trigger, grooved receiver for scope, rifled barrel, adj. rear sight, hooded front sight with interchangable inserts, automatic safety. Mfg. in Spain. Mfg. 2001-04.

	$195	$160	$125	$95	$65	N/A	N/A

Last MSR was $227.

GRADING	100%	95%	90%	80%	60%	40%	20%

MODEL 312 - .177 cal., BBC, SP, SS, 900 FPS, black finish, beech stock, hooded front and adj. rear sights, automatic safety. Mfg. 2002-04.

	100%	95%	90%	80%	60%	40%	20%
	$70	$55	$45	$35	$25	N/A	N/A

Last MSR was $87.

MODEL 320 - .177 cal., BBC, SP, SS, 1000 FPS, black finish, beech stock, hooded front and adj. rear sights, manual safety. New 2002.

MSR $152	$130	$105	$85	$55	$45	N/A	N/A

MODEL 512 - .177 cal., BBC, SP, SS, 490 FPS, 17.7 in. barrel, black finish, synthetic stock, hooded front and adj. rear sights, scope rail, automatic safety. 6.2 lbs. Mfg. 2002-04.

	$80	$60	$50	$40	$30	N/A	N/A

Last MSR was $97.

MODEL 514 - .177 cal., SLC, SP, SS, 490 FPS, five-shot mag., 17.8 in. barrel, black finish, adj. black synthetic pistol grip stock, hooded front and adj. rear sights, automatic safety. 6.4 lbs. Mfg. 2002-04.

	$90	$70	$60	$50	$40	N/A	N/A

Last MSR was $106.

MODEL 516 - .177 cal., BBC, SP, SS, 1000 FPS, 17.7 in. barrel, black finish, synthetic stock, hooded front and adj. rear sights, scope rail, automatic safety. 6.2 lbs. Mfg. 2002-04.

	$115	$90	$70	$60	$50	N/A	N/A

Last MSR was $147.

MODEL CA 100 - .177 cal., PCP, 22 in. barrel, diopter sight, match trigger, adj. laminated stock, 11 lbs. 6 oz. Disc. 1998.

	$1,000	$750	$600	$450	$300	N/A	N/A

Last MSR was $2,200.

MODEL CA 200 TARGET - .177 cal., PCP, 22 in. barrel, adj. rear sight, hooded front sight, match trigger, laminated stock with adj. cheekpiece, adj. recoil pad, available in right- or left-hand variation, 11 lbs. 6 oz.

	$350	$275	$200	$135	$95	N/A	N/A

Last MSR was $570.

This model was also listed as CR 200 in some catalogs.

CA-707 - .22, .25, or 9mm cal., PCP, LA, eight-shot repeater or side-loading single shot, 1200 FPS at high-power setting, three-position power setting, built-in pressure gauge to monitor remaining shots, 16 (carbine) or 23 in. barrel, Western-style straight heel stock, high-gloss blue finish, Indonesian walnut stock with checkered forearm and hand grip, 7.75 lbs. New 1999.

courtesy Howard Collection

MSR $730	$560	$475	$380	$290	$195	N/A	N/A

CA-710T - .22, or .25 cal., PCP, LA, eight-shot repeater or side-loading single shot, similar to Model CA-707, except has interchangeable cylinder, 16 (carbine) or 19 in. barrel, Western-style straight heel stock, high-gloss blue finish, Indonesian walnut stock with checkered forearm and hand grip, 7 lbs. New 2000.

MSR $850	$630	$535	$440	$350	$225	N/A	N/A

CA-715 - .22 cal., CO_2 refillable from tank or 12-gram capsule, BA, SS, 1200 FPS, 20 in. barrel, open rear sight fully adj., hooded front sight with post, Indonesian walnut stock with rubber buttplate, raised cheekpiece, hand checkered hand grip, includes ten rechargeable cartridges, pellet seater, cartridge holder to refill cartridge with air, optional adaptor for scuba tank or pump. 6.5 lbs. Mfg. 1999-2000.

	$500	$425	$340	$270	$165	N/A	N/A

Last MSR was $685.

RA-800 BREAKBARREL (BY THEOBEN) - .177, .20, or .22 cal, 1110-1150 FPS, 12.25 in. barrel with integral extended muzzle brake, two-stage adj. trigger (from 1.75 to 3.25 lbs.), Deluxe African Hyedua stock with high cheekpiece and fine checkering on pistol grip and forearm. Mfg. 2000-2001.

	$1,000	$800	$600	$450	$300	N/A	N/A

Last MDSR was $1,400.

This gas-spring model was built in conjunction with Theoben, and featured a match grade Anschütz barrel.

RADCLIFFE

Previously manufactured by C.H. Radcliffe, located in Chicago, IL.

RIFLES

RADCLIFFE - appears to be a .25 cal. air rifle, but it is designed to shoot water back into the eyes of the shooter, 20.5 in. barrel, walnut buttstock with heavy steel buttplate, marked "Patd. June 17, 1902. No. 702478". For Masonic initiation rites; it predates the light (2.8 lbs.), little Daisy "back squirters," 38.5 in. OAL, 5.8 lbs. Value over $1,000.

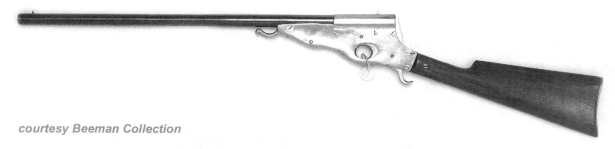

courtesy Beeman Collection

RANCO

For information on Ranco, see "Targ-Aire" in the "T" section.

courtesy Beeman Collection

RANDALL BROTHERS

Previous trademark manufactured by Myron Randall located in Waupaca, WI, circa 1924-29 under U.S. patent #1,509,257 (9/23/24).
Very high quality and design. Estimated production 20-25 guns. Extreme rarity prevents current price evaluation. Ref: AI, Oct. 2002.

RIFLES

RANDALL REPEATER AIR RIFLE - .22 cal., SP, LA moves sliding breech block, tapered steel barrel, tubular magazine under barrel for ten diabolo pellets, blue finish, walnut quarter stock with steel buttplate, walnut forearm, unmarked except for serial number stamped in several places, 38 in. OAL, 6 lbs. Current retail values are in the $1,000-$2,000+ range.

courtesy Hannusch Collection

RANDALL SINGLE SHOT AIR RIFLE - similar to repeater, except without magazine. Current retail values are in the $1,000-$2,000+ range.

courtesy Hannusch Collection

GRADING	100%	95%	90%	80%	60%	40%	20%

RANGER

Previous tradename of American Tool Works located in Chicago, IL.

For information on Ranger, see American Tool Works in the "A" section.

Also used as a tradename for Erma ELG-10 lever action air rifles sold under the Webley brand, circa 1980s.

RAPIDE

For information on Rapide airguns, see Relum Limited in this section.

RAPID

For information on Rapid, refer to Cycloid/Rapid in the "C" section.

REAMES, MIKE

Current custom airgun maker located in Lima, OH.

Mike Reams typically designs and builds CO_2 and PCP single shot and repeater ball reservoir pistols. Most examples come in a custom fitted wood case with accessories. Prices range from $600 to $2,500 depending on complexity of the design.

courtesy Mike Reames

RECORD

For information on Record, refer to FB Record in the "F" section.

RELUM LIMITED

Previous London distributor of several lines of Hungarian products including airguns, founded by George Muller in 1954.

Relum is a reverse version of the name Muller. Brands included Relum, Jelly, FEG Telly (sometimes misread as Jelly), Rapide, Taurus, and Super Tornado. Most are heavily built economy line air rifles with .177 MV in the 500FPS area. Relum Limited was still in business as of 1980. Resale values generally well under $100.

REMINGTON ARMS COMPANY, INC.

Current manufacturer established in 1816, with factory currently located in Ilion, NY. Originally founded by E. Remington, and previously located in Litchfield, Herkimer County, NY circa 1816-1828. Remington moved to Ilion, NY in 1828, where they continue to manufacture a variety of sporting arms. Corporate offices were moved to Madison, NC in 1996. Beginning 2003 Remington licensed Crosman to use the Remington Trademark.

For more information and current pricing on both new and used Remington firearms, please refer to the *Blue Book of Gun Values* by S.P. Fjestad (also available online).

RIFLES

MODEL 26 REPEATING AIR RIFLE - .177 cal. for lead shot (early) or steel, SS pump action, spring air rifle with unique geared system, 21 1/8 in. barrel, adj. rear sight, blue (early) or black painted finish, plain varnished walnut pistol grip buttstock, ten-groove forearm, 4 lbs. Approx. 19,646 total mfg. by Remington circa 1928-1930.

courtesy Beeman Collection

N/A	N/A	$995	$750	$650	$550	$450

1930 retail was approx. $7.50.

Add 15% for first model w/ blue finish.

GRADING	100%	95%	90%	80%	60%	40%	20%

AIRMASTER MODEL AM77 - BB.175 or .177 cal., pump pneumatic, 20.8 in. barrel, 725 FPS, adj. rear sight, brushed nickel barrel and black reciever finish, black synthetic pistol grip buttstock, imported, 39.75 in. OAL. New 2003.

courtesy Remington

MSR $145	$125	$95	$80	$60	N/A	N/A	N/A

GENESIS 1000 MODEL R1K77PG - .177 cal., BBC, SP, SS rifled steel barrel, two stage adj. trigger, 1000 FPS, adj. rear sight, 3-9X40 scope (Model R1K77PGX new 2005), blue finish, ergonomic soft synthetic pistol grip stock, vented recoil pad. New 2004.

MSR N/A	$195	$165	$140	$115	N/A	N/A	N/A

✪ *Genesis 1000 Model R1K77PGX* - .177 cal., BBC, SP, SS rifled steelbarrel, two stage adj. trigger, 1000 FPS, adj. rear sight, 3-9X40mm scope, blue finish, ergonomic soft synthetic pistol grip stock, vented recoil pad. Mfg. 2005-current.

courtesy Remington

MSR $402	$365	$285	$225	$165	N/A	N/A	N/A

MODEL RW1K77X SUMMIT - .177 cal., BBC, SP, SS rifled steelbarrel, 1000 FPS, two stage adj. trigger, 3-9X40mm Center point scope, blue finish, checkerd high-gloss finish Monte Carlo style withg pistol grip stock, vented recoil pad. New 2006.

courtesy Remington

MSR $330	$285	$235	$185	$125	N/A	N/A	N/A

Add 10% for 3-9x40 scope (Model R1K77PGX).

GRADING	100%	95%	90%	80%	60%	40%	20%

REN GUN COMPANY

Previous manufacturer located at PO Box 454, Richmond VA, ca. 1946 - 1950.

PISTOL

SERG'T REN BB gun, 16.5 OAL, SS, cardboard tubing with wood grip. Operates by sliding one end of the tubing over the other. Rare in good condition.

courtesy J. Groenewold

$125	$110	$95	$80	$50	$30	N/A

RIPLEY RIFLES

Current manufacturer of PCP rifles, located in Derbyshire, United Kingdom.

The authors and publisher wish to thank Tim Saunders for his valuable assistance with the following information in this edition of the *Blue Book of Airguns*.Owned and operated by Steve Wilkins, son of late Joe Wilkins who manufactured the Predator rifle and had a significant role in developing the modern PCP. High end regulated PCP rifles, mainly FT. Sporting rifles were available as XL series, .22 cal. SS or with nine-shot rotary magazine (XL9) or twenty-five-shot version (XL25) with spring-loaded linear magazine feeding the rotary magazine.

Most production is custom; all typical airgun calibers. Many actions fitted with very high end stocks from Paul Wilson and other custom stockmakers. Finishes include blue, nickel, colored, and camo. These air rifles typically will retail in the $1,500-$2,000 range.

courtesy Neil MacKinnon

RO

For information on RO airguns, see Gun Toys SRL in the "G" section.

ROBINSON, GEORGE CO.

Previous manufacturer of the O'Connell Gas Rifle located in Rochester, NY circa 1947-49.

During WWII, the Robinson Co. produced munitions for the U.S. Government. Shortly after the company turned to the production of toy tools, an engineer by the name of O´Connell approached George Robinson with a design for a single shot CO_2 rifle. At about the same time, Crosman Arms Corporation was promoting their CG (Compressed Gas) series rifles via indoor shooting leagues, one of which was in East Rochester, NY. It is probably no coincidence that the O´Connell rifle so closely resembles a Crosman CG rifle that collectors who have seen one of these very rare rifles often think that it a prototype or a version of the Crosman CG rifles. The complete lack of any markings on the O´Connell rifles helps promote this error. However, the internal design is considerably different and the quality is higher.

GRADING	100%	95%	90%	80%	60%	40%	20%

RIFLES

O´CONNELL GAS RIFLE - .22 cal., CO_2, SS, rifled barrel, with removable, vertically attached 4 oz. CO_2 tank (tanks are not interchangeable with Crosman CG guns), aperture rear sight only, safety gas by-pass lever on right side of receiver, breech loading by pulling a knob at the rear of the receiver, valve similar to a Schimel gas pistol, approx. 540 FPS, dark stained hardwood stock, machined steel parts, 41.5 in. OAL, 6 lbs. Approx. 100-200 mfg. 1947-49.

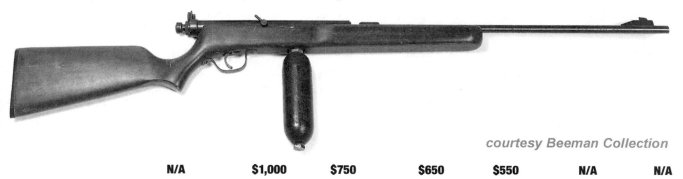

courtesy Beeman Collection

N/A	$1,000	$750	$650	$550	N/A	N/A

ROCHESTER

Previous tradename of air rifles previously manufactured by the Monroe Gasket and Manufacturing Company located in Rochester, NY circa 1948.

The Rochester Air Rifle is the only model, a swinging air pump pneumatic, BA, SS, two-piece wooden stock, with a black crackled paint finish. Probably the direct ancestor of the Kessler Two Piece Stock Model (see Kessler in the "K" section) with which it is identical except for the names stamped on the barrel. Research is ongoing with this trademark, and more information will be included both online and in future editions. Average original condition specimens are typically priced in the $100-$300 range. MSR was $10.

courtesy Beeman Collection

ROGER

For information on Roger airguns, see MMM - Mondial in the "M" section.

ROGUNZ

For information on Rogunz airguns, see Philippine Airguns in the "P" section.

courtesy Beeman Collection

RÖHM GmbH

Current manufacturer located in Sontheim an der Benz, Germany. Currently imported by Airguns of Arizona/Precision Airgun Distribution, located in Mesa, AZ.

For more information and current pricing on both new and used Röhm firearms, please refer to the *Blue Book of Gun Values* by S.P. Fjestad (also available online).

PISTOLS

TWINMASTER ACTION CO_2 MODEL - .177 cal., CO_2, eight-shot mag. repeater, 8.58 in. rifled Walther barrel, black frame with brushed barrel finish, molded grip, adj. trigger, adj. rear sight, trigger safety, 1.96 lbs.

MSR N/A	$462	$390	$315	$250	N/A	N/A	N/A

GRADING	100%	95%	90%	80%	60%	40%	20%

TWINMASTER ALLROUNDER MODEL - .177 cal., PCP, eight-shot mag. repeater, 8.58 in. rifled steel Walther barrel, black frame with brushed barrel finish, molded grip, adj. trigger, adj. rear sight, trigger safety, built-in gauge, 2 lbs.

	100%	95%	90%	80%	60%	40%	20%
MSR N/A	$646	$545	$485	$395	N/A	N/A	N/A

TWINMASTER COMBAT TRAINER CO$_2$ MODEL - .177 cal., CO$_2$, eight-shot mag. repeater, 8.58 in. rifled Walther barrel, black frame with brushed barrel finish, universal contoured grip, adj. trigger, adj. rear sight, trigger safety, 11 in. OAL, 2.4 lbs. New 2005.

	100%	95%	90%	80%	60%	40%	20%
MSR N/A	$572	$480	$425	$350	N/A	N/A	N/A

TWINMASTER MATCH MODEL - .177 cal., PCP, SS, 8.58 in. rifled steel Walther barrel, black frame and barrel finish, adj. walnut grip, adj. trigger, adj. rear sight with extra blades, trigger safety, built-in gauge, balance weights, tool kit, hard case, 2 lbs. New 2005.

	100%	95%	90%	80%	60%	40%	20%
MSR N/A	$1,063	$895	$845	$750	N/A	N/A	N/A

TWINMASTER MATCH TRAINER CO$_2$ MODEL - .177 cal., CO$_2$, eight-shot mag. repeater, 8.58 in. rifled Walther barrel, black frame with brushed barrel finish, adj. laminate grip, adj. trigger, adj. rear sight, trigger safety, 11 in. OAL, 2.4 lbs. New 2005.

	100%	95%	90%	80%	60%	40%	20%
MSR N/A	$651	$548	$495	$425	N/A	N/A	N/A

TWINMASTER SPORT MODEL - .177 cal., PCP, SS, 8.58 in. rifled steel Walther barrel, black frame and barrel finish, adj. molded grip, adj. trigger, adj. rear sight with extra blades, trigger safety, built-in gauge, balance weights, tool kit, hard case, 2 lbs.

courtesy Precision Airgun Distribution

	100%	95%	90%	80%	60%	40%	20%
MSR N/A	$952	$800	$745	$650	N/A	N/A	N/A

TWINMASTER TOP MODEL - .177 cal., PCP, eight-shot mag. repeater, 8.58 in. rifled steel Walther barrel, black frame with brushed barrel finish, adj. wood grip, adj. trigger, adj. rear sight, trigger safety, built-in gauge, 2 lbs.

courtesy Precision Airgun Distribution

	100%	95%	90%	80%	60%	40%	20%
MSR N/A	$762	$641	$575	$475	N/A	N/A	N/A

RUBI

For information on Rubi airguns, see Venturini in the "V" section.

RUTTEN AIRGUNS SA

Current manufacturer located in Herstal-Liege, Belgium. Previously imported on a limited basis by Pyramyd Air, located in Pepper Pike, OH. Previously imported by Cherry's Fine Guns, located in Greensboro, NC, and by Compasseco, located in Bardstown, KY.

The Browning Airstar, built by Rutten, was the first air rifle with a battery-powered electronic cocking system. Less than 800 were manufactured. Please refer to the Browning section in this text for more information. Rutten also builds three other models sold through selected Rutten dealers.

For more information and current pricing on both new and used Rutten firearms, please refer to the *Blue Book of Gun Values* by S.P. Fjestad (also available online).

GRADING	100%	95%	90%	80%	60%	40%	20%

PISTOLS

J&L RUTTEN WINDSTAR HS550 TARGET PISTOL - .177 cal., BBC, SP, SS, 550 FPS, automatic safety, fully adj. rear sight, checkered beech grips, 2.35 lbs. Disc. 2002.

	100%	95%	90%	80%	60%	40%	20%
	$200	$190	$155	$115	$75	N/A	N/A

Last MSR was $235.

RIFLES

BROWNING AIRSTAR - please refer to the Browning section.

AIRSTAR - .177 cal., electronic cocking mechanism powered by rechargeable Ni-Cad battery (250 shots per charge), 780 FPS, flip-up loading port, warning light indicates when spring is compressed, electronic safety with warning light, 17.5 in. fixed barrel, hooded front sight with interchangeable sight inserts, adj. rear sight, frame grooved for scope mount, beechwood stock, 9.3 lbs.

MSR $490	$375	$325	$265	$215	$175	N/A	N/A

J&L RUTTEN WINDSTAR MACH 1 D.E. - .177 cal., UL, SP, SS, 870 FPS, safety integrated with cocking lever, 18 in. barrel, hooded front sight with interchangeable inserts, fully adj. rear sight, frame grooved for scope mount, beechwood stock, 9.7 lbs. Disc. 2002.

	100%	95%	90%	80%	60%	40%	20%
	$450	$405	$335	$275	$225	N/A	N/A

Last MSR was $525.

J&L RUTTEN WINDSTAR PRO 2000 D.E. TARGET - .177 cal., UL, SP, SS, 570 FPS, safety integrated with cocking lever, 18 in. barrel, hooded front sight with interchangeable inserts, fully adj. rear peep sight, frame grooved for scope mount, beechwood target stock with adj. buttplate, 10 lbs.

MSR $510	$465	$420	$345	$280	$230	N/A	N/A

NOTES

S SECTION

S G S (SPORTING GUNS SELECTION)

Previous trademark imported by Kendell International.

GRADING	100%	95%	90%	80%	60%	40%	20%
RIFLES							
DUO 300AP - .177 or .22 cal., TL, SP, 455/430 FPS.							
	$135	$115	$70	$50	$40	N/A	N/A
DUO 300AR - .177 or .22 cal., TL, SP, 455/430 FPS, with extra stock and barrel assembly to create a three-in-one gun.							
	$195	$135	$85	$65	$50	N/A	N/A

SAINT LOUIS

For information on Saint Louis airguns, see Benjamin in the "B" section.

SAULS, RON

Current custom airgun maker and dealer located in Anderson, SC. Ron Sauls occasionally imports airguns from RP (Republic of the Philippines). Ron Sauls, in his spare time makes a variety of unique and unusual design air rifles and pistols. Mr. Sauls also produces a wide variety of aftermarket accessories and spare parts for current and discontinued airguns. Contact Mr. Sauls (see Trademark Index) directly for pricing and availability.

PISTOLS

B & A REPEATING PISTOL - .22 cal., CO_2 bulk fill or powerlet, 24-shot repeater.

courtesy Ron Sauls

RIFLES

B & A REPEATERE RIFLE - .22 cal., CO_2 bulk fill, 24-shot gravity fead repeater.

courtesy Ron Sauls

BALL RESERVOIR RIFLE - .375 cone head darts cal., CO_2, Ball reservoir, tap loader, SS, 24 in. smoothbore BBL, 41.75 in. OAL, 5lbs.

courtesy Ron Sauls

GRADING	100%	95%	90%	80%	60%	40%	20%

BUTT RESERVOIR RIFLE - .38 cal. round ball or pellet, CO$_2$ or 2200 psi compressed air, butt reservoir, tap loader, SS, 31.87 in. half octagon/ half round rifled barrel, 46.75 in. OAL, 8.5 lbs.

courtesy Ron Sauls

SAVAGE ARMS

Current manufacturer and importer located in Westfield, MA.

A century-old manufacturer of rifles and shotguns (more than two hundred different models since 1895), Savage brought its expertise to air rifles in 1999 with five imported sporting models in .177 caliber.

For more information and current pricing on both new and used Savage Arms firearms, please refer to the *Blue Book of Gun Values* by S.P. Fjestad (also available online).

RIFLES

PLAY RIFLE - .38 cal., SP, pump action, sheet metal construction, spring-fed tubular magazine, fixed sights, marked "SAVAGE" in large letters on RHS of receiver, with SVG in circle, barrel stamped: "SAVAGE PLAY RIFLE MANUF. BY SAVAGE ARMS CORP, UTICA, N.Y. PAT. APPLIED FOR", black Japan finish, 34.1 in. OAL, 3.0 lbs.. Mfg. circa 1920-1930s, may be up to three variations.

courtesy Beeman Collection

	N/A	N/A	$225	$200	$185	$165	$145

MODEL 560F - .177 cal., BBC, SP, two-stage trigger with manual safety, adj. rear sight, grooved receiver, 18 in. rifled steel barrel, velocity 560 FPS, black polymer stock with metallic finish, 5.5 lbs. Mfg. 1999-2001.

	$73	$62	$50	$35	$25	N/A	N/A

Last MSR was $93.

MODEL 600F - .177 cal., similar to Model 600FXP, except without scope and rings, 6 lbs. Mfg. 1999-2001.

	$100	$85	$70	$45	$30	N/A	N/A

Last MSR was $128.

MODEL 600FXP - .177 cal., BBC, SP with twenty-five-shot mag., two-stage trigger with manual safety, adj. rear sight, hooded front sight, grooved receiver, includes 2.5x20 scope and rings, 18 in. rifled steel barrel, 600 FPS, black polymer stock with lacquer finish and rubber recoil pad, 6.5 lbs. Mfg. 1999-2001.

	$105	$90	$70	$50	$35	N/A	N/A

Last MSR was $135.

MODEL 1000G - .177 cal., similar to Model 1000GXP, except without scope and rings, 7.1 lbs. Mfg. 1999-2001.

	$145	$125	$100	$85	$65	N/A	N/A

Last MSR was $186.

MODEL 1000GXP - .177 cal., BBC, SP with anti-bear trap mechanism, two-stage adj. trigger with manual safety, adj. rear sight, hooded front sight, grooved receiver, includes 4x32 scope and rings, 18 in. barrel, 1000 FPS, walnut stained hardwood stock with vent. rubber recoil pad, 7.5 lbs. Mfg. 1999-2001.

	$169	$144	$119	$95	$70	N/A	N/A

Last MSR was $216.

GRADING	100%	95%	90%	80%	60%	40%	20%

SAXBY PALMER

Previous manufacturer located in Stratford-Upon-Avon, England. Previously imported/distributed by Marksman Products, located in Huntington Beach, CA.

Saxby Palmer developed a cartridge loading air rifle. This is not a CO_2 or other type of compressed gas gun. The cartridges are pressurized (2250 PSI) and reusable, facilitating speed of loading and much greater velocities. Rifles were supplied with the table pump (for reloading brass or plastic cartridges) and ten cartridges. These accessories are necessary in order to operate air rifles or pistols. See Brocock introduction in the "B" section for information on the British 2004 ban on production and sale of air cartridge airguns.

REVOLVERS

Subtract 50% if without accessories.

ORION AIR REVOLVER - .177 cal., six-shot, compressed air cartridges (reusable), 550 FPS, 6 in. barrel, 2.2 lbs. Disc. 1988.

courtesy Beeman Collection

	N/A	$450	$375	$300	$225	$150	$95

Add 20% for chrome finish.
This model was manufactured by Weihrauch of Germany and included a Slim Jim pump and twelve reusable cartridges. It also came with a 30 grain .38 cal. zinc pellet to allow cartridges to be used in a .38 Special pistol for practice.

MODEL 54 - .177 cal., five-shot, compressed air cartridges (reusable), 4 in. barrel, 1.35 lb. Disc. 1988.

courtesy Beeman Collection

$195	$145	$110	$85	$65	N/A	N/A

This model was manufactured by Weihrauch of Germany and included a Slim Jim pump and twelve reusable cartridges.

WESTERN 66 - .177 or .22 cal., compressed air cartridge, styled after Colt SAA (Peacemaker), blue finish, 11.6 in. OAL, 2.4 lbs.

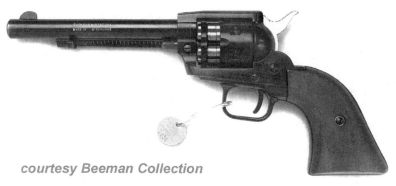

courtesy Beeman Collection

	N/A	$450	$395	$295	$225	$150	N/A

GRADING	100%	95%	90%	80%	60%	40%	20%

RIFLES

Subtract 50% if without accessories.

ENSIGN ELITE - .177 or .22 cal., compressed air cartridge, BA, 1000/800 FPS automatic safety.

	$225	$150	$120	$95	$75	N/A	N/A

Last MSR was $175.

ENSIGN ROYAL - .177 or .22 cal., compressed air cartridge, BA, 1000/800 FPS automatic safety, walnut stock.

	$195	$145	$110	$85	$65	N/A	N/A

Last MSR was $275.

GALAXY - .177 or .22 cal., compressed air cartridge, BA, 1000/800 FPS, automatic safety, walnut stained hardwood stock, 6.5 lbs.

	$175	$125	$90	$75	$65	N/A	N/A

SATURN - .177 or .22 cal., compressed air cartridge, BA, 1000/800 FPS, automatic safety, black polymer stock, 6.5 lbs. Disc. 1987.

	$225	$165	$115	$80	$65	N/A	N/A

Last MSR was $175.

SBS

For information on SBS, see Shark.

SCALEMEAD

For information on Scalemead airguns, see Gun Toys SRL in the "G" section.

SCHIMEL

Previous trademark manufactured by Schimel Arms Company located in California circa 1952-54, and A.C. Swanson located in Sun Valley, CA, circa 1956-58.

The Schimel was the first of a series of pistols made from the same general design by Orville Schimel. Due to undercapitalization and a number of design flaws in the Schimel, the small company went bankrupt. In 1955, the manufacturing fixtures were acquired by the American Weapons Corporation, headed by Hy Hunter. The unsatisfactory seals were replaced by a one-seal unit and an ingenious eight-shot magazine for .22 cal. lead balls was added. The improved design was marketed as the American Luger. Stoeger arms had U.S. ownership of the Luger trademark and quickly forced these "American Lugers" from the market, making them very rare pistols.

PISTOLS

Smith (1957) heralds these as the first American-made CO_2 production pistol and the first to use disposable CO_2 cylinders.

MODEL GP-22 - .22 cal., CO_2, SS, close copy of the German Luger, toggle action, 6 in. barrel, 380 FPS, die-cast body, blue finish, 9.3 in. OAL, 2.5 lbs. Ref.: Ronald Kurihara (1986) Airgun News & Report 1:3- June.

courtesy Beeman Collection

	$225	$195	$160	$125	$100	$60	$40

Add 15% for factory box. Subtract 5% for Model P-22 marking.
A pneumatic version, the Model AP-22 was presented in catalogs but no specimens are known.
Two U-shaped cup seals highly prone to failure.

GRADING	100%	95%	90%	80%	60%	40%	20%

AMERICAN LUGER - .22 cal., CO_2, similar to Model GP-22, except is an eight-shot repeater. Ref: AGNR - Jan. 1989.

courtesy Beeman Collection

	N/A	$900	$750	$600	$400	$300	$150

Add 15% for factory box. Subtract 15% for black grips. Add 25% for Swanson variable power version.
Information sheet included in box with "American Luger" guns may refer to Model V822 and Model HV822, however the guns are marked "American Luger" on the LHS and have the "AL" logo on each grip.

CARBO JET - Smith (1957) and others have reported a repeating CO_2 pistol, supposedly related to the American Luger. Smith illustrates a Schimel and an American Luger as the Carbo Jet. Despite almost a half century of looking, no verified specimens of the CarboJet are known.

SCOUT

For information on Scout airguns, see Milbro in the "M" section.

SEARS ROEBUCK AND CO.

Catalog merchandiser that, in addition to selling major trademark firearms, also private labeled many configurations of airguns and firearms (mostly longarms) under a variety of trademarks and logos (i.e., J.C. Higgins, Ted Williams, Ranger, etc.). Sears discontinued the sale of all firearms circa 1980, and the Ted Williams trademark was stopped circa 1978.

A general guideline for Sears Roebuck and related labels (most are marked "Sears, Roebuck and Co." on left side of barrel) is that values are generally lower than those of the major factory models from which they were derived. Remember, 99% of Sears Roebuck and related label airguns get priced by their shootability factor in today´s competitive marketplace, not collectibility. A crossover listing (see "Storebrand Cross-Over List") has been provided in the back of this text for linking up the various Sears Roebuck models to the original manufacturer with respective "crossover" model numbers.

SELECTOR

Previous trademark used by SGL Industries of Rockville, MD (formerly GL Industries in Westville, NJ) for Special Purpose CO_2 pistols. Circa 1969-1970.

PISTOL

SELECTOR .68 cal., CO_2, 6 shot semi-automatic, fires special purpose projectiles, mainly for law enforcement work. Projectiles include: Stinger, noise/confusion, CN tear gas, CS tear gas, and fluorescent dye.

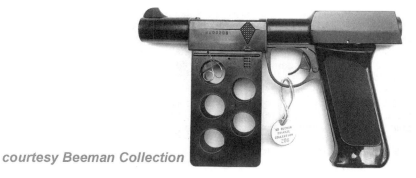

courtesy Beeman Collection

	$125	$100	$90	$80	N/A	N/A	N/A

Add 20% for SGL factory box. Add 30% for GL factory box.

GRADING	100%	95%	90%	80%	60%	40%	20%

SETRA

Previous trademark of unknown maker in Spain, less than 200 imported into England after WWII, a few of these went to New Zealand.

RIFLES

AS 1000 - .22 cal., pump pneumatic, SS, similar in design to American-made Sheridan air rifles, checkered pump handle and pistol grip, 37.3 in. OAL.

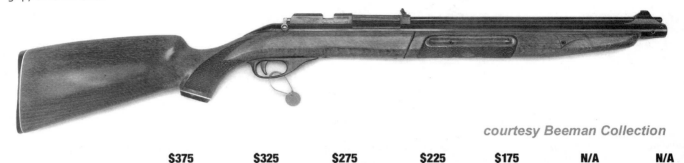

courtesy Beeman Collection

	100%	95%	90%	80%	60%	40%	20%
	$375	$325	$275	$225	$175	N/A	N/A

AS 2000 - .22 cal., bulk fill CO_2 or cartridge.

	100%	95%	90%	80%	60%	40%	20%
	$375	$325	$275	$225	$175	N/A	N/A

SETTER

Previous trademark for 28 gauge pneumatic shotgun made by Armibrescia, Italy ca. 1935-1947. Ref: Hannusch (2001).

There may be a pneumatic rifle version. Additional information is solicited from readers, please contact BBAinput@Beemans.net. Late 1930s.

SHARK MANUFACTURING CO.

Current manufacturer located in Buenos Aires, Argentina. Currently imported by Sunshine Airguns located in FL.

The authors and publisher wish to thank Mr. Eduardo Poloni for much of the following information in this edition of the *Blue Book of Airguns*.

Shark began in 1975, producing underwater spear guns, using elastic bands or a gas-spring mechanism. The great power and ease of power regulation in the underwater gas-spring guns led to the development of air rifles for use on land. Two years of research resulted in the Shark Model CD 455 (Caño Deslizable de 455mm or "455mm Sliding Barrel") in .22/5.5mm caliber. The barrel of this rifle slides through a bushing when an underlever is activated to move the piston back and compress the gas spring. As with the Theoben gas-spring airguns (sometimes inappropriately referred to as gas ram airguns), independently developed later in England, the mainspring consists of a trapped body of gas. The gas, in this case air, which does not exit with the shots, is supplied from a separate manual air pump. This system was granted Argentina patent number 213,908 (application 22 June 1978, granted 30 March 1979) and USA patent number 4,282,852 (granted 11 August 1981).

To take advantage of the great power, special Shark ogival projectiles of 1.6 grams were developed. With these projectiles, muzzle velocity could be adjusted to more than 300 MPS at various levels suitable for the smallest game at close range or larger game to more than 50 meters.

In 1979, a unique application of this gas-spring mechanism was used in the development of the Shark CQ air rifles which use a conventional barrel cocking system but have a very interesting, special multiple cocking capability. A single barrel-cocking stroke compresses the gas-spring to ordinary power potential; two strokes triples the power.

In 1985, Shark introduced an unusual CO_2 powered rifle/shotgun combination. These were charged from separate CO_2 storage bottles. It features instantly interchangeable .22 cal., (5.5mm) rifle and 13 mm shotgun barrels. In the shotgun mode it uses shot charges in plastic or metal cases and is claimed to be effective to 25 meters for hunting of birds and small mammals. In 2003 this model was produced with a horizontally attached buddy-style CO_2 bottle. Caliber .25 (6.35mm) and a rifled 13 mm barrel were also made available. This gun has been used, with arrow projectiles, to take water buffalo in Argentina!

In the early 1990s, Shark switched most of its production to a light, handy CO_2 carbine with a Mauser-type bolt in either .22 (5.5mm) or .25 (6.35mm) caliber. Sturdy, handy SP pistols of the same arrangement were also produced in much smaller numbers.

In 1997, Shark began production of a semiautomatic carbine powered by a horizontally attached buddy-style CO_2 bottle. A 17.5mm paintball version was produced for the newly arrived paintball games.

The Shark airguns have been virtually handmade in a small plant which has grown to only ten employees. Because of this extremely limited production and the fact that these guns normally are produced only for Argentina and Chile, they are rarely seen in most countries. Their rarity and unusually interesting, very well built mechanisms make them highly desirable to collectors. The early, independently developed, complex gas-spring mechanism is especially interesting. Shark guns with the gas spring system now are of special interest to collectors because the factory has decided that they are too expensive to make more of them.

Only a very few of the total production runs of Shark airguns have ever left Argentina. Local specimens may show extremely hard usage.

GRADING	100%	95%	90%	80%	60%	40%	20%

PISTOLS

MODEL SP 95 STANDARD - .177 or .22 (13mm new 2002) cal., CO_2, quick change barrel. Approx. 700 mfg. 1995 to date.

courtesy Beeman Collection

	N/A	N/A	$250	$175	$100	$50	N/A

MODEL SP 95 MAGNUM - .25 cal., CO_2. Approx. 185 mfg. 2002 to date.

courtesy Beeman Collection

	N/A	N/A	$250	$175	$100	$50	N/A

MODEL SP 95 REPEATER - .174/BB cal., spring-fed internal magazine.

courtesy Beeman Collection

	N/A	N/A	$300	$225	$1500	$75	N/A

RIFLES

MODEL CD 405 - .22 cal., GS, hand pump, 16 in. barrel. Approx. 519 mfg. 1980-85.

courtesy Beeman Collection

	N/A	$400	$35	$250	$175	N/A	N/A

GRADING	100%	95%	90%	80%	60%	40%	20%

MODEL CD 455 - .22 or 8mm (shot) cal., GS, hand pump, 17.9 in. barrel. Approx. 1252 mfg. 1979-85.

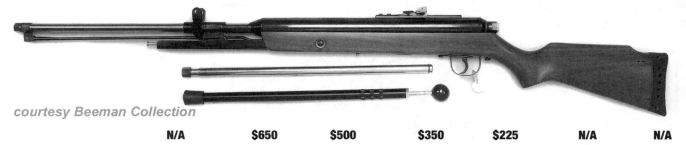

courtesy Beeman Collection

	N/A	$650	$500	$350	$225	N/A	N/A

MODEL CQ-1E - .22 cal., GS, single cocking action with hand pump, identified by rear of receiver being a large flat disc. with a large coin slot, removing the disc exposes the charging valve. Approx. 636 mfg. 1997-2001.

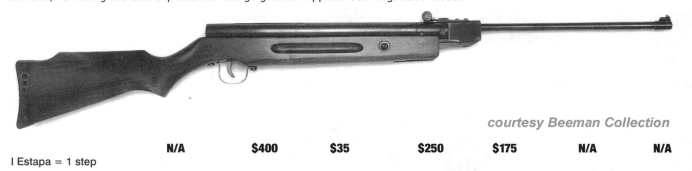

courtesy Beeman Collection

	N/A	$400	$35	$250	$175	N/A	N/A

I Estapa = 1 step

MODEL CQ-2E - .22 cal., GS, double cocking action (one cocking action provides standard power, two cocking actions provide maximum power) allowed by the captive charge of the gas spring system, rear end of receiver is conical with visible opening for air charging with hand pump. Approx. 850 mfg. 1982-86.

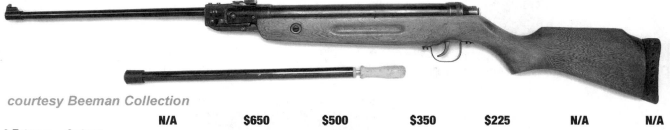

courtesy Beeman Collection

	N/A	$650	$500	$350	$225	N/A	N/A

2 Estapas = 2 steps

MODEL CARBINE CERROJO - .22 or .25 (new 2002) cal., CO_2, manual slide action. Approx. 8350 mfg. 1991 to date.

	$250	$200	$180	$170	$150	$125	$75

MODEL REPEATING CARBINE - .22 or 13 mm (dart) cal., CO_2, interchangeable barrels, Mauser-style bolt action. Approx. 4500 mfg. 1993 to date.

	$250	$200	$180	$170	$150	$125	$75

Also made in 17.5 mm paintball and tranquilizer versions.

MODEL SEMI-AUTOMATIC CARBINE - .22 lead round ball only cal., CO_2, thirty shots. Approx. 650 mfg. 1998-2003.

courtesy Beeman Collection

	$250	$200	$180	$170	$150	$125	$75

GRADING	100%	95%	90%	80%	60%	40%	20%

MODEL SEMI-AUTO QC - all basic airgun cals., similar to Semi-Auto Model except has quick change barrels, bolt slot RHS of stock., approx. thirty shots. New 2004.

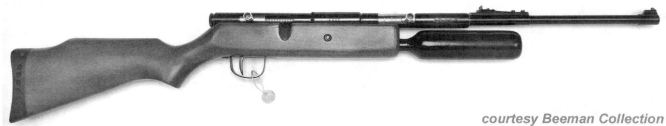

courtesy Beeman Collection

	$325	$275	$225	$175	$125	$75	N/A

MODEL BOLT ACTION - .25 cal., BA, CO_2, ambidextrous Monte Carlo stock with rubber recoil pad, sling swivels, scope grooves, no safety, 37.4 in. OAL, 4.8 lbs. New 2004.

	$250	$200	$175	$125	$85	$50	N/A

SHOTGUNS

MODEL SHOTGUN - .22, .25 (new 2003) pellet or 13 mm (shot) cal. CO_2, quick change rifled barrels. Approx. 3000 mfg. 1989-90. Reintroduced in 2003.

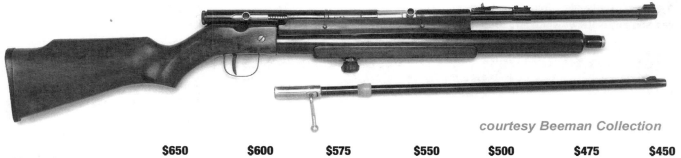

courtesy Beeman Collection

	$650	$600	$575	$550	$500	$475	$450

Add 25% for pre-1990 version.

SHARP

Current tradename of Sharp Rifle Manufacturing Company, Tokyo, Japan. Current manufacturer of air rifles and pistols. Previously imported by Beeman Precision Airguns, then of San Rafael, CA, and perhaps by others.

Founded by Kensuke Chiba, an airgun marksman and inventor, in 1952 as the Tokyo Rifle Laboratory. Name changed in 1955 to Tokyo Rifle Company and then to Sharp Rifle Manufacturing Company in 1960. Over twenty H models of gas and pneumatic guns have been developed by this firm; most of these were produced for Asian markets. This listing shows main Sharp models seen in USA. Other models, to be detailed later, include: Full Mark, Veteran, Victory, Champion, Champion Tiger, Export, Eagle, Pan-Target 700, Ace Hunter, U-SL, Mini- UD-I and II. Research is ongoing with this trademark, and more information will be included both online and in future editions. Ref: AAG - Jan. 1999.

PISTOLS

MODEL U-FP - .177 cal., 545 FPS, CO_2, SS, black finish, hardwood grips, 8 in. BBL, 12 in. OAL. Intro. 1969.

courtesy Beeman Collection

	$650	$600	$550	$425	$350	N/A	N/A

Add 10% for factory box.

GRADING	100%	95%	90%	80%	60%	40%	20%

RIFLES

ACE SPORTER - .177 or .22 cal., swinging forearm pump pneumatic, BA, SS, leaf rear sight, hardwood stock, rubber buttplate with white spacer, 23.9 in. BBL, 920/750 FPS, manual safety catch, 38.4 in. OAL, 6.3 lbs. Mfg. circa 1981-1987. Ref: AR1 (1997): pp. 36-38.

courtesy Beeman Collection

$350	$300	$250	$225	$175	N/A	N/A

Last MSR was $295.

ACE TARGET - .177 or .22 cal., SL, BA, SS, similar to Ace Sporter except, sidelever, more massive stock, adjustable buttplate, and match diopter sights. Mfg. circa 1981-1987. Ref: AR1 (1997): pp. 36-38.

N/A	$1,000	$825	$750	$575	$350	$225

Last MSR was $450

GR-75 .177, CO_2, pump action loading repeater, two 12 gm CO_2 cylinders, 19.6 in. rifled bbl., deep blue steel parts, wood stock, grip cap and buttplate w/ white line spacers, manual cross bolt safety, 39 in. OAL, 6.7 lbs.

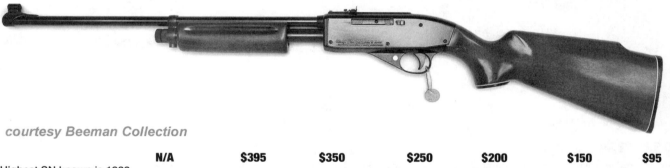

courtesy Beeman Collection

N/A	$395	$350	$250	$200	$150	$95

Highest SN known is 1933.

INNOVA - .177 or .22 cal, swinging forearm pump pneumatic, BA, SS, 20 in. BBL, 920/720 FPS, smooth wood stock and forearm, bolt catch serves as safety. 34.6 in. OAL, 4.3 lbs. Disc. 1988. Innova Special has side lever pump handle and one-piece stock. New 1985.

courtesy Beeman Collection

$250	$200	$165	$115	$80	N/A	N/A

Last MSR was $175.

GRADING	100%	95%	90%	80%	60%	40%	20%

TIGER 500 TARGET - similar to Ace, except has double set trigger, palm rest, special match sights and thumbhole match stock, adj. buttplate, match sling, and fitted case.

courtesy Beeman Collection

	N/A	$1,500	$1,150	$800	$500	$300	$200

USL - .177 cal., CO_2, BA, SS, sporter or thumb-hole wood stock, approx. 620 FPS, 32 in. OAL. Mfg. beginning 1969.

	$200	$175	$150	$100	$70	N/A	N/A

SHARPSHOOTER

For information on Sharpshooter airguns, see Bulls Eye in the "B" section.

SHERIDAN PRODUCTS, INC.

Current trademark marketed by Crosman Corp. located in East Bloomfield, NY.

In 1994 through 1995, after their purchase by Crosman Air Guns, some of the separate lines of the Benjamin and Sheridan airgun companies were merged into one.

The Sheridan Company of Racine, WI was started in 1945 by E.H. Wackerhagen, who teamed up with fellow airgun enthusiast Robert Kraus, who had engineering skills.He stated that their objective was to best the Benjamin Air Rifle Company by producing what they planned would be the best possible pneumatic air rifle.Mr. Kraus related to Robert Beeman that they felt that,becausethat Wackerhagen and Kraus would not be too catchy a name for an air rifle, they named the company after Sheridan Street, a road in Racine which they traversed almost daily as they went between their respective garages during the development of the new gun. Their first model, the Model A, was produced in March 1947. The first paid advertisements evidently appeared about 1948. The perfection of the Model A required a retail price of $56.50 in 1948. Sales were very poor. A less expensive model, the Model B, introduced in October 1948 at a retail price of $42.50, was even less successful. Good sales did not begin until after the introduction of the Model C, which sold for $23.95 in 1949.

See the introduction to the Benjamin section for information on manufacturing locations and the names under which these guns have been marketed in the 1990s.

All Sheridan air rifles and pistols are single shot, bolt action, breech-loading, and .20 (5 mm) caliber. Muzzle velocity figures are for Sheridan´s standard weight pellets of 14.3 grains.

For more information and current pricing on the Sheridan firearms, please refer to the *Blue Book of Gun Values* by S.P. Fjestad (also available online).

PISTOLS

Values listed below assume good working order with no missing parts. If finish has been removed, and the brass polished, the value is reduced to approximately one half of the 90% value.

MODEL E - .20 cal., 12 gm CO_2 cylinder, 5.85 in. barrel, 400 FPS, high polish nickel finish, walnut grips, special serial range of EOOxxxx. Limited mfg. 1990 only.

	$135	$110	$95	$85	$65	N/A	N/A

Add 25% for box and owner´s manual.

MODEL EB - .20 cal., 12 gm CO_2 cylinder, 5.85 in. barrel, 400 FPS, matte black finish, brown plastic grips. Mfg. 1977-1989.

courtesy Beeman Collection

	$85	$75	$65	$55	$50	N/A	N/A

Add 25% for Sheridan box and owner´s manual.

GRADING	100%	95%	90%	80%	60%	40%	20%

⚙ *Model ED Dart Pistol* - .50 (13mm) cal., CO₂, SS, similar to Model EB except is tranquilizer dart version, matte black finish.

courtesy Beeman Collection

	100%	95%	90%	80%	60%	40%	20%
	$200	$175	$150	$125	$100	N/A	N/A

MODEL HB - .20 cal., multiple stroke forearm pneumatic, matte black finish, walnut forearm, brown plastic grips, 8.75 in. barrel, 400 FPS, marked "Sheridan 1982-1990". Mfg. in Racine, WI until 1994, and in E. Bloomfield, NY from 1995 to 1998.

	$100	$90	$75	$65	$55	$50	$45

Add 15% for Sheridan box and owner´s manual. Add 5% for later box and owner´s manual.

This design has been marketed under the Sheridan name, the Benjamin/Sheridan name, and the Benjamin name. Also marketed as the Sheridan HB20, it cannot be distinguished from identical pistols under the Benjamin HB20 heading in the Benjamin section (please refer to names used in the 1990s in the introduction to the Benjamin section).

MODEL H20PB - .20 cal., multiple stroke forearm pneumatic, polished brass plated, 5.85 in. barrel, 400 FPS, commemorates the 50th Anniversary of Sheridan. Mfg. 1998 only.

	$160	$145	$120	$100	$75	N/A	N/A

Add 15% for box and owner´s manual.

This model was marketed only under the Sheridan name.

RIFLES

Values listed below assume good working order with no missing parts. If finish has been removed, and the brass polished, value is reduced by approx. 50%.

MODEL A SUPER GRADE - .20 cal. (first specimen of the Model A may be .22 cal.), multiple stroke forearm pneumatic, blue finish, walnut half stock with raised cheekpiece, aluminum receiver, peep sights, 20.15 in. barrel, 700 FPS. Approx. 2,130 mfg. 1947-1953. Ref: AR 1 (1997): pp. 41-42.

courtesy Beeman Collection

	N/A	$1,000	$800	$700	$500	$450	N/A

Add 60% for box and owner´s manual. Add 15% for first production version without serial numbers, Sheridan logo engraved, felt lining in forearm cocking handle.

Serial numbers on this model were not consecutive, up to about no. 4000 have been observed. Early production had a long handle and felt lined forend. Later production had short handle and no felt lining.

MODEL B SPORTER - .20 cal., multiple stroke forearm pneumatic, black painted finish, walnut half stock, soldered, "ventilated" barrel/pump tube construction, heavy aluminum receiver, peep sights, 20.15 in. barrel, 700 FPS, not serial numbered. Approx. 1,051 mfg. 1948-1951.

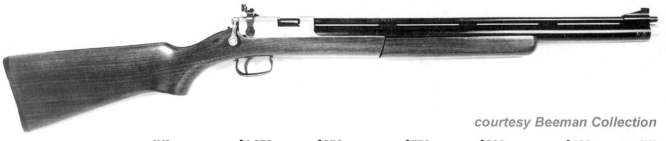

courtesy Beeman Collection

	N/A	$1,250	$950	$750	$600	$400	N/A

Add 60% for box and owner´s manual.

GRADING	100%	95%	90%	80%	60%	40%	20%

MODEL C SILVER STREAK/MODEL CB BLUE STREAK - .20 cal., multiple stroke forearm pneumatic, nickel or black finish, walnut full stock, open sights, 19.5 in. barrel, 675 FPS, rotating safety. Ref: AR (1997): pp. 22-24.

courtesy Beeman Collection

	$185	$160	$135	$85	$65	N/A	N/A

Add 10% for Silver Streak. Add $30 for Models CW and CBW with Williams peep sight. Add 15% for Sheridan box and owner´s manual. Add 20% highly polished original finish, plus 20% for box and owner´s manual. Add 25% for "hold-down" automatic safety models (mfg. 1952-1963 only), and 25% for box and owner´s manual. Subtract 25% for disabled automatic safeties; such guns should be repaired or put into non-firing condition. Add 200% for early Silver Streaks with knurled windage knobs (mfg. 1949-1952) and 30% for box and owner´s manual. Add 150% for earliest Silver Streak "slab stock" model (mfg. in 1949 only) and 35% for original box and owner´s manual. Add 300% for left-handed models, approx. 400 mfg.

This model was marked "Sheridan" from 1949 to 1990. Serial numbering began in 1972 with #000000. Also marketed later as the Sheridan C9 Silver Streak and the CB9 Blue Streak. (See introduction of Benjamin section for information on manufacturing locations and names used in 1990s.)

MODEL C9 SILVER STREAK - .20 cal., multi-pump pneumatic, BA, SS, 19.38 in. rifled brass barrel, 675 FPS, nickel finish, adj. rear sight, American hardwood stock and forearm, 6 lbs.

courtesy Howard Collection

MSR $311	$250	$175	$125	$95	$65	N/A	N/A

✿ *Model CB9 Blue Streak* - .20 cal., multi-pump pneumatic, BA, SS, 19.38 in. rifled brass barrel, 675 FPS, black finish, adj. rear sight, American hardwood stock and forearm, 6 lbs.

courtesy Sheridan Products Inc.

MSR $286	$235	$185	$135	$75	$50	N/A	N/A

MODEL C9PB - .20 cal., polished brass plating, multiple stroke forearm pneumatic, 675 FPS, medallion inset into stock (1998 only) to commemorate the 50th Anniversary of Sheridan. 1999-2000.

courtesy Howard Collection

	$150	$125	$110	$90	$70	N/A	N/A

Add 20% for medallion in stock. Add 20% for box and owner´s manual.
This model was marketed only under the Sheridan name.

GRADING	100%	95%	90%	80%	60%	40%	20%

MODEL F/FB - .20 cal., 12 gm CO_2 cylinder, nickel (Model F) or black (Model FB) finish, walnut half stock, open sights, 19.5 in. barrel, 515 FPS, rotating safety.

courtesy Howard Collection

	N/A	$175	$135	$95	$75	N/A	N/A

Add 50% for Model F. Add 25% for early production, highly polished original finish. Add 15% for Sheridan box and owner´s manual. Add 300% for left-handed models. Add 30% for Models FW and FBW with Williams 5D-SH peep sight.

This model was marked "Sheridan 1975-1990". It was later marketed as the Model F9 under the Benjamin/Sheridan name. (See information on 1990s marketing in the introduction to the Benjamin section.)

SHINBISHA AIR RIFLE CO.

Previous Japanese manufacturer.

Shinbisha manufactured break barrel cocking spring piston air rifles and a .22 caliber rimfire rifle. Rifles are marked S.A.R. with a crossed arrows logo.

SHIN SUNG INDUSTRIES CO. LTD.

Current manufacturer located at 201-6, Samjung-Dong, Ohjeong-Ku, Buchon-City, Kyungki-Do, Korea. Currently imported and distributed by Pyramyd Air located in Cleveland, OH. Previously imported by RWS Precision Products located in Closter, NJ, also distributed by ARS located in Pine City, NY.

Manufacturer of a wide variety of amazing, usually very large, pre-charged pneumatic airguns, often of great power, ranging from the trumpet look-alike confetti/ribbon-shooting, which advertises that "It is real action for your unforgettable moment" up to large bore rifles, such as Career 707, Ultra, Carbine, Tanker Carbine, and Fire 201 for which the maker claims: "It is a real action to chase the fascinated target" or "Become an explorer in the jungle, run for the freedom with your instinct." The guns are very well built and as interesting as the copy. The shiny brass Celebration trumpet model has a current value above $1,200 in excellent condition. Several simple versions without the trumpet's slide and mouthpieces are known. For more information on these airguns, also see ARS in the "A" section, and RWS in the "R" section.

courtesy Howard Collection

RIFLES

ADVENTURE DB - .22 cal., PCP, removable mag., PG stock, 41.3 in OAL, 8.2 lbs. Mfg. 1990s.

courtesy Beeman Collection

$550	$500	$450	$350	$275	N/A	N/A

GRADING	100%	95%	90%	80%	60%	40%	20%

VAN STAR 505 - .22 cal., BA, SS, Brocock-type air cartridges (about size of 20 ga. shell), barrel concentric with receiver. 46.2 in. OAL, 6.7 lbs.

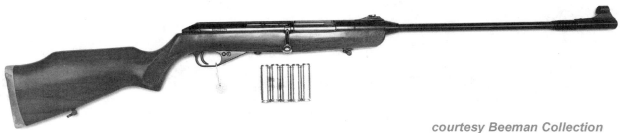

courtesy Beeman Collection

	$500	$400	$350	$275	$200	N/A	N/A

CAREER ULTRA - 9 mm, PCP, SS, under lever cocks gun and moves transverse loading bar, adj. power dial, pressure gauge, hand checkered high grade stock, cross bolt manual safety, 9.4 lbs.

courtesy Beeman Collection

	$500	$400	$350	$275	$200	N/A	N/A

SHOTGUNS

CELEBRATION - full-size, trumpet-look-alike PCP shotgun firing several kinds of projectiles including confetti/ribbon. Advertised that "It is real action for your unforgettable moment". High polish brass. Several simple versions w/o a trombone-style slide and mouthpiece are known.

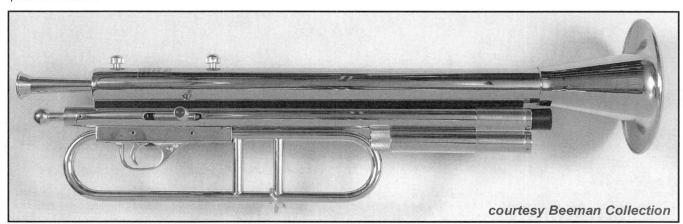

courtesy Beeman Collection

Rarity precludes accurate pricing.

SHOOTING STAR

For information on Shooting Star airguns, see Feltman Products in the "F" section.

SHUE

Previous trademark of Shue High Pressure Air Rifle Company located in Milwaukee, WI circa 1912-14. Ref: AR2:57-60.

RIFLES

SHUE HYPRESURE AIR RIFLE - .173 steel/ 4.4 lead balls cal., BBC, SP, SS, 423 FPS with steel BB, sheet metal, break action BB gun. 33.4 in. OAL, 2.6 lbs. Ref: AR 2 (1998): pp. 57-60.
   Rarity precludes accurate pricing.
   Only two specimens are known: one fine, one poor.

GRADING	100%	95%	90%	80%	60%	40%	20%

SIMCO

For information on Simco airguns, see Apache in the "A" section.

SKAN AR

Current manufacturer located at PO Box 3342, White Colne, Colchester CO6 2RA, England 1991 to present.

Current manufacturer of chronographs (chronoscopes) and bullpup PCP air rifles. Owned and operated by Mike Childs. Extruded aluminium frames with small air reservoir in, or forming, the buttstock. Stock parts usually plastic or rubber; walnut offered from 1995.

RIFLES

Skan rifles vary greatly. Older versions will be detailed in later issues of this guide. Models included: Mk 1 with flat 'pipe organ' magazines holding stacked pellets, cocked with side knob. Mk 2 with horizontal, cylindrical magazine with chambers holding about ninety pellets. From 1992 to 1998 cocked with sliding forearm. Forearm cocking discontinued due to concern that British government would ban such actions as slide action weapons. Normally set to UK 12 ft./lb. limit. Single stage trigger on all but most recent guns. Black or brushed anodized silver finishes.

R32 MILLENIUM - .177 or .22 cal., PCP, thirty-two-shot mag., Bullpup style, air cylinder in walnut stock, extended forearm with flush fitting bipod, grey anodised aluminium, nickel finished steel components, removable silencer, 33 in. OAL, 7.5 lbs. 10 mfg. 1999.

MSR $1,800	$1,550	$1,150	$895	$750	$600	N/A	N/A

Add 5% for case.

MINI M32 MK3 - .177 or.22 (cal., PCP, two vertical drums total thirty-two-shot mag., bullpup style, bottle forms part of buttstock, rubber fittings, two-stage adj. trigger, rear grip slides backwards and forwards to cycle action, built-in sound moderator, bipod, 25 in. OAL, 0.75 lbs.

MSR $1,125	$950	$775	$650	$495	$375	N/A	N/A

Add 15% for laser sight. Add 5% for case.

R32 ULTRA - .177 or .22 cal., PCP, thirty-two-shot mag., similar to Mini except with walnut fittings, leather cover on bottle, built-in laser, spare magazine slot under buttstock.

MSR $1350	$1,095	$895	$750	$625	$500	N/A	N/A

Add 5% for case.

SLAVIA

For information on Slavia, see CZ in the "C" section.

courtesy Beeman Collection

SMITH & WESSON

Current manufacturer located in Springfield, MA. Dealer sales. Currently imported and distributed by Umarex USA located in Fort Smith, AR beginning 2006.

In 1965, Smith & Wesson was purchased from the Wesson family by the conglomerate Bangor Punta. A major diversification program led to the in-house design of an airgun line. With the aid of a former Crosman engineer, four airgun models were developed: the Models 77A, 78G, 79G, and 80G ("A" for "air"; "G" for "gas"). The Model 77A was a .22-caliber pump pneumatic pellet rifle with a less-than-sleek wood stock and forearm-pump lever.

The Model 78G was a single-shot .22 caliber pellet pistol designed to resemble the popular Smith & Wesson Model 41 target automatic. The Model 79G is the .177 caliber version. Both had adjustable rear sights and power. Early versions had adjustable triggers; adjustable for sear engagement; later models had non-adjustable trigger mechanisms. A few problems included gas leakage through porous frame castings.

Smith & Wesson´s Air Gun Division introduced their fourth and final model in 1972, the Model 80G rifle. It was designed by Roger Curran, formerly with Remington. This autoloader fired .175 caliber BBs from a tubular magazine below the barrel. In 1973 the Air Gun Division moved from Tampa, Florida to Springfield, Massachusetts. Some early Model 80G rifles are marked with the Florida address, as are some Model 77A rifles.

In 1978, the Air Gun Division returned to Florida in a part of the former Westinghouse complex and the Model 77A was dropped. Due to changing from a sprayed paint finish to a baked powder-coat finish, Springfield production pistols have a duller, more uniform finish than earlier production. Also around this time, Curran began to develop a CO_2pellet revolver, although Smith & Wesson was not destined to complete development of this model.

Around 1980, Bangor Punta decided that Smith & Wesson should concentrate more on its core handgun business. The Air Gun Division was sold to Daisy. Daisy renamed the Smith & Wesson Models 78G and 79G as the Daisy Powerline Models 780 and 790. A nickel-plated model .177 caliber version was introduced as the Power Line Model 41– in honor of the original Smith & Wesson Model 41 firearm.

Smith & Wesson again entered the airgun field in 1999, when they introduced two models made for them by Umarex of Germany: the .177 caliber ten-shot CO_2 pellet revolvers, Models 586 and 686. These were close copies of the .357 Magnum Smith & Wesson revolvers bearing the same numbers.

For more information and current pricing on both new and used Smith & Wesson firearms, please refer to the *Blue Book of Gun Values* by S.P. Fjestad (also available online).

GRADING	100%	95%	90%	80%	60%	40%	20%

PISTOLS

MODEL 78G - .22 cal., CO_2, SS, styled after S&W Model 41 semiautomatic pistol, gun blue finish, brown plastic grips, 8.5 in. barrel, fully adj. sight, 42 oz. Mfg. 1971-80.

courtesy Beeman Collection

	$135	$115	$100	$85	$60	N/A	N/A

Last MSR was $53.45.

Add 50% for orig. box with can of S&W pellets and box of CO_2 cylinders. Add 30% for orig. box with plastic envelope of pellets and CO_2 cylinders. Add 25% for early pistols with adj. trigger. Add 10% for Model 78G guns stamped "80G".

MODEL 79G - .177 cal., CO_2, SS, styled after S&W Model 41 semiautomatic pistol;, gun blue finish, brown plastic grips, 8.5 in. barrel, fully adj. sight, 42 oz. Mfg.1971-80.

	$135	$115	$100	$85	$60	N/A	N/A

Last MSR was $53.45.

Add 50% for orig. box with can of S&W pellets and box of CO_2 cylinders. Add 30% for orig. box with plastic envelope of pellets and CO_2 cylinders. Add 25% for early pistols with adj. trigger.

M&P - .177 cal., CO_2, DA, 19-shot drop-out mag., 4.25 in. BBL, 480 FPS, integrated accessory rail, fixed front and rear fiber optic sights, manual safety, 7.5 in. OAL, 1.5 lbs. Mfg. 2008-current.

MSR $42	$40	$35	$30	$25	N/A	N/A	N/A

REVOLVERS

MODEL 586B4/586B6/586B8 - .177 cal., CO_2, SA and DA, ten-shot cylinder, 450 FPS, replica of Smith & Wesson Model 586 .357 Mag. revolver, high gloss black finish, black rubber grips, 4, 6, or 8 (disc. 2004), in. interchangeable barrels, 40-48 oz. New 1999.

MSR $241	$195	$165	$135	$85	$70	N/A	N/A

Add 10% for 6 in. barrel Model 586B6. Add 15% for 8 in. barrel Model 586B8.

MODEL 686N4/686N6/686N8 - .177 cal., CO_2, SA and DA, ten-shot cylinder magazine, 450 FPS, replica of Smith & Wesson Model 686 .357 Mag. revolver, 4 (disc. 2004), 6, or 8 (disc. 2004), in. interchangeable barrel, satin nickel finish, checkered black rubber grips, 40-48 oz. New 1999.

MSR $283	$265	$195	$145	$115	$70	N/A	N/A

Add $22 for 8 in. barrel Model 686N8.

RIFLES

MODEL 77A - .22 cal., swinging forearm, multi-stroke pump pneumatic, wood buttstock and forearm/pump handle, sliding wedge elev. adj. rear sight, trigger guard drops for loading breech, SS, black oxide blue finish, 22 in. rifled barrel, 6.5 lbs. Mfg. 1971-78.

courtesy Howard Collection

	$150	$130	$115	$100	$70	N/A	N/A

Last MSR was $46.50.

Add 10% for Springfield address.

GRADING	100%	95%	90%	80%	60%	40%	20%

MODEL 80G - .175/BB cal. CO_2, semi-automatic, brown plastic stock, sliding wedge elev. adj. rear sight, 22 in. barrel. Mfg. 1972-80.

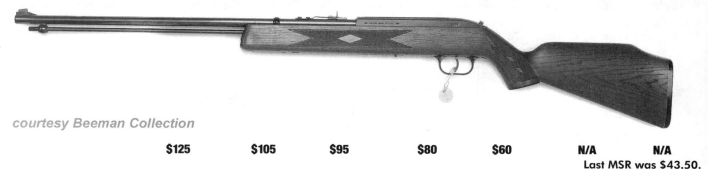

courtesy Beeman Collection

	$125	$105	$95	$80	$60	N/A	N/A

Last MSR was $43.50.

Add 10% for Springfield address.

SNIDER AIR PISTOL

For information on Snider airguns, see Hubertus in the "H" section.

SNYDER, RUSS

Current model and tool maker.

Manufacturedtwelve each museum quality firing replicas of the original St. Louis 1899 and 1900 air rifles circa 1997.

RIFLES

In 1997, collector Marv Freund persuaded Russ Snyder, a highly noted model maker and toolmaker, to make only twelve masterpiece replicas - museum quality, firing copies of his original St. Louis 1899 air rifle. On a whim, Snyder also made five double-barrel versions of the airgun – something that had never existed in the historical record. In 2002, Russ Snyder produced just a dozen copies of the St. Louis 1900 model air rifle for the purchasers of the 1899 model reproductions. Ref: AR 2 (1998): 76-78.

ST. LOUIS 1899 REPLICA - these replicas are virtually perfect copies of the original, right down to the St. Louis Air Rifle Company logo impressed into the wooden buttstock. Eleven were finished with the original Japan black enamel and nickel plating. One replica was given special decoration, including gold plating. Twelve mfg. circa 1997. Ref: ARZ: 1976-78.

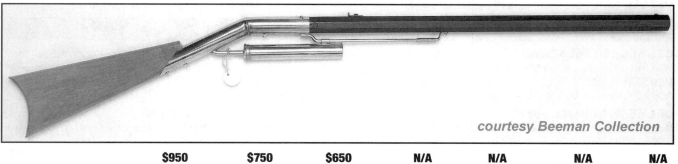

courtesy Beeman Collection

	$950	$750	$650	N/A	N/A	N/A	N/A

Original price was $750.

⊘ **St. Louis 1899 Replica Doouble (SxS)** - similar to St. Louis 1899 Replica except, double barrel (SxS). Five mfg. circa 1997. Rarity precludes accurate pricing.

ST. LOUIS 1900 REPLICA - copy of the original St. Louis Air Rifle Company logo stamped into the LHS of the slab wood stock. 33.8 in. OAL. Twelve mfg. circa 2002.

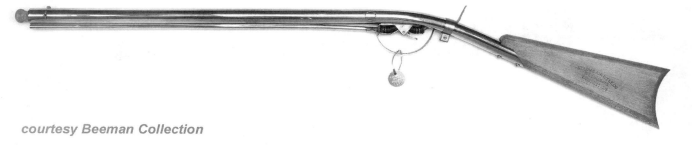

courtesy Beeman Collection

	$950	$750	$650	N/A	N/A	N/A	N/A

Original price was $850.

ST. LOUIS 1901 REPEATER REPLICA - ten mfg. 2007.
Original price was $1,900.

GRADING	100%	95%	90%	80%	60%	40%	20%

SPITFIRE

For information on Spitfire airguns, see Philippine Airguns in the "P" section.

SPLATMASTER

For information on Splatmaster tranquilizer guns, see Palmer Chemical & Equipment Co. in the "P" section.

SPORTSMATCH

Current manufacturer of scope mounts located in Leighton Buzzard, Bedfordshire, UK.

Sportsmatch started around the early 1980s by founder John Ford. Sportsmatch is now run by his son, Matthew Ford.

In its day, the GC2 was probably the most coveted rifle a shooter could own; it was akin to owning a Ferrari. Most were sold for use in UK field target competitions, but some were fitted with sporting stocks. The name was derived from 'Gerald Cardew', the famous airgun engineer who designed the GC2 air regulating mechanism. 'GC1' was a testbed for the regulator and not a production rifle. The GC2 was produced in three marks from 1986 to 1993. In all, around 350 guns were produced, some were sold as 'action only' and were married to custom-built stocks from the likes of John Welham. Weight varies accordingly, but these guns have alloy cylinders and are quite light for their size. The two-stage flat blade trigger is fully adjustable. The Lothar Walther barrel was fitted with a fluted muzzle brake to prevent barrel lift on firing. Most were .177 caliber, although any caliber was available. A bullpup version called the Scimitar was available, although only twelve were made.

The GC2 value is in the $1,750 range with basic walnut stock. Add up to 100% for finest quality custom walnut. The Scimitar value is in the $2,100 range.

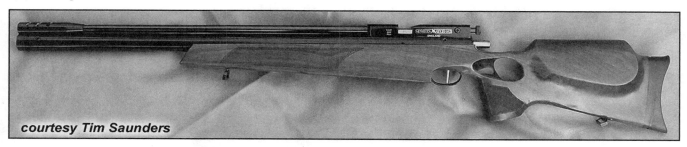

courtesy Tim Saunders

STANLEY AIR RIFLE COMPANY

Previous manufacturer located in Northville, MI circa 1889.

Merritt Stanley, a former employee of the Markham Air Rifle Company was granted at least three patents for BB guns, starting in 1890. He produced a BB gun under his own name circa 1889 in Northville, Michigan, then moved into the Dubuar Manufacturing Company of Northville which produced the Globe air rifles from the early 1890s. In 1908 Daisy consumed the Stanley and Dubuar BB gun production. Stanley may also have been involved in producing designs used by the Plymouth Air Rifle Company. See the Plymouth, Globe, and Decker sections of this guide.

STARFIRE

For information on Starfire airguns, see Feltman Products in the "F" section.

ST. LOUIS AIR RIFLE CO.

For information on St. Louis Air Rifle Co. air rifles, see Benjamin Air Rifle Co. in the "B" section.

STEINER

Previous trademark for pellet pistols made by a firm presently known only from markings on the guns as BBM located in Italy.

PISTOLS

STEINER-S - .177 cal., BBC, SP, 14 in. OAL, 7.25 in. rifled barrel, SS. Die-cast construction, but sturdily built. Brown plastic grips. Front sight very distinctively placed at forward end of receiver, perhaps in the mistaken notion that consistent sight alignment has any significance if the barrel has irregular positioning. No safety or anti-barrel snap mechanism. Black or bright nickel finish. Average original condition specimens on most common (Steiner) models are typically priced in the $35 range for black finish and $40 range for nickel finish.

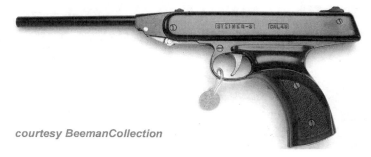

courtesy BeemanCollection

GRADING	100%	95%	90%	80%	60%	40%	20%

STELLA

Previous trademark of Kovo AS of Prague, Czechoslovakia.

This firm mainly made spring piston, barrel-cocking air rifles in the early 1950s. The line may have moved into the Slavia brand.

PISTOLS

MODEL 551 - .177cal., smoothbore, BBC, SP, SS, marked with "STELLA" (pierced by an arrow) and "Made in Czechoslovakia" on top of the barrel, 7.9 in OAL, 1.7 lbs. Mfg. circa 1950.

courtesy Kenth Friberg

Rarity precludes listing a value at this time.

GAT STYLE - .177 in cal., smoothbore, push-barrel cocking, folded metal construction, blued, SP, SS. Marked "STELLA" in round logo on grip and "Made in Czechoslovakia" on side of the barrel.

courtesy Beeman Collection

Estimated value about $65 in 90% condition.

STERLING

Previous trademark manufactured by Sterling in England.

Design and trademark purchased by the Benjamin Air Rifle Company, located in East Bloomfield, NY, in 1994. After Benjamin was purchased by Crosman Air Guns in 1994, the manufacture of the Sterling line was discontinued.

RIFLES

HR 81 - .177, .20, or .22 cal., UL, SP, 700/660 FPS, adj. V-type rear sight, 8.5 lbs.

$295	$250	$200	$155	$115	$80	N/A

Last MSR was $250.

Add $50 for original English markings. Add $10 for .22 cal. Add $20 for .20 cal.

HR 83 - .177, .20, or .22 cal., UL, SP, 700/660 FPS, adj. Williams (FP) peep sight, walnut stock, 8.5 lbs.

courtesy Howard Collection

$325	$275	$240	$195	$150	$95	N/A

Last MSR was $300.

Add $50 for original English markings. Add $5 for .22 cal. Add $20 for .20 cal.

GRADING	100%	95%	90%	80%	60%	40%	20%

STERLING/UPTON

Previous tradename of American Tool Works located in Chicago, IL. Previous manufacturer of BB guns under the Sterling and Upton names circa 1891-1928.

For information on Sterling and Upton, see American Tool Works in the "A" section.

STEYR SPORTWAFFEN GmbH

Current manufacturer located in Austria. Currently imported by Pilkington Competition Equipment, LLC, located in Monteagle, TN. Previously imported and distributed by Nygord Precision Products, located in Prescott, AZ. Dealer or consumer direct sales.

For more information and current pricing on both new and used Steyr firearms, please refer to the *Blue Book of Gun Values* by S.P. Fjestad (also available online).

PISTOLS

LP-1/LP-1P/LP-C - .177 cal., CO_2 or PCP, UIT pistol with compensator, 15.33 in. overall, 2 lbs. 2 oz. Disc. 2002.

	100%	95%	90%	80%	60%	40%	20%
	$850	$800	$750	$600	$450	N/A	N/A

Last MSR was $995.

Add 10% for colored tank variations (red, blue, green, or silver - marked "LP1-C"). Add 100% for limited edition models. Subtract 15% for CO_2. The Limited Edition consists of 250 units, engraved and signed Barbara Mandrell LP-1 USA Shooting Team, in red, white, and blue, and complete with lined walnut presentation case and certificate of authenticity.

LP-2 - .177 cal., CO_2 or PCP, SS, UIT pistol, 9 in. BBL with two-port compensator, 530 FPS, two-stage adj. trigger, adj. sights, adj. Morini grip, 15.3 in. OAL, 2 lbs. New 2003.

courtesy Steyr Collection

MSR $1,300	$1,250	$1,050	$895	$695	$595	N/A	N/A

Subtract 15% for CO_2.

✪ **LP-2 Junior** - .177 cal., CO_2 or PCP, SS, UIT pistol, similar to LP-2, except 13.2 in. OAL, 1.8 lbs. New 2004.

courtesy Steyr Collection

MSR $1,300	$1,250	$1,050	$895	$695	$595	N/A	N/A

Subtract 15% for CO_2.

LP-5/LP-5P/LP5C - .177 cal., CO_2, PCP (LP-5P), match pistol, five-shot semi-auto.

	$1,000	$900	$800	$650	$500	N/A	N/A

Last MSR was $1,150.

Subtract 15% for CO_2.

GRADING	100%	95%	90%	80%	60%	40%	20%

LP-10 - .177 cal., CO_2 or PCP, SS, UIT pistol with internal stabilizer, 15.25 in., adj. trigger, adj. sights, adj. Morini grip, four ten-gram barrel weights, 2 lbs. 2 oz. New 1999.

courtesy Steyr Collection

MSR $1,575	$1,550	$1,375	$1,150	$975	$795	N/A	N/A

Subtract 15% for CO_2.

LP-50 - .177 cal., PCP, CO_2 or PCP, five-shot semiautomatic, match pistol, similar to LP-5, except LP-10 style BBL shroud with three ports. New 2003.

courtesy Steyr Collection

MSR $1,675	$1,650	$1,450	$1,250	$1,050	$850	N/A	N/A

Subtract 15% for CO_2.

RIFLES

LG-1/LG-1P - .177 cal., SL/SSP (LG-1) or PCP (LG-1P), target model, micrometer sight and adj. stock. Disc. 1998.

	$900	$800	$700	$550	$475	N/A	N/A

Last MSR was $995.

MODEL LG-10/LG-10P - .177 cal., similar to LG-1, except has stabilizer and distinctive anodized red frame. Disc. 2000.

	$1,110	$935	$740	$585	$495	N/A	N/A

Last MSR was $1,139.

MODEL LG-20 - .177 cal., PCP, SS, radial adj. Alu butt plate and cheekpiece, laminated wood stock, Steyr stabilizing system, single stage trigger, dry fire action. New 2005.

MSR $1,785	$1,695	$1,595	$1,350	$1,150	N/A	N/A	N/A

MODEL LG-100 - .177 cal., PCP, aluminum two-piece stock, 17 in. barrel, 27 in. steel barrel shroud, 570 FPS, match sight set, 9.5 lbs. Mfg. 2001-06.

	$1,665	$1,500	$1,150	$975	$800	N/A	N/A

Last MSR was $1,850.

MODEL LG-110 - .177 cal., PCP, match rifle, dry fire cocking lever action, single stage trigger, SS, take down Alu-stock, infinitely adj. butt plate, pistol grip, cheek piece, front and rear sights, Steyr stabilizer system with barrel and stocks weights. New 2005.

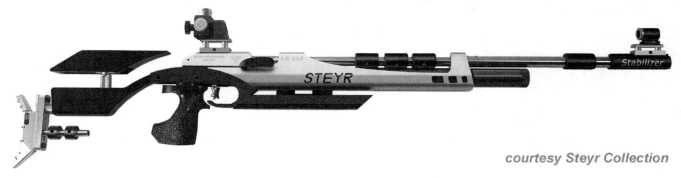

courtesy Steyr Collection

MSR $2,200	$2,150	$1,850	$1,650	N/A	N/A	N/A	N/A

GRADING	100%	95%	90%	80%	60%	40%	20%

MODEL LG-110 FIELD TARGET - .177 cal., PCP, SS, field target rifle, 17.5 in. barrel, dry fire cocking lever action, single stage trigger, take down Alu-stock, infinitely adj. butt plate, pistol grip, cheek piece, no sights, Steyr stabilizer system, comes with plastic case and without scope and weaver rail, 37 in. OAL, 10 lbs. New 2005.

courtesy Steyr Collection

MSR $1,950	$1,850	$1,650	$1,450	N/A	N/A	N/A	N/A

MODEL LG-110 HIGH POWER - .177 cal., PCP, SS, field target rifle, 17.5 in. barrel, dry fire cocking lever action, single stage trigger, Alu-stock w/ thumbhole polymer butt stock, no sights, Steyr stabilizer system, comes with plastic case and without scope and weaver rail, 34.7 in. OAL, 8.3 lbs. New 2005.

MSR $1,675	$1,550	$1,250	$995	N/A	N/A	N/A	N/A

MATCH 88 - .177 cal., CO_2, match rifle with precision receiver sight and adj. buttplate. Mfg. 1991-1995.

	$650	$500	$400	$300	$225	N/A	N/A

MATCH 91 - .177 cal., CO_2, match rifle with precision receiver sight and adj. buttplate. Mfg. 1991-1995.

	$750	$650	$500	$400	$300	N/A	N/A

Last MSR was $1,400.

Add $50 for left-hand variation. Add $100 for Running Target.

LGB1 BIATHLON - .177 cal., PCP, five-shot repeater, Fortner-type action, adj. match trigger, adj. snow sights, 40 in. OAL, 9.6 lbs. New 2004.

courtesy Steyr Collection

MSR $2,525	$2,350	$2,050	$1,850	N/A	N/A	N/A	N/A

Comes with one-shot and five-shot magazine.

STIGA

Previous tradename of Stig Hjelmqvist AB located in Trånas, Sweden.

Makers of firearms, sporting goods, and may be maker or distributor only of a Zenit-style top-lever air pistol. Research is ongoing with this trademark, and more information will be included both online and in future editions.

GRADING	100%	95%	90%	80%	60%	40%	20%

PISTOLS

ZENIT - 4.5mm cal., TL, SP, SS, 5 in. smooth bore barrel. First variant: wood grips with Stiga shield on left-hand side, the name "Zenit" is stamped on the left side of cocking lever, rear sight incorporoated in cocking lever, mfg. 1949-1961.Second variant: uses the Zenit action with a brown plastic grips Stiga name molded into bottom of grip on both sides, mfg. 1962-65.Third variant: Stiga action with blue-grey plastic grips with heavy-duty reinforced sheet metal cocking lever with wings for easier grip, rear sight is at the end of the action, 11 in. OAL, approx. 1.5 lbs. Mfg. 1965-69. Ref: AR 2 (1998): pp. 16-20.

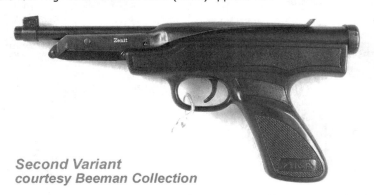

Second Variant
courtesy Beeman Collection

	$350	$300	$250	$175	$125	$75	N/A

Very similar to Zenit single shot, top lever air pistol patented by Franz Moller, Zella-Mehlis, Germany for Em-Ge (See the "E" section) in 1937 and discontinued in 1939 due to WWII. (Also copied by Milbro Bros. as the British Diana Model 4.)

CADET - 4.5mm cal., SP, SS,push-barrel, similar to Diana Model 2, loaded from rear of action, 7.9 in. OAL, .66 lbs.Mfg. 1949-1969.
Current values not yet determined

RIFLES

MODEL 99 (JUNIOR) - .177 cal., BBC, SP, SS, smooth bore steel barrel with beech stock. Mfg. 1948-1960.
Current values not yet determined.

MODEL 100 - 4.5mm cal., BBC, SP, SS, 17.4 in. smooth bore solid steel barrel, adj. rear and blade front sights, PG wood stock with Stiga shield on LH side, marked "STIGA TRANAS SWEDEN" on spring tube, 40 in. OAL. Mfg. 1948-1960.
Current values not yet determined.

ORIGINAL - 6 1/3mm cal., BBC, SP, SS, 20.5 in. smooth bore octagon steel barrel, blue or chrome finish, adj. rear and blade front sights, english style straight grip beech stock with Stiga shield on LH side, marked "STIGA TRANAS SWEDEN" on spring tube, 40 in. OAL. Mfg. 1952-1960.
Current values not yet determined.

STURM, RUGER & CO., INC.

Current manufacturer with production facilities located Newport, NH and Prescott, AZ. Previously manufactured in Southport, CT 1949-1991 (corporate and administrative offices remain at this location). A second factory was opened in Newport, NH in 1963, and still produces single action revolvers, rifles and shotguns. Beginning early in 2008 Ruger partnered with Umarex to manufacture and market airguns under the Sturm, Ruger & Co. Inc. trademark.

On July 6, 2002, the legendary William B. Ruger, Sr. passed away in his home in Prescott, AZ. He is remembered for his visionary efforts in firearms manufacturing and marketing, exceptional design skills, and his philanthropic donations in support of the firearms industry. For more information and current pricing on both new and used Sturm, Ruger, And Co., Inc. firearms, please refer to the *Blue Book of Gun Values* by S.P. Fjestad (now online also). Please refer to the *Blue Book of Modern Black Powder Arms* by John Allen (also online) for more information and prices on Sturm Ruger black powder models.

RIFLES

AIR HAWK - .177 cal., BBC, SP, SS, 18.7 in. in. rifled steel BBL w/ muzzel break, blue finish, 490 or 1000 FPS, adj. rear and fixed front fiber optic sights and 4x32 scope, adj. trigger automatic safety, Monti Carlo wood stock w/ PG and rubber recoil pad, 44.8 in OAL, 8.16 lbs. Mfg. 2008-current.

courtesy Umarex USA

MSR $126		$115	$85	$65	$45	N/A	N/A	N/A

GRADING	100%	95%	90%	80%	60%	40%	20%

○ *Air Hawk Elite* - .177 cal., BBC, SP, SS, 18.7 in. in. rifled steel BBL w/ muzzel break, blue finish, 1000 FPS, 3-9x40mm scope, adj. trigger automatic safety, ambidextrous wood thumbhole stock w/ vented rubber recoil pad, 44.8 in OAL, 9 lbs. Mfg. 2008-current.

courtesy Umarex USA

	100%	95%	90%	80%	60%	40%	20%
MSR $205	$165	$135	$95	$65	N/A	N/A	N/A

SUSSEX ARMORY

For information on Sussex Armory airguns, see Gun Toys SRL in the "G" section.

SUPER TORNADO

For information on Super Tornado airguns, see Relum Limited in the "R" section.

SWISS ARMS MANUFACTURE (SAM)

Current manufacturer located in Davesco, Switzerland. No current US importation, previously imported and distributed by Nygord Precision Products, located in Prescott, AZ. Dealer or consumer direct sales.

Please contact the factory directly for more information and current pricing (see Trademark Index).

PISTOLS

MODEL M5 JUNIOR - .177 cal., PCP, similar to Model M10, except shorter and lighter.

	100%	95%	90%	80%	60%	40%	20%
	$600	$500	$400	$300	$200	N/A	N/A

MODEL M10 - .177 cal., PCP, 492 FPS, 9.50 in. barrel with compensator, adj. trigger, sights and pistol grip, special dry firing mechanism, walnut grips. Mfg. 1998-2000.

	100%	95%	90%	80%	60%	40%	20%
	$700	$550	$475	$400	$300	N/A	N/A

MODEL SAM K-9 .177 cal., PCP, 492 FPS, 7.8 in. barrel with compensator, adj. trigger, adj. sights, ergonomic walnut grip, special dry firing mechanism.

	100%	95%	90%	80%	60%	40%	20%
MSR N/A	$1,066	$875	$750	$550	$400	N/A	N/A

MODEL SAM K-11 - .177 cal., PCP, 492 FPS, 9.45 in. barrel with compensator, adj. trigger, sights and pistol grip, two rod counter-balancing system, special dry firing mechanism, walnut grips, 2.34 lbs. New 2000.

	100%	95%	90%	80%	60%	40%	20%
	$900	$800	$700	$550	$400	N/A	N/A

MODEL SAM K-12 - .177 cal., PCP, 492 FPS, 9.45 in. barrel with compensator, adj. trigger, sights and pistol grip, one rod counter-balancing system, special dry firing mechanism, walnut grip, 2.34 lbs. New 2002.

	100%	95%	90%	80%	60%	40%	20%
	$850	$750	$650	$500	$350	N/A	N/A

MODEL SAM K-15 - .177 cal., PCP, 492 FPS, 9.45 in. barrel with compensator, adj. trigger, sights and pistol grip, one rod counter-balancing system, special dry firing mechanism, adj. ergonomic walnut grip, 2.34 lbs. New 2006.

	100%	95%	90%	80%	60%	40%	20%
MSR N/A	$1,231	$950	$800	$600	$450	N/A	N/A

SWIVEL MACHINE WORKS, INC.

Current manufacturer of AIRROW trademark CO_2 and PCP powered pellet and arrow firing rifles. For information on the AIRROW airguns, see AIRROW in the "A" section.

NOTES

T SECTION

TAHITI

For information on Tahiti airguns, see Dianawerk in the "D" section.

TAIYO JUKI

Current trademark of Miroku Firearms Manufacturing Company (Miroku Taiyo Zuki) located in Kochi, Japan. Airguns manufactured from circa 1970s.

For more information and current pricing on both new and used firearms, please refer to the *Blue Book of Gun Values* by S.P. Fjestad (also available online).

GRADING	100%	95%	90%	80%	60%	40%	20%

RIFLES

BOBCAT - .177 or .22 cal., CO_2, SS, similar to Crosman Model 160.

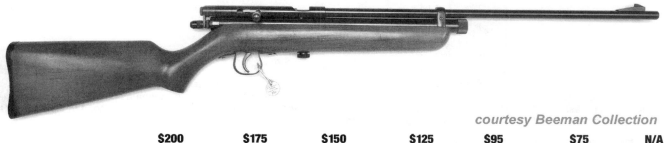

courtesy Beeman Collection

	100%	95%	90%	80%	60%	40%	20%
	$200	$175	$150	$125	$95	$75	N/A

JUNIOR - .177 cal., CO_2, similar to Bobcat.

courtesy Beeman Collection

	100%	95%	90%	80%	60%	40%	20%
	$200	$175	$150	$125	$95	$75	N/A

GRAND SLAM - .22cal., CO_2, BA, five-shot repeater.

	100%	95%	90%	80%	60%	40%	20%
	$300	$265	$225	$185	$150	N/A	N/A

GRAND SLAM II - .177 or .22cal., CO_2, BA, five-shot repeater.

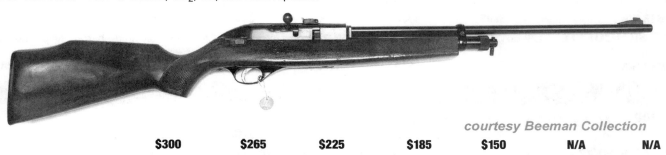

courtesy Beeman Collection

	100%	95%	90%	80%	60%	40%	20%
	$300	$265	$225	$185	$150	N/A	N/A

GRADING	100%	95%	90%	80%	60%	40%	20%

TARG-AIRE (AND RANCO)

Previously manufactured by Targ-aire Pistol Co., located at 120 S. La Salla St. Chicago, IL.

PISTOLS

TARG-AIRE PISTOL - .177, or .22 cal., BBC, SP, 4.25 in. rifled barrel, 10.5 in. overall, blue finish, Tenite or cast aluminum grips, backstrap cocking lever, "Targ-aire" molded in circle around grip screw, large protruding thumbrest top left side of grip, 2.8 lbs. Mfg. 1946-47.

courtesy Beeman Collection

	N/A	N/A	$450	$375	$275	$200	$125

Add 40% for factory box. Add 10% for cast aluminum grips. Add 25% for Ranco markings.
When Targ-aire production ceased, Randall Tool Co. continued production of identical guns for short time using existing Targ-aire marked grips and compression tubes. Thus, some Targ-aire marked guns are found in Ranco boxes. Ranco marking began in Nov. 1947. Ranco manufacture ceased in 1951. See Ranco in the "R" section for image.

TAU BRNO, spol. s r.o.

Current manufacturer located in Brno, Czech Republic. Currently imported and distributed by Pilkington Competition Equipment, LLC located in Monteagle, TN, Top Gun Air Guns Inc. located in Scottsdale, AZ. Currently distributed by Airguns of Arizona/Precision Airgun Distribution, located in Mesa, AZ. Dealer or consumer direct sales.

PISTOLS

TAU-7 - .177 cal., CO_2, SS, UIT target model, attaché case, extra seals, and counterweight, 2.3 lbs. Mfg. by Aeron. Disc. circa 1997.

	$260	$200	$155	$110	$85	N/A	N/A

TAU-7 STANDARD - .177 or .22 cal., CO_2, SS, UIT target model, 10.25 in. barrel, 426 FPS, adj. trigger and sights, attaché case, extra seals, and counterweight, 2.3 lbs. Disc. 2004.

	$265	$200	$155	$110	$85	N/A	N/A

Last MSR was $315.

TAU-7 SPORT - .177 or .22 cal., CO_2, SS, UIT target model, 10 in. barrel, 426 FPS, adj. trigger and sights, attaché case, extra seals, and counterweight, 2.3 lbs.

MSR N/A	$151	$375	$275	$230	$185	N/A	N/A

TAU-7 MATCH - .177 or .22 cal., SS, CO_2, similar to TAU-7 Sport, except has select grade barrel, compensator.

MSR N/A	$695	$435	$360	$265	$225	N/A	N/A

TAU-7 SILHOUETTE - .177 or .22 cal., SS, CO_2, similar to TAU-7 Match, except has 12.6 in. select grade barrel, scope mount, and compensator.

MSR N/A	$840	$650	$475	$395	$295	N/A	N/A

RIFLES

TAU-200 - .177 cal., CO_2, SS, UIT target model, synthetic adj. stock. Mfg. by Aeron. Disc. circa 1997.

	$210	$185	$150	$115	$85	N/A	N/A

TAU-200 JUNIOR - .177 cal., CO_2, SS, UIT target model, 400 FPS, adj. sights, adj. trigger adj. laminated stock, 40 in. OAL, 7 lbs.

MSR N/A	$660	$550	$395	$325	$285	N/A	N/A

TAU-200 ADULT - .177 cal., CO_2, SS, UIT target model, 512 FPS, adj. sights, adj. trigger adj. beech stock, 46 in. OAL, 7 lbs.

MSR N/A	$695	$575	$425	$350	$295	N/A	N/A

TAURUS

For information Taurus on airguns, see Relum Limited in the "R" section.

GRADING	100%	95%	90%	80%	60%	40%	20%

T. DIANA

Probably an illegal trademark previously used by manufacturer of unauthorized copy of the Dianawerk Model 5 air pistol.

The most interesting feature is the logo stamped in the top of the receiver – it shows Diana, the Goddess of Hunting, holding her bow and arrow. (Over the curved stamping: T. DIANA). The maker used this classical view of Diana instead of Dianawerk's humorous and protected trademark which shows Diana holding her air rifle aloft while discarding her bow and arrow. This switch in logos was done either out of ignorance or as a clever attempt to avoid trademark prosecution. Solidly made, blued, two-step barrel, wooden grip with coarse hand checkering. .177 cal., 13.3 in. OAL, BBC, SP, SS. Value of this novel Diana airgun collection item estimated to be about $175.

courtesy Beeman Collection

TELL

Previously manufactured by Venuswaffenwerk, located in Zella, Mehlis, Germany.

Venuswaffenwerk was formed by Oskar Will in 1844, and made both air rifles and pistols for nearly one hundred years. The Tell 1 was most likely designed by Will as a companion to his popular rifles. The design of Tell 2 & Tell 3 are very different and more elegant. They were not companions to any rifle and were designed after Wilhelm Foss took over the company about 1919. The company ceased operations in late 1950s.

PISTOLS

TELL 1 - .177 cal., BBC, SP, rifled 9.75 in. blue barrel, 300 FPS (.177 cal.), nickel plated body, rounded wood grips, 21 in. overall, nickel plated trigger guard with finger rest. Its ungainly size and style suggests that it was a pistol version of the original Will-style air rifle. At least two versions: one unmarked, the other marked "TELLOW" - for Tell and the initials of Oskar Will. 2.9 lbs. Mfg. 1912-1930s.

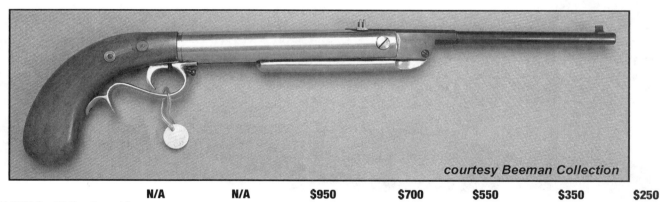

courtesy Beeman Collection

		90%	80%	60%	40%	20%
N/A	N/A	$950	$700	$550	$350	$250

Add 20% for "Tellow" marking.

TELL 2 - .177 cal., SP, concentric-piston, 5 in. rifled barrel, 220 FPS (.177 cal.), 5.75 in. overall, blue or nickel finish, grip backstrap folds out to aid cocking which isaccomplished by front of trigger guard engaging piston, checkered wood grips, 0.9 lbs. Mfg. 1925-1940.

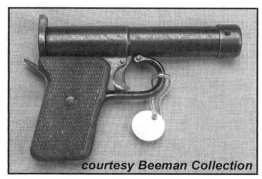

courtesy Beeman Collection

		90%	80%	60%	40%	20%
N/A	N/A	$300	$250	$200	$150	$100

Add 35% for nickel finish (rare). Add 50% for factory box, pellet tin, and paperwork.
The Tell 2 and the Clarke's Bulldog apparently are the world's smallest spring piston airguns.

GRADING	100%	95%	90%	80%	60%	40%	20%

TELL 3 - .177 cal., BBC, SP, unique cocking link above air chamber, 5.38 in. rifled barrel, 280 FPS, 10 in. overall, blue finish, brown checkered Bakelite grips with Tell emblem in center, 2.2 lbs. Approx. fifty mfg. 1936-1940. Ref: AW - June 2003.

courtesy Beeman Collection

N/A	N/A	$950	$700	$550	$350	$250

Add 40% for factory box, accessories, and paperwork.

RIFLES

MARS 86 - 4.4mm lead round ball cal., SP, BA, youth sized, full length hardwood stock, gravity-fed mag. loads through gate on barrel sleeve, swinging safety, 34.1 in. OAL, 3.6 lbs.

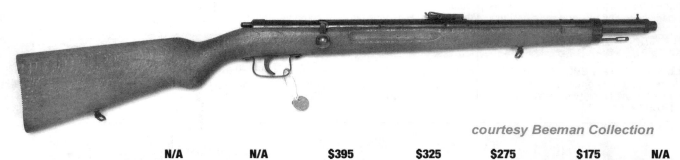

courtesy Beeman Collection

N/A	N/A	$395	$325	$275	$175	N/A

MARS 110 - .4.4mm round lead ball cal., SP, BA, paramilitary-style trainer based on Schmeisser design of Anschütz Model 275, styled very closely to Mauser 98 paramilitary rifle w/full length stock, top wooden hand guards and side slot in buttstock for leather sling, paramilitary type rear sight marked 6 to 12 meters, repeating mechanism with gravity-fed magazine, Mauser wing-type manual safety, 43 in. OAL, 7.3 lbs.

courtesy Beeman Collection

$425	$375	$325	$250	$175	$125	$75

Produced for German Hitlerjugend training. Related military-style models reported: 1935-40 (perhaps some later during Soviet occupation; these would be much lower quality).

MILITIA MODEL - .177, BBC, SP, SS, milita-style rifle, part-round/part-octagonal BBL, walnut buttstock, blue steel buttplate. 5.4 lbs.

$450	$400	$350	$275	$200	N/A	N/A

MARS 100 - 4.4mm lead round ball cal., SP, BA, similar to Mars 85 except, over-all-length.

N/A	N/A	$395	$325	$275	$175	N/A

TELLY

For information on Telly airguns, see Relum Limited in the "R" section.

TEXAN

For information on Texan airguns, see Apache in the "A" section.

GRADING	100%	95%	90%	80%	60%	40%	20%

THEOBEN ENGINEERING

Current manufacturer located in England. Currently imported and destributed by Theoben USA located in Garden Grove, CA beginning 2004 and beginning 1992 by Beeman Precision Airguns, located in Huntington Beach, CA, and previously imported by Air Rifle Specialists located in Pine City, NY. Dealer and consumer direct sales.

Models built for Beeman Precision Airguns can be found in the Beeman section of this text. Please contact Theoben USA directly for more information and prices of their products (see Trademark Index listing).

RIFLES

The U.S. importation of the models listed below was discontinued during 1993 (unless otherwise marked).

Add $150 for Theoben pump applicable for some models listed below.

SIROCCO COUNTRYMAN - .177 or .22 cal., BBC, 1100/800 FPS, pre-charged sealed gas spring, includes scope rings, barrel weight, walnut stained beechwood stock, 7 1/2 lbs. Importation disc. 1987.

	100%	95%	90%	80%	60%	40%	20%
	$360	$285	225	$175	$125	N/A	N/A

Last MSR was $585.

SIROCCO DELUXE - similar to Countryman, except has hand checkered walnut stock. Importation disc. 1987.

	100%	95%	90%	80%	60%	40%	20%
	$540	$450	$395	$245	$195	N/A	N/A

Last MSR was $650.

SIROCCO CLASSIC - similar to Sirocco Deluxe, except has updated floating inertia system in piston chamber and automatic safety, 900/1100 FPS. Mfg. 1987.

	100%	95%	90%	80%	60%	40%	20%
	$665	$565	$465	$385	$295	N/A	N/A

Last MSR was $830.

Add $60 for left-hand variation.
This model was available with either a choked or unchoked Anschütz barrel as standard equipment.

SIROCCO GRAND PRIX - similar to the Sirocco Classic, except has checkered walnut thumbhole stock.

	100%	95%	90%	80%	60%	40%	20%
	$750	$655	$565	$430	$345	N/A	N/A

Last MSR was $940.

Add $60 for left-hand variation. Subtract 50% for older models without safety and new piston design.
In 1987, this model was updated with a floating inertia system in piston chamber, automatic safety, and variable power.
This model was available with either a choked or unchoked Anschütz barrel as standard equipment.

ELIMINATOR - .177 or .22 cal., barrel cocking, 1400/1100 FPS, deluxe checkered thumbhole stock with cheekpiece and pad, 9 1/2 lbs.

	100%	95%	90%	80%	60%	40%	20%
	$825	$750	$490	$410	$325	N/A	N/A

Last MSR was $1,500.

Add $60 for left-hand variation.
This model incorporated an improved barrel design featuring pronounced rifling for the higher velocity pellets.

IMPERATOR - .22 cal., UL, SP, 750 FPS, walnut hand checkered stock, automatic safety. Mfg. 1989.

	100%	95%	90%	80%	60%	40%	20%
	$825	$750	$490	$410	$325	N/A	N/A

Last MSR was $1,500.

IMPERATOR SLR 88 - similar to Imperator, except has a seven-shot magazine. Very limited importation.

	100%	95%	90%	80%	60%	40%	20%
	$1,200	$900	$750	$490	$410	N/A	N/A

Last MSR was $1,680.

RAPID 7 - .22 cal., PCP, 19 in. Anschütz barrel, stippled walnut stock, seven-shot bolt action design, 6 3/4 lbs.

	100%	95%	90%	80%	60%	40%	20%
	$1,000	$850	$750	$650	$550	N/A	N/A

Last MSR was $1,300.

Add $60 for left-hand variation. Add $120 for scuba tank adaptor.

THUNDERBOLT

For information on Thunderbolt airguns, see Produsit in the "P" section.

TIGER

For information on Tiger airguns, see F.I.E. in the "F" section.

GRADING	100%	95%	90%	80%	60%	40%	20%

TITAN (CURRENT MFG.)

Current tradename resurrected by a current British airgun maker who seems to have operated under several names and perhaps several ownerships circa 1990 to present.

Products include high quality air rifles and pistols, including PCP and pump pneumatic power plants. Additional research is being done on this maker and their guns. Research is ongoing with this trademark, and more information will be included both online and in future editions. Average original condition specimens on most common Titan models are typically priced in the $400-$1,200 range. See also Beeman and Falcon sections in this edition.

courtesy Beeman Collection

TITAN (DISC.)

Previous trademark of air pistols patented and probably manufactured by Frank Clarke located in Birmingham, England circa 1916-1926.

Note that there are a considerable number of variations from these basic models; variations which do not seem to merit model level status at this time. These model numbers have been proposed by noted airgun researcher John Atkins (Airgun Editor, *Airgunner Magazine*) and do not represent model designations of the maker. Numbers on guns probably are not serial numbers. The authors and publisher of the *Blue Book of Airguns* wish to express their appreciation to John Atkins and Ingvar Alm for their valuable assistance with the following information in this edition of the *Blue Book of Airguns*.

PISTOLS

Unless otherwise noted, all air pistols noted below are .177 cal., SP, SS, rear rod-cocking, blue finish steel, with walnut grip plates fitted into the sides of the grip frame.

MARK 1 - 9.25 in BBL, bolt action, nickel finish, one-piece grip frame and breech block with black hard rubber grip plates, front sight sleeves muzzle, rear sight is a notch on the bolt handle, cocking plunger in front of compression chamber, angled hard rubber grip plates with "FC" for Frank Clark and "B" for Birmingham on the right side, and "Titan" imprinted on the left side, a crown is stamped over "MADE IN ENGLAND" on back of breech block, 10 in. OAL. approx. 1.1 lbs. Mfg. 1916-17.

courtesy Loke Collection

Rarity precludes accurate pricing.
To aid cocking, a device, made of twisted steel wire, could be attached to the cocking plunger and then held down by the user's toe.

MARK 2 - similar to Mark 1 except, iron grip frame and air chamber cast in one piece, no grip plates, cocked by plunger rod (apparently removable) from rear, bolt attached to BBL, BBL slides forward to load, nickel plated finish. Mfg. 1917.
Rarity precludes accurate pricing.
The spring is compressed by means of a plunger and rod operated from the rear of the action.

MARK 3 - similar to Mark 1 and Mark 2 except, one-piece cast iron compression tube and vertical grip frame, barrel bands with with rearband acting as sight, front sight on barrel, twist breech block rotated counter-clockwise for loading, cocking rod folds into grooved back strap, three pins mounting trigger guard, black painted finish, cocked by pushing a rod in from the rear. Mfg. 1918.
Rarity precludes accurate pricing.
Establishes the basic Titan pattern of cocking and loading found in all later Titan air pistols.

MARK 4 - similar to Mark 3 except, more streamlined, BBL support lugs cast into body tube, pinned cap at forward end allows forward removal of mainspring, vertical grip frame with checkered wood grip plates inset into frame. 10.5 in. OAL. Mfg.1919-1923.

	100%	95%	90%	80%	60%	40%	20%
	N/A	N/A	N/A	$900	$650	$550	$450

GRADING	100%	95%	90%	80%	60%	40%	20%

MARK 5 - similar to Mark 4 except has7 in. barrel, mainspring removes from breech end, front sight caston top of front barrel band, checkered hard rubber grips, roll stamped LH side compression chamber 'THE "TITAN" AIR PISTOL' over 'PATENT 110999/17', approx. 1.9 lbs. Most common model. Mfg. circa 1920.

courtesy Beeman Collection

	N/A	N/A	N/A	$695	$550	$450	$350

MARK 6 - similar to Mark 5 except, trigger sear adj. screw through rear of trigger guard, four pins mounting trigger and guard, roll stamped LH side 'THE "TITAN" AIR PISTOL' over 'PATENT 110999/17', approx. 1.8 lbs. Mfg. circa 1921.

courtesy Loke Collection

	N/A	N/A	N/A	$695	$550	$450	$350

MARK 7 - similar to Mark 6 except, without trigger sear adj. screw, internal grip safety disengaged when cocking rod is depressed into frame slot, checkered hard rubber grip with "T" inside of a circle molded on top half, roll stamped LH side 'THE "TITAN" AIR PISTOL' over 'PATENT 110999/17', approx. 1.7 lbs. Mfg. circa 1923-1925. Ref: AG July, Aug, Sept 1987, Oct 1988, Oct 1991.

courtesy Loke Collection

	N/A	N/A	N/A	$850	$650	$550	$450

Only turning-breech, folding-cocking-rod Titan w/ slanted grips. Evolved into the Clarke-designed Webley Mk 1 which replaced it.

GRADING	100%	95%	90%	80%	60%	40%	20%

TOKYO

Previous manufacturer of barrel cocking air rifles in Japan.

RIFLES

INDIAN JUNIOR - .177 cal., BBC, SP, SS, one-inch dia. receiver tube, copy of BSA barrel cocking air rifle, 17 in. barrel, marked with outline letters "INDIAN" and an Indian head on top of receiver, stamped across receiver: Made by TOK O. 39.4 in. OAL, 3.7 lbs.

courtesy Beeman Collection

	100%	95%	90%	80%	60%	40%	20%
	$250	$200	$150	$100	$75	$50	$25

Research is ongoing with this trademark, and more information will be included both online and in future editions.

INDIAN SENIOR - .177 cal., BBC, SP, SS, similar to Indian Junior except, larger.

	100%	95%	90%	80%	60%	40%	20%
	$250	$200	$150	$100	$75	$50	$25

Research is ongoing with this trademark, and more information will be included both online and in future editions.

TONG IL

Tong Il Industrial Co. Ltd. of Seoul, South Korea. Apparently active.
Relationship to Yewha and National brands are not clear at this time.

RIFLES

GARAND MODEL MT 1 - .177 cal., SS, UL, swinging lever pump pneumatic, very realistic, slightly oversized replica of Garand military rifle. Same bolt action to load. Flash suppressor. Parkerized finish. Marked "TONG IL MT 1" on top rear of receiver. 28.5 in. round BBL, 46.7 in. OAL, 9.8 lbs.

courtesy Beeman Collection

	100%	95%	90%	80%	60%	40%	20%
	N/A	N/A	$1,800	$1,500	$1,000	$650	$300

MI CARBINE MODEL CT 2 - .177 cal., SP, SS, SL, sidelever very suggestive of Feinwerkbau 300 side lever. Very realistic replica of US M1 Carbine military rifle. Same bolt action to load. Web sling with oiler sling retainer; some other original M1 parts. Parkerized finish. Marked "MOD. CT 2." 36.3 in. OAL, 7.3 lbs.

courtesy Beeman Collection

	100%	95%	90%	80%	60%	40%	20%
	N/A	N/A	$1,600	$1,100	$850	$500	$200

TOPGUN

For information on Topgun airguns, see Philippine Airguns in the "P" section.

TRIDENT

For information on Trident airguns, see Philippine Airguns in the "P" section.

GRADING	100%	95%	90%	80%	60%	40%	20%

TyROL

Previous brand name of previous manufacturer, Tiroler Sportwaffenfabrik und Apparatenbau GmbH ("TyROL Sport Weapon Makers and Appara-tus Factory"), Kufstein, Austria. Circa 1939 to 1970s.

Many airgun collectors think that non-match CO_2 rifles were made only in the United States. Here are some wonderful exceptions. The rifles below bear the same TyROL brand name (in the same unusual font printed in this unique way), same Austrian eagle logo, and "MADE IN AUSTRIA" marking. Production of these airguns sometimes has been attributed to Tiroler Waffenfabrik ("Tyrol Weapon Makers") Peterlongo, Richard Mahrhold & Sohn, Innsbrück, Austria, founded in 1854 and reportedly still making airguns into the 1970s, but Richard Mahrhold's Waffenlexikon (Weapon Dictionary) edition of 1998 notes that they are the product of the firm presently known as Tiroler Sportwaffenfabrik und Apparatebau GmbH ("Tyrol Sport Weapon Makers and Apparatus Factory Inc.") (aka Tiroler Jagd undSportwaffenfabrik or "TyROL Hunting and Sport Weapon Makers") of Kufstein, Austria, a gun maker associated with Voetter & Co. of Vöhrenbach/Schwarzwald ("Black Forest"), Germany. The Tiroler Jagd und Sportwaffenfabrik Company name was established in 1965, but the firm was known as the Tiroler Maschinenbau und Holzindustrie ("TyROL Machine Factory and Wood Works") in the 1950s when the TyROL COmatic and CM1 CO_2 rifles were produced and prior to that as Tiroler Waffenfabrik H. Krieghoff (probably unrelated to H. Kreighoff of Suhl and then Ulm, Germany). These airguns, especially the M1 Carbine-style trainer, may have been supplied to Voetter & Co. who reportedly was the official supplier of arms to the Austrian Army. Voetter also used the well-known brand name of Voere. The M1 Carbine version known officially as the Österreichischen Übungskarabiner KM 1 or "ÜK" is one of the most sought-after military arms among European arms and airgun collectors.

The association of the Austrian TyROL CO_2 rifles and the Italian Armigas "OLYMPIC" CO_2 rifles is a puzzle. While the civilian COmatic version of the TyROL gas rifle and the Armigas "OLYMPIC" appear to be the same, close examination shows that while virtually every part is similar, with almost identical styling, none actually are the same and they certainly are not interchangeable! Perhaps the TyROL CO_2 repeater was the inspiration for the OLYMPIC from Armigas. The TyROL CO-Matic rifle obviously was also the model for Venturini's Golondrina COMatic CO_2 pellet rifle, not surprising, considering the past ties of Germany and Argentina. The Golondrina repeater was in turn the model for the Golondrina repeating CO_2 pistol.

The TyROL COmatic and CM1 rifles may have additional special significance in the historical development of airguns as the maker claimed that they were the first semi-automatic CO_2 rifles to be developed commercially. (Ref: Amer. Rifleman Sept 1959:62-3; DWJ March 1992:401-3).

RIFLES

TyROL GAS RIFLE ("COmatic" MODEL) - .177 cal., CO_2 bulk feed, charging valve by muzzle, semi-automatic; spring-fed removable eighty-shot magazine for lead balls, combination cocking tab/manual safety cannot be reset to safe after cocking, 21.2 in. rifled barrel, blue finish, date stamped LHS, 38 in. OAL, 5.3 lbs.Mfg. 1959.

courtesy Beeman Collection

N/A	$750	$600	$500	$400	$300	$200

TyROL MODEL CM1 - .177 cal., CO_2 bulk feed, 21 in. barrel, long removable spring-fed magazine for lead balls on right side of bar-rel, stock styled exactly after U.S. M1 Carbine, complete with web sling retained by regulation oiler tube, military style adj. peep rear and blade protected front sight, LH receiver marked TyROL and with Austrian eagle logo, rear edge of receiver marked 4,5 mm DPH. supplied with four actual M1 carbine magazines loaded with dummy .30 cal. carbine cartridges, gas charging device, cleaning rod, regulation canvas magazine pouches, and canvas case, 36 in. OAL, 5.7 lbs. Approx. only 340 mfg. circa 1950s.

courtesy Beeman Collection

N/A	N/A	$1,200	$1,000	$800	$600	$500

Subtract 40% for "demilitarized" versions. Subtract 25% if missing accessories.

Spring-fed magazine reportedly designed to take approx. the same time to replace as a box magazine of cartridges on the actual U.S. M1 Carbine. Original U.S. M1 carbine magazines fit into the gun in the conventional manner, but did not function. Reportedly used for training of Austrian and Dutch troops who had received large quantities of the U.S. M1 Carbines after WWII, most were destroyed by military authorities. Specimens remaining in Germany usually were modified to a "non-military configuration" by removing the military style sights, regulation sling and oiler, and filling in the sling slot in the stock.

GRADING	100%	95%	90%	80%	60%	40%	20%

TyROL MODEL 51 - .177 cal., SP, BC, SS, conventional sporter-style stock, open sights, TyROL and eagle logo markings.

	$100	$75	$60	$50	$35	$25	$20

TyROL TOURNIER 53 - .177 cal., SP, BC, SS, 17.7 in. rifled barrel, blue finish, precision diopter (match aperture sight), match style stock with carved grip cap, marked on barrel "Tournier 53", "TyROL" plus a large Austrian eagle logo enclosing a large stylized letter "M" on top of receiver, and ."MADE IN AUSTRIA" and serial number on LH side of barrel block, no safety, 42 in. OAL, 9.6 lbs.

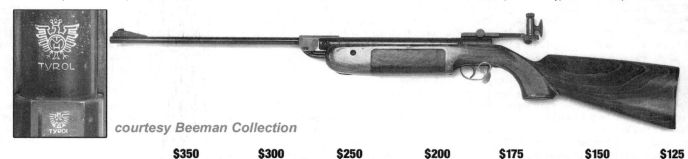

courtesy Beeman Collection

	$350	$300	$250	$200	$175	$150	$125

Stylized letter "M" may indicate an association with Richard Mahrholdt.

U SECTION

ULTI-SHOT

Previous trademark of Ultimate Force in England the manufacturer of UltiShot air shotgun designed by Luke Cammilleri and Martin McManus of Merseyside, England.

Research is ongoing with this trademark, and more information will be included both online and in future editions.

GRADING	100%	95%	90%	80%	60%	40%	20%

SHOTGUN

ULTISHOT - .38 caliber air shotgun (or .375 lead balls or .38 cal. 110 gr. HP slugs), PCP, smoothbore. British FAC version produces about 30 ft./lb. ME (9 mm rifled barrel version made in at least prototype form).Tilting breech block, takes .38 cal. Crosman shot cartridges. 37.2 in OAL, 19.3 in BBL, 6.9 lbs, checkered walnut straight grip stock. Appears to be based on Falcon PCP action. Serial numbers to 6 known. Produced only in 1996. Disc.

courtesy Beeman Collection

$1,200	$995	$800	N/A	N/A	N/A	N/A

ULTRA-HI PRODUCTS

Previous Pioneer BB76 BB gun distributor located in Hawthorne, NJ.

Made in Japan.

RIFLES

PIONEER BB76 - 4.4 mm cal. lead balls (bore too large for American steel .173 in BBs), SP, fifty-shot spring-fed magazine similar to Daisy 25, copy of a Kentucky rifle for the 1976 US Bicentennial. Underlever charging lever. 45.0 OAL, 4.1 lbs. Velocity with 7.8 gr lead balls = 304 FPS, with 5.4 gr Daisy Quick Silver BBs 372 FPS.Three stage adjustable trigger. Hammer is the safety. US Patent 238780. Manufactured in 1976 only. Ref: AR 6:7-10.

courtesy Beeman Collection

$350	$300	$225	$150	$100	N/A	N/A

UMAREX SPORTWAFFEN GMBH & CO. KG

Current manufacturer of private label airguns sold under the Beretta, Colt, Hämmerli, Magnum Research Inc., RWS, Smith & Wesson, Sturm, Ruger & Co., Inc., and Walther names, located in Arnsberg, Germany. These airguns are imported and distributed in the United States beginning 2006, by Umarex USA located in Fort Smith, AR.

UMAREX was founded in 1972 as the "UMA Mayer & Ussfeller GmbH" first manufacturing tear-gas and signal pistols and later air rifles. This was followed by the acquisition of the "Reck Sportwaffenfabrik Karl Arndt." UMA was first reorganized as UMARECK and then as UMAREX. The success story began in 1978 with the introduction of the RECK PK 800 tear-gas and signal pistol, a perfect replica of the renowned Walther PPK. Today UMAREX is Europe's largest importer of air rifles, marketing brands such as Crosman, Marksman, and Norica and at the same time is the world's largest maker of replicas. Famous makers such as Smith & Wesson, Colt, Beretta, FN Browning, Magnum Research Inc. and Walther have awarded UMAREX licenses to construct tear-gas/signal guns and CO_2 weapons.

Umarex is the present owner of Walther. Umarex does not sell directly to the general market, and the various private label models produced are listed under their respective trademark names. Please refer to the Beretta, Colt, Hämmerli, Magnum Research Inc., RWS, Smith & Wesson, Sturm, Ruger & Co., Inc., and Walther listings in this text.

For more information and current pricing on both new and used Umarex firearms, please refer to the *Blue Book of Gun Values* by S.P. Fjestad (also available online).

GRADING	100%	95%	90%	80%	60%	40%	20%

UMAREX USA, INC.

Current importer and distributor of private label airguns sold under the Beretta, Colt, Hämmerli, Magnum Research Inc., RWS, Smith & Wesson, Sturm, Ruger & Co., Inc., and Walther names, located in Fort Smith, AR.

Umarex USA began with the acquisition of Ruag Ammotec USA, marketers of the RWS trademark (manufactured by Dianawerk) adult airguns. Combined with the world class products from German based Umarex, the parent company of Walther Firearms, Umarex USA has become one of the premier providers of airguns and airgun accessories to North America. Please refer to the Beretta, Colt, Hämmerli, Magnum Research Inc., RWS, Smith & Wesson, Sturm, Ruger & Co., Inc., and Walther listings in this text.

UNICA

Manufacturer status is unknown at time of printing.

Details of construction, including cast aluminum receiver, indicate that the one known model is a regular production item.

SHOTGUNS

UNICA AIR SHOTGUN - .25 cal., SP, BBC, SS, breech opening. Appears to be an over/under shotgun, but bottom barrel-like tube is open near barrel pivot, side sling swivels, blued steel and aluminum, rib runs full length of barrel and receiver (serves as scope base on receiver), threaded muzzle ring removes to receive muzzle brake or suppressor, walnut stock. "Unica" in molded type and winged eagle logo on white plastic buttplate – matching grip cap. No safety. 18.3 in. BBL, 41.5 in. OAL, 6.5 lbs.

courtesy Beeman Collection

	100%	95%	90%	80%	60%	40%	20%
	N/A	N/A	$1,100	$850	$700	$550	$200

Information on this gun is actively solicited – please contact BlueBookEdit@Beemans.net or Blue Book Publications.

UPTON

For information on Upton airguns, see Sterling/Upton in the "S" section.

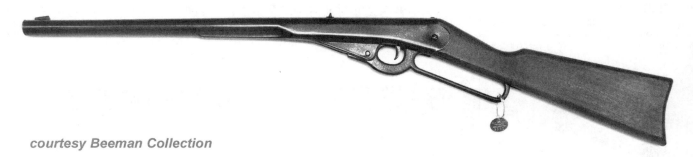

courtesy Beeman Collection

V SECTION

VALESQUEZ

For information on Valesquez airguns, see Philippine Airguns in the "P" section.

courtesy Beeman Collection

VALIENTE

For information on Valiente airguns, see Philippine Airguns in the "P" section.

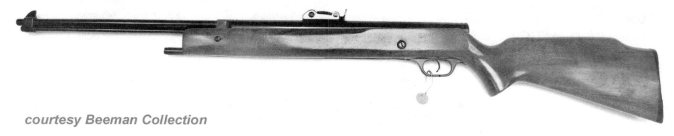

courtesy Beeman Collection

VALMET

Previous tradename of Valmet Oy located in Jyväskylä, Finland. Manufacture of Valmet firearms was replaced by Tikka circa 1989.

Former governmental engineering works, later famous for fine sporting and military firearms, such as the Model 58 Kalashnikov assault rifle. Fused with Sako in 1987 to become Sako-Valmet. Formerly produced BBC air rifles of especially high quality. For more information and current values on used firearms, please refer to the *Blue Book of Gun Values* by S.P. Fjestad (also available online).

GRADING	100%	95%	90%	80%	60%	40%	20%

RIFLES

AIRIS - .177 cal., BBC, SP, SS, steel parts, fwd. sling swivel mounted into outside of barrel, blue finish, hardwood stock with finger-grooved forearm, 39.5 in. OAL, 5.0 lbs.

courtesy Beeman Collection

100%	95%	90%	80%	60%	40%	20%
$425	$375	$325	$250	$200	$150	N/A

VENOM ARMS CUSTOM GUNS

Previous manufacturer/customizer located in the Birmingham, England. No current U.S. importation. Venom Arms Custom Guns was a division of Webley & Scott. The Custom Shot officially closed December, 2005.

Venom Arms specialized in customizing Weihrauch air rifles manufactured in Germany. For more information on their current model lineup, pricing, and U.S. availability, please contact the company directly (see Trademark Index). See also Weihrauch and Webley & Scott in the "W" section. Pricing for Venom Arms Custom Guns models may run 100%-300% over the initial cost of a standard gun.

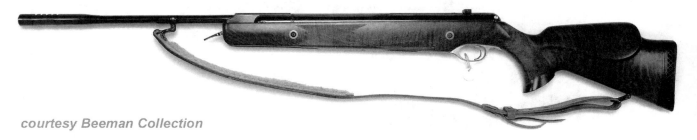

courtesy Beeman Collection

VENTURINI

Previous airgun manufacturer located in Argentine. Produced airguns under Venturini, Rubi, and Golondrina brands. Circa 1970-1980s.

PISTOLS

GOLONDRINA ("C-O-MATIC") - .177 cal., CO_2, repeater, removable spring-fed magazine along barrel, bulk feed, no safety, unusual pistol version of Golondrina "C-O-matic" rifle.

courtesy Beeman Collection

100%	95%	90%	80%	60%	40%	20%
$500	$400	$350	$300	$250	$200	N/A

RIFLES

GOLONDRINA ("C-O-MATIC") - .177 cal., CO_2 repeater, removable spring-fed magazine along RH length of barrel, bulk feed, almost surely copied from the German Tyrol "C-O-matic" repeater, also similar to the Spanish ArmiGas "Olympic" and Brazilian "Fionda".

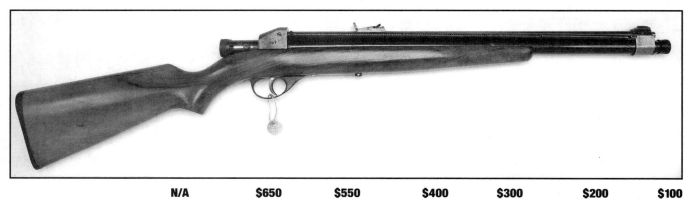

100%	95%	90%	80%	60%	40%	20%
N/A	$650	$550	$400	$300	$200	$100

GRADING	100%	95%	90%	80%	60%	40%	20%

RUBI - .177 cal., BBC, SP, SS, birch stock with finger grooved forearm.

courtesy Beeman Collection

	$200	$165	$130	$95	$70	$50	N/A

VENUSWAFFENWERK

For information on Venuswaffenwerk airguns, see Tell in the "T" section.

VINCENT

Previously manufactured by Frank Vincent, located in Hillsdale, MI.

Metal pump lever handle under barrel. Designed to be pumped to high pressure with seventy strokes. Would shoot many times with one fill, but with diminishing power unless pumped about thirty strokes between shots. Original instructions warned to use only "automobile brake fluid" to lubricate pump. Walnut stocks are handcrafted and metal parts are painted black. Mfg. circa 1930s.

Dennis Quackenbush (see the Q section of this guide) has recently manufactured some working replicas of the Vincent airguns.

RIFLES

RIFLE - .177 cal., BA, rifled brass barrel, 39.75 in. OAL, 700+ FPS, 5 lbs.

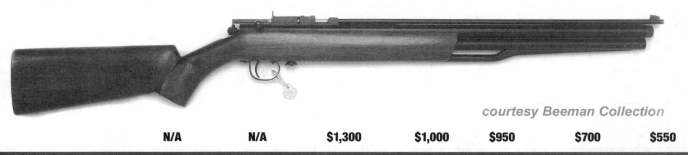

courtesy Beeman Collection

	N/A	N/A	$1,300	$1,000	$950	$700	$550

SHOTGUNS

SHOTGUN - .410 cal., bolt action, smoothbore steel barrel, 44.6 in. overall, very powerful. With brass shot shells, wad cutter, and shell filling tools, 6.4 lbs.

courtesy Beeman Collection

	N/A	N/A	$1,400	$1,150	$800	$500	N/A

Add 25% for tool kit and spare cartridges.

VINTAGE PNEUMATICS

For information on Vintage Pneumatics airguns, see Feltman Products in the "F" section.

VZ

For information on VZ airguns, see CZ in the "C" section.

NOTES

W SECTION

WAFFENTECHNIK JONISKEIT

For information on Waffentechnik Joniskeit airguns, see Joniskeit in the "J" section.

WALTHER

Current manufacturer located in Ulm, Germany. Currently, Match/Target model airguns imported and distributed by Champion´s Choice, located in La Vergne, TN. Currently, Sport model airguns imported and distributed by Umarex USA located in Fort Smith, AR. Previously, Sport model airguns imported by Crosman Corp., located in East Bloomfield, NY. Previously imported by Walther USA located in Springfield, MA, and Interarms, located in Alexandria, VA. Dealer or consumer direct sales.

For more information and current pricing on both new and used Walther firearms, please refer to the *Blue Book of Gun Values* by S.P. Fjestad (also available online).

GRADING	100%	95%	90%	80%	60%	40%	20%

PISTOLS

CP 2 - .177 cal., CO$_2$, 9 in. barrel, adj. sights and trigger, UIT target model, 2.5 lbs. Mfg. 1985-90.

	100%	95%	90%	80%	60%	40%	20%
	$550	$450	$400	$350	$275	N/A	N/A

Last MSR was $850.

Subtract 10% for left-hand variation.

CP 3 - .177 cal., CO$_2$, adj. sights and trigger, UIT target model. Importation 1987-93.

	100%	95%	90%	80%	60%	40%	20%
	$550	$450	$400	$350	$275	N/A	N/A

Last MSR was $1,360.

CP 5 - .177 cal., CO$_2$, target model. Mfg. 1989-95.

	100%	95%	90%	80%	60%	40%	20%
	$700	$600	$450	$375	$350	N/A	N/A

Last MSR was $1,650.

CP 88 - .177 cal., CO$_2$, SA and DA, 4 in. rifled barrel, 393 FPS, 8 shot mag., blue or nickel finish, adj. rear sight, 2.25 lbs. Marked Umarex USA beginning 2006. New 1996.

MSR $198	100%	95%	90%	80%	60%	40%	20%
	$165	$130	$90	$70	$50	N/A	N/A

Add 10% for nickel finish. Add 20% for wood grips.

⊙ **CP88 Competition** - .177 cal., similar to CP 88, except has 6 in. barrel with compensator, 450 FPS, adj. rear sight, 2.5 lbs. Marked Umarex USA beginning 2006.

courtesy Umarex USA

MSR $215	100%	95%	90%	80%	60%	40%	20%
	$195	$165	$135	$95	$70	N/A	N/A

Add 10% for nickel finish. Add 20% for wood grips.

CP88 TACTICAL - .177 cal., similar to CP 88, except has 6 in. barrel with compensator, 450 FPS, adj. rear sight, 2.5 lbs. Marked Umarex USA beginning 2006. Mfg. 2005-current.

MSR $277	100%	95%	90%	80%	60%	40%	20%
	$250	$185	$140	$100	$75	N/A	N/A

GRADING	100%	95%	90%	80%	60%	40%	20%

CP 99 - .177 cal., CO$_2$, eight-shot rotary magazine at breech, 320 FPS, 3.3 in. rifled barrel, slide action for first shot or single action firing, single or double action trigger, manual safety and decocking system, black polymer frame and black or nickel slide finish, adj. rear sight, 1.7 lbs. Marked Umarex USA beginning 2006. New 2000.

courtesy Beeman Collection

MSR $170	$135	$90	$70	$50	N/A	N/A	N/A

Add 10% for nickel finish slide. Add 15% for Class III laser (CP99BLS mfg. 2005-06).

The CP99 is designed for police, military and civilian training, where the actual feel, weight, and action of a firearm are necessary. The CO$_2$ capsule is loaded in a removable cartridge-style magazine.

⊕ **CP 99 Compact** - .177 cal., CO$_2$, 17 shot mag., 345 FPS, 3 in. rifled barrel, slide action for first shot or single action firing, manual safety and decocking system, black polymer frame and black or nickel slide finish, adj. rear sight, 1.7 lbs. Marked Umarex USA beginning 2006. New 2006.

MSR $75	$65	$50	$40	$30	N/A	N/A	N/A

Add 10% for nickel finish slide. Add 15% for CP99 Compact with Laser mfg. 2006-current.

⊕ **CP 99 Compact Recon** - .177 cal., CO$_2$, 17 shot mag., 345 FPS, 3.6 in. rifled barrel, slide action for first shot or single action firing, manual safety and decocking system, black polymer frame and slide finish, bridge mount, Walther Shot Dot green illuminated point sight and compensator, 2.3 lbs. Mfg. 2008-current.

courtesy Umarex USA

MSR $128	$110	$85	$65	$50	N/A	N/A	N/A

⊕ **CP 99 Military** - .177 cal., similar to CP 99, except green polymer frame with black slide finish, adj. rear sight. 1.7 lbs. Marked Umarex USA beginning 2006. New 2001.

MSR $178	$145	$95	$70	$50	N/A	N/A	N/A

⊕ **CP 99 Trophy** - .177 cal., similar to CP 99, except black polymer frame and black or nickel slide finish, includes bridge mount, red dot optical sighting system and case, 1.7 lbs. Mfg. 2001-06.

	$250	$185	$140	$100	$75	N/A	N/A

Last MSR was $300.

Add 10% for nickel finish slide.

CPM-1 - .177 cal., CO$_2$, adj. sights and trigger, UIT target model. New 1992.

	$650	$600	$550	$500	$425	N/A	N/A

CP SPORT(CPS) - .177 cal., CO$_2$, SA and DA, 3.3 in. rifled barrel, 360 FPS, eight-shot mag., black, orange, or yellow polymer frame with blue slide, adj. rear sight, 1.7 lbs. Marked Umarex USA beginning 2006. New 2001.

courtesy Umarex USA

MSR $105	$90	$65	$50	$40	N/A	N/A	N/A

Add 25% for Class III laser (CP Sport Laser new 2005).

GRADING	100%	95%	90%	80%	60%	40%	20%

✪ **CPS Trophy** - .177 cal., similar to CPS, except has red dot scope and mount included. New 2002.

	100%	95%	90%	80%	60%	40%	20%
	$150	$115	$90	$65	$50	N/A	N/A

LP 2 - .177 cal., SSP using linked lever around trigger and grip. Mfg. 1967-72.

	100%	95%	90%	80%	60%	40%	20%
	N/A	N/A	$450	$350	$300	N/A	N/A

Add 25% for fitted case.

LP 3 - .177 cal., SSP, 405 FPS, 2.8-3.0 lbs. Mfg. 1973-85.

courtesy Beeman Collection

	100%	95%	90%	80%	60%	40%	20%
	N/A	N/A	$450	$375	$275	N/A	N/A

Add 15% for shaped barrel (shown) rather than round. Add 20% for fitted case. Add 20% for match grade (adjustable wooden grips).

LP 53 - .177 cal., BBC, with SP system in grip, 9.45 in. rifled BBL, adj. sights with two sets of extra inserts, smooth blue (until circa SN 23,200) black crinkle enamel finish, brown or black plastic grips w/ Walther logo, wood cocking block, early versions with curved receiver back, later versions are straight, 40.6 oz. Mfg. 1952-83. Ref: AAG - Oct. 1991.

courtesy Beeman Collection

	100%	95%	90%	80%	60%	40%	20%
	N/A	$350	$300	$225	$150	N/A	N/A

Add 35% for fitted case, blue and gray inside. Add 25% for fitted case, maroon inside. Add 10% for original brown factory cardboard box. Add 30% for original smooth blue finish. Add 25% for straight back receiver. Add 15% for barrel weight. Subtract 5% for missing sight inserts.

Early versions of the fitted case are blue and gray inside; later versions are maroon.
This pistol was made famous by appearing in a James Bond poster.

LPM-1 - .177 cal., SSP, 9.15 in. barrel, 2.25 lbs. Mfg. 1990-04.

	100%	95%	90%	80%	60%	40%	20%
	$750	$700	$550	$400	N/A	N/A	N/A

Last MSR was $1,050.

LP 200/CP 200 - .177 cal., PCP (CO_2 on CP 200, disc. March 1996), 450 FPS., 9 1/8 in. barrel, adj. grips, sights, and trigger, UIT target model, 2.5 lbs.

	100%	95%	90%	80%	60%	40%	20%
	$800	$700	$575	$500	N/A	N/A	N/A

Last MSR was $1,100.

Subtract 35% for CO_2.

LP 201/CP 201 - .177 cal., PCP (CO_2 on CP201, disc. March 1996), 450 FPS., 9.15 in. barrel, adj. grips, sights, and trigger, UIT target model, 2.5 lbs. New 1990.

	100%	95%	90%	80%	60%	40%	20%
	$800	$700	$575	$500	N/A	N/A	N/A

Last MSR was $1,065.

Subtract 35% for CO_2.

LP 300 - .177 cal., PCP (integral pressure gauge in cylinder), integrated front sight with three different widths, adj. rear sight, 450 FPS, 9.15 in. barrel, adj. grips, and trigger, UIT target model, 2.2 lbs. New 2001.

MSR $1,295	100%	95%	90%	80%	60%	40%	20%
MSR $1,295	$1,295	$975	$800	$650	$500	N/A	N/A

GRADING	100%	95%	90%	80%	60%	40%	20%

⚙ *LP 300 Ultra Light* - .177 cal., PCP (integral pressure gauge in cylinder), integrated front sight with three different widths, adj. rear sight, 450 FPS, 8.19 in. barrel, adj. grips, and trigger, UIT target model, 1.9 lbs. New 2004.

MSR $1,140	$965	$865	$675	$525	$375	N/A	N/A

⚙ *LP 300 XT* - .177 cal., PCP (integral pressure gauge in cylinder), integrated front sight with three different widths, adj. rear sight, 450 FPS, 9.15 in. barrel, adj. grip, adj. trigger, UIT target model, 15.75 in. OAL, 2.2 lbs. New 2007.

MSR $1,360	$1,360	$1,195	$875	$700	N/A	N/A	N/A

NIGHTHAWK - .177 cal., CO_2, DA, semiautomatic, 3.3 in. rifled steel barrel, 360 FPS, synthetic body, eight-shot mag., srth red dot sight, 11.5 in. OAL, 1.63 lbs. Marked Umarex USA beginning 2006. New 2004.

courtesy Umarex USA

MSR $200	$169	$135	$100	$75	N/A	N/A	N/A

PPK/PPK/S/PPK/S LASER - BB/.175 cal. or .177 cal., CO_2, SA and DA, 3.5 in. smooth bore barrel, 295 FPS, fifteen-shot mag., blue frame with blue or nickel slide, fixed sights, Class III laser (PPK/S Laser new 2005), 1.25 lbs. Marked Umarex USA beginning 2006. New 2000.

MSR $72	$65	$55	$45	$30	N/A	N/A	N/A

Add 10% for Sports Kit including PPK/S pistol, shooting glasses, 2 - 12g CO_2 cylinders, 5 - targets, 250 steel BBs. Add 15% for nickel finish slide (PPK/S). Add 30% for PPK/S Laser (New 2005).

RED HAWK - .177 cal., CO_2, DA, semi-auto, eight-shot mag., 3.3 in. rifled steel BBL, 360 FPS, synthetic body, red dot sight, 7.1 in. OAL, 1.39 lbs. Mfg. 2004-06.

	$145	$125	$95	$65	N/A	N/A	N/A

Last MSR was $170.

RED STORM - .177 cal., CO_2, DA, semi-auto, eight-shot mag., 3.3 in. rifled steel BBL, 360 FPS, synthetic body, red dot sight, 7.1 in. OAL, 1.39 lbs. Marked Umarex USA. Mfg. 2007.

	$145	$125	$95	$65	N/A	N/A	N/A

Last MSR was $170.

RED STORM RECON - .177 cal., CO_2, DA, semi-auto, eight-shot mag., 3.3 in. rifled steel BBL, 420 FPS, synthetic body, red dot sight and RS compensator, 11.5 in. OAL, 1.5 lbs. Marked Umarex USA. New 2007.

courtesy Umarex USA

MSR $170	$145	$125	$95	$65	N/A	N/A	N/A

Add $18 for red or blue grips.

GRADING	100%	95%	90%	80%	60%	40%	20%

RIFLES

During 2006 Walther introduced new anti-vibration system, absorber, modified pressure reducer, Centra front sight, and MEC Contact III butt plate on all aluminum or carbon stocked match/target air rifles. These changes are indicated by the "XT" (ie. LG 300 XT) added to model names.

CG 90 - .177 cal., CO_2, 18.9 in. barrel, 10 lbs. 2 oz. Mfg. 1989-1996.

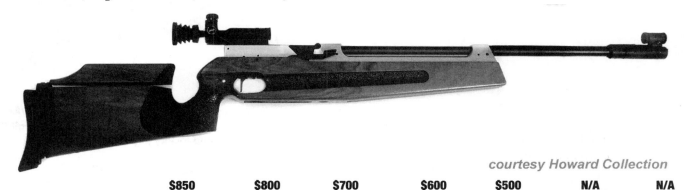

courtesy Howard Collection

	$850	$800	$700	$600	$500	N/A	N/A

Last MSR was $1,750.

CGM - .177, CO_2, target model, laminated stock, similar to LGM-2. Disc. 1997.

	$1,000	$950	$850	$750	$650	N/A	N/A

Last MSR was $1,270.

Add 10% for junior model. Add 10% for running target model.

FALCON HUNTER EDITION - .22 or .25 cal., BBC, SP, SS, 19.75 in. rifled steel BBL w/ muzzel brake, black finish, checkered Mossy Oak Break-Up synthetic Monte Carlo stock w/ adj. rubber recoil pad, automatic safety, adj. rear fixed front Truglo fiber optic sights, 3-9x44mm scope, 49 in. OAL, 8.25 lbs. Mfg. 2008-current.

courtesy Umarex USA

MSR $304	$275	$225	$175	$115	$85	N/A	N/A

JAGUAR - .177 cal., SL, SP, tap loading, 16.4 in. barrel, stained beech adj. stock (for comb, buttplate, and pull), adj. trigger, adj. rear sight, fixed front sight with interchangeable inserts. 7.5 lbs. New 1994.

	$250	$200	$150	$100	$65	N/A	N/A

Add 25% for aperture sight. Add 20% for box, accessories, and factory papers.

LEVER ACTION CARBINE - .177 cal., CO_2, eight-shot rotary mag., similar to lever action rifle, except with 15 in. rifled steel barrel, 34.5 in. OAL, 7 lbs. Mfg 2003.

	$250	$210	$185	$150	N/A	N/A	N/A

Last MSR was $255.

LEVER ACTION RIFLE - .177 cal., CO_2, eight-shot rotary mag., 18.9 in. rifled steel barrel, 630 FPS, wood stock, adj. front and rear sights, cross bolt safety, 38.3 in. OAL, 7.5 lbs. Marked Umarex USA beginning 2006.New 2002.

courtesy Howard Collection

MSR $407	$350	$285	$225	N/A	N/A	N/A	N/A

Add 10% if w/ 4x32mm scope and mount (new 2006). Add 20% for Wells Fargo Edition w/ stage coach scene on gold color receiver (new 2006).

GRADING	100%	95%	90%	80%	60%	40%	20%

LG 51 - .177 cal., BBC, SP, 17.75 in. smoothbore barrel, adj. rear sight, blue finish, walnut color beech stock, steel (early) or plastic buttplate, grooved forearm, pistol grip, 5.7 lbs. Mfg. 1951-53.

courtesy Beeman Collection

	$235	$200	$175	$110	$75	N/A	N/A

Approx. 1951 Retail $34.

Add 10% for steel buttplate. Add 25% for aperture sight. Add 20% for box, accessories, and factory papers.

⚙ LG 51 Z - .177 cal., similar to LG 51, except has rifled barrel. Mfg. beginning in 1953. Disc.

	$200	$175	$110	$75	$50	N/A	N/A

Approx. 1953 Retail $30.

Add 25% for aperture sight. Add 20% for box, accessories, and factory papers.

LG 52 - .177 cal., BBC, SP, beech stock, grooved forearm, checkered pistol grip, adj. trigger, 17.75 in. barrel, steel buttplate, 15 mm steel post inset in stock behind receiver for optional aperture sight. Mfg. 1953.

	$275	$225	$200	$130	$120	N/A	N/A

Add 20% for box, accessories, and factory papers. Add 40% for aperture sight.

LG 53 - .177 cal., similar to Model LG 51, except has plastic buttplate. Aperture sight. Mfg. 1952-76.

	$225	$175	$150	$100	$80	N/A	N/A

Add 20% for box, accessories, and factory papers. Add 40% for aperture sight.

⚙ LG 53 M - .177 cal. similar to Model LG 53, except has match-style stock, front sight with interchangeable inserts, stock and barrel weight. Mfg. 1956.

	$325	$275	$250	$180	$150	N/A	N/A

Add 20% for box, accessories, and factory papers. Add 40% for aperture sight.

⚙ LG 53 ZD - .177 cal., similar to Model LG 53, 5.7 lbs. Mfg. 1951-53.

	$325	$275	$250	$180	$150	N/A	N/A

Add 20% for box, accessories, and factory papers. Add 40% for aperture sight.

LG54 MG - .177 cal. lead balls, similar to Model LG 51, except six-shot rotery magazine for lead balls. Mfg. 1954.

	$575	$525	$475	$375	$250	N/A	N/A

Add 20% for box, accessories, and factory papers. Add 25% for aperture sight. Add 20% for blank magazine for shooting pellets.

LG 55 - .177 cal., BBC, SP, deep leaded forearm, checkered pistol grip. adj. trigger, aperture sight, cresent rubber buttplate. Mfg. 1955-67 (was available through 1974).

courtesy Beeman Collection

	$375	$325	$300	$280	$250	N/A	N/A

Add 20% for box, accessories, and factory papers. Add 25% for aperture sight. Add 20% for walnut stock. Add 10% for barrel weight. Add 100% for Tyrolean stock. Add 50% for double triggers.

LG 90 - SL, target model, 11 lbs. New 1989. Disc.

	$850	$750	$700	$600	$500	N/A	N/A

Last MSR was $1,320.

LGM-1 - .177 cal., SL, 19 in. barrel, approx. 10 lbs. Mfg. 1991. Disc.

	$900	$850	$650	$600	$550	N/A	N/A

Last MSR was $1,890.

GRADING	100%	95%	90%	80%	60%	40%	20%

LGM-2 - .177 cal., SL, similar to LGM-1, laminated stock, 10 lbs. Mfg. 1993-98.

	$900	$850	$650	$600	$550	N/A	N/A

Last MSR was $1,890.

Subtract 15% for junior model. Add 10% for running target model.

LGR RIFLE - .177 cal., SL, 580 FPS, target model, 10 lbs. 8 oz. Mfg. 1974-89.

courtesy Beeman Collection

	$750	$650	$550	$400	$250	N/A	N/A

Last MSR was $1,250.

Add 15% for Running Boar Model. Add 15% for universal. Subtract 10% for left-hand variation.

LGV MATCH RIFLE - .177 cal., BBC, SP, match rifle, barrel latch, heavy barrel sleeve, aperture sight with Walther banner on left, cresent shaped, fixed rubber buttplate, beech stock with cheekpiece and stippled grip. Mfg. 1963-68.

	$600	$500	$400	$300	$200	N/A	N/A

Add 20% for box, accessories, and factory papers. Add 15% for later version with adjustable buttplate, new style aperture sight with Walther banner on top. Add 15% for walnut stock.

⊙ **LGV Special** - similar to LGV Match Rifle, except more massive beech stock, receiver diameter increased to allow direct milling of aperture sight dovetail, double mainspring system. Mfg. 1968-72 (was available through 1985).

courtesy Beeman Collection

	$650	$550	$450	$350	$250	N/A	N/A

Add 10% for box, accessories, and factory papers. Add 40% for Tyrolean stock. Add 10% for Junior version. Add 15% for Junior 3 position version.

MODEL LG 210 - .177 cal., SL, pneumatic, 16.5 in. barrel, laminated wood stock with anatomic pistol grip, rubber butt plate, adj. cheek piece, inline compensator, chrome-molybdenum steel trigger, and peep sight with twenty-click-adjustment. 11.5 lbs. Mfg.1998-2004.

	$1,175	$950	$825	$700	$600	N/A	N/A

Last MSR was $1,393.

Add $85 for fully adj. light metal buttplate.

⊙ **LG 210 Junior** - .177 cal., SL, pneumatic, similar to Model LG 210, except scope rail for the three-position competition and an anatomical metal buttplate, 9.92 lbs. Mfg. 1999-2004.

	$1,150	$970	$800	$725	$650	N/A	N/A

Last MSR was $1,314.

MODEL 30 UNIVERSAL SPECIAL - .177 cal., PCP, manometer, 16.5 in. barrel, ambidextrous aluminum stock, adj. cheekpiece, butt pad., adj. chrome-molybdenum steel trigger, precision diopter rear sight, 42.6 in. OAL, 10.5 lbs. New 2007.

MSR N/A	$975	$850	$695	$500	N/A	N/A	N/A

GRADING	100%	95%	90%	80%	60%	40%	20%

MODEL 1250 DOMINATOR - .177 OR .22 cal., PCP, BA, eight-shot rotary mag., 23.62 in. rifled steel BBL, adj. fiber optic sights, ambidextrous synthetic Monte Carlo stock with checkering, automatic safety, vented rubber recoil pad, 40.94 in. OAL, 5.73 lbs. Mfg. 2008-current.

courtesy Umarex USA

MSR $829	$765	$695	$625	$525	N/A	N/A	N/A

◎ *Model 1250 Dominator FT* - .177 or .22 cal., PCP, BA, eight-shot rotary mag., 23.62 in. rifled steel BBL w/ compensator, quick mount adj. bipod, adj. fiber optic sights, 4-16x56mm Walther FT scope, ambidextrous synthetic Monte Carlo stock with checkering, automatic safety, vented rubber recoil pad, 40.94 in. OAL, 5.73 lbs. Mfg. 2008-current.

courtesy Umarex USA

MSR $1,000	$925	$865	$700	$625	$545	N/A	N/A

MODEL LG 300/LG 300 XT - .177 cal., PCP (integral pressure gauge in cylinder), carbon fiber barrel jacket and absorber (dampener) system eliminates perceptible recoil, 16.5 in. barrel, laminated wood stock with adj. cheekpiece, adj. and tiltable alloy buttplate, adj. chrome-molybdenum steel trigger, precision diopter rear sight, 9.7 lbs. New 2001.

MSR N/A	$1,515	$1,375	$1,095	$965	$850	N/A	N/A

Add $35 for left-hand model. Subtract $200 for Beech stock.

◎ *Model LG 300 Alutec/LG 300 XT Alutec* - .177 cal., similar to Model LG 300, except has aluminum stock with adj. cheekpiece, adj. and tiltable alloy buttplate, interchangeable, adj. pistol grip, adj. forearm, adj. chromolybdenum steel trigger, precision diopter rear sight, 9.7 lbs. New 2001.

MSR N/A	$1,885	$1,595	$1,395	$1,095	N/A	N//A	N/A

Add $50 for left-hand model.

◎ *Model LG 300 XT Alutec Evolution* - .177 cal., similar to Model LG 300 Alutec, except has all black finish w/ non-slip film coating, aluminum stock with adj. cheekpiece, adj. and tiltable alloy buttplate, interchangable, adj. pistol grip, adj. forearm, adj. chrome-molybdenum steel trigger, precision diopter rear sight, 9.7 lbs. New 2006.

MSR N/A	$1,885	$1,595	$1,395	$1,095	N/A	N//A	N/A

◎ *Model LG 300 FT Dominator (Field Target)* - .177 cal., similar to Model LG 300, except 19.3 in. barrel and 9.48 lbs. laminated wood stock or 10.7 lbs. aluminum stock. New 2001.

MSR N/A	$1,470	$1,295	$995	$865	N/A	N/A	N/A

Add $280 for aluminum stock.

◎ *Model LG 300 Hunter/LG 300 XT Hunter* - .177 cal., similar to Model LG 300, except with brown laminated wood stock with adj. cheekpiece, no sight, 935 FPS, 7.6 lbs. New 2004.

MSR N/A	$1,365	$1,195	$975	$795	$695	N/A	N/A

◎ *Model LG 300 Junior/LG 300 XT Junior* - .177 cal., similar to Model LG 300, except has beech stock with adj. cheekpiece, adj. and tilting alloy buttplate, interchangable, adj. pistol grip, adj. forearm, chrome-molybdenum steel trigger, precision diopter rear sight, 9.7 lbs. New 2001.

MSR N/A	$925	$865	$700	$625	$545	N/A	N/A

Add $35 for left-hand model.

GRADING	100%	95%	90%	80%	60%	40%	20%

⊙ **Model LG 300 XT Carbontec** - .177 cal., similar to Model LG 300, exceptanti-vibration system, 25.5 in. rifled steel barrel with carbon fiber sleeve, scaled BBL weight, Centra front sight, 41.7 in. OAL, carbon stock, 10.7 lbs. New 2004.

MSR N/A	$2,775	$2,500	$2,295	$1,995	N/A	N/A	N/A

PANTHER - .177 cal. , similar to Jaguar, except barrel cocking. New 1994.

	$225	$175	$125	$75	$50	N/A	N/A

Add 25% for aperture sight. Add 20% for box, accessories, and factory papers.

TALON MAGNUM - .177 cal., BBC, SP, SS, 19.75 in. rifled steel BBL w/ muzzel brake, black finish, checkered black synthetic Monte Carlo stock w/ adj. rubber recoil pad, automatic safety, adj. rear fixed front Truglo fiber optic sights, 3-9x32 scope, 49 in. OAL, 8.25 lbs. Mfg. 2008-current.

courtesy Umarex USA

MSR $256	$225	$175	$125	$85	$65	N/A	N/A

WARRIOR

For information on Warrior, see Accles & Shelvoke Ltd. in the "A" section.

WEBLEY & SCOTT, LTD.

Current trademark established in 1906, with manufacturing facilities located in West Midlands, England beginning early 2006. Previously located in Birmingham, England, Webley & Scott. LTD. went into receivership late 2005. In March, 2006 the Webley & Scott. LTD. trademark was purchased by Airgunsport, a leading airgun supplier for the UK. Since the re-organization and re-location Webley has released improved versions of a limited number of models. Currently exclusively imported/distributed by Legacy Sports International, located in Reno, NV. Previously imported by Airguns of Arizona, located in Mesa, AZ, by Beeman Precision Airguns, located in Huntington Beach, CA, and by Pyramyd Air International, located in Pepper Pike, OH.

Webley joined with Venom Arms Company to form the Webley Venom Custom Shop that operated out of the Webley factory until it was closed in December 2005. The Custom Shop partnership opened a host of new design developments and manufacturing capabilities, offering airgun products and services including custom air rifles and tuning accessories. The Webley Venom team claimed that no project in the airgun market could be too daunting.

The authors and publisher wish to thank Gordon Bruce for his valuable assistance with the air pistols section, as well as John Atkins, Peter Colman, and Tim Saunders for their assistance with the rifle section information in this edition of the *Blue Book of Airguns*. Bruce's 2001 book, *Webley Air Pistols*, is required reading. Ref: Hannusch, 1988 and AGNR - July 1988, Atkins, AG April, May, & June 1996.

For more information and current pricing on Webley & Scott firearms, please refer to the *Blue Book of Gun Values* by S.P. Fjestad (also available online).

Webley & Scott, LTD. 1790-1932

Webley reports that their roots go back to about 1790. The name Webley has been associated with a wide variety of firearms, ranging from early percussion pistols and centerfire revolvers to much later military and police self-loading pistols. The current name dates to 1897, when the company amalgamated with shotgun manufacturers W & C Scott and Sons, becoming The Webley and Scott Revolver and Arms Company Ltd of Birmingham. The name was shortened in 1906 to the now familiar name of Webley and Scott Ltd.

Webley's airgun history began in 1910 when an interesting air pistol, with an in-line spring piston and barrel, was designed and patented by William Whiting, then director of Webley & Scott. At least one working example was constructed, but the gun never went into production. The first production Webley airgun was the Mark I air pistol designed by Douglas Johnstone and John Fearn. It was patented and appeared in 1924 and became an immediate success. Like the Webley & Scott firearms, these pistols were built of interchangeable parts of superior quality and the designs were internationally patented. In these new pistols, placing the barrel over the spring chamber allowed a relatively long barrel in a compact gun. The Mark I was soon followed by a target model, the Mark II Deluxe version. A smaller air pistol, the Junior, was introduced in 1929 to give younger shooters a more economical version. It had a smoothbore barrel for firing reusable darts for economy of use. These young users soon were eager to acquire the more advanced Webley models. Shortly after the Junior air pistol had been launched, Webley & Scott brought out the more powerful Senior air pistol which established a basic pattern for future manufacture. Its improved method for cocking the air chamber piston, plus the use of the stirrup barrel latch, now a Webley hallmark, contributed to the enduring popularity of the design.

Success of the Webley air pistols encouraged Webley to introduce the Mark I air rifle, basically an extended version of the Mark II Target air pistol. The Mark I air rifle was well received but was produced in limited numbers only from 1926 to 1929. A much improved, larger version, the Service Air Rifle Mark II, was introduced in 1932. Acknowledged to be the finest of its type, it dominated the British airgun scene for many years. The new model featured an airtight barrel locking collar and an additional safety sear, but its most outstanding feature was a quick-change barrel system.

GRADING	100%	95%	90%	80%	60%	40%	20%

Webley & Scott, LTD. 1932-1979

A major shift in appearance of the Mark I and Senior air pistols occurred in 1935 when Webley & Scott introduced the "New Model" series. The key difference was an increase in the vertical grip angle from 100 to 120 degrees. This, and a slightly shorter barrel, created a more contemporary look and considerably improved their balance and gave them a much more natural pointing characteristic. The advent of war in 1939 caused a sudden end to commercial manufacture at the Webley plant and created a five-year gap in all commercial manufacture until the production of airguns was resumed in 1946. The New Model pistol styling, but with a grip angle of only 110 degrees, was extended to the Junior air pistol when airgun production resumed.

Post-WWII activities also included new designs for the Webley air rifles. The original barrel-cocking linkage design was replaced in 1947 by an under lever cocking system in the Mark III, Junior, and Jaguar air rifles. These were followed by the introduction of the Ranger air rifle in 1954. The original Webley factory site at Weaman Street, Birmingham, which had survived two world wars, was vacated during 1958 and the entire operation moved to Park Lane, Handsworth. In 1960, the Senior air pistol was replaced by the Premier. The Premier was virtually identical to its predecessor but featured a series of minor refinements. These series were identified in an alphabetical sequence, starting with model A in 1960 and progressing to model F in 1975. A redesigned version of the Junior air pistol, using new lighter alloy castings, was designated the Junior Mk. II. This was followed by the Premier Mk.II, of similar construction. That model enjoyed only a brief production run.

During the 1970s, Webley introduced the barrel-cocking Hawk, Tomahawk, Victor, Vulcan and Valiant air rifles and the side-lever cocking Osprey and Supertarget air rifles. An improved piston seal development, which helped to reduce piston rebound, was patented in 1979. The improved seal become an important feature of the Vulcan and subsequent rifle models.

To compete with new foreign models, more modern styling was added to the air pistol line in the mid-1970s with the introduction of the Hurricane and its slightly less powerful junior mate, the Typhoon. In 1977, Webley's largest customer at that time, the Beeman Precision Airgun Company in the United States, requested a more compact version. The resulting Tempest, designed by Paul Bednall in the Webley technical department, that more closely followed the size and balance of the more traditional Webley air pistols was introduced in 1979 and soon became the most popular model of the series.

Webley & Scott, LTD. 1979-To Date

As noted by Walther (1984 - see "Airgun Literature Review" section in the 3rd edition, *Blue Book of Airguns*), Webley and Beeman mutually benefited by forming additional links in the 1980s. Beeman expanded their Webley offerings and helped design some Webley airguns, most notably the Beeman C1 air rifle. Webley incorporated Beeman Silver Jet pellets and several of their accessories, such as special air pistol grips, into the Webley international promotions. The Beeman/Webley association became even closer as Webley's president, Keith Faulkner, became Beeman's vice president and Harold Resuggan, then Webley's very talented head engineer, moved up to head Webley.

A basic shift in Webley's business base was completed in 1979 when the company discontinued the manufacture of all firearms. The manufacture of Webley airguns continued at Handsworth until 1984, when the company moved to a modern industrial site at Rednal, South Birmingham, England. Various additions to the Webley line of air rifles during the 1980s included the Viscount, Tracker, Omega, Airwolf, and Eclipse models, while manufacture of air pistols was limited to the Hurricane and Tempest. These two pistols continue to feature the same forward-swing barrel-cocking system as those produced more than seventy years earlier, a sound testament to its efficiency. In 1994, Webley expanded into the mass market arena by adding completely fresh designs, the Nemesis, a single-stroke pneumatic air pistol and the Stinger, a spring-piston, repeating BB pistol in 1996.

The twenty-first century finds Webley rapidly evolving. Air rifles, ranging from conventional barrel-cocking, spring piston models to the latest pre-charged pneumatic and CO_2 guns are now the mainstay of the company. The latest state-of-the-art, computer-driven production stations have replaced the cumbersome networks of separate huge machines powered by noisy forests of immense overhead shafts, wheels, and belts.

PISTOLS

All pistols have rifled barrels, unless otherwise noted. Webley airguns are a large and complex group. This introductory material cannot be complete, and its concise nature may result in some inaccuracies of identification and information. It is strongly advised that you consult the *Webley Air Pistols* book mentioned above for additional details and illustrations.

Add 25-40% for original factory box. Add 50-100% for fitted case. Add 100-200% for factory cut-away display models with moving parts. Add 50-100% for factory nickel plating, not offered in all models, unless otherwise noted. Add 25-75% for factory etching.

GnAT - .177 darts, slugs, pellets, or corks, SP, SS, push-barrel cocking, black alloy and plastic, smoothbore barrel, muzzle nut for shooting corks. Mfg. 2004-05.

courtesy Beeman Collection

	$35	$30	$25	$20	$15	N/A	N/A

GRADING	100%	95%	90%	80%	60%	40%	20%

HURRICANE - .177 or .22 cal., TL, SP, SS, 420/330 FPS, plastic grips with RH thumbrest, adj. rear sight with replacement adapter for scope mounting, hooded front sight, aluminum grip frame cast around steel body tube, RH manual safety, black epoxy finish, 8 in. button rifled barrel, 11.2 in. OAL, 38 oz.

⊙ *Hurricane Variant 1* - forearm marked "HURRICANE", barrel housing (under front sight) 2.75 in. Mfg. 1975-1990.

	100%	95%	90%	80%	60%	40%	20%
	$225	$185	$145	$100	$60	N/A	N/A

Add 5% for simulated wood grips (not available in USA). Add 10% for wood grips. Add 15% for finger groove Beeman "combat" wood grips. Add 20% for Beeman factory markings with San Rafael address. Add 10% for Beeman factory markings with Santa Rosa address. Add 10% for lack of F in pentagon mark ("little hut") which indicated lower power for European market. Add 20% for large deluxe factory box with form fitting depressions, including depression for mounted scope, in hard plastic shell with red flocked surface. Add 10% for factory box with molded white foam support block.

⊙ *Hurricane Variant 2* - forearm marked "WEBLEY HURRICANE", barrel housing 2.187 in. with full length flattop. Mfg. 1990-2005.

	100%	95%	90%	80%	60%	40%	20%
	$220	$195	$150	$115	$90	N/A	N/A

Add 5% for simulated wood grips (not available in USA). Add 10% for wood grips. Add 15% for finger groove Beeman "combat" wood grips. Add 20% for Beeman factory markings with San Rafael address. Add 10% for lack of F in pentagon mark ("little hut") which indicated lower power for European market. Add 20% for large deluxe factory box with form fitting depressions, including depression for mounted scope, in hard plastic shell with red flocked surface. Add 10% for factory box with molded white foam support block.

JUNIOR - .177 cal., TL, SP, SS, metal grips with screw head on RH side, 100-degree grip slant ("straight grip"), fixed rear sight, sliding barrel latch, no safety, 6.5 in. smoothbore barrel for darts, 287 FPS, 7.75 in. OAL, 24 oz. Mfg. 1929-1938.

courtesy Bruce Gordon

	100%	95%	90%	80%	60%	40%	20%
	N/A	$325	$200	$165	$120	$85	N/A

Add 20% for adjustable rear sight. Add 20-50% for original wood grips with vertical grooves, grip screw head on LH side. Subtract 5% for final version with 6.25 in. barrel (protrudes beyond body tube).

⊙ *Junior New Model* - .177 cal., TL, SP, SS, Bakelite grips, 110-degree grip slant, adj. rear sight, sliding barrel latch, 6.125 in. smoothbore barrel for darts, 290 FPS, blued, no safety, 7.75 in. OAL, 24 oz. Mfg. 1945-73.

courtesy Bruce Gordon

	100%	95%	90%	80%	60%	40%	20%
	N/A	$200	$175	$125	$95	$75	N/A

Add 5% for early versions with grip plate "spur" that extends about 0.25 inches from the upper forward edge of the Bakelite grip plates. Add 5% for good condition leather breech seal (barrel joint washer) in pre-1960 production. Subtract 20% for Suncorite 243 paint finish (post-1970). Add 40% for factory nickel or chrome finish (uncommon on Junior models).

GRADING	100%	95%	90%	80%	60%	40%	20%

○ **Junior Mark II** - .177 cal., TL, SP, SS, aluminum grip frame cast around steel body tube, Bakelite grips, rhombus-shaped logo with "BIRMID" mark and a casting number under grips, stirrup barrel latch, black epoxy coating, adj. rear sight, no safety, 6.125 in. barrel, 290 FPS, 8 in. OAL, 23 oz. Approx. 31,750 mfg. 1973-76.

courtesy Bruce Gordon

	100%	95%	90%	80%	60%	40%	20%
	N/A	$150	$115	$85	$55	$45	N/A

Add 50% for low rear sight (barrel latch visible thru aperture), caused pre-Sept 1973 pistols to shoot low. Add 10% for smoothbore (pre-August 1975). Add 15% for seven-groove broached rifling (special order, pre-August 1975).

Introduced the massive aluminum grip frame cast around steel body tube characteristic of Webley pistols. BIRMID mark for Birmingham Aluminium Casting Company Ltd.

MARK I - .177 or .22 cal., TL, SP, SS, 367/273 FPS, wood grips, adj. rear sight, 100-degree grip slant ("straight grip"), manual safety, 8.5 in. OAL, 30 oz. Mfg. 1924-35.

○ **Mark I First Series - Variant 1** - single spring clip barrel catch on right side of breech block, no trigger adj. screw on forward edge of trigger guard.
Rarity precludes accurate pricing.

○ **Mark I First Series - Variant 2** - dual spring clip barrel catch on each side of breech block, no trigger adj. screw on forward edge of trigger guard.
Rarity precludes accurate pricing.

○ **Mark I Second Series** - sliding barrel catch on top of breech block, no trigger adj. screw on forward edge of trigger guard.

courtesy Bruce Gordon

	100%	95%	90%	80%	60%	40%	20%
	N/A	$370	$275	$200	$150	$95	N/A

○ **Mark I Third Series** - trigger adj. screw on forward edge of trigger guard.

courtesy Beeman Collection

	100%	95%	90%	80%	60%	40%	20%
	N/A	$370	$275	$200	$150	$95	N/A

○ **Mark I Fourth Series** - trigger adj. screw on forward edge of trigger guard, U.S. Patent notice on RS, barrel hinge screw with retainer.

	100%	95%	90%	80%	60%	40%	20%
	N/A	$370	$275	$200	$150	$95	N/A

GRADING	100%	95%	90%	80%	60%	40%	20%

⚙ *Mark I Fifth Series* - locking screw on LH side for cone-head trigger adj. screw.

	N/A	$370	$275	$200	$150	$95	N/A

⚙ *Mark I Sixth Series* - flanged screw plug at front end of body cylinder provided front end access to mainspring and piston assembly.

	N/A	$370	$275	$200	$150	$95	N/A

MARK I NEW MODEL - .177 and .22 cal., TL, SP, SS, 345/293 FPS, Bakelite grips, blued, adj. rear sight, introduced the "New Model" 120-degree angle grip, 8.5 in. OAL, 30 oz. Mfg. 1935-64.

⚙ *Mark I New Model Pre-WWII* - blued trigger, barrel without thicker section ahead of rear sight.

courtesy Bruce Gordon

	N/A	$275	$225	$175	$125	$75	N/A

Add 20% for smooth bore barrel. Add 5% for diamond knurling on barrel. Late 1939. Add 10% for unmarked rear breech cap with small retaining screw below sight. Add 10% for black bakelite grips without Webley name.

⚙ *Mark I New Model Post-WWII* - introduced batch numbers instead of serial numbers (none exceed approx. 6000), barrel with 2.4 in. thicker reinforced section with straight knurling.

	N/A	$185	$155	$125	$95	$55	N/A

Add 5% for unmarked rear breech cap.

MARK II TARGET - .177 or .22 cal., TL, SP, SS, 410/325 FPS, vulcanite grips, adj. rear sight, barrel latch secured by screw instead of pin, 100-degree grip slant ("straight grip"), improved piston seal, sliding barrel latch, manual safety, 8.5 in. OAL, 28 oz. Mfg. 1925-30.

⚙ *Mark II Target - First Pattern* - spring guide recessed into front end of body tube, fillister head trigger adj. screw without locking screw.

courtesy Bruce Gordon

	N/A	$660	$495	$350	$250	$185	N/A

Add 30-50% for minor factory engraving (usually done to hide imperfections). Add 100-200% for special order models made in 1928, chased with scroll engraving, silver plated, mother-of-pearl grips.

⚙ *Mark II Target - Standard Pattern* - spring guide with flange to match diameter of front end of body tube, cone head trigger adj. screw with LH locking screw.

	N/A	$450	$395	$350	$250	$185	N/A

Add 30-75% for minor factory etching (usually done to hide imperfections). Add 100-200% for special order models made in 1928, chased with scroll engraving, silver plated, mother-of-pearl grips.

GRADING	100%	95%	90%	80%	60%	40%	20%

⊙ *Mark II Target - Final Pattern* - walnut grips, Stoeger address on RH side.

courtesy Howard Collection

	N/A	$660	$495	$350	$250	$185	N/A

Add 30-50% for minor factory engraving (usually done to hide imperfections). Add 100-200% for special order models made in 1928, chased with scroll engraving, silver plated, mother-of-pearl grips.

NEMESIS - .177 or .22 cal. pellets, TL, SP, SS, 385/300 FPS, two-stage adj. trigger, black or brushed chrome finish, manual safety, adj. sights, integral scope rail, 2.2 lbs. Mfg. 1995-2005.

courtesy Bruce Gordon

$167	$135	$110	$75	N/A	N/A	N/A

Add 10% for brushed chrome finish.

PREMIER - .177 or .22 cal., TL, SP, SS, 350/310 FPS, Bakelite grips, blued finish, adj. rear sight, no safety, 8.5 in. OAL, 37 oz. Last of the traditional forged steel blued Webley air pistols. Six variation series were produced, fortunately each series was marked with a capital letter, starting with A and ending with F, stamped on the LH side of the frame, usually near the trigger guard. Details of each series are given in Bruce (2001). Plated finishes were not provided by the factory during the period of Premier production. Mfg. 1964-1975.

courtesy Beeman Collection

	N/A	$275	$225	$180	$125	$85	N/A

Subtract 20% for painted finish on series E and F.

GRADING	100%	95%	90%	80%	60%	40%	20%

○ *Premier MKII* - .177 or .22 cal., TL, SP, SS, 350/310 FPS, Bakelite grips, blued finish, adj. rear sight, no safety, 8.5 in. OAL, 37 oz. series A through F, production date stamped (LH side of grip frame under grips). Mfg. 1964-1975.

courtesy Beeman Collection

	N/A	$325	$275	$225	$150	$95	$50

Add 25% for barrel forged from one piece of steel (identified by ring-like raised area about 1 in. behind front sight), only 1,700 produced in 1976. Most production had muzzle end of barrel in a 1.48 in. muzzle shroud which incorporates the front sight. Add 20% for Beeman factory markings.

SENIOR - .177 or .22 cal., vulcanite grips, blued, adj. rear sight, stirrup barrel latch, 100-degree grip slant ("straight grip"), no safety, 416/330 FPS, 8.5 in. OAL, 33 oz. Mfg. 1930-35.
   Introduced the stirrup barrel latch from Webley revolvers to the air pistols.

○ *Senior First Pattern* - trigger adj. screw at forward end of trigger guard.

courtesy Bruce Gordon

	N/A	$450	$375	$265	$185	$125	N/A

Add 25% for A.F. Stoeger marking on RH side of air cylinder with checkered walnut grip. Add 10% for flat cocking links which obscured hole in top of air cylinder. Replaced by forward link with wings which operated upon wedge-shaped small rear link.

○ *Senior Second Pattern* - no trigger adj. screw.

courtesy Bruce Gordon

	N/A	$525	$375	$265	$185	$125	N/A

Add 25% for A.F. Stoeger marking on RH side of air cylinder with checkered walnut grip. Add 10% for flat cocking links which obscured hole in top of air cylinder. Replaced by forward link with wings which operated upon wedge-shaped small rear link.

GRADING	100%	95%	90%	80%	60%	40%	20%

⚙ ***Senior New Model*** - .177 or .22 cal., TL, SP, SS, 416/330 FPS, Bakelite grips, blue finish, adj. rear sight, no safety, 8.5 in overall, 33 oz. 1935-64.

courtesy Bruce Gordon

Judged to be the best of the pre-WWII Webley air pistols. Over the thirty-year production span of this model, there were at least fourteen variations, different finishes, barrels, etc. Consult Bruce (2001) for details.

◆**Senior New Model Pre-WWII** - plain exterior of barrel ahead of rear sight - a few 1939 guns had knurled barrels, slim trigger, grips w/o Webley name.

	N/A	$475	$345	$234	$165	$115	N/A

Add 30% for original nickel plating. Add 5% for unmarked rear breech cap. Add 30% for extra long target barrel.

◆**Senior New Model Post-WWII** - cross knurling on barrel, thick trigger, Webley name on grips.

	N/A	$275	$225	$175	$125	$65	N/A

Add 30% for original nickel plating. Add 5% for unmarked rear breech cap. Add 30% for extra long target barrel.

STINGER - BB/.175 cal., slide action dual-cocking, SP, 220 FPS, forty-five-shot internal mag.,smoothbore, fixed sights with integral scope rail, black finish. Mfg. 2001-05.

	$60	$45	$35	$30	N/A	N/A	N/A

TEMPEST - .177 or .22 cal., TL, SP, SS, 420/330 FPS, plastic grips with RH thumb rest, adj. rear sight, aluminum grip frame cast around steel body tube, compact version of Hurricane, RH manual safety, 6.87 in. button rifled barrel, black epoxy finish, 9.2 in. OAL, 32 oz.

Tempest bodies were produced by grinding off the rear section of Hurricane castings. Bruce (2001) refers to the Tempest as "the most charismatic of all Webley air pistols." (Webley offered "Beeman Accessories," such as special grips, for the Tempest and Hurricane in their factory leaflets in England and other world markets.)

⚙ ***Tempest Variant 1*** - forearm marked "TEMPEST". Mfg. 1979-1981.

	N/A	$195	$175	$125	$85	N/A	N/A

Add 5% for simulated wood grips (not sold in USA). Add 10% for Beeman wood grips. Add 15% for finger groove Beeman "combat" wood grips. Add 20% for Beeman factory markings with San Rafael address (rare). Add 20% for large factory box 11.6 x 8.6 inches, black with logo. Add 10% for medium factory box 10.2 x 6.6 inches, black with logo.

⚙ ***Tempest Variant 2*** - forearm marked "WEBLEY TEMPEST", Beeman versions of this variation marked with Beeman name and address and "TEMPEST". Mfg. 1981-2005.

	N/A	$195	$175	$125	$85	N/A	N/A

Add 5% for simulated wood grips. (not sold in USA) Add 10% for Beeman wood grips. Add 15% for finger groove Beeman "combat" wood grips. Add 20% for Beeman factory markings with San Rafael address (rare). Add 10% for Beeman factory markings with Santa Rosa address. Add 20% for large factory box, 11.6 x 8.6 inches, black with logo. Add 10% for medium factory box, 10.2 x 6.6 inches, black with logo.

TYPHOON - .177 or .22 cal., TL, SP, SS, similar to Hurricane, except intended for youth and persons with smaller hands, 360/280 FPS, plastic grips, adj. rear sight, 11.2 in. OAL, 37.5 oz. Approx. 14,214 mfg.1987-1992.

courtesy Bruce Gordon

$200	$160	$130	$100	$60	N/A	N/A

Uncommon in USA, not regularly imported. Warning: early versions could fire upon release of safety; guns should be returned to Webley distributor for correction. Corrected guns have a satin chrome finish on the trigger.

GRADING	100%	95%	90%	80%	60%	40%	20%

TYPHOON (NEW 2008) - .177or .22 cal., BBC, SP, SS, 420/330 FPS,synthetic grip frame around steel body tube, 6.87 in. rifled steel BBL, blue finish, 14.5 in. OAL, 3.2 lbs. Mfg. 2008- current.

courtesy Webley

MSR $139	$120	$100	$80	$60	N/A	N/A	N/A

RIFLES

AXSOR - .177 or .22 cal., PCP, bolt action loading, eight-shot rotary magazine, 1000/800 FPS, 19.7 in. barrel, walnut or beech Monte Carlo stock, recoil pad, two-stage adj. trigger, integral scope grooves, 39.5 in. overall, 6 lbs. Mfg. 1998-2000.

courtesy Howard Collection

	$550	$475	$400	$325	$250	N/A	N/A

Last MSR was $625.

Add 10% for walnut stock.

BEARCUB - .177 cal., BBC, SP, SS, 915 FPS, 13 in. barrel, single stage adj. trigger, manual safety, beech stock with PG, cheekpiece, forearm ends at barrel pivot, threaded muzzle weight, PTFE, nylon Spring Tamer spring guide, 37.8 in. OAL, 7.2 lbs. Mfg. for Beeman 1995-1998.

	$255	$215	$175	$135	$100	N/A	N/A

Last MSR was $325.

Muzzle weight threaded for silencer on this model (if silencer/sound moderator is present), transfer to qualified buyer requires $200 federal tax in USA.

CARBINE C1 - .177 or.22 cal., SP, BBC, SS, 830/660 FPS, slim stock with straight wrist, PTFE, "Spring Tamer" nylon spring guide, rubber buttplate, scope grooves, no safety, 38.2 in. OAL, 6.3 lbs. Mfg. 1981-1996.

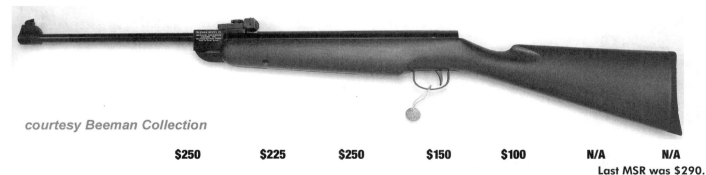

courtesy Beeman Collection

	$250	$225	$250	$150	$100	N/A	N/A

Last MSR was $290.

Subtract 10% for manual safety in later versions.
Designed by Robert Beeman for fast handling in the hunting field. USA serial numbers began at 800,000.

DOMIN8TOR - .177 or .22 cal., BBC, SP, SS 1250/1000 FPS, 17.5 in. barrel, two-stage adj. trigger, integral scope grooves, low-profile sights, checkered wood or TH synthetic Monte Carlo stock with recoil pad, 46.5 in. OAL, 8.2 lbs. Mfg. 2008- current.

MSR $460	$425	$375	$325	$275	$225	N/A	N/A

Add $90 for wood stock.

GRADING	100%	95%	90%	80%	60%	40%	20%

ECLIPSE - .177, .22, or .25 cal., SP, UL, SS, fully opening breech loading hatch allows direct seating of pellet in chamber, 975/710/620 FPS MV, deluxe Monte Carlo stock, cut checkering, rubber buttplate and grip cap w/white line spacers, PTFE, muzzle threaded for Beeman Air Tamer or Webley Silencer, automatic safety, 44 in. OAL, 7.9 lbs. Mfg. 1990-96.

	$350	$300	$250	$200	$150	N/A	N/A

Last MSR was $510.

Add 25% for .25 caliber. Add 10% for Air Tamer (muzzle unit without baffles). Add 10% for Webley Silencer.
Muzzle threaded for silencer on this model (if silencer is present), transfer to qualified buyer requires $200 federal tax in USA.

EXCEL - .177 or .22 cal., BBC, 870/660 FPS, 11.37 (carbine) or 17.5 in. barrel, integral scope grooves, open sights, beech stock, 7 lbs. Disc. 2000.

	$175	$145	$115	$85	$65	N/A	N/A

Last MSR was $215.

FALCON - .177 or .22 cal., SP, BBC, SS, 550/500 FPS, SN hidden by cocking arm when closed, scope ramp welded to body tube, all metal parts, Webley medallion inletted into LHS buttstock, no safety, 41 in. OAL, 6 lbs. Mfg. 1960-70.

	$150	$130	$110	$100	$80	N/A	N/A

Subtract 10% for no medallion.

FX2000 - .177 or .22 cal., PCP, 1000/800 FPS, bolt action loading, eight-shot magazine, 19.7 in. match quality choked barrel, beech or walnut stock, two-stage adj. trigger, integral pressure gauge, 6.6 lbs. New 2000.

courtesy Howard Collection

	$1,054	$825	$750	$550	$450	N/A	N/A

Add 15% for walnut stock.

☉ **FX2000 Field Target** - .22 cal., similar to FX2000, except has Field Target competition black walnut stock with adj. cheekpiece and buttplate, 1000 FPS. Mfg. 2002-04.

	$1,100	$875	$700	$575	$475	N/A	N/A

☉ **FX2000 Hunter SK** - .22 cal., similar to FX2000, except threaded for noise suppressor, two-stage adj. trigger, walnut skeleton stock. New 2000.

	$1,100	$875	$700	$575	$475	N/A	N/A

Add 15% for High-Power model (suppressor requires $200 federal tax in the USA).

HAWK - .177 or .22 cal., BBC, SP, SS, interchangeable barrels, 40-41 in. OAL, approx. 6.5 lbs.

☉ **Hawk Mk I** - angular stock lines, forearm with forward bulge, interchangeable barrels. Mfg. 1971-74.

	$160	$135	$100	$75	$50	N/A	N/A

Add 20% for extra interchangeable barrel.

☉ **Hawk Mk II** - smooth stock lines, interchangeable barrels. Mfg. 1974-77.

courtesy Beeman Collection

	$160	$135	$100	$75	$50	N/A	N/A

Add 20% for extra interchangeable barrel.
Most specimens in USA were diverted by Beeman Company from shipments which failed to reach agents of the Shah of Iran.

☉ **Hawk Mk III** - fixed barrel. Mfg. 1977-79.

	$160	$135	$100	$75	$50	N/A	N/A

GRADING	100%	95%	90%	80%	60%	40%	20%

JAGUAR - .177 or .22 cal., SP, BBC, SS, 500 FPS .177, sheetmetal "tinplate construction," sheetmetal barrel shroud, scope ramp (early with dumb-bell shape, later with parallel sides), early versions with finger grooves on forearm, no safety, 36.25 in. (early), 39 in. (later) OAL, 3.75 lbs. Mfg. 1940s to late 1970s.

courtesy Beeman Collection

	$150	$130	$110	$100	$80	N/A	N/A

Subtract 10% for early versions.
  Some parts interchangeable with Webley Junior and Milbro Diana 22 air rifles.

JAGUAR (2008) - .177 or .22cal., SP, BBC, SS, 1000/800 FPS, rifled steel BBL, adj. TruGlo fibeer optic sights, anti bear-trap cocking safety, OD green molded synthetic stock w/ recoil pad, 44 in. OAL, 7.3 lbs. Mfg. 2008- current..

MSR $167	$150	$130	$110	$100	$80	N/A	N/A

JUNIOR - .177 cal., SP, BBC, SS, smoothbore (early) or rifled brass inner barrel, 405 FPS, sheetmetal barrel shroud, sheetmetal "tin-plate construction," blued, no safety, 36.25 in. OAL, 3.25 lbs. Mfg. late 1940s to late 1960s.

	$150	$130	$110	$100	$80	N/A	N/A

Subtract 10% for smoothbore.
  May have been made by Millard Bros.

LONGBOW/LONGBOW DELUXE - .177 or .22 cal., SP, BBC, SS, 850 FPS, short cylinder and barrel version of Tomahawk, scope grooves, no sights, Venom designed removable adj. trigger system, beech or walnut (Longbow Deluxe) checkered PG Monte Carlo stock with vented recoil pad, blue finish, ported muzzle brake. 39 in. OAL, 7.3 lbs. New 2003.

	$400	$300	$250	$175	$125	N/A	N/A

Add 15% for Longbow Deluxe w/Walnut stock.

LONGBOW (2008) - .177 or .22 cal., SP, BBC, SS, 800/600 FPS, short cylinder and barrel version of Tomahawk, scope grooves, no sights, adj. trigger system, beech checkered PG Monte Carlo stock with vented recoil pad, blue finish, ported muzzle brake. 39 in. OAL, 7.3 lbs. Mfg,.. 2008- current.

courtesy Webley

MSR $399	$365	$325	$275	$225	$175	N/A	N/A

MARK I - .177 or .22 cal., BBC, SP, SS, a small rifle version of the Webley Mark I air pistols, barrel swings forward over compression chamber for cocking, interchangeable barrels, wood half stock, 34 in. OAL, 5.3 lbs. Approx. 1500 mfg. 1926-29.

courtesy Beeman Collection

	N/A	N/A	$800	$550	$300	$200	$100

GRADING	100%	95%	90%	80%	60%	40%	20%

MARK II - .177, .22, or .25 cal., similar to Mark I, except larger, quick change barrels, bolt handle turns to open action and to cam barrel back into airtight connection with air vent, wood half stock, typical size: 43.8 in. OAL, approx. 6.8 lbs.

Important Note: there are many variations of the Webley Mark II rifles, rare versions add to the value. Essential information is available in Atkins, AG April, May, and June 1996.

☼ *Mark II Version 1* - .177 or .22 cal., L-shaped aperture sight, dovetail mounted barrel, leaf spring ahead of receiver which secures the barrel. S serial number prefix. Approx. 1000 mfg. in 1932.

courtesy Beeman Collection

	N/A	N/A	$795	$695	$495	$295	$195

Add 10% for extra .177 or .22 cal. barrel. Add 100% for original factory box with inserts. Add 150% for fitted factory case.

☼ *Mark II Version 2* - .177 or .22 cal., L-shaped aperture sight, side mounted push button for quick release of interchangeable barrels, S serial number prefix. Approx. 1000 guns mfg. early 1933-34, approx. 2000 total of version one and two mfg. circa 1935-38.

	N/A	N/A	$695	$495	$295	$195	$95

Add 10% for extra .177 or .22 cal. barrel. Add 20% for extra .25 cal. barrel (as added after 1937). Add 100% for original factory box with inserts. Add 150% for fitted factory case.

After 1937 Mark II Version 3 .25 cal. barrels were added to some Mark II Version 2 sets.

☼ *Mark II Version 3* - .177, .22, or .25 cal., U-shaped folding aperture sight mounted in center of receiver frame, push button barrel release, S serial number prefix from S2001 forward. Approx. 13,700 mfg. 1934 -1945 (sales ceased during WWII).

courtesy Beeman Collection

	N/A	N/A	$550	$350	$250	$150	$50

Add 10% for extra .177 or .22 cal. barrel. Add 20% for .25 caliber (The Webley "Rook and Rabbit Rifle", only mfg. 1937 and later). Add 100% for original factory box with inserts. Add 150% for fitted factory case.

MARK III SERIES - .177 or .22 cal., UL, SP, SS, tap loader. 42.25 to 43.5 in OAL, 6.8 lbs. Mfg. 1947-1975.

Many British airgun enthusiasts consider the Mark III as one of the finest air rifles ever produced. Became less complex and detailed as it evolved. Made in great numbers and great variety, this guide can only introduce this model. Fortunately, the basic variations generally can be identified by serial number. Additional info is available in the literature, esp. Hiller (1985).

☼ *Mark III Series I* - SN 1-2500. Standard: straight grooving in forearm, ribbed butt. Deluxe: hand checkered stock, ribbed buttplate. Mfg. 1947-49.

	$450	$375	$300	$225	$175	$125	$75

Add 50% for Mark III Series I Deluxe.

☼ *Mark III Series II* - SN 2501-6000. Mfg. 1949-1957.

	$360	$300	$240	$180	$145	$120	$95

☼ *Mark III Series III* - SN 6001-42857. Mfg. 1957-1961.

	$330	$275	$220	$165	$135	$110	$85

☼ *Mark III Series IV* - SN 42858-46289. Mfg. 1961-64.

	$300	$250	$200	$150	$125	$100	$80

☼ *Mark III Late Model Series* - SN 46290 on. Mfg. 1964-1975.

	$300	$250	$200	$150	$125	$100	$80

MARK III SUPERTARGET (MODEL 2) - .177 or .22 cal., UL, SP, SS, tap loader, similar to Mark III, except fitted with Parker Hale micrometer aperture sight, stamped "SUPERTARGET" on receiver (body tube, air chamber), 9.4 lbs. Mfg. 1963-1975.

	$500	$450	$400	$275	$175	$100	$50

NIMBUS - .177 cal., BBC, SP, SS. 570 FPS. Beech stock with contoured comb, plastic buttplate, pressed steel trigger guard. Adj. sights, scope grooves. Push-button manual safety. Junior size, economy level air rifle, imported from China. Intro. 2004.

As this edition went to press, retail pricing had yet to be established.

OMEGA - .177 or .22 cal., SP, BBC, SS, PTFE and O-ring piston seal, 830/675 FPS, scope grooves, auto/manual safety, 42 in. OAL, 7.8 lbs. Mfg. 1989-92.

	$225	$200	$175	$150	$125	N/A	N/A

Last MSR was $430.

Add 20% for Beeman marking.

GRADING	100%	95%	90%	80%	60%	40%	20%

OSPREY - .177 or .22 cal., SL, SP, SS, tap loader, manual safety, 43 in. OAL, 7.3 lbs. Mfg. 1975-1990s.

	$150	$125	$100	$75	$50	$35	N/A

Add 20% for Supertarget version with semi-match style stock, heavier.

PATRIOT - .177, .22 or .25 cal., BBC, 1170/920/820 FPS, 17.5 in. barrel, two-stage adj. trigger, integral scope grooves, low-profile sights, walnut Monte Carlo stock with hand-checkered grip, recoil pad, 9 lbs.

	$566	$515	$465	$385	$285	N/A	N/A

Add 15% for Venom Edition with black walnut stock and gold plated trigger guard.

PATRIOT (2008) - .177, .22 or .25 cal., BBC, SP, SS, 1170/920/820 FPS, 17.5 in. barrel, two-stage adj. trigger, integral scope grooves, low-profile sights, walnut Monte Carlo stock with hand-checkered grip, recoil pad, 46.5 in. OAL, 9.6 lbs. Mfg. 2008- current.

MSR $450	$425	$385	$285	$225	$175	N/A	N/A

RAIDER - .177 or .22 cal., PCP, 1000/800 FPS, BA, SS or two-shot magazine (.22 cal. only), Venom Custom designed beech or walnut stock, 7 lbs. New 2000.

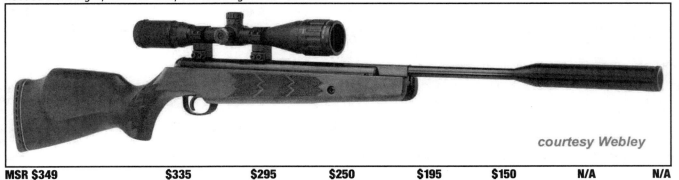

courtesy Webley

	$495	$425	$350	$275	$195	N/A	N/A

Add 15% for walnut stock. Add 10% for two-shot version.

RANGER - .177 cal., SP, BBC, SS, rifled or smoothbore steel barrel, scope ramp (late versions), full length stock, no safety, blued, 38.25 in. OAL, 3.5 lbs. Mfg.1950-1970.

	$450	$400	$350	$300	$250	$225	$200

Add 10% for no code or scope ramp.

Variations: four minor changes indicated with code letter stamped LHS barrel: no code = early, A, B, C. Ranger (grip lever cocking). Ranger name also used as a Webley private label version of Erma ELG10 grip lever Winchester-carbine-style pellet rifle: see Erma section.

SPECTRE - .22 cal., PCP, BA, eight-shot rotary magazine indexed and cocked by RHS cocking lever, neoprene pads inletted into grip and forearm, pressure gauge in synthetic stock, two-stage adj. trigger, free floating barrel, 36.2 in. OAL, 5.5 lbs. Mfg. 2004.

	$900	$725	$575	$475	N/A	N/A	N/A

Joint design with Axelsson of Sweden.

STINGRAY (2008) - .177 or .22 cal., BBC, SP, SS, 800/600 FPS, two-stage trigger, beech oMonte Carlo-style stock, adj. rear sight, hooded front sight, 41.1 in. OAL, 7.3 lbs. Mfg. 2008- current.

courtesy Webley

MSR $349	$335	$295	$250	$195	$150	N/A	N/A

STINGRAY RIFLE - .177 or .22 cal., BBC, 870/660 FPS, two-stage trigger, beech or walnut (Deluxe) Monte Carlo-style stock, adj. rear sight, hooded front sight, 44 in. overall. New 2001.

	$360	$295	$250	$195	$150	N/A	N/A

Add 15% for checkered walnut stock (Deluxe).

✪ *Stingray KS (Carbine)* - .177 or .22 cal., similar to Stingray Rifle, except 38 in. overall. New 2001.

	$295	$255	$210	$170	$130	N/A	N/A

Add 15% for checkered walnut stock (Deluxe).

GRADING	100%	95%	90%	80%	60%	40%	20%

SPORT - .22 in. cal., BBC, SP, SS. 490 FPS. Beech stock, plastic buttplate and trigger guard. adj. sights, scope grooves. No safety. Junior size, economy level air rifle, imported from England. New 2004.

	$235	$210	$180	$145	$105	N/A	N/A

Last MSR was $235.

TOMAHAWK - .177 or .22 cal., BBC, 845/622 FPS, 15 in. barrel with Venon designed ported barrel brake, two-stage adj. trigger, automatic safety, beech or walnut (deluxe) stock with dual cheekpiece, 7.5 lbs. New 2001.

	$463	$405	$325	$260	$215	N/A	N/A

Add 15% for checkered walnut stock (Deluxe).

TRACKER/CARBINE - .177 or .22 cal., SL 750/600 FPS, 11.37 (carbine) or 17.5 in. barrel with removable muzzle weight, single-stage "hunter" adj. trigger, integral scope grooves, Black Nighthunter, Camo Fieldshooter, or beech Monte Carlo stock with recoil pad, optional stocks, 7.2-7.4 lbs. Disc. 2000.

	$240	$195	$165	$125	$85	N/A	N/A

Last MSR was $300.

Add 5% for .22 cal. model. Add 15% for Black Nighthunter or Camo Fieldshooter stocks.

VENOM VIPER - .177, .20 or .22 cal., PCP, similar to Raider, except 6.2 lbs. New 2001.

	$784	$675	$550	$485	$405	N/A	N/A

Add 15% for walnut stock.

VICTOR - .177 or .22 cal., SP, BBC, SS, 720/580 FPS, PTFE and O-ring piston seal, no safety, 40.1 in. OAL, 7 lbs. Mfg. 1981.

	$150	$130	$120	$100	$80	$60	$50

Junior version of Vulcan II.

VISCOUNT/VISCOUNT DELUXE - .177 or .22 cal., SP, SL, SS, tap-loading, 830/650 FPS, PTFE and O-ring piston seal, Italian beech or European walnut (Viscount Deluxe) Monte Carlo full stock, black plastic PG cap, rubber buttplate with white line spacer, manual safety. 43.5-43.8 in. OAL, 7.6-7.7 lbs. Mfg. 1982.

	$300	$250	$200	$175	$150	$130	$110

Add 75% for Viscount Deluxe.

Viscount Deluxe included oil-finished European walnut stock with hand checkering, sling swivels, and vent. rubber buttplate. Intro. Aug. 1982.

VULCAN I - .177 or .22 cal., SP, BBC, SS, 810/630 FPS, PTFE and O-ring piston seal, PG beech stock with angular forearm, shallow cheekpiece, black rubber buttplate, adj. trigger (to 3 lbs.) with constant sear engagement, manual safety, 40.8 in. OAL, 7.1 lbs. Mfg. 1979-81.

	$125	$110	$90	$80	$60	N/A	N/A

Introduced "Webley Power Intensification System" PTFE and O-ring piston seal.

⚙ *Vulcan I Deluxe* - similar to Vulcan I, except .177 cal. only, special walnut stock, hand checkered forearm and PG, soft rubber buttplate with white line spacer, gold plated trigger and manual safety. 43.8 in OAL, 7.65 lbs. Mfg. 1980-81.

	$350	$295	$225	N/A	N/A	N/A	N/A

VULCAN II - .177 or .22 cal., SP, BBC, SS, 830/650 FPS, PTFE and O-ring piston seal, PG beech stock with rounded forearm and plastic grip cap, shallow cheekpiece, ventilated rubber buttpad with white line spacer, adj. trigger (to 3 lbs.) with constant sear engagement, manual safety, 43.6 in. OAL, 7.65 lbs. Mfg.1981-84.

	$175	$150	$125	$100	$75	$N/A	N/A

⚙ *Vulcan II Deluxe* - similar to Vulcan II, except special walnut stock, hand cut checkering, sling swivels. Optional: Special Sporter or Tyrolean stocks of select French Walnut, oil finished. 43.8 in OAL, 7.85 lbs. 1981-84.

	$295	$250	$195	N/A	N/A	N/A	N/A

Add 75% for Special Sporter or Tyrolean stocks of select French Walnut, oil finished.

VULCAN III - .177, .22, or .25 (carbine) cal., BBC, 870/660/620 FPS, 11.37 (carbine) or 17.5 in. barrel with threaded muzzle-brake, single-stage "hunter" adj. trigger, integral scope grooves, open sights, beech Monte Carlo stock with recoil pad, 7.6 lbs. Mfg. 1984-2000.

	$225	$195	$165	$125	$95	N/A	N/A

Last MSR was $300.

Add 10% for .25 cal. model. Add 5% for Carbine version in .177 and .22 cal. Add 10% for noise suppressor (requires $200 federal tax in the USA).

⚙ *Vulcan III Deluxe* - similar to Vulcan III, except has special walnut stock with hand cut checkering and sling swivels.

	$280	$230	$180	N/A	N/A	N/A	N/A

XOCET RIFLE - .177, or .22 cal., SP, BBC, 870/660 FPS, beech Monte Carlo stock, adj. rear sight, hooded front sight, 39 in. overall. New 2001.

	$290	$250	$195	$160	$130	N/A	N/A

XOCET CARBINE - .177, or .22, cal., similar to Xocet Rifle, except 36 in. overall. New 2001.

	$290	$250	$195	$160	$130	N/A	N/A

TOMAHAWK (2008) - .177 or .22 cal., BBC, 1000/800 FPS, 15 in. barrel ported barrel brake, two-stage adj. trigger, automatic safety, walnut (deluxe) stock with dual cheekpiece, 43.5 in. OAL, 7.2 lbs. Mfg. 2008- current.

MSR $399	$365	$325	$275	$225	$175	N/A	N/A

WEIHRAUCH SPORT

Current manufacturer located in Mellrichstadt, Germany. Formerly known as Hans-Hermann Weihrauch. Currently imported and distributed by Beeman Precision Airguns, located in Huntington Beach, CA, and by Pyramyd Air, located in Pepper Pike, OH. Dealer sales.

The authors and publisher wish to thank Mr. Ulrich Eichstädt for the following information in this edition of the *Blue* Book of Airguns.

The world-wide success of Weihrauch airguns is still based on the motto which the company has used for over a century: "Quality - Made in Germany." International gun expert John Walter noted that "Weihrauch is rightly regarded as one of the last bastions of traditional airgunsmithing." It is interesting and instructive to compare the details of their airgun design and quality with any other sporting airguns.

Note that guns stamped with an "F" in a pentagon are low velocity versions intended for the German and other markets with strict power limits. Without that mark the guns generally are designed for the English market with its 12 ft./lb. limit for air rifles and 6 ft./lb. limit for air pistols.

Beeman/Weihrauch guns: For those special models and versions of Beeman brand airguns made by Weihrauch, see the Beeman Precision Airguns section of this book.

For more information and current pricing on Weihrauch firearms, please refer to the *Blue Book of Gun Values* by S.P. Fjestad (also available online).

HISTORY 1899-1970

The Hermann Weihrauch company was founded in 1899 in Zella-Mehlis, the same small German town where several other famous gun manufacturers such as Walther, Sauer & Sohn, and Anschütz also began. Hermann Weihrauch, Sr. was well-known for making excellent hunting rifles. His three sons, Otto, Werner, and Hermann, Jr., soon joined the family-based company. Several new models were introduced after WWI, including the HWZ 21 smallbore rifle (HWZ stands for Hermann Weihrauch, Zella-Mehlis). This was the first mass-produced German .22 rimfire rifle and soon developed an excellent match record. Double and triple barrel shotguns, over and under shotguns, and large bore hunting rifles rounded out the line and established an excellent reputation for quality.

In 1928, Weihrauch began a large international sale of bicycle parts and mechanical door closers. During WWII, Weihrauch was the only German factory to continue production of spare parts for bicycles. At the end of the war, Zella-Mehlis became part of the Soviet occupation zone. In 1948, the Weihrauchs were forced out of their homes and factories by the communist government.

Otto Weihrauch became a mechanic and later a gunsmith in Zella-Mehlis. Werner went to work at the Jagdwaffenwerk (Hunting Weapon Factory) in nearby Suhl. Hermann Weihrauch, Jr. moved to the little German village of Mellrichstadt in Bavaria. There, with the help of his long-time hunting club friends and former customers, and his son Hans, he started the Weihrauch business all over again in the barracks of a pre-war laundry. Spare parts for bicycles were their first and main products.

When German companies were again allowed to manufacture airguns in the early 1950s, Weihrauch made the their first air rifle, the HW Model 50V. This airgun had to have a smooth bore because the Allied Occupation Government would not allow rifled barrels. Finally, after the German Shooting Federation ("Deutscher Schützenbund") was re-established, the allied government allowed the production of rifled barrels. However, because they were not allowed to produce firearms, they put their efforts into making the finest sporting airguns in the world. Even after the firearm manufacturing ban finally was withdrawn, the Hermann Weihrauch KG company continued to produce sporting air rifles of the highest quality. The little HW 25 was slanted towards the youth market while versions of the HW 30 and HW 50 continued as solid mid-market air rifles. The HW 55 was one of Europe´s leading barrel-cocking target rifles. The rather uncommon HW 55T version with its ornate Tyrolean-style stock, usually sporting fine walnut of exceptional grain, has always been a favorite among offhand shooters and collectors. The big HW 35 sporting air rifle was their main and most successful model.

After Hermann Weihrauch, Jr. died in 1967, a new era in the company began under the leadership of Hans Weihrauch, Sr. (born in 1926 and the father of today´s directors Stefan and Hans-Hermann.) The company celebrated 1970 with the introduction of the HW 70 air pistol.

The company had begun plans, and first production, of a repeating air pistol before WWII, but the war aborted its regular production. Although pre-war HWZ sales literature shows an illustration of that thirty-shot top-lever spring piston air pistol, only one specimen of that HWZ LP-1 air pistol is now known. It had survived both the war and the Russian occupation by having safely gone overseas as a sales sample to the Hy-Score Arms Company in the USA. The Hy-Score president, Steve Laszlo, had given it to his friend, Dr. Robert Beeman. Dr. Beeman surprised Hans, Sr. and Christel Weihrauch, the husband/wife directors of the new HW company, when they were visiting the Beeman home, in San Anselmo, CA, by showing them this Weihrauch airgun which was completely unknown to them!

HISTORY 1970-1990

The close connection between the owners of the Weihrauch company and Beeman Precision Airguns led to one of the first (if not the first) joint ventures between a German-based manufacturer and an American airgun distributor. After a period of importing Weihrauch-designed airguns, the Beemans had decided that they needed to introduce a German-made air rifle with American styling and features. They had determined that their main need, in addition to new styling, was a power level above anything that had been known before in the airgun field. They had been very impressed with the quality of the HW 35, but puzzled by its power, which was lower than that of the Feinwerkbau Model 124. That gun, for which Beeman had developed a large market in the U.S., had a lighter spring and smaller compression chamber.

Based on their computer simulation studies, the Beemans proposed a new air rifle model with the quality of the HW 35. This cooperative development program resulted in the Beeman R1 (sold outside of the USA as the Weihrauch HW 80 in a lower power version with a more European-style stock). The new model quickly became the best-selling adult sporting air rifle; it is credited with bringing the American airgun market into the world of adult airguns. Ironically, due to delivery problems with the longer, more complex R1 stock, the first HW 80 rifles were available some weeks earlier than the R1. This led to the incorrect conclusion made by some that the R1 was a copy of the HW80. Tom Gaylord also has written about that coincidence in his book The Beeman R1 and pointed out that clearly Dr. Beeman was the main force behind the invention of the R1/HW80 and that Weihrauch did an outstanding job of production engineering and manufacture.

Almost the same thing happened with the introduction of the next Weihrauch air pistol, the very successful Beeman P1 (sold outside of the USA as the Weihrauch HW 45). Although the Beemans provided the full specifications and design features of this pistol, there was an initial misunderstanding about the external appearance. The factory presented a rather bulky, high top, "Desert Eagle-like" design which the Beemans did not think would appeal to the American market. They felt that it should follow the very popular and trim lines of the Colt 1911 automatic pistol. So the Beeman Company quickly made a plaster-of-paris, life-sized 3D model which the Weihrauch technicians used as a model for the final design. Ironically, the Weihrauch engineers were far ahead of their time in a different way because of another misunderstanding: they thought that, because the Beeman plans were blank in the powerplant area, that Beeman had suggested a single-stroke pneumatic air system instead of the desired, more powerful spring-piston action. These pneumatic models came some years later, when the Beeman P2/Weihrauch HW 75 was introduced. The huge commercial success of the P1 design was aided by its many features: high power, accuracy, solid metal construction, three caliber choices, different choices of finish, and especially its great flexibility: the ability to fire at two

GRADING	100%	95%	90%	80%	60%	40%	20%

power levels, integral scope rail, and the availability of a Beeman-designed shoulder stock.

The R1/HW80, and its several variations, gave rise to a lighter, easier to cock model: the R10/HW85. Weihrauch then produced an under-lever spring piston rifle, the HW77. This gun opened fully for loading directly into the breech of the barrel, like a Feinwerkbau match rifle. This was a great improvement over barrel-cocking air rifles which utilized a loading tap from which the pellet had to leap into the barrel. The HW77 and HW77 Carbine, with their rigid barrel and easy cocking and loading, became extremely popular in countries where their lower power was under the legal limit. However, these models had very disappointing sales in the USA, where shooters still preferred the R1/HW80 and R10/HW85 barrel-cockers, by a margin of over 20 to 1, due to their higher power.

The field-style air rifle designs for the American market were a great success because only a very small minority of adult airgun shooters were involved in any competition or group shooting activities. Field target shooting was the most popular of the American group airgun shooting sports, but even that involved much less than one percent of adult airgun shooters. Almost the exact opposite was true of airgun shooters in Germany; there, most such shooters were involved in 10 meter competition. Nevertheless, in 1989, the leading German gun magazine, VISIER, discovered from a survey that a large number of German airgun shooters would be willing to pay more than 500 DM (about 300 U.S. dollars) for an air rifle which was equipped with a sporting-style stock and designed for scope use. Many Germans responding to the poll also submitted useful suggestions for new designs to be added to the many new stock designs being developed by Weihrauch.

The reunification of Germany in 1990 resulted in many changes for every German citizen and manufacturer. Weihrauch began a cooperation with Theoben Engineering in England which resulted in the introduction of the first German/English air rifle design: the Weihrauch HW 90 (the Beeman versions are the RX and RX-1). This was the first Weihrauch rifle using the patented Theoben gas-spring system (sometimes inappropriately called "gas ram"). These new rifles sold very well in Great Britain where field target shooting had originated in the early 1980s and also were well received there and in the USA for small game hunting.

The great optimism of that period of the company´s development was dampened by the unexpected death of Hans Weihrauch, Sr. on April 3, 1990 at the age of only 63. His business accomplishments were so admired that he was posthumously decorated with the Federal Cross of Merit. His wife, Christel, and sons, Stefan and Hans-Hermann, took the reins of the company. Fortunately, Christel Weihrauch had shared the management of the firm for decades and the preparation of the two sons for their expected future management roles was well advanced. Both had been involved with the company all of their lives and had nearly finished their engineering and marketing training as well. Director-to-be Hans-Hermann had even spent several months as an apprentice executive in the Beeman Precision Airguns business in America and had polished his English language skills by living with Robert and Toshiko Beeman in their California home during that time.

The fall of the German wall right by their little village of Mellrichstadt suddenly placed them "in the middle of Germany." This opened new markets for their surface engineering branch. They added new machines for electroless nickel plating and bronzing (and made the floors slip-proof with expanded mesh, stainless-steel fencing panels supplied from the nearby fallen "Iron Curtain!").

PISTOLS

MODEL HWZ - LP 1 - .177 lead balls, thirty-shot repeater, TL, SP, walnut single-piece grip, front sight acts as BB magazine retainer, blue finish. Extremely rare. Mfg. 1939.

courtesy Beeman Collection

Rarity precludes accurate pricing.
Weihrauch's first airgun, production was halted by WW II.

MODEL HW 40 PCA - .177 cal, CO₂, SS, styled like semi-auto firearm, 410 FPS, adj. rear sight.

MSR N/A	$155	$130	$110	$90	$60	N/A	N/A

MODEL HW 45 LP - .177, .20, or .22 cal, SP, 600/500 FPS, adj. rear sight, blue or matte nickel finish. Developed from Beeman P1.

MSR N/A	$340	$290	$230	$195	$150	N/A	N/A

Add 10% for matte nickel finish. Add 50% for shoulder stock.

MODEL HW 70 - .177 cal., BBC, SP, SS, 410 FPS, 2.25 lbs.

	$155	$130	$110	$90	$60	N/A	N/A

Last MSR was $170.

Add 30% for chrome.

GRADING	100%	95%	90%	80%	60%	40%	20%

○ **Model HW 70-A** - similar to HW 70, except has improved rear sight suitable for scope mount, improved trigger and safety.

courtesy Beeman Collection

MSR N/A	$185	$160	$140	$115	$90	N/A	N/A

Add 10% for stylized black grip and silver finish. Add 10% for early versions without safety.

○ **Model HW 70 LP** - .177 cal., BBC, 440 FPS, 2.25 lbs.

MSR N/A	$185	$160	$140	$115	$90	N/A	N/A

MODEL HW 75 M - .177 cal, SSP, 435 FPS, adj. rear sight, manual safety, walnut target grips.

MSR N/A	$440	$390	$340	$290	$240	N/A	N/A

RIFLES

MODEL HW 25 L - .177 cal., BBC, SP, 590 FPS.

courtesy Beeman Collection

MSR N/A	$185	$155	$125	$95	$75	N/A	N/A

MODEL HW 30 - .177 or .20 cal., BBC, SP, 660/600 FPS, 17 in. barrel, 5.3 lbs.

courtesy Beeman Collection

MSR N/A	$175	$150	$120	$90	$70	N/A	N/A

Add 10% for .20 cal.

○ **Model HW 30 M/II** - .177 or .22 cal., BBC, SP, 660/450 FPS, match trigger, automatic safety, 17 in. barrel, 5.3 lbs.

MSR N/A	$210	$180	$145	$120	$90	N/A	N/A

Add 15% for Monte Carlo cheekpiece. Add 20% for Beeman factory markings.

○ **Model HW 30 S** - .177 or .22 cal., BBC, SP, 660/450 FPS, Rekord match trigger, 17 in. barrel, tunnel front sight.

courtesy Beeman Collection

MSR N/A	$220	$190	$155	$125	$95	N/A	N/A

Add 15% for Monte Carlo cheekpiece. Add 20% for Beeman factory markings.

GRADING	100%	95%	90%	80%	60%	40%	20%

MODEL HW 35 - .177 or .22 cal., BBC, SP, 790/600 FPS, Rekord match trigger, walnut, beech or stained beech Safari stock, matte blue finish barrel and receiver.

courtesy Beeman Collection

	100%	95%	90%	80%	60%	40%	20%
MSRN/A	$370	$325	$260	$230	$200	N/A	N/A

Add 10% for Safari Model with safari finish stock. Add 25% for walnut stock. Add 20% for thumbhole stock. Add 15% for Safari Model - matte blue, safari finish stock. Add 20% for Beeman factory markings.

☼ **Model HW 35 EB** - .177 or .22 cal., BBC, SP, walnut stock with special cheekpiece, checkered pistol grip with white spacer under grip cap, rubber buttplate, 755/660 FPS, 20 in. barrel, 8 lbs. Disc. 1985.

			90%	80%	60%		
	$350	$305	$250	$210	$175	N/A	N/A

Last MSR was $450.

Add 20% for chrome. Add 5% for .22 cal. Subtract 10% for 35L. Add 20% for Beeman factory markings.

MODEL HW 50 - .177 or .22 cal., BBC, SP, 705 FPS, 17 in. barrel, 6 lbs. 9 oz.

MSR N/A	$255	$215	$185	$150	$90	N/A	N/A

Add 40% for Beeman factory markings with up-grade stock, and rubber buttplate.

☼ **Model HW 50 M/II** - .177 or .22 cal., BBC, SP, 850/620 FPS, 17 in. barrel, 6.6 lbs.

courtesy Beeman Collection

MSR N/A	$280	$225	$175	$135	$105	N/A	N/A

Add 10% for HW50S with Rekord trigger. Add 20% for Beeman factory markings.

MODEL HW 50V - .177 cal., smoothbore, BBC, SP, SS, beech stock with rounded grip end, grooves across butt, cast trigger guard, knurled and threaded rear end cap, marked "H.W.50" with image of soaring bird over that marking, no safety, 42.1 in. OAL, 5.6 lbs. Mfg. early 1950s

courtesy Beeman Collection

	N/A	N/A	$750	$650	$500	$350	$200

Weihrauch's first airgun, smoothbore because the Allied Occupation Government would not allow German civilians to own rifled guns after WWII.

HW BARAKUDA EL 54 - .22 cal., BBC, SP, SS, power augmented by diesel ignition of ether vapors from ether-injection tube affixed to right side of main body tube, 19.7 in. barrel, approx. 600-700 FPS without ether; much higher with ether, early versions with steel trigger guard and simple steel trigger system, later versions with cast aluminum trigger guards and Rekord trigger system, 8.4 lbs. Mfg. 1954-81.

courtesy Beeman Collection

	N/A	N/A	$750	$650	$500	$350	$200

Add 25% for Beeman markings. (Factory stamped with RDB for Robert David Beeman serial number - value N/A.) Add 30% for high gloss factory chrome plating. Subtract 20% for Standard Model with beech stock. Ether injection attachment only = $295.

Only a few hundred were made under cooperation of Weihrauch Company and Barakuda Company in Hamburg, Germany. Twenty specially made for Beeman Precision Airguns in 1981 from last remaining parts.

GRADING	100%	95%	90%	80%	60%	40%	20%

Caution: Specimens are not authentic unless factory stamped "BARAKUDA". Air rifles with ether-injection tubes, but marked HW 35, or with other model numbers, are fakes; compromised specimens of other models. Handle ether with care.

MODEL 55 - .177 cal., BBC, SP, 660-700 FPS, 7.5 lbs.

courtesy Beeman Collection

	100%	95%	90%	80%	60%	40%	20%
	$440	$375	$295	$225	$175	N/A	N/A

Last MSR was $610.

Add 10% for left-hand variation. Add 20% for Match (squarish forearm with lower line equal to bottom of trigger guard). Add 30% for Tyrolean stock. Add 10% for Beeman factory markings.

☼ *Model HW 55 SM* - .177 cal., BBC, SP, 590 FPS, adj. match target rear sight, hooded front sight, match trigger.

MSR N/A	$460	$390	$315	$235	$185	N/A	N/A

MODEL HW 57 - .177 and .22 cals., UL, SP, beech stock, rubber buttplate, Rekord trigger, 14.2 in. (360 mm) barrel, 820/570 FPS MV, 7 lbs. (3.8 kg). (An economy version of the HW97 with a pop-up loading tap.)

MSR N/A	$295	$245	$195	$150	$115	N/A	N/A

MODEL 77/77 CARBINE - .177, .20, or .22 cal., UL, SP, 830/710 FPS, 8.6 lbs.

courtesy Beeman Collection

MSR N/A	$385	$330	$250	$175	$125	N/A	N/A

Add 10% for left-hand version. Add 10% for deluxe version. Add 10% for .20 cal. Add 25% for Tyrolean stock.

MODEL HW 80 - .177, .20, .22, and .25 cals., BBC, SP, SS, barrel length 19.7 in. (500 mm) (16.1 in., 410 mm for Carbine), 965-570 FPS, Rekord trigger, beech stock does not cover barrel pivot, checkered pistol grip, rubber buttplate. 8.8 lbs. (4.0 kg).

MSR N/A	$395	$350	$295	$245	$175	N/A	N/A

Add 5% for .20 cal. Add 15% for .25 cal.

MODEL HW 85 - similar to Model HW 80 except 7.7 lbs (3.5 kg) and plain stock.

	$250	$215	$170	$135	$90	N/A	N/A

Add 5% for .20 cal. Add 20% for .25 cal. in USA. Add 15% for Deluxe Model with fine checkered pistol grip with cap and white spacers.

MODEL HW 90 - .177, .20, .22, or .25 cal., Theoben gas spring system, 1120/790 FPS.

MSR N/A	$545	$460	$370	$300	$250	N/A	N/A

Add 15% for .20 and .25 cal. models.

MODEL HW 97 - .177, .20, .22, and .25 cals., UL, SP, 930 FPS in .177; 9 lbs (4.1 kg), laminated stock, designed for scope use only. Replaced by HW 97K in 2001.

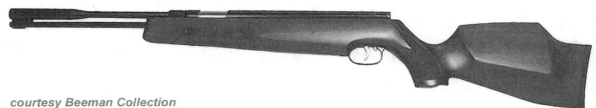

courtesy Beeman Collection

	$465	$395	$310	$250	$195	N/A	N/A

Add 10% for .20 cal. Add 20% for .25 cal. in USA.

GRADING	100%	95%	90%	80%	60%	40%	20%

◎ **Model HW 97 K** - .177, .20, .22, and .25 cals. UL, SP, designed for field target and silhouette. 930 FPS in .177 cal., brown laminated stock, 9 lbs. (4.1 kg.).

MSR N/A	$465	$395	$310	$250	$195	N/A	N/A

Add 5% for .20 cal. Add 20% for .25 cal. in USA. Add 10% for blue laminated stock in USA. Add 15% for green laminated stock in USA. Add 25% for HW Centennial model, marked "100 Jahre Weihrauch" (Germany) or "100 years Weihrauch" (UK version) in USA.

MODEL HW 98 - .177 cal., BBC, SP, 930 FPS, automatic safety, Field Target Competition model with adj. cheekpiece, buttplate.

MSR N/A	$530	$450	$360	$295	$225	N/A	N/A

MODEL HW 100 - .22 cal., PCP, side lever action, fourteen-shot rotary mag., 16.25 in. BBL, no sights, blue finish, two stage adj. trigger, walnut thumbhole target stock with stippled grip, 38.6 in. OAL, 8.6 lbs. New 2004.

MSR N/A	$950	$775	$695	$595	N/A	N/A	N/A

MODEL HWB CHAMP - .177 cal., BBC, SP, 590 FPS, adj. match target rear sight, hooded front sight, youth model.

MSR N/A	$460	$395	$310	$250	$195	N/A	N/A

MODEL HW 95 - .177, .20, .22, and .25 cals., BBC, SP, SS, barrel length 19.7 in. (500 mm) (16.1 in., 410 mm for Carbine), 965-570 FPS, beech stock, checkered pistol grip, rubber buttplate. 7.8 lbs. New 2005.

MSR N/A	$315	$265	$225	$195	$145	N/A	N/A

Add 5% for .20 cal. Add 15% for .25 cal.

WELLS

Previous airgun designer located in Palo Alto, CA.

William Wells may be one of the greatest airgun innovators of the twentieth century. Born in 1872, he apparently started designing and producing experimental airguns in the 1930s. He became a design consultant to Daisy in 1947. He also produced many dozens of designs, mostly repeating pneumatic rifles, but his work also included air pistols and spring piston airguns. These designs are represented by actual working specimens. Identification may not be easy; the interested reader must refer to Hannusch´s paper, cited below. Many are marked "Cde P" on the base of the grip. The base of the stock usually is marked with his favorite .180 caliber (true BB shot), but several other calibers are known, including .187. Many models were produced in the election year 1952 and are marked with a small elephant emblem engraved with the 52 date. Many of Wells´ designs are incorporated into Daisy and other brand airguns. William Wells died in October 1968, still very alert at the age of 96. It is not possible to assign values to the wide variety of Wells´ experimental airguns, but collectors should be on the lookout for his products. Ref: Larry Hannusch, 1999, *Airgun Revue 4*.

courtesy Beeman Collection

WESTERN AUTO

Catalog sales/retailer that has subcontracted various manufacturers to private label airguns.

To date, there has been very little interest in collecting Western Auto airguns, regardless of rarity. Rather than list Western Auto models, a general guideline is that values generally are under those of their "first generation relatives." As a result, prices are ascertained by the shooting value of the airgun, rather than its collector value. See "Store Brand Crossover List" located in the back of this text.

WESTINGER & ALTENBURGER

For information on Westinger & Altenburger, see Feinwerkbau in the "F" section.

WESTLEY RICHARDS & CO. LTD.

Current manufacturer located in Birmingham, England, and previously located in London, England.

Westley Richards previously manufactured the "Highest Possible" air pistols circa 1907 to late 1920s. Airgun production was quite limited; the highest known airgun serial number is 1052. For more information and current pricing on Westley Richards firearms, please refer to the *Blue Book of Gun Values* by S.P. Fjestad (also available online).

PISTOLS

TOP BARREL MODEL - .177 cal., BBC, SP, SS, rifled 9.7 in. barrel on top of compression tube/body tube, marked (WESTLEY RICHARDS "HIGHEST POSSIBLE" AIR PISTOL) on tube, piston moves rearward during firing, horn or bakelite grips, blue or nickel finished, 11.9 in. OAL, 3.1 lbs., patented 1907, marketed Dec. 1909 to late 1914.

GRADING	100%	95%	90%	80%	60%	40%	20%

⊙ **Top Barrel Model First Variant** - some with heart-shaped opening in frame behind trigger, with smooth horn grip plates.

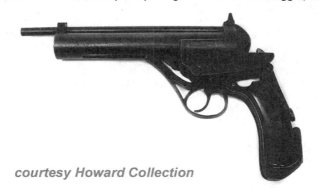

courtesy Howard Collection

		N/A	N/A	$1,300	$1,000	$750	$500	$350

Add 25% fornickel finish. Add 15% for barrel over 10 inches.

⊙ **Top Barrel Model Second Variant** - vertically curved rear sight screwed to frame, frame behind trigger closed, checkered hard rubber grip plates.

courtesy Howard Collection

		N/A	N/A	$1,000	$750	$600	$450	$300

Add 10% for horn grips (transitional Model). Add 25% nickel finish.

CONCENTRIC PISTON MODEL - .177 cal. BBC, SP, SS, piston concentric around central rifled 7.2 in. BBL, piston moves rearward during firing, 9.4 in.OAL, 2.3 lbs, patented 1921, marketed in 1924.

courtesy Beeman Collection

		N/A	N/A	$2,000	$1,650	$1,050	$750	$400

Designed by Edwin Anson. Blued (two known in nickel). The length of the sleeve ("shoe") covering the rear of the body tube varies. Ref: AG:Dec.1998, May 1999, Dec. 2004.

WHISCOMBE

Current manufacturer of Whiscombe Opposed Piston Air Rifles. Situated at 'Runways,' Stoney Lane, Ashmore Green, Thatcham, Berkshire, RG18 9HG, England. Direct sales.

High-end, spring-piston rifles with twin pistons opposing each other rather than moving in opposite directions as in Giss patent airguns manufactured by Dianawerk where one piston is a dummy. The opposing action eliminates almost all recoil and intensifies power. Each piston has a pair of springs, the total of four springs gives up to 650 lbs. loading.

The authors and publisher wish to thank Tim Saunders for his valuable assistance with the following information in this edition of the *Blue Book of Airguns*.

GRADING	100%	95%	90%	80%	60%	40%	20%

RIFLES

MODELS JW50-JW80 - .177, .20, .22 or .25 cal., field target and hunting air rifles with high recoilless power without resorting to precharged gases or pumping. The model numbers, ranging from JW50 to JW80, indicate the piston stroke in millimeters. Smaller stroke guns usually are cocked by two stokes of an underlever. Larger stroke guns (70/80 mm) use three strokes. The large JW80 version, which requires a FAC license in Britain, produces up to 28 ft./lb. ME in .22 caliber and 30 ft/lb. ME in .25 caliber, blued or silverized steel finish, sporter or thumbhole stocks, action design, and standard or match trigger. 15 in. polygonal rifled barrel. About 450 rifles produced, most stocked for field target. Estimated about 2/3 sold into USA. Sporting stock versions about 9.8 lbs; thumbhole versions about 10.5 lbs. All guns hand built by John Whiscombe. Mfg. 1987 to present.

MSR $2,200-$2,600	$2,000	$1,800	$1,600	$1,250	N/A	N/A	N/A

Add 10% for extra barrel.

Many upgrades and extras available. Please contact the company directly for more information and prices of their products (see Trademark Index listing).

WILKINS, JOE

Previous custom maker of the Predator PCP repeating air rifle located in England.

Sometimes incorrectly referred to as the Ripley Predator. However, Ripley Rifles, the small firm which produced the Ripley AR-5 rifle, is owned by Steve Wilkens, Joe's son. The Wilkens Predator was discontinued to a large degree because slide action guns are considered politically incorrect in Britain and the maker did not want to stimulate the Home Office into further control of airguns.

RIFLES

PREDATOR - .22 cal.,PCP, Field Target rifle, fifteen- or sixteen-shot repeater, slide action loads and cocks with a single rapid stroke, power regulator, most set at 12 ft./lb., one at 18 ft./lb., and one at 26 ft./lb. 20 mfg. 1987-1999.

courtesy Tim Saunders

	$2,000	$1,750	$1,500	$750	$500	N/A	N/A

One was made in .177 cal.

WILL

Previous tradename of Oskar Will of Zella-Mehlis, Thüringen, Germany, established in 1844.

His son, Oskar Will The Younger, was one of the most famous airgun makers in Germany before 1914. Circa 1923, the company was sold to Wilhelm Foss who operated it as Venuswaffenfabrik until 1945. Especially famous for air rifles, with large diameter central compression chambers, which used the extended trigger guard as a cocking lever("Bügelspanners") . These guns carried on the tradition of the large receiver gallery airguns made in the USA in the mid-1800s. Such trigger guard lever guns (Bügelspanners) continued to be listed in European gun wholesaler catalogs into the 1960s. (See American Gallery Airguns section in the "A" section.) Actual old specimens of Will and Original Will airguns currently retail in the $500-$750 range, while newer copies, marked "Original", or without markings, retail in the $250-$400. Crank style air rifles (Kürbelspanners) from the Wills usually retail in the $650-$1,250 range. Crank style pistols retail in the $1,500-$3,500.

courtesy Beeman Collection

GRADING	100%	95%	90%	80%	60%	40%	20%

WINCHESTER

Current manufacturer located in New Haven, CT.

Beginning 2001, airguns under the Winchester label were imported again; this time from Spain. Sales and service are through Daisy Outdoor Products, located in Rogers, AR.

Between 1969 and 1975 Winchester imported eight rifle models and two pistol models into the United States from Meyer & Grammelspacher located in Germany. A total of 19,259 airguns were imported through 1973. See Dianawerk in the "D" section for a table of Winchester airguns made by M&G in Germany.

For more information and current pricing on both new and used Winchester firearms, please refer to the *Blue Book of Gun Values* by S.P. Fjestad (also available online).

PISTOLS

MODEL 353 - .177 or .22 cal., BBC, SP, SS, 7 in. rifled steel barrel, 378 FPS, blue finish, composition plastic stock, hooded bead front and adj. rear sights, 2.75 lbs.

100%	95%	90%	80%	60%	40%	20%
N/A	$300	$250	$200	$150	N/A	N/A

1974 retail was $42.

MODEL 363 - .177 cal., BBC, SP, SS, 7 in. rifled steel barrel, 378 FPS, double piston recoilless design, micrometer rear and interchangeable front sights, fully adj. trigger, match grade composition plastic stock with thumb rest, 16 in. overall, 3 lbs.

100%	95%	90%	80%	60%	40%	20%
N/A	$300	$250	$200	$150	N/A	N/A

1974 RP was $64.

RIFLES

MODEL 333 - .177 cal., BBC, SP, SS, 576 FPS, diopter target sight, fully adj. trigger, double piston recoilless action, checkered and stippled walnut stock, 9.5 lbs.

100%	95%	90%	80%	60%	40%	20%
N/A	$600	$425	$300	$150	N/A	N/A

MODEL 416 - .177 cal., BBC, SP, SS, smooth bore barrel, blue finish, double pull-type trigger, wood stock, 363 FPS, fixed front and adj. rear sights, 33 in. overall, 2.75 lbs.

100%	95%	90%	80%	60%	40%	20%
$50	$40	$30	$20	$15	N/A	N/A

1974 RP was $21.

MODEL 422 - .177 cal., BBC, SP, SS, rifled barrel, blue finish, wood stock, double pull-type trigger, 480 FPS, fixed front and adj. rear sights, 36 in. overall, 3.75 lbs.

100%	95%	90%	80%	60%	40%	20%
$65	$50	$40	$30	$20	N/A	N/A

1974 retail price was $30.

MODEL 423 - .177 cal., similar to Model 422, except fixed ramp front and adj. rear sights, 36 in. overall, 4 lbs.

100%	95%	90%	80%	60%	40%	20%
$85	$65	$50	$40	$30	N/A	N/A

1974 retail price was $37.

MODEL 425 - .22 cal., similar to Model 423, except with 543 FPS, adj. double-pull type trigger, dovetail base for scope, non-slip composition buttplate, 38 in. overall, 5 lbs.

courtesy Beeman Collection

100%	95%	90%	80%	60%	40%	20%
$125	$85	$70	$55	$40	N/A	N/A

1974 retail price was $42.

MODEL 427 - .22 cal., similar to Model 425, except with 660 FPS, micrometer rear and hooded front sight, 42 in. OAL, 6 lbs.

100%	95%	90%	80%	60%	40%	20%
$195	$150	$125	$100	$75	N/A	N/A

1974 retail price was $48.

MODEL 435 - .177 cal. similar to Model 427, except with 693 FPS, micrometer rear and interchangeable front sight, checkered stock and adj. trigger, 44 in. OAL, 6.5 lbs.

100%	95%	90%	80%	60%	40%	20%
$225	$195	$150	$125	$100	N/A	N/A

1974 retail price was $70.

GRADING	100%	95%	90%	80%	60%	40%	20%

MODEL 450 - .177 cal., UL, SP, SS, rifled steel barrel, blue finish, 693 FPS, micrometer rear and interchangeable front sight, dovetail base for scope, checkered Schutzen style stock, rubber buttplate, 44.5 in. OAL, 7.75 lbs.

	100%	95%	90%	80%	60%	40%	20%
	$350	$300	$250	$200	$150	N/A	N/A

1974 retail price was $100.

MODEL 500X - .177 cal., BBC, SP, SS, 490 FPS, rifled steel barrel, micro-adj. rear sight, hooded front sight with blade and ramp, grooved receiver, sporter-style select walnut stock, 5.7 lbs. Mfg. in Turkey. New 2003.

MSR $147	$120	$95	$70	$60	N/A	N/A	N/A

Add 40% for Model 500XS with 4x32 Winchester scope new 2004.

MODEL 600X - .177 cal., BBC, SP, SS, 600 FPS, rifled steel barrel, micro-adj. rear sight, hooded front sight with blade and ramp, grooved receiver, sporter-style select walnut stock, 5.9 lbs.Mfg. in Turkey. Mfg. 2001-06.

	$85	$75	$60	$50	$40	N/A	N/A

Last MSR was $90.

Add 30% for Model 600XS with 4x32 Winchester scope new 2004.

MODEL 722X - .22 cal., BBC, SP, SS, 700 FPS, rifled steel barrel, micro-adj. rear sight, hooded front sight with blade and ramp, grooved receiver, rear safety button, sporter-style select walnut stock, 6.6 lbs. Mfg. in Turkey 2001-03.

	$115	$95	$75	$60	$50	N/A	N/A

Last MSR was $170.

MODEL 800X - .177 cal., BBC, SP, SS, 800 FPS, rifled steel barrel, micro-adj. rear sight, hooded front sight with blade and ramp, grooved receiver, rear safety button, sporter-style select walnut stock, 6.6 lbs. Mfg. in Turkey. New 2001.

MSR $165	$135	$105	$95	$75	$50	N/A	N/A

Add 20% for Model 800XS with 4x32 Winchester scope new 2004.

MODEL 1000X - .177 cal., BBC, SP, SS, 1000 FPS, rifled steel barrel, micro-adj. rear sight, hooded front sight with blade and ramp, grooved receiver, rear safety button, sporter-style select walnut stock, 6.6 lbs. New 2001.

MSR $229	$195	$165	$115	$95	$75	N/A	N/A

Add 15% for Model 1000XS with 3-9x32 Winchester scope new 2004.

MODEL 1000B - .177 cal., BBC, SP, SS, 1000 FPS, rifled steel barrel, micro-adj. rear sight, hooded front sight with blade and ramp, grooved receiver, rear safety button, black sporter-style composite, recoil pad, 44.5 in. OAL, 6.6 lbs. New 2004.

MSR $185	$155	$135	$100	$85	$65	N/A	N/A

Add 15% for Model 1000SB with 3-9x32 Winchester scope (new 2004).

MODEL 1000C - .177 cal., BBC, SP, SS, 1000 FPS, rifled steel barrel, micro-adj. rear sight, hooded front sight with blade and ramp, grooved receiver, rear safety button, camo sporter-style composite stock, recoil pad, 44.5 in. OAL, 6.6 lbs. Mfg. 2004-2007.

	$140	$125	$95	$85	$70	N/A	N/A

Last MSR was $150.

Add 15% for Model 1000SC with 3-9x32 Winchester scope (new 2004).

MODEL 1894 - BB/.174 cal., lever action, SP, 300 FPS, fifteen-shot mag., smooth bore steel barrel, micro-adj. rear sight, blade and ramp front sight, crossbolt trigger safety, western-style wood stock and forearm, 3.4 lbs. Imported from Turkey. New 2003.

MSR $100	$95	$85	$65	$50	$35	N/A	N/A

WINSEL

Previously manufactured by Winsel Corporation of Rochester, NY.

PISTOLS

JET PISTOL - .22 cal., CO_2, SS, breech loading, brass barrel, button safety behind trigger, cocked and breech opened by pushing lever at bottom of grip, black plastic grips, aluminum frame, 12 in. overall, with cylinder attached, black crinkle paint finish on receiver and rear of barrel housing, glossy black elsewhere. Supplied with two CO_2 cylinders, one in a slim cardboard "mailing box" for returning cylinders to factory for refill, 2.3 lbs. Mfg. 1948.

courtesy Beeman Collection

	100%	95%	90%	80%	60%	40%	20%
	N/A	$1,350	$1,050	$750	$600	$400	$200

Add 30% for original maroon factory box and papers. Subtract 20% for each missing cylinder.
Most specimens are without one or both cylinders because the manufacturer went out of business while holding many customers' cylinders. They were destroyed.

GRADING	100%	95%	90%	80%	60%	40%	20%

WISCHO

For information on Wischo air guns, see B.S.F. in the "B" section.

WRIGHT MFG. CO.

Previous Manufacturer located in Burbank, CA.

PISTOLS

WRIGHT TARGET SHOT JR. - .177 cal., SP, SS, rear plunger pulls out to cock, 2.5 in. smoothbore barrel unscrews for rear loading of pellet, shot, or dart. Diecast body includes checkered grip panels. 8.1 in. OAL, 1.0 lbs.

	N/A	N/A	$45	$40	$35	$30	$25

WYANDOTTE

Previous tradename of American Tool Works located in Chicago, IL.

For information on Wuandotte, see American Tool Works in the "A" section.

NOTES

Y-Z SECTION

YEWHA

Previous tradename of airguns manufactured in South Korea.

Yewha (Ye-Wha), reported to have been made by Tong-Il Industrial Co. Ltd. of Seoul, South Korea, but that may be only a trading company. Yewha may be the name of the maker. Distributed in United States by Beeman Precision Airguns in 1970s. These airguns apparently made only in 1970s. Due to anti-firearm laws in Korea, whole gun clubs may be equipped with these guns; club pictures show huge piles of ringneck pheasant taken with the B3 Dynamite airgun. Ref: AGNR - Oct. 1987, www.beemans.net (see also the "A Shot of Humor" section in this book and on the www.beemans.net website).

GRADING	100%	95%	90%	80%	60%	40%	20%

RIFLES/SHOTGUN

3-B OR B3 DYNAMITE - .25 cal., pump pneumatic (pump-rod-at-the-muzzle), SS, 28.7 in. smoothbore barrel, breech loaded with plastic cartridge loaded with birdshot or single lead balls, parkerized finish, hardwood stock, twenty or more pumps can produce up to 1000 FPS, 41.3 in. OAL, 5.75 lbs.

courtesy Beeman Collection

N/A	$500	$450	$350	$300	$200	$100

REVOLVING RIFLE - .177 cal., DA, similar to B3 Dynamite, except has six-shot revolving cylinder for pellets, exposed hammer, rifled barrel, parkerized finish.

courtesy Beeman Collection

N/A	$1,000	$900	$700	$600	$400	$200

TARGET RIFLE - PUMP ROD MODEL - similar to revolving rifle, except SS.

courtesy Beeman Collection

N/A	$900	$800	$550	$400	$250	$150

TARGET 200 - .177 cal., SL, SP, recoilless match target air rifle.

N/A	$350	$300	$250	$150	$75	$50

An unauthorized copy of the Feinwerkbau Model 300 of much lower quality and reliability.

ZENITH

Previous trademark manufactured by Nick Murphy of Sileby, Loughborough, England from about 2001 to 2003.

Nick Murphy developed and produced top level Field Target air rifles. All are .177 caliber Walther or Career barrels. All barrels are sleeved and free floating. Most stocks are made by custom stock maker Paul Wilson. All are built with special Zenith regulators. Ripley and Zenith air rifles were among the outstanding field target guns in German and English FT competition during 2003 and 2004. These were produced with a wide variety of features and finishes. Production stopped at a total of sixteen rifles. The most recent sale was for $3,100.

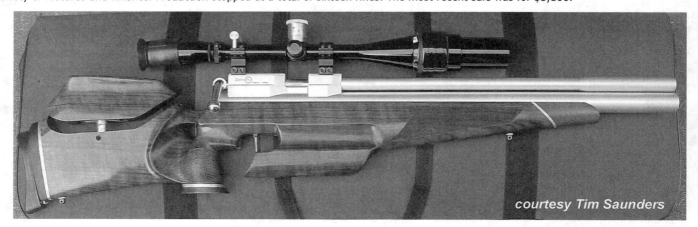

courtesy Tim Saunders

TRADEMARK INDEX

The listings below represent the most up-to-date information we have regarding airgun manufacturers (both domestic and international), trademarks, importers, and distributors (when applicable) to assist you in obtaining additional information from these sources. Even more so than last year, you will note the addition of website and email listings whenever possible—this may be your best way of obtaining up-to-date model and pricing information directly from the manufacturers, importers, and/or distributors. More and more companies are offering online information about their products and it pays to surf the net!

As this edition goes to press, we feel confident that the information listed below is the most up-to-date and accurate listing possible. Remember, things change every day in this industry, and a phone/fax number that is current today could have a new area code or be gone tomorrow. International fax/phone numbers may require additional overseas and country/city coding. If you should require additional assistance in "tracking" any of the current airgun manufacturers, distributors, or importers listed in this publication, please contact us and we will try to help you regarding these specific requests.

10-RING-SERVICE, INC.

1737 Birdsong Rd.
Thomaston, GA 30286
Phone: 706-647-5941

AERON CZ s.r.o.

Importer - see Top Gun Air Guns Inc.
Factory - Aeron CZ s.r.o.
Svitavske Nab. 27
602 00 Brno
Czech Republic
Phone/Fax: 420 (5) 4557-3080
Website: www.aeron.cz
Email: info@aeron.cz

AIR ARMS

Importer - see Pyramyd Air, Inc.
Importer - see Pomona Air Guns
Importer - see Top Gun Air Guns Inc.
Factory - Air Arms
Hailsham Industrial Park
Diplocks Way, Hailsham
E. Sussex, BN27 7TN, ENGLAND
Phone: 01323 845853
Fax: 01323 440573
Website: www.air-arms.co.uk
Email: sales@air-arms.co.uk

AIR GUN INC.

9320 Harwin Dr. #201
Houston TX 77036
Phone: 713-780-2415
Fax: 713-780-4831
Email: agi2001a@hotmail.com

AIRFORCE AIRGUNS

4841 Freeman Dr., P.O.B. 2478
Ft. Worth, TX 76113
Phone: 817-451-8966
Fax: 817-451-1613
Website: www.airforceairguns.com
Email: staff@airforceairguns.com

AIRGUN EXPRESS, INC.

26800 Fargo Ave., Unit #L
Cleveland, OH 44146
Phone: 216-896-0893
Fax: 216-896-0896
Website: www.pyramydair.com
Email: sales@pyramydair.com

AIRGUNS OF ARIZONA

26 N Gilbert Rd.
Gilbert, AZ 85234
Phone: 480-461-1113
Fax: 480-461-3928
Website: www.airgunsofarizona.com
Email: mail@airgunsofarizona.com

AIRHOG

3600 Osuna Rd. N.E. Ste. 406
Albuquerque, NM 87109
Fax: 505-341-3164
Website: www.airhog.com
Email: sales@airhog.com

AIR RIFLE SPECIALISTS

P.O. Box 138
Pine City, NY 14871
Phone: 607-734-7340
Fax: 607-733-3261
Email: gusto@stny.rr.com

AIRROW

See Swivel Machine Works.

ALFA PROJ

Importer - see Top Gun Air Guns Inc.
Factory - ALFA Proj
Sumavska 416/15
602 00 Brno
Czech Republic
Phone/Fax: 420 (5) 45 120-667
Website: www.alfa-proj.cz
Email: info@alfa-proj.cz

ANICS CORP.

Importer – see European American Armory Corp.
Importer - see Compasseco Inc.
Factory - Anics Corp.
7 Vorontsovo Pole St.
Moscow, 105062, RUSSIA
Phone: 7095-917-7405
Fax: 7095-917-1766
Website: www.anics.com
Email: anics@anics.com

ANSCHÜTZ

Importer - see Champions Shooter's Supply
Importer - see Gunsmithing Inc.
Warranty Repair/Gunsmithing Services - see 10-Ring-Service, Inc.
Factory - ANSCHÜTZ, J.G. GmbH & Co. KG
Daimlerstrasse 12
D-89079 Ulm, GERMANY
Fax: 011-49-731-401-2700
Website: www.anschuetz-sporters.com
Email: JGA-Info@anschuetz-sport.com

ARMSCOR (ARMS CORPORATION OF THE PHILIPPINES)

Factory - Arms Corp. of the Philippines
Armscor Ave., Bgy Fortune
Marikina City, PHILIPPINES 1800
Phone: 632-941-6243
Fax: 632-942-0682
Website: www.armscor.com.ph
Email: armscor@info.com.ph

BSA GUNS (UK) LTD.

Importer - see Precision Airgun Distribution
Factory - BSA
Armoury Rd., Small Heath
Birmingham, W. Mids, B11 2PP, ENGLAND
Phone: 0121-772-8543
Fax: 0121-7730845
Website: http://www.bsaguns.co.uk
Email: sales@bsaguns.com

BAIKAL

Importer – see European American Armory Corp.
Importer - see Compasseco Inc.
Importer - see Pyramyd Air, Inc.
Factory - Baikal
Izhevsky Mekhanichesky Zavod
8, Promyshlennaya str.
Izhevsk, 426063 RUSSIA
Fax: 011-95-007-341-276-765830
Website: www.baikalinc.ru
Email: worldlinks@baikalinc.ru

BAM (BEST AIRGUN MANUFACTURER IN CHINA)

Importer - see Xisico USA, Inc.
Factory - BAM
37 ZhongNan Road
WuXi, JiangSu Province, China 214024
Phone: 0510-5404803 or 5403117
Fax: 0510-5401258
Email: BAM@china-bam.com

BARNES, GARY

P.O. Box 138
New Windsor, MD 21776
Website: www.glbarnes.com
Email: mail@glbarnes.com

BEC INC. (BEC EUROLUX AIRGUNS)

1227 West Valley Blvd.
Alhambra,CA 91802
Phone: 626-281-5751
Fax: 626-281-2960
Email: becline@yahoo.com

BEEMAN PRECISION AIRGUNS

Division of S/R Industries (Maryland Corp.)
5454 Argosy Dr.
Huntington Beach, CA 92649-1039
Phone: 714-890-4800
Phone: 800-227-2744 (orders only)
Fax: 714-890-4808
Website: www.beeman.com

BENJAMIN AIR RIFLE COMPANY

See Crosman Corp.

BENELLI

Importer - see Larry's Guns Inc.
Factory - Benelli Armi S.p.A
Via della Stazione, 50
61029 Urbino (PU) ITALY
Fax: 011-39-722-30-7207-307227
Website: www.benelli.it

BERETTA, PIETRO

Importer - see Umarex USA
Factory - Fabbrica d'Armi Pietro Beretta S.p.A
Via Pietro Beretta 18
25063 Gardone Val Trompia
Brescia, ITALY
Phone: 011-39-30-8341-1
Fax: 011-39-30-8341-421
Website: www.beretta.it

BRENZOVICH FIREARMS & TRAINING CENTER

22301 Texas Hwy. 20
Ft. Hancock, TX 79839
Phone: 877-585-3775
Fax: 877-585-3775
Website: www.brenzovich.com

BROCOCK

Previous Importer - see Airguns Of Arizona
Factory
Unit 32 Heming Road
Washford Industrial Estate
Redditch, Worcestershire
England B98 0DH
Phone: 44-152-7527800
Fax: 44-152-7527850
Website: www.brocock.co.uk
Email: sales@brocock.co.uk

C Z (CESKA ZBROJOVKA)

Administration Offices - Ceska Zbrojovka
Svatopluka Cecha 1283
CZ-68827 Uhersky Brod
CZECH REPUBLIC
Fax: 011-420-572-655 012
Website: www.czub.cz
Email: info@czub.cz

CHAMPIONS CHOICE, INC.

201 International Blvd.
LaVergne, TN 37086
Phone: (Orders Only) 800-345-7179
Phone: 615-793-4066
Fax: 615-793-4070
Website: www.champchoice.com
Email: champchoice@nashville.com

CHAMPIONS SHOOTER'S SUPPLY

P.O. Box 303
New Albany, OH 43054
Phone: 800-821-4867
Fax: 614-855-1209
Website: www.championshooters.com
Email: sales@ShootersCatalog.com

COLT'S MANUFACTURING CO., INC.

Importer - see Umarex USA
P.O. Box 1868
Hartford, CT 06144-1868
Phone: 800-962-COLT
Fax: 860-244-1449
Website: www.colt.com

COMPASSECO, INC.

151 Atkinson Hill
Bardstown, KY 40004
Phone: 800-726-1696
Fax: 502-349-9596
Website: www.compasseco.com
Email: staff@compasseco.com

CROSMAN CORP.

7629 Routes 5 & 20
East Bloomfield, NY 14443
Phone: 800-7-AIRGUN
Fax: 716-657-5405
Website: www.crosman.com
Email: info@crosman.com

DAISY OUTDOOR PRODUCTS

400 W. Stribling Dr.
P.O. Box 220
Rogers, AR 72757-0220
Phone: 479-636-1200
Fax: 479-636-1601
Website: www.daisy.com
Email: info@daisy.com
Daisy repair - Jim & Ann Coplen
P.O. Box 7297
Rochester, MN 55903
Phone: 507-281-2314

DAYSTATE LTD

Importer - see Daystate America/Precision Airgun Dist.
Factory
Birch House Lane
Cotes, NR. Stone
Staffordshire ST15 0QQ UNITED KINGDOM
Phone: 44-1782-791755
Fax: 44-1782-791617
Website: www.daystate.co.uk
Email: admin@daystate.co.uk

DIANAWERK, GmbH & Co. KG MAYER & GRAMMELSPACHER

Importer - see Umarex USA
Importer - see Dynamit Nobel - RWS
Repair/Gunsmithing Services - see 10-Ring-Service, Inc.
Factory Dianawerk, Gmbh & Co. KG Mayer & Grammelspacher
Postfach 1452
D-76404 Rastatt GERMANY
Phone: 49-7222-7620
Fax: 49-7222-762-78
Website: www.diana-airguns.de
Email: info@diana-airguns.de

DYNAMIT NOBEL-RWS INC.

A division of RUAG Ammotec USA Inc.
81 Ruckman Road
Closter, NJ 07624
Phone: 201-767-1995
Fax: 201-767-1589
Website: www.dnrws.com
Factory - Dynamit Nobel RWS
Postfach 12 61
Troisdorf D-53839 GERMANY
Email: RWS@dynamit-nobel.com

EURO IMPORTS

2221 Upland Ave. South
Phrump, NV 89048
Phone/Fax: 775-751-6671
Email: mrbrno@yahoo.com

EUROPEAN AMERICAN ARMORY CORP.

P.O. Box 560746
Rockledge, FL 32956
Phone: 321-639-4842
Fax: 321-639-7006
Website: www.eaacorp.com
Email: eaacorp@eaacorp.com

EXCELLENT AIRGUNS OF MINNESOTA

2979 Edgerton Street
St. Paul, MN 55117
Phone: 651-481-8631

FX AIRGUNS AB

Importer - see Airguns of Arizona
Factory - FX Airguns AB
Fagerlid 548 92 Hova
Sweden
Website: www.fxairguns.com
Email: info@fxairguns.com

FALCON

Importer - see Airhog.
Factory - Falcon Pneumatic Systems Limited
Unit 20, The Gateway Estate
Birmingham B26-3QD ENGLAND
Phone: 011-121-782-2808
Fax: 011-121-782-2886
Website: www.falcon-airguns.com
Email: sales@falcon-airguns.co.uk

FEINWERKBAU WESTINGER & ALTENBURGER GMBH

Importer - see Beeman Precision Airguns
Importer - see Brenzovich Firearms & Training Center
Repair/Gunsmithing Services - see 10-Ring-Service, Inc.
Factory - Westinger & Altenburger GmbH
Neckarstrasse 43
D-78727 Oberndorf/Neckar GERMANY
Fax: 011-49-7423/814-200
Website: www.feinwerkbau.de
Email: info@feinwerkbau.de

GAMO USA CORP.

3911 S.W. 47th Avenue, Suite 914
Ft. Lauderdale, FL 33314
Phone: 954-581-5822
Fax: 954-581-3165
Website: www.gamousa.com
Email: info@gamousa.com

GUN POWER STEALTH

See Air Force Airgun.

GUNSMITHING, INC.

30 West Buchanan St.
Colorado Springs, CO 80907
Phone: 800-284-8671
Fax: 719-632-3493
Website: www.nealjguns.com
Email: neal@nealjguns.com

HAENEL

Importer - see Pilkington Competition Equipment LLC

HÄMMERLI AG

Importer - see Umarex USA
Importer - see Brenzovich Firarms & Training Center
Importer – see Larry's Guns Inc.
Importer - see Wade Anderson
Warranty Repair/Gunsmithing Services - see 10-Ring-Service, Inc.
Factory - Hämmerli AG
Industrielplatz
CH-8212 Neuhausen, SWITZERLAND
Fax: 011-41-52-674-6418
Website: www.haemmerli.ch
Email: info@haemmerli.ch

HATSAN ARMS COMPANY.

Izmir - Ankara Karayolu 28. km. No.289
Kemalpasa 35170 Izmir - TURKEY
Phone: 90-232 878 9100
Fax: 90-232 878 9102 - 878 9723
Website: www.hatrsan.com.tr
Email: info@hatrsan.com.tr

IAR, INC.

33171 Camino Capistrano
San Juan Capistrano, CA 92675
Phone: 877-722-1873
Fax: 949-443-3647
Website: www.iar-arms.com
Email: sales@iar-arms.com

INDUSTRY BRAND

Importer - see Compasseco
Importer - see Air Gun Inc.
Factory - Industry Brand
Shanghai Air Gun Factory
625 Yaoha Rd.
Pudong Shanghai CHINA 200126
Phone: 0086-021-68630290 58743300
Fax: 0086-021-58837175 68582880
Website: www.airrifle-china.com
Email: shairg@public.sta.net.cn

LARRY'S GUNS INC.

56 West Gray Rd.
Gray, ME 04039
Phone: 207-657-4559
Fax: 207-657-3429
Website: www.larrysguns.com
Email: info@larrysguns.com

LOGUN

Importer - see Straight Shooters Precision Airguns
Importer - Pyramyd Air, Inc.
Factory Logun
Universe House
Key Industrial Park
Willenhall, West Midlands UK WV13 3YA
Phone: 44 1902 722144
Fax: 44 1902 722880
Website: www.logun.com
Email: sales@airgunsport.com

MAC1 AIRGUN

13974 Van Ness Ave.
Gardena, CA 90249
Phone: 310-327-3581
Fax: 310-327-0238
Website: www.mac1airgun.com

MAGNUM RESEARCH, INC.

Importer - see Umarex USA
7110 University Ave. N.E.
Minneapolis, MN 55432
Phone: 763-574-1868
Fax: 763-574-0109
Website: www.magnumresearch.com

MARKSMAN PRODUCTS

5482 Argosy Drive
Huntington Beach, CA 92649
Phone: 714-898-7535
Fax: 714-891-0782
Website: www.marksman.com
Email: sales@marksman.com

MATCHGUNS srl

Via Cartiera 6/d
43010 Vigatto
Parma, ITALY
Phone: 011-39-0521-632020
Fax: 011-39-0521-631973

MAUSER

No current U.S. importation.
Factory - Mauser Jagdwaffen GmbH
Zeigelstadel 1
D-88316 Isny, GERMANY
Fax: 011-4190-368-4750794
Website: www.mauserwaffen.de
Email: info@mauserwaffen.de

MENDOZA S.A. de C.V.

Importer - see Crosman Corp.
Importer - see Compasseco, Inc.
Factory - Mendoza S.A. de C.V.
Prolongacion Constitucion No. 57
Xochimilco, 16210, Mexico, D.F.
Phone: 5255 1084-1122
Fax: 5255 1084-1155
Website: www.pmendoza.com.mx
Email: pmendoza@mail.internet.com.mx

MORINI

Importer - see Champion's Choice
Importer – see Pilkington Competition Equipment LLC
Factory - Morini Competition Arm SA
Via AiGelsi II
CH-6930 Bedano SWITZERLAND
Fax: 011-41-91-9-35-2231
Website: www.morini.ch
Email: morini@morini.ch

NORICA-FARMI S.L.A.

Avda. Otaola, 16
Eibar, Guipuzcoa, SPAIN 26000
Fax: 011-34-943-207-449
Website: www.norica.es
Email: farmi@norica.es

PALMER CHEMICAL & EQUIPMENT CO., INC.

P.O. Box 867
Palmer Village
Douglasville, GA 30133
Phone: 928-717-2315
Fax: 928-717-2198

PARDINI, ARMI S.r.l.

Importer - see Larry's Guns Inc.
Factory - Armi Pardini S.r.l.
154/A Via Italica
I-55043 Lido di Camaiore, ITALY
Fax: 011-39-584-90122
Website: www.pardini.it
Email: info@pardini.it

PARK RIFLE COMPANY

Unit 68A, Dartford Trade Park
Powder Mill Lane
Dartford, Kent
ENGLAND DA1 1NX

PILKINGTON COMPETITION EQUIPMENT LLC

P.O. Box 97
#2 Little Tree's Ramble
Monteagle, TN 37356
Phone: 931-924-3400
Fax: 931-924-3489
Website: www.pilkguns.com
Email: info@pilkguns.com

PIPER PRECISION PRODUCTS

Box 95
Lamposa, TX 76550

PNEUDART, INC.

1 West 3rd St. Ste. 212
Williamsport, PA 17701
Website: www.pneudart.com

POMONA AIR GUNS

15555 Main Street Ste. D-4 #496
Hysperia, CA 92345
Phone: 760-244-8271
Website: www.pomona-airguns.com

PRECISION AIRGUN DISTRIBUTION

22 N. Gilbert Rd.
Gilbert, AZ 85234
Phone: 480-539-4750
Fax: 480-461-3928

PRECISION SALES INTERNATIONAL, INC.

14 Coleman Ave.
P.O. Box 1776
Westfield, MA 01086
Phone: 413-562-5055
Fax: 413-562-5056
Website: www.precision-sales.com
Email: info@precision-sales.com

PYRAMYD AIR, INC.

26800 Fargo Ave., Unit #L
Cleveland, OH 44146
Phone: 216-896-0893
Fax: 216-896-0896
Website: www.pyramydair.com
Email: sales@pyramydair.com

QUACKENBUSH AIR GUNS

2203 Hwy. AC
Urbana, MO 65767
Phone: 417-993-5262
Website: http://ns.connext.net/~daq/

RWS PRECISION PRODUCTS

Importer - see Umarex USA
Importer - see Dynamit Nobel-RWS

RÖHM GmbH

Importer - see Airguns of Arizona
Factory - Röhm GmbH
Postfach 1161
Sontheim/Benz GERMANY d-89565
Phone: 49-073-25-160
Fax: 49-073-25-16-492
Website: www.roehm.rg.de
Email: inforg@roehm.rg.de

RUTTEN HERSTAL

Importer – see Compasseco
Factory - Rutten Herstal
Parc Industriel des Hauts-Sarts
Premiere Avenue, 7-9
B-4040 Herstal, BELGIUM
Fax: 011-32-41/648589

Ron Sauls

P.O. Box 5772
Anderson, SC 29623
Phone: 864-261-6810
Website: www.bryanandac.com
Email: bryanandac@aol.com

Email: info@pilkguns.com

SAVAGE ARMS, INC.

100 Springdale Road
Westfield, MA 01085
Phone: 413-568-7001
Fax: 413-562-7764
Website: www.savagearms.com

SIG ARMS, INC.

18 Industrial Park Drive
Exeter, NH 03833
Phone: 603-772-2302
Customer Service Fax: 603-772-4795
Website: www.sigarms.com
Factory - SIG - Schweizerische Industrie-Gesellschaft
Industrielplatz
CH-8212 Neuhausen am Rheinfall, Switzerland
Fax: 011-41-153-216-601

SMITH & WESSON

Importer - see Umarex USA
2100 Roosevelt Avenue
P.O. Box 2208
Springfield, MA 01102-2208
Phone: 413-781-8300
Fax: 413-781-8900
Website: www.smith-wesson.com

STEYR SPORTWAFFEN GmbH

Importer – see Pilkington Competition Equipment LLC

Factory - Steyr Mannlicher A.G. & Co. KG

Hauptstrasse 40
A-4432 Ernsthofen AUSTRIA
Fax: 01143-7435-20259-99
Website: www.steyr-sportwaffen.com
Email: office@steyr-sportwaffen.com

STRAIGHT SHOOTERS PRECISION AIRGUNS

2000 Prairie Hill Rd.
St. Cloud, MN 56301
Phone: 320-240-9062
Fax: 0041 91 930 8356
Website: www.staightshooters.com
Email: shooters@staightshooters.com

SWISS ARMS MANUFACTURE SA (SAM ARMS SA)

Via alla Roggia 9a
LUGANO Viganello
CH-6962
Phone: 0041 79 415 6869
Fax: 320-259-0759
Website: http://www.samarms.ch
Email: marco@dolina.ch

SWIVEL MACHINE WORKS

11 Monitor Hill Rd.
Newtown, CT 06470
Phone: 203-270-6343
Website: www.swivelmachine.com
Email: swivelmachine@swivelmachine.com

TAU BRNO, spol. s r.o.

Importer – see Pilkington Competition Equipment, LLC

Importer – see Top Gun Air Guns Inc.

Stará 8, 602 00
Brno, Czech Republic
Phone: 420-5-4521-2323
Fax: 420-5-4521-1257
Website: www.taubrno.cz
Email: info@taubrno.cz

Tim Jones

412 Church St.
Hawley, PA 18428

THEOBEN LTD

Importer - see Theoben USA

Importer - see Beeman Precision Airguns

Factory - Theoben LTD.

West Newlands
Somersham,Cambridgeshire
ENGLAND PE28 3EB
Fax: 011-44-1487-740040
Website: www.theoben.co.uk
Email: sales@theoben.co.uk

THEOBEN USA

Garden Grove, CA
Phone: 931-565-4841
Website: www.theobenusa.com

TOP GUN AIR GUNS INC.

8442 East Hackamore Dr.
Scottsdale, AZ 85255
Phone/Fax: 480-513-3778
Website: www.topgunairguns.com

UMAREX SPORTWAFFEN GmbH & CO. KG

Importer - Umarex USA

Factory - Umarex Sportwaffen GmbH & Co. KG

Postffach 27 20
D-59717 Arnsberg GERMANY
Fax: 011-49-2932-638222
Website: www.umarex.de

UMAREX USA

6007 South 29th Street
Fort Smith, AR72908
Phone: 479-646-4210
Fax: 479-646-4206
Website: www.umarexusa.com

V-MACH CUSTOM RIFLES LTD.

P.O. Box 4582
Stourbridge, West Midlands
DY8 3WT U.K.
Phone: 44 7850-296-360
Fax: 208-979-2848
Email: v-mach@blueyonder.co.uk

WADE M. ANDERSON

19296 Oak Grove Circle
Groveland, CA 95321
Phone: 209-962-5311
Fax: 209-962-5931
Email: hammerliusa@msn.com

WALTHER

Importer - see Umarex USA

Importer - see Champion's Choice Inc.

German Company Headquarters

Carl Walther Sportwaffen GmbH
Postfach 2740
D-59717 Arnsberg GERMANY
Fax: 011-49-29-32-638149

Factory - Carl Walther, GmbH

Sportwaffenfabrik
Postfach 4325
D-89033 Ulm/Donau, GERMANY
Fax: 011-49-731-1539170
Website: www.carl-walther.de
Email: sales@carl-walther.de

WEBLEY & SCOTT LTD.

Importer - see Straight Shooters

Importer – see Pyramyd Air

Factory - Webley & Scott LTD.

Universe House
Key Industrial Park
Willenhall, West Midlands
ENGLAND WV13 3YA
Phone: 44-1902-722144
Fax: 441-1902-722880
Website: www.webley.co.uk
Email: guns@webley.co.uk

WEIHRAUCH SPORT GmbH & CO. KG

Airgun Importer - See Beeman Precision Airguns

Airgun Importer - See Pyramyd Air, Inc.

Firearms Importer - See European American Armory

Factory - H. Weihrauch, Sportwaffenfabrik

Postfach 25 Industriestrabe 11
D-97638 Mellrichstadt, GERMANY
Fax: 011-49-977-6812-281
Email: info@weihrauch-sport.de

WINCHESTER (U.S.REPEATING ARMS)

Importer - Umarex USA

Administrative Offices
275 Winchester Avenue
Morgan, UT 84050-9333
Customer Service Phone: 800-945-1392
Fax: 801-876-3737
Website: www.winchester-guns.com

WISCHO JAGD-UND SPORTWAFFEN

Dresdener Strasse 30,
D-91058 Erlangen, GERMANY
Postfach 3680
D-91024 Erlangen, GERMANY
Fax: 011-91-31-300930
Website: www.wischo.com
Email: info@wischo.com

XISICO USA, INC.

16802 Barker Springs, Ste. 550
Houston, TX 77084
Phone: 281-647-9130
Fax: 208-979-2848
Website: www.xisicousa.com
Email: xisico_usa@yahoo.com

STORE BRAND CROSS-OVER LIST

Many companies sell airguns under their own name but which have been made by others. In many cases all of the models sold under a given brand may be made by another company and it may be impossible or difficult to know who is the actual maker. In other cases a known maker will produce "private label" or "store brand" models for various sellers based on models which they produce under their own name. Only rarely will the private label version be "just the same as" the original base model. The value of comparable models may differ, even hugely, from the base models. Rarely the private label will be a lesser grade version of the base model, but in many cases the private label gun will be an improved version and/or have different cosmetic features. In some cases the private label model will be almost an entirely different gun, only using many of the parts of the base model. Values may differ due to different features and variations, including power levels (higher or lower depending on regulations and demand in the selling area), stock designs, stock material and quality, calibers, sights, trigger mechanisms, etc. In some cases quality control will be higher on the private labels, simply because when the maker sells the guns under their own name returns will come back one by one, but when they make them in huge groups for another company, they may get returns of entire production runs, even thousands of guns, if there is a problem.

This table lists the actual manufacturer and the manufacturer's model that comes closest to the private label brand name and model numbers which will be found on the airgun. Once the name and model of the base model is determined, the reader should find the description of the base model to gather possible information on parts interchangeability, base specifications, and an idea of value range.

(NOTE: These tables are not complete; more information will be added in future editions. Readers are encouraged to submit information on known comparable models not yet listed.)

MONTGOMERY WARDS STORES, HAWTHORN BRAND

"Wards" number	Actual Manufacturer	Equivalent model	Notes
1414A	Crosman	V350	
M180	Crosman	180	
1415	Crosman	99	
1412	Crosman	140	
1447	Crosman	38C	
1448	Crosman	38T	
1435	Crosman	MK I	
1445	Crosman	45	
1434	Crosman	760	
1438	Crosman	130	

J. C. PENNY'S STORES, PENNEY'S BRAND

Penny's number	Actual Manufacturer	Equivalent model	Notes
7236	Daisy	1894	Wood stock and forearm

SEARS STORES, J. C. HIGGINS, SEARS, AND TED WILLIAMS BRANDS

Sears number	Actual Manufacturer	Equivalent model	Notes
126.10294	Crosman	V350	
126.1930	Crosman	140/1400	
126.1931	Crosman	180	
126.1932	Crosman	400	
126.1933	Crosman	166	
126.1934	Crosman	130	
126.1935	Crosman	150	
126.1936	Crosman	600	
126.1937	Crosman	45	
126.1938	Crosman	SA6	
126.1909	Crosman	150	
126.1910	Crosman	160	
126.294	Crosman	V350	
126.1923	Crosman	760	
126.2831	Crosman	180	
126.10349	Crosman	38C	
126.10350	Crosman	38T	
126.19041	Crosman	V350	
126.19131	Crosman	45	
126.19141	Crosman	166	
126.19151	Crosman	180	

Sears Stores, J. C. Higgins, Sears, and Ted Williams Brands, cont.

Sears number	Actual Manufacturer	Equivalent model	Notes
126.19161	Crosman	400	
126.19171	Crosman	160	
126.19181	Crosman	SA6	
126.19191	Crosman	150	
126.19201	Crosman	600	
123.19211	Crosman	130	
126.19241	Crosman	140	
126.19221	Crosman	38C	
126.19231	Crosman	38T	
126.19391	Crosman	M1	
126.19331	Crosman	760	
799.10276	Daisy	25	
799.19020	Daisy	111	
799.19025	Daisy	177	
799.19052	Daisy	1894	Octagon barrel "Crafted by Daisy"
799.19054	Daisy	1894	
799.19062	Daisy	300	
799.19072	Daisy	880	
799.1912	Daisy	1894	Black, round barrel, no scope rail
799.203	Daisy	94	
799.9009	Daisy	105	
799.9012	Daisy	111	
799.9045	Daisy	25	
799.9048	Daisy	1938	
799.9051	Daisy	1894	With scope bracket
799.9052	Daisy	1894	
799.9054	Daisy	1894	
799.9057	Daisy	1914	
799.9061	Daisy	572	
799.9062	Daisy	300	
799.9068	Daisy	840	
799.9072	Daisy	880	
799.9073	Daisy	1938	
799.9076	Daisy	822	
799.9078	Daisy	922	
799.9079	Daisy	922	
799.9082	Daisy	880	

Sears Stores, J. C. Higgins, Sears, and Ted Williams Brands, cont.

Sears number	Actual Manufacturer	Equivalent model	Notes
799.9083	Daisy	880	
799.9085	Daisy	850	
799.9093	Daisy	880	
799.9113	Daisy	900	
799.9115	Daisy	130	
799.9166	Daisy	95	
799.9215	Daisy	545	
799.9224	Daisy	7800	
799.924	Daisy	111	
799.9306	Daisy	557	
799.9313	Daisy	40	
799.9323	Daisy	562	
799.9355	Daisy	1880	
799.9382	Daisy	1880	
799.9393	Daisy	1880	
799.9478	Daisy	1922	
799.9498	Daisy	499	
799.9499	Daisy	499	
799.19083C	Daisy	880	Gold Receiver
799.19383C	Daisy	880	Gold Receiver and scope
799.19385C	Daisy	850	With scope
799.19478C	Daisy	922	
79919085C	Daisy	850	

WESTERN AUTO STORES, REVELATION BRAND

Revelation number	Actual Manufacturer	Equivalent model	Notes
GC3376	Crosman	760	First variation
GC3370	Crosman	73	
GC3375	Crosman	788	
GC3377	Crosman	766	
GC3360	Crosman	V350	
GC3367	Crosman	99	
GC3379	Crosman	140	
GC3416	Crosman	45	
GC3412	Crosman	38T	
GC3375	Crosman	166	

DIANAWERK COMPARABLE MODEL NUMBERS

Only airguns made by Dianawerk of Rastatt, Germany are considered here. The Diana brand name was taken to Scotland as war reparations after WWII. Scottish Dianas were made by Milbro. Some were imported to the USA as economy airguns under the Daisy label. Important note: Comparable models often have different values due to different demand by collectors, different levels of rarity, and, because distributors of private label guns often specified different power levels (for different markets, and not just mainspring differences), stock design, stock material and quality, calibers, sights, trigger mechanisms, etc. may differ from the basic manufacturer´s model. Beeman-marked and pre-1970 Winchester-marked guns generally sell for a premium. Early models of the same number may differ from more recent model.

Diana, RWS Original*	Geco, Peerless	Beeman	Hy-Score	Winchester	Crosman
1					
2			814		
5*			815T	353	
5G		700	825T		
6*			816M	363	
6G		800	826M		
6M		850	827M		
10		900	819SM		
15			808		
16			805	416	
22			806	422	
23 w/receiver rails			813 Mark1		
25 / 25D			801	425	
27*		100	807	427	
35*		200	809	435	
45		250	828		Challenger 6100
50				450	
60			810M		
65			810SM	333	
66			811SM		
75		400, 400 Univ.	820SM		

* Also produced as Beeman´s "Original" series under the same model number.

AIRGUN LITERATURE
AN ANNOTATED PARTIAL REFERENCE LIST
By Dr. Robert D. Beeman

Largely limited to separate publications such as books, periodicals, and booklets, rather than individual airgun articles. (For a large listing of airgun articles prior to 1990 see Groenewold [1990]). For more information and a detailed analysis of the references listed below, see the Literature Review section of www.Beemans.net and a less up-to-date analysis in the Second Edition of the *Blue Book of Airguns*.

PERIODICALS:

The latest contact and subscription information is available on www.Google.com. Older issues sometimes available at secondary book markets, eBay, Doug Law (dlaw1940@yahoo.com, PO Box 42, Sidney, NE 69162); FSI at 906-482-1685; gunshows, etc.

Airgun Ads (Box 1534, Hamilton, Montana 59840, airgunads@brvmontana.com). Small monthly, only ads for airguns and accessories.

Addictive Airgunning. Jan. to Oct. 2004. Online format allowed large articles and color pictures. For both collectors and shooters.

Airgun Hobby (www.airgunhobby.com). October 2004 to date. Now America's only airgun periodical. Quarterly, published by airgun enthusiasts Ron Sauls and Jim Giles. Less glitzy than some previous airgun periodicals, but far superior in reporting airgun events and info on airgun collecting and use.

Airgun Illustrated. August 2002 to January 2004. The first five issues, with Tom Gaylord's input, were truly wonderful.

Airgun Journal (Beeman Precision Airguns). Small, only 1979 to 1984. Edited by Robert Beeman. Many articles valuable to airgun shooters and collectors. One of the rarest of all airgun publications. Less than 500 copies of each of the six issues were printed. Beautifully printed on heavy, textured deep tan paper with green and brown masthead; extremely difficult to scan or photocopy because of the dark paper. Back issues available at www.Beemans.net.

Airgun Letter. Monthly newsletter of 12-16 pages, plus Airgun Revue 1-6 of about 100 pages each, perhaps the world's best reference material on adult airguns. Closed August 2002 when editor Tom Gaylord moved to Airgun Illustrated.

Airgun News & Report (later as *American Airgunner*). Valuable articles, out of print.

Airgun World and Airgunner (both by Romsey Publishing Co., 4 The Courtyard, Denmark St., Workingham, Berkshire RG402AZ, England). British monthlies. *Airgun World* articles of Roy Valentine (under pen name "Harvey" in 1970s) and later, those of John Atkins in *Airgunner* and Tim Saunders in *Airgun World*, are especially valuable to collectors.

Guns Review. British gun magazine formerly carried excellent articles on airguns; especially the pioneer research of John Walter and the late Dennis Commins around 1970s.

New Zealand Airgun Magazine. Pub. by Trevor Adams from February 1986 to April 1988.

Philippine Airgun Shooter. Only four quarterly issues, plus an annual, in 1989.

Shotgun News. Newspaper format, mainly firearm ads, but also airgun ads and America's only airgun column - by outstanding airgun writer Tom Gaylord.

U.S. Airgun (last issue as *Rimfire and Airgun*). Valuable articles for airgun shooters and collectors, out of print.

VISIER, Das Internationale Waffen-Magazin. Lavishly illustrated, prestigious slick German language magazine. Basically a firearm publication, but contains some of the best written, best illustrated airgun articles ever. VISIER Specials, such as 1996 Special Number 4, may have only airgun articles.

Other gun periodicals sometimes have airgun articles: *Precision Shooting* and *The Accurate Rifle*, perhaps the best shooting magazines in the English language, frequently present excellent articles on airguns. *The Rifle* and *Guns* previously featured airgun columns. Most American gun magazines such as *American Rifleman*, *Arms and the Man*, *Guns and Ammo*, *Sports Afield*, etc. only have occasional airgun articles.

REFERENCES:

Adler, Dennis. 2001. (Edited by Dr. Robert D. Beeman and S.P. Fjestad) *Blue Book of Airguns*, First Edition. 160 pp. Blue Book Publications, Inc., Minneapolis, Minnesota. Now rare collectors' item (hardbound sell for $100+).

Atkinson, R. Valentine 1992. *Air Looms*. Gray's Sporting Journal. Sep 1992: 35-41. Beautifully illustrated report on some of the Beeman collection. Some garbled information.

Baker, Geoffery and Colin Currie. 2002, 2003, 2006. Vol 1:Revised 2nd Ed., *The Construction and Operation of the Austrian Army Repeating Air Rifle*, 102 pp.; Vol. 2, The Walking Stick Air Gun 79 pp., info and direct from geoffrey.baker@virgin.net. Detailed photos, full-scale drawings, and measurements. Everyone even slightly interested in these amazing airguns and certainly anyone who contemplates opening one should have these guides. More guides in planning.

Beeman, Robert D., 1977. *Air Gun Digest*. 256 pp. DBI Books, Northfield, IL. Airgun collection, selection, use, ballistics, care, etc. When I did this volume way back in the 20th century, when the field of adult airgunning hardly existed, I never dreamed that someday it would be called a classic collectible, but I'm not going to fight it.

Beeman, Robert D. 1977. *Four Centuries of Airguns*, pp. 14-26. The Basics of Airgun Collecting. Pp. 218-235 (Later reprinted together as The Art of Airgun Collecting by Beeman Precision Arms in 1986, 23 pp.). Considered as the first guide to airgun collecting. A key work. Should be teamed with the "Rare Air" airgun collecting article by R. Beeman in the First Edition of the *Blue Book of Airguns*.

Beeman, Robert and M.J. Banosky, John W. Ford, Randy Pitney, Joe Sexton. 1991. *Air Guns, A Guide to Air Pistols and Rifles*. National Rifle Association, Washington, D.C. Abbreviates and revises the original Beeman manuscript, but very useful introduction to airgun shooting and programs.

Beeman, Robert D. 1995. *The Odyssey of the Beeman* R1. Chapter in *The Beeman R1 - Supermagnum Air Rifle*, pp. 1-9. GAPP. The real story of the gun that brought America into the adult airgun world - and gave rise to the HW 80.

Beeman, Robert D. and John Allen. 2002-2007. *Blue Book of Airguns*. Second through Sixth Editions. Blue Book Publications, Inc., Minneapolis, Minnesota. Price is not the primary purpose of these guides. Model ID and information are. From 19th century to latest guns. Valuable to all airgunners. Every volume has valuable articles; serious airgunners should have a complete set of all editions!

Beeman, Robert D. 2006. Meriwether *Lewis's Wonder Gun*. We Proceeded On May 2005: 29-34. Lewis and Clark Trail Heritage Association. On the Beeman Girandoni: "*this rifle, in fact, was the one carried on the expedition*."

ᵉehling, Larry. 2006. *Air Machine Guns*. 324 pp. Pub. by L. Behling. rte6larry@alltel.net. Huge, wonderfully illustrated on a group of airguns that previously were very poorly known and understood by most airgun collectors. A must.

ᵇruce, Gordon. 2000. *Webley Air Pistols*. 224 pp. Robert Hale, London. The bible on Webley air pistols.

ᵇrukner, Bruno, 2000. *Der Luftpistole*. Second edition, 230 pp. Journal Verland Schwend. Outstanding book on air pistols. All air pistol fans, not just those reading German, should have it. Just the diagrams are worth the price of admission.

ᵇrychta, Frank S. 1994 a. *FSI Airgun Ballistic Tables*. 88 pp. 1994b. FSI *Advanced Airgun Ballistics*. 52 pp. Firearms & Supplies, 514 Quincy St., Hancock, MI 49930.Absolutely essential pair of books for all who are interested in airgun ballistics, field target shooting, and airgun hunting ballistics. Mainly very useful tables.

ᶜardew, G.V. & G.M. Cardew, E.R. Elsom. 1976. *The Air Gun from Trigger to Muzzle*. 96 pp. Martin Brothers, Birmingham, England. Highly technical. The best guide to internal airgun ballistics.

ᶜardew, G.V. & G.M. Cardew. 1995. *The Airgun from Trigger to Target*. 235 pp. Privately published. ISBN 0 9505108 2 3. Extension of Cardew's pioneer book to include external ballistics. Reveals how much and how little we know about airgun ballistics.

ᶜhapman, Jim. 2003. *The American Airgun Hunter*. 234 pp. Chapman, Jim and Randy Mitchell, 2003. *The Airgunners Guide to Squirrel Hunting*. 128 pp. Jaeger Press, 67 Sentinel, Alviso Viejo, CA. www.geocites.com/echochap/airgun_hunter.html. The "American" book actually covers airgun hunting in several countries. Entertaining gab mixed into an essential guide - these fellows are most interested in results while I would lean more towards the quality of the gun. Great.

ᶜhurchill, Bob & Granville Davies. 1981. *Modern Airweapon Shooting*. 196 pp. David & Charles, Devon, England. Authors should be shot for using the word "weapon." Excellent introduction to formal airgun target shooting.

ᴰarling, John. 1988. *Air Rifle Hunting*.160 pp. Crowood Press, Wilshire, England. Excellent, but now rather dated w/o good coverage of PCP guns, night lights, etc.

ᴰieter, Ernst 2002. *Luftgewehre und Luftpistolen nach 1945 aus Suhl und Zella-Mehlis*. 143 pp. WTS Waffentechnik in Suhl GmbH, Lauter 40, 98528 Suhl, Germany. Writing under a pseudonym, a former top engineer at Haenel presents invaluable information on almost 60 models - some not previously known to collectors.

ᴰunathan, Arni T. 1971. *The American BB Gun: A Collector's Guide*. 154 pp. A.S. Barnes and Co., Cranbury, New Jersey. The pioneer work on BB gun collecting. Now badly out of date, but forever essential! The 1970 prices will bring tears to your eyes!

ᴱichstädt, Ulrich 2007. *Corpus delicti, Die Suche nach der Lewis & Clark Windbüchse*. (Body of Evidence -The Search for the Lewis & Clark Airgun), *VISIER* Jan.2007:135-143. Europe's leading airgun historian and author says: "*the puzzle about the legendary airgun carried by Captains Meriwether Lewis and William Clark from 1803 to 1806 appears to have been solved.*".

ᴱlbe, Ronald E. 1992. *Know Your Sheridan Rifles & Pistols*. 79 pp. Blacksmith Corp. The best review of the Sheridan guns.

ᶠletcher, Dean. 1996-98. *The Crosman Arms Handbooks*, 259 pp.; and *The Crosman Rifle 1923-1950*, 265 pp., *The Crosman Arms Model "160" Pellgun*, 144 pp., *75 Years of Crosman Airguns*, 223 pp., *Crosman Arms Library* (CD). Pub. by D.T. Fletcher, 6720 NE Rodney Ave, Portland, Oregon 97211. (For more Crosman info see Eichstädt, Ulrich and Dean Fletcher. 1999. *Eine Unbekannte Größe*. Visier, Feb.

1999:52-57 and Oakleaf, Jon B. 1979. *Vintage Crosmans. The Airgun Journal* 1(1): 1-3, 1980. *Vintage Crosmans II. The Airgun Journal* 1(2):1-7.)

Fletcher, Dean. Undated. *The Crosman Arms Library*. CD with 888 full color scans of Crosman literature. 1998c. *The Chronology of Daisy Air Guns 1900 - 1981 and Daisy Toy and Metal Squirt Guns*. 18 pp.; 1999. *The St. Louis and Benjamin Air Rifle Companies*, 305 pp. Pub. by D.T. Fletcher.

Friberg, Av Kenth. 2001. *Luftvapen*. 191 pp. Karlshamn\Göteborg, Sweden. (K. Friberg, Ekbacken 3, 37450 Asarum, Sweden). In Swedish; one of several guides to some airguns not generally known to Americans.

Galan, Jess I. 1988. *Airgun Digest*, 2nd Edition; 1995. *Airgun Digest*. 3rd Edition. 288 pp. DBI Books, Northbrook, IL. Classic books, all aspects of airgunning. Outstanding author.

Garber, Gary. 2007. *An Encyclopedia of Daisy Plymouth Guns*. 8.5 in. x 11 in., 414 pp. Published by author at BBgunBook@aol.com. Finally, the much-waited, huge "bible" on Daisy airguns made at Plymouth, MI from late 1880s to 1958 and a few latter ones from Rogers, AK.

Gaylord, Tom. 1995. *The Beeman R1- Supermagnum Air Rifle*. 174 pp. GAPP. One of the classic, best books on airguns. Highly recommended by many airgun writers. Includes a chapter by R. Beeman on the Beeman Rl as the precursor of the HW 80. The most useful book on the market for understanding the function and use of ANY spring piston airgun.

Groenewold, John. 1990. *Bibliography of Technical Periodical Airgun Literature*. 28 pp. Pub. by John Groenewold, Box 830, Mundelein, IL 60060. A great listing. John promises to go beyond 1990 "someday"!

Groenewold, John. 2000. *Quackenbush Guns*. 266 pages. Pub. by John Groenewold, Box 830, Mundelein, IL 60060-0830. Phone 847-566.2365. The definitive guide to the wonderful antique Quackenbush guns.

Hannusch, Larry. 2001. *Pneumatic Reflections*. 280 pages. Self published by L. Hannusch, 5521-B, Mitchelldale, Houston, TX 77092 or lhannusch@netscape.net. Compilation of last twenty years of interesting and valuable articles on airgun collecting by one of the world's leading authorities.

Herridge, Les. 1987. *Airgun Shooting*. 96 pp. A & C Black, London. Herridge, 1994. *Airgun Shooting Handbook*., 80 pp. Herridge, Les and Ian Law. 1989. *Airgun Field Target Shooting*. 100pp. Peter Andrew Publishing Co. Basic introductions to British field target airgun shooting.

Hiller, Dennis E. 1982. *The Collector's Guide to Air Pistols*, Revised Second Edition. 187 pp. Published by Dennis Hiller. Rather dated, depressed values, but invaluable model info - mainly European models. An almost essential item to pair with *Blue Book of Airguns*, but sadly out of print.

Hiller, Dennis E. 1985. *The Collectors' Guide to Air Rifles*, Enlarged Third Edition. 276 pp. Published by Dennis Hiller. See above note. Again, lots of invaluable information.

Hoff, Arne. 1972. *Air Guns and Other Pneumatic Arms*. 99 pp. Barrie and Jenkins, London. A classic that everyone interested in the history of airguns simply must have!

Hoff, Arne, 1977. *Windbüchsen und andere Druckluftwaffen*. 105 pp. Parey, Berlin. Updated version of above; in German.

Holzel, Tom. 1991. *The Air Rifle Hunter's Guide*. 159 pp. Velocity Press, 52 Lang St., Concord, MA 01742. Simply the best book on hunting with an air rifle. Presents crow hunting as philosophically similar to fly fishing. The "Killing as a Sport" chapter is one of the best ever presentations on the morality and ethics of hunting. Includes outstanding, practical material on field ballistics of airguns.

Hough, Cass S. 1976. *It's A Daisy!* 336 pp. Daisy Division, Victor Comptometer Corp., Rogers, Arkansas. Delightful history of the Daisy Company by one of its longest term executives. Rare, a very desirable collectors' item - softbound.

House, James E. 2002. *American Air Rifles*. 208 pp., 179 black and white illus. 2003. *CO2 Pistols & Rifles*. Krause (www.krause.com). Both softbound books press the theme that pellet guns from Daisy, Crosman, etc. should be seriously considered by adults also. Some of the best ballistic info available for airguns of this level.

Hughes, D.R. 1973. *An original handbook for the model 35D, 27, 35 & 50 air rifles*. 77 pp. Pub. by D.R. Hughes, England. (Original brand = Diana, RWS, Gecado, some Winchester, some Beeman, some HyScore). Delightful guide to assembly, etc.

Hughes, D.R. 1981. *HW 35. A Handbook for Owners and Users of the HW35 Series Air Rifles*. 65 pp. Optima Leisure Products, 75 Foxley Lane, Purley, Surrey, England. Another delightful Hughes tour through a famous airgun.

Janich, Michael D. 1993, *Blowguns, The Breath of Death*. 81 pp. Paladin Press, Boulder, Colorado. Basic info on the most basic of airguns.

Johnson, Bill 2003. *Bailey and Columbian Air Rifles*. 38 pp. Book plus CD. Bill Johnson, PO Box 97B, Tehachapi, CA 93581. The definitive work on some of America's most interesting and solid airguns (formerly known as Heilprin airguns). 1/4 and 1/2 scale detailed drawings.

Kishi, Takenobu. 1999. *The Magnum*, 303 pp. Printed in Japan. ISBN 4-7733-6563-3 C0075. In Japanese. Detailed info on airgun ballistics.

Kersten, Manfred. 2001. *Walther - A German Legend*. 400 pp. Safari Press, 15621 Chemical Lane B, Huntington Beach, CA 92649-1506 USA. This gorgeous masterpiece covers all Walther guns, including excellent coverage of the airguns. Also available in German.

Knibbs, John. 1986. *B.S.A. and Lincoln Jefferies Air Rifles*. 160 pp. Published by John Knibbs Publications, Birmingham. Another classic British work on the history and models of a leading airgun maker.

Kolyer, John M. 1969. *Compilation of Air Arm Articles and Data* 130 pp. John Kolyer, 55 Chimney Ridge Drive, Convent, New Jersey 07961. Primarily older airgun ballistic material. Pioneer work.

Kolyer, John M. & Ron Rushworth. 1988. *Airgun Performance*. 157 pp. Sangreal Press, Newport Beach, California. Updated version of Kolyer's 1969 work. Even includes blowgun and slingshot data.

Law, Robert. 1969. *The Weihrauch Handbook*. 44 pp. Air Rifle Monthly, Grantsville, West Virginia. One of a series of how-to-do-it airgun maintenance and tuning booklets by one of America's early adult airgun hobbyists. Verbose but very useful. Last supply available in Sale section www.Beemans.net .

Lawrence, Andrew. 1969. *Development of the Hy-Score Air Pistol*. Engineering Case Library No. 134. Department of Mechanical Engineering. Leland Stanford Jr. University. Extremely rare paper on the origin of the American HyScore concentric piston air pistols.

Marchington, James. 1988. *Field Airgun Shooting*. 200 pp. Pelham Books/London (Penguin). Basic guide to British field target shooting.

Moore, Warren, 1963. *Guns, the Development of Firearms, Air Guns, and Cartridges*. 104 pp., Grosset and Dunlap, New York, N.Y. Contains a wonderful, well-illustrated section on antique airguns.

Munson, H. Lee. 1992. *The Mortimer Gunmakers, 1753-1923*. 320 pp. Andrew Mowbray, Lincoln, Rhode Island. Includes excellent material on the elegant large bore airguns made by the Mortimer family, 1700s to early 1900s.

Nonte, George C. 1970, *Complete Book of the Air Gun*. Stackpole, Harrisburg, PA. Somewhat lightweight and dated, but very useful.

Oscar Will-Catalogue *Venus Waffenwerk Reprint of 1902/03 catalog*. 9? pp. Journal-Verlang in Schwäbish Hall.

Parks, Michael R. 1992, 1994. *Pneumatic Arms & Oddities*, Vol. 1 an? Vol. 2. 245 and 211 pp. Southwest Sports, 1710 Longhill Road, Ber?ton, AR 72015. Fascinating collection of older American airgun pa?ents.

Punchard, Neal. 2002. *Daisy Air Rifles & BB Guns, The First 100 Year?* 156 pp., 300 color illustrations, MBI Publishing. Not really a guid? but a beautiful celebration of Daisy air guns!

Reno, Brett, (2004). *Airgun Index and Value Guide*. 13th edition, 150? unnumbered pages in three-ring binder. Brett Reno, RR2 Box 6? Heyworth, IL 61745. No illustrations, descriptions, history, mode? details, etc. but invaluable for its literature references!

Robinson, Ron, (1998) *The Manic Compressive* 125 pp.; (2001) *Airgu? Hunting and Sport*, 138 pp.; (2003) *A Sporting Proposition*, 126 p? Ron Robinson, 4225 E. Highway 290, Dripping Springs, Texas 7862? Three thoroughly Texan tomes on airgun hunting. Loves hunting wit? airguns, from his favorite Beeman R1 to latest oriental big bore ai? guns. A real hunter, real character, real ego! Every airgun hunter shou? have all three.

Saunders, Tim. 2006. *History Maker, Airgun World* Oct. 2006, pp. 47-5? British report on the Beeman Girandoni: "*The weight of new evidence such that few doubt that it is indeed the actual Lewis and Clark rifle.*"

Schreier, Philip 2006. *The Airgun of Meriwether Lewis and the Corps of Discover? American Rifleman* Oct.2006: pp. 66-69, 86, 97-99. Senior Arms Curator at t? prestigious National Firearms Museum of the NRA reports on the Beema? Girandoni as the Lewis airgun: "*the circumstantial evidence is overwhelming*".

Skanaker, Ragnar and Laslo Antal. 2001. *Sportliches Pistolen-schieße? (Competitive Pistol Shooting)*. In German. 194 pp. Motorbuch Ve? lang, Postbox 103743, Stuttgart70032, Germany. Includes a chapt? on air pistol target shooting.

Shepherd, Arthur. 1987. *Guide to Airgun Hunting*. 123 pp. Argus Book? London. Very interesting, but severely British.

Smith, W.H.G. 1957. *Smith's Standard Encyclopedia of Gas, Air, an? Spring Guns of the World*. 279 pp. Arms and Armour Press, Londo? and Melbourne. The initial bible of airguns, badly dated and wit? many errors, but absolutely indispensable.

Støckel, Johan F., 1978-82. Revision edited by Eugene Heer: *Heer d? Neue Støckel. Internationales Lexikon der Büchsenmacher, Feurwaffenfa? rikanten und Armbrustmacher von 1400-1900*. 2287 pp. Journal-Ve? lang, Schwend GmbH, Schwäbish Hall, Germany. Extreme? expensive, extremely useful three volume guide to virtually all gu? makers from 1400 to 1900. In German, but that is not much of ? handicap for those speaking other tongues when looking up names an? dates.

Thomas, James F., 2000. *The BB Gun Book - A Collectors Guide*. 75 p? Self-published. (Basically a brief update of the classic 1971 Dunatha? book).

Townshend, R.B. 1907. *The Complete Air-Gunner*. 88 pp. I. Upcott Gi? London and Chas. Scribner's Sons, New York. (reprinted). Delightf? insight to airgunning at the beginning of the 20th century.

Traister, Robert J. 1981. *All About Airguns*. 306 pp. Tab Books, Blu? Ridge Summit, PA. Pot-boiler, largely derived from 1980 Beeman catalog.

Tyler, Jim. 1988. *Vermin Control with an Air Rifle*. Andrew Publishin? Company, Ltd. Controlling what Americans call "varmints" or pests.

Wade, Mike, 1984. *The Weihrauch HW 80 and Beeman R1 Air Rifle, A User's Guide to Higher Performance.* 19 pp. Techpress, Mike Wade Engineering, 87 Elgin Rd., Seven Kings, Ilford, Essex, England. Technical, excellent.

Walter, John. 1981. *The Airgun Book.* 146 pp. Arms and Armour Press, London. British based register of then current airguns. Excellent.

Walter, John. 1984. *The Airgun Book*, 3rd Edition. 176 pp. Arms and Armour Press, London. Contains best ever survey of airgun manufacturing history from 1900 to 1984.

Walter, John. 1985, *Airgun Shooting, Performance Directory and Index of Suppliers from A to Z.* 96 pp. Lyon Press Ltd., West Hampstead, London. Tall, little guide to fit the vest pocket.

Walter, John. 1987. *The Airgun Book*, 4th Edition. Arms and Armour Press, London. Broadened the scope of this series. The last of an excellent series.

Walter, John. 2002, *Greenhill Dictionary of Guns and Gunmakers.* 576 pp. Greenhill Books, London and Stackpole Books, PA. Indispensable guide includes amazing amount of airgun information. Covers 1836 to 2000.

Wesley, L. and G.V. Cardew. 1979, *Air-Guns and Air-Pistols.* 208 pp. Cassell, London. Updated revision of a British classic on all aspects of airgunning and airguns.

Wolff, Eldon G. 1958. *Air Guns.* 198 pp., Milwaukee Public Museum Publications in History 1, Milwaukee, WI. A classic work on antique airguns. Try to find an original museum edition!

Wolff, Eldon G. 1963. *Air Gun Batteries.* 28 pp. Milwaukee Public Museum Publications in History 5, Milwaukee, Wisconsin. Concise guide to how airgun mechanisms, from early to modern, work. Rare, valuable. Photocopies available in Sale section of www.Beemans.net.

Wolff, Eldon G. 1967. *The Scheiffel and Kunitomo Air Guns.* 54 pp. Milwaukee Public Museum Publications in History 8, Milwaukee, WI. A rare booklet on an unusual pair of antique airguns. Rare collectors' item

OTHER LITERATURE:

In addition to following the current airgun periodicals and latest books, one cannot remain current, or develop understanding of older models, without consulting the latest and old catalogs from Beeman Precision Airguns, Dynamit-Nobel (RWS), Air Rifle Specialties, etc. There is a wealth of information in factory bulletins and ads. Beeman Precision Airguns was especially productive: look for pre-1993 *Beeman Technical Bulletins*, and the early *Beeman Precision Airgun Guide/Catalogs*, starting with Edition One (only 500 were printed!) in 1974, and *Beeman's Shooter's News*, basically a sales bulletin to its retail customers. Especially interesting to airgun collectors are the Beeman Used Gun Lists (the "UGL") published in the 1970s to 1990s. They hold a wealth of information on the large numbers of vintage and antique airguns sold by the company over that period. The former prices of the collectors' items will make today's collectors pale. Old Crosman manuals are also highly collectible.

Finding and Collecting Airgun Literature: Astute collectors, most notably Dean Fletcher and Doug Law, have realized that airgun literature itself has become a key field of collecting. Unlike the airguns themselves, the literature, especially the airgun company literature, generally is quickly lost. Thus the literature becomes both a challenge to collect and a vital link to the special history of the field, which, like so many histories, soon becomes very hazy. As every year passes, this literature becomes harder to find and more valuable in several ways. Many readers will find that many of the references mentioned here have been printed in only limited editions and can be purchased "not for love nor money." Try gunshows and the special order desks of Barnes and Noble and Brothers book stores, and the search services of their websites and those of www.Amazon.com, www.Alibris.com, and especially www.Add-ALL.com for used and out of print books. Check the website of Ray Rieling of New York for the world's largest selection of out of print gun books; sometimes he has a few airgun books. Generally these books are not going to be easy to find, so act fast if you do find any. Some airgun literature is available in the "Sale and Wanted" section of www.Beemans.net. Doug Law dlaw1940@yahoo.com (PO Box 42, Sidney, NE 69162) specializes in the sale of airgun literature. (The *Blue Books of Airguns* themselves have become a very collectible series. Hardbound editions are the most sought. They can sell for up to 100 dollars and more.)

INDEX

A

S

T